10 mi

10 km

4

205 580

LIVERMORE VALLEY

Pleasanton

Livermore

101

Morgan Hill

129

Walnut Creek

680

San Leandro

Hayward

Fremont

680

680

Santa Clara

San Jose

SANTA CLARA VALLEY

82

Los Gatos

Aptos

17

Capitola

Berkeley

Oakland

580

880

84

85

Saratoga

Santa Cruz

Alameda

San Francisco Bay

92

280

Palo Alto

9

Ben Lomond

Sausalito

101

SANTA CRUZ MOUNTAINS

1

80

San Francisco

280

Pacifica

1

Half Moon Bay

84

San Gregorio

Napa

Farallon Islands

NAPA VALLEY

CHILES VALLEY

128

ATLAS PEAK

STAGS LEAP

Yountville

OAK KNOLL

29

CARNEROS

Pope Valley

Angwin

RUTHERFORD

OAKVILLE

Oakville

YOUNTVILLE

MT VEEDER

12

HOWELL MOUNTAIN

ST HELENA

Rutherford

Glen Ellen

Sonoma

Calistoga

St Helena

SPRING MOUNTAIN

29

128

DIAMOND MOUNTAIN

12

BENNETT VALLEY

SONOMA MOUNTAIN

SONOMA VALLEY

116

© AVALON TRAVEL PUBLISHING, INC.

CONTENTS

Discover Northern California Wine Country

Explore Northern California Wine Country

Know Northern California Wine Country

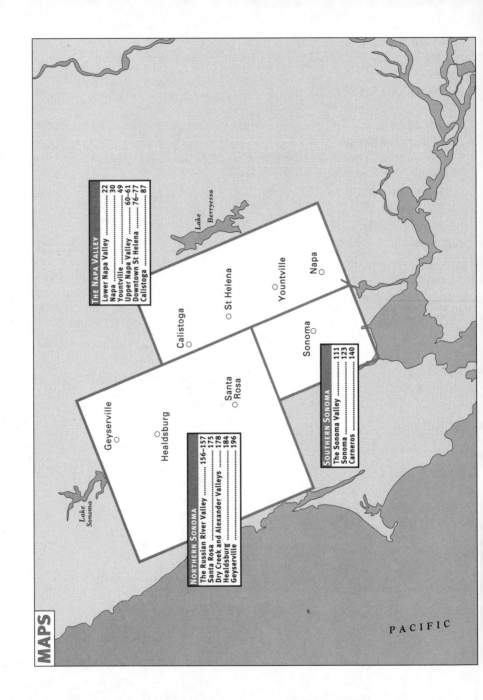

MAPS

THE NAPA VALLEY
Lower Napa Valley 22
Napa 30
Yountville 49
Upper Napa Valley 60–61
Downtown St Helena 76–77
Calistoga 87

NORTHERN SONOMA
The Russian River Valley 156–157
Santa Rosa 175
Dry Creek and Alexander Valleys 178
Healdsburg 184
Geyserville 196

SOUTHERN SONOMA
The Sonoma Valley 111
Sonoma 123
Carneros 140

Geyserville

Healdsburg

Santa
Rosa

Calistoga

St Helena

Sonoma

Yountville

Napa

Lake
Sonoma

Lake
Berryessa

PACIFIC

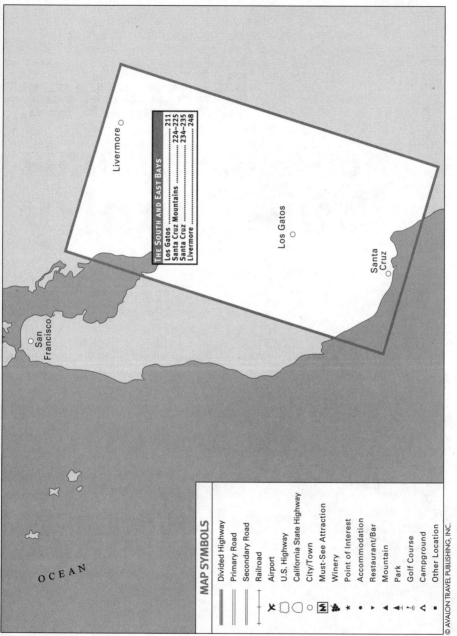

OCEAN

San Francisco

Livermore

Los Gatos

Santa Cruz

MAP SYMBOLS

	Divided Highway
	Primary Road
	Secondary Road
┼┼	Railroad
✈	Airport
⬭	U.S. Highway
⬭	California State Highway
○	City/Town
Ⓜ	Must-See Attraction
♣	Winery
★	Point of Interest
•	Accommodation
▶	Restaurant/Bar
◀	Mountain
◀	Park
⌐○	Golf Course
◁	Campground
■	Other Location

© AVALON TRAVEL PUBLISHING, INC.

Discover
Northern California
Wine Country

As you unwind at the end of another perfect summer day in the Wine Country, sitting on a winery patio sipping a glorious cabernet while surrounded by fragrant lavender and bathed in the golden glow of the late afternoon sun as it casts long shadows over the endless green corduroy of the vineyards, it's hard not to dream of picking up and moving here.

You wouldn't be the first. As the wine and nature have worked their magic over the centuries, people from all over the world have been lured by the lush forests, tall mountains, abundant rivers, and warm valleys that make up Northern California's Wine Country, creating a rich historical, cultural, and agricultural tapestry.

In the 1800s, early winemakers chose this giant, geographically diverse area of the then-largely unpopulated state to grow grapes—a testament to just how ideal the conditions and climate are. Ever since fine wine production took off almost 150 years ago, it has remained the center of California's wine industry, flourishing in Victorian times as other popular wine growing regions came and went. Even as wine making has spread up and down the California coast in the past few decades, Napa,

Sonoma, and the Santa Cruz Mountains remain the center of it all, able to boast some of the best (some maintain *the* best) growing conditions in the state for virtually every major type of wine grape.

Despite its well-earned position as California's Wine Country jewel, the Napa Valley accounts for less than five percent of the wine produced in the state. As more visitors saturate the Napa Valley in search of its wine, food, and luxury accommodations, attention is turning to neighboring Sonoma County and the many other important wine producing areas that are within easy reach of the Bay Area's gateway cities. It is these other areas where the diversity of the Wine Country and its wines can really be seen.

Yet Northern California is more than just the source of world-class wines. From the hot lowlands of Sonoma to the foggy heights of the Santa Cruz Mountains, Northern California's wine lands are as culturally diverse as they are geographically varied. Visitors can indulge in hedonistic pleasures far removed from their daily lives, sampling the fine wine and food that have made Napa and Sonoma famous around the world, being pampered in spas, soaking up the sun on sandy beaches, exploring the great outdoors, or shopping in unique boutiques.

The appeal is that there's a lifestyle for every dream. This Wine Country lifestyle can be as diverse as the land, people, and history of the region it draws from. A little corner of Tuscany with sumptuous Mediterranean meals drenched in fresh olive oil and shared with your family on a warm, brick patio with a bottle of sangiovese. A personal retreat while hiking through redwoods and past waterfalls to picnic on a lofty meadow overlooking peaceful, verdant valleys. Enjoying a cosmopolitan atmosphere as you indulge in a luxurious spa treatment followed by an afternoon of shopping at designer boutiques before finishing off the evening with signature cocktails and late-night jazz.

But it is the wine that brings people here, and there's no better place in the world to learn about this mysterious libation than in Northern California's Wine Country. There are a greater variety of styles and types of red and white wines made here in just a few hundred square miles than in almost any other place on earth. And just as there's a lifestyle for every taste, there's a wine to suit every palate.

In many ways Northern California's Wine Country shares the same characteristics as some of its world-class wines. There are numerous layers of bold, complex flavors and nuances to discover, from the aromas of fresh spring flowers to the dusty hints of rich earth on a warm fall day. These layers continue to develop and change with time, revealing a few new surprises in every taste and visit. The Wine Country and its wines undoubtedly leave those who come here remembering some unique feature more appealing than any other, planting the desire to return or perhaps even the dream to pick up and move here.

The mind-boggling range of activities, wines, scenery, and foods that makes this such a diverse part of the world also ensures that seeing and doing the Wine Country will mean different things to different people.

The key to visiting the region is planning. In the hedonistic Wine Country, it's hard not to have fun whatever you do, but it can be made all the more enjoyable if you come up with a plan—any plan—however rudimentary, otherwise it's easy to feel overwhelmed. Often it's more fun to let tasting room staff, hotel concierges, or fellow travelers help flesh it out with local knowledge and experiences. It needn't be a detailed or rigid schedule. A crucial part of Wine Country lifestyle is relaxation and indulgence, neither of which should be worked at too hard.

If you try to visit too many wineries, the day will seem a blur with few lasting memories except the frustration caused when heavy traffic wrecks an over-optimistic schedule. Take note of how long tours last or how many wines there are to taste, and allow plenty of time to linger and chat with the winemaker or tasting room staff. Mix big wineries and small wineries to experience the full spectrum of the wine-making world, or focus on a particular style of wine. And pepper any visit with healthy doses of non-wine-related activities, such as hiking or cooking classes, to keep in touch with all of the many aspects of the Wine Country that make its lifestyle unique.

When you finally open that expensive bottle of Napa cabernet you'll have some far more interesting dinner table anecdotes to tell.

WHEN TO GO

Summer and fall are the most popular seasons to visit, and for perfectly good reasons. This is when the weather is at its best and the wineries are at their most active, laying out lavish food and wine events, preparing for harvest, and releasing new vintages.

The problem is, everyone seems to be here at this time of year. Hotel prices jump, if you can get a room, and restaurant reservations can be hard to come by. Weekends can be particularly bad as local day-trippers from San Francisco and other Bay Area cities swell the already bulging tourist traffic, potentially turning a weekend getaway into a weekend of purgatory.

Even visiting midweek at this time of year can make a huge difference. St. Helena, Healdsburg, and Sonoma can feel positively deserted on an August or September weekday. Experiences will also vary depending on location. The Napa Valley is the most popular part of Wine Country by far, and St. Helena is best avoided on summer weekends. The Santa Cruz Mountains and Dry Creek Valley are often much quieter.

Consider visiting at another time of year altogether for a more fulfilling experience. Almost every season in Wine Country has something going for it, if not the weather.

After October, things quiet down a little bit, hotel rates drop, and the weather can still be fine. Vineyards turn glorious hues of red and gold. It's finally cool enough to drive through the valley vineyards with the air conditioning off, yet still warm enough to have the windows down and smell the aromatic, dusty fall air.

December–April is the wettest period, and although there can still be stretches of warm, sunny weather, gray and foreboding clouds are more common. Wineries can also be blissfully quiet during the winter, giving you plenty of one-on-one time with tasting room staff, who are usually more than happy to spend an hour talking about their wines and maybe slip a few free pours under the table. This is also a perfect time of year to try port or other powerful, warming red wines that might otherwise induce instant headaches on a hot summer day.

In May and June the rainy season comes to an end, the weather warms up, and the valley and mountains are a fresh, vivid green. Although spring is becoming a more popular time to visit parts of the Wine Country, it's still possible to sneak in ahead of the worst summer crowds.

WHAT TO TAKE

The Wine Country is generally a rather civilized place to visit, but nature likes to keep everyone guessing. November–May, be sure to pack an umbrella and plenty of wet-weather gear, particularly if you plan any outdoor activities.

Though wet, winter is a great temperature equalizer throughout the region. Almost every part of Wine Country, from the coast to the heart of the Alexander Valley, will be about the same temperature—usually 55–65°F during the day. Summer is a different story. The coast tends to be cool June–October while the inland valleys are hot, with significant temperature differences often experienced in just a half-hour drive.

The key to staying comfortable in such conditions is to bring plenty of layers of clothing that can be shed during the drive from the cool coast to the cauldron of Calistoga. Be prepared to put some back on in the evening, as temperatures in many places can drop sharply after dark. The Russian River Valley, Carneros, and Santa Cruz Mountains tend to have variable summer weather. It might be hot and sunny, windy and partly sunny, or windy and foggy, or sometimes all three in one day.

Farther inland, the summer sun shines virtually every day and it can get extremely hot, so be well prepared with sunscreen, a hat, and sunglasses. Remember to drink plenty of bottled water to ward off dehydration from drinking wine or from any strenuous exercise like hiking.

Whatever the time of year, this is essentially an outdoorsy, agricultural area, so casual clothing and good walking shoes are recommended for tramping up to picnic spots or through vineyards on tours. Very few restaurants require anything more than smart-casual attire, so unless you're planning to eat at the ones that do it's fine to leave heels and ties behind.

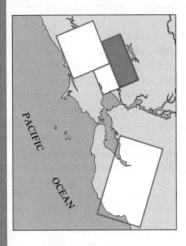

NAPA VALLEY

This *is* California Wine Country as far as many people are concerned—arguably the most important wine-making region in the state with a name recognized around the world. The 30-mile-long Napa Valley is a valley of contrasts with hundreds of wineries ranging from the historic big names like Niebaum-Coppola and Beringer, which produce millions of cases of wine a year, down to more modest wineries turning out some of California's best cabernet sauvignon, such as in the more rural regions of Stags Leap District and Spring Mountain. Most visitors head for the cultural center of the valley around upscale St. Helena, but there's a slower pace of life along the Silverado Trail on the other side of the valley and farther north near the laid-back, historic spa town of Calistoga.

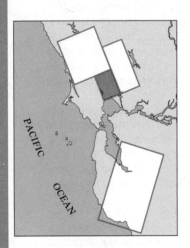

SOUTHERN SONOMA

Living in the shadow of the Napa Valley is just fine for neighboring Sonoma Valley, the historical center of California's modern wine industry. The notable town of Sonoma is thoroughly at peace with itself, as though worn out from the tumultuous series of events more than 150 years ago that gave birth to the state of California. Wineries, too, feel more laid-back here, even those like Buena Vista and Gundlach Bundschu that witnessed California's wine industry beginnings back in the late 1800s. Travel north to the sleepy town of Glen Ellen, near where writer Jack London found his nirvana, and where wineries like Chateau St. Jean and Benziger turn out red and white wines to rival those over the mountains in Napa. Or head south from Sonoma down to the cool flatlands of Carneros, where sparkling wine houses like Gloria Ferrer and Domaine Carneros work wonders with chardonnay and pinot noir.

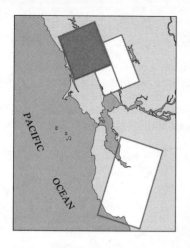

NORTHERN SONOMA

If any region epitomizes the diversity of California's Wine Country it is northern Sonoma, where scenery and wines often have little in common other than their Sonoma County address. The cool, lush **Russian River Valley** is home to the easy-going town of **Guerneville** and countless recreation opportunities in the mountains or on the Russian River. It's also the source of some of California's best pinot noir and chardonnay. The hotter **Alexander Valley** farther north is the land of big velvety cabernet sauvignons, while the **Dry Creek Valley** is home to dozens of modest, family-run wineries making jammy zinfandels and some more unusual wines. Between them both is the upscale town of **Healdsburg,** known for its antique shops and increasing number of tasting rooms. It's an easy day trip beyond northern Sonoma into **Mendocino,** where the **Anderson Valley** is making a name for its pinot noir and white wines.

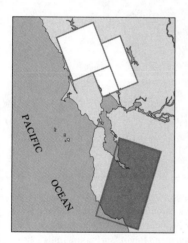

THE SOUTH AND EAST BAYS

Challenging the Russian River Valley for sheer scenic and cultural diversity, the Santa Cruz Mountains stretch from the hot western fringes of Silicon Valley up to elevations of over 3,000 feet before sloping gently down toward the ocean. Historic and moneyed towns like **Los Gatos** and **Saratoga** anchor wineries on the hot eastern slopes, where **Ridge Vineyards** and **Mount Eden Vineyards** produce some of California's best chardonnay and cabernet sauvignon. The cool western slopes are prime pinot noir territory, where small pockets of vineyards belonging to such famous wineries as **David Bruce** mingle with groves of ancient redwoods and thousands of acres of parkland. Where the mountains meet the sea, the city of **Santa Cruz** is more summer beach town than wine destination, with the only roller coaster within walking distance of a tasting room.

Most people bypass the suburbs of **Livermore Valley** in the East Bay without realizing that this is one of the most historic wine-growing regions in California. Fine wine grapes were planted here long before those in Sonoma and Napa, and wineries like **Wente** produce chardonnays to rival those from the Sonoma Valley.

One Week in Wine Country

There's more than wine to the Wine Country, and some of the best sights and activities are not wine-related at all. This week-long tour of the major wine regions will give a taste of the diversity on offer, taking in a mix of wineries, sights, and outdoor activities. Driving is the best way to get around, or rent a bike in Sonoma or Healdsburg to explore some of the local attractions.

DAY 1

In the city of Napa visit Copia, America's first museum devoted to food and wine. Tour the exhibits, sit in on a seminar, and have lunch at the café. In the afternoon, visit nearby wineries, including the Hess Collection, home to contemporary art as well as good wine, and the Persian palace of Darioush. Drive north on the Silverado Trail to Frog's Leap Winery, an organic wine and produce wonderland, before continuing to Calistoga.

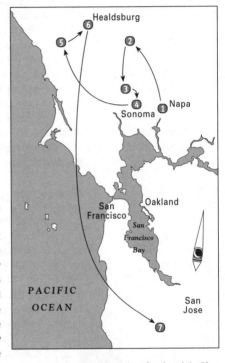

DAY 2

Explore Calistoga by visiting the Sharpsteen Museum, which showcases the town's colorful Victorian history. Take a tour of the caves at the nearby Schramsberg winery, a champagne house with its own unique Victorian history. Buy picnic supplies in Calistoga and drive south to Bothe-Napa Valley State Park for a picnic and maybe a short hike through the redwoods. Drive farther south to St. Helena, stopping off for one of the cooking demonstrations at the Culinary Institute of America. From St. Helena, take the scenic drive up Spring Mountain Road to the top, where Pride Mountain Vineyards makes some wonderful mountain wines. Spend the night in Sonoma Valley.

DAY 3

Take a fun, motorized tour around the Benziger Family Winery vineyards, one of the few biodynamic wineries in California. After tasting some of their classic Sonoma cabernets, head for the nearby Olive Press just south of Glen Ellen to taste some diverse olive oils. After lunch in Glen Ellen, hike around the scenic Jack London State Historic Park, once part of the Victorian author's giant ranch and full of fascinating ruins. Those with enough energy can expend plenty of it in Sugarloaf Ridge State Park on the other side of the valley, where redwoods and sunny ridges offer ample outdoor choices and spectacular views. End the day tasting reserve wines on the peaceful patio overlooking the valley vineyards at Chateau St. Jean.

DAY 4

While browsing the shops and sights around historic Sonoma Plaza, explore some of the equally historic wineries nearby, such as Gundlach Bundschu. Lunch in Sonoma, before heading south to Carneros to the artistic wonderland of the di Rosa Preserve. Visit nearby wineries like Carneros Creek and Domaine Carneros to taste some of the area's fine pinot noirs and champagnes before dining in Sonoma at one of the town's many superb restaurants.

DAY 5

Drive north to Santa Rosa, then head west into the Russian River Valley (1 hour) for fine champagne tastings at Iron Horse Vineyards and Korbel Champagne Cellars. After lunch in Guerneville, head for the cool forests of nearby Armstrong Redwoods State Reserve for a hike through the redwoods, or rent a canoe and float through the trees on the Russian River, stopping at one of the many small beaches. In the afternoon, drive north on West Side Road to Healdsburg (30 minutes), calling in at the Hop Kiln Winery to taste some unusual wines and see the giant kilns that once dried hops for beer. You'll be spoiled for choice for dinner in Healdsburg and might be able to catch a show at the town's Raven Theater that evening.

DAY 6

Explore the many downtown tasting rooms of Healdsburg, then drive or bike into the nearby Dry Creek Valley to visit some small wineries that produce some big zinfandels. Ridge Vineyards has an environmentally friendly winery building as organic as its wines, and Michel-Schlumberger produces some of the best cabernet in a valley otherwise dominated by zinfandel. Cross over into neighboring Alexander Valley, where cabernet is king. Visit Alexander Valley Vineyards, one of the most historic in the valley. That evening, drive south to Saratoga in the Santa Cruz Mountains (3 hours).

DAY 7

From Saratoga, drive northwest to the wineries of Monte Bello Road, stopping off the see the peacocks at the rustic Picchetti Winery before continuing up to the highest ridge at Ridge Vineyards, maker of some of the best Santa Cruz cabernets and home to stunning views. Loop back through Saratoga and up U.S. 9 to Skyline Boulevard. Turn left on Skyline and take it all the way to its narrow, winding end (30 minutes), then turn right on Bear Creek Road. The first winery is David Bruce, which makes outstanding pinot noirs from virtually all the best pinot-growing regions of California. Continue west, visiting the palatial Byington Vineyard & Winery, until you reach the small mountain town of Boulder Creek, an ideal place for a late lunch. Drive a little farther north to Big Basin Redwoods State Park, an 18,000-acre wilderness of forests, ridges, streams, and waterfalls that is a hiking mecca. Alternatively, drive south from Boulder Creek through Felton to Santa Cruz (45 minutes) and get the adrenaline pumping on the roller coasters at the Beach Boardwalk before kicking back and watching the sun set over the ocean from one of the many seafood restaurants on the wharf.

Most wineries make a whole host of wines, but many are particularly well known for just one or two varietals. In addition, certain grapes grow best in specific parts of the Wine Country, so planning a trip to taste a particular style of wine can mean focusing on just one or two regions.

If you're a fan of a particular type of wine, it's worth planning a trip to the regions that specialize in it. Some wines, like pinot noir for example, are best in cooler regions suited to growing that grape, such as the Russian River Valley, Carneros, or the Santa Cruz Mountains. Grapes for other wines, like cabernet sauvignon, can be grown almost anywhere, creating countless styles that reflect the growing conditions in each location.

Classic Cabernets

Cabernet sauvignon is the king of California wines, and the Napa and Sonoma Valleys are where some of the best Californian cabernets are made. Some classic examples can be sampled in just a 10-mile drive that also takes in some of the best scenery in Wine Country. Limit yourself to just four of these wineries and the trip can easily be completed in a day.

Start in the eastern hills of the Napa Valley in the Stags Leap District, where beautifully structured cabernets are made. Make an appointment for a tour at Shafer Vineyards, tucked away in its own private canyon, where you might be lucky enough to taste its Hillside Select cabernet. A short drive away is Stags' Leap Wine Cellars, home to one of the most famous cabernet vineyards in the valley. That vineyard produced the wine that beat the best in the world in the famous Paris tasting of 1976, and it still makes outstanding wine today.

Drive west to Rutherford, where bigger, bolder cabernets are laced with the appellation's distinct flavor of "Rutherford dust" a term made famous by the valley's most famous winemaker, André Tchelistcheff, who helped put the historic Beaulieu Vineyard on the world's wine maps. Not far away, the equally historic Niebaum-Coppola Estate produces the great Rubicon wine from its Rutherford-area vineyards as well as

one of the best winery shows in the valley, courtesy of owner and Hollywood director Francis Ford Coppola.

From Rutherford, drive north to St. Helena, stopping for a takeout lunch at the bistro Market on Main Street before heading west on Madrona Road and up Spring Mountain Road into the Spring Mountain appellation.

The road winds up the mountain, through for-

© PHILIP GOLDSMITH

the Stags Leap District, home of blockbuster cabernets

ests and past steep vineyards until reaching the summit at **Pride Mountain Vineyards,** an ideal place for a picnic with views of both the Napa and Sonoma Valleys. A taste of the elegant cabernet up here will reveal just how different these highly extracted mountain wines can be from their valley-floor competitors.

From Pride Mountain, continue west and drop down into the Sonoma Valley, turning left on Calistoga Road and heading south toward Kenwood and **Chateau St. Jean.** Sit on the reserve tasting room patio and watch the sun set over the valley while sipping the exquisite Cinq Cepages bordeaux blend.

Pleasures of Pinot

Santa Barbara County in Southern California might have had the best pinot publicity in recent years from the movie *Sideways,* but the cooler parts of Northern California are home to arguably the best pinot noirs in the state. In just a day or two, you can experience just how diverse and complex the wines made from this fussy little grape can really be.

In cool **Carneros,** discover how not only the region but also the vine clone can subtly affect the wine at **Carneros Creek Winery.** One of the winery's founders was a pinot pioneer, and the winery makes not only vineyard-designate pinot noir, but even wine from specific clones of the vine.

Carneros is also a big champagne-producing region, and pinot noir is one of the most im-

portant champagne grapes. At the palatial **Domaine Carneros** winery learn how champagne is made on an educational tour, then sit out on the terrace and enjoy the brut cuvée, a bubbly made with 65 percent pinot noir, followed by the winery's flagship Avant Garde pinot noir, a Carneros classic.

From Carneros, head north to Sonoma, stopping at the **Basque Boulangerie Café** on historic Sonoma Plaza for a simple lunch before continuing to Kenwood. **Landmark Vineyards** is worth a stop to taste its highly regarded Kastania and Grand Detour pinot noirs, sourced from coastal vineyards.

Continue west through Santa Rosa and on into the Russian River Valley, another of California's great pinot-producing appellations. Try the wines from one of the valley's best pinot noir vineyards, Dutton Ranch, at the **Sebastopol Vineyards** winery in Graton. A little farther north, the **Hartford Family Winery** is as beautiful a location as any to taste some highly praised, vineyard-designate Russian River pinots.

If there's time, cross the river to the **Davis Bynum** winery, founded by a former journalist in the 1970s in an old hop kiln building. Bynum's vineyard-designate pinot noirs are some of the best in this area.

Finish the day with a sumptuous dinner among the redwoods at the **Applewood Inn** just south of Guerneville, where the wine list is full of wonderful pinot noirs to pair with exquisite local cuisine.

A Romantic Weekend

What better way to spend a long weekend in the Wine Country than by experiencing the best champagne, food, art, and pampering that the Napa and Sonoma Valleys have to offer. This long weekend trip illustrates the diversity and hedonism of Wine Country, and most locations are within easy drives of the countless inns, B&Bs, and resorts in the southern end of the Napa Valley.

Depending on what time your day gets started, there are plenty of opportunities to stop in at additional wineries in the Napa and Sonoma Valleys or Carneros. Alternatively, cut out a few wineries from the itinerary along the way and spend more time simply soaking up the atmosphere or soaking in a mud bath.

DAY 1

Get acquainted with the Napa Valley, its history, and its wines at the **Napa Valley Museum** just outside Yountville before toasting your arrival in the Wine Country with some luxuriously rich blanc de noirs champagne at nearby **Domaine Chandon**. Have lunch at the winery's renowned restaurant, then take a tour or simply explore the sculpture-filled gardens.

In the evening, head down to the old redbrick Napa Mill on the river in downtown Napa for a classic Wine Country dinner on the patio at **Celadon**, followed by an after-dinner cocktail and dance at **DG's** jazz and blues bar right next door.

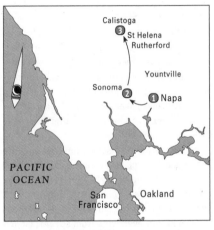

DAY 2

Drive south into Carneros to the **di Rosa Preserve** and see some whimsical contemporary art at the Gatehouse Gallery. Before you get to Napa, make an appointment for one of the morning tours of all the galleries and beautiful gardens that are home to one of California's biggest collections of contemporary art.

Afterward, head across the road to the palatial **Domaine Carneros** and contemplate art with a glass of fruity Brut Rosé champagne and hors d'oeuvres on the terrace overlooking the vineyards, or in front of a blazing fire on a chilly winter day.

Drive a little farther west to Sonoma and enjoy a light gourmet lunch before spending the afternoon exploring the historic sights and boutique shops around pretty **Sonoma Plaza**, perhaps even taking a stroll past flower-filled front yards to the **Sebastiani** winery to taste some of the more unusual Italian-varietal wines.

In the evening, enjoy a glass of wine while watching the plaza's wildlife—from ducks to humans—at the **Ledson Hotel** before driving north for dinner in Glen Ellen at the cozy and romantic bistro **Saffron**. If you're in the mood for some nighttime stargazing, drive east from Glen Ellen up into the dark Mayacamas Mountains on Trin-

© PHILIP GOLDSMITH

Domaine Carneros, a taste of French glamour in Carneros

ity Road, then descend back into the Napa Valley via the Oakville Grade.

DAY 3

Begin the day with breakfast or brunch at Gordon's Café & Wine Bar in Yountville. If it's not too late in the morning, drive north to the winery that has come to symbolize the Napa Valley like no other—the Robert Mondavi Winery. Be sure to take one of the regular tours to see the best of the sprawling mission-style buildings and taste some classic Napa wines.

Continue north to the V. Sattui Winery just outside St. Helena to buy a cheap, fruity bottle of Gamay Rouge and picnic supplies (including a corkscrew and picnic cups) before continuing north to the Bothe-Napa Valley State Park, where you can be in the redwoods within minutes and find a perfect picnic spot.

After a relaxing lunch, and perhaps a short hike to appreciate some of the park's valley views, it's time for some pampering, Calistoga style. Drive north to the famous spa town in time for your appointment for a couple's restorative mud bath at the Lincoln Avenue Spa. Since it's a wine-themed weekend, choose the antioxidant-laden mud containing wine, grape seed oil, and green tea.

Later in the afternoon, head south from Calistoga along the pretty Silverado Trail to Rutherford and the Mumm Napa Valley champagne house. There's usually a fascinating exhibition of art or photography that can be enjoyed with glass of bubbly in hand.

Stay in Rutherford or return later in the evening for the culinary highlight: a sunset dinner overlooking the valley at the Auberge du Soleil resort, high up in the hills. Book well in advance to secure a table on the terrace for a memorable experience.

More Than Wine

Tasting wines is certainly not the only reason to visit the Wine Country. To lure more people through their doors, wineries have become skilled at differentiating themselves from their neighbors and competitors using attractions besides wine, which is great for you. Take an entertaining tour, explore the region's history, peruse famous artwork, or simply learn more about wine. The Wine Country also excels at producing fine food. There was a rich agricultural heritage in the region even before the modern wine industry took root, and food lovers will find ingredients to make their mouths water.

Standout Tours

Wineries in the Napa Valley lay on some pretty impressive tours of their equally impressive properties. This is the place to go for the most ostentatious tour to accompany the pretty good wines.

Architecture buffs should check out the free tour at the futuristic Opus One winery to see the opulence that comes from being created by two of the world's most famous winemakers. Farther north in the valley, the angular Clos Pegase winery has a bolder, more brash postmodernist style. Tours here take in not only the architecture but the founder's big art collection.

At the historic Far Niente winery, car fanatics can admire the private vintage car collection of late owner Gil Nickel and visit the huge network of caves under the main house. For the ultimate showoff tour, the Niebaum-Coppola Estate features a museum devoted not only to the winery's storied history, but also to the Hollywood history of its current owner, Francis Ford Coppola.

Getting to some wineries can be as much fun as touring them. To visit Long Meadow Ranch high in the hills above Rutherford, visitors are driven to its pastoral location in a curious-looking Swiss military vehicle called

© PHILIP GOLDSMITH

Clos Pegase winery, bold architecture in a sea of vines

a Pinzgauer. To reach the monastery-like Sterling Vineyards perched on a knoll outside Calistoga, visitors board gondolas more at home at a ski resort. Once you're at the top, the self-guided tour is unique.

History Highlights

Some of the most fascinating wine-related history can be found in the town of Sonoma. This is where the State of California was born and where modern Northern California wine-making got its start. Rent a bike at Sonoma Cyclery to visit some of the historic wineries at the edge of town.

The Buena Vista Winery and neighboring Bartholomew Park Winery are both on land originally farmed by wine-making pioneer Agoston Haraszthy. Both have fascinating, small museums telling Haraszthy's story, and both have plenty to keep history buffs happy. The Gundlach Bundschu Winery was winning awards for its wines more than 100 years ago, and Sebastiani Vineyards & Winery was founded in 1904 by Italian immigrant Samuele Sebastiani, who also built many buildings in the town, including the Sebastiani Theater on the plaza.

Explore other historic sites around the Sonoma Plaza, some dating from the early 1800s. Mission San Francisco de Solano was California's 21st (and last) Spanish mission. The Sonoma Barracks, dating from the 1840s, once housed soldiers of the Mexican army. Their commander, General Vallejo, built his opulent house, Lachryma Montis, nearby.

Wine Education

Many wineries offer tours of their wine-making facilities, but some teach more about wine and how it's made. For a thorough understanding of how to appreciate wine, sign up for one of the Saturday morning Wine Basics classes at Goosecross Cellars in Yountville and do some swirling and sniffing on the lawn next to the vineyards.

Champagne houses often have the most educational tours to help visitors understand the complex process of making sparkling wines. Just outside Calistoga, the historic Schramsberg winery offers one of the more entertaining and educational champagne tours through its spooky Victorian caves. It finishes with a tasting of the J. Schram champagne, considered by some to be California's best.

Visiting smaller, appointment-only wineries can also be rewarding. Owner and winemaker Chris Loxton might have time to take you on a tour of his Loxton Cellars vineyards in the Sonoma Valley. If you can find the Medlock Ames winery in the Chalk Hill region near Healdsburg, Ames Morrison would be happy to take you on a tour of the vineyard and the modern winery building to explain how everything is done.

Culinary Adventures

Fresh produce is the key to Wine Country cuisine. Visit one of the many farms that sell seasonal fruit and vegetables, from the small Rutherford Gardens in the Napa Valley to one of the many fruit farms in the Russian River Valley, including Kozlowski Farms and Twin Hill Ranch. Many of the region's top chefs shop at farmers markets. Two of the best are held weekly in Healdsburg and Sonoma during the summer and fall.

Discover that there are potentially as many styles of olive oil as there are wines at the tasting bars of the Olive Press in the Sonoma Valley or at the St. Helena Olive Oil Company in the Napa Valley. Staff at both will help you learn how different olives produce oils with different tastes—from grassy styles perfect for salads to richly flavored oils that can add strong flavors to almost any dish.

Some of the secrets to cooking with these ingredients can be learned at the Culinary Institute of America in the imposing Greystone Winery building near St. Helena. It is the leading West Coast cooking school and offers several cooking demonstrations a day Friday–Monday.

Much of the Wine Country is rural, and excellent opportunities for outdoor recreation abound. Escaping the winery crowds in summer is surprisingly easy in one of the many parks and preserves, or even on the rivers and lakes of the region. The Santa Cruz Mountains and Russian River Valley have perhaps the most open space of all, with giant redwood forests and hundreds of miles of hiking and biking trails weaving through trees, past waterfalls, and over ridges with spectacular views. But the rest of northern Sonoma is also blessed with great swaths of wilderness to explore, and even the crowded Napa Valley has some outstanding parks.

Armstrong Redwoods State Reserve

This 800-acre forested reserve is just a few miles from the bars and restaurants of Guerneville in the Russian River Valley, yet offers some of the most diverse hiking in the area. Take a stroll through the cool, damp redwoods and take in some local history on the Pioneer Trail or a two-hour hike on the East Ridge or Pool Ridge Trails.

The more adventurous can drive or hike from Armstrong reserve up to the 5,700-acre wilderness of Austin Creek State Recreation Area. Camp at either the main Bullfrog Pond campground or hike about four miles to one of the primitive creekside campgrounds.

Big Basin Redwoods State Park

Stretching over 18,000 acres of the Santa Cruz Mountains, Big Basin is perhaps the ultimate outdoor location in the Wine Country. Anyone exploring the mountain wineries or en route from Saratoga to Santa Cruz can stop by for a quick taste of what this park is all about on the short Redwood Trail, which passes by the 329-foot-tall Mother of the Forest tree.

Otherwise this is a park for adventurers. A half-day hike on the Meteor Trail takes you to a spectacular outlook 1,600 feet up with views all the way to the ocean. The best full-day hike takes in three picturesque waterfalls, including Berry Creek Falls and Golden Falls, named for the gold-colored sandstone rock it cascades over.

Camp at one of the many hike-in campsites in the park, such as the Sunset Camp not far from the falls. Alternatively, stay in a tent cabin at the main campground near park headquarters. Despite the perfect setting, backcountry camping is not permitted.

Swimming and Boating

The Russian River has plenty of beaches, most unmarked but still easily accessible from the road. The best place to swim is in the roped-off area at Memorial Beach in Healdsburg, while the best place for a summer beach party is Guerneville's Johnson's Beach. In between there are countless other beaches, some clothing-optional, with swimming holes, including the family-friendly Sunset Beach near Rio Nido.

Another way to access Russian River beaches is by renting an aluminum canoe at Burkes Canoe Trips in Forestville and paddling up- or downstream through the forests and vineyards. The more adventurous can rent a sporty kayak at Russian River Outfitters in Duncans Mills and paddle all the way to the ocean.

Anyone in the Alexander Valley or Dry Creek Valley wanting a cool plunge should head for Lake Sonoma at the top of Dry Creek Valley. The

COURTESY OF THE SKYLINE WILDNERNESS PARK

Get out of the car and explore the mountains and parks of Wine Country on a bike.

lake is a recreation hub for the area, with several swimming beaches and powerboat rentals available at the marina.

Biking

Several parts of Wine Country offer relatively flat and quiet roads well suited to biking between wineries. The Dry Creek Valley in northern Sonoma is compact, easy to navigate, and full of wineries, though it tends to get hot in the summer. Rent bikes in nearby Healdsburg. Just as flat, but a little cooler and with longer distances between wineries, is Carneros. Rent bikes in Sonoma and take a 35-mile loop past some of the best wineries in the wetlands.

Experienced mountain bikers have plenty of world-class trails to choose from. In the Sonoma Valley, many head for the trails of Annadel State Park, including the fast downhill single-track Lawndale Trail and the rocky, technical Orchard Trail. Just south of Napa, Skyline Wilderness Park has hosted several mountain-biking world cup competitions, and much of the competition loop can still be ridden today, including the Manzanita Trail, which was described as one of the best single-tracks on the world cup circuit.

Explore
Northern California
Wine Country

The Napa Valley

Mention California wines and most people will think of the Napa Valley, usually abbreviated to simply "Napa." Mention that you're writing a travel guide to Wine Country and almost everyone will ask about your favorite Napa wineries. There's no escaping it—the Napa Valley is regarded as the center of everything wine in California, much as Sonoma, Santa Barbara, or Mendocino might jump up and down for attention.

Napa put California wine firmly on the international map in the 1970s with the oft-mentioned Paris tasting of 1976, which pitted the valley's wines in a blind tasting against France's best. It led the premium wine revolution in the 1980s and saw the building of some of California's most ostentatious wineries in the 1990s. This little valley is now home to more than a quarter of all the wineries in California, despite the fact that it accounts for only about 5 percent of all the wine made in the state. The statistics speak for themselves—the Napa Valley turns out some of the best wine in California.

The valley is also a marketing manager's dream. Natural beauty, colorful history, some of the biggest names in world wine, and $200 bottles of cabernet all serve to draw hordes of visitors—almost five million a year at last count. They in turn are entertained by top chefs, luxury pampering, and lavish winery

© PHILIP GOLDSMITH

Must-Sees

Look for M to find the sights and activities you can't miss and N for the best dining and lodging.

M **Darioush:** In a valley full of palaces to wine, the Khaledi brothers created one of the most unique. Their sandstone palace, inspired by their Persian roots, is fit for a sultan (page 32).

M **The Hess Collection:** Located in the mountains above Napa, this part gallery, part winery brings new meaning to the expression "the art of wine making" (page 34).

M **Copia:** There's a cornucopia of culinary fun to experience at the country's first museum devoted to food and wine, from tastings to seminars and interactive exhibits (page 36).

M **Frog's Leap Winery:** Revel in the laid-back vibe at this organic winery. In addition to good wine, there's an organic garden and plenty of places to just chill out in the sun (page 63).

M **Pride Mountain Vineyards:** Straddling the Napa and Sonoma border, this mountaintop winery has some of the best views in the valley and some of the best mountain wines (page 75).

M **Culinary Institute of America:** The West Coast's next star chefs are born inside this fortresslike former winery, and you can get a taste of their training at regular cooking demonstrations (page 78).

M **Bothe-Napa Valley State Park:** Take a break and stroll back in time through the redwoods in this gem of a park (page 80).

M **Schramsberg:** If you plan to visit just one champagne cellar, why not make it the most historic one in the valley? Take a tour through the spooky cellars once visited by Robert Louis Stevenson (page 90).

M **Sharpsteen Museum:** Learn about Calistoga's early days at this quirky little museum next to one of the original cottages from the first-ever hot springs resort in the town (page 93).

The Napa Valley

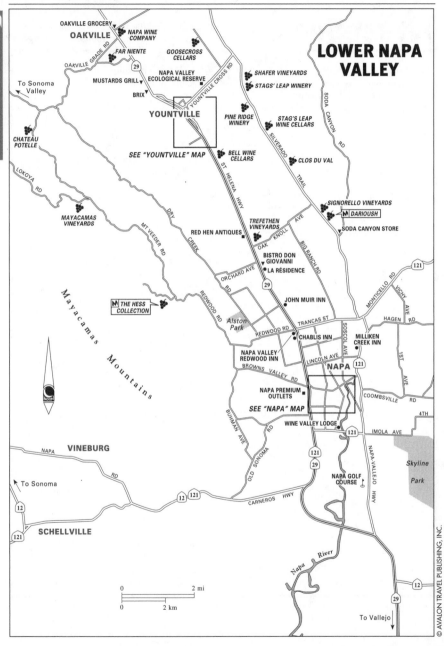

OAKVILLE GROCERY
OAKVILLE
NAPA WINE
COMPANY
FAR NIENTE
GOOSECROSS
CELLARS
OAKVILLE GRADE RD
29
MUSTARDS GRILL
NAPA VALLEY
ECOLOGICAL RESERVE
To Sonoma
Valley
BRIX
YOUNTVILLE
YOUNTVILLE CROSS RD
SHAFER VINEYARDS
STAGS' LEAP WINERY

LOWER NAPA
VALLEY

PINE RIDGE
WINERY
STAG'S LEAP
WINE CELLARS
SODA CANYON RD
CHATEAU
POTELLE
SEE "YOUNTVILLE" MAP
BELL WINE
CELLARS
ST. HELENA HWY
SILVERADO TRAIL
CLOS DU VAL
LOKOYA RD
SIGNORELLO VINEYARDS
DARIOUSH
MAYACAMAS
VINEYARDS
DRY CREEK
MT VEEDER RD
RED HEN ANTIQUES
TREFETHEN
VINEYARDS
OAK KNOLL AVE
BIG RANCH RD
SODA CANYON STORE
BISTRO DON
GIOVANNI
LA RÉSIDENCE
ORCHARD AVE
29
REDWOOD RD
THE HESS
COLLECTION
JOHN MUIR INN
MONTICELLO RD
121
VICHY AVE
Mayacamas Mountains
Alston
Park
REDWOOD RD
TRANCAS ST
HAGEN RD
CHABLIS INN
SOSCOL AVE
MILLIKEN
CREEK INN
NAPA VALLEY
REDWOOD INN
LINCOLN AVE
NAPA
121
Moon
BROWNS VALLEY RD
1ST AVE
BUHMAN AVE
OLD SONOMA RD
NAPA PREMIUM
OUTLETS
SEE "NAPA" MAP
COOMBSVILLE RD
WINE VALLEY LODGE
121
IMOLA AVE
4TH
VINEBURG
NAPA RD
Skyline
Park
To Sonoma
121
NAPA GOLF
COURSE
NAPA-VALLEJO HWY
12
121
12
121
CARNEROS HWY
Napa River
SCHELLVILLE
12
29
29
To Vallejo

0   2 mi
0   2 km

© AVALON TRAVEL PUBLISHING, INC.

shows like no others in California, or probably anywhere else in the world.

It can all seem a bit like a giant wine theme park at times, especially when lining up at yet another ticket booth for the privilege of being herded around another winery by guides who are probably as bored as they look. It's not a great stretch to imagine that one day there will be giant gates at either end of the valley where all-inclusive passes will be sold to the "Greatest Wine Show on Earth" (the Sonoma Valley would be the parking lot if some competitive types had their way).

Although many visitors flock lemming-like to the same big wineries, there are hundreds of others to choose from in the valley, big and small, glamorous and rustic. Such diversity is one of Napa Valley's big draws.

Art lovers could easily spend an entire vacation visiting the many wineries with art or sculpture displays. Photosensitive souls can hunt down all the wineries with cool, dark underground caves. Architecture buffs will have a field day at some of the more outlandish wineries.

And that's before even considering wine itself. The valley is home to boutique wineries, making just a few hundred cases of wine a year, to corporate behemoths turning out millions. The multitude of microclimates has given rise to a patchwork of 14 distinct appellations (and counting) where just about every major type of grape can be grown. Although this is a red-wine-lover's paradise, there's bound to be a wine here for almost every palate.

The valley's diversity extends well beyond wine: At one end of the valley are the hot springs and spas of Calistoga, while Napa at the other end contains some big-city entertainment. In between, nature offers plenty of diversions from wine, and plenty of fodder for some restaurants that would put many in world capitals to shame.

The locals are remarkably sanguine about the semipermanent invasion of their valley. Clearly, they are wise enough not to discourage the hands that ultimately feed them. But they also get to experience the beauty and di-

versity of the valley, the quality of the food, and the strong sense of community when the rest of us are long gone.

And, of course, they get to toast their good fortune with some of the best wines in the world.

ORIENTATION

The Napa Valley, including Carneros (see the *Southern Sonoma* chapter), is roughly 35 miles long with two main roads running up each side of the valley and about half a dozen roads traversing the 2–4 miles between them. As far as major world wine-making regions go, this is baby-sized, so don't be intimidated.

Just north of Carneros is the city of **Napa** itself, the biggest settlement in the valley, home to many of the workers that make the wine industry function. It's a bit of a sprawl and has traditionally been bypassed by tourists speeding to the big-name wineries farther north, but Napa has recently made an effort to cash in on its Victorian history and riverside setting.

There are decades of neglect to counter, however, and the downtown revitalization is definitely a work in progress, still lacking the compactness and style of other Wine Country destination towns like Sonoma, Healdsburg, or even St. Helena farther north.

From Napa, the two main valley roads begin. The St. Helena Highway (U.S. 29) is the well-beaten path up the valley. It passes the town of Yountville, dominated by shops, restaurants, and inns, then whistles past sleepy **Rutherford** before hitting what has become almost the spiritual heart of the valley, **St. Helena.** This is the town that all others in Wine Country aspire to be. Pretty, upscale, full of boutiques and restaurants, yet still a fairly down-to-earth, functional place—except on those weekends when the world comes knocking and traffic slows to a crawl.

With St. Helena and its big-name wineries the main draw of the valley, rural tranquillity quickly returns as the St. Helena Highway continues north to the narrow top of the valley, where sleepy **Calistoga** has an almost frontier-town feel to it—seemingly torn between

NAPA'S SILLY-MONEY WINES

At the Napa Valley Wine Auction in 2004, three bottles of Screaming Eagle sold for $220,000. They were three-liter bottles, but that still works out to more than $18,000 for a regular bottle. Granted, the auction is a charity event and therefore encourages big spending for a good cause, but there are probably no other wines that would be bid so high, whatever the occasion.

Make that *few* other wines. There were 10 bottles of Harlan Estate wine that sold for $180,000. And then there were seven bottles of Dalle Valle Vineyards wine that sold for $150,000. Just those three lots illustrate the power of Napa's so-called cult wines to open the wallets of both serious collectors and those simply with more money than they know what to do with.

The cult wine phenomenon started in the early 1990s and reached a crescendo during the dot-com boom years when a lot of people really did have more money than they knew what to do with. They bought the beautifully made, limited-production Napa Valley cabernets, like those from Screaming Eagle and Harlan Estate, probably as much to gain the cachet of owning something so rare as to resell for a profit a few years later. As with any rare commodity, lots of bidders will push up the price.

The dot-com bubble burst, but the cult wine bubble never really did. Retailers report that sales of such silly-money wines remain as solid as their prices. There's no doubting that they are good wines, made by some of the best winemakers and sourced from some of the best vineyards. Whether they're worth hundreds of dollars or more is a question often asked though ultimately somewhat irrelevant because there are plenty of people still willing to pay and to wait years to get on the exclusive mailing lists to even get a chance to pay.

A little more troubling is that the cult term is now bandied about a little too casually. It is now commonly used as a marketing tool or for bragging rights, so it's no surprise that calling even the Screaming Eagles of the world a cult wine these days is as likely to elicit a roll of the eyes as an opening of the wallet.

maintaining its slumber and being awoken by attracting more tourists to its up-and-coming wineries and famous volcanic hot springs.

Calistoga is also where the other main valley road, the Silverado Trail, ends. Named for a silver mine that it once served north of Calistoga, it runs from Napa along the foot of the eastern hills and is the shortcut used to get up and down the valley by locals in the summer when the other side of the valley is clogged. Anyone in a hurry to get to a spa appointment in Calistoga or a restaurant in Napa should seriously consider cutting across the valley to the Silverado Trail if there is heavy traffic on the St. Helena Highway.

This undulating, winding two-lane road remains almost eerily quiet at times, and feels like it's in another valley altogether. It's a road along which smaller wineries turn out some of the best wines in the valley with none of the hoopla of the big showoffs farther west. It's also a road down which serious wine lovers might prefer to travel, sampling famous cabernet sauvignons in the Stags Leap or Rutherford appellations before heading up into the hills to some hidden gems on Howell Mountain or in the rural Chiles Valley.

Napa Valley Wines

The Napa Valley appellation probably has more microclimates and soil types along its 35-mile length than any other valley in the Wine Country, and this is what makes it so important.

As you're driving from the city of Napa up to Calistoga in the middle of summer, the temperature can rise by several degrees, though it's far from an even change. On the valley floor, the hills around Calistoga and in the Stags Leap appellation farther south create their own localized climates, as do the slopes and canyons rising up the mountain ranges on each side of the valley.

Geologists have identified a staggering 33 different types of soil in the valley, laid down over millions of years by volcanoes, rivers, and the earth's shifting crust. The combined soils and microclimates create a patchwork of growing conditions that could keep winemakers happy for centuries more, and that is why there are so many subappellations in the Napa Valley.

The Napa Valley north of Carneros is predominantly a red-wine-growing region, due primarily to the hot climate that ripens just about anything on a vine. White grapes can get by in cooler climates because they generally don't need to get as ripe to make great wines. Red grapes, on the other hand, need the hot sun to get sweet enough, otherwise they'll end up creating the sort of wine that strips the lining off the inside of your throat.

None more so than the one red grape the Napa is most famous for—cabernet sauvignon. In 2003, there were about 44,000 acres of vineyards in Napa County, about three-quarters of which were planted with red grape varietals. About half that red grape acreage was cabernet. That means cabernet accounts for 40 percent of all the vineyards in Napa County, and probably closer to 50 percent of all the vineyards in the Napa Valley north of Carneros, where pinot noir and chardonnay are the more dominant grapes.

That's not to say that other wines are not important here. Far from it. The Napa Valley is where some of California's most distinct chardonnay and sauvignon blanc are produced, together with increasing amounts of syrah, sangiovese, and many other minor varietals. But cabernet always has, and probably always will, dominate the scene.

Most wineries in the valley own or buy from vineyards all over the valley, however, so white wine drinkers need not despair. There will usually be plenty of whites on offer, even at wineries in the cabernet-dominated appellations like Rutherford and Stags Leap.

PLANNING YOUR TIME

So how can visitors make sense of all those wineries and avoid all the crowds? It's a $10,000 question with about 10,000 different answers. Many visitors seem to follow a similar pattern, never making it much farther north than St. Helena and sticking to the western side of the valley. If you can avoid that pattern, you're halfway to lowering your blood pressure.

The other key to enjoying the valley rather than being frustrated by it is plenty of planning. There's so much to do and so many wineries to visit that anyone simply turning up without even a vague plan will end up with a headache even before drinking too much wine in the sun. Visitors can get away with no planning in many other parts of Wine Country but not here.

Research the type of wine that wineries make before choosing which to visit, especially if you're not a big red-wine drinker. This is, after all, the land of endless cabernet sauvignon, but it is also a land where plenty of stunning white wines, including champagne, are made. And if you are a big cabernet drinker, this can be the place to learn much more about the king of wines—how and why a Spring Mountain cabernet is different from a Rutherford cabernet, for example.

Alternatively, pick a non-wine-related theme for a day of touring. Wineries in Napa have necessarily become adept at distinguishing themselves from all their competitors to try to attract increasingly jaded visitors, a form of Wine Country evolution. Some rely on the reputation of their wines, others on art, caves, car collections, architecture, gardens, tours, history—the list is almost endless, and the marketing people have endless employment opportunities.

If the crowds or choices all get too much, simply head for the hills, where healthy doses of nature help make the hidden wineries in the Mt. Veeder, Spring Mountain, or Chiles Valley appellations that much more enjoyable.

Or just try to avoid the peak season, which roughly runs July–October and brings peak crowds and peak daytime temperatures. March–May is perhaps the best time to visit, when the wet winter weather is finally drying out, the hills are green, the creeks flowing, and the vineyards are full of vivid yellow wild mustard or the bright green of fresh vine buds.

TOURS

One way of visiting wineries and not having to worry about traffic, drinking, or cooking an expensive wine in a sun-baked car is to take a daylong organized wine tour. Someone else does the driving, you can drink until you can no longer stand, and any precious wine purchases will get transported back to your hotel probably in better shape than you.

Another advantage is that the local tour guides are knowledgeable about the valley, the wineries, and often about wines, too, making an organized tour an option worth considering if you have no idea where to start.

There are two tour companies, each offering different experiences. The **Napa Winery Shuttle** (707/257-1950, www.wineshuttle.com) is basically a hop-on, hop-off minibus that picks up at any of a long list of local hotels at about 10 A.M. (though they can often pick up at any hotel not on the list) and runs among 10 different wineries between Oakville and St. Helena, plus a couple of Yountville restaurants for those who want a sit-down lunch. Those wineries represent a good cross section of the valley and include a handful of smaller producers, a champagne house, and some of the big names, including Mondavi, Niebaum-Coppola, and Beaulieu Vineyard. Visit as many or as few of them as you want during the day for $45 a person.

Beau Wine Tours (707/257-0887 or 800/387-2328, www.beauwinetours.com) is more of a custom touring company, and often the owner of the limos seen parked at some of the bigger wineries. Rent a chauffeured car, van, or limousine for 3–14 people for $50–135 an hour plus tax, tip, and (depending on gas prices) a fuel surcharge, and plan your own itinerary. The only thing to consider is that the size of the stretch limos and vans means they sometimes cannot visit smaller wineries at all, or only by prior arrangement. Beau Wine Tours has plenty of knowledge of the valley, however, and can offer plenty of advice. It also offers private, pre-planned, day-long tours starting and finishing in either the Napa Valley or San Francisco.

Napa Valley Wine Train

The age of the steam trains that first brought the masses to the valley's Victorian spas and early wineries has long gone, but a tiny reminder remains in the Napa Valley Wine Train (1275 McKinstry St., Napa, 707/253-2111 or 800/427-4124, www.winetrain.com), kept alive by what the valley does best—good food and wine.

The idea of being cooped up on a glorious fall day watching the vineyards and wineries through the windows of an old Pullman rail car might not seem appealing, but it's a little better than it sounds. The only problem is that it eats into your day. Think of it as taking a four-hour lunch or dinner at a gourmet, if slightly unusual, restaurant. The food is beautifully prepared, the wine first class, and the restaurant dripping with brass and mahogany. No Amtrak comparisons allowed.

Lunch and dinner trips are offered daily with an additional brunch excursion on weekends. Rates range from $75 for the Gourmet Express brunch menu up to $140 for a five-course dinner with specially paired wines. In reviving the old rail cars the Wine Train also revived the old railroad class system too—each car caters to a different class of diner, so you won't be jealously eyeing your neighbor's five-course spread when you've already polished off your three courses.

The train runs 20 miles from Napa up to St. Helena and back. Reservations are essential.

GETTING THERE

As with the Sonoma Valley, there were far more ways to get to the Napa Valley a century ago, when trains and riverboats brought the visitors and goods that made the valley so successful. The car has long since become the main transportation mode, though the more adventurous can still get here on public transport.

By Car

The Napa Valley is almost the same driving distance from three major international airports—Oakland, San Francisco, and Sacramento. Driving from them to the city of Napa itself will take 1–2 hours, depending on traffic, though from downtown San Francisco and Oakland it's closer to an hour of driving time.

The most direct route from Oakland and Sacramento is on I-80 (west from Sacramento, east from Oakland), exiting at American Canyon Road, which connects with U.S. 29, which runs north into Napa. From Sacramento, a slightly more direct route is to exit at Jamieson Canyon Road (U.S. 12), a little farther north of American Canyon. This also heads west to U.S. 29.

From the San Francisco airport and city (especially downtown), it takes about the same amount of time to drive across the Bay Bridge to I-80 and north to Napa as it does to go the more usual and prettier route through Marin. This route crosses the Golden Gate Bridge on U.S. 101 to Marin County, past Novato then west on U.S. 37, which links with U.S. 121 though Carneros, past the turnoff to the Sonoma Valley, and eventually to U.S. 29 just south of Napa.

The Napa Valley is also easily accessible from other parts of the Wine Country thanks to the numerous roads that cross the Mayacamas Mountains down the western side of the valley.

From the Sonoma Valley, just north of Glen Ellen, Trinity Road winds its way east into the mountains, becoming Dry Creek Road in the Mt. Veeder appellation, before coming down into the Napa Valley to Oakville as the Oakville Grade. Farther north in the Sonoma Valley, just east of Santa Rosa, Calistoga Road heads to the hills and eventually to Calistoga, or turn off on St. Helena Road after about three miles to cross into the Napa Valley down through the Spring Mountain appellation and into St. Helena.

From the Russian River Valley, just north of Santa Rosa, take Mark West Springs Road east, eventually turning onto Porter Creek Road, which leads down into Calistoga. And from the Alexander Valley, U.S. 128 runs south through Knights Valley to Calistoga.

Try not to be in a rush if you take these routes, because they are narrow, winding, and slow, but a lot of fun if time is not of the essence.

By Boat and Bus

The most unusual way to get to the valley without driving, short of an epic bicycle ride, is on the **Baylink Ferry** from San Francisco via Vallejo. The speedy catamarans leave San Francisco's Ferry Building about every hour 7 A.M.–10 P.M. during the week and every couple of hours 9 A.M.–10 P.M. on weekends for the 55-minute crossing to Vallejo, which is about 12 miles south of Napa. The one-way fare is $9.50. For a detailed seasonal schedule, contact Baylink Ferries (707/643-3779 or 877/643-3779, www.baylinkferry.com).

From the Vallejo ferry terminal, route 10 of Napa Valley's **Vine** bus service runs directly to downtown Napa about every hour until 8 P.M. during the week, every two hours until 6:50 P.M. on Saturday, and just four times a day on Sunday with the first bus leaving at 10:15 A.M. and the last at 5:30 P.M. It's about a 65-minute journey to Napa (except for a few times of the day when the bus makes stops) and is a bargain at $1.50. Route 10 also continues to the valley through Yountville and St. Helena to Calistoga. For more information on schedules and routes contact Vine (707/255-7631 or 800/696-6443, www.napavalleyvine.net).

Taking the ferry and bus to the valley, then renting a bike in downtown Napa, St. Helena, or Calistoga for a couple of days, would certainly make for a memorable Wine Country experience.

GETTING AROUND

By Car

Seemingly everyone drives to the Napa Valley, so you'd think everything would be geared up for the cars transporting those five million annual visitors to this part of the world. Wrong! This is essentially agricultural land that its custodians battle to protect, so the mighty vine and strict planning laws limit a lot of development. Including, evidently, road widening.

The 28-mile drive from Napa to Calistoga up the St. Helena Highway takes about 45 minutes in the middle of a winter day. Try that same drive on a summer weekend or a weekday during the evening rush hour and it might take well over an hour, possibly longer.

The sheer volume of traffic is really what slows things down, especially around the destination town of St. Helena, but the traffic situation is not helped by the countless turnoffs for wineries from Rutherford to St. Helena. Make your life easier and use the empty middle lane of the road to turn left into wineries or when turning left out of wineries to merge into traffic. That's what it's there for.

That's when the Silverado Trail is worth discovering, though it too can get a little slow when some valley visitors are unfamiliar with its dips and bends or simply get lost. Usually, however, this is the domain of merciless local speed demons zipping up and down the valley at 60 mph, a feat sometimes possible even when the road through St. Helena across the valley is at a standstill.

Napa is the only city in the valley to have made an effort to smooth traffic flows with its brief stretch of freeway and frustrating one-way system downtown. Perhaps one day they'll build a monorail linking Napa and St. Helena, with stops for all the major wineries along the way. And perhaps one day snow will fall on the vines in August!

By Bike

Whether you plan a long bike ride up the Silverado Trail or a short hop around a handful of Rutherford-area wineries, there are places to rent bicycles up and down the valley. A couple of companies will do all the work for a bike tour, except the pedaling, for you.

St. Helena Cyclery (116 Main St., St. Helena, 707/963-7736, 9:30 A.M.–5:30 P.M. Mon.–Sat., 10 A.M.–5 P.M. Sun.) rents basic hybrid bikes for $10/hour or $30/day and more advanced bikes from $60/day but takes no reservations, so get there early. **Calistoga Bike Shop** (1318 Lincoln Ave., Calistoga, 707/942-9687 or 866/942-2453, 10 A.M.–6 P.M. daily, www.calistogabikeshop.com) does take reservations and rents hybrids for $25/day and both road and mountain bikes from $40/day.

To plan an entire vacation centered around biking in the valley, try **Getaway Adventures** (1117 Lincoln Ave., Calistoga, 707/568-3040 or 800/499-2453, www.getawayadventures.com), which offers day, weekend, and weeklong all-inclusive packages, including hotel, meals, bike, tour guide, and shuttle van. Weekend packages are $700–1,000, and four- to six-day packages range $1,000–2,300, with prices depending on both luxury and the number of days. They are usually offered once a month and take in the Napa Valley and parts of northern Sonoma. The day trips cost $115 and include the bike, helmet, water, lunch, and a guided tour of about five wineries in the Calistoga area.

Napa Valley Bike Tours (4080 Byway St. E., Napa, 707/255-3377 or 800/707-2453, www.napavalleybiketours.com), based at the other end of the valley, also offers three- and four-day all-inclusive packages that stay within Napa Valley. The two-night, three-day Romantic Getaway packages are $750–950, depending on accommodations and time of the week (weekends are more expensive), and the longer packages start at $715. Day tours are also offered at $115 for the day, lunch and group tour guide included. Plain old bike rentals to go it alone start at $10 per hour or $30 a day.

Napa and Vicinity

Many people bypass Napa, heading up to the middle of the valley to start their wine-tasting day, but there's plenty happening this far south as well. Napa is chock-full of tasting rooms, the city is bordered by one of the best mountain appellations in the valley, and the newest valley appellation is home to both historic and brand-new wineries.

Just north of the city of Napa is the newest of the Napa Valley's 14 appellations, **Oak Knoll.** As in the Yountville appellation farther north, the climate is a blend of the cooler weather in Carneros to the south of Napa and the hotter midvalley temperatures. Just about every major grape varietal is grown here, though the appellation is probably best known for whites, such as chardonnay and sauvignon blanc. Being such a new appellation it does not yet have much name recognition, so don't expect to see many wines with Oak Knoll identified on the label.

West of the Oak Knoll appellation is the **Mt. Veeder** appellation, stretching all the way from Napa up the middle of the valley on the slopes of the Mayacamas Mountains. A handful of wineries craft some delicately structured cabernets and age-worthy chardonnays from vines struggling away on the steep slopes.

TASTING ROOMS IN NAPA

You could spend a whole day, or even two, sampling wines from the dozen tasting rooms in the city of Napa itself—a process that's made a lot cheaper with the **Taste Napa Downtown Wine Tasting Card.** For $15 (available at all participating tasting rooms and shops), it is valid at all the bigger tasting rooms and many stores that offer wine tasting, including J.V. Wine and Spirits, Copia, and the Napa General Store.

If you taste all the wines offered at all the establishments, the cost of the card works out to about 10 cents per taste. Without it, tasting prices range from a couple of dollars up to $15 at the larger collectives (though you can keep the quality Riedel tasting glass at the Vintner's Collective). The three main tasting rooms are the only places to taste the wine of some of the valley's smallest wineries, and the winemakers themselves will sometimes be pouring the wines on weekends.

One of the most central participating tasting venues is the café-style **Wineries of Napa Valley** in the Napa Town Center shopping mall on 1st Street (1st St. and Randolph St., 707/253-9450 or 800/328-7815, www.napavintages.com, 11 A.M.–6 P.M. daily, until 7:30 P.M. summer weekends). Managed by Goosecross Cellars, it is also the outpost of a half dozen other small valley producers, including Zahtila up in Calistoga, Baldacci Family Vineyards in Stags Leap, and Ilona, which makes some good cabernet from the Howell Mountain.

Nearby is **Napa Wine Merchants** (1146 1st St., 707/257-6796, www.napawinemerchant.com, 10 A.M.–5 P.M. Mon.–Sat.), which used to be a wine shop until a cooperative of wineries took it over and created the tasting room in 2002. Wines from 10 different wineries are poured here, including GustavoThrace, which makes some good zinfandel and a Chiles Valley appellation cabernet; Crichton Hall Vineyard, which sources its pinot noir and merlot from Carneros vineyards; and Z52, a new winery making zinfandel from vineyards in the Sierra foothills. Also ask about the wine appreciation classes held on Tuesday evenings.

The biggest tasting room is the **Vintner's Collective** in the historic stone Pfeiffer Building (1245 Main St., at Clinton St., 707/255-7150, www.vintnerscollective.com, 11 A.M.–6 P.M. Wed.–Mon., Tues. by appointment), once a house of ill repute during its Victorian youth. It represents 15 different wineries, most notably Frazier, which makes a good cabernet sauvignon from nearby Lupine Hill; the zinfandel specialist, D-Cubed; Patz & Hall, which specializes in pinot noir and chardonnay from Sonoma and Mendocino; and Caldwell

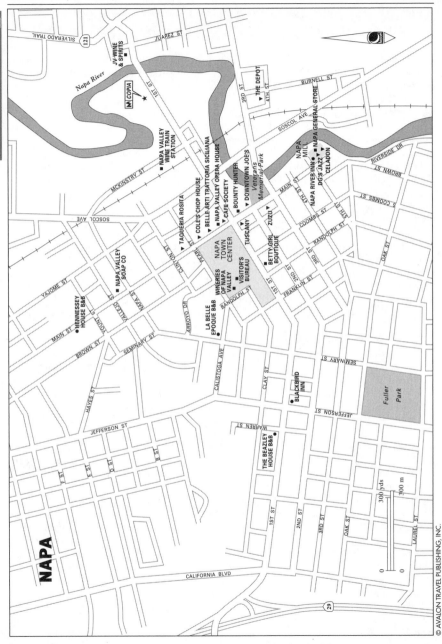

NAPA

Napa River

SILVERADO TRAIL
121
JUAREZ ST
JV-WINE & SPIRITS
COPA
THE DEPOT
BURNELL ST
3RD ST
4TH ST
SOSCOL AVE
NAPA VALLEY WINE TRAIN STATION
MCKINSTRY ST
TAQUERIA ROSITA
COLE'S CHOP HOUSE
BELLE ARTI TRATTORIA SICILIANA
CAFÉ SOCIETY
NAPA VALLEY OPERA HOUSE
BOUNTY HUNTER
DOWNTOWN JOE'S
Veterans Memorial Park
NAPA MILL
NAPA RIVER INN
DG'S JAZZ
CELADON
NAPA GENERAL STORE
RIVERSIDE DR
MAIN ST
4TH ST
5TH ST
COOMBS ST
S COOMBS ST
BROWN ST
OAK ST
SOSCOL AVE
NAPA VALLEY SOAP CO
CLINTON ST
PEARL ST
NAPA TOWN CENTER
TUSCANY
ZUZU
BETTY GIRL BOUTIQUE
RANDOLPH ST
3RD ST
2ND ST
FRANKLIN ST
WINERIES OF NAPA VALLEY
VISITOR'S BUREAU
YAJOME ST
NAPA ST
VALLEJO ST
YOUNT ST
ARROYO DR
LA BELLE EPOQUE B&B
BANDOLPH ST
HENNESSEY HOUSE B&B
MAIN ST
BROWN ST
SEMINARY ST
HAYES ST
JEFFERSON ST
CALISTOGA AVE
CLAY ST
BLACKBIRD INN
WARREN ST
THE BEAZLEY HOUSE B&B
SEMINARY ST
Fuller Park
JEFFERSON ST
1ST ST
2ND ST
3RD ST
OAK ST
LAUREL ST
E ST
E ST
D ST
B ST
A ST
300 yds
300 m
0
0
CALIFORNIA BLVD
29

© AVALON TRAVEL PUBLISHING, INC.

FREE TOURS AND TASTINGS

Wine tasting in the Napa Valley can be expensive—but it doesn't have to be. Many wineries now charge $10 to taste fewer than five wines, many costing not more than $20 a bottle. That's the equivalent of $10 for a standard glass of mediocre wine—worth it if the tasting comes with a decent tour or attention from knowledgeable staff, but there's no guarantee of that in the crowded summer months when many tasting rooms are mobbed. With a bit of planning and research, there are ways to have an entirely free touring and tasting experience in the valley.

First, a handful of wineries still offer free tasting as part of a free tour, usually by appointment only. They include **Frog's Leap** (which also offers free organic produce if you're lucky), **Shafer Vineyards** (weekdays only), **Caymus Vineyards, Mayacamas Vineyards** high up in the Mount Veeder appellation, **Pride Mountain Vineyards,** equally high up on Spring Mountain, and **Reverie Vineyard** on Diamond Mountain.

Free tasting without a tour is also available at **V. Sattui Winery,** though you'll have to endure crowds most of the year, and at **Frank Family Vineyards** in the historic Larkmead winery building. At **Goosecross Cellars,** there is a free Wine Basics seminar every Saturday that usually includes a couple of tastings as part of the fun.

Second, many wineries offer free tours that are often entertaining or educational enough even without wine. At one end of the spectrum is **Opus One,** which is happy to tour visitors (by appointment) around its opulent facility for free but charges $25 to taste its opulent wines. At the other end are smaller boutique wineries where simply asking will often get visitors a quick, unofficial tour if it's a quiet time of day. Some large and small wineries that schedule free tours (often by appointment only) include **ZD Wines, Trefethen Vineyards,** and **Clos Pegase.**

A third way to save money is to drop in to the local chamber of commerce or any other tourist information center; they sometimes have vouchers for free tasting at various wineries hidden among the piles of free brochures and magazines. On one midweek trip to the tiny **Spa Information Center** on Lincoln Avenue in Calistoga, I found vouchers for free tasting for two at both Goosecross Cellars, some 20 miles away in Yountville, as well as nearby wineries.

If no vouchers are lying around, don't despair quite yet. Browse a few of the free magazines, like **Vine** or **Wine Country This Week,** available at wineries and information centers, paying special attention to the advertisements, which often include vouchers or offers for free tasting. I've found complimentary tasting vouchers for Goosecross, Catacula Lake Winery, the Napa Wine Company, Bell Wine Cellars, and the Wineries of Napa Valley tasting room, as well as a money-off voucher for Copia in Napa. That represents about one full day of touring and tasting for free.

Finally, talk to the concierge or owner of wherever you're staying. Many hotels and inns arrange free tastings for their guests at local wineries, or at least have a few vouchers for free tastings. In general, the more you pay per night, the more likely the concierge or B&B owner will be able to help you save some money.

If you can't avoid paying to taste the wines at a favorite winery, then check if the cost of the tasting can be deducted from wine purchases. Many wineries offer this courtesy, especially with their more expensive reserve tasting fees.

Hopefully you can discover that wine always tastes better after beating the system.

Vineyard, which specializes in a small-production red bordeaux-style blend. There's also a free parking lot.

OAK KNOLL WINERIES

Darioush

One of the newest wineries in the Napa Valley is also one of the most unusual to behold, a Persian palace plunked down just outside Napa. Darioush and Shahpar Khaledi came to America from Iran in the 1970s and after a stint in the grocery business set about creating their dream winery. They made their first wines in 1997, but the visitor center, with its unique mix of Persian and contemporary architecture, didn't open until 2004.

This is a hard-to-miss winery, thanks in part to the 16 giant sandstone pillars, each topped with a double-headed bull, that take the place of more traditional trees in front of the main entrance. The theme is continued in the luxurious interior, where carved sandstone, which looks like it's straight from the set of *Raiders of the Lost Ark,* blends seamlessly with designer furnishings more often seen in a contemporary art museum.

About half the winery's total production of 9,000 cases is the Signature cabernet sauvignon, a luxurious wine made with all five bordeaux varietals. Other wines include (appropriately) a shiraz made from the grape named for the Shiraz region of Iran where it is believed to have originated, and where the Khaledis grew up. Merlot, chardonnay, and viognier round out the wines offered, and all are made with grapes from the winery's 75 acres of vineyards spread throughout the Napa Valley (4240 Silverado Trail, Napa, 707/257-2345, www.darioush.com, 10:30 A.M.–5 P.M. daily, $10 tasting fee).

Signorello Vineyards

Originally a grower of predominantly white grapes, Signorello started making its own wine in the mid-1980s and by the early 1990s had planted red grapes and started making the bordeaux-style wines that it is best known for today. Visiting here is a nice reassurance that small wineries can still thrive

Signorello Vineyards thrives among its big-name neighbors.

COURTESY OF TREFETHEN VINEYARDS

This 19th-century winery at the Trefethen family's vineyard is listed on the National Historic Register. The building not only houses the tasting room and wine library, but is still used for barrel-aging the Bordeaux-style wines.

in the big-time Napa Valley even without attaining cult status.

The estate cabernet sauvignon now dominates the winery's 5,000-case annual production, but limited-production estate chardonnay and syrah are also made, together with some highly rated pinot noir from the Las Amigas vineyard in Carneros, and zinfandel from hotter vineyards up near Calistoga (4500 Silverado Trail, Napa, 707/255-5990, www.signorellovineyards.com, tastings 10:30 A.M.–5 P.M. daily by appointment).

Trefethen Vineyards

Not far from U.S. 29 is the huge wooden building that was built in 1886 as the Eshcol Ranch winery. It contained an early version of a gravity-flow wine-making system that is now commonplace in modern wineries. The winery was briefly owned by Beringer before being bought in 1968 by the Trefethen family and was briefly used by Domaine Chandon to produce sparkling wine while its current home near Yountville was built.

The old Eshcol Ranch name is still maintained as a cheaper, second wine label (not available at the winery), and the Eshcol history is also lovingly preserved in the building itself, which is on the National Register of Historic Places. Rather than housing wine-making equipment, however, the building is now used mainly for barrel storage and hospitality, but free, appointment-only tours shed more light on its storied past.

Trefethen is perhaps best known for its chardonnay, which grows well in this slightly cooler southern end of the valley, but also makes outstanding cabernet sauvignon and a host of other wines, including both a dry and a sweet riesling (a pour of the dry riesling is often free, but tasting four other estate wines costs $10). The more expensive tasting option ($20) next to aging barrels in the wood-paneled Wine Library includes three older vintages. All told, the winery makes about 65,000 cases a year.

The Trefethens were also the driving force behind the decade-long quest to have Oak Knoll designated as an official subappellation in the Napa Valley. The federal Bureau of Alcohol, Tobacco, and Firearms finally bestowed AVA status on the area in 2004 (1160 Oak Knoll Ave., Napa, 707/255-7700, www.trefethen.com, 10 A.M.–4:30 P.M. daily).

MOUNT VEEDER WINERIES

⋈ The Hess Collection

The art is probably going to be more memorable than the wines at this mountain estate just 15 minutes from downtown Napa and right next door to the Christian Brothers' Mont LaSalle Novitiate. That's not to say the art of wine-making has not been perfected here. It certainly has, but the soaring four-story gallery linking the two historic stone winery buildings is the biggest draw. It houses part of the private contemporary art collection of winery founder and Swiss entrepreneur Donald Hess.

Most of the contemporary paintings and sculptures are by lesser-known European artists discovered by Hess through his artistic grapevine, though works by some big names like Francis Bacon and Frank Stella are also there. While lost in the art it would be easy to forget this is a winery but for a couple of large windows looking from the gallery onto the inner workings of the winery itself, one framing a bottling line that, if running, could itself almost be called a piece of industrial art.

There are no organized tours, so take yourself on a free tour of the gallery and also the cool, dark barrel room off the lobby, which is open to visitors and offers a glimpse at the inside of one of the original winery buildings. A winery was first built here in 1903 and later sold to Christian Brothers in 1930. Hess secured a 99-year lease on the property in the 1980s and rebuilt the winery to produce wine from the mountain vineyards he had started planting in the 1970s.

Hess now owns about 300 acres of vineyards in the Mt. Veeder appellation, which provide the core of the Hess Collection wines, augmented by hundreds more acres elsewhere in the Napa Valley and farther south in Monterey County that provide grapes for the cheaper Hess Estate and Hess Select labels.

A few of the Hess Collection wines, including the cabernet and chardonnay, are the only ones usually available to taste, but on weekends you might also be treated to impromptu tastings of some of the rest of the huge portfolio here, including perhaps the beautifully structured Mountain Cuvee red blend or even some of the Peter Lehman wines from South Australia that are distributed in the U.S. by Hess and sold at the winery (4111 Redwood Rd., Napa, 707/255-1144, www.hesscollection.com, open 10 A.M.–4 P.M. daily, $5–10 tasting fee).

Chateau Potelle

The location of Chateau Potelle in a peaceful mountain valley down a long, private road, together with its French-inspired name, conjures up images of a grand country estate, but the reality is a little more modest.

The small wooden tasting room is part of a cluster of buildings that the Fourmeaux family calls home, decades after first visiting Napa on a fact-finding mission for the French wine regulators. That mission convinced them of the quality of the local wines, and they started looking for a mountain vineyard to get in on the action.

Chateau Potelle is perhaps best known for its outstanding zinfandel but also makes chardonnay, cabernet sauvignon, and syrah from its Mt. Veeder vineyards. Also available to taste at the winery are cheaper wines from the sister winery near Paso Robles in California's Central Coast appellation.

This is the farthest north of the wineries in the Mt. Veeder appellation, reached from Napa via Redwood Road and Mt. Veeder Road, or from Oakville via the Oakville Grade to Mt. Veeder Road (3875 Mt. Veeder Rd., Napa, 707/255-9440, www.chateaupotelle.com, 11 A.M.–6 P.M. daily, $5 tasting fee).

Mayacamas Vineyards

Down the road from Chateau Potelle is tiny Lokoya Road, leading to the historic stone winery of Mayacamas Vineyards, which dates from the 1880s but was abandoned soon after. It was bought in 1941 by Jack Taylor, who brought the abandoned winery back to life and named it after the Mayacamas Mountains it stands on. He is said to have issued stock and paid dividends of winery picnics and chardonnay, a concept that might not fly so well in today's cash-driven world.

The current owners, Robert and Elinor Travers, bought the winery in 1968 and now produce an earthy cabernet sauvignon with great aging potential, and a crisp, oak-free chardonnay that will also improve with age. Those two wines account for the bulk of the 4,000-case production, though Mayacamas also produces smaller quantities of sauvignon blanc, merlot, and pinot noir from its mountain vineyards, which rise up to 2,400 feet, making them some of the highest in Napa (1155 Lokoya Rd., Napa, 707/224-4030, www.mayacamas.com, tasting and tours by appointment 10 A.M. and 2 P.M. Mon.–Fri. only).

SIGHTS

In an attempt to lure St. Helena–bound visitors to the valley, Napa has recently made a big push to recast itself as a hip and historic place that's a Wine Country destination rather than a series of exits off the freeway. In doing so, however, it has also had to avoid alienating its big population of local residents and valley workers, who would prefer the city remain as cheap and functional as possible.

It's a tough balancing act, and the results to date been mixed. The main anchor downtown is the Napa Town Center shopping mall, a pastel-colored 1980s concoction generally worth avoiding other than for the city's visitor center and neighboring Wineries of Napa Valley tasting room. In the streets around the Town Center, the sense of being in the center of any sort of dynamic downtown area quickly fizzles.

One attempt by the city to liven up the downtown scene is an ongoing program to have local artists paint **murals** depicting scenes from the valley's history. The effort is noble but the sites could be better. Look for them on walls on Randolph Street at 1st Street (opposite a gun shop), outside the visitor center hidden at the back of the Town Center shopping center, and opposite the Opera House on Main Street.

The city was originally called Nappa City when it was laid out in grand style by Nathan Coombs in 1848 on a bend in the Napa River. The river connected the city to San Francisco and was pivotal to its rapid growth over the subsequent decades. It has also been pivotal to the city's ongoing modern revival since it embarked on a huge flood defense program after disastrous floods wiped out downtown businesses in the 1980s and '90s.

Napa River Front District

The most obvious result of the flood defense work is the revitalization of the historic commercial area north of 1st Street and east of Main Street to lure valley visitors, though empty storefronts testify to the loss of momentum in this project since the 2002 recession. Nevertheless, this is the area where many of the newer downtown attractions and restaurants are making a

© PHILIP GOLDSMITH

Napa's Italianate Opera House now hosts theater, not opera.

go of it and could eventually generate the sort of critical mass needed to lure more tourists.

The cultural anchor of the River Front District is the recently restored **Napa Valley Opera House** (1030 Main St., 707/226-7372, www.napavalleyoperahouse.com). La Scala it isn't, but the 1880 Italianate building is a reminder of Napa's Victorian boom times. The opera house is one of a handful of pre-1890 buildings scattered around downtown. In fact, Napa has more buildings that survived the 1906 earthquake than any other city or town in this part of the Wine Country. At one end of the spectrum is the fabulous Gothic Victorian **First Presbyterian Church** at 3rd and Randolph Streets (1333 3rd St.), built in 1875, and at the other is the 1888 **Semorile Building** (975 1st St.), just around the corner from the opera house and now home to Bounty Hunter (see *Food*). An easy-to-follow walking tour of Napa's historic buildings is available from the Napa Valley Conference & Visitors Bureau (see *Information*).

Farther south right at the end of Main Street is the southern anchor of the River Front District, the restored **Napa Mill.** This riverside complex in a redbrick Victorian building used to be where steamships docked before the automobile age. It now houses upscale restaurants and shops including the Napa General Store. The Riverbend Performance Plaza here hosts free music and art shows on weekends and summer performances by the **Napa Shakespeare Company,** though it had to cancel its 2004 schedule due to lack of funding, so its future is uncertain. Also at the mill is **Gondola Servizio** with its gondolas and gondoliers looking like they're fresh from Venice. Sure, it's touristy but there are few places in the world where you can visit a winery and go for a gondola ride all in the same day. The 30-minute trips start at $55 per couple, or for $135 you can float and drink some wine (540 Main St., 707/257-8495 or 866/737-8494).

Copia

The most ambitious attempt in Wine Country to capture the spirit of California's wine industry is at The American Center for Wine, Food, and the Arts, also known as Copia, the first museum in the country devoted entirely to the culture of food and wine (500 1st St., Napa, 707/259-1600 or 888/512-6742, www.copia.org, open 10 A.M.–5 P.M. daily except Tues., adults $12.50, kids $10, half price on Wed.).

The impressive contemporary building on the bank of the Napa River was the brainchild of Robert Mondavi, who bought the land and donated it to the nonprofit organization that today runs the museum. The museum was slow to generate respectable visitor numbers when it first opened but finally seems to have found a winning combination of exhibits and events.

Some of the exhibits upstairs try their hardest to teach visitors about the science, history, and art behind food and wine, but the scope of some is so broad they tend to fall a little flat. The main reasons to come here (other than the free copy of *Wine Spectator* magazine) are for the regular special exhibits and films, the formal fruit and herb gardens around the building, and the hundreds of events, from themed wine tastings to a mouthwatering array of hundreds of food and wine courses and demonstrations, some free with the entrance price, others costing extra. A couple of Napa's best eateries, Julia's Kitchen and the American Market Café, are located here.

ENTERTAINMENT

There's usually something going on in the bars and restaurants along bustling Main Street in downtown Napa's River Front District, especially on the **Third Thursday Night** event each month, when many places stay open until 9 P.M. with accompanying music and other events.

Not far away, one of the best casual jazz venues is **Uva Trattoria** (1040 Clinton St., at Brown St., Napa, 707/255-6646, www.uvatrattoria.com)—not a bad place to eat either. Wednesday–Saturday 6:30–9 P.M. there is music from the Leo Cavanaugh Trio and the big-band sound of The Gentlemen of Jazz, together with some occasional visiting artists, mainly on Saturday nights. Another Napa eatery with live music Thursday–Sunday evenings is **Downtown Joe's** brewery and grill (902 Main St., at 2nd St., 707/258-2337, www.downtownjoes.com). Music is varied and ranges from rockabilly to Latin to jazz.

Jazz and more can be heard at the Napa Mill complex in **DG's Jazz, Blues and Salsa,** the nighttime incarnation of the M. J. Schaer gallery in the Napa Mill complex (530 Main St., 707/253-8474, 6:30 P.M.–1:30 A.M. Thurs.–Sun.). Cocktails, wines, and a small plate menu add to the cool ambience though might also add to indigestion if you decide to take the Thursday evening Latin dance lesson ($15).

Almost across the river from the Napa Mill is Napa's newest (and only) cabaret venue, the **Rainbow Room,** opened in 2004 as an extension of The Depot, an Italian restaurant (806 4th St., off Soscol, 707/252-4477, performances Tues.–Sat. until after midnight). The classic cocktail lounge was actually fashioned from an old porch area at the restaurant.

Napa might not be the center of the valley's wine scene, but it is the cultural center where most of the performance art can be found. The **Napa Valley Opera House** (1030 Main St., Napa, 707/226-7372, www .napavalleyoperahouse.com) is home to just about every performance art except opera. It is the home of the **Napa Valley Repertory Theater** (707/251-9126, www.naparep.com), which usually has about four programs each season, and also has its own wide range of music, dance, and theater throughout the year. Call for more information or check the website for a schedule of programs.

Every Friday night at 8 P.M. is **Friday Night Flicks at Copia** (500 1st St., Napa, 707/259-1600 or 888/512-6742, www.copia.org, films start 8 P.M., $6), with most of the classic films having absolutely no connection to food and wine but enjoyable nonetheless. On Saturday nights at the same time, Copia's theater hosts a live performance of a musical or theatrical bent, often held outdoors on the riverside terrace in the summer. A full schedule of performances and films is listed on Copia's website.

Copia also has a huge variety of other events going on, from wine tastings to the popular **cooking demonstrations**—well worth checking out if for no other reason than to fill up on the samples of the chef's creations at the end. Demonstrations usually cost $35. Check the website for details.

SHOPPING

The city of Napa is a slightly schizophrenic place as far as shopping goes, having to cater to its large working-class population, downtown office workers, and visitors alike. It manages with some aplomb, herding visitors with the promise of a historic backdrop and free rides on the **Napa Downtown Trolley** to a relatively compact downtown area where many of the best shops are located.

The maroon-colored trolleys that resemble San Francisco's historic cable cars run in two loops, both of which circle the downtown area bordered by 1st, Oak, and Main Streets. On Friday and Saturday trolleys run about every half hour 11 A.M.–11 P.M., but the services are staggered on each loop so you won't have to wait more than 15 minutes if you're sticking to the downtown area. The rest of the week the services run until 6 P.M. (Mon.–Wed.) or 8 P.M. (Thurs. and Sun.) there's a 45 minute gap between services, or just over 20 minutes downtown. For a schedule and map, visit www.nctpa.net/trolley or call 707/251-2800.

The red loop also heads east, down 1st Street and across the freeway to **Napa Premium Outlets,** a typical modern outlet mall containing 50 stores including Ann Taylor, Timberland, J Crew, Bennetton, and Izod (all open 10 A.M.–8 P.M. Mon.–Thurs., until 9 P.M. Fri., and Sat., and until 6 P.M. Sun., located at 629 Factory Stores Dr., right off U.S. 29, 707/226-9876, www.premiumoutlets.com).

The other trolley loop runs a little farther west to Copia. Both routes go past the **Napa Town Center** shopping center. The shops are rather unremarkable, but it is also home to the Napa Valley Conference & Visitors Bureau and the Wineries of Napa Valley tasting room.

NAPA VALLEY FESTIVALS AND EVENTS

January–April
The year in the Napa Valley kicks off with the **Napa Valley Mustard Festival,** a celebration of food and wine in the valley that lasts from the end of January to early April, roughly coinciding with the blazing yellow flowers of wild mustard that brighten up the otherwise bare, leafless vineyards.

The festival is as much about drumming up business for valley businesses during the tourism off-season as raising dollars for local charities. There are countless events throughout the two months in towns up and down the valley, most notably **Savor St. Helena,** usually held on the last Saturday of February; **Mustard, Mud, and Music** in Calistoga on the first Saturday in March; and the **Taste of Yountville,** usually held on the third Saturday of March. All are essentially big street parties featuring local restaurants, entertainment, wineries, and stores. For more information and tickets for these events and others during the Mustard Festival, contact the festival organizers in Yountville (707/944-1133, www.mustardfestival.org).

June
Summer begins with big blowout sales at the **Napa Valley Wine Auction,** usually a three-day event over the first weekend in June. The annual charity event brings together the valley's biggest wine names and some very big wallets to wine, dine, and bid sometimes crazy prices for barrels and bottles of wine, all for a worthy cause. Most of the pricey tickets are sold by invitation only, and the few available to the general public usually sell out early in the year. Contact the Napa Valley Vintners for more information (707/963-3388, www.napavintners.com/auctions).

July–September
The **Robert Mondavi Summer Music Festival** (888/769-5299, www.robertmondavi-winery.com) in July and August has become a summer institution in the Napa Valley and features big name rock, jazz, blues, and Latin music artists (Julio Iglesias, Tears for Fears, Aimee Mann, and India Arie, for example). The outdoor concerts are held Saturday evenings in the Robert Mondavi winery grounds, usually from the beginning of July through mid-August. Tickets cost $50–90 depending on the concert.

On 1st Street at the shopping center is the quirky vintage clothing store **Betty's Girl Boutique** (1239 1st St., 707/254-7560), far more original than most of the clothing stores downtown. A block east on Main Street in the River Front District is the curious **Café Society** (1000 Main St., 707/256-3232, www.cafesocietystore.com), the place to go if you're planning to re-create a classic French café or bistro in your own home, from the furniture to the food. It's also a good place for a relaxing coffee, early breakfast, or for the $5 French conversation lessons for all comers that are held every Monday evening at 6 P.M. A little farther north on Main Street is the **Napa Valley Soap Company** (1506 Main St., 707/257-1151), a source of local handmade soaps, potions, and fragrances.

One of the best wine shops in town is **J.V. Wine and Spirits,** just down the street from Copia (426 1st St., 707/253-2620, 10 A.M.–7 P.M. daily), which sells a huge selection of wine and beer and can ship wine to most states. It also offers afternoon tasting of wine (Friday) and beer (Thursday) for $2. It also takes part in the Taste Napa Downtown Wine Tasting Card program.

Antique shoppers shouldn't miss **Red Hen**

The celebration of music continues in August with the monthlong **Music in the Vineyards** series of chamber music concerts (707/258-5559, www.napavalleymusic.com). The festival kicks off at the Napa Opera House in early August and then features a concert every couple of days at wineries and other venues up and down the valley.

Not to be left out of the music action, Calistoga throws a big blues party in the fall (usually late August). **Calistoga Downtown Blues** (866/306-5588, www.calistogajazz.com) includes local and national blues artists playing on stages set up along Lincoln Avenue. This being Wine Country, wine tasting is a big part of the fun, too. It's free to attend, though the wine tasting and the biggest evening events require tickets.

Downtown Napa is also host to a couple of other annual fairs. The **Napa Town & Country Fair** in early August at the Napa Valley Expo Fairgrounds (www.napavalleyexpo.com) is a kid-friendly arts, crafts, and (of course) culinary celebration, though distinct from the free **Annual Napa Wine and Crafts Faire** (call 707/257-0322 for information) that takes over streets in downtown Napa in early September.

November

It might seem strange to have a wine festival in the Napa Valley, a place where wine seems to be celebrated every day of the year. But the **Napa Valley Wine Festival,** held in early November at the Napa Valley Expo in downtown Napa, has a higher purpose than simply indulgence—it raises money for local schools. Some 50 wineries pour their wines to accompany food from countless valley restaurants, making it the best place to sample the wines of the valley without spending hours in a car. Tickets ($40) and information can be obtained from the festival sponsor, Napa Valley Unified Education Foundation (707/253-3511).

December

The valley's wine caves are great for aging wine but also have pretty good acoustics, as you can discover at one of the weekend **Carols in the Caves** concerts from late November through December. Visit www.cavemusic.net or call 707/224-4222 for more information on the wineries hosting the concerts.

Antiques, Napa's oldest antiques market, where 70 dealers peddle their wares. Look for the big rooster perched on top of the old red barn west of St. Helena Highway just north of Napa (5091 St. Helena Hwy. S., Napa, 707/257-0822, 11 A.M.–5 P.M. Thurs.–Mon.).

RECREATION

Skyline Wilderness Park

Most people don't associate Napa Valley with serious mountain biking, but just outside the city of Napa is Skyline Wilderness Park, which hosted the U.S. round of the Mountain Bike World Cup three years in a row in the late 1990s. It's not the prettiest park in the valley—that distinction goes to Bothe-Napa Valley State Park near St. Helena—but it does offer 16 miles of trails for bikers, hikers, and horseback riders through its 850 acres of meadows and woodland. Spring is probably the best time to come, when the meadows are full of wildflowers doing their stuff before the dry season turns the grassland to golden brown.

The park is reached from downtown Napa on Imola Avenue. The day-use fee is $5, and be sure to pick up a map when you arrive because the trail system is more complex than

MORE THAN JUST HOT AIR

Hot-air balloons have become so synonymous with the Napa Valley that locals barely even blink when they float overhead in the early morning. There are still plenty of people willing to pay to get up before dawn for this unique adrenaline rush and silent aerial view of the valley and its spectacular wineries, though perhaps fewer than in recent years; mergers between ballooning companies have reduced the number offering rides to less than half a dozen.

Most are farther south in the valley, especially around Yountville, but a couple farther north can float the bleary-eyed over some of the volcanic scenery at the northern end of the valley. Early-morning winds tend to be southerly, so pick a company that launches north of any place you really want to see from the air, but also bear in mind that balloons generally don't float far—often only a few miles over the course of a flight.

The drill is more or less the same for any ballooning adventure, whatever the company: get up before the sun rises and starts to generate unstable warm air that balloon pilots hate; get to a prearranged pickup point by 6–7 A.M. (depending on the season), usually a hotel near the launch site (some companies will also collect customers staying locally); drive to the launch site and watch, sometimes take part in, the inflation of the balloon; then finally take off with the roar of the burners for an hour-long silent drift at elevations ranging from treetop to several thousand feet, depending on the conditions. Brunch usually follows, either at a local restaurant or alfresco in a meadow, and the whole experience usually lasts about four hours.

Plenty of variables, however, can make a balloon trip less than perfect. The obvious one is the weather, which can either cancel a trip outright (fog, rain, and high winds especially) or, in the case of more localized fog, cause the launch site to be moved to somewhere where the skies are clearer, sometimes even outside the valley.

Some companies will also do a "double hop," leaving those unfortunate enough to be assigned to the second hop, or flight, of the day following behind the balloons in a van to the landing spot before finally getting a flight. The drawback of the second flight (apart from the feeling of having woken up early for nothing) is that air currents can die down after the sun rises, and the balloon might not float very far. Ask if a double hop is planned—they tend to be more common during the busy summer and fall seasons. If it is, insist on being on being a first hopper.

Also ask how big the basket is and how many groggy souls will be crammed in with you. Some companies limit riders to eight or even four people; others take up to sixteen per flight. For a large premium, most also offer the option of a private flight for two.

Farthest north in the valley is **Calistoga Balloons** (888/995-7700, www.calistoga-balloons.com, $190), which launches from the Calistoga area and offers brunch afterward at the Hydro Grill in town. **Napa Valley Aloft** (www.napavalleyaloft.com) owns three Yountville-area ballooning companies with three different prices, and can be visited in the Vintage 1870 building in Yountville. One of the three is **Above the West Ballooning** (800/627-2759, $220), which offers a free shuttle from anywhere in the valley, guarantees no more than four people to a basket, and in summer has its post-flight brunch alfresco in a vineyard. The cheapest is **Balloon Aviation** (800/367-6272, $195), which has no shuttle but still guarantees no double hops.

The **Bonaventura Balloon Company** (707/944-2822 or 800/359-6272, www.bonaventuraballoons.com, $175–220) offers flights in the northern half of the valley and a variety of brunch options, from the most expensive at the Meadowood Resort to a cheaper picnic option. Also check the website for special rates. **Balloons Above the Valley** (707/253-2222 or 800/464-6824, www.balloonrides.com, $190–210) launches from near the Domaine Chandon winery in Yountville and offers a private brunch after the flight. It also sometimes has good online deals, including no-frills flights that are shorter, foodless, and cheaper.

COURTESY OF SKYLINE WILDERNESS PARK

Skyline Wilderness Park

most. Hikers should also look out for bikers and horses—all users share all the trails. The park is open 9 A.M.–dusk (707/252-0481, www.ncfaa.com/skyline/skyline_park.htm).

Mountain bikers wanting to try their skills on the world cup route should ride from near the park's entrance for about a mile up Lake Marie Road before turning right onto the murderous ascent of Passini Road before descending on the rocky, sometimes steep single-track of the Bayleaf Trail. The next stage of the cup was the Manzanita Trail, reached by climbing back up Lake Marie Road to the fig tree. The two-mile, undulating trail was described as one of the best single-tracks on the cup circuit.

Horseback riding in the park is offered by the Sonoma Cattle Company all year (707/255-2900, www.napasonomatrailrides.com, $90 per person). Wet weather in the winter or very hot weather in summer might cause a cancellation of the two-hour ride, as might a lack of riders to make up the required group of 4–5 people.

Disc golf offers some less traditional exercise. You might know it as Frisbee golf, but the Professional Disc Golf Association would prefer you use the D word instead. It is played exactly as you might think, like golf but throwing a Frisbee instead of hitting a little white ball. There is an 18-hole course, and (in case you don't always travel with one) Frisbees (sorry, discs) are available at the entrance kiosk, along with course maps. The dress rules are also a little more relaxed than on most traditional golf courses—no collared shirts or fancy shoes are required. In fact, you don't even have to wear shirts or shoes.

Those who'd prefer to expend less energy can find **picnic areas** near the park entrance and about 2.5 miles up the Lake Marie Road at the lake itself.

Alston Park

Untouched by either vineyards or development, Alston Park instead has sweeping views of both from the western fringe of the city of Napa. The park is off Dry Creek Road, reached by driving west from the St. Helena Highway from either Redwood Road or Trower Avenue. There's no entrance fee and the park is open dawn to dusk, though the only map is on an information board.

It's not on quite the same scale as Skyline

but still offers plenty of picnicking, hiking, and biking possibilities in its 150 acres of rolling hills and meadows and along five miles of trails. There are also picnic tables and a canine common where dogs can be let off the leash—a rarity in the relatively dog-unfriendly valley. Just avoid the park during the middle of hot summer days unless you're training for a desert trek, because there are few trees and little shade.

Golf

The southern end of the valley is where all the biggest and most exclusive golf courses are, many of them not open to the public. Among those that are, the biggest is the 18-hole **Napa Golf Course** at Kennedy Park a couple of miles south of the downtown area on Soscol Avenue, which eventually becomes the Napa-Vallejo Highway (2295 Streblow Dr., Napa, 707/255-4333, www.playnapa.com, call for tee times). The par-72, 6,500-yard championship course costs $31 to play during the week for nonresidents and $41 at weekends. It also has a driving range, practice putting greens, and a fully stocked golf shop.

ACCOMMODATIONS

Although it feels a little removed from all the wine action in the valley, and is not the most attractive Wine Country town in this part of the world, the city of Napa provides the widest choice of accommodation options. Many major chain hotels can be found here, as well as cheap independent motels, Victorian B&Bs, and a new, riverside boutique hotel. Best of all, rooms are generally cheaper here than anywhere else in the valley, especially at the low end of the market.

Another advantage of staying in Napa, particularly if you're not a cabernet sauvignon fan, is its proximity to the Carneros region—the land of pinot noir and chardonnay (see the *Southern Sonoma* chapter). It's just a 15-minute drive south to many wineries in the eastern half of Carneros, or a 15-minute drive north to some of the Napa Valley's best cabernet pro-

ducers. And for those traveling to or from Oakland or San Francisco, Napa has the shortest drive time of any of the valley's towns—a full 45 minutes closer to San Francisco than Calistoga, for example.

Under $100

The **Wine Valley Lodge** (200 S. Coombs St., Napa, 707/224-7911, www.winevalleylodge.com) is a simple, clean, and bargain-priced independent motel let down only by its location about a mile south of downtown Napa, putting it just out of walking distance to most good restaurants and shops. It is, however, just off Imola Avenue, which provides a quick connection to the St. Helena Highway and wineries to the north and south. The rooms are simply but tastefully furnished, though still with the ubiquitous bulletproof synthetic bedspreads that no motel seems to be without. All have TVs, air-conditioning, and private bathrooms with showers, and cost $69–89 midweek, $89–109 on weekends.

A little north of downtown Napa is **Napa Valley Redwood Inn** (3380 Solano Ave., off Redwood Rd., Napa, 707/257-6111 or 877/872-6272, www.napavalleyredwoodinn.com). Some big-hotel touches (newspapers, free high-speed Internet access, free HBO, a decent-sized outdoor pool) sweeten the appeal of the otherwise plain and somewhat small motel-style rooms. Its location right next to the St. Helena Highway puts it in easy reach of wineries but also means there's some traffic noise to contend with, and you must drive to local restaurants in Napa and Yountville. Nothing too unbearable considering the rates are as low as $70–90 midweek and $80–130 on weekends, depending on the season.

Right next door to the Redwood Inn is the **Chablis Inn** (3360 Solano Ave., off Redwood Rd., Napa, 707/257-1944 or 800/443-3490, www.chablisinn.com). It's a bit more upscale than its neighbor but still a glorified motel with prices that squeak in at just under $100 midweek for the basic rooms (with the bulletproof bedspreads). The deluxe rooms are only $20 more a night and a little more luxurious, with comforters, CD players, and whirlpool tubs in the bathrooms. Weekend rates are considerably higher, starting at $140 a night.

$100–200

For just a few dollars more a night than the nearby motels you could stay in the **John Muir Inn,** a fairly plain, modern building cheered up with lots of trelliswork and foliage, just off the St. Helena Highway on the northern outskirts of Napa (1998 Trower Ave., Napa, 707/257-7220 or 800/522-8999, www.johnmuirnapa.com). The clean and comfortable rooms here are a step up from most motel rooms, with Internet access and desks, and some have refrigerators and microwaves or full kitchenettes. Three of the deluxe king rooms also have whirlpool tubs. Standard rooms cost $105–135 a night midweek, depending on season, and $120–155 on weekends. Deluxe rooms are usually only $10 more a night. As with most inns and hotels, a free continental breakfast is included but guests can instead choose a money-off voucher for breakfast or brunch at the neighboring Marie Callendar's restaurant.

Napa's first and only boutique hotel, the **Napa River Inn,** has perhaps the best location in the city at the historic, redbrick Napa Mill, a small riverside food and entertainment complex only a 10-minute walk to more shops and restaurants in downtown Napa (500 Main St., Napa, 707/251-8500 or 877/251-8500, www.napariverinn.com). The 66 rooms are spread among three buildings—two part of the historic mill itself and one (the Embarcadero building) built in 1997. All are furnished in an eclectic mix of contemporary and either Victorian or nautical style, many with fireplaces, balconies, or views, though the views vary wildly from a parking lot to the river, which still bears some ugly scars of recent flood-control construction work. Staying here is not as pricey as the location and luxury might suggest. Smallish standard rooms cost $160–180 midweek and only about $20 more on weekends. The most expensive deluxe rooms are double that, though there are plenty of options in between.

The Napa Mill itself has everything a hotel guest might need: Choose between two of the city's best restaurants (Celadon and Angèle) for dinner, washed down by cocktails at DG's jazz club. In the morning, after the hotel breakfast from Sweetie Pies bakery, buy picnic supplies at the Napa General Store and book an evening spa treatment before setting off for a day of wine tasting.

The choice of Victorian B&Bs in Napa can be a bit bewildering. One establishment that has some of the cheaper rates and plenty of room options, from flowery frills to ornate antiques, is **Hennessey House** (1727 Main St., Napa, 707/226-3774, www.hennesseyhouse.com), about six blocks north of downtown Napa. Six rooms in the main Queen Anne-style Victorian house cost $129–229 depending on season, all with private bathrooms and some with four-poster beds and claw-foot tubs. Four larger, more ornate rooms, with fireplaces, whirlpool tubs, and CD players, are in the Carriage House and cost $189–299. The full gourmet breakfast is enough to soak up plenty of wine during those morning wine tastings, and the sauna is a place to relax tasting-weary feet at the end of a winter day. Allergy sufferers be warned: The resident cat has full reign of the common areas.

Anyone fed up with Victorian frills should check out the **M Blackbird Inn,** a unique Arts and Crafts–style shingled house dating from the 1920s with furnishings to match the era's relatively clean and simple lines (1755 1st St., 707/226-2450 or 888/567-9811, www.blackbirdinnnapa.com). It's just a few blocks from downtown Napa, and, unusually for a B&B, there are TVs in every room with DVD players (the walls supposedly have some decent soundproofing, unlike those at many B&Bs) and free wireless Internet access in addition to the more common fireplaces and whirlpool tubs in some rooms. Rates range from $135 midweek to $185 on weekends for the smallest room, though most are in the $160–200 range. The teddy bears on each bed are a trademark of the Four Sisters group, which owns this and a handful of other small Wine Country inns, not that there's any chain feel to the place. The only disadvantage is that there are no owners living there to take care of any late-night problems.

Just a block from the Blackbird Inn and touted as Napa's first B&B when it opened in the 1980s, **The Beazley House** (with its own feline resident) is in another big shingled mansion, this one dating from 1906 (1910 1st St., Napa, 707/257-1649 or 800/559-1649, www.beazleyhouse.com). Rooms contain the usual mix of what look like your great-grand-mother's best furnishings. The five in the main house have private bathrooms, though only one of the five has a claw-foot tub, and cost $155–225. The other five rooms are in the Carriage House and are more luxurious, with whirlpool tubs, fireplaces, individual air-conditioning, and views of the lush garden. They cost $195–300.

Over $200

Arguably one of the finest Victorian B&Bs in Napa is **La Belle Époque** (1386 Calistoga Ave., Napa, 707/257-2161 or 800/238-8070, www.labelleepoque.com), a gloriously ornate Queen Anne–style mansion built in 1893 with an antique-stuffed interior that looks like the movie set for an Agatha Christie mystery. The six rooms are all unique, most with stained-glass windows, some with canopy beds, and others with fireplaces or whirlpool tubs. Standard amenities include TV with VCR, high-speed Internet access, and CD players, and all guests are invited to evening wine receptions featuring wines from local wineries or from the inn's own big wine cellar. All this pampering and history, plus a very central location, comes at a higher cost than at many B&Bs. Rates range from just under $200 for a couple of the rooms midweek in midwinter up to $275–295 on summer weekends. Two suites in a separate Victorian house across the street go for about $100 more.

Less Victorian chintz and more privacy than at most B&Bs are part of a stay at **La Résidence,** on the northern edge of the city (4066 St. Helena Hwy., also known as Howard Ln., Napa, 707/253-0337 or 800/253-9203, www.laresidence.com). It's actually more of an exclusive inn, with 23 rooms spread among three buildings set in two acres of wooded grounds with a hot tub and a small pool. The smallest and cheapest rooms ($175–235 depending on season) are in the main Victorian mansion house dating from 1870, furnished with queen beds and antiques, though the plumbing in the old house can reportedly be temperamental. The larger rooms in the more modern French Barn building ($225–275) have a touch of French country style to them, plus balconies or patios and fireplaces. The newest and biggest rooms ($300–350) are in the new Cellar House and add TVs, stereos, wet bars, and giant bathrooms into the mix. A couple of suites are also similarly luxurious. Although the inn is nowhere near downtown Napa, it does offer easy access to the rest of the valley and is next door to the excellent Bistro Don Giovanni.

There are luxurious resorts in the valley with views, others with wooded privacy, some with vineyards, but the **Milliken Creek Inn** (1815 Silverado Trail, Napa, 707/255-1197 or 888/622-5775, www.millikencreekinn.com) has another twist—its riverside setting, understated mix of Victorian and colonial Asian furnishings, relaxing earth tones, and the sense of exclusivity that comes from having just 12 rooms to share the lush gardens and fountains.

Relax on the lawn by the riverbank or lounge in the room in front of a fireplace or on a private deck and have yourself a peaceful, zen experience. All rooms also come with full entertainment systems, luxurious linens, and wireless Internet access should work intrude. The cheapest are the two Milliken rooms at $300–425, depending on season and time of the week. The premium rooms starting at $400 a night (and going up to more than $600) include extras ranging from Jacuzzis and canopied beds to plasma-screen TVs and expansive private decks.

Worth noting is that the inn is a gratuity-free zone but, as a reminder that nothing is free in the Napa valley, a 10 percent service fee is added to your bill each day. Unless you want to complain and have the fee removed or reduced (and feel like a grinch) be sure make full use of the helpful staff and the evening wine tastings to get your money's worth.

FOOD
River Front District

"Global comfort food" is how the culinary creations at **Celadon** have been described, and the surroundings in the historic Napa Mill buildings are equally comfortable (500 Main St. Napa, 707/254-9690, lunch and dinner daily, dinner entrées $16–26). The shabby-chic exterior and huge sheltered patio give way to a pure bistro-chic interior, the perfect match for the internationally influenced Californian menu. The wine list offers about the same balance of California and the rest of the world.

The Napa General Store in the riverside Napa Mill is at night transformed into the **General Café,** serving Asian-Californian food designed by Nam-Pham, the former chef at San Francisco's Slanted Door Vietnamese restaurant (540 Main St., 707/259-0762, dinner Wed.–Sun., entrées $10–14). Creations

like Coca-Cola–braised short ribs sit alongside more traditional Asian dishes like Vietnamese crepes on the inventive menu.

Cole's Chop House (1122 Main St., Napa, 707/224-6328, dinner daily, entrées $18–46) is the baby brother to Celadon, offering a slightly less refined but equally well-designed (though short) menu featuring steakhouse dishes, from oysters to well-aged beef, in a classic steakhouse setting, rich with dark wood and contrasting white tablecloths.

Belle Arti Trattoria Siciliana (1040 Main St., Ste. 104, 707/255-0720, lunch weekdays, dinner daily, dinner entrées $12–26) is a little hard to find behind the Main Street Exchange building but is worth hunting out for its riverside setting and food that seems straight from mama's Sicilian kitchen. Fish features prominently on the menu (Sicily is an island, after all), but there are plenty of creative pasta dishes and less creative meat dishes to balance things out. The wine list includes more than two dozen Italian wines, though just a few from Sicily.

Another of Napa's standout Italian joints, with food emanating from the other end of

The Napa Mill complex is a food and entertainment hub.

that country, is **Tuscany** (1005 1st St., Napa, 707/258-1000, lunch weekdays, dinner daily, dinner entrées $14–25). The atmosphere is just as casual as Belle Arti, perhaps more so given its location on busy 1st Street, with a farmhouse-like setting and blazing rotisserie ovens that turn out the rich stews and roasted meats typical of Tuscan cooking.

The River Front District is the main food center in downtown Napa, and one of its most inventive recent additions is **ℕ Bounty Hunter** (975 1st St., off Main St., Napa, 800/943-9463, lunch and dinner daily, plates and entrées $6–18), a wine shop, tasting bar, and (most recently) a casual restaurant serving small plates to help the wine go down. The setting, in a historic brick-walled Victorian building with knotty wood floors, a copper ceiling, and wine barrels for table bases, is as relaxed as the comfort food served here. It includes gumbo, the beer-can chicken (a Cajun-spiced chicken impaled on a Tecate beer can), and chili. Alternatively, just order some cheese and settle down at the wine bar with one of the 400 wines sold here (40 by the glass) or a tasting flight. Since it's a wine shop too, you'll only pay retail price for wines bought with a meal and there'll be plenty of advice available from the entertaining staff.

With the amount of critical praise heaped on **ZuZu** (829 Main St., at 2nd St., Napa, 707/224-8555, lunch weekdays, dinner daily, plates $5–13) you'd think it was competing with French Laundry for title of the valley's best restaurant. Thankfully, it's a refreshingly down-to-earth tapas bar that's a great place to end a stressful day of touring without having to worry about reservations or the bill. The cozy interior with its exposed brick, beams, and tile is the perfect setting for the Spanish-inspired small plates, none of which (except the Moroccan glazed lamb chops) costs over $10. The fact that lunch is only served during the week indicates it's a popular local hangout.

Downtown Joe's American Grill and Brewhouse (902 Main St., 707/258-2337, lunch and dinner daily, breakfast weekends, dinner entrées $9–21) is a hopping alternative to the swanky restaurants and endless wine of the Napa Valley. Sure it has a wine list (a short one), but most people come here for the more than half dozen microbrews with the usual comical microbrew names, like **Tantric India Pale Ale** and **Catherine, The Great Imperial Stout.** The menu is pretty normal though slightly pricey grill fare, but there's also a cheaper pizza and pub grub menu. Thursday–Sunday there is live music every night.

What The Depot does for Italian food, tiny **Taqueria Rosita** does for Mexican (1210 Main St., Napa, 707/253-9208, lunch and dinner Mon.–Sat., $3–10). The fairly standard taco and burrito fare can be either ordered to go or eaten in the cozy, tile-floored restaurant.

Copia

The legacy of celebrity chef Julia Child lives on in **Julia's Kitchen,** tucked away in a corner at Copia where the cold minimalism of the modern building is softened by drapes and carpet (in Copia, 500 1st St., Napa, 707/265-5700, lunch Wed.–Mon., dinner Thurs.–Sun., dinner entrées $20–30). Watching the chefs work their magic in the open kitchen of this highly rated restaurant is touted as an extension of Copia's food education mission, though most people seem too engrossed in the French-Californian dishes and Napa-centric international wine list to care much. One great advantage Julia's Kitchen has over other upscale restaurants is Copia's extensive gardens, which grow some of the produce for the kitchen. Copia's giant, free parking lot comes in handy, too.

The **American Market Café** at Copia (500 1st St., Napa, 707/265-5700) can be a relaxing, out-of-the-way place to have lunch as long as crowds aren't too thick. Order soup, salad, a sandwich, or other delights from the big circular deli counter and grab a table outside on the patio overlooking the pretty garden.

Vicinity of Napa

A few miles north of downtown Napa is the popular Italian restaurant **Bistro Don Giovanni** (4110 St. Helena Hwy., also known as Howard Ln., Napa, 707/224-3300, lunch and dinner daily, dinner entrées $14–28). It's hard to miss on the east side of the St. Helena Highway and is a favorite of locals looking for moderately priced Italian bistro food with a bit of Californian flair, all in a relaxed and cheery setting, especially on a warm summer night when the huge, tiled outdoor patio is bustling. Anything from the wood-fired oven is worth trying here, especially the pizzas and oven-roasted fish. The wine list is dominated by Napa and Sonoma, but there's a good choice from the mother country too, and an unusually wide selection by the half bottle.

Bring your own pot to the back door of **The Depot** (806 4th St., off Soscol, Napa, 707/252-4477, dinner Tues.–Sun., entrées $14–19) and you can take some down-home American-Italian cooking of this Napa landmark back to your hotel room for a few dollars. Alternatively, go in the front door and enjoy its trademark malfatti pasta, said to have been invented by former owner Teresa Tamborelli (who established the restaurant in 1925) when she ran out of ravioli but had to feed a hungry San Francisco baseball team.

Picnic Supplies

If you're in Napa and heading to the hills for lunch, the **Napa General Store** in the Napa Mill complex is about as gourmet as you can get for takeout food in the town (540 Main St., 707/259-0762). You'll have to battle your way past all the other non-food trinkets and gifts it sells, though. At Copia, the **American Market Café** also serves up some luxury foods ideal for picnics.

Just south of the Darioush winery is the **Soda Canyon Store,** just about the only decent place to buy deli food, cheeses, and wine along the Silverado Trail (4006 Silverado Trail, at Soda Canyon Rd., Napa, 707/252-0285).

Farmers Markets

Napa might not instantly bring to mind bucolic country farms, but farm-fresh produce (and craft stalls) can still be found at **Napa Downtown Market** May–October, on Tuesday mornings until noon in the parking lot of Copia on 1st Street.

A sort of mini Taste of Napa is the **Napa Chef's Market,** open 4–9 P.M. each Friday Memorial Day–Labor Day (at 1st St. and Napa Town Center, 707/257-0322). Line up at your favorite stand to buy tasty snacks like barbecued oysters.

INFORMATION AND SERVICES

First stop for any visitors without a plan—whether staying in Napa, heading up to Calistoga, or simply doing some online research—should be the **Napa Valley Conference & Visitors Bureau** (1310 Napa Town Center, 707/226-7459, www.napavalley.com, 9 A.M.–5 P.M. daily). The staff know the valley like the backs of their hands and can usually rustle up some useful printed information.

The nearby **Napa Chamber of Commerce** (1556 1st St., Napa, 707/226-7455, www.napachamber.com, 8:30 A.M.–5 P.M. Mon.–Fri.) sells packages of information from maps to directories and touring guides, although you might be able to find some of the same information for free at the visitors bureau.

The Napa Valley

Yountville and Vicinity

The appellations in the southern half of the Napa Valley encompass some of the best cabernet-growing regions in California but can also be cool enough for growing many other varietals, both red and white, most notably in the **Yountville** appellation, where chardonnay, sangiovese, zinfandel, sauvignon blanc, and even the picky pinot noir seem to thrive.

The **Stags Leap** appellation on the eastern side of the valley along the Silverado Trail is exposed to more of the cool air that rolls in from the San Francisco Bay than are the appellations farther north, though its own little range of hills keeps things just sheltered enough that it doesn't get too cold. The cabernets are more subtle and aromatic than their bolder, fuller hot-climate cousins, and some of the best known in the valley—especially those from Stag's Leap Wine Cellars. For wineries that make such renowned wines, however, the wineries are refreshingly low-key.

North of Yountville is the **Oakville** appel-lation, warmer and home to some of the most famous cabernet sauvignon vineyards and wineries, including Robert Mondavi and Far Niente. Although this is where the land of big, bold Napa cabernets begins in the valley, the appellation also turns out some excellent sauvignon blanc and chardonnay.

YOUNTVILLE WINERIES
Domaine Chandon

The first big French champagne house to come to California was Moët-Hennessy in 1973, and its Domaine Chandon winery has some of the most beautiful grounds in the valley. The winery also blends into the hillside and is almost invisible from the road, not the sort of modesty that one expects from such a big, glamorous operation producing several hundred thousand cases of sparkling and still wines each year.

Those wines include everything from the basic Chandon labeled wines, including the

COURTESY OF DOMAINE CHANDON

Domaine Chandon, the modest home to some of the valley's best champagne and food.

popular, bone-dry Riche, up to the most expensive—Étoile sparklers that are bottle-aged for years to give them a rich, toasty aroma. Some of the reserve wines offer perhaps the best bargains, however, with more complexity than the nonreserve wines for not much more money. Domaine Chandon also makes still wines from the three most important champagne grapes—pinot noir, chardonnay, and petite meunier—that are worth trying, though a little over-priced.

All can be tried inside in the salon or out on the sunny terrace, but the experience here is about more than just the wines. Art is everywhere, both inside and out in the gardens (some of it for sale), and free tours taking in all stages of champagne making run on the hour until 5 P.M. at weekends, or every two hours during the week (1 California Dr., off U.S. 29, Yountville, 707/944-2280, www.domainechandon.com, 10 A.M.–5 P.M. daily or to 6 P.M. in summer, tasting $9–14).

Goosecross Cellars

Anyone lamenting that nothing much wine-related in the Napa valley is free anymore should head on over to Goosecross on a Saturday morning during the summer for the fun and informative (and totally free) Wine Basics class (at 11 A.M. Sat. May–Oct., reservations essential). The hour-long session is held on a shady lawn and pitched at just the right level for novices and wine buffs alike to learn some fascinating facts (and myths) about wines and the best ways to savor them. And, of course, there are a couple of wines to taste as part of the education.

The cozy Goosecross tasting room is squeezed in next to the barrels and offers all 10 wines

that this family-owned winery makes, including the standout Howell Mountain cabernet sauvignon, the juicy syrah sourced from vineyards in southern California, and the crisp but fruity Napa Valley chardonnay. In total, Goosecross produces only about 9,000 cases of wine, making it one of the valley's smaller wineries that is open to the public. Although there's a tasting fee, those lucky enough to get in the Wine Basics class will get a discount coupon for the wines (1119 State Ln., Yountville, 707/944-1986 or 800/276-9210, www.goosecross.com, 10 A.M.–4 P.M. daily by appointment only, $5 tasting fee).

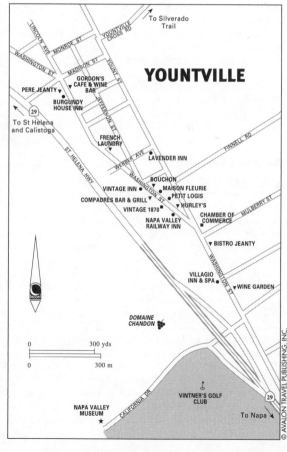

Bell Wine Cellars

It's not surprising that a former assistant wine-maker at Rutherford's Beaulieu Vineyard now makes his own critically acclaimed cabernet sauvignon from Rutherford-area vineyards.

Anthony Bell established Bell Wine Cellars in the early 1990s, first making wine at other wineries before buying the former Plam Vineyards winery near Yountville in 1998. The cabernet from Baritelle Vineyards in Rutherford, which is Bell's signature wine, was first made in 1991 and was then Napa Valley's first ever single-vineyard cabernet made from just one clone of the vine.

Other wines include a well-priced (and multi-clone) cabernet, merlot, chardonnay, and syrah from vineyards in the Sierra foot-hills a hundred miles east. As the tasting bar squeezed between the barrels suggests, this is a small winery. It makes about 6,000 cases a year and the appointment-only tastings offer the chance to talk to people who really know their wines (6200 Washington St., Yountville, 707/944-1673, www.bellwines.com, tastings daily by appointment, $15).

STAGS LEAP WINERIES

The Stags Leap Duo

A trip down the Silverado Trail would not be complete without visiting at least one of the two wineries that share the name of one of the best known Napa appellations—one that helped put California on the international wine map in the 1970s.

If you're wondering how two unrelated wineries can use the name in this age of strongly protected trademarks, it's probably no surprise that there was a lengthy legal battle involved. These neighbors fought over the use of the Stags Leap name as it became associated with world-class wines in the 1970s and '80s, and the case was finally settled in 1985 when the court ruled that the term Stags Leap referred simply to a geographical area and both wineries agreed to let each other use it (each also kept the apostrophe in a different position). Not long after the dust had settled, Stags Leap

became an official appellation with no apostrophe at all.

The most famous of the duo is **Stag's Leap Wine Cellars** (5766 Silverado Trail, Napa, 707/944-2441 or 866/422-7523, www .cask23.com, 10 A.M.–4:30 P.M. daily), which made the cabernet sauvignon that beat out the best French bordeaux in the now-famous 1976 blind tasting in Paris. It still makes outstanding single-vineyard cabernet from that same S.L.V. vineyard as well as the older Fay vineyard next to it. Such renowned wines command high prices, none more so than the Cask 23 cabernet, which uses the best grapes from both the S.L.V. and Fay vineyards.

These three estate cabernets, together with an equally impressive chardonnay, can be tasted for $30. Non-estate wines from other Napa vineyards offer a cheaper tasting option ($10) and might include the excellent Artemis cabernet, which has some Fay vineyard grapes in it; the merlot; or the sauvignon blanc (you might also be able to steal a taste of these non-estate wines if you indulge in the more expensive tasting option). Appointment-only tours that take in the pristine-looking cave system and its fascinating Foucault pendulum (for measuring the earth's rotation) are also available and include a tasting.

Although a magnet for serious wine enthusiasts and a fairly large producer (about 50,000 cases including the cheaper Hawks Crest label), this family run winery exudes an unassuming and friendly atmosphere, making it far less intimidating for the casual day-tripper than many of the valley's other big names. The small tasting room is off to the left of the main winery building and can get crowded, so plan to get here early.

Farther north on the Silverado Trail, set well back from the road, is the original winery to bear the area's now-famous name. **Stags' Leap Winery** (6150 Silverado Trail, Napa, 707/944-1303 or 800/640-5327, www.stagsleap.com) was founded in 1893, taking its name from the old Native American legend of a stag that evaded its hunters by leaping across the crags overlooking the winery.

In 1909 the winery's original owner sold out, and the stone Manor House became a hotel and then a navy camp before being abandoned in 1953. It wasn't until 1970 that it was brought back to life as a winery and the vineyard was replanted to include cabernet sauvignon, merlot, and petite sirah, alongside some of the original Sirah vines that are said to be some of earliest plantings of that grape in the United States. Those three varietals still dominate the winery's production of about 60,000 cases today, with perhaps the most noteworthy wine being the inky, full-bodied petite sirah.

Since 1997 the winery has been owned by multinational Beringer Blass. Few people realize it's open to the public, but a limited number of appointment-only tours are available (Fri. and Sat. only, 10:30 A.M. and 2:30 P.M.) and include the original Victorian caves, which were rediscovered in the 1970s and have since been extended.

Clos Du Val

Cofounder Bernard Portet wanted to create a winery to rival the best in Bordeaux, where he grew up and learned his wine-making skills, and he settled on this prime 120-acre chunk of Napa Valley in 1972, adding another 180 acres in Carneros a few years later. The winery has always produced wines to rival some of the best in Bordeaux, though the rather plain, concrete winery building itself seems to take more inspiration from 1970s design aesthetics than a Bordeaux chateau and is livened up only by its pretty gardens.

Almost half the 80,000 cases of wine made here each year are cabernet sauvignon, and this is the wine Clos Du Val is best known for. The generic Napa cabernet is good, but the Stags Leap estate cabernet is outstanding and comes from the vineyard right outside the winery door. Chardonnay is the other large-production wine in the portfolio and comes from the Carneros vineyard, as does a pinot noir. Another estate wine worth trying is the white bordeaux blend of semillon and sauvignon blanc called Ariadne.

There's plenty to do here other than taste wine, from a self-guided tour around the demonstration vineyard that illustrates all the different trellis systems used in vineyards (the tour provides an accompanying explanation), to playing a game of pétanque, the French version of bocce ball. Tours are also available by appointment only (5330 Silverado Trail, Napa, 707/259-2200 or 800/993-9463, www.closduval.com, 10 A.M.–5 P.M. daily, tasting $5, tour and tasting $10).

Pine Ridge Winery

Nestled in a small dell with its trademark ridge of pine trees above is another of Stags Leap's big cabernet houses, established by Gary Andrus in 1980. He has since expanded the winery to 65,000 cases and increased his vineyard holdings to about 200 acres throughout the valley, helping make Pine Ridge one of the few wineries to make highly rated wines from most of Napa's finest cabernet appellations—Stags Leap, Rutherford, Oakville, and Howell Mountain. The flagship is the Andrus Reserve, a bordeaux-style blend made with grapes from almost all those appellations.

The smallish tasting room is virtually devoid of merchandise, putting the wines firmly center stage. The regular tasting option covers the white wines and cheaper reds, and might include a Carneros- or Rutherford-sourced chardonnay, viognier, merlot, or cabernet franc. The reserve and some of the cabernets can only be tried with the more expensive tasting option ($20) or as part of the appointment-only barrel tasting in the Hillside Room, offered three times a day for $30.

Tours of the vineyard and aging caves, followed by a barrel tasting, are also offered three times a day by appointment (10 A.M., noon, and 2 P.M., $20), and there's a small, picnic area under the trees above the winery (5901 Silverado Trail, Napa, 707/252-9777 or 800/575-9777, www.pineridgewinery.com, 10:30 A.M.–4:30 P.M. daily, tasting $10 or $20, tours by appointment, $20).

Shafer Vineyards

Tasting wine here is about as close as many visitors might get to one of Napa's much-hyped

© PHILIP GOLDSMITH

History is on display at plenty of Napa wineries.

cult wines without forking over hundreds of dollars for the rare bottles that do make it beyond the waiting lists. Schafer's limited-production Hillside Select cabernet sauvignon is regularly compared to the highly extracted wines from small producers like Screaming Eagle, Harlan Estate, and Bryant Family that are critically acclaimed and rare enough to command their cult status. About 2,000 cases of Hillside Select are made each year out of about 32,000 for the winery as a whole.

The secrets to success here are the rocky, hillside vineyards behind the modest winery, which produce limited quantities of powerfully flavored grapes that go into the Hillside Select cabernet. Some of these grapes also make it into the lower-priced but equally plush cabernet, supplemented by grapes from vineyards farther south that also provide fruit for the acclaimed syrah (called Relentless) and merlot. Schafer's chardonnay is sourced from the winery's Carneros vineyards. A small vineyard on the hillside behind the winery is planted to sangiovese, which provides the fruit for the limited-production Firebreak blend of sangiovese and cabernet.

An informative tour followed by tasting is offered twice a day on weekdays by appointment only. The Hillside Select is sometimes not available for tasting, but a cabernet port that is only available at the winery usually is. Visitors will also probably meet John Shafer's canine grape tester, Tucker.

Space on the tour is limited to 10 people and demand is high, so booking weeks in advance is sometimes necessary, as is a tolerance of the serious enophiles who tend to flock here. There's also no sign for the winery on Silverado Trail, so just look for the cluster of property numbers at the end of the private road (6154 Silverado Trail, Napa, 707/944-2877, www.shafervineyards.com, sales weekdays 9 A.M.–4 P.M., free tour and tasting by appointment weekdays 10 A.M. and 1:30 P.M. only).

OAKVILLE WINERIES
Napa Wine Company
The modest Cellar Door of the Napa Wine Company a few yards from the Oakville Grocery does not suggest that this is a huge winemaking operation. The tasting room is a

cooperative of 25 small wineries, all of which use the Napa Wine Company's custom-crush facilities to make their wines.

In fact, the venture makes more than 1.5 million cases of wine for wineries ranging from tiny boutiques making a few hundred cases up to some of the giants of the valley, like Pine Ridge and Mondavi (who would probably prefer that people didn't know they have to outsource some production). Between all those jobs, the Napa Wine Company manages to make about 10,000 cases of its own label wine as well, including a highly regarded cabernet sauvignon. It manages all this using equipment bought from the wine conglomerate Heublein in 1993, including what used to be the white-wine production facility for the Inglenook Winery.

Some of the small wineries represented in the tasting room have links to some major valley figures. Independent winemaker Heidi Barrett of Screaming Eagle fame, for example, makes wines for several small wineries here, including La Sirena, and former Inglenook winery president Dennis Fife and his wife, wine writer Karen MacNeil-Fife, also use the facilities for their Fife Vineyards wines. Other wineries here are simply small- or medium-sized family affairs (7830 U.S. 29, Oakville, 707/944-1710 or 800/848-9630, www.napawineco.com, 10 A.M.–4 P.M. daily, tasting $7).

Opus One

Only serious wine lovers need go out of their way to visit Opus One, the monolithic tribute to red bordeaux wine that was formed in 1979 by Robert Mondavi and the late, legendary French winemaker Baron Philippe de Rothschild, head of famed Château Mouton-Rothschild in France.

The concierge escort to the tasting room and $25 tasting fee to taste just the single type of wine made here (it's a generous pour) are reminders that Opus One was California's very first ultra-premium winery, and it still tries hard to retain that edge with its wines and its attitude, producing among the best cabernet in the valley. As well as the signature wine at

$160 a bottle, Opus One also makes a cheaper nonvintage cabernet called Overture that sells for about a third that price.

The hour-long, appointment-only tour is free, however, and takes in some of the striking features of the winery. The building, completed in 1991, is a half-buried architectural tribute to the contemporary and old-school heritages (and wines) of the two founders, resembling a spaceship that landed in Rome. Inside, antique European furniture blends with minimalist design touches and state-of-the-art wine-making elements like the semicircular barrel aging room. Despite the opulence, this is a relatively small winery by Napa standards, making about 35,000 cases a year (7900 U.S. 29, Oakville, 707/944-9442, www.opusonewinery.com, 10 A.M.–4 P.M. daily, tasting $25, tours 10:30 A.M.).

Far Niente

One of the most highly regarded wineries in the valley opened to the public only in 2004, but the appointment-only tour and tasting is among one of the best in the valley for the price, not least because Far Niente makes only two highly regarded (and expensive) wines—cabernet sauvignon and chardonnay—so the tasting of five wines will always include some older, library wines.

Far Niente was established as a winery in the late 1800s, and the name is Italian for "without a care," which was appropriate considering the place was abandoned before Prohibition in 1919. Oklahoma businessman Gil Nickel bought the elegant old stone buildings in 1979 and has since transformed the winery into a Napa wine-making powerhouse (he also established the nearby Nickel & Nickel winery). Far Niente now produces just over 30,000 cases of wine a year, around a third of it cabernet from the Oakville appellation, and is known for its consistently high ratings from critics.

Among the highlights of the tour are a walk through aging caves under the main house, which have been extended into a 40,000-square-foot labyrinth over the decades, and a chance to see Nickel's classic cars in the Carriage House, many of which he raced at some point, including a rare prototype Ferarri (known as the Yellow Beast). Those lucky enough to visit in April and May will also see some of the 8,000 azaleas in bloom in the 13 acres of gardens with a sweeping view of the valley (1350 Acacia Dr., off the Oakville Grade, Oakville, 707/944-2861, www.farniente.com, tours10 A.M.–4 P.M. Mon.–Sat. by appointment, $40).

Nickel & Nickel

Almost opposite the lavish Mondavi winery is the rather quaint Victorian farmstead of Nickel & Nickel, sister winery to Far Niente just down the road. Gil Nickel of Far Niente fame founded the winery in the mid-1990s to make only wines made entirely from one type of grape rather than containing small percentages of blending grapes that never get mentioned on the bottle.

The collection of beautifully restored cottages, barns, and centerpiece 1884 Sullenger House opened to the public in 2003 and can be seen on the appointment-only tour, which culminates with the tasting of five wines. Considering that the winery only makes about 15,000 cases of wine a year it has a big portfolio, including vineyard-designate chardonnay, merlot, cabernet, zinfandel, and syrah (8164 U.S. 29, Oakville, 707/967-9600, www.nickelandnickel.com, tasting and tours daily by appointment, 10 A.M.–2 P.M. Mon.–Fri., until 3 P.M. weekends, $30).

Robert Mondavi Winery

This sprawling mission-style complex with its distinctive giant archway and bell tower is considered by some to be the temple of Napa wine-making, with Robert Mondavi himself as high priest, and by others as an example of the over-commercialization of the Napa wine industry.

The winery itself is the crown jewel of the Robert Mondavi Corporation, which acquired many other Californian and international wineries since Mondavi established his winery in the 1960s and helped shape the valley's modern-day wine industry. The Robert Mondavi stable now includes Arrowood Vineyards over

in the Sonoma Valley; the Woodbridge winery in central California, which makes a cheaper range of wines; a share of the exclusive Opus One winery just down the road, and several Italian wineries. Annual production for all the Mondavi labels is measured in the millions of cases rather than the thousands.

At the time it was built in 1966, this was the first new winery in the valley since Prohibition, and the ever-growing company remained family-controlled until 2004, when it was bought by the multinational Constellation Brands.

The Robert Mondavi labeled wines available here are generally the company's premium wines, and all are from the Napa Valley. They include mostly red and white varietals, including single-vineyard wines and some highly regarded reserves. Unfortunately, the opportunities to taste them are relatively limited.

A comprehensive $20 tour of the vineyards and winery includes a tasting of three wines and is offered nearly every hour, with reservations taken for those at 10 A.M., noon, and 2 P.M. Otherwise, the only tasting option is in the Kalon Room, where sampling a flight of four reserve wines costs $30, though it's free to wander around the courtyard and giant shop (7801 U.S. 29, Oakville, 707/226-1395 or 888/766-6328, www.robertmondaviwinery.com, 10 A.M.–5 P.M. daily).

SIGHTS

Napa Valley Museum

More about the history of Napa and the entire valley can be found at the Napa Valley Museum, in Yountville (55 Presidents Circle, off California Dr., Yountville, 707/944-0500, www.napavalleymuseum.org, 10 A.M.–5 P.M. daily except Tues., adults $4.50, kids $2).

It usually has a fascinating mix of exhibits exploring the valley's natural and cultural heritage, from the modern wine industry back to Native American life, together with an interactive, high-tech exhibit on the science of wine-making. From the St. Helena Highway north of Napa take the Veteran's Home exit and head west on California Drive.

SHOPPING

Yountville, population about 3,500, is the little valley town that can—can separate you from your money better than any other. It seems to have more shops and restaurants per capita than any other place in the valley.

Most are in and around the giant brick **Vintage 1870** building (6525 Washington St., Yountville, 707/944-2451, 10 A.M.–5:30 P.M. daily) that was once a winery and distillery, built in (you guessed it) 1870 by German immigrant Gottlieb Groezinger, who made most of his fortune decades before in the gold rush.

His huge winery was left abandoned after Prohibition, and just over a century after it was built it was transformed from a temple of wine to a temple of consumerism. Groezinger might turn in his grave to know that his winery estate's mansion next to the main building is now home to the boisterous Mexican restaurant Compadres Bar & Grill. Then again, not every shopping center can boast being on the National Registry of Historic Places.

The building has been tastefully restored inside, with the exposed brick and giant wooden beams lending an air of sophistication to the 36 mostly unsophisticated little boutique shops selling everything from clothes and accessories to toys, art, and the usual silly gifts.

Most of them clearly thrive on tourist dollars, but it's still fun to get lost for half an hour exploring the nooks and crannies of the three floors. Some of the more memorable shops include **Cravings,** on the ground floor near the back entrance, which sells some gourmet food that could be useful for a picnic as well as some interesting gourmet cookware; **Domain Home & Garden** and **Gami's Scandia Imports,** which both sell some fun items for the home and garden; and **The Barrel Cellar,** just off the courtyard, which sells plenty of overpriced wine-related paraphernalia. Just across the courtyard is the **Vintage 1870 Wine Cellar,** a decent and fairly large wine shop that sells a lot of local and international wines and has occasional tastings.

Arts and crafts lovers should cross Washing-ton Street to the rather undistinguished and equally touristy **Beard Plaza,** which is where some of the town's galleries can be found, including **RAS Galleries** (707/944-9211), which features contemporary ceramic, glass, and sculpture artists.

RECREATION

Napa River Ecological Reserve

They saved a small patch of land next to the river in Yountville from the vineyards and it's now a great place to see wildlife other than the flocks of tourists most commonly sighted in these parts. Almost 150 types of bird and 40 types of butterfly call this peaceful 70-acre patch of the valley home.

The small paved parking lot is on the north side of Yountville Cross Road, about halfway between the St. Helena Highway and the Silverado Trail. There's just one trail, about a mile long, that dives into woodland, crosses the river (only possible during the dry summer and fall months), and eventually loops back on itself.

Golf

Just south of the Domaine Chandon winery is the 9-hole, 2,800-yard **Vintner's Golf Club** in Yountville (7901 Solano Ave., off California Dr., 707/944-1992, www.vintnersgolfclub.com, call for tee times). Fees range from $18 midweek to $28 weekends for 9 holes, and up to $36 to play 18 holes.

ACCOMMODATIONS

The small town of Yountville just eight miles north of Napa, halfway to St. Helena, has an impressive number of restaurants, shops, and places to stay, and is right on the St. Helena Highway and a major cross-valley road, bringing it that much closer to most of the valley's major wineries.

Those advantages make the town both blessed and cursed, however. Easy access and plentiful services make it a great base from which to explore the valley, but Yountville also attracts hordes of visitors during the day and suffers from almost constant traffic noise near the St. Helena Highway, destroying much of the rural charm and often making it feel more like a suburban mall than a historic town of 3,000 residents. You might wonder where all the locals actually are—they tend to emerge at night after the shops close.

Curiously, Yountville has a high preponderance of French-themed inns and restaurants, not that this part of the valley is more connected to France than any other—just another example of how the Napa Valley still struggles to carve out a unique identity for itself.

Under $150

The Orient Express it is not but it is the only place in the valley where you can sleep on a train. Sort of. The nine railcars and cabooses that constitute the affordable **Napa Valley Railway Inn** (6503 Washington St., Yountville, 707/944-2000) took their last trip many decades ago and are now fitted out with king or queen beds, air conditioning, skylights, and private bathrooms, making surprisingly comfortable accommodations right in the middle of Yountville ($110–130 winter and spring, $130–145 summer and fall). The downside is that they are stranded in the middle of a sea of blacktop that is the parking lot for the Vintage 1870 shopping center (there'll certainly be no problem parking here). The odd-numbered red rooms back onto the main parking lot and St. Helena Highway beyond. The blue rooms are a bit quieter and back onto a smaller parking lot and downtown Yountville. In any of the rooms, just remember to draw the curtains at night.

$150–200

The **Burgundy House Inn** (6711 Washington St., Yountville, 707/944-0889, www .burgundyhouseinn.com) is a half mile from the busy center of Yountville in an old stone building with pretty window boxes that looks like it's been transported straight from a French country village. Just try to ignore the bland, modern restaurant building next door. Most of the five rooms ($135–175 a night) have raw stone walls

inside, too, creating an unusually rustic contrast to the French country-style furnishings. One has its own private entrance. Just as rustic is the lack of televisions, and the central air conditioning—you'll have to ask the inn to crank it up if it gets too hot in summer. Breakfasts are adequate but nothing to write home about, though one of Yountville's best breakfast cafés, Gordon's, is right opposite if you fancy something more substantial to start the day.

In the heart of Yountville is the **N Maison Fleurie** (6529 Yount St., Yountville, 707/944-2056 or 800/788-0369, www .maisonfleurienapa.com), which also does its best to be more French than Californian. The old, ivy-covered stone and brick buildings around a pretty courtyard certainly evoke the French countryside, as does the vineyard right across the street. Inside the cozy lobby and the 15 rooms the French country theme continues, though it tends to go a little over the top with the flowery fabrics and faux antiques. Cozy is also the word used by the hotel to describe its smallest and cheapest rooms—the Cozy Double is just 50 square feet. They start at $130 and at that price sell out quickly despite their diminutive floor space. Plan on spending time outside by the small pool to prevent claustrophobia if you do get one. The biggest rooms ($200–285) are in the adjoining Carriage House and Bakery buildings, and include fireplaces, views, and spa tubs in some.

The teddy bears on the beds of Maison Fleurie are a feature of the small chain of hotels owned by Four Sisters Inns, which also owns the **Lavender Inn** (2020 Webber St., Yountville, 707/944-1388 or 800/522-4140, www.lavendernapa.com). The nine spacious rooms here are similarly themed in French country style, though with a little more of a contemporary feel, and cost $200–250 a night. All have fireplaces, and a few have private hot tubs and patios to take in the smell of the lavender gardens on warm summer nights. Guests can also use the pool at Maison Fleurie down the road.

The French theme continues (in name, at least) at the tiny **Petit Logis,** tucked away in a one-story building next to Maison Fleurie

(6527 Yount St., Yountville, 877/944-2332, www.petitlogis.com). The five rooms in a row of former shops have their own outside entrances and are decorated in fairly minimal but comfortable France-meets-New-England country style. They include private bathrooms with whirlpool tubs ($150–180 a night midweek depending on season, $225 on weekends). Rates are $20 less without breakfast, but the extra is worth paying because the inn smartly defers to the cooking skills of two nearby restaurants—Pacific Blues across the street or Gordon's Café a short drive (or long walk) away—far better than picking over the less-than-impressive breakfast options at many other inns in the valley.

Over $200

The Yountville area has more than its fair share of upscale lodgings, many of which seem to be competing for conference and meeting business. That roughly translates to some slightly unjustified prices for the average visitor.

Two that are probably more worth the top dollar they charge than most are **Villagio Inn & Spa** and **Vintage Inn,** large, resort-style properties on either side of the Vintage 1870 shopping center that are spacious, luxurious, and far more service oriented than lower-priced inns. The concierges are actually able to get reservations at top local restaurants when your own attempts might fail.

The Vintage Inn (6541 Washington St., Yountville, 707/944-1112 or 800/351-1133, www.vintageinn.com) has a French theme and is the smaller and more attractive of the two, with rooms arranged around gardens, fountains, and pools. The Villagio Inn (6481 Washington St., 707/944-8877 or 800/351-1133, www.villagio.com) has Tuscan-themed decor and similar amenities, plus an on-site spa (that can also be used by Vintage Inn guests) but is in a cluster of buildings that looks like an extension of the neighboring apartment complex, despite the faux Roman gardens. Neither Euro-theme is terribly convincing, but both inns have very similar, spacious rooms with fireplaces and sunken tubs, and a small out-door patio area or balcony. Rates are identical and determined in part by position. A first floor, exterior room starts at $230 midweek in the winter ($330 in the summer) and the midweek price increases for courtyard rooms, peaking with the giant suites ($375–500). Add 10–20 percent for weekend nights throughout the year.

FOOD

Downtown Yountville

Good luck trying to get a reservation at **French Laundry** (6640 Washington St., Yountville, 707/944-2380, dinner daily, lunch weekends). The world-famous restaurant is usually booked up two months in advance for much of the year, despite its astronomical prices and the fact that you can't book any farther in advance than two months. You'll probably remember the seven- or nine-course, set-price dinner as your best meal all year, but you'll want to forget the $175 price in a hurry.

Touched by the same magic, however, is French Laundry's little cousin down the road, **Bouchon** (6534 Washington St., Yountville, 707/944-8037, lunch and dinner daily until 1 A.M., entrées $16–27), a French bistro that gives Bistro Jeanty a run for its money in terms of both food and setting. There's a little more bustle here than at Jeanty, perhaps because of the French Laundry connection or proximity to Yountville's thriving downtown scene (if there is such a place as downtown Yountville), but the brief menu still evokes a relaxed Parisian hole helped by a smattering of French wines on the otherwise Napa-dominated list.

What was once Yountville's most popular casual breakfast hangout, The Diner, closed in 2004 (reportedly to much local dismay), but in its place opened the **Wine Garden Food and Wine Bar** (6476 Washington St., Yountville, 707/945-1002, lunch, dinner, and wine sales daily, plates $6–12), which brought the equally casual small-plate phenomenon to Yountville. Choose from any number of small plates of internationally influenced modern American

a hidden courtyard begging for lunchtime diners near the Bouchon Bakery in Yountville

food, all grouped into categories on the menu and made from local organic ingredients. Then either buy a bottle of local wine from the 70 available here (30 by the glass), or pick one of the tasting flights of three wines before settling down to eat in the clean, modern interior or the pretty picnic garden. This place knows its wines intimately. It was established by the Nord family, long-time valley grape growers and vineyard managers who have connections with countless local wineries, big and small. In homage to a specialty of the restaurant this replaced, the dessert menu also includes Ode to the Diner—two rich, flavored buttermilk shakes.

Tucked behind a rickety wooden storefront next to a dive bar is **Gordon's Café & Wine Bar** (6770 Washington St., Yountville, 707/944-8246, lunch $6–12), a refreshingly low-key little eatery behind the brash modern buildings of Washington Square at the northern end of Yountville. With the demise of The Diner, Gordon's has assumed the mantle of Yountville's breakfast destination and is the sort of place you would certainly not be embarrassed to drag your hungover, unkempt self to on a Sunday morning. It also serves lunches

popular with locals and dinner on Friday nights. Alternatively, just while away an afternoon with a glass or two of the well-priced wines and watch the lost tourists go by.

Opposite Gordon's is the steakhouse Père Jeanty (6725 Washington St., 707/945-1000, dinner daily, entrées $18–39), relative of the cozy little **Bistro Jeanty** (6510 Washington St., Yountville, 707/944-0103, lunch and dinner daily, dinner entrées $14–22) a mile down the road. While the younger Père has reportedly struggled to find the right recipe for success, the original Bistro Jeanty remains as popular as ever thanks to its familiar French bistro menu, which still uses superb ingredients but has resisted getting too fancy, sticking instead to classics like coq au vin and crêpes suzette.

A couple of the most unpretentious places in Yountville are on either side of the Vintage 1870 complex. **Compadres Bar & Grill** (6539 Washington St., 707/944/2406, lunch and dinner daily, dinner entrées $8–20) serves regular Mexican fare under a giant oak tree, which shades both the big restaurant and equally large patio, though does not help much with the road noise. Forget wine here—try one of the 50 or so tequilas, or a big margarita.

Cross Washington Street and walk a hundred yards south to **Hurley's** (6518 Washington St., Yountville, 707/944-2345, lunch and dinner daily, entrées $10–28). It might lack the Frenchified charm of some of its neighbors, but the spacious restaurant has won a loyal following for its Mediterranean-inspired food prepared by renowned Valley chef Bob Hurley. It also stays open far later than other local restaurants, serving from a smaller bar menu 10 P.M.–midnight every day.

Along St. Helena Highway

One of the first big roadside restaurants north of Napa is **Brix** (7377 St. Helena Hwy., Yountville, 707/944-2749, lunch and dinner daily, set-price dinners $40–60), a cavernous place with a little bit of an expense-account atmosphere but which serves some interesting Asian-American food—somewhat of a rarity in the valley. A standout feature of the restaurant is the big patio overlooking vineyards, marred only by traffic noise.

Mustards Grill (7399 St. Helena Hwy., Yountville, 707/944-2424, lunch and dinner daily, dinner entrées $16–24) is considered the king of the valley grills, as illustrated by the line waiting for a table on busy weekends. It might not look like much from the outside, but unlike the Napa Valley Grille and the Rutherford Grill, which are both now part of a chain, Mustards is a thoroughly Napa Valley affair. It has spawned a cookbook and grows many of its own vegetables in its garden as only a Napa restaurant could. The menu is filled with the sort of rich, roasted and grilled meats that scream for a powerful Napa cabernet sauvignon, of which there are several dozen on the international wine list.

Picnic Supplies

In Yountville, the **Bouchon Bakery** (6528 Washington St., Yountville, 707/944-2253), opposite Vintage 1870, has a limited selection of very good sandwiches for under $10, as well as fresh bread and some sweeter bakery delights (try the macaroons). Behind Vintage 1870 and next to the Wine Cellar is the little **Cucina a la Carte** (707/944-1600, 11 A.M.–2 P.M. daily), a café that serves lunch to eat in or take out, including salads and sandwiches.

Farther up the St. Helena Highway is the hard-to-miss **Oakville Grocery** (7856 St. Helena Hwy., Oakville, 707/944-8802, 9 A.M.– 6 P.M. daily). Just look for the line of cars parked at the side of the road next to a rather underwhelming-looking building with only a giant vintage Coca-Cola sign on one wall to brighten it up. Although it lacks the modern glamour of its spin-offs in Healdsburg and Palo Alto, this original is one of the best picnic supply stops in the valley (some say in the entire country) and has certainly stood the test of time.

Farmers Market

Those who really want to assemble a picnic from scratch might want to pick through **Yountville's farmers market,** which operates May– October in the giant Vintage 1870 parking lot (where else?) on Wednesdays 4 P.M.–dusk.

INFORMATION AND SERVICES

The tiny **Yountville Chamber of Commerce** (6516 Yount St., Yountville, 707/944-0904, www.yountville.com, 10 A.M.–3 P.M. daily) is awash with guides, leaflets, magazines, and advice about the local area. The concierge desk at the **Vintage 1870** shopping center is also worth stopping at for some local tips and information.

Rutherford

This is a part of the valley where the weather starts to get seriously warm in the summer and the cabernets get seriously sumptuous. In fact, 70 percent of the vineyards in this appellation are planted to cabernet sauvignon. Try to taste the mysterious "Rutherford dust," a slightly mineral flavor said to be present in some of the classic cabernets from the likes of Beaulieu Vineyard and Niebaum-Coppola.

RUTHERFORD AREA WINERIES
Peju Province Winery
The slightly overstated French provincial architecture here hints at the roots of owner An-

thony Peju, who arrived in the Napa Valley in the 1980s from his homeland of Azerbaijan by way of France, England, and Los Angeles. He was initially a grape grower in the valley, selling fruit to other valley winemakers before finally making his own wine.

He also inadvertently helped smaller winemakers in the late 1980s by successfully suing Napa County when it tried to prevent him from selling wine out of his garage before his new winery had been completed. He won thanks to a state law that allows a grower to sell his product where it is grown, and his victory subtly redefined what the term "winery" actually meant.

The Napa Valley

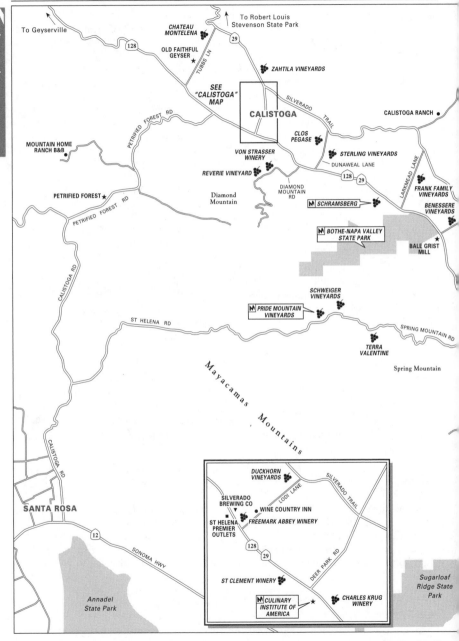

To Geyserville

To Robert Louis
Stevenson State Park

CHATEAU
MONTELENA

OLD FAITHFUL
GEYSER

128

29

ZAHTILA VINEYARDS

TUBBS LN

SEE
"CALISTOGA"
MAP

SILVERADO TRAIL

CALISTOGA

CALISTOGA RANCH

PETRIFIED FOREST RD

MOUNTAIN HOME
RANCH B&B

CLOS
PEGASE

VON STRASSER
WINERY

STERLING VINEYARDS

DUNAWEAL LANE

128

29

LARKMEAD LANE

FRANK FAMILY
VINEYARDS

PETRIFIED FOREST

REVERIE VINEYARD

Diamond
Mountain

DIAMOND
MOUNTAIN
RD

SCHRAMSBERG

BENESSERE
VINEYARDS

PETRIFIED FOREST RD

CALISTOGA RD

BOTHE-NAPA VALLEY
STATE PARK

BALE GRIST
MILL

ST HELENA RD

SCHWEIGER
VINEYARDS

PRIDE MOUNTAIN
VINEYARDS

SPRING MOUNTAIN RD

TERRA
VALENTINE

Spring Mountain

Mayacamas Mountains

CALISTOGA RD

SANTA ROSA

12

SONOMA HWY

Annadel
State Park

DUCKHORN
VINEYARDS

SILVERADO
BREWING CO

LODI LANE

SILVERADO TRAIL

Wine Country Inn

ST HELENA
PREMIER
OUTLETS

FREEMARK ABBEY WINERY

128

29

DEER PARK RD

ST CLEMENT WINERY

CULINARY
INSTITUTE
OF
AMERICA

CHARLES KRUG
WINERY

Sugarloaf
Ridge State
Park

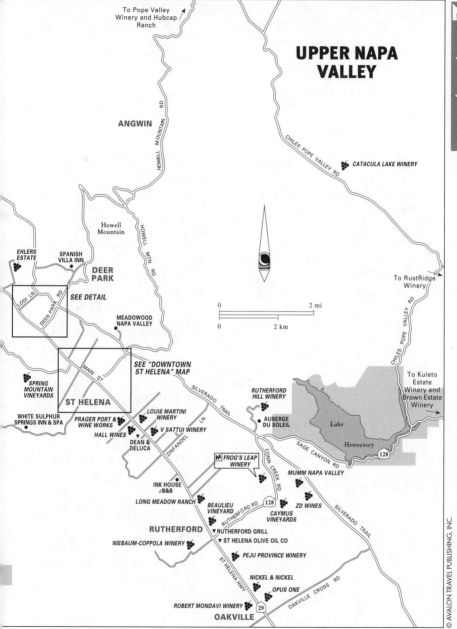

UPPER NAPA VALLEY

To Pope Valley
Winery and Hubcap
Ranch

ANGWIN

HOWELL MOUNTAIN RD

CHILES POPE VALLEY RD

CATACULA LAKE WINERY

Howell
Mountain

HOWELL MTN RD

EHLERS
ESTATE

SPANISH
VILLA INN

DEER
PARK

To RustRidge
Winery

LODI LN

DEER PARK RD

SEE DETAIL

MEADOWOOD
NAPA VALLEY

0   2 mi

0   2 km

To Kuleto
Estate
Winery and
Brown Estate
Winery

SPRING
MOUNTAIN
VINEYARDS

MAIN ST

SEE "DOWNTOWN
ST HELENA" MAP

ST HELENA

SILVERADO TRAIL

RUTHERFORD
HILL WINERY

Lake
Hennessey

CHILES POPE VALLEY RD

128

WHITE SULPHUR
SPRINGS INN & SPA

PRAGER PORT &
WINE WORKS

HALL WINES

LOUIS MARTINI
WINERY

V SATTUI WINERY

DEAN &
DELUCA

ZINFANDEL LN

CONN CREEK RD

AUBERGE
DU SOLEIL

SAGE CANYON RD

MUMM NAPA VALLEY

SILVERADO TRAIL

FROG'S LEAP
WINERY

INK HOUSE
B&B

LONG MEADOW RANCH

BEAULIEU
VINEYARD

RUTHERFORD RD

128

ZD WINES

CAYMUS
VINEYARDS

RUTHERFORD

ST HELENA HWY

RUTHERFORD GRILL

ST HELENA OLIVE OIL CO

NIEBAUM-COPPOLA WINERY

PEJU PROVINCE WINERY

NICKEL & NICKEL

OPUS ONE

OAKVILLE CROSS RD

ROBERT MONDAVI WINERY

29

OAKVILLE

TAKING TOURS TO ANOTHER LEVEL

There are already gondolas and balloon rides, buildings full of art and others full of history, Hollywood connections and classic car collections. What could possibly upstage such a diverse collection of attractions in this giant theme park of viticultural hedonism?

How about a ride around a mountain ranch on a Swiss military vehicle that looks like a six-wheeled roller-coaster car and has a name that's tough to pronounce even before tasting the wine at the top?

It might sound unlikely, but that is the latest and perhaps greatest (for now at least) tour in the valley, offered not by a big-money winery funded by Disney but by the humble **Long Meadow Ranch,** a tranquil 650-acre organic farm looking down from the Mayacamas Mountains to the traffic-choked highway below.

Ted Hall, a former management consultant who grew up on a farm in Pennsylvania, bought the historic ranch in 1989 and has since transformed it into a farming business that could probably fill every stall at the nearby St. Helena farmers market all year long. Lean beef (from shaggy-looking Highland cattle), eggs, vegetables, and olive oil are all part of the organic bounty. The ranch also breeds and sells horses and cattle.

This being Napa, of course, wine also gets a hook in. In fact, vineyards were planted up here as far back as the late 1800s by some accounts. The ranch's cabernet sauvignon has taken its place alongside some of the best in the valley in recent years, and a sangiovese was added to the portfolio in 2000. The couple of acres of merlot grapes planted in the late 1990s go into the proprietary Ranch House Red blend.

Tasting the wines and a couple of olive oils is the culmination of the unusual, two-hour tour in those Swiss army vehicles called Pinzgauers, which roll up into the hills from Rutherford, through vineyards, olive orchards, and meadows, to the spectacular building containing the winery and olive press. The building itself is a model of sustainable practices, with walls made from compressed earth dug out during construction of the caves, and all its power provided by solar panels.

If the Pinzgauer sounds a little too gimmicky you can also get ferried up the hill and follow a hiking trail around the ranch, though you won't see as much and won't save any money—both tour options cost $75 and take about two hours. For an additional $75, you can taste just about everything the ranch produces, including some library wines, with a gourmet picnic after the main tour (picnic is perhaps too modest a term—multicourse lunch would be a better description).

The organic farming spread down the hill when Ted Hall also bought a six-acre parcel of land next to Highway 29 in Rutherford and, instead of planting vines like all his neighbors, turned it into a vegetable garden. Produce is sold at the farmers market, to local restaurants, and also at a roadside stand that's open May–October. Rutherford Gardens, as it's called, is also where the tours start from, and is right across from the Grgich Hills winery (1796 St. Helena Hwy. S, Rutherford).

For more information about the tours and to book a spot, contact Long Meadow Ranch (707/963-4555, www.longmeadowranch.com) at least 48 hours before you'd like to take a tour. There doesn't seem to be a fixed schedule for the tours, though most apparently happen on weekends.

Peju's winery, with its manicured gardens, sculptures, curiously shaped trees, and classy tasting room with giant stained-glass window, was finally completed in 1990 and now produces about 30,000 cases of wine, though there are plans to eventually increase this threefold.

It is perhaps best known for its cabernet franc, but that's one wine that is not available for tasting due to its almost cult-like status. It sells out within months of its release each year, but Peju eventually plans to expand production and offer both reserve and vineyard-designate cabernet franc in the tasting room.

Instead, visitors can taste the equally outstanding estate cabernet sauvignon and the unusual Provence table wine, a dark rosé blend of almost all the other varietals Peju grows—merlot, cabernet franc, and syrah, plus the white colombard and sauvignon blanc. Those varietals, together with zinfandel, are also available as separate wines, many sold only through the winery (8466 U.S. 29, Rutherford, 707/963-3600 or 800/446-7358, www.peju.com, 10 A.M.–6 P.M. daily, tasting $5).

Frog's Leap Winery

Unlike many of his haughty neighbors, owner John Williams injects some fun into the often staid Napa wine scene, from the name of the winery and its classy, black-and-white deco-style wine labels, to a wine called Leapfrogmilch (a blend of riesling and chardonnay, and a perfect picnic wine) and the ever-present winery motto "Time's fun when you're having flies."

Frog's Leap was actually formed by Williams and partner Larry Turley in 1981 near St. Helena on a former frog farm that once supplied the little amphibians' legs to restaurants throughout California. The winery's name was also a take on Stags' Leap, that famous winery farther south where Williams was once winemaker (and from where he reportedly spirited away grapes to make his first independent wines). It was not until 1994 when the partnership ended that Williams moved the winery to Rutherford and restored the huge red barn that was home to the Adamson winery a hundred years before.

All along, organic farming practices were used by Williams, and Frog's Leap is now regarded as a champion of organic practices in the valley. It also has a big organic vegetable and fruit garden, and visitors can usually help themselves to produce or simply picnic on the huge expanses of grass. Even on a busy summer weekend, Frog's Leap never really feels crowded.

Although you can visit the winery free and taste the wine of the day (and perhaps luck out with some fresh fruit), an appointment is required for the two or three free tours each day, which highlight organic farming and end with a tasting of four wines. Almost half the 60,000 cases of wine made here each year are the excellent and well-priced sauvignon blanc, but Frog's Leap is also known for its cabernet sauvignon, zinfandel, and the flagship Rutherford, a bordeaux-style red blend that highlights the unique fruit-meets-earth characteristics of Rutherford appellation wines.

The portfolio also includes merlot, chardonnay, syrah, and a wine called (appropriately enough) Pink, which is another fun and cheap picnic wine (8815 Conn Creek Rd., off Silverado Trail, Rutherford, 707/963-4704 or 800/959-4704, www.frogsleap.com, 10 A.M.–4 P.M. Mon.–Sat., free tours twice daily).

Caymus Vineyards

This is a great example of how wineries on this side of the valley turn out some of the best wines with little fanfare. The Caymus family has been farming in the valley for more than 100 years but was ahead of the modern wine-making crowds when they ripped up their prune orchards to plant vines in the early 1970s.

Since then, Caymus gained a reputation under the ownership of the late Charlie Wagner for producing one of the best Napa cabernets, the Special Selection, made with the best grapes from the estate vineyard in Rutherford. The only other wine made here now, by Charlie's son, Chuck, is a nonreserve cabernet, equally impressive but at half the price (8700 Conn Creek Rd., Rutherford, 707/967-3010, www.caymus.com, free tasting 10 A.M.–4 P.M. daily by appointment).

Beaulieu Vineyard

It's not very fitting for such a historic valley winery to have a tasting room squeezed behind the Rutherford Grill and surrounded by a giant parking lot, but the giant, ivy-clad winery building itself is a reminder of the huge role Beaulieu Vineyard (BV) played in the modern Californian wine industry.

Founded in 1900 by Frenchman Georges de Latour, BV was one of the few wineries to maintain production during Prohibition. After repeal, Latour brought a young wine expert over from France to help him refine his wines and ensure they would not spoil while being shipped to the East Coast markets. That man was the late **André Tchelistcheff,** a Russian emigré who ended up transforming the way wine was made in California while he was winemaker at Beaulieu from 1938 to 1973.

Tchelistcheff helped modernize the winemaking process and improved vineyard management at Beaulieu. Where he led, others followed. BV wines were soon winning awards, and the quality of the valley's other wines drastically improved as Tchelistcheff's methods became commonplace. He is also said to have coined the term "Rutherford dust" for the area's soils, an expression still used today by critics who claim to be able to taste the soil's characteristics in the wines.

BV has long since passed into the hands of multinational wine conglomerates (it is currently owned by Diageo) and now makes over a million cases of wine a year. It is perhaps best known for its powerful, dusty cabernet sauvignons, in particular the flagship Georges Latour Private Reserve and the more approachable Tapestry blend, plus the cheaper nonreserve Rutherford. BV also makes a full range of other red and white wines from its Napa Valley vineyards, five of which can always be tasted from the ever-changing tasting menu ($5). Alternatively, try a horizontal or vertical tasting of the reserves for $25 in the new reserve tasting room (1960 U.S. 29, Rutherford, 707/967-5200, www.bvwines.com, tastings and tours 10 A.M.–5 P.M. daily).

Rutherford Hill

Arguably the best merlot for the price and certainly the best winery picnic grounds can be found at Rutherford Hill, just off the Silverado Trail overlooking the valley. This was once the sister winery to what is now Chateau Souverain in Sonoma's Alexander Valley, when both were briefly owned by the Pillsbury food company in the early 1970s. The Rutherford Hill name dates from 1975, when a group of investors bought the winery, and since then it has carved out a name for making excellent and consistent merlot. That varietal now accounts for about three-quarters of the 100,000 cases of wine made here.

Rutherford Hill also makes small quantities of a lot of other, less highly praised wines. They include cabernet sauvignon, syrah, sangiovese, and chardonnay from its Napa Valley vineyards and a gewürztraminer from Mendocino vineyards, which is a perfect wine to have with a picnic on the acre of beautiful wooded hillside picnic grounds.

In the 1980s the winery also carved out some of the most extensive aging caves in the valley, with more than a mile of tunnels that can store about 8,000 barrels of wine. They can be seen as part of the short tour offered three times a day at 11:30 A.M. and 1:30 and 3:30 P.M., for $10 including a regular tasting or $15 with a reserve tasting (200 Rutherford Hill Rd., off Silverado Trail, Rutherford. 707/963-1871, www.rutherfordhill.com, 10 A.M.–5 P.M. daily, tasting $10 or $15 for reserves).

Niebaum-Coppola Estate Winery

It was probably inevitable that when one of the most storied of the historic Napa Valley wineries was bought by a fabled Hollywood director the result would be one of the most ostentatious winery shows in the valley. And so it is at the Niebaum-Coppola Estate, where stretch limos idle in the parking lot and a giant red velvet curtain greets visitors as they enter the historic ivy-clad stone mansion nestled at the foot of the scenic hills.

Try to ignore the pergolas and fountains outside—they are modern additions that manage to turn the otherwise beautiful mansion into just part of a fake-looking film set. Inside, a small museum highlights the history of the former Inglenook Estate, which Francis Ford Coppola and his wife, Eleanor, bought in sections between 1975 (a year after *The Godfather II* was released) and 1994, and which they have since transformed into a huge tourist and wine-making presence in the valley. And with this being part Hollywood production, there's also plenty of ego-massaging museum space devoted to the Coppolas themselves, including the film careers of Francis, Eleanor, and their children Sofia and Roman.

The Inglenook Estate was originally established in 1871 by the son-in-law of George Yount, the first white settler in Napa Valley who was also credited with planting the first vineyard in the valley in 1838. Inglenook, its vineyard, and some surrounding land were bought in 1879 by Alaskan fur trader Gustave Niebaum, who set about becoming a serious wine producer, albeit as more of a hobby than a business. Niebaum died in 1908, but the winery and its mission to make world-class wines lived on in fits and starts in the hands of Niebaum's widow, friends, and relatives (including Niebaum's great-nephew, renowned valley winemaker John Daniel), until it was sold to United Vintners in 1964, which eventually became Heublein in 1969.

What the Coppolas bought in 1975 was not actually the Inglenook winery operation but part of the estate's land and Niebaum's mansion. Nevertheless, a new winery was born in 1978 and called Niebaum-Coppola in homage to Gustave Niebaum and his pursuit of wine perfection. Legendary winemaker André Tchelistcheff helped the Coppolas create their first wine, called Rubicon, a powerful bordeaux blend that is still made today.

The entire Inglenook Estate was eventually reunited almost 20 years later when the Coppolas bought much of the rest of the Inglenook winery and its vineyards from Heublein in 1994 (one of the Inglenook production facilities was sold to the Napa Wine Company in Oakville).

Despite its grand surroundings and history, Niebaum-Coppola makes a modest 20,000 cases of estate wines, including the flagship Rubicon; its white equivalent, called Blancaneaux; and cabernet franc, merlot, zinfandel, cabernet, and an unusual sparkling wine called Sofia blanc de blancs. It's made using pinot blanc, muscat, and sauvignon blanc, giving it a richer fruit flavor than traditional sparklers (there's no mention of whether the wine's character matches Sofia Coppola's).

The Coppola name is attached to many other cheaper wine labels, however, and production of Coppola-branded wines amounts to about 750,000 cases a year. The Director's Reserve label is one of those available in the three spacious tasting rooms, where most of the wines can be sampled or bought by the glassful. Basic tasting of four wines costs $15, but for just $10 more there is a worthwhile tour of the mansion three times a day (10:30 A.M. and 12:30 and 2:30 P.M.) that includes a tasting session. Separate appointment-only tours of the vineyards and wine-making facilities are also available, but times vary, so call for more information (1991 U.S. 29, Rutherford, 707/968-1100, www.niebaum-coppola.com, 10 A.M.–5 P.M. daily).

Mumm Napa Valley

A late starter among the French champagne houses to set up here in California, Mumm Napa was established in 1985 by France's G. H. Mumm and Seagram, though it has been owned by Allied Domecq (which also owns G. H. Mumm) since 2002. The unassuming, barn-like winery building was completed on the Silverado Trail in 1988 and now makes about 200,000 cases of sparkling wine from more than 50 vineyards all over Carneros and the Napa Valley.

They range from the classic and reasonably priced Brut Prestige, a dry blend of pinot noir and chardonnay, up to the more fruit-forward and expensive DVX, which comes in white and rosé styles. Mumm also makes a winery-only pinot gris still wine, which is perfect for a picnic but tends to sell out quickly.

Like all the big champagne houses in the valley, Mumm puts on quite a show for visitors and has a bewildering array of options for tasting the wines. Relax on the big patio and have someone bring you a sampling of four sparklers. Or buy a glass of champagne and wander through the small art gallery, which features a permanent collection of Ansel Adams prints and another photography exhibit that changes several times a year. Those who prefer to learn more about what they are drinking should take the informative (and free) tour, which runs on the hour until 3 P.M. and illustrates the art and science behind the bubbles. Private tours are also available by appointment (8445 Silverado Trail, Rutherford, 707/967-7700, www.mummcuveenapa.com, 10 A.M.–5 P.M. daily, tasting $5–12).

ZD Wines

People leave all sorts of professions to establish wineries, though perhaps one of the more unusual is the aeronautical engineering business that Gino Zepponi (the "Z" in the name) and Norman de Leuze (the "D") eventually left to concentrate on the winery they had started as a hobby in Carneros in 1969. By the time they had put ZD on the map as a producer of high-quality chardonnay and pinot noir, wine-making was a full time profession. Their winery moved to its current location in Rutherford in 1979.

ZD is now owned by the de Lueze family and still makes outstanding chardonnay and pinot from its Carneros vineyards, including reserves. Those two varietals also still account for the majority of the 30,000 cases made each year but have been joined by a rich cabernet sauvignon from other Napa appellations, together with a reserve cabernet from ZD's own three acres of vineyards in Rutherford. All are available in the tasting room but can also be tried at the $20 wine and cheese pairing offered every Saturday morning by appointment. Free tours of the small winery are also offered about three times a day by appointment.

Taking pricey Napa cabernet to the extreme, ZD also makes limited quantities of its Abacus wine each year from a blend of all its previous vintages of reserve cabernet, starting from 1992. In 2005, Abacus VII was released, containing 13 former vintages. The idea is to combine the best aspects of aged wine with the fruit of more youthful wine. You'll have to pay upwards of $325 per bottle to find out if it succeeds, however, because Abacus is not available for tasting (8383 Silverado Trail, Napa, 800/487-7757, www.zdwines.com, 10 A.M.–4:30 P.M. daily, regular tasting $5, reserve $10).

SHOPPING

Yountville and St. Helena have done a pretty good job of sucking the retailing life from elsewhere in the midvalley area with the exception of the **St. Helena Olive Oil Company** (8576 St. Helena Hwy. S., Rutherford, 707/967-1003 or 800/939-9880, 10 A.M.–5 P.M. daily), which is orphaned a few miles south of its namesake town in Rutherford. Don't be put off by the modest storefront while tooling up the road toward St. Helena. This place has a cavernous interior and sells far more than olive oils. In fact, almost every condiment a gourmet cook might need (and some they never knew they needed) is probably here, from balsamic vinegar to honey by way of strange concoctions like apricot pepper and stone-ground cabernet mustard. Take a break from wine tasting and try some of the 20 or so olive oils lined up on the counter. Then end the break and wash the oils down with more wine at the tasting counter of **Off the Map Wines** (www.offthemapwines.com, tasting fee $10), which represents more than a dozen of the valley's small, high-end wine producers.

ACCOMMODATIONS

High up in the eastern hills of the valley, bathed in afternoon sun, is **Ⅺ Auberge du Soleil,** or the Inn of the Sun, one of the valley's most luxurious resorts (180 Rutherford Hill Rd., Rutherford, 707/963-1211 or 800/348-5406, www.aubergedusoleil.com). This is a place totally at ease with itself, where the decor plays a relaxed second fiddle to the stunning location rather than competing. Terracotta tiles, natural woods, fireplaces, leather, and earth tones hint at some French country style, but it's the views from almost everywhere that dominate. Work out in the gym with views, eat with views at the acclaimed restaurant, swim with views, or step out of your room's French doors onto a balcony with views. Just be prepared to pay dearly for those views.

There are 50 rooms and suites in cottages spread throughout the 33 lush acres of this former olive grove, and all have the word "view" in their descriptions. The cheapest and smallest are the Hilltop View rooms ($450 in winter, $550 summer/fall) in the main building upstairs from the restaurant and bar, though they "may be inappropriate for light sleepers," the resort suggests. Slightly larger rooms in better locations start at $500–650, and the mammoth suites that are the size of most apartments range $800–1,600 a night.

FOOD

If a special occasion requires a special restaurant (and French Laundry is not answering the phone), there's probably no better place in this part of the valley than **Auberge du Soleil** (180 Rutherford Hill Rd., off Silverado Trail, Ruth-

erford, 707/967-3111 or 800/348-5406, reservations required, lunch and dinner daily). You don't need to be a guest to see why this resort restaurant has been wowing diners with its menu and stunning views of the valley since 1981. The wow factor is still as strong as ever and might make you want to stay at the resort on your next visit (after saving up, that is).

The exquisitely prepared French-Californian food is not as expensive as you'd think—the $79 set price buys you a four-course dinner with plenty of choices for every course. Just make sure you choose a fine day, and try to get a table out on the terrace for the best views, especially at sunset. And casual as it might be, don't turn up in board shorts and flip-flops.

For some more down-to-earth dining, often without the need for a reservation, the **Rutherford Grill** (1180 Rutherford Rd., next to Beaulieu Vineyard's winery, Rutherford, 707/963-1792, lunch and dinner daily, dinner entrées $15–40) offers traditional steakhouse fare in a rather corporate setting that hints at the fact it is owned by the Houston's restaurant chain. It's a great place for a steak to pair with a Rutherford cabernet, but not the place to go for cutting-edge California cuisine. There's also a nice patio, though it's too close to the road to be peaceful.

St. Helena and Vicinity

St. Helena has been the center of the valley's wine industry from the very beginning, when George Crane first planted grapes in the area in 1861 followed by Charles Krug a few years later. With the new wine industry springing up all around, the town grew rapidly and was incorporated in 1876, only a few years after Napa and many years before Calistoga in 1885.

St. Helena's history has been inextricably linked to the valley's wine industry ever since. Calistoga to the north had its spas to draw visitors, and Napa to the south became a thriving commercial port city, gateway to the valley. St. Helena has to a certain extent always been a tourist town. Wealthy weekenders came here

to wine and dine in the early 1900s, an influx of European immigrants created the thriving Italian and French heritage, and the town was the epicenter of the valley's bootlegging industry during Prohibition, making the St. Helena Highway almost as busy in the 1930s as it is today.

This might be a town with the dubious distinction of having a name used disparagingly as a verb—"St. Helena-ization" being the process of a pretty town selling its soul to tourism—but it also boasts active civic leaders who fight hard against overdevelopment in an attempt to keep some semblance of the town's historic and rural charm intact.

The Wines

As the Napa Valley gets narrower farther north and the mountains ever more sheltering, the weather gets hotter. The **St. Helena** appellation includes the narrowest point of the valley and also some of the biggest and most historic winery names, like Beringer, Charles Krug, and Louis Martini.

West of St. Helena is the **Spring Mountain** appellation, where an increasing number of wineries are making quite a name for their well-balanced and supple red wines, none more so than Pride Mountain Vineyards, which straddles the Sonoma-Napa border along the crest of the mountain range.

ST. HELENA WINERIES

V. Sattui Winery

To say this place gets crowded in the summer is a slight understatement. Sattui can resemble a supermarket the night before Thanksgiving, an appropriate description considering that food is one of the major draws.

This is picnic central (and often party central) for this part of the valley, though after eating enough free deli samples you might not need to buy picnic supplies. The pungent smell of the dozens of cheeses and countless other gourmet foods fills the tasting room of the stone winery building, while on summer weekends hardly an inch of grass is visible outside in the big picnic area, despite the constant drone of traffic from the main road.

V. Sattui is an old wine business but the winery itself is not that old. Vittorio Sattui started making wine in San Francisco in the late 1800s using grapes from St. Helena vineyards. But it wasn't until 1975 that a winery was built here by great-grandson Daryl Sattui. The wines and delicatessen were instant hits.

Sattui now makes about 45,000 cases of wine each year, with most bottles costing less than $20. Rave reviews from critics are few and far between, but the wines still fly off the shelves by the caseload. They include a host of great picnic wines, like the popular Gamay Rouge rosé (both still and sparkling forms), a

dry riesling, and a remarkably cheap pinot noir from Carneros, though cabernet sauvignon in both blended and vineyard-designate styles is what the winery is perhaps best known for. All can be tasted for free.

Also worth trying are the dessert wines, including delicious madeira and juicy muscat. Buy a case of any wine and you instantly become a member of the Cellar Club, which has its own tasting bar. The winery has some of the longest opening hours in the valley (1111 White Ln., St. Helena, 707/963-7774, www.vsattui.com, 9 A.M.–5 P.M. daily, to 6 P.M. in summer).

Hall

The is the classy public face of one Napa Valley's rising stars, which has been snapping up prime vineyards since it was established in Rutherford in 1995 by entrepreneurs Kathryn and Craig Hall. It is also likely to become one of the most talked-about wineries in the valley once its new Frank Gehry–designed home is completed.

Hall is the second label currently occupying the old Napa Valley Cooperative Winery, which will eventually be transformed by Gehry and local architect John Lail into a big, modern facility. The Halls promised local residents that there would be "no curvy metal," a trademark of Gehry's designs, and had to tone down some of the more ambitious aspects of the $70 million plan. As of early 2005 those plans were still being revised, so the construction is not likely to be finished until 2006 or beyond.

Once the new winery is completed, production of Hall wines will probably increase from the current 25,000 cases to take full advantage of the hundreds of acres of vineyards the Halls now own in the Napa and Alexander Valleys. Until then, the tasting room is in a shabby-chic stone barn with a bright red awning, pretty courtyard, and sculpture from the Halls' private collection all around.

Kathryn Hall Vineyards in Rutherford, which is not open to the public, makes high-end cabernet sauvignon from its estate vineyards, while the Hall label brings the same style of powerful but easy-drinking wines to the masses for some very reasonable prices, including vineyard-designate cabernet sauvignon, merlot, and sauvignon blanc (401 St. Helena Hwy. S., St. Helena, 866/667-4255, www.hallwines.com, 10 A.M.–5:30 P.M. daily, tasting $10).

Louis M. Martini Winery

The hulking winery of Louis M. Martini just north of Sattui is another piece of Napa's wine-making history, established here in the 1930s by Louis Martini himself, who had previously been making his wines in the Central Valley. Shortly after setting up in the Napa Valley he also bought 240 acres of vineyards in the Mayacamas Mountains above the Sonoma Valley, and that Monte Rosso vineyard has been responsible for Martini's best wines ever since.

The winery was family owned right up to 2002, when it was bought by the even bigger family wine business, the giant E&J Gallo, and became Gallo's first Napa Valley outpost. Gallo pumped millions into upgrading the rather tired old winery, and all eyes are now on Martini to see how its wines will improve as a result. One anticipated change is that the focus will probably shift even more toward cabernet sauvignon, but for now Martini still makes plenty of other wines among the 300,000 cases it churns out each year.

Many of the best wines come from the Monte Rosso vineyard, including a cabernet, several zinfandels, and an unusual white wine made with folle blanche grapes, which are normally used to make brandy and have a curious, apple-like aroma. Another wine worth trying (sometimes offered as a free tasting appetizer) is the dry, creamy gewürztraminer from Martini's Russian River vineyards.

Tasting options in the very businesslike tasting room range from $7 for some generic cabernets up to $15 for a flight of Monte Rosso wines. If there are no white wines on the tasting menu, just ask and the staff will happily set you up with a $5 selection. A sheltered patio provides tables and chairs for those who

want to linger (254 St. Helena Hwy., St. Helena, 707/968-2736, www.louismartini.com, 10 A.M.–4:30 P.M. daily, tasting $7–15).

Prager Wine & Port Works

Right opposite the entrance to Martini is the little wooden sign and driveway leading to a funky, family-owned port producer that is a refreshing change from the commercial atmosphere of most wineries in the area. The closest you'll find to a winery museum here is the Web Window, a masterpiece of spider web engineering that's supposedly been untouched since 1979.

The Prager family makes a few regular wines here (a couple are usually included in the tasting), but most of the 3,500-case annual production is an unusual selection of ports, including a fruity white port made from chardonnay and the more usual vintage and tawny ports made predominantly with cabernet sauvignon and petite sirah grapes. Bring a cigar to enjoy with port out in the garden (1281 Lewelling Ln., St. Helena, 707/963-7678 or 800/969-7678, www.pragerport.com, 10 A.M.–4:30 P.M. daily, tasting $10).

Beringer Vineyards

The oldest continuously operated winery in Napa Valley is now a huge tourist attraction that often contributes to St. Helena's summer traffic jams, though it is still worth a visit (ideally midweek when it's a bit quieter) for its significance in the valley's wine history and for some good wines.

It was started by a couple of German brothers, Jacob and Frederick Beringer, who already knew a bit about wine making by the time they reached California. Jacob arrived first, working briefly for Charles Krug before he bought land nearby. By 1878 his winery was said to be making 100,000 gallons of wine a year (about 45,000 cases by today's measure) and he was eventually joined by his brother, who built the curious Rhine House to remind him of home.

The winery operated through Prohibition and shortly after repeal was making an astonishing 200,000 gallons of wine a year. It was

© PHILIP GOLDSMITH

The Rhine House at Beringer Vineyards harks back to the Beringer family's German roots.

good wine, too. Beringer is one of a handful of historic wineries in the valley (others include Inglenook, Beaulieu, and Larkmead) credited with helping modernize the wine industry after Prohibition by introducing European-style production techniques rather than making cheap, bulk wines.

In the 1970s, the winery was bought by food giant Nestlé, which poured millions into restoring both the property and the reputation of the winery. It is now owned by Fosters Wine Estates and makes several million cases of wine each year under numerous labels (at a modern facility over the road) but is still known for turning out some of the best, most consistent premium wines in California, most notably its Private Reserve chardonnay and cabernet sauvignon.

Beringer was the first Napa winery to offer reserve wine tasting back in the 1980s. It is now offered in the Rhine House and priced depending on the wine you want to taste rather than on a flat-fee basis. The regular tasting in the old winery building costs just $5 for one of several themed flights of wine.

The whole estate was put on the National

Register of Historic Places in 2001, helping to draw the crowds to the ticket booths that make the place feel more like a wine theme park at times. Nevertheless, it still has some of the better tours in the valley (if you can get on them).

The basic tour every hour includes the old stone winery and 19th-century hand-dug caves, plus tasting of a couple of wines, and is a bargain at $5 (no reservations are taken, so come early to buy tickets for a later tour). Twice a day there is also a longer Vintage Legacy Tour ($30, 12:30 and 3 P.M.), which includes a barrel tasting and glass of reserve chardonnay. Another option is the Historic District Tour ($18, daily at 10:30 A.M.), which focuses on the historic significance of the buildings on the estate and includes tasting of four wines. Reservations are essential for the longer tours during the summer. The ultimate experience here is probably the picnic (every Saturday, July–Sept., $65, reserve in advance), which includes barrel tasting followed by a three-course feast in the redwood grove (2000 Main St., St. Helena, 707/963-7115, www.beringer.com, 10 A.M.–5 P.M. daily, till 6 P.M. in summer).

Charles Krug Winery

It's probably fitting that the winery founded by the grandfather of the Napa Valley wine industry, Charles Krug, was also the winery that helped start the modern-day wine dynasty of the Mondavis. Most of the historic parts of the winery are off-limits to the public, however, making a visit a little anticlimactic.

Krug arrived in California in the heady days after the gold rush and fell in with the likes of Agoston Haraszthy, credited with being the first serious winemaker in the state. He planted his first vineyard in the Sonoma Valley in the 1850s next to Haraszthy's ranch and was soon making wine for friends and acquaintances in the Napa Valley, including George Yount (father of Yountville) and Edward Bale (who built the nearby Bale Grist Mill). He eventually sold up in Sonoma and moved to the winery's present-day location in the 1860s, using the land belonging to his new wife, Carolina Bale, to set up the valley's first large-scale winery.

Krug made a lot of wine there, and made quite a reputation for himself both as a winemaker and pillar of the local community. When he died in 1892, his winery was run by his business associate, local banker James Moffit, who maintained its reputation before Prohibition sent it reeling.

Enter the Mondavis. In 1943, the Krug winery was saved from its post-repeal life as a bulk wine producer when Cesare Mondavi bought it and built a new family wine business around it, creating one of the leading wineries in the valley. After his death in 1959, however, there was a bitter feud between his two sons, Robert and Peter, a feud that resulted in Robert establishing his own, separate winery (which has since become an empire), while Peter's side of the family held on to and still controls the Charles Krug business.

With a history like that, it's hardly surprising that parts of the winery are historical landmarks, including the stately old Carriage House. Due to renovations to some of the earthquake-unsafe buildings, however, there are currently no tours, and no one seems to know when they will start again. Visitors instead can see the buildings from afar and taste wines in a far less glamorous tasting room that resembles a modest postwar bungalow, though it is said to have been the first dedicated tasting room in the valley when it was built in the 1950s. The winery owns over 800 acres of vineyards throughout Napa and produces about 80,000 cases of just about every major varietal, though it specializes in cabernet (2800 Main St., St. Helena, 707/967-2200 or 800/682-5784, www.charleskrug.com, 10:30 A.M.–5 P.M. daily, tasting $5).

St. Clement Winery

After passing the big boys of Napa wine like Beringer, Krug, and Markham, it's hard not to miss the quaint, turreted Victorian house perched up on a knoll west of the main road. That is St. Clement, a small winery that used to be Spring Mountain Winery before those owners moved their operation farther up the hill in the 1970s and sold this place.

It is now owned by Fosters Wine Estates, making it the little sister to Beringer Vineyards just down the road. The winery is as small as its home suggests, making about 25,000 cases of wine a year, three-quarters of which is cabernet sauvignon and the proprietary Orropas red meritage. The popular sauvignon blanc and a merlot are two other wines worth tasting, though they may or may not be on the tasting menu of five wines. For picnics, the rosé wine called La Vache is a steal at under $10 a bottle.

Although the small, businesslike tasting room lacks some of the Victorian charm of the exterior and surrounding gardens, the stone cellars under the house, where its original owner used to make wine, can be seen as part of the appointment-only tour. There's also a pretty porch overlooking the valley, though traffic noise spoils what would otherwise be an idyllic view (2867 St. Helena Hwy. N., St. Helena, 800/331-8266, www.stclement.com, 10 A.M.–4 P.M. daily, tasting $5).

Freemark Abbey

Despite the name, there is no religious connection with the weathered stone barn sandwiched between a brewpub and an unremarkable group of small office buildings. Freemark Abbey instead got its current identity in the 1940s from the nickname of Albert "Abbey" Ahern and the names of partners Charles Freeman ("Free") and Markquand Foster ("Mark"), who bought the former Lombarda Winery and its old stone building dating from 1899.

That wine-making era lasted only 20 years, however. After a brief stint as a candle factory and a restaurant, the place once again became a winery in 1967 when it was bought by a new set of partners. Today, Freemark Abbey is probably best known for its cabernet sauvignon, from the generic Napa Valley version to a couple of vineyard designates, including the flagship from the Bosche Vineyard near Rutherford.

Plenty of other wines are available to try in one of the most comfortable tasting rooms in the valley, though it's in the decidedly unhistoric building next to the winery. The portfolio includes merlot, sangiovese, chardonnay, and viognier, which may or may not be on the five-wine tasting menu. Cabernet lovers should visit at weekends when a more expensive red-only tasting option is offered (3022 St. Helena Hwy. N., St. Helena, 800/963-9698, www.freemarkabbey.com, 10 A.M.–5 P.M. daily, regular tasting $5, $10 reds only).

Duckhorn Vineyards

Up the road from St. Clement on the left is Lodi Lane, which cuts across the valley to the Silverado Trail and the pretty Victorian-style home of Duckhorn, a winery known for some outstanding merlot and cabernet sauvignon. Those two wines were the first to be made when the winery was established in the mid-1970s, and they still account for most of the 50,000 cases of wine made each year. Sauvignon blanc is the only white wine in the portfolio.

Duckhorn also makes about 10,000 cases of its Paraduxx wine, a proprietary blend of zinfandel, cabernet, and merlot, and built a custom Paraduxx winery to the south near Yountville that opened at end of 2005.

The stylish entrance lounge of the winery

and the big circular tasting bar beyond, surrounded by neatly arranged tables and chairs, resemble an upscale restaurant, so it's no surprise that trying the wines can be pricey. But the personal service, quality wines, and peaceful veranda overlooking the vineyards make the tasting experience far more relaxing and fulfilling than at some other wineries.

Tasting starts at $10 for three Napa Valley wines, and $5 more also buys a taste of two of the highly praised estate cabernet sauvignons from the Howell Mountain and St. Helena appellations. More of the estate wines, including the best merlots, can be tasted on the appointment-only estate tasting (11 A.M., 1 P.M., and 3 P.M., $25), which also includes some food pairings. Free tours are available once a day at 12:15 P.M., and although reservations are not required they are usually needed (1000 Lodi Ln., at Silverado Trail, St. Helena, 888/354-8885, www.duckhorn.com, 10 A.M.–4 P.M. daily, tasting $10–15).

Ehlers Estate

Moderate wine consumption is believed to be good for your heart but moderate consumption of Ehlers Estate wines is definitely good for your heart. This historic stone winery just north of St. Helena is owned by the Leducq Foundation, a French charity that funds cardiovascular research projects at high-profile medical schools around the world including Harvard, Columbia, and the University of California.

The winery was established in 1886 by Bernard Ehlers but lasted only until prohibition. It languished until the 1960s when the first of a series of well-intentioned owners brought the estate back to life as a winery under various names for the next two decades.

French businessman Jean Leducq and his wife Sylviane bought part of the estate in the late 1980s and continued acquiring other parts as they became available. In 2001, they bought the winery building thus reuniting the entire 42-acre estate for the first time since prohibition. (Jean died the following year.) Since then, the beautiful stone building has been enhanced by a tasteful architectural makeover and now sits peacefully among the vines in the middle of the valley.

Unlike many valley wineries, the Ehler's Estate makes only estate wines from those surrounding vineyards, many of which have been replanted over the last decade. About 10,000 cases of wine are made now, including a worthy cabernet sauvignon, merlot, and sauvignon blanc, but that will undoubtedly increase. One thing that won't change: a portion of the sales generated by the winery go to the Leducq Foundation to support its research programs (3222 Ehlers Ln., St. Helena, 707/963-5972, www.ehlersestate.com, daily 10 A.M.–5 P.M., tours by appt., tasting $5).

Benessere Vineyards

The family that established Benessere in 1994 does not publicize the fact that the winery used to be owned by **Charles Shaw,** a name that will now forever be associated with the Two-Buck Chuck phenomenon of cheap and cheerful wines. Shaw owned the winery from the 1970s but eventually went bankrupt, and his brand (essentially his name) was bought by the Bronco Wine Company, which now churns out those cheap wines.

Bronco bought the name, but John and Ellen Benish bought the 42 acres of vineyards and the winery itself, and have since transformed it into a producer of increasingly good sangiovese and zinfandel with the help of some expert Italian wine-making consultants.

The wines here are a nice diversion from the cabernet and chardonnay that dominate the Napa Valley scene, and the winery itself is at the end of a small road far off the beaten path of the St. Helena Highway. Sangiovese and zinfandel dominate the 5,000-case production, but Benessere also makes a small amount of sauvignon blanc and the proprietary Phenomenon, a blend of sangiovese, cabernet sauvignon, syrah, and merlot. An appointment for tasting is technically necessary but calling ahead by even an hour is usually fine (1010 Big Tree Rd., St. Helena, 707/963-5853, www.benesserevineyards.com, 11 A.M.–5 P.M. daily in summer, 10 A.M.–4 P.M. winter, tasting $7.50).

SPRING MOUNTAIN WINERIES

Exploring this lesser-known appellation makes an interesting diversion from St. Helena and is a beautiful drive. From the St. Helena Highway turn onto Madrona Road and Spring Mountain Road is three blocks up on the right. Alternatively, just south of Beringer Vineyards, Elmhurst Road also leads to Spring Mountain Road.

From there the road follows a creek as it climbs steeply through redwoods and oak trees, past terraced mountain vineyards and orchards, to the many small wineries that often have stunning views of the valley far below.

Spring Mountain Vineyards

Not far out of St. Helena is one of the oldest Spring Mountain wineries. It is as famous for its Hollywood connection as for its history and wines. It was established in the 1880s as the Miravalle estate by businessman Tiburcio Parrot, who also built the ostentatious Victorian mansion that is said to have been inspired by the Rhine House built down the hill by his friends the Beringer brothers.

The estate became Spring Mountain Vineyards when it was bought in the 1970s by Michael Robbins. He built a modern winery on the grounds, but his wines were somewhat forgotten when the grounds and mansion were used as the set for the 1980s' television soap opera *Falcon Crest.* Although Robbins tried to cash in by releasing wines under the Falcon Crest label, the winery never regained its former glory and eventually went bankrupt in 1990.

It has since been brought spectacularly back to life after it was bought in 1992 by a Swiss banker, Jaqui Safra, who bought several surrounding vineyards (including part of the historic La Perla vineyard) and built a new winery. The winery reopened to the public in 2003 after Safra's investments had paid off and the quality of the wines, along with the grounds, had been restored. Spring Mountain is now perhaps best known for its sauvignon blanc and cabernet sauvignon, in particular the meritage blends called Elivette and Reserve, which are both predominantly cabernet and get consistently high ratings. The winery also makes a good syrah.

Tours of the beautiful grounds and some of the historic buildings, including the famous Miravalle mansion and caves, are now offered twice a day by appointment (10 A.M. and 2 P.M.). Tours are followed by a tasting of four wines, though there's also a tasting-only option at noon and the fee can be applied to any purchase (2805 Spring Mountain Rd., St. Helena, 877/769-4637 or 707/967-4188, www.springmountainvineyards.com, tours and tasting $25).

Terra Valentine

One man's remarkable stone folly of a building is reason alone to visit this winery, which was established in 1999 on the former Yverdon Vineyards property. Yverdon itself was founded in the 1970s by a reclusive eccentric, Fred Aves, who built himself a Gothic-style dry stone and concrete winery replete with stained-glass windows (he made those, too), statues, and curious features like fish-shaped door knobs and a sculpted spiral staircase.

Terra Valentine still makes wine in the building and is known mainly for its cabernet sauvignon, which accounts for much for the 7,000-case annual production, and the best cabernet is the flagship bottling from the Wurtele vineyard. It also makes a Russian River Valley pinot noir and a couple of limited production wines, including a sangiovese and cabernet blend called Amore.

Appointment-only tours are offered three times a day (10:30 A.M. and 12:30 and 3:30 P.M.); although a bit pricey at $20, they are worth it to see the fabulous building and for the sit-down tasting of wines paired with cheese and chocolate (3787 Spring Mountain Rd., St. Helena, 707/967-8340, www.terravalentine.com, open daily, tour and tasting $20).

Schweiger Vineyards

A little farther up the hill on the right is another of Spring Mountain's small makers of highly regarded cabernet sauvignon and another with spectacular views from its vineyards. Schweiger used to sell its fruit to other wineries in the Napa Valley but started making its own wines in the mid-1990s, gradually

COURTESY OF SCHWEIGER VINEYARDS

Schweiger Vineyards, high up on Spring Mountain

increasing production to the current level of about 5,000 cases and building a new winery along the way.

Winemaker Andy Schweiger used to ply his trade at Chateau St. Jean in the Sonoma Valley and Cain Vineyards near St. Helena before he started making wine for his family's label. He is also the winemaker for several of Napa Valley's smallest boutique wineries.

The vast majority of the wine is cabernet, but Schweiger also makes small amounts of merlot and chardonnay, all from the estate vineyards at about 2,000 feet in elevation. The flagship wine is the reserve cabernet, called Dedication, which competes with the best from Spring Mountain, and there is also a small amount of sauvignon blanc made from Sonoma Valley fruit (4015 Spring Mountain Rd., St. Helena, 707/963-4882 or 877/963-4882, www.schweigervineyards.com, tours and tasting by appointment 10 A.M.–3 P.M. Mon.–Sat., $10).

Pride Mountain Vineyards

This is just about as far as you can drive up Spring Mountain without entering the Sonoma Valley appellation, and, in keeping with its lofty location, Pride Mountain has been getting some lofty reviews for its wines in recent years.

The former Summit Ranch was bought by the Pride family in the late 1980s and has since grown to make about 15,000 cases of wines a year, most notably big, supple examples of cabernet sauvignon and merlot that account for about two-thirds of the winery's production. Other wines that regularly score over 90 points with the critics include a cabernet franc, chardonnay, and viognier. Many Pride wines sell out quickly, particularly the limited production reserves.

Grapes have been grown here since 1870 by some accounts, and the size of the burned-out shell of the Summit winery building, constructed in 1890, suggests a fair amount of wine was produced, too, until Prohibition ended the party.

The 80 acres of vineyards that Pride owns

straddle the Sonoma-Napa border at about 2,000 feet of elevation and offer stunning views over the two valleys and toward the ocean. Some wines are made from Napa grapes, others from both Napa and Sonoma grapes. All taste pretty good.

The views and wines can be enjoyed on the free tour and tasting offered once a day at 10 A.M., but be sure to book well in advance. You can also book picnic tables and eat literally on top of the wine world. Appointment-only tastings are offered the rest of the day and cost $5, though that's still a bargain considering the quality of the wines that generally cost upwards of $50 a bottle (4026 Spring Mountain Rd., St. Helena, 707/963-4949, www.pridewines.com, open 10 A.M.–3:30 P.M. daily except Tues. by appointment, tasting $5).

SIGHTS

Much of St. Helena's Victorian heyday is on display on Main Street (mainly between Hunt and Adams Streets), in the residential area stretching a few blocks west, and just one block east on Railroad Avenue. Even the unusual street lamps on Main Street are antiques, dating from 1915.

At **1302 Main Street** (at Hunt Street), a brass inlay in the sidewalk is the only sign that the wonderfully named Wonderful Drug Store had its home for half a century in this building constructed in 1891 by local businessman Daniel Hunt (as a sign of the times, the building is now home to a plus-size clothing store and real estate agent).

North up that block is the retro-looking **Cameo Theater** (1340 Main St.), the latest of a long line of theaters to inhabit the 1913 building with its pressed-steel ceilings and classy deco exterior, both now complemented by state-of-the-art seating, sound, and projection.

At the end of that block is the former **Odd Fellows Hall** (1350 Main St.), built in 1885 as Lodge 167 of the Independent Order of Odd Fellows, the social fraternity established in 1810 in England. The building is said to still have a sealed granite memorial stone containing a time

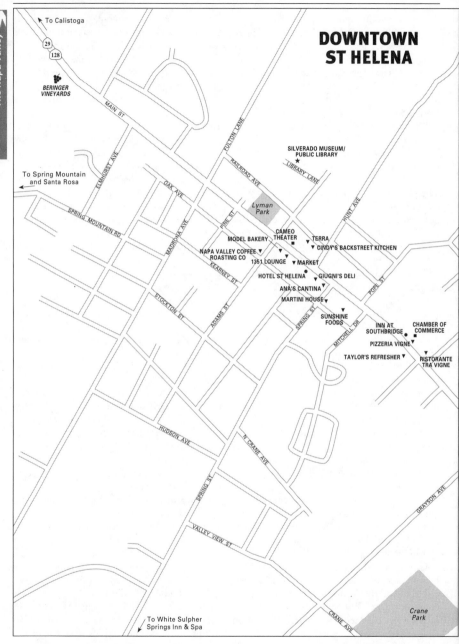

The Napa Valley

To Calistoga

29
128

BERINGER
VINEYARDS

MAIN ST

ELMHURST AVE

To Spring Mountain
and Santa Rosa

SPRING MOUNTAIN RD

OAK AVE

MADRONA AVE

PINE ST

KEARNEY ST

STOCKTON ST

ADAMS ST

SPRING ST

FULTON LANE

RAILROAD AVE

LIBRARY LANE

HUNT AVE

POPE ST

MITCHELL DR

**DOWNTOWN
ST HELENA**

SILVERADO MUSEUM/
PUBLIC LIBRARY
★

Lyman
Park

MODEL BAKERY
CAMEO
THEATER
NAPA VALLEY COFFEE ▼
ROASTING CO
1351 LOUNGE   ▼ MARKET
HOTEL ST HELENA   ▼ GIUGNI'S DELI
ANA'S CANTINA ▼
MARTINI HOUSE ▼
SUNSHINE
FOODS

▼ TERRA
▼ CINDY'S BACKSTREET KITCHEN

INN AT   CHAMBER OF
SOUTHBRIDGE   COMMERCE
●
PIZZERIA VIGNE ▼   ■
TAYLOR'S REFRESHER ▼   RISTORANTE
TRA VIGNE

HUDSON AVE

N CRANE AVE

SPRING ST

VALLEY VIEW ST

GRAYSON AVE

To White Sulpher
Springs Inn & Spa

CRANE AVE

Crane
Park

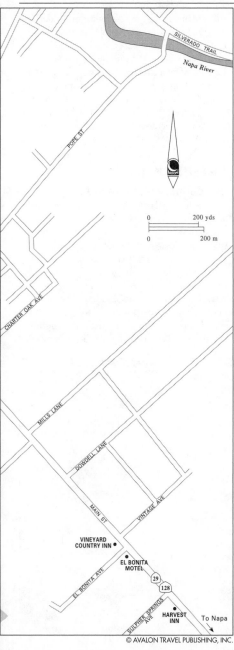

capsule of articles from the era. It was also once home to the neighboring **Steves Hardware,** itself founded in 1878.

Almost opposite at 1351 Main Street is what used to be the **Bank of St. Helena,** established and built in the 1880s by a group of local winemakers, including Charles Krug. A lot of the original interior features and stone walls are still evident, though many of the patrons of the **1351 Lounge** might not notice through the alcohol haze. Farther south is another 1880s building (this one made of wood) that is home to the **Hotel St. Helena** (1305-09 Main St.).

Silverado Museum

One of the Valley's most famous literary visitors, the Scottish writer Robert Louis Stevenson, spent his honeymoon in the valley just as St. Helena's Victorian building boom was getting underway in 1880. His life and visit is celebrated in the compact Silverado Museum (1490 Library Ln., off Adams St., 707/963-3757, noon–4 P.M. daily except Mon.), right next to the small library a few blocks from Main Street.

There are more than 9,000 of Stevenson's personal artifacts on display, including original manuscripts of some of his many books. The most famous in these parts is *The Silverado Squatters,* published in 1883, which chronicles his Napa Valley travels and meetings with early wine industry pioneers. Stevenson is probably best known elsewhere in the world for some of his other books, including *Treasure Island* and *The Strange Case of Dr. Jekyll and Mr. Hyde.*

Bale Grist Mill

About two miles north of St. Helena is one of the more unusual sights in a valley long dominated by the wine industry, the Bale Grist Mill (3801 St. Helena Hwy. N., 707/942-4575, mill grounds open 10 A.M.–5 P.M. daily, tours weekends only at 11:30 A.M. and 1, 2:30, and 3:30 P.M.). The small, rickety-looking redwood mill building with its oversized, 36-foot-high waterwheel is now part of a small State Historic Park. It was built in 1846 by Edward Bale on a tiny part of the 10,000 acres of land he was granted by the

Mexican government as thanks for his role as surgeon-in-chief for the Mexican army in California (it also probably helped that he had married the niece of the army's regional commander, General Mariano Vallejo, a few years earlier).

He bartered away chunks of his land for money and services to help build both this mill and a separate sawmill not far away. It originally had a 20-foot waterwheel, but a later owner made a few power upgrades, adding the bigger wheel and iron cogs in the 1850s, a few years after Bale died. This was all before the age of wine, so the mill became a big part of valley life and people from far and wide brought their grist (grain) to be milled here.

The weekend-only tours shed more light on both the man and the milling. The wheel turns sporadically these days, subject to the vagaries of its age and park budget cuts. When it is operating (usually only during the summer), there is usually some "run of the mill" flour for sale, ground between the giant millstones that literally weigh a ton. If it's not operating, the only real reason to visit (unless you're a water mill junkie) is the setting. The mill itself and a hand-

ful of picnic tables are reached from the parking lot along a quarter-mile trail that ends looping back to the main road, so traffic noise and the rather sad state of the mill building itself make for a bit of an anticlimax. Instead, turn left before reaching the mill to take the pretty mile-long hike through the madrone woods and past the remains of the valley's first church and the old Pioneer Cemetery into neighboring Bothe-Napa Valley State Park.

ENTERTAINMENT

M Culinary Institute of America

The Napa Valley takes food very seriously, so it's fitting that the West Coast outpost of the Culinary Institute is housed in one of the grandest old winery buildings in California, the fortresslike former **Greystone Winery** just north of downtown St. Helena (2555 Main St., St. Helena, 707/967-2320). Built in 1890, it later found fame as the Christian Brothers winery until a new corporate owner put it up for sale in the late 1980s. The institute bought the building in 1992 and spent $15 million reno-

Culinary Institute of America

vating it to its former glory. It still makes some wine under the Greystone label from a small estate vineyard nearby.

Chefs and sommeliers are busy being trained behind the imposing stone walls, but you don't need the dedication they have to learn a secret or two from the Napa Valley's top chefs. Hour-long cooking demonstrations are open to the public Friday–Monday (1:30 and 3:30 P.M. Mon. and Fri., 10:30 A.M. and 1:30 and 3:30 P.M. weekends, $12.50, reservations 707/967-2320) and include a tasting of the finished dish, so the fee makes it worthwhile, especially at lunchtime. Don't expect to go more than once over a weekend though, because the same demonstration is given on all four days.

A small exhibit just beyond the huge, carved redwood entrance doors illustrates the history of the Greystone Winery with some of the original Christian Brothers barrels, casks, and brandy-making stills. Most intriguing of all is a display of over a thousand corkscrews, some of them hundreds of years old and miniature marvels of engineering, all collected by Brother Timothy, a wine chemist and renowned winemaker at Christian Brothers 1935–1989.

Nightlife

It might seem like this part of the valley goes to sleep after the restaurants have closed down for the evening, a handful of bars provide some alcohol- and music-fueled entertainment into the wee hours just in case the wine-tasting hangover has not set by bedtime.

One that bills itself as the valley's premier nightspot (it's all relative) is the **1351 Lounge** in St. Helena (1351 Main St., 707/963-1969), where there's live music Thursday–Saturday until about 1:30 A.M., from local DJ sessions to country and rock ($5 cover on weekend nights), to help the vodka-soaked cocktails go down. The last Sunday of each month is open mic night, and the third Monday is trivia night. The Victorian bankers who built this stone-walled building in the 1800s are probably turning in their graves.

The 1351 is fairly casual, but just down the street is an even more casual venue, **Ana's Cantina** (1205 Main St., 707/963-4921), a Mexican restaurant by day and bar by night, when beer and margaritas are the drinks of choice, and pool, karaoke, and live weekend music provide the entertainment, usually until 1 A.M.

More live music from Bay Area bands of varying quality can be heard on weekend nights at the **Silverado Brewing Company** (3020 St. Helena Hwy. N., 707/967-9876), a couple of miles north of St. Helena.

SHOPPING

It's hardly surprising in a valley that was built on the guilty pleasures of consumption that shopping is a close third to eating and drinking for many visitors. St. Helena is dominated by small boutiques that tend to cater to tourists—locals head south to the big box stores around Napa or Santa Rosa for any major shopping trips.

The short stretch of Main Street in downtown St. Helena is quick and easy to explore, with an eclectic mix of shops catering mainly to the visitors that jam the streets in the summer. Countless gift shops sell everything from soap to wine trinkets; some of the more eclectic gifts are to be found at **Findings** (1269 Main St., 707/963-6000). Fashionable St. Helena dogs must shop for gifts and clothes at **Fideaux** (1312 Main St., 707/967-9935), which has been described as the Eddie Bauer for pets and sells the latest fashions for Fido, as well as other pricey, pet-related paraphernalia. Down the southern end of Main Street next to the gas station is **Lolo's Second to None** (1120 Main St., 707/963-7972), a consignment store stuffed with St. Helena's version of pre-owned junk, from designer labels to collectible crockery.

Another St. Helena–style shopping experience is the outlet mall about 1.5 miles north of the town itself (just before the Freemark Abbey winery), which is an altogether more relaxing affair than most of the modern malls stuck next to a freeway. **St. Helena Premier Outlets** (3111 St. Helena Hwy. N., St. Helena, 707/963-7282, 10 A.M.–6 P.M. daily) has more greenery than parking-lot asphalt between the handful of low-key wooden buildings that house stores including Brooks Brothers, Tumi, Coach, and Escada.

Probably the valley's best kitchen store, the **Spice Islands Marketplace** (2555 Main St., St. Helena, 707/967-2309, 10 A.M.–6 P.M. daily) in the Culinary Institute of America supplies all those trainee chefs and sommeliers (and you) with the best culinary equipment, spices, and other essentials from around the world. It is also the place to go to pick up a cookbook memento of the Wine Country. It carries thousands of wine and cookery books, including every Napa Valley title under the sun, and some might even be signed by the authors, who also teach courses here.

Foodies might drool on entering the only West Coast outpost of New York's super-deli, **Dean & Deluca,** just south of downtown St. Helena (607 St. Helena Hwy. S., 707/967-9980, 7:30 A.M.–7 P.M. Mon.–Sat., 9 A.M.–7 P.M. Sun.). This being the Wine Country, of course, it stocks some 1,400 wines plus countless local cheeses, meats, and produce, all alongside the already unmatched selection of gourmet foods from around the world.

The best olive oil in town is undoubtedly at the **Napa Valley Olive Oil Manufacturing Company,** though it no longer presses its oils here (835 Charter Oak Ave., St. Helena, 707/963-4173). Despite being in the heart of the valley's food scene it retains a decidedly small-time family feeling, selling its organic oils and thoroughly Italian deli items out of a colorful and chaotic small store.

RECREATION

The Napa Valley might seem to be covered with vineyards, but around its fringes there are still hundreds of acres as yet untouched by the mighty vine, some only minutes away from the Wine Country hordes.

M Bothe-Napa Valley State Park

This is the most accessible place upvalley to escape wine and the inside of the car, just a few miles north of St. Helena and right off the main highway (3801 St. Helena Hwy. N., 707/942-4575, open sunrise to sunset, $4 day-use fee). Proximity to the wineries and shops of St. Helena makes the park a popular picnic spot, but most picnickers don't venture far beyond the shady picnic area just beyond the parking lot near the Pioneer Cemetery (and the road). They miss the best reason to come here, which is to experience the relative wilderness that's so close to the beaten path and home to some of the most easterly stands of coastal redwood trees.

Most of the best hiking trails start from the **Redwood Trail,** which runs from the main parking lot through the cool redwood forest along Ritchey Creek for just over a mile before meeting the **Ritchey Canyon Trail.** That trail more or less follows the creek for about another mile to the site of an old homestead, an ideal destination for adventurous picnickers.

More strenuous hikes start from the Redwood Trail and climb steeply into the heat to some rewarding lookout points. The closest is Coyote Peak, accessed via the **Coyote Peak Trail** and just under a mile from the creek. From the lookout spur, the trail continues to the **South Fork Trail.** Turn right here to head back down to the creek for a loop of about four miles, or go left to climb again to another lookout. These trails are not for the faint-hearted, especially in the summer when it can get very hot, so don't underestimate the dehydrating power of too many glasses of wine.

Mountain bikers (or anyone on a Wine Country bike tour tired of dodging weaving rental cars) also have a few miles of trails to explore here, but only those that start north of the creek near the campground. Those same trails are also open for horseback riding, offered during the summer and fall by the **Triple Creek Horse Outfit** for those without their own steed (reservations 707/933-1600 or www.triplecreekhorseoutfit.com). A 1.5-hour ride costs $50.

Golf

If driving a golf ball is preferable to driving from winery to winery, there are a couple of

9-hole golf courses upvalley. Serious golfers should head south to the Napa area, where all the valley's 18-hole courses are.

The **Mt. St. Helena Golf Course** at the Napa County Fairgrounds in Calistoga (14435 N. Oak St., 707/942-9966) has green fees of $16 during the week and $22 at weekends. The **Aetna Springs Golf Course,** up in the Pope Valley (1600 Aetna Springs Rd,. from the Silverado Trail via Deer Park Rd. and Howell Mountain Rd., 707/965-2115, $16 weekdays, $22 weekends) is a little farther to drive to, but the pretty, par-70 course bills itself as the oldest golf course west of the Mississippi.

The **Meadowood Country Club & Resort** (900 Meadowood Ln., off Silverado Trail, St. Helena, 707/963-3646, www.meadowood.com) has a 9-hole par-62 course open only to guests or guests of guests of this exclusive 250-acre hideaway.

ACCOMMODATIONS

This part of the valley has a far wider range of accommodations than Calistoga, but at far higher prices, justified perhaps by the convenient location in the middle of the valley, the pretty Main Street, the thriving restaurant scene, and simply because it's St. Helena and can get away with it.

It's all relative. The cheapest accommodations in this area might be pricier than the low end in either Napa or Calistoga, but don't expect that extra cost to result in more luxury. The low end is still the low end, where rooms will generally be clean and comfortable but not as luxurious as their price might suggest. At the other end of the scale are some truly luxurious rooms but at prices that might make you choke on a glass of cabernet, especially on summer weekends.

Under $150

The 1940s-era **El Bonita Motel,** with its retro neon sign, is not the most glamorous place to stay in St. Helena but is one of the cheapest and still relatively glamorous for a motel (195 Main St., St. Helena, 707/963-3216 or 800/541-3284). The rooms are laid out around a small pool, though the cheapest Poolside rooms are just a stone's throw from the main highway, which seems to be busy day and night. Slightly quieter are the Garden rooms set a little farther back from the road. All contain modern but fairly sparse furnishings and include air-conditioning and microwave ovens. Rates for the Poolside rooms start at $90 on winter weekdays and go as high as $190 on summer and fall weekends ($135 during the week). The Garden and Homestead rooms are quieter but less of a bargain with rates starting at $120 during winter weeks and rising to $230 on peak-season weekends.

The **Ⓜ White Sulphur Springs Inn & Spa** is well off the beaten track, a couple of miles west of St. Helena in a wooded canyon (3100 White Sulphur Springs Rd., via Spring St., St. Helena, 707/963-8588 or 800/593-8873, www.whitesulphursprings.com). The spa resort was established in the 1850s on 45 acres of pristine land with its own mineral springs, a creek, redwood grove, giant hot tub and unheated pool, and miles of hiking trails. Many people come for the relatively cheap spa treatments (starting at $50) or to stay in one of the eight quaint cottages next to the creek that sleep up to four and have their own kitchenettes with all amenities ($170–210 a night). But for those who don't mind rustic decor with no air-conditioning there are also 29 much cheaper rooms in either the Carriage House (shared baths, $95 weekdays, $120 weekends) or the main inn building (private baths, $115–140). That's about as cheap as they come this close to St. Helena.

One of the more reasonably priced B&Bs in the area is **Ink House** (1575 S. St. Helena Hwy., St. Helena, 707/963-3890, www.inkhouse.com), an 1884 Victorian just south of the town with an unusual observatory room perched on top of the roof where guests can sip wine and watch the world go by. The common areas are chock-full of unusual antiques, from the grand piano and pipe organ to the stained glass in the observatory. The six bedrooms continue the theme and have been lovingly decorated with a mix of antiques, and most have a view of either hills or vineyards. The smallest two ($125) share a bathroom. The others all have private bathrooms and range in price from $175 up to $205–230 for the larger rooms with small sitting areas. Midweek discounts are usually offered during the winter. Breakfasts are something of an event and include the signature bella torta, a northern Italian pie crammed with eggs, cheese, and vegetables.

$150–250

The **Hotel St. Helena** is about as central as can be, down a little alley off Main Street right in the middle of town (1309 Main St., St. Helena, 707/963-4388 or 888/478-4355, www.hotelsthelena.com). The old Victorian building is full of original features and stuffed with knickknacks, including a lot of dolls. The 18 rooms get some of the same treatment (minus the dolls), with brass beds, a smattering of antiques, plush carpeting and fabrics, but limited modern touches—air-conditioning is included, but you'll have to ask for a TV. The four smallest and cheapest rooms share a bathroom and cost from $155 midweek. The best deals are the North Wing rooms, which are still on the small side but have private bathrooms and start at $185 midweek. The larger Windsor rooms start at $225 and the single suite at $325. Weekend prices are 20–40 percent higher.

Right next to El Bonita Motel is the **Vineyard Country Inn** (201 Main St., St. Helena, 707/963-1000, www.vineyardcountryinn.com), a combination of traditional hotel and motel with 21 spacious suites that all cost the same, ranging from a relative bargain of $170 in winter months to less of a bargain of almost $300 during peak summer and fall seasons. All are in a main two-story building or several cottages around the pool area and pretty brick patios—just be sure to ask for a room away from the main road, which is noisy enough to render the balconies of some suites next to useless. All suites have either two queens or one king bed, vaulted or beamed ceilings, fireplaces, refrigerators, and comfortable but unexceptional country-style furniture.

For some true peace and quiet, skip the valley floor and head for the hills. Northeast of St. Helena near the small community of Deer Park is secluded **Spanish Villa Inn,** a small Mediterranean-style B&B set in several acres of beautifully tended grounds, with bocce ball and croquet courts, and roses galore (474 Glass Mountain Rd., St. Helena, 707/963-7483). The six rooms and two suites start at $175 during the winter (sometimes there's a 20 percent discount during slow weeks) and $195 during the summer. All have private bathrooms and unusual touches like hand-painted sinks, plantation-style shutters, and carved headboards. Downstairs rooms open onto a patio overlooking the garden, while one of the upstairs suites has its own balcony.

Over $250

On the southern edge of St. Helena, hidden from the road behind a thicket of trees, is the mock-Tudor mansion of the **Harvest Inn** (1 Main St., St. Helena, 707/963-9463 or 800/950-8466, www.harvestinn.com), set in eight acres of verdant gardens. The place is crammed with stylish antiques and fancy brickwork and other often surreal English country features, though many struggle to gel together and can feel a bit superficial. There's nothing superficial about the luxury of the 53 rooms and suites, however. All have CD and VCR players, featherbeds, and minibars, and some have their own private terrace or views of neighboring vineyards. The smallest queen and king rooms cost from about $250 midweek during the winter, and $315 in the summer. The priciest deluxe rooms with vineyard views start at $400 in the winter and $435 in the summer. Add about $50 to those rates for weekend nights or knock $50–75 off if you've stayed there before (repeat guests get discounts). There are some good special deals during the winter at more reasonable rates.

The **Inn at Southbridge** (1020 Main St., St. Helena, 800/520-6800, www.innatsouthbridge.com) doesn't even try to pretend it's in the middle of Wine Country and instead offers luxurious urban sophistication with barely a hint of faux Tuscan decor or Victorian antiques, all in a refreshingly modern building opposite the Taylor's Refresher diner. The 20 spacious rooms all have vaulted ceilings, understated modern furniture, DVD players, and down comforters. A few also have fireplaces and balconies with a view of either the highway or vineyards. They start at $255 midweek in winter ($355 weekends), though there are often special deals that take the rate closer to $200 midweek. Summer rates start at $350 midweek for the cheapest king rooms ($450 weekends) and shoot up to more than $500 for the suites. In the same complex of buildings is the bargain Pizzeria Tra Vigne and right next door is the Napa Valley Health Spa, with a fitness center and heated outdoor pool (both free for inn guests) and a full-service luxury spa.

Its location surrounded by vineyards a few miles north of St. Helena makes the **Wine Country Inn** a slightly cheaper alternative to some of the other luxury resorts out in the wilds (1152 Lodi Ln., St. Helena, 707/963-7077 or 888/465-4608, www.winecountryinn.com). This family-run establishment offers an unusual down-home atmosphere. Rooms are decorated with a mix of modern and rustic, where CD players and handmade quilts enhance the sometimes plain, antique furniture. You'll either love the combination or wonder why you're paying so much for a riot of flowery fabric. Splurge on a room with a view, though, and there'll be no questioning. Rooms with those views, or a private patio, cost about $240–300 for most of the year, increasing about $30 during the harvest season (Aug.–Oct.). Small suites with added features like balconies with a view, Jacuzzi tubs, and double-headed showers cost $270–400 most of the year, and there are also five luxury cottages with 800 square feet of lounging space starting at $500 a night.

The luxurious **Meadowood Napa Valley** resort is a bit past its prime and facing increasing competition in this astronomical price bracket, but it's still worth considering if you're planning to splurge, not least because of its spectacular setting on 250 lush acres in the hills above the Silverado Trail (900 Meadowood Ln., off Silverado Trail, St. Helena, 707/963-3646 or 800/458-8080, www.meadowood.com).

The rooms are in 20 country-style lodges spread around the grounds and range from the simple two-room studios ($475 Dec.–Mar., $625 the rest of the year) up to the spacious suites ($675–900). All have fireplaces, beamed ceilings, private decks or terraces, and every conceivable luxury trapping. For those who actually venture out of the rooms there are plenty of distractions, including miles of hiking trails, two swimming pools surrounded by vast expanses of lawn, tennis courts, a 9-hole golf course, and croquet. And to make sure visitors never have to venture down into the valley, there's a small spa, wine-tasting events, and two highly regarded restaurants on-site.

Camping

The Napa Valley might be touted by every marketing brochure as a bank-breaking hedonistic playground, but it actually has a couple of remarkably good campgrounds where two people can stay for less than it would cost them to taste wine at most of the nearby wineries. So forget about matching a Napa cabernet with the latest in-season gourmet produce—instead see how it goes with s'mores around a campfire under a warm summer night sky.

You can light your fire and unpack the marshmallows just a few miles north of St. Helena in the leafy **Bothe-Napa Valley State Park** (3801 St. Helena Hwy., 707/942-4575). There are 50 sites, 42 of which can accommodate RVs up to 31 feet long (though there are no hookups). The other eight sites are tent only, and all cost $20 a night. Sites can be reserved through Reserve America (www.reserveamerica.com or 800/444-7275) March–October and the rest of the year are available on a first-come, first-served basis. Most sites offer some shade beneath oak and madrone trees and there's a swimming pool to cool down in, as well as flush toilets and hot showers and that all-important fire ring at every site. The park itself stretches up into the hills and offers miles of hiking trails through the redwoods along the creek or up into the sun for some great views (see *Recreation*).

Further north in Calistoga is a slightly less appealing camping location at the **Napa County Fairgrounds** (1435 Oak St., Calistoga, 707/942-5221.) It's ostensibly an RV park with 78 sites, 32 with sewer hook up ($25 a night) and the other 46 with only water and electricity ($22). Campers are corralled onto a grassy area with 20 tent-only sites ($10). Showers and restroom are provided but for most other amenities you'll have to head to downtown Calistoga.

FOOD

There's an ongoing tug of war between upvalley and downvalley restaurants for the limited tourist food dollars, and the balance seems to shift almost every time one restaurant closes and a new one opens—both common occurrences in the Napa Valley. St. Helena's everchanging restaurant scene with its big-name chefs continues to do battle with towns down south, competing with Yountville for the title of Napa Valley's culinary epicenter.

Californian

The wood, waterfalls and twinkling lights outside might make it seem like a Japanese restaurant, but **Martini House** (1245 Spring St., at Oak St., dinner entrées $25–37, prix fixe menu $40) is actually the latest venture by super-restaurateur Pat Kuleto, celebrating the valley's wine-making and Native American heritages. That roughly translates to some beautifully designed dishes prepared by chef Todd Humphries, who has a tendency to go foraging in the local woods for some of the ingredients, like wild mushrooms (or so we're told). The wine list is suitably stocked with cult classics, but this place has become such a classic itself that it is usually tough to get a reservation. The curious, craftsman-style bungalow just of Main Street is worth a look, however. It was built by an opera singer turned bootlegger, and Kuleto seems to have spared no expense restoring it.

A couple of restaurants are worth discovering on Railroad Avenue, just a block east of

Main Street but a world away from the bustle. The eponymous owner of **☒ Cindy's Backstreet Kitchen** (1327 Railroad Ave., at Hunt St., 707/963-1200, lunch and dinner daily, dinner entrées $13–21) is the same woman behind the ever-popular Mustards Grill in Yountville. She has created a charming hole in the wall here with a side entrance that makes it feel like you're walking into someone's house. The quiet patio is a hive of activity at lunchtime. The menu goes for the same homey charm, with large plates including meatloaf, wood oven duck, and steak frites. The small plates and sandwiches for lunch can be ordered to go.

A few doors from Cindy's in the historic stone Hatchery Building is **Terra** (135 Railroad Ave., 707/963-8931, dinner Wed.–Mon., entrées $18–30), a romantic place that competes with the best restaurants in the valley (with its food and spin-off cookbook) thanks to chef Hiro Stone, who won the prestigious James Beard Foundation award for Best Chef in California. The menu is French and Californian with Asian flourishes, and might include such eclectic creations as sake-marinated Alaskan black cod with shrimp dumplings.

When three partners with résumés that read like the greatest hits of Bay Area restaurants got together in 2002 to create **Market** (1347 Main St., St. Helena, 707/963-3799, lunch and dinner daily, dinner entrées $10–20), the result could well have been another quality Napa Valley dining experience ending with an astronomical bill. That's certainly what the stone walls, Victorian bar, and elegant tables might suggest. Instead, the bill remains firmly on this planet, and jaded locals have grown to love it.

The American bistro-style food is sophisticated yet familiar, with dishes like pan-roasted crispy chicken sharing the menu with mac and cheese made, of course, with the best artisan cheeses. The wine list manages to keep a lid on prices with none of the wide selection more than $14 above retail, beating the corkage fee of most other restaurants. The lunch menu is even more of a bargain, with most of the gourmet sandwiches and salads well under $10, all available to go for a perfect picnic.

Italian

Ristorante Tra Vigne (1050 Charter Oak Ave., 707/963-4444, lunch and dinner daily, dinner entrées $13–26) is a rarity in the valley—a restaurant that has been around since the early 1990s without ever really changing its formula (though it has changed chefs a few times). This is a thoroughly Italian place with a classic Italian/English menu, lots of cool stone and tile, and a wonderful enclosed, leafy patio straight out of Tuscany. The wine list reflects the California-inspired Italian menu, with a good selection of local and Italian wines to go with the exquisite pizzas, pastas, and dinner entrées prepared with the usual high-quality local ingredients. As well as a cookbook, Tra Vigne has spawned a deli, wine bar, and pizzeria in St. Helena.

If getting a reservation at Tra Vigne is a problem there are still plenty of ways to experience its winning formula thanks to its numerous offspring. One is **Pizzeria Tra Vigne** (1016 Main St., 707/967-9999, lunch and dinner daily until 8:30 P.M., pizzas $10–20), which has had many incarnations over the years (like any adolescent) but always the same parent. This being Napa, the pizzas have some unusual and exotic toppings, but perfect thin crusts, and are best enjoyed on the patio. Look for the giant tomato outside the front door opposite the entrance to the Merryvale winery—left over from the restaurant's previous incarnation as Pizzeria Tomatina.

Casual Dining

Although St. Helena's food scene is constantly changing there is one place that the term "institution" could apply to, and that's the half-century old **Taylor's Refresher** (933 Main St., 707/963-3486, lunch and dinner daily until 9 P.M., 8 P.M. in winter, $3–13). This unmistakable old diner just south of downtown is home of the ahi burger and other diner delights, some with a Wine Country gourmet twist and prices with a bit of a Wine Country lift (like the less-than-generous $5 milkshakes). A big grassy picnic area with plenty of tables gives a little respite from the traffic, or perch on a stool at the counter.

The colorful, cavernous interior of **Ana's Cantina** is the perfect antidote to Wine Country burnout (1205 Main St., 707/963-4921, lunch and dinner daily). Nothing on the Mexican menu costs more than $10 and you can play pool and drink beer to your heart's content. This is also a popular live-music venue.

The **Model Bakery** (1357 Main St., 707/963-8192, 7 A.M.–6 P.M. Tues.–Sat., 8 A.M.–4 P.M. Sun., lunch items $4–10) is known for baking some of the best bread in the valley and is the latest incarnation of a bakery that has existed here since the 1920s. It's a great place for quick and easy lunches, including gourmet sandwiches, salads, and pizza cooked in the same brick ovens as the bread. Most can be ordered to go, but you might also be lucky enough to snag one of the few tables dotted around the black-and-white tiled floor like chess pieces.

If quick refreshment is all you need to keep going, the **Napa Valley Coffee Roasting Company** offers some peace and quiet on its patio a block from Main Street (1400 Oak St., 707/963-4491).

A couple of miles north of St. Helena is the **Silverado Brewing Company** (3020 St. Helena Hwy. N., 707/967-9876, dinner daily, entrées $7–15), sprawling right next to the historic stone winery of Freemark Abbey. The menu won't win awards for originality but uses quality local produce and is well priced. The small selection of beers is complemented by an unexpectedly generous wine list.

Picnic Supplies

The ease of finding picnic food in this part of the valley is matched only by the ease of finding a place to eat it, whether at the countless wineries with big and small patches of grass or among the redwoods in the Bothe-Napa Valley State Park.

Several of St. Helena's restaurants offer almost all their lunch menu items to go, including **Cindy's Backstreet Kitchen, Market,** and the **Model Bakery.** But even they cannot compete with the gourmet paradise of **Dean & Deluca** (607 St. Helena Hwy. S., 707/967-9980). Just don't lose track of time while browsing the food you never knew existed. A cheaper and altogether quirkier place to buy sandwiches is the old-fashioned deli counter at **Giugni's Deli** (1227 Main St., St. Helena, 707/963-3421), an old St. Helena institution. Those planning to build their own sandwich can also battle through the crowds to the well-stocked deli at the **V. Sattui Winery** (1111 White Ln., St. Helena, 707/963-7774, www.vsattui.com).

And don't shun the ugly strip mall home of **Sunshine Foods** (1115 Main St., 707/963-7070), next to Wells Fargo bank at the southern end of the downtown zone. It's a quality grocery store with a remarkably broad range of deli sandwiches and salads, wines, and even freshly made sushi.

Farmers Market

The place to buy the local produce direct from the farmers is the **St. Helena Farmer's Market,** held every Friday 7:30 A.M.–noon, May–October, at Crane Park, west of Main Street via Sulphur Springs Road or Mills Lane.

INFORMATION AND SERVICES

Just about every brochure, free magazine, and coupon can be found at the **St. Helena Chamber of Commerce,** at the southern end of Main Street (1010 Main St., 800/799-6456, www.sthelena.com, 9 A.M.–5 P.M. Mon.–Fri., 11 A.M.–3 P.M. Sat.).

Those desperate to look up some obscure wine fact on the fly should head to the small wine annex of the modest **St. Helena Public Library** (1492 Library Ln., off Adams St., 707/963-5244, open daily), a few blocks off Main Street, though it's not nearly as comprehensive as the Sonoma County Wine Library in Healdsburg. Just across the street from Library Lane, on the second floor of the modern office building, is the **Napa Vintners Association** (www.napavintners.com). You can usually pop in to buy one of the excellent maps it publishes of the valley and its wineries.

If you're in town for a few days, the local *St. Helena Star* newspapers are worth picking up at any local café, as much for the latest Wine Country gossip as for information about local events and some entertaining wine-related columns.

Calistoga

No other town in the Napa Valley retains a sense of its Victorian roots more than Calistoga, with the remaining stretch of its old boardwalk and Victorian storefronts framed by views in all directions of distant mountains and forests.

Replace the cars and paving with horses and mud, and things would probably look much like they did a hundred years ago when the spa town was at its peak, drawing visitors from far and wide to its natural hot springs and mud baths. The town was built on mud, literally and figuratively.

San Francisco businessman Sam Brannan bought up thousands of acres of land here in the 1850s, drawn by the development potential of the hot springs. He opened a very profitable general store in the late 1850s (now a historic landmark at 203 Wapoo Ave.) followed

by his lavish Hot Springs Resort in 1868. He was also instrumental in bringing the railroad this far up the valley to transport visitors to his new resort, making the town a destination for the masses and gateway to Sonoma and Lake Counties to the north.

What Brannan is perhaps best known for, however, is an alcohol-induced slip of the tongue. Legend has it that in a speech promoting his resort he planned to say that it would become known as the "Saratoga of California," referring to the famous New York spa town at the time, but his words instead came out as "the Calistoga of Sarafornia."

The Wines

Many visitors never really explore the wineries this far north in the valley, and they are missing

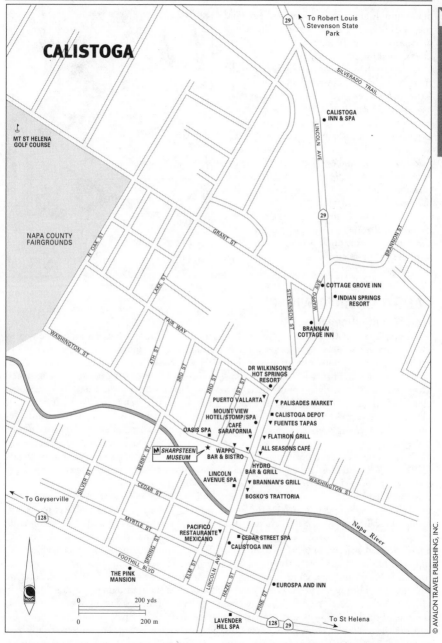

CALISTOGA

To Robert Louis
Stevenson State
Park

SILVERADO TRAIL

CALISTOGA
INN & SPA

MT ST HELENA
GOLF COURSE

NAPA COUNTY
FAIRGROUNDS

GRANT ST

LINCOLN AVE

BRANNON ST

N OAK ST

LAKE ST

FAIR WAY

WASHINGTON ST

COTTAGE GROVE INN

INDIAN SPRINGS
RESORT

STEVENSON ST

WAPPO AVE

BRANNAN
COTTAGE INN

4TH ST

3RD ST

2ND ST

1ST ST

DR WILKINSON'S
HOT SPRINGS
RESORT

PUERTO VALLARTA

▼ PALISADES MARKET

MOUNT VIEW
HOTEL/STOMP/SPA

■ CALISTOGA DEPOT

▼ FUENTES TAPAS

OASIS SPA

CAFÉ
SARAFORNIA

▼ FLATIRON GRILL

ALL SEASONS CAFÉ

BERRY ST

M SHARPSTEEN
MUSEUM

WAPPO
BAR & BISTRO

LINCOLN
AVENUE SPA

HYDRO
BAR & GRILL

▼ BRANNAN'S GRILL

BOSKO'S TRATTORIA

WASHINGTON ST

To Geyserville

128

SILVER ST

CEDAR ST

MYRTLE ST

SPRING ST

PACIFICO
RESTAURANTE
MEXICANO

▼ CEDAR STREET SPA

CALISTOGA INN

Napa River

FOOTHILL BLVD

ELM ST

LINCOLN AVE

HAZEL ST

THE PINK
MANSION

EUROSPA AND INN

PINE ST

0   200 yds

0   200 m

LAVENDER
HILL SPA

128 29

To St Helena

© AVALON TRAVEL PUBLISHING, INC.

out. Not only are crowds thinner up here (and the food cheaper), but the area is a historic hub of wine making in the valley that still has plenty of wine-making action today.

Although the Calistoga area was one of the first places that grapes were grown in the Napa Valley, it has been one of the last to be granted its own subappellations. On the western slopes, home of the historic Schramsberg winery, is the **Diamond Mountain** appellation, which was designated in 2001. Winemakers there are already making a name for their new appellation as they learn to tame the powerful tannins of the mountain grapes to create increasingly impressive and intense wines.

The rest of the Calistoga area is likely to get its own appellation very soon—probably by the time you read this book, thanks to the folks at Chateau Montelena who have been leading the charge.

COURTESY OF FRANK FAMILY VINEYARDS

Frank Family Vineyards

CALISTOGA AREA WINERIES
Frank Family Vineyards
The imposing sandstone building of the historic Larkmead Winery a few miles south of Calistoga has had a more colorful history than most, finding fame for still wines and sparkling wines, and surviving many identities and a big fire in 2000. In its current incarnation it is now perhaps as best known for a fun, free tasting experience as for the wines made there.

The Larkmead area was christened by Lillie Hitchcock Coit (memorialized by San Francisco's Coit Tower) in the 1870s, and a winery was first established here in 1884. It was not until the winery found fame under the ownership of the Italian-Swiss Salima family that the big stone building was constructed in 1906 and Larkmead went on to be known for making some of the valley's best early wines, right up until 1940 when Felix Salima died.

Equally well known was the winery's next identity, Kornell Champagne Cellars, which was one of the biggest producers of sparkling wines in the valley and at one point made close to 80,000 cases of mainly sweeter, German-

style bubbly before bankruptcy ended its run in the early 1990s.

The most recent incarnation of the winery has had its ups and downs. In the early 1990s, the Rombauer family (as famous for Irma Rombauer's book, *The Joy of Cooking*, as for its wines) bought the winery in partnership with Hollywood executive Rich Frank. Both partners made wine there and ran a custom crush business for small wineries up and down the valley until a disastrous warehouse fire in 2000 destroyed an estimated 85,000 barrels of stored wine, wiping out the entire stock of many of those clients.

Now the winery makes about 15,000 cases of Frank Family Vineyards still and sparkling wines. The increasing emphasis is on still wines, particularly cabernet sauvignon from Rutherford-area vineyards and chardonnay from Carneros. Sparkling wine remains an important part of the portfolio, however, and a dry blanc de blancs and blanc de noirs are offered as the first part of the free tasting in the series of modest tasting rooms. Free tours are offered twice a day for most of the year, except when the winemakers are particularly busy around bottling or crush time. If there are no tours, while away some time in the shady picnic area behind the winery (1901 Larkmead Ln., Calistoga, 707/942-0859 or 800/574-9463, www.frankfamilyvineyards.com, 10 A.M.–5 P.M. daily, free tasting).

Sterling Vineyards

When it opened in 1973, this contemporary, monastery-like winery, perched high on a wooded knoll just south of Calistoga, was hailed as one of the most spectacular wineries in the valley by some and lambasted by others. It remains one of the most striking, with whitewashed walls and bell towers that look like they're straight from a Greek travel brochure—hard to miss driving north on the St. Helena Highway into Calistoga.

Such an unusual building with its aerial gondola whisking visitors 300 feet up to the winery was bound to become a serious tourist attraction, and so it has. This far north in the valley, however, it tends to attract those more serious about wines than some of the other big magnets like Beringer and Mondavi. The gondola, ticket booths, and giant parking lot make it feel more like an out-of-season ski resort than a winery at first, but once at the top of the hill it's all about wine.

Sterling was established in the late 1960s by executives Peter Newton and Michael Stone, who owned the Sterling Paper Company that gave the winery its name. Newton added some sounds of his homeland by shipping over the bells from the old St. Dunstan's Church in London, destroyed during World War II.

Since then, Sterling has built up its production and vineyards. It now makes about 400,000 cases of wine a year and has more than 1,200 acres of vineyards in just about every Napa appellation, from Carneros, where it owns the Winery Lake vineyard in the di Rosa Preserve (source of some highly rated pinot noir and chardonnay), to high up in the Diamond Mountain appellation (source of grapes for some excellent cabernet sauvignon). Its growth was helped by the deep pockets of the multinational corporations that have owned the winery since the late 1970s, most recently Diageo.

Once visitors have paid the $15 to get up the hill, everything is pretty much free, including a fun, self-guided tour of the winery, the views, and a sit-down tasting of five wines either inside or out (weather permitting). For an additional $25, three of the better reserve wines can also be tried in the Reserve Room, or $30 buys a reserve wine vertical tasting (those fees can be put toward a purchase). The only thing sometimes missing is the sort of personal service found at smaller wineries, so you might have to persevere to get any detailed information about what you're drinking from the harried staff (1111 Dunaweal Ln., Calistoga, 707/942-3345 or 800/726-6136, www.sterlingvineyards.com, 10 A.M.–4 P.M. daily, visitor fee $15).

Clos Pegase

Sterling might be hard to miss perched up on its hill, but just down the road this place is truly hard to miss. If the giant pink-and-yellow creation reminds you of whimsical home appliances in your local Target store then there's good reason. Clos Pegase was designed in the 1980s by postmodernist architect Michael Graves, better known to avid shoppers now as the designer of some cheerful tea kettles and toasters sold at Target.

Graves won a competition sponsored in the 1980s by the San Francisco Museum of Modern Art to design a "temple to wine and art" for entertaining owner Jan Schrem's wine-making passion and displaying his sizable art collection. The original design, which included a giant statue of the winged horse Pegasus, had to be toned down, but the resulting building, completed in 1987, could easily be mistaken for the Napa outpost of a modern art museum. Giant sculptures seem to lurk around every corner, and postmodern design touches grace almost every part of the building. Look for art by Kandinsky, Ernst, and other big names on the walls.

Schrem, who made his fortune in the publishing business, also bought hundreds of acres of vineyards in the Calistoga area and down in Carneros, and now makes about 40,000 cases of wine each year, from the high-end

Homage reserves down to a local cabernet sauvignon and some reasonably priced, approachable pinot noir, merlot, and chardonnay from Carneros. Free tours of the winery, which include a trip to the extensive caves and a lot of artistic banter, are offered twice a day at 11 A.M. and 2 P.M. (1060 Dunaweal Ln., Calistoga, 707/942-4981, www.clospegase.com, 10:30 A.M.–5 P.M. daily, tasting $10).

Schramsberg

If you plan to visit just one of the valley's big champagne makers, the historic Schramsberg winery should be high on the list. The winery was established on the slopes of Diamond Mountain in 1862 by German immigrant Jacob Schram, who had soon made such a name for himself as a maker of high quality wines that he was paid a visit by a vacationing Robert Louis Stevenson in 1880, a visit memorialized in Stevenson's book *Silverado Squatters.*

Schram made still wines mainly from German grape varietals, and the winery's fame as a sparkling winemaker began in the 1960s when the Davies family bought the old winery and, rather than compete with the makers of sweeter sparkling wines like the nearby Kornell winery and Korbel in the Russian River Valley, opted to make drier wines from traditional French champagne grapes—a risk considering the American palate was better accustomed to sweet white zin than bone-dry champagnes.

The 1965 blanc de blancs was the first American-made champagne to use chardonnay grapes. And the 1969 vintage was served to President Richard Nixon and Premier Zhou Enlai of China in Beijing in 1972 for a toast to the normalization of diplomatic relations.

Today Schramsberg makes about 45,000 cases of wines, ranging from that historic blanc de blancs and a rich, creamy blanc de noirs up to its flagship J. Schram wine, regarded as one of the best Californian champagnes. Tasting the champagnes is the culmination of a fascinating appointment-only tour of the winery that includes a visit to the spooky caves dating from the late 1800s and a lesson on the art of champagne making.

You can also explore Jacob Schram's beautiful Victorian home and gardens.

If the wines taste complex, that could be due to the grapes coming from 67 different vineyards in four California counties, with many in Carneros and the Anderson Valley in Mendocino. The hotter estate vineyard around the winery was replanted mainly to cabernet sauvignon in the late 1990s, and Schramsberg now makes a cabernet (the 2001 vintage was the first release) under the J. Davies label (1400 Schramsberg Rd., via Peterson Rd. off U.S. 29, Calistoga, 707/942-2414 or 800/877-3623, www.schramsberg.com, 10 A.M.–4 P.M. daily, tour and tasting $20).

Reverie Vineyard & Winery

North from Schramsberg is this small winery that's a good introduction to the gutsy, sometimes tannic style of cabernet sauvignon typical of the steep Diamond Mountain appellation.

Reverie released its first wine in 1995 and now produces about 2,500 cases of mainly bordeaux-style red wines, together with small amounts of a delicious cabernet franc, barbera, and tempranillo, all from its 40 acres of rocky, mountain vineyards and with the help of consultant winemaker Ted Lemon, better known for his sought-after Littorai pinot noir and chardonnay wines.

With help from a different winemaker, Reverie also makes small quantities of crisp, nonmalolactic chardonnay from Diamond Mountain fruit, and a sauvignon blanc sourced from vineyards down in the valley—both under the Daydream label.

A quick tour of the small, low-key winery followed by a tasting in the caves (all free) can easily be arranged by calling first. There's no real tour schedule. If someone's there they will probably be happy to show you around (1520 Diamond Mountain Rd., Calistoga, 707/942-6800 or 800/738-3743, www.reveriewine.com, 10 A.M.–4 P.M. daily by appointment).

Von Strasser Winery

Reverie is sandwiched between two of the big names of Diamond Mountain: the Diamond

Creek winery (not open to the public) and Von Strasser, which was established in 1990 by Rudy von Strasser, who also spearheaded the alliance of local growers that, after almost a decade, succeeded in having Diamond Mountain declared its own subappellation within Napa Valley in 2001.

Von Strasser offers a good example of what can be done with Diamond Mountain grapes. It makes a selection of intense, vineyard-designate cabernet sauvignons from its own estate and adjacent vineyards, together with a chardonnay and a few hundred cases of the appellation's only zinfandel. Total production of about 9,000 cases makes it one of the largest of Diamond Mountain's handful of producers.

The Estate Vineyard cabernet is the wine that von Strasser is probably best known for, balancing powerful tannins with equally powerful fruit, resulting in high ratings from critics almost every year. This and a couple of other cabernets are usually available to taste in the flight of five wines. Tours of the grounds and a tasting in the caves are also available by appointment (1510 Diamond Mountain Rd., Calistoga, 707/942-0930, www.vonstrasser.com, 10 A.M.–5 P.M. daily, tasting $15).

Zahtila Vineyards

Across the valley from Diamond Mountain, where the Silverado Trail meets the St. Helena Highway just east of Calistoga, is a little cluster of modest buildings belonging to this family-owned boutique winery. Zahtila makes some fine cabernet sauvignon and zinfandel. Its relaxed atmosphere and smooth-drinking wines offer a nice change of pace (and price) from the Napa Valley crush. Staff in the cozy tasting room are also a mine of information about other small, local wineries. Just don't trip over the chewed toys left lying around by the canine meeter and greeter, Zoe.

The specialty here is zinfandel, which is grown in the small Oat Hill Vineyard next to the winery planted in the 1970s by the previous owners. Most of the fruit, however, is bought from other growers for its 2,000 cases of wine. Cabernet sauvignon comes from the Ruther-

ford and Calistoga areas and goes into the rich, smooth Napa cabernet and flagship Beckstoffer cabernet. Additional zinfandel is bought from the Russian River Valley and sometimes the Dry Creek Valley. There are also plans to make a few hundred cases of chardonnay (2250 Lake County Hwy., Calistoga, 707/942-9251, 10 A.M.–4:30 P.M. daily, tasting $5).

Chateau Montelena

This beautiful French- and Chinese-inspired wine estate was responsible, along with Stag's Leap Wine Cellars, of helping put Californian wines firmly on the international map at the Paris tasting in 1976, when a Chateau Montelena chardonnay beat the best French white burgundies to win its category.

That modern history is what many people talk about, but the winery actually dates back to the 1880s when Alfred Tubbs (after whom Tubbs Lane is named) bought land and built the imposing stone chateau, eventually naming it Montelena after Mount St. Helena, which looms in the distance. The winery prospered until Prohibition, after which it made limited amounts of wine and sold grapes to other growers before the estate was broken up in the 1950s.

The giant, five-acre Jade Lake and curious Chinese flourishes like the lacquered bridges and pavilions were added by Yort Wing Frank, who bought a chunk of the estate in 1958 for a bit of retirement fun. Serious wine making didn't start again until a decade later when the chateau and original vineyards were reunited by Leland Paschich and partner James Barrett, signaling the start of Chateau Montelena's modern-day wine-making heritage.

Soft, plush cabernet sauvignon and a rich chardonnay are the mainstays of the 35,000-case production here, but an estate zinfandel is also made. They can be tasted either as part of an appointment-only, two-hour tour offered twice a day (once in winter) or at a regular tasting. Cabernet fans can also try a vertical tasting of the pricey estate cabernet in the stone-walled Estate Room (1429 Tubbs Ln., Calistoga, 707/942-5105, www.montelena.com,

COURTESY OF CHATEAU MONTELENA

The Chateau Montelena's Estate Room has been created for the exclusive enjoyment of its tour guests.

9:30 A.M.–4 P.M. daily, tasting $10/$25, tours 9:30 A.M. and 2 P.M., $25).

THE EASTERN MOUNTAINS

The oak-studded peaks and valleys hidden in the Vaca Mountains on the eastern side of Napa Valley offer a relaxing diversion and a total change of pace. Grapes have been grown here for over 100 years, and the area was ripe for a new wave of viticultural development until the valley's biggest growers recently turned their attention farther north to Lake County, where land is cheaper and the promise greater.

Nevertheless, there are still some great wines made in these hills, most notably in the Chiles Valley appellation, where zinfandel and sauvignon blanc enjoy the warmer growing conditions, and on Howell Mountain, where cabernet sauvignon reigns supreme in the thin, volcanic soils.

The Chiles Valley offers the best touring possibilities and is easy to reach. Take Highway 128 (Sage Canyon Rd.) up into the hills from the Silverado Trail at Rutherford, past Lake Hennessey, and go either left or right at the junction. Both roads lead to the valley. Just be sure to take lunch, because there's very little apart from farmland and vineyards up there.

Catacula Lake Winery

Turn left at the Lake Hennessey junction onto Chiles & Pope Valley Road and continue for about six miles into the Chiles Valley to this former summer camp. Catacula Lake's first vintage was in 1999, and it now makes about 5,000 cases of wine a year, including some increasingly good zinfandel and sauvignon blanc, at bargain prices.

Considering so few wines are made here, none costing more than $20 a bottle, the $5 fee for the appointment-only tasting might seem a little steep, but a couple of library wines are thrown in and there's also sometimes a two-for-one tasting offer on the winery's website. The peaceful setting next to the lake with an outdoor patio and picnic area also makes it a worthwhile outlay (4105 Chiles Pope Valley Rd., St. Helena, 707/965-1104, daily by appointment, tasting $5).

RustRidge Ranch & Winery

About three miles from Lake Hennessey on Chiles Pope Valley Road, turn right onto Lower Chiles Valley Road to get to this very rustic part winery, part thoroughbred horse breeding ranch. Tastings are held in an old cattle barn that now houses the winery workings, and a visit here is as much about smelling the horses as the wine.

About 55 of the ranch's 440 acres are planted with grapes, and the winery makes about 2,000 cases of zinfandel, both barrel- and tank-fermented chardonnay, cabernet sauvignon, and sauvignon blanc. The rest of the fruit is sold to other wineries. Tours and tastings are offered every day by appointment only, but, with life up here so relaxed, all that's usually required is a call to check that someone's home (2910 Lower Chiles Valley Rd., St. Helena, 707/965-9353, www.rustridge.com, 10 A.M.–4 P.M. daily, tour and tasting $5).

Brown Estate Vineyards

At the far southern end of the Chiles Valley appellation is a relative newcomer to the wine business but one that is already making a name for its zinfandels.

The Brown family bought the land as a vacation home in 1981 and by 1990 had planted 40 acres of vineyards on the former Victorian homestead. The Browns sold their fruit to other wineries until 1996, when they made their first zinfandel vintage, which was lauded by critics along with many of the subsequent vintages.

Brown makes about 4,000 cases of predominantly zinfandel but also small quantities of cabernet sauvignon and chardonnay from the estate vineyards, though it still sells some fruit to other local wineries (3233 Sage Canyon Rd., St. Helena, 707/963-2435, www.brownestate.com, open daily by appointment).

Kuleto Estate

When one of the Bay Area's most successful restaurateurs turns his hand to wine making, you can be sure the resulting winery is going to be quite a destination. Pat Kuleto's hillside estate does not disappoint, from the secret gate code given to visitors who make an appointment to the Tuscan-style house, Villa Cucina, looking down on Lake Hennessey.

Kuleto is the man behind such swank San Francisco restaurants as Boulevard and Fallaron, as well as the popular Martini House down the hill in St. Helena. The winery, completed in 2002, will likely be just as successful, particularly as Kuleto works his culinary contacts to get his wines on the lists of some of the country's top restaurants.

The 90 acres of vineyards planted on the twists and turns of these 800 acres of former grazing land are planted predominantly to cabernet sauvignon and sangiovese, with small blocks of zinfandel, syrah, pinot noir, and chardonnay. Production is about 8,000 cases now but will undoubtedly grow if the success of Kuleto's other ventures is anything to go by.

Tours of the diverse vineyards and modern winery, together with a comprehensive tasting of wines with cheeses, are available twice a day by appointment. And as you enter the gate code and drive onto the estate, you can imagine for a fleeting moment that you've arrived at your own, personal Wine Country estate (2470 Sage Canyon Rd., St. Helena, 707/963-9750, www.kuletoestate.com, tours 10:30 A.M. and 2:30 P.M. Mon.–Sat., $25).

SIGHTS
Sharpsteen Museum

This quirky little place (1311 Washington St., 707/942-5911, 11 A.M.–4 P.M. daily, donations requested) was donated to the city in the 1970s by its creators, Ben and Bernice Sharpsteen, and depicts upvalley life from the days of the Wappo people to the early 1900s. Its main claim to fame is a beautifully painted diorama depicting Calistoga in its hot springs heyday, but it also has some more traditional exhibits, many no doubt enhanced by the skills of Ben Sharpsteen, who was an academy-award winning animator.

Next door is one of the frilly little cottages built by Sam Brannan in the 1860s for his groundbreaking Hot Springs Resort in Calistoga. It was moved here in the 1970s, leaving only one of Brannan's cottages remaining where it was originally built—at the Brannan Cottage Inn on Wapoo Street.

Old Faithful Geyser

Although it's really not worth the time or money, visitors continue to flock to Calistoga's Old Faithful Geyser (1299 Tubbs Ln., Calistoga, 707/942-6463, 9 A.M.–6 P.M. daily, $8), one of only three geysers in the world reliable enough to get the Old Faithful moniker. There must be something hypnotic about the thought of watching water shoot 60 feet or more into the air that keeps people coming. Or perhaps it's the free mud bath that you can sink into if you get too close to the water. Just hope you don't get there right after an eruption has finished or it could be as long as a 45-minute wait until the next one (though the gap between eruptions varies depending on the season). Still, that's time enough to open your faithful wallet for some overpriced Old Faithful gifts. Even the famous fainting goats near the entrance seem bored by the all the fuss and no longer faint on cue, as their "genetic defect" is supposed to guarantee (could be evidence of evolution).

Petrified Forest

Another natural attraction nearby that illustrates the area's volcanic past but with far more scenic value (though no goats) is the Petrified Forest, about half a mile up Petrified Forest Road from Calistoga (follow the signs to Santa Rosa, 707/942-6667, 9 A.M.–6 P.M. in summer, until 5 P.M. in winter, $6). Short trails meander through fallen redwood trees that were long ago turned to stone at such a microscopic level that they still look almost like wood. In the distance looms Mount St. Helena, believed to have been the source of the volcanic eruption that buried the trees millions of years ago and started the long petrifaction process. Guided tours are available on weekends at 11 A.M., and there are plenty of chunks of petrified wood for sale in the rustic visitor center under a very old oak tree (no one knows how old, but probably over 600 years).

Pope Valley

Sleepy Pope Valley is the unlikely setting for California Historic Landmark No. 939. Even more unlikely is that California would designate a collection of thousands of hubcaps strung from posts, fences, and trees as a historic landmark. But such is the importance of this strange collection to the state's eclectic folk art scene (or so someone thought) that the **Hubcap Ranch,** created by Emanuel "Litto" Damonte from the 1950s to his death in 1985, was given its lofty status and Litto immortalized as the Pope Valley Hubcap King.

It is still a private ranch, so don't expect any Wine Country–style tours, though you're welcome to leave a hubcap from the rental car or your own to ensure the collection keeps growing. The ranch's dogs seem to love trying to scare visitors, so don't be surprised when they hurl their snarling bodies at the fence behind the landmark plaque.

Litto's grandson, Mike Damonte, has kept

Old Faithful Geyser in Calistoga

Hubcap donations are always welcome.

up the folk art tradition that his grandfather inadvertently started when he hung lost hubcaps on his fence in case their hapless owners wanted them back. The growing collection proved to be a magnet, and soon neighbors and anonymous visitors were leaving hubcaps rather than taking them. Now, half a century later, there are reportedly about 5,000 of the things glinting in the sun, from lavish chrome 1960s trim to the present-day plastic wannabes.

Hubcap Ranch is easy to get to and easy to spot. From the Silverado Trail, head up Deer Park Road, through the small college town of Angwin, and down through the forest to the auto-repair shop, junkyard, and general store that constitute downtown Pope Valley. At that intersection, turn left onto Pope Valley Road. From the Catacula Lake Winery, continue east along Chiles Pope Valley Road, then bear right at the general store. Hubcap Ranch is about two miles farther, at 6654 Pope Valley Road just past the Pope Valley Winery, though you certainly won't need to look for the number on a mailbox.

While you're in the area, the **Pope Valley Winery** is worth a stop, despite its sprawling,

scrappy-looking setting (6613 Pope Valley Rd., 707/965-1246, 10 A.M.–4 P.M. daily, free tasting). The original three-story winery building was built in 1909 and operated as the Sam Haus Winery until 1959 when it closed. Since then a variety of owners have tried to make a go of it in this remote location, the latest being a group of valley residents who bought the old buildings in 1998 and now make about 4,000 cases of mainly red wines from the 80 acres of Pope Valley vineyards, including zinfandel, cabernet sauvignon, and sangiovese.

ENTERTAINMENT

Calistoga feels decidedly sleepy at night, but a couple of bars are open late. The **Hydro Bar & Grill** (1403 Lincoln Ave., 707/942-9777) sometimes has local live music on weekend nights, and the small pub at the **Calistoga Inn** (1250 Lincoln Ave., 707/942-4101, www.calistogainn.com), where there's live music most nights Thursday–Saturday (and often on Sunday afternoons) plus a popular open mic night on Wednesday. Call the venues for more information.

SHOPPING

Like many things in Calistoga, shopping is a little more down to earth here than elsewhere in the valley. Sure, there are still plenty of gift shops but there's a decidedly artisan feel to most of them, like the **American Indian Trading Company** (1407 Lincoln Ave., next to the Hydro Grill, 707/942-9330, 10 A.M.–6 P.M. daily), which sells arts, crafts, and jewelry from Native American tribes all over the country, including a few local tribes. On U.S. 29 just south of Lincoln Avenue is **Calistoga Pottery** (1001 Foothill Blvd., 707/942-0216, 10 A.M.–5 P.M. daily), another good place to buy something original from local artists who have supplied some of the valley's biggest wineries and restaurants with their stoneware.

At the eastern end of Lincoln is the historic **Calistoga Depot** (1458 Lincoln Ave.), the second-oldest remaining railroad depot in the country, built by Sam Brannan in 1868 and crucial to the success of Calistoga's Victorian spas. It is now home to handful of funky little stores, some of them in six old railroad cars parked on the tracks leading to nowhere. **Calistoga Wine Stop** (707/942-5556, 10 A.M.–6 P.M. daily) is in one of those cars and has a good selection of wines from both Napa and Sonoma, including a few rarities.

Wine aficionados will also probably enjoy sniffing around the small **Enoteca Wine Shop** (1348 Lincoln Ave., 707/942-1117, 11:30 A.M.–5:30 P.M. daily), which specializes in smaller (sometimes cult) producers of wines from California and beyond. Another fascinating wine shop, one that prides itself on selling hard-to-find boutique Californian wines, is the **Wine Garage** on Foothill Boulevard just south of Lincoln Avenue (1020 Foothill Blvd., Calistoga, 707/942-5332, 11 A.M.–7 P.M. Tues.–Sat., noon–5 P.M. Sun.). Owner Todd Miller travels throughout the lesser-known wine regions of Northern California trying and buying wines from small wineries, loading them onto his truck, and bringing them back to the shop. No bottle costs over $25, and many are under $15—a refreshing change in a valley of big wine names and big prices.

The only railroad cars in Calistoga these days are part of the Depot shopping center.

© PHILIP GOLDSMITH

LEAVE WINE (AND CLOTHES) BEHIND

Put away the camera, forget about wineries, leave your cynicism behind, and take off all your clothes (only if you want to) at the historic and decidedly alternative **Harbin Hot Springs** about a half hour north of Calistoga, beyond Mount St. Helena in rural Lake County (Harbin Springs Rd., off Big Canyon Rd., Middletown, 707/987-2477 or 800/622-2477, www.harbin.org).

In some sense this place could be described as a hot springs resort. It has the natural springs and the history of its Calistoga spa cousins to the south, dating from the late 1800s when the sick and infirm sought out the natural waters here. A more accurate description these days, however, would be a new-age eco-resort still running on 1960s flower power. It's a place where you're far more likely to hear about the joy of finding a higher state of consciousness than the joy of savoring the best cabernet in Napa. That's if you hear anything. In some parts of the resort even a whisper will elicit gentle but firm rebukes that might conjure up fears of some bizarre karmic retribution (it also has a bit of a reputation of being a pickup joint, both gay and straight).

Nevertheless, there's enough on offer within the 1,200 acres to please even a wine-hardened cynic—from hiking trails in the hills to the series of indoor-outdoor hot and cold pools among the trees; from the organic food store to the communal kitchen. Best of all is the endless flow of free classes and workshops ranging from dance and yoga classes to meditation and massage. Harbin is perhaps best known for its Watsu massage—a form of Shiatsu massage performed while you float in a pool.

Nearly all the activities are free after paying a day-use fee of $25 (weekdays) or $30 (weekends), though at least one person will need to also buy a $10 trial membership to the nonprofit organization that now runs Harbin. If you only want to sunbathe naked (or clothed) for half a day or take a yoga class, the six-hour fee is $5 less. Check the website for a full schedule of events and classes.

Another reason to come here is for the wide range of accommodations. They range from dorm rooms ($35–50, bring your own towels and bedding) and basic rooms with shared bathrooms ($80–120) up to rooms with full bath (from $110 midweek, $170 weekends) and three cottages tucked away in the woods ($140–170 midweek, $190–230 weekends). Camping in the meadows is also an option and is free with the day-use fee ($25–30), though no fires or camping stoves are allowed so you'll be eating in one of the on-site vegetarian restaurants or using the communal kitchen.

RECREATION

Robert Louis Stevenson State Park

By far the best views in the valley, and perhaps the entire Wine Country, are from the top of ever-visible Mount St. Helena at the northern end of the valley, in the park named for the mountain's most famous Victorian visitor.

Stevenson honeymooned in a cabin here after traveling from his native Scotland to marry Fanny Osbourne, the woman he met at an artists' retreat. The area had just been abandoned by silver miners following the rapid rise and fall of the **Silverado mine** in the 1870s,

after which the Silverado Trail is named, along with Stevenson's account of his brief stay in the valley, *Silverado Squatters*.

The happy couple's cabin is long gone, marked only by a small monument partway up the five-mile trail to the summit. Look out for two big, dirt parking lots on either side of the road about eight miles north of Calistoga on U.S. 29. The **Mount St. Helena Trail** starts from the western lot and has virtually no shade, together with some particularly steep sections— it climbs about 2,000 feet in five miles to the 4,339-foot summit of the mountain—so hiking it in the middle of a hot summer day is not recommended. On the clearest days, usually in spring, the 360-degree views stretch for more than 100 miles, and in winter there is often a dusting of snow near the peak. Those not so determined to get to the summit can take a spur off the main trail at about the 3.5-mile point to the 4,000-foot South Peak, which has impressive views of the valley.

The eastern parking lot marks the start of the **Table Rock Trail,** a shorter and less strenuous 2.2-mile trail that climbs out of the woodland and past volcanic rock outcroppings to a ridge overlooking the flat moonscape known as Table Rock and the entire valley to the south. The more adventurous can connect to the **Palisades Trail,** which crosses Table Rock and eventually meets the Oat Hill Mine Road leading down into the valley, though that turns the hike into a daylong expedition and ends miles from the parking lot.

Calistoga Spas

During his stay here in 1880, Robert Louis Stevenson observed that Calistoga "seems to repose on a mere film above a boiling, subterranean lake." That mineral-laden boiling water fueled the growth of one of the biggest spa destinations in California. Railroad baron Samuel Brannan first cashed in on the endless hot water supply in 1862 with his Hot Springs Resort, and by the late 1860s the new railroad was bringing the fashionable and well-heeled from San Francisco to immerse themselves.

The emphasis of the dozens of spas these days has broadened to include everything from restorative volcanic mud to mineral soaks, wraps, and facials. The clientele has also broadened to include the less well-heeled, drawn by the straightforward, no-nonsense spa treatments here that dispense with the more luxurious (and expensive) frills offered by the bigger Napa Valley and Sonoma super-resorts. Don't go expecting glamorous establishments straight out of a glossy magazine spread—some of the places look like decidedly unglamorous motels in need of some restorative work themselves.

The region's Wappo people were actually the first to discover the unlikely pleasure of soaking in the local mud (one wonders who first had the idea and why). These days the mud is usually a mixture of dark volcanic ash, peat (for buoyancy), and hot mineral water that suspends your body, relaxes muscles, and draws out impurities in the skin, all accompanied by a rather off-putting sulfurous smell. A 10–15 minute soak is usually followed by rinse in crystal-clear mineral water and a steam wrap with or without piped music. Aromatherapies, massages, and other hedonistic treatments can be added afterward but will quickly run up the price. Those worried about lying in someone else's impurities can take comfort from the claims that the mud is regularly flushed with fresh spring water. There is evidently such a thing as clean mud.

Wherever and whatever the treatment, remember that the heat can rapidly dehydrate your body, so lay off the wine beforehand and don't plan to hike to the top of Mount St. Helena afterward, either. Reservations are usually needed but you might luck out just by walking in, especially midweek. Most spas are also open late, making them an ideal way to wrap up a long day of touring (pun intended).

On the site of Brannan's original resort is the **Indian Springs Resort** (1712 Lincoln Ave., 707/942-4913, www.indiansprings calistoga.com, 9 A.M.–8 P.M. daily), which specializes in 100 percent volcanic mud bath treatments ($75), using the volcanic ash from its 16 acres of land, and mineral baths ($65). It also has what is said to be California's oldest continuously operating swimming pool, an Olympic-sized version built in 1913 and fed by warm spring water. In fact, you can usually see the puffs of steam from the natural hot springs onsite. Spa customers can lounge by the pool as long as they want, though it can get crowded and the water is a little too warm for any serious swimming.

Another muddy Calistoga institution announced by its big, red neon sign is the funky **Dr. Wilkinson's Hot Springs** (1507 Lincoln Ave., 707/942-4102, www.drwilkinson.com, 8:30 A.M.–3:45 P.M. daily), founded by an eccentric chiropractor in the 1950s who devel-

a frilly Victorian cottage that was once part of Sam Brannan's original Calistoga spa resort

oped his own secret recipe for the mud that his children still guard closely today. "The Works," a 1.5-hour pampering with mud bath, facial, mineral soak, and blanket wrap, costs the fairly standard $75. For just $35 more, you can finish with a 30-minute massage, and there are plenty of other well-priced packages available.

The **Lincoln Avenue Spa** (1339 Lincoln Ave., 707/942-5296, www.lincolnavenuespa.com, 9 A.M.–9 P.M. daily) offers couples the chance to float in twin tubs of mud for a slight discount ($68 per person compared to $75 for singles). There is a choice of four types of mud, including an Ayurvedic herbal mud and an antioxidant-laden wine mud containing wine, grape seed oil, and green tea. It also offers salt scrubs, with or without accompanying mud, and a full range of massages and facials. No jokes about spa treatments breaking the bank here—this spa is in a solid-looking stone building that was a Victorian-era bank.

Some of the most reasonable prices for being immersed in mud are at the unpretentious (even for Calistoga) **Oasis Spa,** behind the less modest, motel-like Roman Spa Resort (1300 Washington St., 707/942-2122, www.oasisspa.com).

The hour-long mud treatment costs just $55, and there are also interesting mineral bath additions, including Dead Sea salt and mustard powder.

At the **Lavender Hill Spa** (1015 Foothill Blvd., 707/942-4495, www.lavenderhillspa.com, 9 A.M.–9 P.M. daily) the mud is used only once before being discarded and is an international affair, containing Calistoga volcanic ash, French sea kelp, Dead Sea salt, and the trademark lavender oil. Like most treatments here, the mud bath ($68) is available for singles or couples. For the same price there is also a unique Thai milk bath with sea kelp and some fruity essential oils that is part of a whole range of other Thai-inspired massages and facials, all in a relaxing gardenlike setting.

There are no mud baths at the **Mount View Spa** in the namesake hotel (1457 Lincoln Ave., 707/942-5789, www.mountviewhotel.com, 9 A.M.–9 P.M. daily), but there are mud wraps, as well as plenty of mineral bath, massage, and facial treatments in perhaps the classiest setting in Calistoga. Mineral baths ($55, couples $65) might contain grape seeds, aromatherapy essences, or Moor mud added to the water. Massages start at $65, and the huge selection culminates with a three-hour, $300 extrava-ganza called the Head to Toe package, which includes a mineral bath, body polish, Swedish massage, and facial. The hotel's pool can also be used by spa customers.

Another spa that specializes in massage rather than mud baths is the **Cedar Street Spa** (1107 Cedar St., 707/942-2947, www .cedarstreetspa.com). Most massages start at $75 for 50 minutes and include hot stone, deep tissue, Shiatsu, therapeutic, sports, and Swed-ish styles. There's also a $48 "Refresher" mas-sage for either back, neck and shoulders, or tired feet.

ACCOMMODATIONS

Calistoga is the one of the cheapest places in the valley for most purchases, whether food, gas, or a place to stay. This is still Wine Coun-try, however, so cheap is a relative term. Some of the Victorian B&Bs strung along the St. Helena Highway and Foothill Boulevard seem downright reasonable during the week, but rates can almost double on summer week-ends, much like everywhere else in the valley. The best bargains are probably the numerous spa resorts that offer slightly less stylish, motel-style rooms for slightly more reasonable prices. All generally offer free continental breakfast, though with some you might be left wonder-ing which continent manages to function on such limited morning sustenance.

Whatever the accommodation, remember that this end of the valley is the hottest, and sleeping without air-conditioning in the height of sum-mer can be a challenge. As in the rest of the val-ley, there is also a penalty to pay for wanting to stay during a weekend when rates are often 50 percent higher than midweek and a two-night minimum is pretty standard. And that's if you can find a room. As always, book plenty of time in advance from July through October.

Under $100

To use the term "bargain" to describe the **N Calistoga Inn** (1250 Lincoln Ave., Calis-toga, 707/942-4101, www.calistogainn.com)

might be a bit of an overstatement, but this no-nonsense inn right on the creek in the center of town does offer some of the cheapest, if not the most luxurious, accommodations in town. The 18 rooms are spartan compared to those of the Victorian inns in the surrounding blocks—no air-conditioning, no televisions, shared bath-rooms (but an in-room sink), a dose of street or restaurant noise, and often not enough room to swing a proverbial cat. Still, they are clean, comfortable, stylish in their minimalist way, and cost from only $65 a night in the winter or from $75 a night midweek during the sum-mer—that's about as cheap as it gets in Calis-toga. On summer weekends the price shoots up to $125, making the basic rooms far less of a bar-gain, though there is no minimum-stay require-ment so it might still be worth paying. One of Calistoga's better restaurants and a small brew-pub are right downstairs, making for a night of good food, entertainment, and (hopefully) sleep, all in a charming Victorian package.

A more rustic accommodation option is at the **Mountain Home Ranch,** up in the hills a few minutes outside of Calistoga (3400 Mountain Home Ranch Rd., off Pet-rified Forest Rd., Calistoga, 707/942-6616, www.mountainhomeranch.com). This is a down-home family B&B and working ranch with rooms in the main house and separate cot-tages that are more practical than stylish. The cheapest, with shared bathroom, squeak in at just under $80 March–November ($55 during the winter) while regular rooms with private bathrooms are just over $100 during the high season and $80 during the winter. The two-and three-room cottages start at $130 for dou-ble occupancy, though there's an additional $20 charge per person for more than two guests.

Within walking distance of downtown Calistoga is motel row, the eastern stretch of Lincoln Avenue where the chains and cheapies are located. One of the cheaper ones is the **Cal-istoga Inn and Spa** (1880 Lincoln Ave., Cal-istoga, 707/942-0991, www.greatspa.com), which has basic rooms starting at $90 and big-ger rooms and suites, some with roman bath-tubs, from $130 and up. All are decorated in the style of Anywhere, U.S.A., with the ubiquitous flowery bedspreads and plain furniture, though they also have air-conditioning and pools, two essential extras for hot Calistoga summers. A cheap on-site spa offers mud baths for just $50.

$100–200

This is the price range that many of Calistoga's spas and B&Bs fall into. At the low end of the range is the **EuroSpa and Inn,** a motel-style abode on a peaceful residential street just a block from Lincoln Avenue (1202 Pine St., Calistoga, 707/942-6829). Rooms in the small bungalows arranged around a central parking lot are fairly tastefully furnished and come with a long list of standard features including whirlpool tubs, air-conditioning, gas stoves (certainly not needed in summer), and refrigerators. They start at $100 midweek during the summer and $150 on weekends, and go up to $160 midweek ($230 weekends) for the largest rooms with two beds. Being on the edge of town, the inn's pool looks onto vineyards and is where the continental breakfast is usually served in summer.

Staying in a little piece of history is cheaper than you might think at the **Brannan Cottage Inn** (109 Wapoo Ave., Calistoga, 707/942-4200, www.brannancottageinn.com). The Victorian cottage with its white picket fence is the only cottage from Sam Brannan's original Calistoga resort that still stands where it was first built, now on a quiet street just off Calistoga's main drag. It is now on the National Register of Historic Places and contains six rooms furnished in tasteful and restrained Victorian style, all with air-conditioning, private bathrooms, views of the pretty gardens, and a private entrance from the wraparound porch. The smallest room with a four-poster bed costs $145 midweek and $165 weekends. The biggest room, an upstairs minisuite, costs $165 midweek and $185 weekends. Knock about $20 off those prices during the winter.

A Calistoga institution best known for its mud baths, **Dr. Wilkinson's Hot Springs Resort** also has 42 good though basic rooms just a few steps from all the shops and restaurants of Lincoln Avenue (1507 Lincoln Ave., Calistoga, 707/942-4102, www.drwilkinson.com). From the outside this looks like a 1950s motel, but the rooms have a little more going for them with modern and tasteful (if slightly sparse) furnishings, air-conditioning, and fairly standard motel levels of equipment. Don't expect luxury at this price, though the charm of the lively resort more than compensates. The cheapest rooms are arranged around the courtyard or pool area and cost from $110 midweek during the winter up to $180 on summer weekends. A small neighboring Victorian cottage houses some slightly more expensive rooms that range $140–190, though there's little in the way of additional creature comforts to justify the higher prices.

One of the biggest old buildings in downtown Calistoga (though that's not saying much) is home to the **Mount View Hotel,** which brings a bit of urban class within walking distance of almost everything Calistoga has to offer (1457 Lincoln Ave., Calistoga, 707/942-6877 or 800/816-6877, www.mountviewhotel.com). The cheapest queen and king rooms ($159–179 midweek, $20 more on weekends) can be a bit on the small side, but all 29 rooms and suites have a slightly eclectic mix of modern furnishings with Victorian antique and art-deco touches harking back to the hotel's 1920s and '30s heyday. The list of standard features is impressive for Calistoga and stretches to CD players in some rooms and free wireless Internet access. The more expensive suites ($208–289 midweek, $30 more on weekends) have claw-foot tubs and wet bars, and the pricier suites have balconies overlooking the street. Best of all are the three separate cottages, each with its own small outdoor redwood deck and hot tub, though expect to pay upward of $300 a night during the summer. Downstairs is arguably one of Calistoga's best restaurants, Stomp, and a spa that's more luxurious than most in the area.

Even farther up into the eastern hills—in the next valley, in fact—is the **RustRidge Ranch B&B** (2910 Lower Chiles Valley Rd., St. Helena, 707/965-9353, www.rustridge.com), one of the few B&Bs in Wine Country that comes with a winery attached as well as a working ranch. There are just five rooms and 450 rural acres of vineyards, pasture, and woodland, where the only traffic noise is likely to be galloping horses. The cheapest is The Oaks ($150), which has a private bathroom out in the hallway. The biggest room is the Rust-Ridge ($225), with impressive views, a deck, and a fireplace. A small cottage sleeps four and costs $250 a night. All rooms are decorated in a western ranch style with modern, comfortable furnishings, and guests have access to the swimming pool, tennis court, and miles of hiking trails. If you want to ride a horse, however, you'll have to bring your own.

Over $200

Hats off to the owners of **The Pink Mansion** for not even attempting to come up with a chintzy name for their bright pink Victorian pile, which dates from 1875 (1415 Foothill Blvd., Calistoga, 707/942-0558 or 800/238-7465, www.pinkmansion.com). The unique name is matched by some unique features that were added by the last person to live there, the eclectic Alma Simic, like the small heated pool in what looks like a Victorian parlor. She also painted the house pink in the 1930s, the color it has been ever since. The woodsy surroundings, quaint but not overly frilly furnishings, and features like claw-foot tubs and air-conditioning make this one of the pricier establishments along this stretch of road, however. The smallest rooms start at $175 a night, and the gargantuan and luxurious Master Suite, dripping with period features and exotic woods, goes for $300. At $195, the Wine Suite is perhaps the best value, with a fireplace, private garden entrance, and separate sitting area.

One of the prettiest spa resorts to stay at in Calistoga is **Indian Springs** (1712 Lincoln Ave., Calistoga, 707/942-4913, www.indianspringscalistoga.com). The 1940s-era cottages are on the pricey side but made more palatable by the plank flooring, kitchenettes, barbecues on their back porches, and the fact that the summer rates are the same all week with no additional weekend surcharges. The cheapest are the Sam's Bungalows, named for Calistoga's founder, Sam Brannan, who set up his Victorian resort on the same land that Indian Springs now occupies. They start at $235 during the summer (May–Oct.) and on winter weekends but are $185 midweek in winter. The palm-lined driveway is surrounded by the cozy one- and two- bedroom Palm Row cottages that start at $265 during the summer ($235 midweek in winter) and are probably the best bargains with their separate sitting area with a sofabed. Ask for number 16 or 17—they back onto open fields for some extra isolation. Both the Sam's and Palm Row bungalows share front porches and a wall with the neighboring unit, but the more expensive Colbert bungalows are totally detached and can comfortably sleep four. They cost $285 during the summer ($215 midweek in winter).

As its name suggests, the **Cottage Grove Inn** is actually 16 private cottages strung along a small road under a pretty grove of old elm trees on the edge of Calistoga (1711 Lincoln Ave., Calistoga, 707/942-8400 or 800/799-2284, www.cottagegrove.com). The cottages were custom built in 1996 and offer some modernity along a strip dominated by older motels. Despite their slightly clichéd sounding individual names, all 16 are furnished in a similar Mediterranean style with vaulted ceilings, beautiful antique wood floors, and a long list of luxury features including a double Jacuzzi tub, CD and DVD player, fireplace, and front porch on which to sit, sip, and watch the world go by. The price for such personal space and luxury is $250 midweek and $325 on weekends April–November and $215–295 the rest of the year.

A spa resort in a former trailer park might not sound appealing, but the **Calistoga Ranch** is just that and one of the valley's newest and most luxurious places to stay (580 Lommel Rd., off Silverado Trail, Calistoga, 707/254-2800, www.calistogaranch.com). The owners avoided the costly and lengthy process of winning approval for new buildings and instead decided to work with the existing RV permit. So the 47 guest lodges on 150 acres of wooded canyon land really are trailers, albeit with well-hidden wheels and a design aesthetic that is distinctly Manhattan modernism rather than trailer trash.

The lodges are made up of a series of rooms joined by an outside deck with every conceivable luxury bell and whistle, from indoor/outdoor fireplaces and showers to plasma-screen TVs and wet bars. The smallest are 600 square feet, about double the average hotel room size and also double the average price around here, starting at $450 in winter and $550 in the peak fall season. Expect to pay more for views of any kind, and for one of the apartment-sized one-bedroom lodges (starting at $675 without hot tub, $775 with). For those who actually want to leave their luxury hideaways there's the exclusive Bathhouse spa (treatments $65–260), outdoor pool, classes and seminars, and miles of hiking trails around the grounds.

FOOD

Calistoga is often overlooked in the valley's food scene, eclipsed by the culinary destinations of Yountville and St. Helena. But there is probably more diversity in the restaurants along a few blocks of Lincoln Avenue than those other towns can manage, from high end to hole in the wall.

Breakfast

The old-fashioned **Café Sarafornia** (1413 Lincoln Ave., 707/942-0555, 7 A.M.–2:30 P.M. daily) has become almost a destination itself in this destination spa town, serving down-home, no-nonsense breakfast and brunch at bar, booth or table. It also sells sandwiches to go for those on the go or planning a picnic ($8–10). Its name comes from the famous verbal blunder by the town's founder, Samuel Brannan.

Californian

When it replaced much-loved Catahoula in the historic Mount View Hotel in 2004, **Stomp**

Restaurant (1457 Lincoln Ave., 707/942-8272, dinner daily except Mon., lunch weekends, dinner entrées $24–29) was hailed by some reviewers as the harbinger of the rise of haute cuisine in Calistoga. Whether that turns out to be true with the resurgence of down-valley destinations remains to be seen, but the classy Wine Country cuisine served here is without peer in the town. Think of such intricately named dishes as maple-leaf duck breast with root vegetable tower, candied chestnuts, and duck natural. Think also of prices not far off $30 for many dinner entrées. The huge wine list is peppered with cult wines costing many hundreds of dollars but also offers more than 40 wines by the glass. There's also free corkage on some nights during the week, though other times it's $18, waived if you buy a bottle in-house too.

Bistros

The **Ⓜ Wappo Bar & Bistro** (1226 Washington St., 707/942-4712, lunch and dinner daily except Tues., dinner entrées $15–25) is one of the most relaxing places to eat in this part of the valley during the summer thanks to its quiet, unassuming home just off Lincoln Avenue and the small arbor-covered patio that transports you from Wine Country U.S.A. to Wine Country Tuscany. The menu spans the globe and might include such diverse dishes as chicken pot pie or a Thai coconut curry, but the wine list is focused firmly on Napa with a few other California appellations thrown in.

Walking past the **Calistoga Inn** on a cool, dark winter evening, it's tempting to go into the restaurant just for the cozy, rustic atmosphere exuded through its Victorian windows (1250 Lincoln Ave., 707/942-4101, dinner and lunch daily, dinner entrées $15–20). During the warmer months the draw is the creekside patio, but all year the food would probably best be described as reliable, bistro-style comfort food. Next door to the restaurant is an equally relaxed pub that's home to the **Napa Valley Brewing Company,** founded in 1989 and said to be the first brewery established in the valley since Prohibition. It also usually has some sort of entertainment going on, from open mic nights to jazz.

The menu at the **All Seasons Café** (1400 Lincoln Ave., 707/942-9111, 6–9:30 P.M., dinner daily except Mon., lunch Fri.–Sun., dinner entrées $17–27) is, as the name suggests, inspired by local produce currently in season, and the sophisticated dishes attract food lovers from all over the valley, though recent reports suggest quality has slipped a bit. The small wine list at the table is just a sampling of the hundreds of labels available in the wine store at the back of the main restaurant. Buy a bottle to take home or pay the $15 corkage fee to drink it at the table, saving plenty on the usual markup for wines.

Bosko's Trattoria (1364 Lincoln Ave., 707/942-9088, 11:30 A.M.–10 P.M. daily, dinner entrées $10–14) is another Calistoga institution with a local reputation as solid as the stone building it calls home. The simple salads, some of the valley's best pastas, and wood-fired pizzas served in the homey surroundings all cost less than $14, and there's a good selection of delicious, well-stuffed panini sandwiches for less than $9.

Grills

Brannan's Grill (1374 Lincoln Ave., 707/942-2233, lunch and dinner daily, dinner entrées $19–30) brought the big-time Napa food scene right to the heart of Calistoga when it opened in 1998, though its reputation has slipped a bit in recent years. White tablecloths, the 19th-century dark-wood bar, and the giant murals of the valley's past lend an air of elegance to accompany the pricey, all-American menu, which usually includes two or three steaks. Corkage is normally $15 but is waived if you buy at least one bottle of wine in-house from the wine list that offers a smattering of choices from Oregon, Europe, and Australia alongside Napa and Sonoma regulars. Lunch or brunch ($7–12) is a cheaper way to experience the sumptuous interior.

A few doors down the road is Brannan's sister restaurant, **Flatiron Grill** (1440 Lincoln Ave., 707/942-1220, dinner daily, lunch weekends, dinner entrées $11–20), which is an altogether cheaper dining option. In terms of both the food and decor it is almost a baby Brannan's, serving slightly less sophisticated food from the grill in less elegant, though still stylish, surroundings.

Mexican

The best place for Mexican and Latin-themed food in town is **Fuentes Tapas** (1458 Lincoln Ave., at the Calistoga Depot, 707/942-8165) in the Depot building, formerly Wappo Taco and the fun, boisterous sister to the more restrained Wappo Bar & Bistro. Some more traditional Mexican food can also be found at **Pacifico Restaurante Mexicano** (1237 Lincoln Ave., 707/942-4400, lunch and dinner daily), including some regional specialties and weekend brunches. Don't let the bland, strip-mall exterior put you off.

Those who prefer more of a hole-in-the-wall Mexican experience should walk to the other end of Lincoln Avenue to **Puerto Vallarta** (1473 Lincoln Ave., 707/942-6563, lunch and dinner daily until 9 P.M., $5–10), right next to the supermarket. The cheap and cheerful traditional food comes with equally traditional plastic surroundings both inside and out on the patio leading to the entrance.

The roomy, exposed brick interior of the **Hydro Bar & Grill** (1403 Lincoln Ave., 707/942-9777, dinner entrées $9–15) hints at its other life as a live music venue, but it is also a place to get quick meals at the bar, ranging from traditional burgers to Mexican-themed small plates ($4–10), together with plenty of microbrews, and it stays open well after most other eateries have closed.

Picnic Supplies

Picnic central in Calistoga is the **Palisades Market** (1506 Lincoln Ave., 707/942-9549, daily until 6 P.M.). Burritos, salads, wraps, and sandwiches are all available at the giant deli counter with pretty much everything costing less than $7. The rest of the old-fashioned grocery store should also be explored for all the other picnic accoutrements. Just over the road is the less glamorous **Cal Mart** (1491 Lincoln

Ave., 707/942-4545) supermarket, which sells even cheaper deli sandwiches, though it has a more limited selection.

Another alternative is to drop in to **Café Sarafornia** (1413 Lincoln Ave., 707/942-0555) a few blocks down Lincoln Avenue to pick up one of its sandwiches, or go to **Bosko's Trattoria** (1364 Lincoln Ave., 707/942-9088) and order a panini to go.

Farmers Market

The **Calistoga Farmers Market** (Lincoln Ave. at Washington St.), which sells crafts as well as produce, is held 8:30 A.M.–noon on Saturday June–September.

INFORMATION AND SERVICES

The **Calistoga Chamber of Commerce** is right next to the Calistoga Depot at the eastern end of Lincoln Avenue (1458 Lincoln Ave., 707/942-6333, www.calistogafun.com, 9 A.M.–5 P.M., closed Tues. and Sun.).

Also worth checking for information is the tiny **Spa Information Center,** next to the Lincoln Avenue Spa (1339 Lincoln Ave.), with which it seems to share hours (9 A.M.–9 P.M. daily). Although most of the information is about just a handful of spas owned by the same company, there are also some other potentially useful Napa Valley brochures and coupons.

Southern Sonoma

It's difficult to get overexcited in southern Sonoma, and that's a good thing. The Sonoma Valley and neighboring Carneros region are just so darned laid-back and leafy that even sitting in what passes as rush-hour traffic here will barely raise your blood pressure.

Apparently it's always been a pretty good, stress-free life in these parts. Mother Nature might mix things up a bit with the occasional fire or earthquake, but she also provides hot springs, redwood forests, burbling streams, fertile soils, and a friendly climate.

In a sense, southern Sonoma is fairly close to paradise: a place where wine, history, scenery, and some of the best California produce combine in an area small enough to tour in a day or two. A visitor can spend the morning sipping splendid wine then in the afternoon stroll through historic Victorian splendor, or traverse a muddy mountain one hour and spend the next in a spa covered in therapeutic mud.

Hundreds of years ago, these same natural attributes attracted numerous Native American tribes, who lived peacefully side by side without the turf battles common elsewhere. Even author Jack London sensed something intoxicating in the air. He relocated from Oakland to put down deep roots in the Sonoma Valley, transforming

© PHILIP GOLDSMITH

ust-Sees

M Gundlach Bundschu Winery: Witness Shakespeare or Mozart performed on a summer day at the outdoor amphitheater of this historic winery (page 113).

M Benziger Family Winery: See Benziger's biodynamic vineyards from a tractor-drawn tram, the most entertaining tour in the valley (page 116).

M Chateau St. Jean: It's worth it to pay a little extra for the reserve tasting and learn about wine while relaxing on the patio overlooking the valley (page 120).

M Sonoma Plaza: Spend an afternoon exploring the eclectic shops and historic sites of the notable Sonoma Plaza (page 123).

M Sonoma Mission: The last Californian mission has been immaculately restored, and its museum sheds light on the important role it played in the region's history (page 124).

M Sugarloaf Ridge State Park: Meander down the short nature trail or hike to the top of Bald Mountain for the best valley views (page 128).

M Jack London State Historic Park: Scenic hiking trails surround the former residence of the valley's prolific author and adventurer, Jack London (page 128).

M Carneros Creek Winery: Discover the full range of pinot noir wines by tasting the many different clonal varieties and blends (page 142).

M Domaine Carneros: Take a private tour and learn how champagne is made, all with a glass of bubbly in hand (page 142).

M The di Rosa Preserve: Enter a wonderland of art and leave the Wine Country behind (page 146).

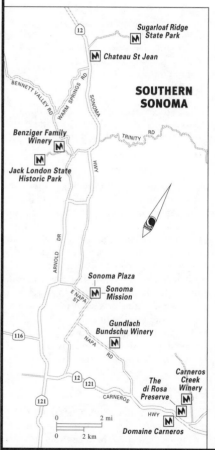

Southern Sonoma

FIGHTING FIRE WITH WINE

On a breezy day in September 1911 a stove exploded in a cobbler's shop on the east side of Sonoma Plaza, setting off what the *Sonoma Index-Tribune* newspaper described as a "disasterous fire" that was eventually extinguished with the help of a quick-thinking wine merchant.

The town's fire truck and 100 firefighters were quickly on the scene of the original fire but were soon overwhelmed when changing winds spread the flames to buildings up and down the street and, at one point, set fire to the grass on the plaza.

When the roof of Agostino Pinelli's wine cellars on Spain Street caught fire, and he saw the fire truck was too far away to help, he and some firefighters connected a hose and pump to a 1,000-gallon tank of his wine and, as reported by the *Index-Tribune*, "A powerful stream of red wine was directed on the burning wine cellar."

Although the fire eventually destroyed most of the other buildings on 1st Street East, Pinelli's red wine was credited with helping firefighters focus on preventing the fire from spreading to even more buildings on the south side of the plaza.

The Pinelli building is still standing today on 1st Street East near Spain Street. It was built in 1891 from local stone quarried by the Pinelli family, which also helped Samuele Sebastiani get his start in the quarrying business before he went on to establish the Sebastiani Winery. Today, the building is home to offices and shops including (rather appropriately) the Sonoma Wine Shop (412 1st St. East, Sonoma, 707/996-1230, open 11 A.M.–6 P.M. daily).

himself from working-class hero to gentleman farmer and land owner. The main characters in his 1913 novel *Valley of the Moon* spent months wandering up and down California in search of their nirvana, the Sonoma Valley.

The lucky locals have worked hard against the odds to keep their valley and flatlands so inviting. In the 1960s, they fought off a plan developed by car-crazed California to drive a freeway down the middle of Sonoma Valley. While fame and freeways brought the heaving masses to Napa and northern Sonoma, the valley became the land that development forgot. By 1980, there was a grand total of two sets of traffic lights—and there aren't many more now. The valley's modern custodians are still a potent force, even defending a few local chickens threatened with resettlement. Such is the passion here to keep "slow" in locally nicknamed Slow-noma.

Can the valley keep its identity amid modern population and development pressures? It's trying hard but is swimming against the tide of tourism. Wineries and hotels are being mopped up by bigger and bigger conglomerates. The succulent local food is transforming into ever-more-expensive ethnic cuisine. An

average family home in the valley now costs over $1.5 million. Visit quickly before Napa hops over the mountains and ends it all.

In the long term, there's more hope for Carneros simply because there is no "there" there. (Ask anyone to name one town in Carneros and most will list Sonoma—a place also claimed by its eponymous valley.) In Carneros, the vineyards that are slowly covering any remaining pastureland not already underwater are effectively spiking future development. Chances are that nothing much will change here anytime soon—except perhaps that rush-hour traffic on the two-lane roads may worsen as more people move to the Napa and Sonoma Valleys.

PLANNING YOUR TIME

The Sonoma Valley and Carneros are two of the easiest parts of Wine Country to visit, each having just one main road running its entire length. A visit to Carneros can be slightly harder to plan due to the lack of major towns, but it's easy enough to stop there for a few hours on the way to or from Sonoma and Napa.

Within the 17-mile-long Sonoma Valley, the

wineries, shops, and hotels are generally centered around the towns of **Glen Ellen** and neighboring **Kenwood,** and Sonoma itself. Without a well-planned strategy it can be time consuming to try to visit wineries at both the northern and southern ends of the valley, especially when the Sonoma Highway (U.S. 12) becomes clogged with northbound rush-hour traffic in the afternoon. You'll find yourself spending as much time in the car as in a tasting room.

It can easily take a full day to visit about five wineries around Sonoma, Kenwood, or in Carneros, and still have enough time for lunch without getting indigestion. An alternative strategy might be to pick four or five wineries that specialize in a particular wine. Or just spend a full day exploring the shops and historic sights of Sonoma, while tasting wine at several dedicated tasting rooms on the Sonoma Plaza.

If you do plan to visit wineries throughout the valley, get an early start. Their busiest times are mid- to late afternoon, especially for the wineries around Kenwood that most visitors only get to toward the end of the day. Most wineries are open from 10 A.M. (a few from 11 A.M.) and close between 4:30 and 5:30 P.M.

Arnold Drive, which runs roughly parallel to the Sonoma Highway up the west side of the valley, is a less scenic but often quicker way to travel between the heart of Glen Ellen and Sonoma. It also runs right down to the junction with U.S. 121 in **Carneros.**

Wineries along the Carneros Highway (U.S. 121) are generally clustered at the eastern and western ends of Carneros. Those at the western end include Roche, Gloria Ferrer, and Shug, and they are on the way from San Francisco to Sonoma. Those farther east are more spread out and generally lie between the road to Sonoma (Napa Rd. or U.S. 12) and the city of Napa. They include Artesa, Carneros Creek, and Bouchaine.

For some reason very few wineries have any sizable trees in their parking lots, preferring instead to plant trees that either look stunted or have minimal leaf cover. Consequently there's usually no shade and for the nine months of

the year that the sun shines parked cars quickly heat up to the temperature of an oven. Take a cooler if you plan a picnic or want to prevent that $100 bottle of wine from trying to become vinegar.

Most wineries charge a $5 tasting fee and $10 for tasting more expensive reserve wines. As in many other parts of the Wine Country, the tasting fee can sometimes be recouped when you buy wine.

GETTING THERE

A century ago there were more ways to get to Sonoma than there are today—by ferry, train, stagecoach, automobile, or plane. The train is long gone, ferries come nowhere near, the tiny local airports have no scheduled services, and there is no direct bus service to Sonoma, just some local connections to Santa Rosa and Petaluma. All of which leaves the car with a monopoly.

Getting there by car is, however, straightforward. From San Francisco the most traveled route is via U.S. 101, U.S. 37, and U.S. 121, which leads to the heart of Carneros and to the junction of U.S. 12 to Sonoma and the Sonoma Valley. The drive from the bridge to Sonoma takes just under an hour, longer if you have to navigate San Francisco local traffic.

To avoid Sonoma and go straight to Glen Ellen, go straight on Arnold Drive at the junction and gas station about five miles after joining U.S. 121. It is a slower road but avoids heavy traffic and leads straight to the heart of Glen Ellen.

Other routes to the area from the north and east include U.S. 12 east into the valley from U.S. 101 at Santa Rosa, or U.S. 37 west from I-80 at Vallejo to the junction of U.S. 121. Be warned that U.S. 121 through Carneros is infamous for nasty accidents due to its unexpected bends, dawdling tourists, and high volume of traffic.

GETTING AROUND

Once again, the car is how most people get around Carneros and the Sonoma Valley. The only real alternative to the tiring car-to-winery-to-car relay is a tiring bike ride. Rent a **bicycle** in either Glen Ellen or Sonoma and stick to the wineries in those areas to avoid long distances, summer heat, and tipsy drivers. Cruising around the empty flatlands of Carneros on two wheels is a rewarding way to get off the beaten track and visit less-crowded wineries, but only for those with the stamina for long distances.

Some hotels and B&Bs have their own bicycles for rent. Otherwise, two shops rent bikes and supply tour maps. **Sonoma Valley Cyclery** (20093 Broadway, Sonoma, 707/935-3377, 10 A.M.–6 P.M. Mon.–Sat., 10 A.M.–4 P.M.

Sun.) rents bikes for $25 a day. For $10 more it offers a packed lunch and self-guided tour from the shop to local Sonoma wineries or a 35-mile roundtrip trek to some Carneros wineries.

There is no physical address for the **Goodtime Touring Company** (888/525-0453 or 707/938-0453), but it will deliver bikes to your hotel. It rents basic bikes for $25 a day, tandems for $35, and full-suspension mountain bikes for $60. The closest thing to biking luxury (short of having someone else pedal) is Goodtime's half-day guided tour of Sonoma- or Kenwood-area wineries, which includes a gourmet lunch and a pack bike to carry the group's purchases. Those tours are $90 and start at 10 A.M.

The Sonoma Valley

They must feed the ducks of Sonoma Plaza something special to make them stick around the car-choked plaza, with its fetid green pools, rather than flying a few miles north to the serenity of the valley. Getting out of Sonoma, as fascinating and historic as it is, is the only way to really get an idea of what valley residents are fighting to preserve.

The road north out of Sonoma passes fast-food outlets and a strip mall, and comes as close to urban sprawl as there is. In keeping with the valley's laid-back nature, it's a spaced-out, relaxed sort of sprawl linking Sonoma and three spring towns: Boyes Hot Springs, Fetters Hot Springs, and Agua Caliente, all of which look like they could do with a rejuvenating spa treatment themselves.

The towns end abruptly and the serene valley lies ahead. Plum, walnut, and peach orchards once shared the valley with cows that must have thought they'd died and gone to heaven to be grazing here. Now the mighty vine has taken over the valley floor, although that's far better than subdivisions. There's really little else but green things along the Sonoma Highway, except the loose-knit community of **Kenwood** (with the valley's cheapest gas) and, at the border of Santa Rosa, the retirement community of Oakmont.

Slightly off the main road southeast of Kenwood, the town of **Glen Ellen** probably has more restaurants and grocery stores per capita then almost any other town in North America. It's a true one-street town, with a curious dogleg halfway down the main street that is the real center of it all, not that there's all that much happening. It has managed to remain quaint without succumbing to the fake frills that so many other old towns in the United States get buried under. One of the biggest buildings is an auto shop, a sign that real life still takes place in this part of the valley.

The Wines

The volcanic soils of the hot mountainsides and the rich alluvial plains of the valley floor make Sonoma an ideal place to grow a plethora of grape varietals, a fact the missionaries and immigrants of the 1800s quickly discovered. The valley doesn't have quite the number of different growing conditions and soils of the larger Napa Valley, but winemakers maintain that its wines can be just as good.

Of the three distinct appellations, Sonoma Valley is the largest and includes some or all of the other two. It stretches from the top of the valley near Santa Rosa all the way down to the bay, bordered by 3,000-foot-high mountains

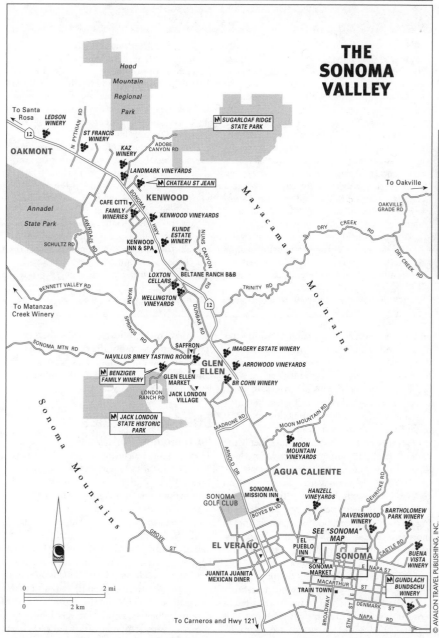

BATTLE OF THE CHICKENS

They are sometimes there, but officially they're not. The saga of the Sonoma Plaza chickens perfectly illustrates Sonoma's enduring small-town quirkiness in the face of the creeping invasion by expensive hotels, restaurants, and other newcomers.

At one point there were more than 100 chickens scratching out a living in the plaza, and they had plenty of local fans who appreciated the hick character they brought to the city. Letters to local newspapers told newcomers to "go home" if they didn't like the chickens. Even a city plan to cull the birds and keep their numbers to a more manageable 40 was met with squawks of protest from supporters.

"You'd see them crossing on the crosswalk. I think they learned from watching people," a reporter at the *Sonoma Index-Tribune* newspaper recalled. There was even one that regularly laid eggs in a plaza crafts store.

In 2000, however, the roosters were implicated in several pecking and scratching attacks on small children, marking the beginning of the end for the chicken population. In May that year, citing safety and liability issues, the city council voted to evict the chickens from the plaza and resettle them at local farms, a move that prompted a "roost in" protest by 100 chicken lovers in front of city hall.

There was an attempt to reintroduce some friendlier breeds of chicken later that year, together with an "egg patrol" to ensure their numbers didn't get out of hand, but four of them quickly fell foul of local dogs, and the rest were rounded up and whisked off to safety.

Now there are officially no chickens, just the plaza's friendly duck population to occasionally hold up traffic. But a small group of unofficial chickens can sometimes be seen scratching around city hall, especially at night, perhaps trying to undermine the council that sent them packing years ago.

on each side and encompassing 116,000 acres of land and about 13,000 acres of vineyards.

The valley acts like a giant funnel, channeling cooler air (and sometimes fog) up from the bay, leaving the mountainsides to bask in warm sunshine. Zinfandel loves the higher, hotter elevations, while cabernet and merlot ripen well on hillsides and the warmer north end of the valley. Pinot noir, chardonnay, and other white varietals prefer the slightly cooler valley floor, especially farther south toward Carneros.

The 800 acres of vineyards in the cooler and rockier Sonoma Mountain appellation just up the hill from Glen Ellen vary widely depending on their exposure, but the region is known mostly for its cabernet, although chardonnay, pinot noir, and other white varietals are also grown here.

The newest appellation is Bennett Valley, created in 2003, which stretches northeast from the Sonoma Mountains toward Santa Rosa and only just overlaps with Sonoma Valley. Its 700 acres of vineyards are primarily planted with merlot and chardonnay and generally have rocky, volcanic-based soils. A gap in low mountains west of the Bennett Valley lets ocean air and fog through and keeps growing conditions cool compared to the Sonoma Valley and the mountains.

SONOMA WINERIES

Bartholomew Park Winery

There seems to be a history competition between Bart Park, as it's known, and the neighboring Buena Vista Winery. Both have links to the Sonoma wine pioneer Agoston Haraszthy, and both are equally entitled to brag about it since they share what used to be Haraszthy's land. While Buena Vista has the original press house and caves from Haraszthy's winery, Bart Park has the site of Haraszthy's Romanesque home (a reproduction now stands there and is open only on Wednesdays and weekends) and most of the vineyard land. Neither of the two wineries that exist today has been operating very long.

Since Haraszthy's day, Bart Park has been home to a cat-loving widower, a home for "delinquent women," a hospital, and finally the Bartholomew family, which bought it in the 1940s and soon started making wine again under Haraszthy's defunct Buena Vista label. They later sold the winery and the Buena Vista name, keeping a large chunk of the vineyards and creating the Hacienda Winery, which they operated until their deaths. In 1994 it became the Bartholomew Park Winery and is now owned by the nearby Gundlach Bundschu Winery and operated as a boutique sibling.

Bart Park's colorful history is detailed in a small but packed museum housed in the old hospital building, along with the small tasting room where you can taste the estate chardonnay, cabernet sauvignon, and merlot, as well as several wines from other vineyards around Sonoma. Only 4,000 cases are produced a year, though for such limited production wines they're not too expensive.

The real charm of Bart Park, however, has nothing to do with history or wine. The winery sits in some glorious open space, including what remains of the formal gardens of an old mansion that was burned down (reportedly by the delinquent women) and the small garden of the reproduction Haraszthy home. You can wander freely throughout as if it's your own private garden and find great shaded picnic spots with sweeping views of the valley. Miles of hiking trails start from the winery and wind up the nearby hillsides, though they're not obvious so ask someone in the winery for directions (1000 Vineyard Ln., Sonoma, 707/935-9511, www.bartpark.com, open 11 A.M.–4:30 P.M. daily, tasting $5).

Buena Vista Winery

Buena Vista boasts that it was California's first premium winery, but that claim should be taken with a pinch of salt. The current Buena Vista sits on some of the land used by the original Buena Vista Winery, established by Agoston Haraszthy in 1858. The old hand-dug caves remain (but are now unsafe and closed), along with the original champagne cellar and stone press-house, which is now the visitor center and helps the site qualify as a California Historic Landmark.

The original Buena Vista Winery did not survive Prohibition, however, and the current winery is a modern incarnation. Some land and the Buena Vista label were bought in 1968 from the Bartholomew family (former owners of the Bartholomew Park winery), and ownership has changed many times since then. One could also argue that Haraszthy's original Buena Vista Winery wasn't actually the first so-called premium winery in California. It all depends on the definition of premium.

The winery is now owned by international conglomerate Allied Domecq and is a thoroughly commercial operation (as it was in Haraszthy's day), producing half a million cases of wine a year and attracting 120,000 visitors. Despite the fact that it gets very crowded in the summer, it's still worth visiting for its historical importance. You can wander around on your own or take a $15 guided tour that includes a historical presentation, an educational stroll through a vineyard, and tasting of some older, library wines. The plentiful picnic tables are shaded, though none of them offer much privacy, especially on summer weekends when the winery can be swamped with visitors.

Although Buena Vista is in the Sonoma Valley, its 1,000 acres of vineyards are now about seven miles south in the Carneros area, apart from a few acres used for demonstrations and tours. The midpriced Carneros estate wines include pinot noir, cabernet, merlot, chardonnay, and a newly released syrah. The cheapest Classics line of wines uses grapes from all over California and includes cabernet sauvignon, merlot, zinfandel, chardonnay, and sauvignon blanc, while the flagship reserve wines are available only at the winery and include cabernet, pinot noir, and chardonnay. They can be tasted for an additional fee, depending on the wine (18000 Old Winery Rd., Sonoma, 800/926-1266, www.buenavistawinery.com, open 10 A.M.–5 P.M. weekdays, until 5:30 P.M. weekends, tasting $5).

Gundlach Bundschu Winery

Not many wineries in California can boast that they won awards for their wines almost 100 years ago, but GunBun, as it's known, is one of them. The 19 Gundlach Bundschu wines entered into the 1915 Panama-Pacific International Exhibition in San Francisco all won medals, and the winery today focuses on squeezing the highest quality wines possible out of its estate vineyards without buying any grapes from anywhere else.

Grapes have been grown in the winery's Rhinefarm vineyard since they were first planted in 1858 by Bavarian-born Jacob Gundlach, a pioneer of the early California wine industry who is credited with planting Sonoma County's first riesling vines. He was joined in the business by his son-in-law, Charles Bundschu, in 1868, and the next generation of Gundlachs and Bundschus established the Gundlach Bundschu Wine Company in the early 1900s. Wine production was stopped during Prohibition and was restarted in 1973 by Jim Bundschu, Gundlach's great-great-grandson, who runs the winery today with his son Jeff.

The 300 acres of Rhinefarm vineyards today principally grow cabernet sauvignon, merlot, pinot noir, chardonnay, and gewürztraminer, together with some zinfandel, tempranillo, and a few other minor varietals. The winery's emphasis is on red bordeaux- and burgundy-style wines, and the cabernets and merlots tend to have plenty of tannic backbone. Some of the cheaper wines are available only from the winery and include the nonvintage Bearitage red blend and the unusual Kleinberger, an aromatic, fruity German wine.

The tasting room is housed in one of the original stone winery buildings, which can feel cramped when full of visitors—but the fun atmosphere makes it more bearable. Browse the historical memorabilia, including old wine posters from the 1800s. A short walk away is the 430-foot-long hillside cave, which is the longest in California and is part of a tour offered on weekends (and weekdays by appointment). GunBun also provides a shady patio, a picnicking area at the top of Towles' Hill overlooking the valley, and even a grassy amphitheater where you can see performances of Shakespeare or Mozart during the summer. Check the website for event schedules (2000 Denmark St., Sonoma, 707/938-5277, www.gunbun.com, open 11 A.M.–4:30 P.M. daily, tasting $5).

Sebastiani Vineyards & Winery

A visit to Sonoma would not be complete without a trip to the Sebastiani winery, founded by one of the city's most important benefactors and philanthropists, Samuele Sebastiani, and the only large winery within walking distance of the Sonoma Plaza.

Samuele Sebastiani arrived in Sonoma from northern Italy in 1895 and worked in local stone quarries before gathering enough money to buy an old winery in 1904. The business grew rapidly and was one of only 10 wineries that stayed open during Prohibition, when it made sacramental and medicinal wines as well as a fortune for Samuele. He spent money lavishly around town, building the Sebastiani theater on the plaza and countless other commercial and residential buildings, most of which survive today in some form or another.

Samuele's son August took over the business in 1934 and transformed Sebastiani into a huge wine empire before his death in 1980. The winery was then managed by August's son, Sam Sebastiani, but a family dispute forced him out in the 1980s, and he went on to establish the Viansa winery in Carneros with his wife (this fact is airbrushed out of the official winery history). The Sebastiani winery is now run by August's daughter, Mary Ann Sebastiani Cuneo.

Sebastiani pioneered the sale of cheap and cheerful half-gallon bottles of wine in the 1970s and developed a slew of additional wine brands in the 1980s, eventually producing a mind-boggling 8 million cases (96 million bottles) of wine a year. With the new millennium came a new strategy to focus only on premium, Sebastiani-labeled wines, and all the other brands were sold off in 2001, reducing production to less than 200,000 cases.

The flagship wine is the $70 Cherryblock cabernet sauvignon sourced from an old vineyard near the winery. Most of the other wines come from vineyards throughout Sonoma County and are reds, including merlot,

THE HUNGARIAN CONNECTION

Although German and Italian families founded some of the oldest wineries still operating in this part of Sonoma, it was a Hungarian immigrant called **Agoston Haraszthy** who became the area's first big commercial winemaker and in doing so helped change the face of the Californian wine industry.

Within a decade of arriving in the state he had established the pioneering Buena Vista Winery in the Sonoma Valley and was producing some of the best wines in America. A decade later he was gone. While his contribution to California's wine industry was important, it was not quite as important as might be suggested by some of the gushing accolades heaped upon him over the centuries.

Haraszthy is often called the Father of California Viticulture, for example, despite the fact that by the time he started bottling wine at Buena Vista the state was already producing about 240,000 gallons of the stuff. He is also sometimes credited with introducing the ubiquitous zinfandel grape to California, but there is some evidence that it arrived in the state before him.

One thing that is safe to say is that Haraszthy helped introduce European grapes and European-style commercial wine production to an industry still dependent on its missionary roots. He also had an entrepreneur's sense of self-promotion, which might explain his larger-than-life image.

His wine odyssey started in Wisconsin, of all places. He arrived there from Hungary and helped create what is now Sauk City, but the harsh Wisconsin winter quickly killed the vines he tried to cultivate. In 1849, like modern-day sunbirds, he headed west to the kinder climate of Southern California.

In San Diego, Haraszthy entered politics as a state legislator, and a combination of political and agricultural aspirations gradually drew him north. The 560-acre plot of land he bought in the Sonoma Valley in 1856 was quickly planted with many European grape varietals, and soon the Buena Vista Winery, with its hand-dug caves, boasted the largest vineyard in America and was producing award-winning wines.

He also reportedly helped plant vineyards for other Sonoma families that became (and still are) big names in the wine industry themselves, including Krug, Gundlach, and Bundschu.

By the 1860s, Haraszthy was combining his political and viticultural interests, promoting Californian wine across America and getting state funding to travel around Europe to study wine-making techniques.

He returned in 1862 with thousands of vine cuttings collected in almost every European country, from Spain to Turkey. Among them were believed to be the cabernet sauvignon, pinot noir, sauvignon blanc, riesling, and semillon varieties that have become mainstays of the California wine industry.

Exactly what he brought back is open to debate, however, since cataloguing and naming conventions in those days were unreliable. Some of those well-known grapes might also have stealthily arrived in California long before, and many others that he brought back never took hold.

Haraszthy's downfall was as sudden as his success. In 1863, facing financial problems, he sold his wine business to the Buena Vista Viticultural Society, a conglomerate in which he held almost half the shares and took a management position. But within three years he was accused of mismanagement and Enron-style fraud in an attempt to create the biggest winemaker in California, and in 1866 he quit.

What happened after this is still a bit of a mystery. Haraszthy left California in 1868 to run a sugar plantation in Nicaragua, but he disappeared in the jungle and is believed to have been killed by a crocodile.

It's hard not to raise a glass to an immigrant who, in the space of 25 years, had been the co-founder of a Wisconsin town, an entrepreneur, successful businessman, politician, and crocodile's meal. But as you raise that glass of mass-produced Sonoma Valley red wine, also consider that it might not taste quite the same (or be as cheap) if not for Agoston Haraszthy.

Southern Sonoma

pinot noir, zinfandel, and cabernet, together with a barbera that reflects Sebastiani's Italian heritage. The only white offered, in both vineyard-specific and Sonoma County styles, is chardonnay. Several wines are also available exclusively at the winery, including a Napa Valley cabernet, the Italian-style red blend Dolcino Rosso, and Eye of the Swan, a pinot noir-based wine with a pale pink color that reminded August Sebastiani (who was an avid amateur ornithologist) of the eyes of a black swan.

The cool, vaulted visitor center is chock-full of Italian-themed gifts, and three times a day there are tours ($5) of the cellars and historic stone buildings during which you can see some of the original wine-making equipment from the early 1900s. If you're what the winery calls a novice wine customer you can also make an appointment to take an instructive tasting seminar for $25 (389 4th St. E., Sonoma, 707/933-3230 or 800/888-5532, www.sebastiani.com, open 10 A.M.–5 P.M. daily, tasting $5).

Castle Vineyards

A newly opened tasting room just off the Sonoma Plaza is the public face for this local winery, which was established in 1994. Vic McWilliams, winemaker and founder, focuses on producing fruit-driven, mainly red wines from the 9 acres of vineyards owned by the winery in Sonoma and Carneros, together with another 30 acres it manages in the valley. Castle makes about 3,500 cases of wine each year, making it one of the smallest wineries in the valley with a public tasting room.

Highlight wines include several pinot noirs from the highly regarded Durell and Sangiacomo vineyards, merlot, and Rhône-style syrah and cinsault. The only white wine produced is late-harvest viognier, and none of the wines costs more than $35. Castle also has a guest cottage available to rent next to its winery about a mile away on Castle Street, which gave the winery its name but is not open to the public (tasting room at 122 W. Spain Street, Sonoma, 707/996-4188, www.castlevineyards.com, open 10 A.M.–5 P.M. daily, tasting $5).

Wineries by Appointment

Many of the wineries open to the public in the Sonoma Valley are those of big producers that can attract big crowds. For a more personal (and free) experience of some Valley wines, call ahead to visit an appointment-only winery.

Moon Mountain Vineyard (1700 Moon Mountain Dr., Sonoma, 707/996-5870) is high up in the Mayacamas Mountains on a site that has been planted with vineyards since the 1800s. The winery's current 74 acres of organic vineyards grow bordeaux varietals for its cabernet sauvignon, sauvignon blanc, and cabernet franc wines, as well as grapes for its dense, concentrated zinfandel. The parent company's Dynamite brand wines can also be tasted here.

Hanzell Vineyards (18596 Lomita Ave., Sonoma, 707/996-3860 or 800/393-4999), just north of Sonoma, was established in 1948 and is renowned for its luxury-priced but limited-production chardonnays and pinot noirs that regularly score over 90 points in reviews. A new winery facility was recently opened, and Hanzell will eventually double its existing production to 7,000 cases a year from its 42 acres of estate vineyards.

GLEN ELLEN WINERIES
Benziger Family Winery

With vines poking out from the hillside grass, free-range cockerels crowing, and its collection of ramshackle wooden buildings hidden among the trees, this mountainside winery seems like an old family farm rather than a commercial wine business, and in some ways it is. The Benziger family came from New York in the 1980s to this former hippy ranch and transformed it into the valley's only biodynamic winery while managing to keep three generations of Benziger happy on its 800 acres. Some 30 Benziger folk now call this land their home, many of them working in the winery.

Biodynamic farming principles go beyond plain organic, focusing as much on the positive forces of nature as on the elimination of chemicals. The overgrown look of the vineyards is deliberate (cover crops in biodynamic

Benziger Family Winery's Sonoma Mountain estate

terms), as are the 30 acres of woods and wetlands. The colorful Insectory is a garden in the middle of the vineyards planted with native flowers to attract dynamic, pest-fighting insects. The nonnative peacocks had to be fenced in, however, because they were playing havoc with the vines.

All this and more can be seen on an entertaining, 45-minute, tractor-drawn tram tour that winds through the vineyards giving information on vines, local nature, and biodynamic principles, before delivering you to the hillside storage cave. Tours are $10, which includes tasting, and leave four times a day from the parking lot. The tram isn't big, so when it gets crowded in the summer you should buy a same-day ticket as far in advance as possible.

Almost two-thirds of the 45 acres of vineyards is planted with cabernet sauvignon, taking advantage of the natural sun trap created by the surrounding hillsides. Other bordeaux varietals are also planted, plus some zinfandel and sauvignon blanc. The Sonoma Mountain estate wines are biodynamic and are priced from about $25 and up. The Family and Reserve ranges of wines, together with some more pricey vineyard designates, are made with grapes from vineyards all over Sonoma and Northern California, and most can be tried in the often-crowded tasting room. Benziger's Imagery brand of small-lot wines, with its unique label art, has its own home in the nearby Imagery Winery (1883 London Ranch Rd., Glen Ellen, 888/490-2739, www.benziger.com, open 10 A.M.–5 P.M. daily, tasting $5 or $10 for reserves.).

B. R. Cohn Winery

If you're a cabernet lover then you have something in common with founder and owner Bruce Cohn. He is so fond of cabernet that he has planted all 100 acres on a former dairy with cabernet sauvignon. His Olive Hill vineyard has its own microclimate warmed by an underground geothermal aquifer (the same one that feeds the valley's hot springs) and shielded from cool air by Sonoma Mountain.

Cohn used to sell his grapes to other wineries in the valley but started bottling under his own label after an Olive Hill vineyard wine produced by the Gundlach Bundschu Winery was chosen to accompany President Reagan on a trip to China in the 1980s. Cohn had help from famed winemaker Charlie Wagner at Napa's Caymus Winery, and the rest, as they say, is history.

The highly regarded Olive Hill wines are priced $40 and up. Cohn also buys chardonnay, zinfandel, and merlot grapes from elsewhere in Sonoma for some of his cheaper blends priced from $20.

The olive trees surrounding the buildings and lining the driveway not only give the vineyard its name but also some award-winning olive oil that is available in the tasting room. The French picholine olive trees are relatively young by olive standards—only 130 years old—and the eight acres around the winery form the largest picholine orchard in the valley. The estate oil is 100 percent picholine, and various blended oils are also available, together with some unusual vinegars, such as raspberry champagne vinegar and cabernet vinegar. Many can be tasted at the winery.

As you walk from the parking lot up to the tasting room you might also hear Doobie Brothers songs wafting over the patio, giving away Bruce Cohn's other profession as the manager of the Doobies since the early 1970s and some other bands in the 1980s, including Bruce Hornsby and Night Ranger. Also look out for Moose, a black Bulldog-Labrador cross, in the winery and on a label (15000 Sonoma Hwy., Glen Ellen, 800/330-4064, www.brcohn.com, open 10 A.M.–5 P.M. daily, tasting fee $5, tours by appointment).

Imagery Estate Winery

The world's largest collection of wine label art by some well-known contemporary artists (including Sol LeWitt and Terry Winters) is one reason to visit Imagery. Another is the wide variety of small-lot wines that are available only at the winery itself. Imagery was established as a boutique offshoot of the Benziger Family Winery in the 1980s when art labels were catching on and winemaker Joe Benziger met the art director at nearby Sonoma State University, Bob Nugent. That relationship helped spawn the Imagery brand and the unique labels.

Artists have free reign apart from two rules:

There can be no nudity on the label (for legal reasons), and every label has to include an image, however abstract or small, of the Greek Parthenon, a small replica of which stands on a hillside at parent winery Benziger and was evidently the site of some wild parties before the Benziger family bought the ranch. The Parthenon is also now the symbol for Imagery, and a Greek theme is seems to have been worked into almost every aspect of the winery.

Nugent, who has painted some of the labels himself, is now curator of the collection, charged with finding new up-and-coming artists. Benziger focuses on creating unusual wines from vineyards on the 20-acre estate and other vineyards throughout Sonoma, including Ash Creek, the highest vineyard in Sonoma County. Imagery produces fewer than 6,000 cases of wine a year. The Artist Series includes sangiovese, barbera, malbec, petite sirah, viognier, and a white burgundy, while the Vineyard Collection includes more traditional wines like cabernet sauvignon, merlot, and zinfandel. All are priced $20–40 (14335 Sonoma Hwy., Glen Ellen, 707/935-4515 or 877/550-4278, www.imagerywinery.com, open 10 A.M.–4:30 P.M. daily, Fri. and Sat. until 5:30 P.M. in summer, tasting fee $5).

Matanzas Creek Winery

It's worth the 10-minute drive up scenic Bennett Valley Road (off Warm Springs Road) from Glen Ellen to visit Matanzas Creek, especially in May and June when the lavender is in full bloom. The winery is in Sonoma's newest appellation, nestled at the foot of the hills surrounded by woods, flower-filled gardens, and the largest planting of lavender in California, which provides the raw material for the vast array of aromatic products on sale in the tasting room.

The former dairy became a winery in 1977, although the current barnlike building was built in 1985. Former owners Sandra and Bill MacIver led the drive to get the Bennett Valley classified as its own appellation, and in December 2003 it became the 13th AVA in Sonoma County, with Matanzas Creek one of only four wineries.

The winery's 216 acres of vineyards are planted with chardonnay, merlot, cabernet sauvignon, sauvignon blanc, and syrah, all benefiting from cooling influences of the ocean air that never makes it over the mountains into the Sonoma Valley. More grapes are now brought in from elsewhere in Sonoma and Mendocino Counties as the new owner, Kendall-Jackson, ramps up production to 60,000 cases a year. All the estate's grape varietals are represented in the wines, together with a sangiovese, and prices start at $20 for some of the whites and go up to $150 for the limited release Journey meritage, a blend of merlot and cabernet. Matanzas Creek is particularly well known for its chardonnays.

Tours are available by appointment twice a day, and printed guides to the surrounding flower and lavender gardens are available in the tasting room. The last Saturday in June is also the Lavender Harvest Party, with wine and barrel tastings, food, and a celebration of all things lavender. Tickets are $75 and can be booked in advance (6097 Bennett Valley Rd., Santa Rosa, 707/528-6464 or 800/590-6464, www.matanzascreek.com, open 10 A.M.–4:30 P.M. daily, tasting fee $5).

Navillus Birney Winery

This boutique winery is one of only four located in the Sonoma Mountain appellation and was established in 1998 by two former PR executives, Jonelle Birney and Rick Sullivan. Just over 2,000 cases of award-winning chardonnay and pinot noir are made each year with grapes from its 72 acres of vineyards in Sonoma Mountain, just up the hill from Glen Ellen, and also farther south in Carneros. In 2002 it also started making a small amount of syrah.

The small, dedicated tasting room opened next to the Garden Court Café in Glen Ellen in 2003 and offers complimentary tasting of the three chardonnays and two pinot noirs, together with plenty of information about the wines and local Glen Ellen history and gossip from the tasting room manager.

The wines, priced at around $30, have very distinct styles reflecting the stark differences between the warm and cool vineyards

they come from. The winery was originally called Sullivan Birney but changed its name to Navillus Birney (reversing the spelling of Sullivan) in 2004 to avoid confusion with Sullivan Vineyard in Napa. (tasting room at 13647 Arnold Dr., Glen Ellen, 707/933-8514, www.navillusbirney.com, open 10:30 A.M.–5 P.M. daily).

Wineries by Appointment

A visit to **Loxton Cellars** (11466 Dunbar Rd., Glen Ellen, 707/935-7221) usually includes a personal tour of the vineyards with Australian owner Chris Loxton, who used to be a winemaker at neighboring Wellington Vineyards. He focuses on syrah and zinfandel wines made from both Sonoma Valley and Russian River Valley grapes, including a shiraz from Australian vine clones, a syrah port, and a dry rosé wine. With just 1,500 cases made each year, the wines are some of the best values among appointment-only wineries.

KENWOOD AREA WINERIES
Kunde Estate Winery

The Kunde Estate sprawls across 2,000 acres of valley land, making it the largest family-owned winery in the west and providing enough space for a whopping 800 acres of estate vineyards where 20 varietals of grape are grown from the valley floor up to elevations of 1,000 feet on the terraced hillsides. In fact the winery has the vineyards and varied enough growing conditions to make only estate wines without the need for grapes from elsewhere in California. It even sells surplus grapes to neighboring wineries.

Grapes have been grown here by the Kunde family since 1904, when Louis Kunde acquired the historic Wildwood Vineyard, which was first planted in 1879 by some of the valley's wine pioneers. There is still a patch of zinfandel vines dating from 1882 happily growing here, grapes from which go into the limited production Shaw Vineyard zinfandel.

The current incarnation of the winery was built in the late 1980s to resemble a giant version of an old dairy barn that stood nearby and

Southern Sonoma

is run by the fourth wine-making generation of the family. Kunde makes fine examples of just about every wine that can be made from Sonoma Valley grapes, though is perhaps best known for its zinfandel, cabernet sauvignon, and vineyard-designate chardonnays. It also makes a few unusual wines among its bargain-priced Tasting Room series, available only at the winery, including a fruity gewürztraminer, a strawberry-laced grenache rosé (both perfect picnic wines), and an intriguing blend of cabernet and zinfandel called Bob's Red.

Tours of the aging caves stretching half a mile under the hillside behind the winery are offered on the hour Friday–Sunday. Groups of six or more can also go on one of many appointment-only tours to see parts of the huge estate. Contact the winery for more information (10155 Sonoma Hwy., Kenwood, 707/833-5501, www.kunde.com, open 10:30 A.M.–4:30 P.M. daily, tasting $5–10).

© PHILIP GOLDSMITH

Ledson Winery, known locally as "The Castle"

Chateau St. Jean

If you were to build your own personal chateau in the Sonoma Valley you couldn't pick a much better location than this. A long driveway through the vineyards leads up to the white, turreted mansion at the foot of the mountains. The walk from the parking lot to the tasting rooms leads through a manicured, formal garden, and on the other side of the reserve tasting room is a patio area and expanse of lawn overlooking the valley vineyards.

The winery itself was once a private residence surrounded by walnut groves, built as a palatial summer home by a family of Michigan mining barons in the 1920s. The only signs now of its Michigan roots are the two fishponds shaped like the Great Lakes Michigan and Huron.

The chateau was almost bought by Bruce Cohn, founder of B. R. Cohn Winery, in the 1970s but ended up being acquired by a group of investors and who opened it as a winery in 1975 with Richard Arrowood as the winemaker. He went on to establish his own Arrowood Vineyards & Winery just down the road, and St. Jean is now owned by the multinational Fosters Wine Estates.

The winery pioneered the production of vineyard-designate wines in Sonoma in the 1970s and now has four in its portfolio—two chardonnays, a pinot blanc, and a fumé blanc. Grapes for all the wines are sourced from vineyards all over Sonoma County, but 80 acres of estate vineyards around the chateau are planted principally with chardonnay.

Although St. Jean is best known for its white wines (which include multiple chardonnays, viognier, gewürztraminer, pinot blanc, riesling, and fumé blanc), it also has its share of big reds, including Cinq Cepages, a bordeaux-style red blend of five grapes that is always rated highly by critics. Other red wines are Sonoma County cabernet sauvignon, merlot, and pinot noir, as well as reserve versions priced up to $100. Tasting room staff love to boast that this is the only Californian winery that (as of 2005) that has had five wines in the *Wine Spectator* Top 100 in one year (which was 1996).

It's worth spending a little extra for a reserve

tasting ($10), especially in summer when the sun-drenched reserve tasting patio is open. For just $5 more than the reserve tasting you can also take a 45-minute tour of the winery and a short course on wine tasting at 11 A.M. and 3 P.M. It is one of several appointment-only educational courses and tours offered (8555 Sonoma Hwy., Kenwood, 707/833-4134, www.chateaustjean.com, open 10 A.M.–5 P.M. daily, tasting fee $5).

Kaz Vineyard & Winery

This is the one winery in the valley where it's guaranteed that the owner will be pouring the wine in the tasting room. Kaz (a.k.a. Richard Kasmier) is also as close as you'll get to a renegade winemaker, producing just 400 cases a year of bizarrely named wine blends and ports, some dominated by relatively rare grapes for California, such as the red alicante bouschet and lenoir, which is a varietal more commonly found in Texas or in tiny amounts in some Californian blends.

Kaz also grows syrah, cabernet franc, chardonnay, and dechaunac in his 2.5-acre organic vineyard (he once grew an unimaginable 15 varietals on 5 acres) and buys other grapes from neighboring wineries. A winery motto, "No harm in experimenting," ensures that many blends will change each year, though some are pretty much constant, including the ZAM (zinfandel, Alicante, Morvedre), Sangiofranc (sangiovese and cabernet franc), and Mainliner (100 percent lenoir). For added flair, all the wine labels are vintage photos hand-colored by Kaz's wife, Sandy.

The winery is open Friday–Monday only and is four driveways up the road from Landmark Vineyards on the left (drive slowly because it's easy to miss). The tiny tasting room doubles as a barrel storage area and can get very full, but Kaz keeps the crowd entertained and you'll quickly get to know everyone around you. The unmarked door at the back of the tasting room opens onto a small garden with just enough room for a private picnic (233 Adobe Canyon Rd., Kenwood, 707/833-2536, www.kazwinery.com, open 11 A.M.–5 P.M. Fri.–Mon., tasting fee $5).

Landmark Vineyards

Landmark was one of the first California wineries to make only chardonnay, though it has since expanded to pinot noir and most recently syrah, all made using grapes from the 11 acres of estate vineyards and others sourced from all over California.

Chardonnay still accounts for the majority of the 25,000 case production, and the wines range in price from the $15 Courtyard chardonnay up to the most expensive Lorenzo Reserve and Damaris Reserve, named after the winery's founder, Damaris Deere Ethridge, the great granddaughter of John Deere (inventor of the steel plow and the name now associated with tractors).

The Deere family heritage is also evident in the red wines, which include four pinot noirs ranging from the cheapest Courtyard up to the reserve Kastania and Grand Detour (named after John Deere's home town in Michigan), and the limited-production Steel Plough syrah.

A large mural behind the tasting bar livens up an otherwise drab room, but the best aspects of the Spanish-style building are outside. The large, shady courtyard outside the tasting room leads to a fountain and gardens with a view straight over the vineyards to Sugarloaf Mountain in the distance. A few picnic tables are available, as is a free bocce ball court to test how straight you can throw after a few glasses of wine (101 Adobe Canyon Rd., Kenwood, 707/833-1144, www.landmarkwine.com, open 10 A.M.–4:30 P.M. daily, tasting $5).

Ledson Winery & Vineyards

It's worth driving almost all the way to the top of the valley just to see the "Castle," as it's known. This is about as ostentatious as the Sonoma Valley gets, and it's still a far cry from Napa Valley's wine palaces.

Steve Ledson, who made his money in the contracting business, set about building this 16,000-square-foot Gothic dream home to get back to his childhood roots of farming and ranching in the Sonoma Valley (and it's literally a dream home—Ledson says its design came to him in dreams). By the time it was finished in 1999, he had decided that it was attracting a little too much attention for his family, so he turned it into a winery and hospitality property and remained instead near Sonoma where he has another vineyard.

When you enter through the grand front door, pass the sweeping staircase, polished oak, and marble fireplaces, you almost feel like you're walking onto the set of some Beverly Hills soap opera. The three tasting rooms and a small marketplace are stocked with the wines and a pungent selection of cheeses and other picnic supplies. You can picnic on the grounds, although there's limited space and you can only eat food bought at the winery itself.

The house is surrounded by 17 acres of merlot vineyards, but Ledson sources grapes from all over the Wine Country to make its white and red wines, which are available only from the winery and the exclusive Ledson Hotel on Sonoma Plaza. Almost every grape varietal is represented, including the estate merlot; cabernet sauvignon from Northern Sonoma; chardonnay, pinot grigio, and pinot noir from the Russian River Valley; and the unusual orange muscat from the Monterey area. Prices range from $16 for some of the whites up to $175 for the oldest estate merlot (7335 Sonoma Hwy., Kenwood, 707/537-3810, www.ledson.com, open 10 A.M.–5 P.M. daily, tasting $5).

St. Francis Winery & Vineyards

Named to honor the Franciscan monks who are widely credited with planting California's first wine grapes, St. Francis is a place for red wine lovers, and particularly merlot fans. Merlot grapes have been grown there since the winery was established in 1971, and St. Francis was one of the first California wineries to bottle merlot as a stand-alone wine rather than as part of a bordeaux-style blend.

The winery has expanded from the original, historic 100-acre Behler Ranch vineyard and now has more than 600 acres of vineyards in the Sonoma Valley and Russian River Valley that supply grapes for its

chardonnay, cabernet, merlot, zinfandel, and syrah wines. They include the Nun's Canyon vineyard high up in the Mayacamas Mountains, which produces some of St. Francis's best cabernets and merlots. All the reserve wines are from single vineyards, while the cheaper Sonoma County wines include grapes from multiple vineyards.

The spacious tasting room is one of the best-designed in the valley, not surprising considering the mission-style winery complex was opened in 2001, making it one of the newest in the valley. Windows running the length of the room look out onto the vineyards and mountains, and you can easily escape into the garden if it gets too crowded.

Tasting the reserve wines costs $10, though for $10 more the winery throws in some food at the appointment-only food and wine pairing session with appetizers from the winery's chef, Todd Muir (100 Pythian Rd., Santa Rosa, 800/543-7713, www.stfranciswine.com, open 10 A.M.–5 P.M. daily, tasting $5).

Family Wineries of Sonoma Valley

This small roadside cooperative tasting room in Kenwood is right on the Sonoma Highway and offers a chance to experience wines from some of the smaller wineries in the Sonoma Valley that are not open to the public. The emphasis is on red wines, and 5–7 wineries are usually represented, including **Noel Wine Cellars,** which produces 500 cases of wine a year; the **Nelson Estate,** which makes about 3,000 cases a year; and **Deerfield Ranch Winery,** which produces 10,000 cases a year and will have its own tasting room at a new winery opening just down the road.

The tasting counter is divided to give a sense of privacy, and owners or winemakers from the participating wineries are just as likely to be pouring the wine as other winery staff. It's also worth waiting until the end of the day to visit because this tasting room is open until 6 P.M., long after other wineries have shut their doors for the day (9200 Sonoma Hwy., Kenwood, 707/833-5504, www.familywineries.com, open 11 A.M.–6 P.M. daily).

SIGHTS

Sonoma is not the only Wine Country town with a rich history stretching back hundreds of years, but it holds the distinction of being ground zero both for the turbulent events that led to the creation of the state of California in the 1840s and for the beginnings of California's booming wine industry. Many of the most important buildings from that active period in the mid-1800s are still standing, making Sonoma one of the most historically alive Wine Country towns in Northern California.

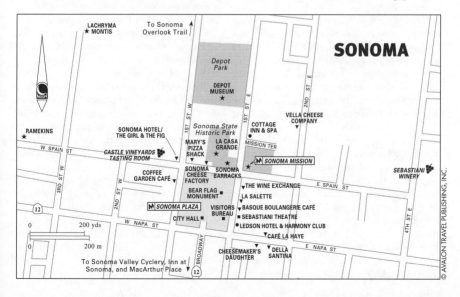 Sonoma Plaza

Sonoma Plaza, the eight-acre square that over the last 180 years has seen religion, uprisings, revolution, fires, and now large numbers of tourists, is at the center of the region's history and is the heart and soul of the valley. Fascinating shops and boutiques selling everything from designer clothes to African handicrafts fill the streets around the plaza, along with galleries and some of the valley's best restaurants, many of them in historic buildings that date from the 1800s.

Sonoma Plaza was created in 1835 by General Vallejo for troop maneuvers and for a long time was little more than a muddy patch of grazing land surrounded by a picket fence. It is now the largest town square in California and, despite being thoroughly gentrified and besieged by cars, still maintains a sense of grace that only somewhere with such a rich history can pull off.

An excellent self-guided walking tour of the plaza's many Victorian-era buildings is buried between the endless pages of advertisements in the free *Sonoma Valley Guide,* copies of which are usually in the **Sonoma Valley Visitors Bureau** on the plaza.

A few yards north of the visitors bureau is the **Bear Flag Monument,** a bronze statue that is roughly where the flag was raised by settlers in 1846 heralding the eventual creation of the State of California and demise of Mexican rule. Smack in the middle of the plaza is **Sonoma City Hall,** built from locally quarried stone with four identical sides—to give equal importance to traders on all four sides of the plaza, so the legend says. Like most civil construction projects today, the building project came in late and way over its budgeted cost of $15,000, delayed by stonemason strikes and the ballooning price of

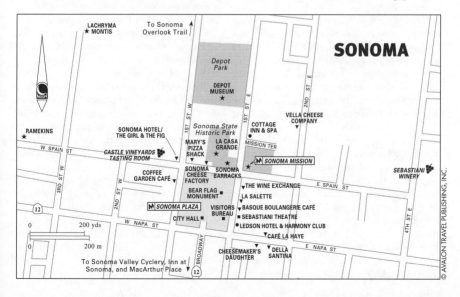

Southern Sonoma

materials following the 1906 San Francisco earthquake. It took five years to build and was finally completed in 1909.

Almost opposite the mission entrance on Spain Street, the wobbly-looking adobe building with a long first-floor veranda is the **Blue Wing Inn,** a gold-rush era saloon and stagecoach stop that is thought to be one of the oldest unaltered buildings in the city. It is currently being renovated.

Sonoma Mission

The north side of the plaza was the first to be developed in the early days of Sonoma and is where the oldest buildings can be found, many now part of the Sonoma State Historic Park. The **Mission San Francisco Solano de Sonoma** (corner of 1st St. and E. Spain St., 707/938-9560, open 10 A.M.–5 P.M., $2), established in 1823, was the last of California's 21 missions but had a short religious life. Its land and buildings were seized by the Mexican government in 1834, along with all the other missions on the West Coast. By the end of the 1800s, Sonoma's once-proud mission had suffered the ignominy of being used as hay barn and a winery, and of having a saloon built right in front of it.

Enter the unlikely figure of newspaper magnate William Randolph Hearst, who helped provide funding that enabled a preservation society to buy the mission in 1903 for $5,000. Restoration didn't start until 1911, however, by which time various collapses had left the building in ruins. The reconstructed building open to the public today has a large cross on the roof where an old bell tower used to be but is otherwise largely the same as the original. The $2 entrance fee buys access to a small museum and the large, dusty courtyard full of giant cacti said to be as old as the mission itself. Just don't touch the cacti or you'll be pulling tiny, hairlike spikes out of your hands for the rest of the day.

The Vallejo Connections

Many of the historic sights in Sonoma that date from the turbulent mid-1800s were built for or

by General Mariano Vallejo, the Mexican army commander who later became an important state politician.

Across 1st Street from the mission is the two-story adobe **Sonoma Barracks** building, which was constructed in stages between 1834 and 1841 by Native American slaves captured by the same Mexican army it eventually housed. In 1860 it was converted to a winery by General Vallejo (many plaza buildings saw service as wine cellars or wineries over the years) and in the late 1800s became a store with an ornate Victorian facade tacked on the front. It was partly restored in the 1930s and was used for private residences and offices until being bought by the state in 1958 and fully restored. The small museum housed there today (open 10 A.M.–5 P.M., $2) contains artifacts from its military history. The courtyard was once the scene of grisly staged animal fights.

Next to the barracks is the old **Toscano Hotel,** which was built in the 1850s. Just across the small square behind the 1940s building that contains the Sonoma Cheese Factory is the site of Vallejo's first home, **La Casa Grande,** built in 1840 and where Vallejo was arrested by the Bear Flag party in 1846. The house itself burned down long ago, and just the two-story, adobe-brick servants' quarters remain.

Vallejo's next home, built in 1850, reflected his new status as a state senator and is on 20 acres of parkland about a 10-minute walk west of the plaza on Spain Street at 3rd Street West. Vallejo called this new home **Lachryma Montis,** Latin for "tear of the mountain," the name given by Native Americans to a nearby spring that once supplied much of the town's water. The Mission, Barracks, and Lachryma Montis are all part of the Sonoma State Historic Park (707/938-9560).

In a display of excess that would put many of today's movie stars to shame, Vallejo spent $150,000 (in 1850 dollars) to build and decorate the ornate, Gothic-style Victorian house, construct numerous summer houses, and plant the huge, 250-acre estate where he lived until his death in 1890. Even the wood-framed **Swiss Chalet** next to the house, originally used to store the estate's fruit (and, of course, used as a winery), was built from materials imported from Europe. Today it is a visitor center and museum (open 10 A.M.–5 P.M., $3). The house itself is open the same times and is still full of Vallejo's decadent marble fireplaces, rosewood furniture, chandeliers, and frilly lace.

The Sebastiani Theatre

Not only was California born in Sonoma, but so was California theater. What was believed to be California's first theatrical presentation, Benjamin Webster's *The Golden Farmer,* was put on by American soldiers in an old adobe storehouse converted to a theater in 1849.

Today, a theater of the silver screen era is one of the most prominent buildings on the plaza. The **Sebastiani Theatre,** built to replace the burned-down Don Theatre, was funded by Samuele Sebastiani, city benefactor and founder of the eponymous winery. It opened its doors

The Sebastiani Theatre dominates Sonoma's plaza just like the Sebastiani family dominated the town's wine-making history.

in April 1934 with the film *Fugitive Lovers* and today has performances of film and live entertainment almost every night. Call 707/996-2020 or visit www.sebastianitheatre.com for current event listings.

Although the most striking, the theater was only one of many buildings Sam Sebastiani built for the city. Others included an apartment building still standing at 28–34 Spain Street, a bus station next door, and a combined bowling alley and skating rink not far away that was originally called the Sebastiani Rollatorium in the 1940s but has long since fallen victim to a strip mall.

Train Town

The scale model trains that haul passengers around a 1.25-mile track at the Train Town amusement park in Sonoma represent all that is left of the once-thriving railroad that brought visitors to Sonoma Valley.

The first stretch of the original Sonoma Valley Railroad opened in 1879 and ran from Vineburg just south of Sonoma to Wingo, three miles south of present-day Schellville, where it connected with boats to San Francisco. It was soon extended down to San Pablo Bay and north to Sonoma Plaza. From the plaza it followed Spain Street and turned right on present-day U.S. 12, running all the way up the valley to Glen Ellen.

Back in 1890, taking the ferry and train from San Francisco's Ferry Building to Sonoma took about two hours, not much longer than it takes by car now. But the rising popularity of cars in the early 1900s and the opening of the Golden Gate Bridge in 1937 eventually led to the demise of the region's railroads.

More about the history of the Sonoma railroads can be found at the small **Depot Museum,** a block north of the plaza (270 1st St. W., 1–4:30 P.M. Wed.–Sun., 707/938-1762). The museum is an exact replica of the original railroad depot, which burned down in 1976, and is surrounded by Depot Park, popular with the city's drunks except on Friday when the farmers market takes over.

Riding the only trains left in town requires a

© PHILIP GOLDSMITH

Southern Sonoma

visit to **Train Town** (20264 Broadway, Sonoma, 707/938-3912). The strange and often crowded combination of amusement park, model railway, and petting zoo is open 10 A.M.–5 P.M. daily June–Labor Day, and on Friday, Saturday, and Sunday the rest of the year. The fare is $3.75 for all ages.

ENTERTAINMENT AND EVENTS

The Sonoma Valley is as much about olives as wine during the winter when the annual **Sonoma Valley Olive Festival** is in full swing (www.olivefestival.com). The festival kicks off with the Blessing of the Olives at Sonoma's mission and the Olive Harvest Tasting in early December, then runs through February. Check the website for a full list of the 30 or more events, including plenty of fun cooking demonstrations, organized at wineries, restaurants, and outdoors to celebrate the oily fruit. Many are free but the biggest events usually require tickets, available at the Sonoma Valley Visitors Bureau on Sonoma plaza.

Late May through June is lavender season in the Sonoma Valley, and the aromatic purple flower is celebrated with the annual **Lavender Festival** next to the Chateau St. Jean winery in Kenwood (usually the third weekend in June, 707/523-4411, www.sonomalavender.com/festival, $5 per car). Learn about growing countless varieties of lavender, how to use the oil, and even how to cook with lavender. There's also a lavender festival held in early June at the Matanzas Creek Winery near Glen Ellen.

Shakespeare in Sonoma celebrates the town's theatrical heritage and its great summer weather from July to September with Sunday evening performances of Shakespeare plays put on by the local Avalon Players group in the outdoor amphitheater at the Gundlach Bundschu Winery. Tickets cost $15–20. For more information contact the Avalon Players (707/996-3264, www.sonomashakespeare.com).

If the silver screen is more your thing, August brings the annual **Wine Country Film Festival** to the historic Sebastiani Theatre

on Sonoma Plaza and several valley wineries. Film screenings are usually accompanied by a range of other Wine Country events during the month, all involving plenty of food and wine. For a schedule of events and ticket prices, visit www.winecountryfilmfest.com.

Among the big wine events in the valley during the year is the annual **Heart of the Valley Barrel Tasting,** usually the third weekend in March at wineries around Glen Ellen and Kenwood (707/939-0708, www.heartofthevalley.com).

Ramekins Sonoma Valley Culinary School

The Napa Valley has the famous Culinary Institute of America, but the Sonoma Valley, not to be outdone, has its own renowned culinary school in **Ramekins** (450 W. Spain St., Sonoma, 707/933-0450, www.ramekins.com), just four blocks from the plaza and voted 2005 Cooking School of the Year by the International Association of Culinary Professionals.

Ramekins has far more in the way of a hands-on cooking experience for casual visitors than the Culinary Institute over in St. Helena. Three-hour classes or demonstrations by sometimes well-known chefs are offered every day over the weekend and on several days during the week, usually in the late morning or evening, and cover almost every style of food imaginable. They don't cost much more than a meal at many local restaurants (generally $50–100), making the evening classes a fun alternative to eating a meal that someone else prepared. Check the website for a constantly updated schedule.

RECREATION

Outside the town of Sonoma and its environs there is little in the way of development—the two other major valley towns of Kenwood and Glen Ellen are compact, to say the least. Vineyards are counted as important residents in this part of the world, and large swaths of the mountains are protected parkland, creating a giant playground for the valley's residents and visitors to bike, hike, and trot to their heart's content in (and also creating a planning nightmare for would-be developers and wineries wanting to expand their vineyards). Even the town of Sonoma has its own little hiking paradise within walking distance from the plaza.

The three largest year-round park areas are the 5,000-acre Annadel State Park (6201 Channel Dr., Santa Rosa), with almost 40 miles of trails; the 2,700-acre Sugarloaf Ridge State Park, with 25 miles of trails; and the neighboring 1,400-acre Hood Mountain Regional Park. All three are just minutes from the wineries at the north end of the Sonoma Valley, though be warned that they all get hot in the summer; come prepared to battle dehydration.

Also worth noting is that dogs are not allowed on any major trails in any of the state parks but are allowed on short leashes in Sugarloaf's neighbor, Hood Mountain Regional Park (although this park is closed during the fire season June–October, so you'll have to walk Fido here in the rainy season).

Annadel State Park

Redwoods, oaks, meadows, and a large, well-stocked lake make this one the most diverse of Sonoma Valley's parks, and it's easily accessible from both Santa Rosa and Kenwood. Most trails start from Channel Drive, which is reached by driving north from Kenwood on U.S. 12; just before the road becomes four lanes turn left on Melita Road then left on Montgomery Drive and left on Channel Drive. The entry fee is $2 per car, and the park is open from sunrise to sunset. For information, call 707/539-3911.

The rocky trails that make Annadel a bone-jarring ride for mountain bikers today also give away its previous life as an important source of obsidian for Native American tools and rock for cobblestones for cities up and down the West Coast in the early 1900s. There's still some evidence of quarrying on many of the trails, including the aptly named Cobblestone Trail, which used to be the route of a tramway carrying rock down the hill to the railroad.

Mountain bikers love the fact that most of the trails are either singletrack or doubletrack and strewn with rocks for a bit of added fear. This is probably not the best place for novice bikers to find their wheels, but it offers some of the best midlevel mountain biking in the Bay Area, with plenty of technical trails and an elevation gain/drop of about 1,000 feet for most loops.

Popular downhills include the Lawndale Trail from Ledson Marsh, a smooth, fast single-track through the forest; the Upper Steve's Trail and Marsh Trail loop; and the rockier Orchard and Cobblestone Trails (including the Orchard Loop). Lake Illsanjo is the pretty much the center of the park and a good start and end point for many biking loops, although it can also be relatively crowded on summer weekends. The best way to reach it from the main parking lot is to ride up the Warren Richardson fire road, saving the single-track for going downhill.

An alternative entrance that avoids the fee and is popular with mountain bikers is on Lawndale Road. From U.S. 12, take a left just north of the Landmark winery, and the unmarked, dirt parking lot is on the right about a mile down the road. Farther up Lawndale Road, forking off to the right, is Schultz Road leading to the Schultz Trailhead. It's better to bike up the Schultz Trail and come down Lawndale.

The best time to go **hiking** in Annadel is spring or early summer when the wildflowers are in full bloom in the meadows around Lake Ilsanjo, named after two former landowners, Ilsa and Joe Coney. The two-mile trek from the parking lot up the Warren Richardson Trail to the lake gives a good cross section of the park's flora, starting in a forest of redwoods and Douglas fir and climbing up through oaks to the relatively flat area around the lake where miles of other trails converge.

Lower Steve's Trail, which branches off and then rejoins the Richardson trail, is one of the few trails off-limits to bikes and therefore worth taking if you've been harassed by speeding bikers. Allow about four hours to make the round-trip and explore the lake area.

The Cobblestone Trail to Rough Go Trail is an alternative but rockier and longer ascent to the lake, and one on which you're more likely to meet bikers hurtling down the hill or some of the park's wild turkeys ambling across your path. At the lake there are picnic areas and restrooms, plus access to the rest of the trail network.

Fishing at the lake is also popular, with black bass and bluegill the most common catch. The Park Service suggests the purple plastic worm as the best bait for bass, and garden worms or grubs are favored by bluegills. Anyone over 16 must have a California fishing license.

Sugarloaf Ridge State Park

Sugarloaf Ridge State Park (2605 Adobe Canyon Rd., Kenwood, 707/833-5712) is perfect for either a quick fix of shady redwood forests or for hikes to some of the best views, both terrestrial and extraterrestrial, in the valley. It's about a 10-minute drive up Adobe Canyon Road from Landmark Vineyards (it's not called Landmark for nothing). The park is open from sunrise until about two hours after sunset, but hours change depending on the time of year. Call to check times. It also has the only campground in the valley.

The somewhat barren hillside near the entrance is deceiving. From winter to early summer, a 25-foot waterfall tumbles just a few hundred yards from the parking lot along the Canyon Trail, and the three-quarter-mile long, shady Creekside Nature Trail runs from the picnic area.

The big **hiking** draw is the seven-mile roundtrip slog up to the summit of 2,729-foot Bald Mountain, rewarded by spectacular 360-degree views of the North Bay. It starts off on paved fire roads, but the paving soon ends as the trail climbs 1,500 feet in about three miles with no shade at all, so take a hat and plenty of water in the summer. From the summit, the Grey Pine Trail offers an alternative route downhill, and on the way up there's a short detour to the peak of neighboring Red Mountain.

To get 12 inches closer to the sun there's an equally long and hot hike from the parking lot to the 2,730-foot summit of **Hood Mountain,** which actually lies in neighboring Hood Mountain Regional Park. The dirt parking lot for the Goodspeed Trailhead is on the left of Adobe Canyon Road next to a stand of redwood trees just before the road starts climbing steeply.

From the lot, the trail crosses and follows Bear Creek through the forest, eventually crossing the creek again and steepening for the next three miles into exposed grass and scrubland. Eventually it reaches a ridge where you can bear left for the sweeping views west from the Gunsight Rock Overlook or turn right and trek the remaining half mile up to the Hood Mountain summit. Allow at least five hours roundtrip. During fire season (June–Oct.) the trail is closed about halfway up but is still a good place to go for a picnic.

Sugarloaf is also home to the **Robert Ferguson Observatory** ($2 for night viewing, under 18 free, daytime solar viewing free, 707/833-6979, www.rfo.org), the largest observatory open to the general public on the West Coast. It's just a short walk from the main parking lot. Check the website or call for a schedule of daytime solar viewing and regular stargazing through 8-, 14-, and 24-inch telescopes. There are usually at least two public day- and night-viewing sessions a month, plus regular astronomy classes throughout the year. A huge, 40-inch refractor telescope is scheduled to open sometime in 2005.

Jack London State Historic Park

The 800-acre Jack London State Historic Park (2400 London Ranch Rd., Glen Ellen, 707/938-5216, open 9:30 A.M.–5:30 P.M. daily, $6 entrance fee per car), past the Benziger Family Winery, offers a unique combination of scenic hiking and self-guided history tours around the buildings that once belonged to one of the valley's best-known authors, Jack London.

From the entrance kiosk, turn left to visit the **House of Happy Walls** (open 10 A.M.–5 P.M. daily, admission free), the former residence of Jack London's widow, Charmian, and now a

© PHILIP GOLDSMITH

the ruins of Jack London's imposing Wolf House, which mysteriously burned down in 1913 just days before being completed

Many of the other buildings once belonged to the 19th-century Kohler and Frohling winery, including a barn, an old distillery building, and the ruins of the winery itself. Others, like the piggery known as the Pig Palace, were built by London himself.

From the Beauty Ranch Trail, the Lake Trail goes uphill past the vineyards and through the redwoods for about half a mile to the forest-fringed lake created by London, where there are picnic spots and restrooms.

From there, explore the oak woods and meadows on a series of looping trails, or take the long Mountain Trail to the park summit next to Sonoma Mountain. That hike is about seven miles round-trip but can be lengthened by taking loops off the main trail. Another long hike is the Ridge Trail, which leaves the Mountain Trail and twists through forests and clearings with sweeping views before reaching the connecting Vineyard Trail leading back to the lake.

Mountain biking is allowed on all the trails in the park except the Cowan Meadow, Fallen Bridge, and Quarry Trails, plus a few around the lake. You might see a member of the Benziger family from the winery down the road hurtling by, but be aware that all trails are shared with hikers and some with horses. The Ridge Trail loop is recommended over the Mountain Trail to the summit, which is a steep uphill and perilously rocky downhill.

museum about the author's life. From there it's only a half-mile walk on a paved trail to London's grave and the ruins of the spectacular **Wolf House,** his 17,000-square-foot dream home that burned down accidentally just before it was completed in 1913. There was speculation that it was arson, though modern-day investigators conducted a forensic arson investigation in 1995 and concluded the fire was probably caused by spontaneous combustion of rags soaked in highly flammable turpentine and linseed oil used during construction. Today, only the monumentally thick stone walls remain in the dappled shade of the surrounding redwoods, but there's a model in the House of Happy Walls of just how impressive the house would have looked had it not met such a fiery fate.

The parking lot for the miles of **hiking** trails is to the right after the entrance. From there, the Beauty Ranch Trail winds around the buildings on London's former ranch, including the cottage where he wrote many of his later books and died at a youthful 40 years old.

Sonoma Overlook Trail

Nowhere is the spirit of Slow-noma better represented than in this three-mile trail just north of Sonoma Plaza that winds through woods and meadows to the top of Schocken Hill, with fine views over the town below. The site almost became home to another Wine Country resort in 1999, but residents banded together to ensure it instead became a city-owned open space.

Grab picnic supplies and head for the trailhead near the entrance to the Mountain Cemetery on West 1st Street about a half mile north of the plaza beyond Depot Park.

Within an hour you'll feel like you're in the middle of nowhere. Dogs, bikes, and smoking are not allowed on the trail.

In spring, the **Sonoma Ecology Center** (707/996-0712, www.sonomaecologycenter.org) offers docent-led weekend hikes along the trail to identify the abundant spring wildflowers and other natural highlights. Contact the center for more information.

Golf

An alternative to hiking miles up a hot, dusty trail is to meander around a lush golf course never far from a glass of crisp chardonnay.

The grande dame of the valley golf scene is the **Fairmont Sonoma Mission Inn Golf Club** (17700 Arnold Dr., Sonoma, 707/996-0300 or 800/956-4653), opened in 1928 and planned by the original investors to rival the famous Del Monte course in Monterey. The 18-hole, par-72 course is on 170 acres bordered by the Sonoma Mountains and vineyards. Only club members and guests at the neighboring Fairmont Sonoma Mission Inn can play here, however.

The closest public course is in Petaluma, a 15-minute drive from Sonoma, at the **Adobe Creek Golf Club** (1901 Frates Rd. Petaluma, 707/765-3000, www.adobecreek.com). The 18-hole, par-72 links course has tee rates from $25 midweek up to $62 on the weekends, and rents clubs and carts. Be sure to check the website for last-minute, discounted greens fees.

Horseback Riding

Rides of 1–3 hours, together with more expensive private rides, are available in Sugarloaf Ridge and Jack London State Parks through the **Triple Creek Horse Outfit** (707/933-1600, www.triplecreekhorseoutfit.com). Rates range from $40 for one hour up to $70 for three hours, and groups don't usually exceed six riders. Reservations must be in advance, and rides are limited to those over eight years old and weighing less than 240 pounds. Wear appropriate footwear, and arrive at the stable (located at the end of the main parking lots in both parks) about a half hour before your date with the horse.

Sonoma Valley Spas

Aware that local Native American tribes had long talked about the healing properties of Sonoma Valley's numerous hot and springs, Captain Henry Boyes spent two years drilling all over his property in search of them. In 1895 he hit what would turn out to be liquid gold—water at 112°F that gushed from the well and ushered in decades of prosperity for the valley's hotel owners.

Within a few months, another source of the hot water had been tapped by the owner of the neighboring Agua Caliente Springs Hotel. By 1900 thousands of visitors were bathing in the new hot mineral baths every year, and developers saw the potential for mass tourism, especially with the increasing popularity of the new railroad that ran from San Pablo Bay to Sonoma and up to Glen Ellen.

Soon the Boyes Springs mineral baths and the Agua Caliente Springs Hotel were transformed into first-class resorts. By 1910 many other hotels and resorts had opened, including Fetters Hot Springs and Verano Springs, complete with vaudeville shows, dances, and concerts. The *Sonoma Index-Tribune* newspaper reported that 23,000 people came in on the railroads for the Fourth of July weekend in 1916, close to the peak of the resort boom. Just seven years earlier there had been no one to witness the annual Fourth of July parade except local residents.

Boyes Hot Springs Hotel (along with several other resorts) burned down in a huge valley fire in September 1923, and an exclusive new resort, the **Sonoma Mission Inn** (100 Boyes Blvd., Sonoma, 707/938-9000, www.fairmont.com/sonoma), with its mission-style architectural touches, opened on the site in 1927.

Today, the inn is the only spa hotel in the valley with its own natural source of hot mineral water. Even if you're not a guest at the Fairmont-owned hotel, basic spa packages are available for $45–85, depending on how many extra salon pamperings are added on. The basic spa includes an exfoliating shower, warm and hot mineral baths, herbal steam room and sauna, interspersed with various cold showers and baths. Various add-on massages, stone treatments, and mud baths are also available to purify and relax you (until you see the bill).

The Kenwood Inn & Spa (10400 Sonoma Hwy., Kenwood, 707/833-1293 or 800/353-6966, www.kenwoodinn.com) might not have its own source of mineral water, but its Caudalie Vinotherapie Spa makes full use of the surrounding vineyards. The wraps, baths, and other treatments use vine and grape seed extracts to purify body and mind. Some might make you feel like a grape yourself, such as the wine barrel bath that exfoliates using bubbling water enriched with crushed grape seeds, skin, stalks, and pulp. For prices and availability for non-hotel guests, contact the hotel.

Though not as grandiose as those at the resort hotels, more reasonably priced spa services are available at Sonoma's **Spa on the Plaza** (457 1st St. W., 707/939-8770). Many of the facials, wraps, and massages are under $50, and packages are available for as little as $70.

ACCOMMODATIONS

Anyone who comes to the heart of Wine Country expecting cheap and cheerful accommodation will be sadly disappointed. The cheapest place to sleep in the valley is with Mother Nature in a campground. Second cheapest is almost $100 a night.

Like the wine made here, the Sonoma Valley is marketed as a luxury destination with luxury bells and whistles and therefore commands premium prices. The pressure to keep the small-town feel of Sonoma doesn't help either, ensuring that most hotels and inns stay small and planning hurdles remain high, thus limiting the number of rooms available.

Many places are selling a Wine Country lifestyle (does anyone actually live a Wine Country lifestyle?), not least the newly opened Ledson Hotel on the plaza, with its package of exclusivity, fine wine and food, and attempt to lead visitors back to the area's romantic Victorian heyday. Granted, things have not quite got to the Napa Valley extremes of wine lifestyle, but then

again the Sonoma Valley doesn't have nearly as many rooms as Napa to keep a balance.

Several sizable new hotels are planned in the valley that might tip the balance in favor of visitors (if their developers can ever jump the numerous planning hurdles and actually get them built). Or they might simply soak up the increase in visitors that's expected after the relative slump in travel from 2001 to 2003.

Apart from a few big hotels, the accommodation scene in Sonoma Valley is one of small, usually independent establishments with a handful of rooms. The smaller the hotel or inn, the more likely there is to be a two-night minimum over weekends, especially during the busiest summer and early fall months. Cancellation policies might also be less than flexible. The peak hotel season is generally from the end of May through October, roughly corresponding to the best weather in the region.

The closest place for true bargain-priced accommodations is along the U.S. 101 freeway corridor across the Sonoma Mountains, where most of the chain motels can be found. Stay around Petaluma or in the Rohnert Park and Santa Rosa areas and it's only a 10–15 minute drive into the valley.

Under $150

The **Sonoma Hotel** (110 W. Spain St., Sonoma, 707/996-2996 or 800/468-6016) is one of the rare bargains in the valley, with some of the cheapest rooms and a superb location in a historic building right on Sonoma Plaza next to the highly rated Girl & the Fig restaurant. Even the four cheapest rooms (from $95 low season, $110 high season) have views of something worthwhile, though don't expect luxury. The rooms are small, dark, and sparsely (though tastefully) furnished, but for this price in this location there's really nothing to complain about. More expensive rooms and junior suites get more light and floor space, plus some additional French country-style furniture, and cost from $160 to $220 a night during the summer. In keeping with the price and the hotel's heritage (the building dates from 1880), there are few amenities and you're likely to hear your neighbor's nighttime antics.

Also be warned that the bathroom for one of the cheapest rooms (room 34), although private, is out in the hallway past the friendly ghost.

El Pueblo Inn (896 W. Napa St., 707/996-3651 or 800/900-8844, www.elpuebloinn.com) is actually more of an upscale motel but offers a lot of rooms for a modest price and is just a 10-minute walk from the plaza. It's also one of the few places with no weekend minimum stay requirements. The cheaper Adobe rooms all have air-conditioning and start at $120 during the summer with two-room suites available for as little as $150. Although they still hint at the 1950s motel rooms they once were, they now open onto a courtyard rather than a parking lot. The larger, more luxurious Sonoma rooms, added during a 2001 reconstruction, feel more hotel-like with DVD players and high ceilings but are generally over $160 a night in the summer. All rooms have access to the small outdoor pool and landscaped gardens.

Most B&Bs in this area tend toward plenty of Victorian frills. Not so the quirky **Sonoma Chalet** (18935 5th St. W., Sonoma, 707/938-3129 or 800/938-3129, www.sonomachalet.com), which is more like Swiss Family Robinson meets the Wild West with its alpine murals, dark wood, and colorful fabrics. There are four individually decorated rooms in the main Swiss-style farmhouse: the two cheapest ($110) share a bathroom, while the larger of other two ($125–170 midweek) has a fireplace and balcony. For more privacy several small cottages in the three acres of wooded grounds have claw-foot tubs and wood-burning stoves and cost from $185 a night. The leafy location on the edge of Sonoma is peaceful but not within easy walking distance of Sonoma's shops and restaurants.

Although located in the relative no-man's land of Boyes Hot Springs just north of Sonoma, the **Sonoma Creek Inn** (239 Boyes Blvd., 888/712-1289 or 707/939-9463, www.sonomacreekinn.com) is one of the cheapest non-chain hotels in the valley, with rooms starting at $89 in the summer and as low as $69 during the winter. In this price range it's more common to see IKEA furniture, but the furnishings here are delightfully quirky, and some look like spoils from local antique stores. The 15 rooms are small and laid out in motel style; all are clean and have air-conditioning, and some have tiny, private patios.

$150–250

The Chapel Suite with its vaulted ceilings and skylight above the bed is one of the more unusual rooms at the **Cottage Inn & Spa** and the neighboring **Mission B&B,** just a block north of Sonoma Plaza (302 1st St. E., 707/996-0719 or 800/944-1490, www.cottageinnandspa.com). This self-styled "micro resort" with its mission-style architectural flourishes is an oasis of calm and style, with a wide range of rooms for all tastes and wallets. The cheapest are the rather plain Courtyard rooms ($140 a night midweek during the summer), but for under $250 some of the quirky suites are available (including the Chapel Suite), many with private patios and fireplaces.

A teddy bear slumbering on the bed greets everyone staying at the **Inn at Sonoma** (630 Broadway, Sonoma, 888/568-9818 or 707/939-1340, www.innatsonoma.com). It is one of Sonoma's newest hotels, opened in 2002, and what it lacks in historic charm it makes up for in functionality, price, and convenience, being only a few blocks from the plaza. The 19 rooms are furnished in slightly pastiche Wine Country style but have all amenities, including fireplaces, DVD players, and luxury bathrooms. The smallest Quaint Queen rooms are $145–200 a night during the summer. The larger queen and king rooms that cost $155–240 a night also have small patios.

The two dachshunds and Nutmeg, the cat, help provide the welcome at the **M Glenelly Inn** (5131 Warm Springs Rd., Glen Ellen, 707/996-6720, www.glenelly.com), a B&B tucked away behind Glen Ellen in a former railroad inn. The six rooms with private bathrooms are relative bargains for such a historic B&B, costing $150–175 a night. All are decorated in cottage style with plenty of floral prints and are relatively small except for the Valley of the Moon room, which has a wood-burning stove. There are also two suites for $185 a night with private decks. As with most well-priced, historic B&Bs the soundproofing is minimal, none of the rooms has a television, and most have no air conditioning. Breakfast is served outside in the pretty gardens during the summer, and there's an outdoor hot tub.

Also near Glen Ellen, the **Beltane Ranch B&B** (11775 Sonoma Hwy., Glen Ellen, 707/996-6501, www.beltaneranch.com) looks like a little piece of the Deep South landed in the vineyards. The Victorian-era house with its New Orleans-style wraparound veranda and lush gardens sits in the middle of the valley at the end of a long driveway, far from the madding crowds of U.S. 12. The five tastefully furnished, white-paneled rooms ($130–200 a night) evoke a bygone era without going over the top, and all open onto the veranda. The ranch is actually 1,600 acres of vineyards, pasture, and woods at the bottom of the Mayacamas Mountains, with miles of hiking trails and a tennis court for guests.

$250–350

MacArthur Place (29 E. MacArthur St., Sonoma, 707/938-2929 or 800/722-1866, www.macarthurplace.com) touts itself as a historic Victorian inn. What it doesn't tell you is that by expanding and transforming itself into an exclusive seven-acre spa resort in 1997 it came to resemble an executive housing development. Nevertheless, the cookie-cutter, faux Victorian cottages and landscaped gardens that now fan out from the original 1850s building provide 64 luxurious rooms, making it one of the larger hotels in Sonoma. Some occasional good deals can push the price for a standard room a touch under $250. All rooms are sumptuously furnished in a cottage style that makes it seem more like a luxurious B&B, and all have the usual mod-cons for this price range. Other amenities include an outdoor pool, free DVD library, complimentary breakfast, and some free evening cheese and wine. Suites and cottages also come with a fireplace and hydrotherapy tub. Try to avoid the rooms that overlook the neighboring high school or noisy Broadway.

An alternative to the big-name spa resorts in the area is the luxuriously appointed

Gaige House Inn (13540 Arnold Dr., Glen Ellen, 707/935-0237 or 800/935-0237, www.gaige.com), where serenity, contemporary Asian-inspired furnishings, gourmet breakfasts, and a big outdoor pool help soften the financial blow. Eight of the rooms cost $275 for a midweek summer night, from the airy Gaige rooms in the main Victorian house to the smaller Garden rooms, some with fireplaces and their own little Japanese gardens. The more expensive suites include fireplaces and truly indulgent bathrooms, while the Creekside rooms add a private patio overlooking the Calabazas Creek to the package. Also vaulting into the next price category are the stunning, Asian-minimalist spa suites added in late 2004, each with its own granite soaking tub, sliding glass walls, and contemporary furnishings. The inn also manages four luxury rental cottages in the area.

Over $350

The **Ledson Hotel** (480 First St.E. on Sonoma Plaza, Sonoma, 707/996-9779, www.ledsonhotel.com), a sibling to the Ledson Winery up the valley, made the Hot List of *Condé Nast Traveler* magazine in its first full year of operation, 2004. The ornate, Victorian-style brick building looks as old as the plaza itself despite the fact it was built this century. The six rooms ($350–375) are all the first floor, three of them with balconies looking onto the plaza, and all include just about every luxury feature possible, from state-of-the-art entertainment systems and high-speed Internet access to marble bathrooms with whirlpool tubs. Unusually for a hotel in this category, there is no dedicated reception area; guests either check in while sipping wine at the bar downstairs in the Harmony Club restaurant or slip in through a side door.

At the other end of the scale to the intimate Ledson Hotel is the 228-room **Sonoma Mission Inn** (100 Boyes Blvd., Sonoma, 707/938-9000, www.fairmont.com/sonoma), which dates from 1927 and is now owned by Fairmont Hotels. It is luxurious, even by Fairmont standards. The well-heeled are drawn by the 40,000-square-foot, full-service spa, use of the exclusive Sonoma golf club next door, and one of the best (and most expensive) restaurants in the valley (called Santé). Many of the rooms have tiled floors and plantation-style wooden shutters to complement their colonial-style furnishings, some have fireplaces, and they generally cost from $300 and up in the summer. The 60 suites, including the newest Mission suites, are priced upward of $500. Despite the exclusivity, the in-room amenities are typical of chain hotels, albeit a high-end chain.

Cottages

For a more private getaway, or for groups of more than two people, there are a lot of cottages available for rent in the valley, many owned by wineries. Although most charge an extra small fee for more than two people, they usually have full kitchens and still work out cheaper than booking multiple hotel rooms. For a romantic weekend some cottages available that cost less than some midpriced hotels or B&Bs.

Some of the wineries listed earlier in this chapter that have rental properties on their grounds include **Castle Vineyards** in Sonoma, the **Kaz Winery** near Kenwood, and **Landmark Vineyards** next door to Kaz. A couple of the local inns also have rental management companies, including the **Glenelly Inn,** with over 10 local cottages on its books, and the **Gaige House Inn,** which manages several local properties including one on the **Navillus Birney Winery** estate.

Camping

With cheap rooms at a premium in the valley and not a drop of rain falling for about five months of the year, camping starts to look attractive, especially when the campground also happens to be just 10 minutes from many wineries and a stone's throw from some of the best hiking trails in the area.

The year-round **Sugarloaf Ridge State Park** campground is the only one in the valley and has a lot going for it if you can stand the summer heat (it does get cooler at night). It's a somewhat typical state park campground,

with a small ring road serving the 49 mostly shady sites for tents and small RVs (up to 27 feet), drinking water, restrooms, fire pits, and picnic tables.

Sites 1–11 and 26–28 back onto a small creek, across which is the start of a popular hiking trail. Most of the rest of the sites are at the foot of a hill and get the most shade, although none can be described as truly secluded. Year-round reservations can be made through www.reserveamerica.com or by calling 800/444-7275. Fees are $19 during the summer, $14 the rest of the year. For directions and hiking information, see the *Recreation* section.

FOOD

There's no better illustration of Sonoma's changing food scene than the closure of a local favorite, Rob's Rib Shack, in 2003 and the departure of its founding chef to become partner in a tiny, chic French restaurant, La Poste.

Despite the gradual change in the food scene, Sonoma's resistance to change is still alive and well. Some high-profile chefs and eateries have been sent packing in recent years after their restaurants flopped. Even the Viansa Winery's once-successful Sonoma Plaza outpost, Cucina Viansa, closed in 2005 after 10 years. Many of the most successful establishments are small and relaxed, retaining a degree of intimacy that some of their cousins in the Napa Valley seem to have lost.

There's a strong European theme to food in the valley, but ingredients will likely be fresh and local, representing the giant produce basket that is Sonoma County. Expect to see menus change throughout the year as vegetables, fish, and meats come in and out of season.

Sonoma itself offers a huge variety of places to eat, from cheap to chic. Most of the other notable restaurants are around Glen Ellen at the other end of the valley.

Downtown Sonoma

Ask any of the valley's winemakers where they like to eat and the list will likely include the family-owned Italian trattoria **Della Santina** (133 E. Napa St., 707/935-0576, lunch and dinner daily, dinner entrées $12–19). The outdoor patio and the simple, Italian country food garner consistently good reviews, so reservations are usually essential despite the otherwise casual atmosphere. Prices for the pastas, daily fish, and spit-roasted meats range $10–18, and if the excellent local wine list does not satisfy there's a $12 corkage fee, lower than the $20 charged by many other restaurants.

Almost opposite Della Santina is another trusted and well-loved restaurant, **Café La Haye** (140 E. Napa St., 707/935-5994, 5:30–9 P.M. Tues.–Sat., Sun. brunch). Local ingredients are the backbone of the simple yet polished dishes like house-smoked wild salmon ($8), pan-roasted Wolfe Ranch quail ($18), and a daily risotto, while the wine list is dominated by smaller wineries from all over Sonoma and farther afield. The uncluttered, split-level dining room is small, so either book well in advance or be prepared to sit at the bar in front of the tiny kitchen. The café is part of La Haye Art Center, which contains studios and the work of several local artists.

N The Girl & the Fig (110 W. Spain St., 707/938-3634, 11:30 A.M.–10 P.M. lunch and dinner daily, brunch 10 A.M.–3 P.M. Sun., dinner entrées $15–25) is somewhat of a valley institution, having moved to the Sonoma Hotel on the plaza from its previous home in Glen Ellen, spawning a cookbook and also a wine bar in its old Glen Ellen digs. The French country menu includes main courses like free-range chicken and seafood stew ($18–25), an excellent cheese menu, and delicious salads, including the signature arugula, goat cheese, pancetta, pecan, and grilled fig salad. To match the Provençal cuisine, the wine list focuses on Rhône varietals, so don't expect a huge number of local wines. The restaurant usually closes at 10 P.M., but a brasserie menu is offered until 11 P.M. on Friday and Saturday.

Portuguese is Sonoma Plaza's latest culinary influence. It arrived in mid-2004 when popular restaurant **La Salette** moved from Boyes Hot Springs to its new location (452 1st St. E., Ste. H, 707/938-1927, lunch and dinner until 9 P.M. daily except Mon., dinner entrées $16–25). The menu reflects Portugal's old history of world domination, with traditional dishes such as the Portuguese national soup, caldo verde ($7), and unusual international influences like the pan-roasted Mozambique prawns ($20). The wine list includes a wide range of both local and Portuguese wines, plus 12 different madeiras and 19 ports.

Not the best place for a relaxed dinner but fun for some wine, light evening food, and people-watching is the **Ledson Hotel & Harmony Club** on the plaza (480 1st St. E., 707/996-9779, lunch and dinner daily except Tues., $6–18), where a beautifully detailed and ornate (but faux) Victorian-style dining room opens out onto the sidewalk. Small plates of internationally inspired food, ranging from fries to dishes like tropical lobster salad and marinated skirt steak with foie gras truffle butter ($18), can be washed down with Ledson wines that are available only here and at the winery itself. On weekend evenings the restaurant is open until 11 P.M., and there's often live music.

Pay attention after ordering anything at the **Basque Boulangerie Café** (460 1st St. E., Sonoma, 707/935-7687, open 7 A.M.–6 P.M. daily), because customer names are only called once when food is ready. The long ordering line moves quickly and the wide selection of soups, salads, and sandwiches can also be bought to go, which is handy because table space is usually scarce.

There are more seating options at the unassuming **Coffee Garden Café** (415 1st St. W., 707/996-6645, open 7 A.M.–6 P.M. daily) across the plaza. It has a fairly basic selection of cheap beverages and sandwiches, but the real gem is a big patio hidden at the back of the neighboring, historic adobe home of Captain Salvador Vallejo (brother of General Vallejo), an oasis of greenery with plenty of tables.

Glen Ellen and Kenwood

The intimate and cozy **N Saffron** in Glen Ellen (13648 Arnold Dr., 707/938-4844, dinner

Tues.–Sat., entrées $16–27) describes its daily menu as "eclectic," but the emphasis is firmly on Sonoma with a hint of Spain. Main course options might include saffron-laced paella alongside roasted pork with winter vegetables. The wine list is certainly eclectic, with both Californian, Spanish, and other international wines together with an unusual selection of beers.

The decor inside the **Kenwood Restaurant and Bar** (9900 Sonoma Hwy., 707/833-6326, lunch and early dinner Wed.–Sun., dinner entrées $12–24) is a little on the homey side, but the outdoor patio open during the summer is one of the most idyllic places to eat in the valley, looking onto vineyards and surrounded by flowers. The small plates (up to $15) and main courses ($16–28) are simple and unpretentious combinations of local ingredients like goat cheese with red beets and grilled lamb chops with mushroom raviolis. The wine list is also dominated by locals and includes wines from almost every valley winery as well as the rest of Sonoma, plus a few bottles from Napa, France, and Italy for some variation.

If you're nursing a wine-tasting hangover on a Saturday or Sunday morning, the Ⓜ **Cellar Cat Café** (14301 Arnold Dr. #23, 707/933-1465) just south of Glen Ellen in Jack London Village is a soothing place to recover over brunch. It has three tranquil, shady outdoor decks overlooking the Sonoma Creek and serves up brunch on the weekends (11 A.M. to 3 P.M.), dinner Wednesday–Sunday (5–11 P.M.), and live jazz on Sunday nights. The midpriced seasonal dinner menu combines French, Italian, and Asian influences matched to a wine list of local and international wines. The three cats tend to keep a low profile and will probably be hunting for their own dinner in the historic mill next door. The great outdoor spaces can also be used to eat lunch bought at neighboring Olive & Vine.

The Fig Café and Wine Bar (13690 Arnold Dr., Glen Ellen, 707/938-2130, dinner Thurs.–Mon., weekend brunch, dinner entrées $12–18) is the north valley offshoot of the popular Girl & the Fig restaurant in Sonoma and serves up some of the same fig-accented French dishes

in its colorful, tiled dining room. The emphasis here is on lighter (and cheaper) food: thin-crust pizzas (including one with figs), sandwiches, and main courses like braised pot roast. The Sonoma-dominated wine list is also more compact, and corkage is a reasonable $12.

For all the local praise heaped on its relaxed atmosphere and Northern Italian food, **Café Citti** (9049 Sonoma Hwy., 707/833-2690, daily lunch and early dinner) could be related to Sonoma's popular trattoria, Della Santina. The roadside cottage in Kenwood is well known for its moderately priced rotisserie chicken dishes and risottos but also offers tasty foccacia sandwiches and pizzas that you can eat on the small patio with a glass of Italian wine or take out for a picnic.

Just south of Glen Ellen in Jack London Village you can buy gourmet soups, salads, sandwiches, and entrées at **Olive & Vine** (14301 Arnold Dr. #3, 707/996-9150). Owner and chef Catherine Driggers has cooked at numerous local wineries and restaurants, so don't be surprised to find luxurious picnic options like parmesan basil picnic chicken with fresh peach chutney on the seasonal menu. The cavernous room has a few tables inside (along with a tasting bar for the Eric Ross winery in northern Sonoma), but the best place to eat is the big, shady deck out back overlooking Sonoma Creek, where you might also be able to pick some wild plums during summer.

Casual Valley Dining

Sonoma's Italian heritage is not only represented by fancy trattorias. **Mary's Pizza Shack,** founded by Italian New Yorker Mary Fazio in 1959, has been around longer than many other Sonoma restaurants and now has 15 branches throughout the North Bay. The traditional or build-your-own pizzas are consistently good, and there's a big selection of traditional pasta dishes, including spaghetti with baseball-sized meatballs. Local branches are on the plaza (8 W. Spain St., 707/938-8300) and in Boyes Hot Springs (18636 Sonoma Hwy., 707/938-3600).

Some inventive red (with tomato sauce) and

white (no tomato sauce) pizzas at **The Red Grape** (529 1st St. W., Sonoma, 707/996-4103) include a pear, gorgonzola, and hazelnut pizza ($11), and another using local Sonoma Sausage Company meat ($11). There are plenty of less inspiring, but cheap, pizza and pasta options, and it's worth trying to escape the rather drab interior to the outside patio.

For a monster burrito to soak up excess wine or to refuel after a long bike ride, try the roadside Mexican diner **Juanita Juanita** on the west side of Arnold Drive just north of Sonoma (19114 Arnold Dr., 707/935-3981, 11 A.M.–8 P.M. daily). Although it isn't the cheapest Mexican food in Sonoma ($6–12, cash only), it can be mind-blowingly spicy. The menu warns that "Food isn't properly seasoned unless it's painful to eat."

Other non-gourmet food for those with burger-hungry kids can be found at the **Filling Station** diner (18709 Arnold Dr., 707/939-3855, 11 A.M.–9 P.M., closed Tuesday), just south of the Sonoma Golf Course. It has the usual diner selection of burgers, fries, and fountain drinks, and also serves beer and wine for the grownups. Nothing on the menu is over $7, and you can escape the plasticky interior to sit in the large patio out back, just a stone's throw from golfers on the driving range.

A cosmopolitan town shouldn't be without an Irish pub, and Sonoma has **Murphy's Irish Pub** (464 1st St., 707/935-0660, 11 A.M.–11 P.M. daily) just off the plaza behind the Basque Boulangerie. It's one of the few places in the valley where beer trumps wine and live, usually Irish, music gets people dancing four nights a week. The food includes pub standards like fish and chips, shepherd's pie, and Irish stew, as well as sandwiches and a kids' menu. Nothing comes in over $13, and most dishes are under $10.

Picnic Supplies

The Sonoma Valley is like one giant picnic ground. Many of the wineries have large open spaces or picnic tables. The more adventurous can drive up into the hills for some additional seclusion and maybe the company of a few insects.

Many wineries now offer a limited selection of deli-style food in their visitor centers or gift stores, but some offer more than most, including the **Ledson Winery,** with its pungent selection of cheeses, and the **Viansa Winery** in Carneros, which sells a broad range of Italian-themed deli foods and sandwiches.

Bread can usually be found at most delis, though many places run out by lunchtime. Two bakeries supply most of the valley's bread, both centrally located. The **Basque Boulangerie Café** on the plaza (460 1st St. E., Sonoma, 707/935-7687, open 7 A.M.–6 P.M. daily) sells not only sandwiches and salads to go but also freshly baked breads. It is one of the leading suppliers of bread to grocery stores in the area. The other big local bread supplier is **Artisan Bakers,** in a nondescript building about half a mile from the plaza (750 W. Napa St., 707/939-1765). It also sells a limited selection of sandwiches and pastries.

Three good cheese shops are around the plaza. On the north side is the **Sonoma Cheese Factory** (2 Spain St., 800/535-2855, open daily), which is easy to spot: just look for the ugliest building. It is the home of Sonoma Jack cheese and also sells other strangely flavored cheeses (which you can usually, thankfully, taste first) as well as a limited selection of salads and fancy sandwiches. A less-crowded place to buy cheese is the **Vella Cheese Company** (315 2nd St. E., 707/938-3232 or 800/848-0505, open Mon.–Sat.), a block north of the plaza in a former brewery building. A third option at the other end of the plaza is the more upscale **Cheesemaker's Daughter** (127 E. Napa St., 707/996-4060, closed Mon.), which also sells a selection of other picnic-compatible foods and sandwiches.

Other places to stock up on picnic supplies that are on well-traveled roads include the **Vineburg Deli & Grocery** (997 Napa Rd., 707/938-3306, daily) just south of Sonoma not far from the Gundlach Bundschu Winery. At the north end of the valley are **Olive & Vine** (14301 Arnold Dr. #3, 707/996-9150) and **Café Citti** (9049 Sonoma Hwy., 707/833-2690), both of which sell a big selection of picnic-ready food in addition to being great sit-down dining destinations.

Perhaps the easiest option for getting everything in one place is to visit one of the valley's favorite, upscale grocery stores. The **Sonoma Market** (500 W. Napa St., 707/996-3411), not far from the plaza, and the **Glen Ellen Market** (13751 Arnold Dr., Glen Ellen, 707/996-6728) are both owned by the same partners and sell a wide variety of basics including a decent local wine selection. They each have an extensive deli that includes hot and cold foods, sandwiches, and a salad bar.

Fresh Produce

Just south of Glen Ellen in the Jack London Village, **The Olive Press** (14301 Arnold Dr., Glen Ellen, 707/939-8900 or 800/965-4839, www.theolivepress.com, open 10 A.M.–5 P.M. daily) is the place to discover that olive oils can be as diverse in taste as wines. A small tasting bar usually features six oils ranging from a light and grassy taste up to a rich, mellow one, with flavors generally determined by the olives used and where they're grown (sound similar to wine grape lore?). The Olive Press is also a functioning production center, processing olives from growers across Northern California, including the nearby B. R. Cohn Winery, and it sells a full range of gifts, from cookbooks to oil containers and even olive trees.

Seasonal produce from the organic Oak Hill Farm and some fabulous freshly cut flowers are sold in an old dairy barn known simply as the **Red Barn Store,** off U.S. 12 just north of Madrone Road near Glen Ellen (15101 Sonoma Hwy., Glen Ellen, 707/996-6643, open 10 A.M.–5 P.M. Wed.–Sun. from May to Christmas).

The Sonoma Valley's prolific farmers congregate at the **farmers market** in Depot Park, a block north of the plaza on 1st Street West, every Friday morning year-round. April–October there's an additional market in front of city hall on Tuesday evenings, 5:30 P.M.–dusk.

INFORMATION AND SERVICES

First stop for visitors to the Sonoma Valley should be the **Sonoma Valley Visitors Bureau** (453 1st St. E., Sonoma, 707/996-1090, www.sonomavalley.com, open 9 A.M.–5 P.M. daily) in the Carnegie Library building in the middle of the plaza right next to city hall and across from the Sebastiani Theatre. It publishes a free valley guide and its staff is happy to dispense all sorts of local information for nothing more than an entry in the visitor's book. There's a branch of the visitors bureau just through the gates of the Viansa Winery in Carneros.

If you're staying in the valley, be sure to pick up a copy of the *Sonoma Index-Tribune* newspaper, which has been published for over 100 years and now comes out twice a week. It is full of local news, gossip, event information, and reviews.

For wine-related information, including events at individual wineries, check the website of the **Sonoma County Wineries Association** (www.sonomawine.com), which represents all of Sonoma's wineries, including those in the valley. The **Heart of Sonoma Valley Association** (www.heartofthevalley.com) represents only those wineries around Glen Ellen and Kenwood and organizes plenty of local events throughout the year.

Carneros

Replace the vineyards with grass, throw in a few more cows, and Carneros would probably look a lot like it did 100 years ago. *Carneros* is Spanish for sheep or ram, and grazing has been the mainstay of the region for hundreds of years. In fact, it has more of a Wild West feel to it than much of the region and was home to the annual Sonoma Rodeo until 1950.

In addition to the grazing land, there were once fruit orchards growing every type of soft fruit. The first vineyards were thought to have been planted in 1830s, and by the end of the 1800s the advent of the ferries and railroad had made Carneros a veritable fruit and wine basket.

Phylloxera and Prohibition wiped out the small wine industry in Carneros, and it didn't get back on its feet again until the 1960s. By then, the fruit growers had moved elsewhere and the march of the vineyards across the pastureland began.

Today, the western part of Carneros primar-ily resembles grazing land, and huge marshes still merge at the edge of the bay with the low-lying flatlands. Drive east, and hills are now covered with vineyards as far as the eye can see, a sign that cows will probably not return here anytime soon.

The Wines

The 39,000-acre Carneros appellation borders San Pablo Bay and straddles the county line dividing Napa and Sonoma Counties, though the majority of its vineyards are actually on the Sonoma side of that line. The cool winds that blow off the bay and the murky cloud cover that often takes half the morning to burn off in the summer help make this one of the coolest appellations in California, ideal for creating crisp, acidic pinot noir and chardonnay grapes.

Not surprisingly, those two varietals fill 85 percent of the vineyards, but more winemakers are now discovering that very distinctive wines can be made from syrah and merlot

© PHILIP GOLDSMITH

A roadside sign in Carneros extols the virtues of the humble grape.

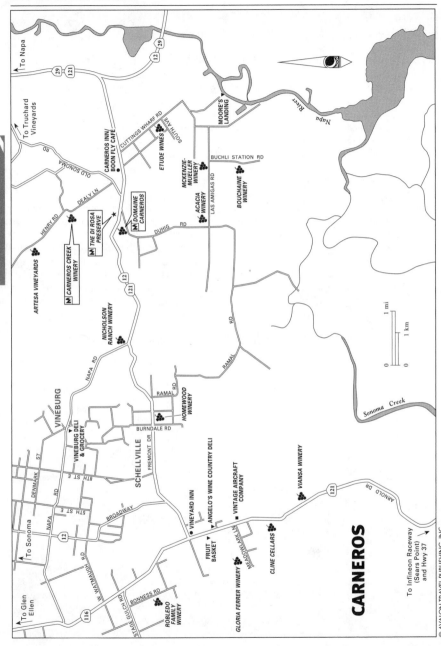

To Napa

29

12 29

121

To Truchard
Vineyards

OLD SONOMA RD

CUTTINGS WHARF RD

CARNEROS INN/
BOON FLY CAFE

SOUTH AVE

MOORE'S
LANDING

ETUDE WINES

McKENZIE-
MUELLER
WINERY

BUCHLI STATION RD

HENRY RD

DEALY LN

THE DI ROSA
PRESERVE

DOMAINE
CARNEROS

DUHIG RD

LAS AMIGAS RD

ACACIA
WINERY

BOUCHAINE
WINERY

ARTESA VINEYARDS

CARNEROS CREEK
WINERY

121

NICHOLSON
RANCH WINERY

NAPA RD

RAMAL RD

RD

RAMAL RD

Napa River

Sonoma Creek

1 mi

1 km

0

0

VINEBURG

VINEBURG DELI
& GROCERY

HOMEWOOD
WINERY

BURNDALE RD

SCHELLVILLE

FREMONT DR

8TH ST E

DENMARK ST

RD

5TH ST E

NAPA

BROADWAY

12

To Sonoma

VINEYARD INN

ANGELO'S WINE COUNTRY DELI

VINTAGE AIRCRAFT
COMPANY

FRUIT
BASKET

MEADOWLARK LN

VIANSA WINERY

121

ARNOLD DR

CLINE CELLARS

116

To Glen
Ellen

W WATMAUGH RD

STAGE GULCH RD

BONNESS RD

ROBLEDO
FAMILY
WINERY

GLORIA FERRER WINERY

CARNEROS

To Infineon Raceway
(Sears Point)
and Hwy 37

© AVALON TRAVEL PUBLISHING, INC.

grapes grown here. Carneros is about as cool as it can be for merlot to ripen completely, and the resulting wines have a greater softness and subtlety than their hot-climate cousins.

Despite its cool, damp appearance, Carneros actually gets less annual rainfall than any other part of Napa or Sonoma County. In addition, the fertile-looking topsoil is usually only a few feet deep and sits on top of a layer of dense, cold clay.

There are far fewer wineries in the Carneros region than its size might suggest. Its prized, cool growing conditions mean that most of the vineyards seen from the road are either owned by, or sell their grapes to, wineries based outside the area. Those that are open range from international champagne houses to tiny, family-owned businesses where you're more likely to experience informative (and free) tasting sessions that used to be the norm in Napa and Sonoma.

Finding some of the wineries can be a test, best taken when sober. Plenty of big, white signs mark the vineyard owners, but they're of absolutely no help in actually finding a winery, so a sharp eye is needed to spot the tiny signs tied to trees and posts. Most of the bigger wineries are fairly obvious from the main road, however.

EASTERN CARNEROS WINERIES
Artesa Vineyards & Winery

A sure sign of how close this part of Carneros is to the Napa Valley, both geographically and culturally, is the marriage of wine, art, and design at this outpost of the historic Spanish sparkling wine producer Codorníu. The grass-covered winery was designed by Barcelona architect Domingo Triay to blend in with the surrounding land, and to a certain extent he succeeded: driving up tiny Henry Road through the vineyards, the only sign of the winery's presence is that one of the low hills happens to be square.

Art is everywhere, from the sculptures and reflecting pools around the parking lot up to the gallery-like interior of the winery, and much of it was created by the winery's artist-in-resi-

CHAMPAGNE CENTRAL

The French fiercely guard the word *champagne*, and over the last few decades they have forced much of the rest of the world to accept that a champagne can only be called Champagne if it comes from the Champagne region of France located just east of Paris. Not so in California, where the term champagne can still be legally used to describe wine made using traditional methods.

Champagne-style wines have popped up all over the world over the centuries, from the sophisticated cava wines of Spain that have been made for hundreds of years to the more recent rise of sparkling wines in California, where Carneros is the center of it all.

In the 1980s and '90s, the world's top producers of cava and champagne saw the potential of Carneros to produce world-class sparkling wines, and many set up shop in the area. The two biggest cava makers in Spain, Freixenet and Codorníu, are represented by the Carneros wineries Gloria Ferrer and Artesa, while Domain Carneros is the American outpost of champagne house Taittinger.

The local wineries of many other big French champagne houses, including Mumm, Krug, and Moët & Chandon, might be located in the nearby Napa Valley, but all grow a large proportion of their champagne grapes in Carneros.

The cool climate of Carneros is ideally suited for growing the two most important champagne grape varietals, chardonnay and pinot noir. Brisk winds and overcast summer mornings might not be the best conditions for touring with the top down, but a taste of some crisp, local champagne more than makes up for the morning chill.

dence, Gordon Huether, who also has his own gallery in Napa. The airy tasting room has a spacious indoor seating area and large (if breezy) patio overlooking the Carneros vineyards, and a small museum gives some history of champagne making and the Codorníu family.

Like those of most Carneros wineries, Artesa's 350 acres of vineyards are planted primarily with chardonnay and pinot noir, and the wine list reflects this. The winery also makes cabernet sauvignon, merlot, and syrah from Napa and Sonoma County grapes. Despite being owned by one of the world's great producers of cava sparkling wines, however, Artesa currently makes only one sparkler, although it does offer tasting of two others from Spain.

Rather than paying a flat tasting fee, visitors can taste one wine for $2 or six for $8. Reserve wines can be tasted for $4 each or $10 for four, and trying one champagne costs $5, though for that you get a full glass. Free tours are offered at 11 A.M. and 2 P.M. daily (1345 Henry Rd., Napa, 707/224-1668, www.artesawinery.com, open 10 A.M.–5 P.M. daily, tasting $2–8).

Carneros Creek Winery

Just down the road from the fake hill of Artesa is the more modest Carneros Creek Winery, which was founded in 1972 and claims to be the oldest continually owned and operated winery in Carneros (Bouchaine claims title of oldest winery site but has had a few breaks in its wine-producing history). One of the founders of Carneros Creek, Francis Mahoney, was a pioneer in researching and planting many of the pinot noir clones grown in Carneros today, and the winery offers tasting of both blended pinots together with those made from specific clones grown on its 148 acres of Carneros vineyards.

Six pinot noir wines are usually available, ranging from the light and fruity Gamay Beaujolais clone up to the earthier Carneros blends. The winery also makes a chardonnay, syrah, and merlot from its Carneros vineyards, together with a zinfandel using grapes from the hot foothills of the Sierra Nevada. Prices range from $16 up to $26 a bottle, and most can be tasted in one of three different tasting flights (1285 Dealy Ln., Napa, 707/253-9463, www.carneroscreek.com, open 10 A.M.–5 P.M. daily, tasting $5–10).

Domaine Carneros

The French heritage of one of California's premier champagne houses is obvious when you see the glistening chateau and its formal gardens on the hill. The Domaine Carneros chateau was built in the style of the 18th-century Chateau de la Marquetterie, home of one of the winery's principal founders, Champagne Taittinger.

When it opened in 1990 it was the first Carneros winery devoted to champagne production and now produces more than 40,000 cases a year of sparkling wines, including a brut cuvée, brut rosé, and the 100 percent chardonnay blanc de blancs flagship bubbly.

In 2003 it achieved another first, opening the first Carneros wine-making facility dedicated to pinot noir production right behind the chateau. On its roof, the facility has the largest solar panel array at a winery in the U.S.; it provides about 40 percent of the power to the entire winery. The new building was designed to look like a carriage house to fit with the chateau theme, and it produces about 15,000 cases of the winery's three pinot wines.

All the wines are made using grapes from the 110 acres of vineyards around the winery and range in price from $18 for the cheapest pinot to $55 for the blanc de blanc sparkler. On the hour (until 4 P.M.) there are free, informative tours that let visitors peer into the squeaky-clean, modern production and bottling areas. Alternatively, just chill on the huge patio area around the chateau and let the bubbles do their work. There is no traditional tasting of multiple wines here. Instead, when you buy a glass of any of the champagnes ($5–10) you get a few morsels to eat, too (1240 Duhig Rd., Napa, 707/257-0101, www.domainecarneros.com, open 10 A.M.–6 P.M. daily).

Bouchaine Vineyards

Before turning into the palatial grounds of Domaine Carneros, continue on Duhig Road for about a mile into the flatlands, turn left on Las Amigas Road, and then right on Buchli Station Road to get to this historic spot out on the flatlands of Carneros close to the bay.

The current Bouchaine winery was established in 1981, but there has been a winery on the site since 1934, when the Garetto Winery started up, and grapes were first grown here in 1899. Not much remains of the old building following a 1990s renovation, although the old redwood tanks were recycled to create the sidings of some of the current buildings. The cozy tasting room is refreshingly free of Wine Country paraphernalia and has a veranda and small picnic area overlooking San Pablo Bay not far away. It's also one of the few wineries in Carneros not to charge for tasting (unless you're in a big group).

Bouchaine grows pinot noir, chardonnay, and a small amount of viognier in its 90 acres of Carneros vineyards, providing grapes for its six blended and vineyard-specific wines, which include the cheaper Buchli Station–labeled chardonnay and pinot selling for only $12. Viognier accounts for only 500 cases of the 27,000 produced annually. The winery's old, concrete open-top fermenters, used instead of more modern stainless steel to produce the pinot noir wines, can be seen on an appointment-only tour of the facility (1075 Buchli Station Rd., Napa, 707/252-9065, www.bouchaine.com, open 10:30 A.M.–4 P.M. daily, free tasting).

Homewood Winery

Just a mile or so from the grandeur of Domaine Carneros, down well-hidden Burndale Road, is the homey Homewood Winery, where owner and winemaker Dave Homewood produces just 3,000 cases of reasonably priced wines from grapes he buys all over Carneros, Napa, and Sonoma, together with a couple of acres of pinot noir around the winery that should start producing wines in the 2005 vintage.

The focus here is on small batches of a variety of mainly red wines like zinfandel, merlot, barbera, and bordeaux-style red blends sourced from vineyards elsewhere in Sonoma and Napa. There are also some excellent Napa and Carneros chardonnays available, and a couple of bottlings of pinot noir sourced from a neighboring Carneros vineyard.

The staff will happily spend an hour or more with visitors in the tiny tasting room explaining the wines, conducting some vertical tastings, and teaching some tasting tricks, like how to identify the oak used in the barrels.

Be sure to check out the olive oils also sold at the winery (23120 Burndale Rd., Sonoma, 707/996-6353, www.homewoodwinery.com, open 10 A.M.–4 P.M. daily, free tasting).

Wineries by Appointment

Tucked away off the well-beaten path of the Carneros Highway are some notable, appointment-only wineries that give more opportunities to discover the nuances of cool-climate Carneros wines.

The **McKenzie-Mueller** winery (2530 Las Amigas Rd. Napa, 707/252-0186) is the family-run operation of Napa Valley wine veterans Bob and Karen Mueller. From their 50 acres of estate vineyards they produce limited quantities of a broad range of wines, including merlot, pinot noir, cabernet sauvignon, and pinot grigio, while a large proportion of the vineyard grapes are sold to other wineries. The winery is on Las Amigas Road at the junction with Buchli Road, just up the road from Bouchaine.

Just down Las Amigas Road from McKenzie-Mueller is the large **Acacia Winery** (707/226-9991 or 877/226-1700, open by appointment 10 A.M.–4 P.M. daily), which has produced pinot and chardonnay wines since 1979 and now owns 150 acres of local vineyards. The rather inelegantly named but powerful-tasting Marsh chardonnay is worth buying just for the fact that proceeds support the restoration of the nearby Napa-Sonoma Marsh. Acacia is at 2750 Las Amigas Road, near the junction with Duhig Road.

At the eastern end of Carneros close to Napa is **Etude Wines** (1250 Cuttings Wharf Rd., Napa, 707/257-5300), which is well known for its refined but pricey Carneros pinot noir. It also produces pinot blanc and pinot gris from local Carneros vineyards together with some Napa Valley merlot and cabernet. Limited tastings and tours are available Monday to Friday only.

The highly acclaimed wines made by **Truchard Vineyards** (3234 Old Sonoma Rd., Napa, 707/253-7153) come from its huge 270-acre Carneros vineyard, where 10 varietals are grown, including cabernet, tempranillo, and zinfandel grapes that reflect the vineyard's location near the border with the warmer Napa Valley. Truchard uses just 20 percent of its estate grapes to make its wide range of premium, limited-release wines (the rest are sold to other wineries). A tour and free tasting also gives the chance to see the winery's 100-year-old barn.

WESTERN CARNEROS WINERIES

Nicholson Ranch

Though just outside the Carneros appellation boundary by literally a few yards (it's technically in the Sonoma Valley appellation), the mission-style Nicholson Ranch winery, opened in 2001, is perched on a hill right at the junction of the Carneros Highway and Napa Road, putting it on the route of most Carneros visitors.

It makes 3,000 cases of predominantly pinot noir and chardonnay wines, with very limited production of estate syrah and merlot, using grapes from its 31 acres of vineyards. Tasting is pricey at $10, but you can usually sample two or three vintages of some of the five chardonnays and four pinot noir wines available, all highly rated.

Several chardonnays are also available in half bottles, ideal for a picnic for two in the sheltered courtyard or on the veranda overlooking the surrounding hills. A small gallery upstairs in the visitor center features local artists. The small, replica amphitheater on the hillside opposite the parking lot is a reflection of the Greek heritage of the Nicholson family that founded and owns the winery (4200 Napa Rd., Sonoma, 707/938-8822, www.nicholsonranch.com, open 10 A.M.–6 P.M. daily, tasting $10).

Cline Cellars

Though surrounded by some big names in Sonoma wine, Cline Cellars is actually a transplant from across the bay and the little-known wine region of Contra Costa County. It moved to its new home in 1991 and brought some of its newfangled East Bay ideas with it, planting syrah, viognier, marsanne, and roussanne instead of the more usual pinot noir and chardonnay. Add the wines made from its East Bay vineyards, and Cline is one of Sonoma's biggest makers of Rhône-style wines.

Despite being a relatively new member of the winery set in Carneros, Cline sits on some historic land, and some of that history comes to life on one of the three tours offered daily at 11 A.M., 1 P.M., and 3 P.M. The wooden house that doubles as the tasting room dates from 1850, and the land was once used by Father Altimira as a forward camp while investigating a site for what would become the Sonoma mission. Natural springs feed the ponds and water the lush gardens that make the winery worth visiting for a picnic.

The highly rated, spicy Los Carneros syrah is worth tasting, as is the unusual Carignane, sourced from old vines at Cline's original home in Oakley across the bay. Many other East Bay wines are also available, including some powerful zinfandels and a lush mourvèdre (24737 U.S. 121, Sonoma, 707/940-4000 or 800/546-2070, www.clinecellars.com, open 10 A.M.–6 P.M. daily, free tasting).

Robledo Family Winery

If you ever wondered about the fate of the laborers who hand-pick the grapes throughout the Wine Country, a visit to this winery will provide one answer. In the 1970s, Mexican immigrant Reynaldo Robledo was working in local vineyards. He eventually formed a successful vineyard management company and finally created his dream winery, making his first commercial vintage in 1998.

Grapes for the merlot, pinot noir, chardonnay, and sauvignon blanc wines come from Robledo's three separate estate vineyards in Carneros, totaling 30 acres, as well as several other vineyards managed by the winery, including the Oak Ranch vineyard up in Lake County. Grapes are also sold to other wineries in the region, so production at Robledo is limited, but the wines are reasonably priced between $15 and $37.

The small winery with its tasting room furnishings from Michoacán, Mexico, is on Bonness Road, reached from U.S. 116 (Arnold

Dr.) just north of the junction with U.S. 121 (21901 Bonness Rd., Sonoma, 707/939-6903, www.robledofamilywinery.com, open 10 A.M.–5 P.M. Mon.–Sat., 11 A.M.–4 P.M. Sun.).

Gloria Ferrer

At one end of Carneros is Artesa, California outpost of one of the giants of cava production in Spain. At the other end is Gloria Ferrer, representing the other historic Spanish bubbly producer, Freixenet, now the largest sparkling wine producer in the world.

Gloria is the wife of José Ferrer, latest in a long line of Ferrers to have made Spanish champagnes. The winery, with its Spanish flourishes and large terrace, opened in 1986 and has the largest selection of champagnes in Carneros, priced from a modest $18. There are now also four pinot noirs available, including the highly rated (and expensive) pinot from the unfortunately named Gravel Knob block of the estate vineyard.

In addition to the pinot noir and chardonnay grown in the estate vineyards to make champagnes and still wines, small lots of merlot and syrah were also planted and the resulting wines first released in 1999 and 2000.

There are three informative tours daily, and the shop sells everything from olive oil to the striking, pop-art inspired posters designed for some of the wines. Wine tasting costs $2–3 per wine, or $4–10 for a glass of sparkling wine (23555 Carneros Hwy., Sonoma, 707/933-1917, www.gloriaferrer.com, open 10:30 A.M.–5:30 P.M. daily).

Viansa Winery & Italian Marketplace

When a family dispute forced Sam Sebastiani out of his family's historic winery in Sonoma in the mid-1980s, he and wife Vicki founded their own operation down in Carneros and used a contraction of their own names (Vicki and Sam) to christen it. The winery is perched on a windswept knoll overlooking the wetlands of Carneros, and the Italian heritage of its founders is obvious from the Tuscan-style architecture of the terracotta-roofed buildings and from the 15,000 cases of Cal-Ital wines made there each year.

Cabernet sauvignon and chardonnay are about the only non-Italian wines you'll find. The long tasting menu is instead filled with red Italian varietals like sangiovese, barbera, dolcetto, nebbiolo, and freisa, and whites including pinot grigio, arneis and vernaccia. Most of those grapes are grown in Viansa's own estate vineyards and elsewhere in Sonoma.

If you've never heard of most of those grapes then the $5 tasting of four wines will be a good introduction. The premier tasting option ($10) includes reserve cabernet sauvignon and the Samuele Cabernet France, named for the founder of the Sebastiani wine-making heritage in Sonoma.

As your mouth waters from the crisp, food-friendly reds and whites, the vast array of deli foods also sold in the tasting room will seem all the more appealing. Just be warned that this is a popular destination for busloads of visitors, so you might end up feeling more like a Mediterranean sardine than part of an exclusive Tuscan club. Many of the wines are also a perfect accompaniment (and price) for a picnic.

The neighboring 90-acre wetlands built by

© PHILIP GOLDSMITH

Tuscan heritage is everywhere at Viansa.

Viansa with the bay in the distance make a fine view from the numerous picnic tables on the long terrace area, marred only by the constant drone of traffic and the sometimes-brisk winds. In the spring (Feb.–May) two-hour **wetland tours** are offered every alternate Sunday for $15, or for $25 including lunch. Call the winery for more details and reservations. Tours of the winery itself are offered twice a day at 11 A.M. and 2 P.M. and are free with the $5 tasting fee. (25200 Arnold Dr., Sonoma, 800/995-4740, www.viansa.com, open 10 A.M.–5 P.M. daily, tasting $5–10).

Wineries by Appointment

The **MacRostie Winery** (21481 8th St. E., Sonoma, 707/996-4480) just south of Sonoma produces 20,000 cases of highly regarded chardonnay, pinot noir, syrah, and merlot from vineyards all over Carneros, including Steve MacRostie's own local Wildcat Mountain vineyard, which was first planted in 1998.

SIGHTS

M The di Rosa Preserve

When writer Rene di Rosa sought rural tranquillity in 1960 and bought some old grazing land in Carneros, locals would probably have thought they were as likely to see cows walking on water than the eventual creation of the biggest collection of Northern Californian contemporary art, and one of the largest regional art collections in the country. Thirty years later, they saw both.

The di Rosa Preserve (5200 Carneros Hwy./ U.S. 121, Napa, 707/226-5991) opened to the public in 1997 and now has more than 2,000 works on display throughout its 217 acres, including a colorful cow that has floated on the 35-acre lake since 1989, although it occasionally tips over.

When he originally bought the land, di Rosa restored a turreted, former winery building as his residence and eventually planted 250 acres of vineyards on the land where grapes were once grown until disease and Prohibition killed the wine industry. The art first came

from local artists through barter arrangements, and di Rosa eventually sold off the vineyards to focus purely on his passion for collecting art.

The Winery Lake vineyards are now owned by Sterling Vineyards (the Winery Lake name can be seen on some of Sterling's premium merlot, pinot noir, and chardonnay wines), and the old winery building is now one of the four indoor galleries on the grounds of the preserve.

Di Rosa himself lives in an apartment above the neighboring tractor shed and still actively collects art from up-and-coming artists all over the greater Bay Area to add to the huge collection of works that date from the 1950s. Visiting the preserve is to enter an eclectic, artistic wonderland, where giant sculptures march up into the hills, a car hangs from a tree, and every indoor space is crammed with photographs, paintings, and video installations of sometimes mind-bending bizarreness. Even nature seems to do its part to maintain the sense of whimsy as the preserve's 85 peacocks (including two albinos) strut, screech, and occasionally crash-land around the galleries.

And don't expect labels to help make sense of the art because there are none, just a numbered catalog in each gallery to ensure viewers approach each piece with no preconceptions.

The only aspects that tie everything together are the Bay Area and di Rosa's love of maximal art over minimal. "The Bay Area is the pond in which I fish. The artists I like use the familiar as a hook to lead you into new realms. The best artists are like shamans who can take us to deeper truths."

The preserve is on the north side of the Carneros Highway (U.S. 121) just west of Napa, almost opposite the Domaine Carneros winery, and is open Monday to Saturday by appointment only (the Saturday tours are at 9:25 and 10:25 A.M. only). The 2.5-hour tours cost $12 but are free on the first and third Wednesdays each month. For reservations call 707/226-5991 or visit www.dirosapreserve.org.

Some overspill of the collection is also on display at the Gatehouse Gallery, which can be visited without a reservation 9:30 A.M.–3 P.M. Tuesday–Friday ($3, free on Wednesday).

EVENTS

Both big and small wineries open their doors during the **April in Carneros** event, usually held on the third weekend in April. Just visit one of the participating wineries for a ticket ($25), which gets you a glass and access to special tastings and events at all the other wineries, including many that are not usually open to the public. For a list of wineries and more information about the event, visit www.carneroswineries.org.

RECREATION

Infineon Raceway

Sleepy Carneros is the unlikely setting for one of the busiest racetracks in the country, the Infineon Raceway (29355 Arnold Dr., Sonoma, 800/870-7223), which usually has some sort of motorized vehicle racing round its two miles of track on 340 days of the year. Born in 1968 as the Sears Point Raceway and rechristened in 2002 after San Jose-based Infineon Technologies bought the naming rights, the track is now part of the circuit for major national motorsport events, including **NASCAR** in June (when the area is choked with traffic and best avoided late afternoon when everyone leaves). It is also home to more than 70 motorsport companies, from racing teams to parts suppliers.

The raceway is en route from San Francisco at the turnoff for Sonoma and Napa, hidden behind the hill at the junction of U.S. 37 and U.S. 121. A full list of events at the raceway can be found on the website at www.infineonraceway.com.

Those who prefer a more hands-on approach to motorsports can try the track out through the **Russell Racing School** (800/733-0345, www.espnrussellracing.com), which is based at the raceway and offers driving, karting, and racing courses, most starting at about $500 for the day. Anyone worried about missing out on the Wine Country experience can buy a pricey Speed and Spa multiday package that includes racing instruction, local hotel room, and spa services to soak out the smell of burned rubber.

Tubbs Island

When the tide comes in, large swaths of lower Carneros disappear underwater, so it's not surprising that the only hike in the area is a wetland hike (waders not required) at Tubbs Island, part of the **San Pablo Bay National Wildlife Refuge.** The eight-mile loop, open to hikers and bikers, is a dirt road that runs through farmland before reaching the edge of the bay and marshes.

It offers little in the way of memorable scenery or strenuous exercise, so the main reason to go is for the wildlife. Legions of migrating wetland birds call the tidal marshes home, particularly in the cold and wet winter months. Even in the slightly warmer summer months there are hawks, pelicans, and plenty of other interesting critters to see, including several endangered species, making the often-bracing, cold wind worth enduring.

The Tubbs Island gravel parking lot where the trail begins is on the right side of U.S. 37, immediately after the traffic lights at the junction with U.S. 121 to Sonoma. For more information on the refuge and its wildlife, contact the Vallejo headquarters of the San Pablo Bay National Wildlife Refuge at 707/562-3000.

Flying

Balloons might be the traditional way to see Wine Country from above elsewhere in the Wine Country, but Carneros has an altogether more adventurous way to take to the air. The **Vintage Aircraft Company** (23982 Arnold Dr. in Schellville, just south of Sonoma, 707/938-2444, www.vintageaircraft.com) offers rides in its fascinating collection of old planes, which includes biplanes and a World War II–era training aircraft.

Simply pick your adrenaline level for the 15–20 minute biplane flights and the FAA-certified pilots can oblige. For a modest adrenaline rush pick the Scenic ride over the vineyards and mountains of the Sonoma Valley ($130 or $190 for two people). To really get the adrenaline pumping, try the Aerobatic ride with a few loops and rolls thrown in for fun ($170–230), and for a heart-stopping experience close your

© PHILIP GOLDSMITH

Discover a different kind of barrel roll in one of the Vintage Aircraft Company's old planes.

eyes and experience the Kamikaze ride. A longer Dawn Patrol trip of 35–40 minutes is also offered, with or without aerobatics, for $250 or $290 for two passengers. Longer rides of up to an hour are also offered in the WWII SNJ-4 training aircraft.

The Vintage Aircraft Company's home is the Sonoma Country Airport, a thriving base for vintage aircraft restoration and flights. You'll probably see an old plane or two parked close to the Carneros Highway as you drive by.

ACCOMMODATIONS

As the drive through the endless vineyards and fields of Carneros might suggest, there's not much in the way of lodging in this part of Wine Country. Carneros thinks of Sonoma as its main town, and that's where most of the "local" hotels can be found. There are, however, a couple of options at opposite ends of the price spectrum for those looking for either an out-of-the-way bargain or some out-of-this-world luxury.

$100–150

The recently refurbished **Vineyard Inn** (23000 Arnold Dr., Sonoma, 707/938-2350 or 800/359-4667, www.sonomavineyardinn.com) is one of the best values in southern Sonoma. The former motel has 17 modern, Spanish-style rooms that cost from just $119 a night, is just minutes from some of the biggest wineries in Carneros, and is only a 10-minute drive from Sonoma. The standard queen rooms are the cheapest, the larger Vineyard rooms start at $149 a night, midweek, and there are a couple of two-room suites and deluxe rooms starting at $179. All have tiled floors, private bathrooms, satellite television, air-conditioning, and access to the small, outdoor pool. One drawback is the inn's location at one of the busiest junctions in Carneros. Other than the constant traffic and a gas station opposite there's really not much else around so you'll be driving to dinner.

Over $150

The **Carneros Inn** (4048 Sonoma Hwy., Napa, 707/299-4900, www.carnerosinn.com) is a new development of 86 individual cottages surrounded by vineyards at the eastern end of Carneros, providing a dose of contemporary luxury on a 27-acre site that ironically used to be a trailer park. As you drive past the place on the Sonoma-Napa Highway (U.S. 121), the stark, tall walls resemble those of a prison, but on the other side of those walls is a luxury planned community with its own manicured streets, a town square, and some privately owned three-bedroom houses sharing the spa, pool, vineyard views, and other amenities with the resort cottages. Not surprisingly there's a hefty price to pay in the Wine Country for a personal cottage that has cherry-wood floors, a plasma-screen TV, a fireplace, an alfresco shower, and a private garden. The cheapest places start at $300 a night, and the price rockets to $500 for a vineyard view. Suites are mini, two-building walled compounds that start at $850. The on-site restaurant is the highly regarded and remarkably cheap (for the inn at least) Boon Fly Café, serving breakfasts that will make you feel instantly at home.

FOOD

The bright red exterior of the **N Boon Fly Café** brightens up the gray walls of the Carneros Inn on the Sonoma-Napa Highway (4048 Sonoma Hwy., Napa, 707/299-4870, breakfast, lunch, and dinner daily, dinner entrées $8–19). The food is rustic and full of fresh ingredients, as might have been eaten by a local known as Boon Fly who used to farm the surrounding land. Breakfast and brunch are the fortes here and are priced low enough to make you want to fill up for the day, but it's also worth making a road stop in the evening to sample the flatbread pizzas or simple but elegant main courses that are equally well priced.

Look for the sign to the Napa River Resorts a little farther east from Boon Fly and take Cuttings Wharf Road as far south as it will go. There are no resorts at the river these days but there is a popular juke-joint next to the boat ramp called **Moore's Landing** (6 Cuttings Wharf Rd., Napa, 707/253-2439, lunch weekdays, breakfast and lunch weekends), which serves American-Mexican comfort food to boaters, anglers, and the occasional stray winery visitor.

Picnic Supplies
Carneros is often chilly and windy compared to the Napa and Sonoma Valleys it borders and so might not be the best place for a picnic, but there are plenty of places to stop for supplies en route to warmer climes.

Angelo's Wine Country Deli (23400 Arnold Dr., 707/938-3688, open 9 A.M.–5 P.M. daily), almost opposite the entrance to the Gloria Ferrer winery, is renowned for its smoked meats but also sells a wide range of other deli food.

Just up the road is the **Fruit Basket** (24101 Arnold Dr., 707/938-4332, open daily), which looks a little like a shack in the middle of its dusty parking lot but is actually one of the best places to buy local, in-season fruit and vegetables (as well as almost every other grocery staple). There's a second Fruit Basket on U.S. 12 in Boyes Hot Springs, too.

Northern Sonoma

There's probably no other wine-producing region in California that has as much to offer visitors as northern Sonoma. Famed Victorian horticulturist Luther Burbank called this part of Sonoma the "chosen spot of all this earth as far as Nature is concerned," and he was pretty well traveled. For a man who tinkered with plants, this was paradise.

This is also a place where living off the land has always been, and still is, a way of life. That land provides some of California's best wine and food and countless recreational possibilities. You can mix wine with almost anything outdoors here: kayaking, mountain hikes, apple picking, camping, fishing, lounging on a sandy beach, flying, or even a safari.

While "Hop Country" and "Prune Country" don't have quite the same ring as Wine Country, those crops and others once dominated the land but have long since vanished. (At one point in the last century a silkworm farm was planned, and a frog farm briefly found fame with its edible amphibians.) There's even a major road named after the slowly disappearing gravenstein apple. It would be easier to name crops that had not at some point been grown on these hills and valleys, helped along by the vast number of microclimates. There

Must-Sees

M Hop Kiln Winery: The towering hop kilns are so well preserved that this small winery could almost produce beer in addition to its unusual range of well-priced wines (page 158).

M Korbel Champagne Cellars: In a forest clearing in Victorian times, two Czech brothers started making wine, and the historic stone winery still makes sparkling wine fit for presidents (page 159).

M Iron Horse Vineyards: An unassuming barn off the beaten track is home to some of the Russian River Valley's best sparkling wines and a flock of wild turkeys (page 160).

M Luther Burbank Home & Gardens: Discover more about the Victorian horticulturist who created hundreds of new plants in his greenhouses and see many of the plants in the historic gardens (page 162).

Hop Kiln Winery, where hops were once dried to make beer

M Armstrong Redwoods State Reserve: Take a break from the car and the heat on a short hike through the cool, damp redwood forest in this historic park (page 166).

M The Russian River: Rent a canoe for a day and drift through the trees on the Russian River, stopping at some of the many secluded beaches (page 167).

M Michel-Schlumberger: Producing some of the best cabernet in a valley dominated by zinfandel, this winery is housed in a beautiful mission revival building tucked away in a scenic canyon (page 181).

M Ridge Vineyards: This is a sister winery to its more famous sibling in the Santa Cruz Mountains, and its building made of rice straw takes the principle of organic wines to a whole new level (page 181).

M Raven Theater: Visit this historic theater for performance art, a movie, or simply a quick lunch, and support the artists that help keep Healdsburg real (page 186).

M Alexander Valley Vineyards: Incorporating part of the homestead of the valley's first settler, Cyrus Alexander, the grounds of this winery are peppered with historic buildings (page 202).

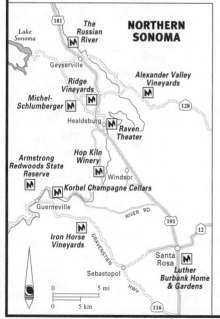

Northern Sonoma

are probably more here than in any other part of the Wine Country—which is saying something in this climate-challenged part of the world. One day vines too might disappear, only to be replaced by the next big agricultural cash generator.

That's not to say that all is peace and rural tranquillity. Far from it. The freeway that was carved through the region in the 1960s has brought with it the kind of suburban sprawl and rush-hour traffic that sucked the soul out of the largest city, Santa Rosa. While Santa Rosa continues to bulge outwards, it doesn't take much to get back to the land and step back in time. Less than a half hour away deep in the woods are towns like Guerneville and Occidental that still retain some feeling of the frontier towns they once were, even as they become overrun in the summer by an unlikely mix of urbanites, hippies, bikers, and ranchers who all seem to happily coexist for a few months.

Even the Victorian town of Healdsburg has managed to keep in touch with its historic past, despite trying ever so hard to sell its soul to those marketing an imaginary Wine Country lifestyle.

The whole area is slowly being dragged upmarket, however, as the burgeoning Bay Area population seeks out bigger backyards. At the southernmost edge of this part of the Wine Country, Sebastopol is starting to resemble a hip San Francisco neighborhood. Property prices everywhere are soaring, slowing down the machine of change that has continually transformed the land since European immigrants first arrived here in the 1800s and carved out a life for themselves in the soil and forests.

Winemakers still produce wines to rival the best in the world, but as the cost of doing so rises the conglomerates are increasingly taking over, much as they have already done in the Napa and Sonoma Valleys. You now have to be big to survive in the wine world here, and many new winemakers are looking farther north in Mendocino and Lake Counties for a chance to get in on the action.

Nevertheless, there is still an amazing diversity of wine, scenery, and activities in northern Sonoma, and there's still plenty of life left in the northern Sonoma scene, of course. There might be trouble in paradise, but it's still paradise to visit.

PLANNING YOUR TIME

Parts of northern Sonoma are easy to get around, others are not. The Russian River Valley is definitely in the not category. This sprawling appellation encompasses forests and mountains, hills and dales, and has the navigational inconvenience of a large river cutting almost straight through the middle of it. A map is essential here, as is a bit of planning to ensure you spend more time in wineries than backtracking on the roads. The Russian River Wine Road publishes one of the best maps, which can usually be found free at wineries.

The **Dry Creek** and **Alexander Valleys** are relatively straightforward to navigate by comparison, with most of the wineries strung along a few long roads. These valleys are almost like miniature Sonoma or Napa Valleys as far as climate, shape, and scenery, and it's easy to get a good feel for the area in a day or even a half day.

The three main appellations are like night and day when it comes to wine, which makes planning a wine route either exciting or daunting. Sample some velvety Alexander Valley cabernets, for example, before crossing into the Dry Creek Valley and tasting the subtly different cabernets there. Or try the warm-climate chardonnays in the Alexander Valley then head down Westside Road to try some leaner, cool-climate versions in the Russian River Valley.

Alternatively, try to find your favorite Dry Creek zinfandel from the hundreds on offer in the valley, or hunt out the next big pinot noir in the Russian River Valley.

If all the possibilities just seem too overwhelming, there's always the option of staying in **Healdsburg,** which has enough tasting rooms to satisfy the most ardent wine critic, as well as plenty of shops and restaurants to occupy those less curious about the region's wines. Healdsburg is also the most central town in the region, with the highest concentration of interesting hotels and restaurants, making it an almost essential staging post for day trips.

As in other parts of the Wine Country, wineries generally open late and close early, so don't expect to get started until late morning, and plan to be finished touring by about 4:30 P.M. Unlike in some other parts of Wine Country, there are usually no tasting fees, except for reserve wines and at a few of the bigger wineries.

GETTING THERE

The railroad came and went to this part of Sonoma before most of us were even born, leaving the car and sporadic bus services as the only real options for getting around.

U.S. 101, which runs down the center of the northern Sonoma Wine Country, might be a bit of an eyesore as it growls up otherwise picturesque valleys, but it's pretty convenient for getting around. It's about a one-hour drive from San Francisco up the freeway to almost every major town in the area.

From the freeway, Highway 116 (west) runs up through Sebastopol to Guerneville. Around Santa Rosa, River Road runs west to Forestville, though it tends to get choked during rush hour. The Healdsburg Avenue exit leads straight into downtown Healdsburg, and the Westside Road exit is the entry to the Dry Creek Valley and Russian River regions. The next four exits serve Dry Creek and Alexander Valleys.

Although most people come to this part of the Wine Country by car, there are other transport options, particularly for those planning to spend a day or two in the self-contained city of Healdsburg. **Greyhound Lines** (800/229-9424, or www.greyhound.com) runs a scheduled bus service from San Francisco to Healdsburg once a day, a two-hour trip. Both Santa Rosa and Sebastopol are well served by **Golden Gate Transit** (415/923-2000 or 707/541-2000, www.goldengatetransit.org), which runs scheduled bus service to and from San Francisco hourly for much of the day. From Santa Rosa, **Sonoma County Transit** (707/576-7433 or 800/345-7433, www.sctransit.com)

runs regular services to Healdsburg, Geyserville, and Guerneville, and from Sebastopol there's service to Guerneville through Graton and Forestville.

GETTING AROUND

The Russian River Valley is roughly square in shape, with an arm stretching from its top right corner up to Healdsburg. The major towns are Guerneville, in the top left corner of the square, Sebastopol on the bottom edge, Occidental on the left edge, and Santa Rosa on the right. In the middle is a patchwork of farmland and vineyards, together with the hamlets of Graton and Forestville. Highway 116, also called the Gravenstein Highway, is the main road running north to south through them.

Wineries are spread mainly along Eastside and Westside Roads, which run on either side of the river from Healdsburg down toward Guerneville, and in the patchwork in the middle.

Many of the region's food and lodging options lie in Healdsburg and around the edge of this Russian River square. Unlike in the Dry Creek and Alexander Valleys farther north, roads here tend to meander as they follow the river and hills, often making driving times longer than anticipated.

In comparison, the Dry Creek Valley could be navigated with your eyes shut. Just two roads run the length of the valley, and the wineries are roughly spread out along them, making it the easiest part of northern Sonoma to visit in a day, even without a map.

Along the other side of the freeway is the longer and wider Alexander Valley. Even here, the wineries are concentrated along Geyserville Avenue on the western side of the valley and along Highway 128 on the eastern side.

Of course, driving is not the only way to get around. Wine Country would not be complete without tourists wobbling along on bikes. The compact, flat Dry Creek Valley and relatively flat Westside Road from Healdsburg down into the Russian River Valley are two of the most bikable routes. The Alexander Valley also is relatively flat, but distances between wineries are greater. In all areas, temperatures get high in the summer, so plenty of water is essential.

The best place to rent bikes is at **Spoke Folk Cyclery** in Healdsburg (201 Center St., 707/433-7171, www.spokefolk.com). The friendly folks will set you up on decent touring bikes for $30 a day (racing bikes and tandems $50/day) and send you off with maps for trips ranging from 12-mile loops in Dry Creek Valley to 40-mile epics down to Guerneville.

The Russian River Valley

The Russian River appellation is one of Sonoma's largest and most diverse. It covers about 150 square miles of forest, orchards, vineyards, and pastureland from trendy Sebastopol in the south to chic Healdsburg in the north, from the suburban freeway sprawl in the east to rural Occidental in the west. And running right through it is the mighty Russian River, shaping the climate, scenery, and recreation opportunities of the region.

The Russian River Valley attracted immigrants in the late 1800s to exploit its almost endless forests, and many of the towns were originally logging or railroad outposts. Once the redwood forests had been largely cleared it was sheep ranches, cattle pasture, orchards, and even hop farms that took over the land. The gravenstein apple, now an endangered piece of local agricultural history, was embraced as the region's very own, though its roots remain somewhat ambiguous.

It wasn't until the 1980s, when the cool growing climate was recognized as ideal for the increasingly fashionable pinot noir and chardonnay grapes, that the area's wine industry took off. It's not an easy part of Wine Country to explore, however, compared to relatively self-contained valleys elsewhere in Sonoma. Roads wind through forests, over hills, and along the snaking river, making wineries sometimes hard to find. Large parts of the region are rural, dotted with small communities like **Forestville** and **Graton,** which hide their already small populations very well in the surrounding hills and woods.

The center of the action is **Guerneville** and neighboring **Monte Rio,** both slightly faded Victorian resort towns that are transformed each summer into a surreal scene of leather-clad bikers, fashionable urban hipsters, plaid-clad outdoorspeople, and country hippies.

The eastern and western edges of the appellation could not be more of a contrast. The suburban sprawl of **Santa Rosa** is just outside the eastern boundary of the appellation. This is by far the biggest city in the region—where culture meets characterless malls—but a far cry from the peaceful and remote Bohemian Highway running along the appellation's western edge, with its dark forests and the picture-postcard town of **Occidental.**

The Wines

Almost a third of all the grapes grown in Sonoma County come from the Russian River Valley, though only about 12,000 (and growing) of the 125,000 acres it covers are planted with vines.

The river provides the region with the unique climate and conditions that are perfect for growing cool-weather grapes. Pinot noir and chardonnay are the dominant varietals here, but syrah, zinfandel, merlot, and cabernet are also grown in some of the warmer, hillside areas.

Fog rolls down the river valley during the summer, keeping the temperature here lower than elsewhere in Sonoma and slowing the ripening of the grapes to create more complex and supple pinot flavors, and crisper, leaner chardonnay. Grapes are usually harvested several weeks later than in some hotter Sonoma regions.

The river is also responsible for the area's unique soils, depositing deep, well-drained sandy and gravelly soils over million of years. These keep the vines hunting for water while providing them with essential, flavor-creating minerals—the perfect combination for good wines.

THE GRAVENSTEIN HIGHWAY

Although almost every imaginable fruit and vegetable seems to be grown in Sonoma, the most celebrated in the Russian River Valley (apart from grapes) is perhaps the apple, and in particular the small, yellow gravenstein with its aromatic taste. Highway 116, which runs through Sebastopol and Graton, is also called the Gravenstein Highway for the large number of orchards it used to run through. The orchards are now disappearing, along with the gravenstein apple itself, as growers favor bigger and more easily transported varieties of apple like fuji and golden delicious.

Nothing specifically links the gravenstein apple to this area (it is believed to have originated in Germany)—it just grows particularly well here and has been doing so for almost 200 years.

The gravenstein is the earliest-ripening apple in the region, so look out for it starting in late July. Others types ripen August–December. Farms offering apples and other seasonal produce are generally clustered around Sebastopol and Graton. Most are open only during the summer and fall.

In Graton they include: **Foxglove Farms** (5280 Gravenstein Hwy. N., 707/887-2759, open daily except Wed. July–Oct.), **Kozlowski Farms** (5566 Gravenstein Hwy. N., 707/887-1587, open daily year-round), **Gabriel Farm** (3175 Sullivan Rd., just off Graton Rd., 707/829-0617, open daily except Sat. Sept.–Oct.), and **Walker Apples** (10955 Upp Rd., off Graton Rd., open daily Aug.–mid-Nov.), which sells a staggering 27 varieties of apple.

Just south of Sebastopol on Bloomfield Road off the Gravenstein Highway is **J. Luis Gudino** farm (1617 Bloomfield Rd., 707/823-7350, open weekends May–Sept.). Continue on Bloomfield to Pleasant Hill Road and **Munch Apples** (2061 Pleasant Hill Rd., 707/824-6939, open by appointment all year) or to **Twin Hill Ranch** (1689 Pleasant Hill Rd., 707/823-2815, open Mon.–Sat. all year).

More information about all the fruits and vegetables grown here and the farms that sell them is available from **Sonoma Country Farm Trails** (707/571-8288, www.farm-trails.org). You might also see the free *Farm Trails* map and guide at wineries and farms in the region.

Within the southwest corner of the Russian River appellation, closest to the ocean, is the even cooler Green Valley appellation. This is just about as cool as a climate can be and still ripen grapes, and it is the source of some of Sonoma's best pinot noir grapes (though Carneros growers might beg to differ).

WINERIES

The Russian River doesn't make it easy to visit wineries in this part of the world. As it curves south and west toward the sea it leaves no neat valleys or straight roads but a complex patchwork of vineyards, redwood forests, orchards, and pastureland.

Many of the Russian River wineries are

down Westside Road from Healdsburg, but that's as easy as it gets. Once that road reaches River Road a map is a good idea in order to find the many wineries that lie in a broad swath from the river down to Sebastopol.

Foppiano Vineyards

The first major winery south of Healdsburg on the Old Redwood Highway is also one of the few historic wineries that continued to operate right through Prohibition. It remains a family-owned affair even though it is more of a corporate-sized business, producing several hundred thousand cases of wine a year under three different labels.

Giovanni Foppiano founded the winery in 1896, and the fourth generation of Foppianos

Northern Sonoma

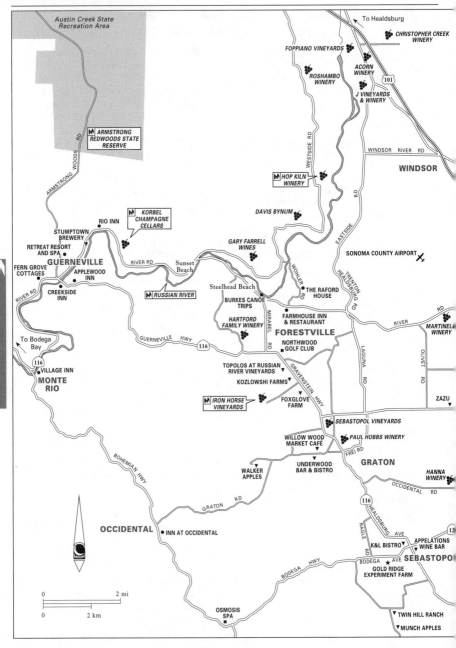

THE RUSSIAN RIVER VALLEY

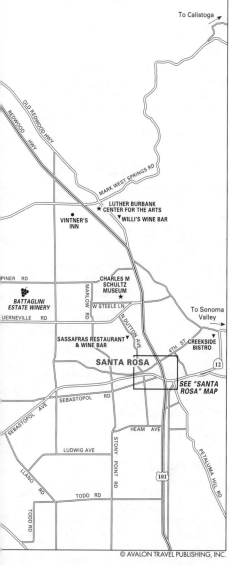

To Calistoga

OLD REDWOOD HWY

REDWOOD HWY

MARK WEST SPRINGS RD

LUTHER BURBANK
★ CENTER FOR THE ARTS
VINTNER'S   ▼ WILLI'S WINE BAR
INN

PINER   RD   CHARLES M
                              SCHULTZ
                              MUSEUM
BATTAGLINI   W STEELE LN   To Sonoma
ESTATE WINERY   Valley
UERNEVILLE RD

SASSAFRAS RESTAURANT ▼
& WINE BAR   ▼ CREEKSIDE
                               BISTRO
SANTA ROSA

                              SEE "SANTA
                              ROSA" MAP   12

SEBASTOPOL   RD

SEBASTOPOL AVE
                 HEAM   AVE

LUDWIG AVE   STONY POINT RD   PETALUMA HILL RD

LLANO RD   101

        TODD RD

TODD RD

© AVALON TRAVEL PUBLISHING, INC.

Northern Sonoma

today runs the business and its 200 acres of estate vineyards. For most of its existence over the last century the winery sold wine in bulk and some cheap and cheerful jug wines. It wasn't until the 1970s that the winery went upmarket and put its product into bottles.

Today, Foppiano is best known for its powerful cabernet sauvignon and inky petite sirah, which has been very highly rated in recent years. It also makes sangiovese, zinfandel, and merlot. White wines, including sauvignon blanc and chardonnay, are sold under the Fox Mountain label. Although there are no official tours, visitors are free to head into the vineyards on a self-guided tour (12707 Old Redwood Hwy., Healdsburg, 707/433-7272, www.foppiano.com, open 10 A.M.–4:30 P.M. daily, free tasting).

Christopher Creek Winery

The family-owned Christopher Creek Winery, until 1992 the Sotoyome Winery, makes about 4,500 cases of wine a year from its 10 acres of estate vineyards and 35 acres in the Dry Creek Valley. They include syrah, petite sirah, and cabernet sauvignon (Dry Creek), and the winery also buys Russian River fruit from other growers to make its chardonnay, viognier, and zinfandel. If it's not too busy you might be treated to an impromptu tour (641 Limerick Ln., off Old Redwood Hwy., Healdsburg, 707/433-2001, www.christophercreek.com, open 11 A.M.–5 P.M. daily, free tasting).

J Vineyards & Winery

Just south of Foppiano, the giant parking lot shared with the neighboring Rodney Strong Winery can be a magnet for busloads of tourists, but there's a relative oasis to be found inside the J's Bubble Room.

Food pairings are part of the tasting experience here. At the main tasting bar, $10 buys a sample of five wines and accompanying morsels of luxurious food prepared by the winery's own chef. If the main bar is overrun, a common occurrence, the more exclusive Bubble Room (open Fri.–Sun. only) takes the tasting experience (and the price) up a notch with table service, heartier bites, and more expensive wine samples.

J specializes in producing wines from cooler-weather grapes—chardonnay, pinot noir, and pinot gris—and is best known for its sparkling wines, which account for almost half the winery's 45,000-case production and consistently score well with critics. The appointment-only tours also focus on the sparkling wine-production process.

The Vintage brut is the signature wine here and was the only wine that owner Judy Jordan (hence the name "J") made when she started the winery in 1986. Of the pinot noir on offer, the limited-release Nicole's Vineyard is perhaps the best (11447 Old Redwood Hwy., Healdsburg, 707/431-3646, www.jwine.com, open 11 A.M.–5 P.M. daily, tastings $10).

Roshambo Winery

Where a lot of winery tasting rooms seem to celebrate an imagined Wine Country lifestyle of country cottage interiors, this one celebrates the art of wine. It's all concrete, blond wood, glass, steel, and strange angles, making the space feel like a gallery interior, especially with the contemporary art and sculpture dotted around the place. Sweeping views over vineyards and the bottles on the minimalist bar are the reminders that it's actually a winery.

Roshambo is shorthand for the rock/paper/scissors game we all used to settle disputes as kids. The winery's owner, Naomi Johnson Brilliant, came up with the name from her father's fondness for such dispute resolution when she was a kid in Japan, where the game originated. If you're here in June you might be lucky enough to take part in the regional Rock Paper Scissors Championship.

The playful atmosphere of the place continues right into the winery's tank room, where each giant stainless steel tank is named for a literary figure that was influential in Naomi's life. This is probably the only place in Wine Country where Kafka meets Willy Wonka over several million glasses of wine.

The wine's not bad either, though some can be a little angular, like the surroundings. Roshambo sits at the border of the Dry Creek Valley appellation, so zinfandel is a big part

of the 16,000-case annual production. Syrah, merlot, and chardonnay also feature strongly, with many of the best wines coming from the nearby Frank Johnson Vineyards, which were established by Naomi's grandfather in the 1970s (3000 Westside Rd., Healdsburg, 707/431-2051, www.roshambowinery.com, open 10:30 A.M.–4:30 P.M. daily, tastings $10).

ⓜ Hop Kiln Winery

Just down the road from Roshambo but a world away from steel and glass modernity is one of Sonoma's best-preserved old hop kilns, a towering wooden building where hops were once dried before being used to make beer. The hops of Sonoma have long since been replaced by vines, but the Hop Kiln Winery has kept much of the cavernous interior of the 1905-era building intact, including the old stone ovens.

Belying its giant home, the winery itself is a fairly small operation, producing about 10,000 cases a year of reasonably priced zinfandel, cabernet sauvignon, chardonnay, and some interesting blends.

Marty Griffin's Big Red (named after the winery owner) is just that—a rambunctious blend of zinfandel, cabernet, and syrah. A Thousand Flowers is a more delicate white blend of chardonnay, gewürztraminer, and riesling. The once-common Napa gamay red grape is also represented under its more accurate name of valdiguié. Very few wineries still make it—it's an acquired taste.

There are plenty of picnic tables around the building, including some next to a rather murky pond, but dogs are not welcome (6050 Westside Rd., Healdsburg, 707/433-6491, www.hopkilnwinery.com, open 10 A.M.–5 P.M. daily, free tasting).

Davis Bynum

After an early career in journalism and a failed attempt to establish a winery in the Napa Valley in the 1970s, Davis Bynum bought this ranch at the southern end of Westside Road and, in the ensuing decades, established himself as one of the region's best pinot noir makers and a champion for Russian River Valley grapes.

In addition to the flagship, single-vineyard pinot noirs, there are some cheaper pinots as well as chardonnay and cabernet sauvignon to taste, all sourced from the Russian River Valley.

The tasting room is in an old hop kiln, true to the "use and reuse" organic philosophy of the winery, and visitors can picnic in a three-acre permaculture garden containing all sorts of edible and ornamental plants that love the local climate (8075 Westside Rd., Healdsburg, 800/826-1073, www.davisbynum.com, open 10 A.M.–5 P.M. daily, free tasting).

Gary Farrell Wines

The last winery on Westside Road before it reaches River Road is also one of the newest. The spacious tasting room at the end of a long driveway (easy to miss when driving east) was completed in 2001 and overlooks some of the Russian River vineyards from which Farrell crafts his renowned chardonnay and pinot noir.

Farrell used to be the winemaker at nearby Davis Bynum, another master of pinot noir, and set up his own winery in the 1980s to pursue his pinot passion. Since 2003, Allied Domecq has owned the winery.

The 10 or so vineyard-specific and Russian River chardonnays and pinot noirs account for about half of the winery's 17,000-case annual production. Don't overlook the beautifully structured merlot, cabernet sauvignon, and zinfandel wines, however, which all have the same understated elegance.

The tasting room is open daily, but appointments are needed for the single tour each morning that ends with a cheese and wine pairing (10701 Westside Rd., Healdsburg, 707/473-2900, www.garyfarrell.com, open 10 A.M.–4 P.M. daily, free tasting).

M Korbel Champagne Cellars

This is one of the most impressive of the 19th-century wineries in Sonoma, from its location at the edge of redwood forests to its solid, imposing stone buildings.

Three Korbel brothers, immigrants from the Bohemia region of what is now the Czech Republic, founded the winery in 1882 after making their money in the local redwood lumber business. They continued making redwood tanks and boxes even after planting vines among the stumps of some of the cleared land. But wine

Drink champagne in the redwoods at Korbel winery.

production gradually took over from their other businesses as the quality of their sparkling wines and brandies improved and word spread.

Now the winery makes close to 1.7 million cases of the fizzy stuff a year, as well as table wines, brandy, and port that can only be bought at the winery.

The Korbel family connection has long since gone, but Korbel wines remain the tipple of presidents and plebians alike. The champagne has been poured at five presidential inaugurations and is claimed to be the most popular premium champagne in the United States.

From the bone-dry, top of the line Le Premier to the sweeter Sec, Korbel's 10 or so champagnes are eminently affordable, as are the cabernet, pinot noir, chardonnay, and zinfandel table wines, and even the barrel-aged port.

How the bubbles get into the wine and how the Korbel brothers got into the wine business are both covered in an entertaining tour offered six times a day—buy tickets in the little shack at the opposite end of the parking lot from the tasting room. A tour of the ornate old rose garden is offered three times a day from mid-April to mid-October, and after all that touring you can lounge under some redwood trees outside the delicatessen, which serves gourmet sandwiches and even beer (13250 River Rd., Guerneville, 707/824-7000, www.korbel.com, open 9 A.M.–5 P.M. daily in summer, until 4:30 P.M. winter, free tasting).

Hartford Family Winery

A little off the beaten track (about a mile up Martinelli Road and surrounded by lush gardens and forest) is the giant but rather plain white winery and mansion of this pinot noir and chardonnay specialist. Hartford makes about 20,000 cases of some serious point-scoring regional and single-vineyard wines from the Sonoma Coast, Russian River Valley, Carneros, and (unusually) Marin County to the south.

If you think this family winery seems a little too big business, that's because it has some big business connections. Part-owner Don Hartford is married to the daughter of Jess Jackson, founder of the Kendall-Jackson wine empire that also owns the majority of Hartford.

The best wines here are the vineyard-designate and limited-production pinots and chardonnays under the Hartford Court label, which cost up to $40 a bottle. The slightly cheaper Hartford-labeled wines are well worth trying and include three zinfandels from some of the oldest vineyards in the Russian River region (8075 Martinelli Rd., Forestville, 707/887-1756 or 800/588-0234, www.hartfordwines.com, open 10 A.M.–4:30 P.M. daily).

Sebastopol Vineyards/ Dutton Estate Winery

The modest little tasting room of the Dutton family, just off Highway 116, barely hints at the renown of their Dutton Ranch vineyards and others in the Green Valley appellation for producing highly rated, limited-production wines.

The family farms about 1,300 acres of vines (and apples) but sells most of the grapes, producing just over 6,000 cases of wine from the remainder for its premium Dutton Estate label wines and slightly cheaper Sebastopol Vineyards label.

Chardonnay, pinot noir, and syrah are the only wines made, but there are lots of different versions of them made from specific vineyards and sometimes specific blocks within a vineyard.

Discovering some of the nuances of the tiny Green Valley subappellation with the more expensive vineyard-specific wines entails a tasting fee, but there is also free tasting of some wines (8757 Green Valley Rd., Sebastopol, 707/829-9463, www.sebastopolvineyards.com, open 11 A.M.–4 P.M. Thurs.–Mon., free tasting or $5 fee).

ⓜ Iron Horse Vineyards

One of the southernmost wineries in the Green Valley appellation is also well off the beaten track down Ross Station Road (off Hwy. 116), a one-lane road that winds through orchards, over a creek, and (perhaps) past some wild turkeys before climbing up to the palm-lined driveway of the winery.

The simplicity of the barnlike building belies the pedigree of the sparkling wines made here—they have been served to presidents and won numerous accolades from wine critics over the last 30 years. Tours are offered by appointment weekdays only.

Today the winery makes about 20,000 cases of sparkling wines a year, most priced at over $30, including the ever-popular Wedding Cuvée and a series of late-disgorged wines, including the flagship Brut LD, which are bottle-aged for four or more years in contact with the dead yeast to give them a rich aroma and flavor.

Iron Horse makes just as much still wine from its vineyards in the cool Green Valley and warmer Alexander Valley appellations, and gets just as many rave reviews. Standouts include the single-vineyard pinot noir and chardonnay, and dry rosé wines made from pinot and sangiovese (9786 Ross Station Rd., Sebastopol, 707/887-1507, www.ironhorsevineyards.com, open 10 A.M.– 3:30 P.M. daily, tasting fee $5).

Martinelli Winery

One of the most noteworthy zinfandels made in the Russian River Valley comes from Martinelli's Jackass Vineyard, planted in the 1800s and still going. That notable vineyard's name has absolutely no historical significance, instead referring to the sort of farmer who would consider farming such a steep and rugged slope.

Those Jackass Martinellis have been a fixture here since the early 1900s as grape and apple growers. In fact, apples can be found alongside the wines and other gourmet food in the rather chaotic winery gift shop.

The family only started making wines in the late 1980s. The winery is in an old hop barn on River Road just west of the freeway and is still a relatively small affair, producing well under 10,000 cases a year. As well as the Jackass and other zinfandels, wines include consistently highly rated gewürztraminer, chardonnay, an aromatic and fruity muscat, and the tasty Bondi Home Ranch pinot noir from the Green Valley appellation, which is the only wine with a tasting fee (3360 River Rd., Windsor, 707/525-0570 or 800/346-1627, www.martinelliwinery.com, open 10 A.M.– 4 P.M. daily, free tasting).

Hanna Winery

From humble beginnings in the 1970s, Hanna has grown to become one of the larger privately owned wineries in northern Sonoma, making 35,000 cases of wine in 2003 at its modest Home Ranch winery here in the Russian River Valley and set to grow even larger with the completion of a new 100,000-case winery at its Alexander Valley location (9280 Hwy. 128, Healdsburg, 707/431-4314).

Hanna's specialty is crisp, steel-fermented sauvignon blanc, but it has a full portfolio of wines from the 250 acres of vineyards it owns around its two winery locations and high up in the Mayacamas Mountains at its Bismark Ranch vineyards above Sonoma Valley— claimed to be the highest-elevation vineyard in Sonoma.

The Bismark red wines, including bordeaux blends, sangiovese, and nebbiolo, are powerful and often highly rated by critics (5345 Occidental Rd., Santa Rosa, 707/575-3371, www.hannawinery.com, open 10 A.M.– 4 P.M. daily).

Wineries by Appointment

Acorn Winery (12040 Old Redwood Hwy., down a gravel driveway just south of Limerick Ln., Healdsburg, 707/433-6440), with its version of a tasting bar propped on two barrels in the corner of Bill and Betsy Nachbauer's garage, couldn't be further from the wine-making behemoths of Rodney Strong and Foppiano nearby. The Nachbauers are former corporate lawyers who bought their 26 acres of vineyards here in 1990 and started making their own wine six years later using equipment at other wineries but barrel aging (and tasting) in their garage. Production now is about 1,800 cases a year and a thoroughly Italian affair. Wines include zinfandel, sangiovese, dolcetto, and field blends including Medley, a blend of 15 varietals that redefines the term "complex."

From Healdsburg via Argentina to Graton might seem like tortuous route for a winemaker, but the founder of **Paul Hobbs Winery** (3355 Hwy. 116, 707/824-9879, www.paul-hobbswinery.com) picked up some valuable wine-making experience along the way from Simi Winery near Healdsburg and Vina Cobos winery in Mendoza, Argentina, before establishing his wine label in 1991. As he built up his vineyard holdings during the 1990s, wines were made at other Sonoma wineries, including Kunde, but a dedicated facility in Graton was opened in 2003. Now Hobbs makes highly rated, vineyard-designate chardonnay and pinot noir from Russian River vineyards, and a cabernet sauvignon using Napa fruit.

Most Italian wine families in northern Sonoma can trace their roots back over a century, but Giuseppe Battaglini and family arrived in the 1950s with the same dream of re-creating his memories of the Italian Wine Country right here in Sonoma. **Battaglini Estate Winery** (2948 Piner Rd., Santa Rosa, 707/578-4091, www.battagliniwines.com) has the advantage of owning vineyards planted by one of those early Italian immigrant families in the 1880s that supply grapes for the intensely flavored zinfandel and petite sirah wines. A more recent planting of chardonnay brought total production up to about 2,100 cases. It's all very much a family affair, and visitors will probably bump into a Battaglini in the tiny tasting room.

SIGHTS

M Luther Burbank Home & Gardens

Apples and pears, grapes and hops, plums and peaches—as Sonoma County's rich agricultural history suggests, pretty much anything will grow here. Pioneering horticulturist Luther Burbank recognized this when he made Sonoma County his home in 1875.

Burbank's cross-breeding experiments at his Santa Rosa and Sebastopol greenhouses are credited with creating over 800 new strains of flowers, fruits, trees, and other plants over his 50-year science career, including the big, white Shasta daisy, a spineless cactus, the blight-resistant Burbank potato, and the plumcot (a cross between an apricot and a plum).

He was also well connected in science circles of the time, counting Thomas Edison and Henry Ford, amongst others, as friends. Ford

sent him the first tractor off the company's production line as a gift in 1918.

Santa Rosa was proud to have Burbank, and he was happy to be part of the city's self-promotion. A Santa Rosa promotional brochure in the 1920s described him as "California's best citizen," and borrowed one of his many famous Sonoma quotes: "I would rather own a piece of land the size of a good healthy house lot in Sonoma County than an entire farm anywhere else on earth."

Burbank's own healthy house lot where he lived until 1906 is preserved, together with a small greenhouse and the gardens, as part of the 1.6-acre State Historic Park in Santa Rosa (on the 200 block of Santa Rosa Ave. at Sonoma Ave., just across the street from city hall, 707/524-5445).

The gardens contain many of Burbank's horticultural creations and are open 8 A.M.–sunset every day. The museum and greenhouse, which include some of his tools and explain the significance of his work, are open April–October (10 A.M.–4 P.M. Tues.–Sun., $4). Guided tours are also available during the summer months.

Also open near Sebastopol is the 15-acre **Gold Ridge Experiment Farm,** where Burbank did many of his horticultural experiments and where there is still a historic collection of some of his creations (7781 Bodega Ave., Sebastopol, 707/829-7041, open year-round, cottage open Wed.). Take a self-guided hike or join a docent-lead tour (Apr.–Oct. by appointment).

Railroad Square

There's a hopping restaurant, shopping, and entertainment scene around the historic Railroad Square district in Santa Rosa, encompassing 3rd, 4th, and 5th Streets downtown, just west of the freeway. The center of the Railroad Square district is the **Northwestern Pacific Railroad Depot,** a small stone station house built in 1904 to replace an earlier wooden structure that burned down. Like many of the basalt stone buildings in the surrounding blocks, the depot is as solid as it looks and withstood the 1906 earthquake that leveled much of downtown Santa Rosa.

Its claim to fame was acting as a backdrop in the Alfred Hitchcock film *Shadow of a Doubt*, and is now home to the **Santa Rosa Convention & Visitors Bureau** (9 4th St., Santa Rosa, 707/577-8674 or 800/404-7673, 9 A.M.–5 P.M. Mon.–Sat., 11 A.M.–5 P.M. Sun.).

Pick up a historic walking map from the visitor's bureau to see some of the other historic buildings made from the locally quarried basalt stone. The buildings now house dozens of **antique stores** and other boutiques; 4th Street is particularly rich in historical storefronts. **Whistlestop Antiques** (130 4th St., Santa Rosa, 707/542-9474, 10 A.M.–5:30 P.M. Mon.–Sat., 11 A.M.–5 P.M. Sun.) is a collective of dozens of antique dealers worth visiting not least because of its antique building—a 1911 brick-and-steel building that won the city's first merit award for historical preservation and is typical of a lot of the surrounding edifices.

Museums

Being the region's biggest city, Santa Rosa also has some worthy cultural attractions. A few miles north of downtown Santa Rosa right next to the freeway is the nonprofit **Luther Burbank Center for the Arts** (50 Mark West Springs Rd., 707/546-3600, www.lbc.com), also handily located at the same freeway exit for River Road that leads into the heart of the Russian River Valley. In addition to the four theaters that host a wide range of music and theatrical performances, it is home to the **Sonoma Museum of Contemporary Art** (707/527-0297, open daily, main galleries Wed.–Sat. only). The MOCA, as it's known, claims to be the only museum between San Francisco and Portland, Oregon, dedicated to contemporary art. Although it has just four galleries and a couple of outdoor sculpture venues, it usually hosts about a dozen shows during the year featuring local and national artists.

A slightly offbeat cultural attraction is the **Charles M. Schulz Museum** (2301 Hardies Ln., off W. Steele Ln., 707/579-4452, www.schulzmuseum.org, closed Tues., $8), also slightly off the beaten track just north of downtown Santa Rosa, which might explain why visitor attendance has been a little lackluster

since it opened. You'd better like Snoopy if you come here as this museum is dedicated to the Snoopy creator, who lived in the city until his death in 2000. Exhibits of original cartoons by Schulz and his peers are on display alongside Snoopy-related art and other dog-related exhibits. The gift shop, of course, sells every conceivable Snoopy toy as well.

Being the biggest city in Sonoma County also means Santa Rosa is home to the **Sonoma Country Museum** (425 7th St., Santa Rosa, 707/579-1500, www.sonomacountymuseum.org, 11 A.M.–5 P.M. Wed.–Sun., $5). Permanent exhibits of historic artifacts and photos help tell the story of the county alongside temporary local art exhibits and an unlikely collection of art from the world-famous artists Christo and Jeanne-Claude that was donated to the museum in 2001 by their longtime assistant Tom Golden, who's from nearby Freestone.

ENTERTAINMENT

Santa Rosa has Railroad Square as its downtown entertainment hub, but Guerneville and its environs have probably the most diverse entertainment scene in the Russian River Valley, befitting the eclectic population that swells in the summer with an influx of both gay and straight revelers.

Much of Guerneville's nightlife caters to the gay scene with a curious mix of rustic bars enhanced with day-glo furnishings, all open late (and a few open unusually early, too) and all along a three-block stretch of Main Street downtown. **The Rainbow Cattle Company** (16220 Main St., 707/869-0206) is one of the oldest, with a big outdoor patio and legendary quarts of Long Island iced tea to get patrons in the mood. The poolside bar at the **Russian River Resort** (also known as the Triple-R) is also a popular drinking location for the gay masses (16390 4th St., 707/869-069).

About 15 minutes west on U.S. 116, Monte Rio is a sort of miniature Guerneville on acid, a self-proclaimed Vacation Wonderland with more going on than its scrappy cluster of downtown buildings suggests.

NORTHERN SONOMA FESTIVALS AND EVENTS

Whatever the time of year there's always some sort of festival or wine-related event going on in this part of the world.

January

Wineries have to think of something to bring in customers in the depths of winter. Hence the **Winter Wineland** event (707/433-4335, www.wineroad.com), held around the middle of the month. Over a hundred of the region's wineries take part. For the ticket price of $30 visitors get the VIP treatment and samples of limited-release wines. There's even a special designated-driver ticket price of $5.

March

The region's annual **Barrel Tasting** (707/433-4335, www.wineroad.com) is a great excuse to visit as many wineries as possible in a day and sample wines straight from the barrel, whether you're interested in buying wine futures or not. Just turn up at a participating winery and buy the official glass for $5, and all tasting is then free. Held on the first weekend of the month.

April

The **Passport to Dry Creek Valley,** held on the last weekend of the month, gets visitors into almost every winery in the valley, even those usually open by appointment only. Every one of them has some sort of theme for the weekend and puts on quite a party, with plenty of food and, of course, wine. The mock passports are stamped at every winery and cost about $100 for the weekend, though numbers are limited so book early. Contact the Winegrowers of Dry Creek Valley for more information (707/433-3031, www.wdcv.com).

May

At the end of the month Healdsburg gets in on the festival action with the **Healdsburg Country Fair,** a weekend-long celebration of the town's community (707/433-1014, www.healdsburg.org). And on Memorial Day weekend, the town's antique sellers set up shop on the plaza for the **Healdsburg Antique Fair** (707/433-1014, www.healdsburg.org).

June

Before wine there was the Wild West, which is celebrated every year at the **Russian River Rodeo,** held the first weekend of the month at the Duncans Mills Rodeo, a 15-minute drive west of Guerneville (707/869-1959).

The town's **Pink Elephant Bar** (9895 Main St., Monte Rio, 707/865-0500, open all day every day) is known to some as simply The Pink and has been a Monte Rio institution for almost half a century. Once a magnet for leather-clad bikers, it is now just as much a magnet for dive-bar aficionados and serves cocktails and local microbrews.

Hard to miss is the brightly painted, neon-signed hump of the **Rio Theater** (20396 Bohemian Hwy., at Hwy. 116, Monte Rio, 707/865-0913, www.riotheater.com, daily in summer, Wed.–Sun. in winter), an old WWII-era Quonset hut, one of 170,000 churned out for emergency housing and warehousing in the 1940s. The theater now shows a program of current films that would put any big-city independent theater to shame. The week-

The **Russian River Blues Festival** in mid-June is the first of two riverside music festivals that bring world-renowned musicians to the beach in Guerneville. Tickets for the weekend event are available beginning in January from the festival organizers (510/655-9471, www.russianriverbluesfest.com). The best seats go early.

July
The big blowout wine event of the year is the **Sonoma County Showcase of Food and Wine,** a three-day wine, food, and arts extravaganza held around the middle of the month at the region's wineries. The main event is the **Taste of Sonoma County,** which is usually held at a winery near Healdsburg. Tickets cost $150 and are available from the Sonoma County Wineries Foundation (707/586-3795, www.sonomawine.com).

August
They named a highway after this apple, so why not have a festival in its honor as well? The **Gravenstein Apple Fair** in Sebastopol is held around the middle of the month at the town's Ragle Ranch Park. It celebrates the increasingly rare little apple that is still grown in orchards along the nearby Gravenstein Highway. The event includes music, crafts, and plenty of apple-flavored fun (800/207-9464, www.farmtrails.org).

September
The **Russian River Food and Wine Fest** is an unashamedly commercial affair in Guerneville celebrating the region's food and wine, with cooking demonstrations and plenty of local artisan food and wine producers. Usually held on the last weekend of the month (707/869-9474, www.russianriverfoodandwinefest.com).

Celebrate the end of summer on the beach in Guerneville at the **Russian River Jazz Festival,** usually held the weekend after Labor Day. Top jazz musicians, fine wine, late summer sun, and the option of simply floating on the river all combine to make a unique experience. Tickets for the weekend event are available starting in January from the festival organizers (510/655-9471, www.jazzontheriver.com).

November
With all the creative names for food and wine events apparently exhausted for the year, this month's reason to eat and drink to excess is called simply **A Food & Wine Affair.** Many of the region's wineries match their wines with all sorts of food on the first weekend of the month. All you have to do is get from one winery to another. Tickets (about $40) and information are available from the Russian River Wine Road (707/433-4335, www.wineroad.com).

end matinees ($5.50) start late afternoon and the main daily show time is 7 P.M. in winter, 7:30 P.M. in summer ($7.50). Check the website or call the theater for the regularly changing schedules.

If you think a movie theater satiates the cultural requirements of tiny Monte Rio, think again. Monte Rio is also home to an active nonprofit theater group, the **Pega-** sus Theater Company, established in 1998 by some veteran regional actors. It puts on plays and readings during the year, most from well-known playwrights (except the holiday variety show). Each runs for about six weeks at the 90-seat Pegasus Theater (20347 Hwy. 116, Monte Rio, 707/522-9043, www.pegasustheater.com). Call for the seasonal schedule.

RECREATION

Two big wilderness areas, miles of river, tracts of forest, and a limited population make almost any sort of outdoor pursuit possible in the Russian River Valley, whether on land, water, or in the air.

Armstrong Redwoods State Reserve

This 805-acre reserve is just a few miles up Armstrong Woods Road from the center of Guerneville and is, as its name suggests, home to some neck-twistingly tall redwoods. The shady and damp forest provides welcome relief from the summer heat and is now the largest remaining old-growth redwood forest in Sonoma.

Some of its trees survived the region's vast 19th-century logging operations and were ironically saved by a lumberman—Colonel James Armstrong—who bought the land in the 1870s to preserve the last tracts of the very same forest he profited from.

Visitors with little time or energy can make a short trek on groomed paths from one of the three parking lots to some fine redwood specimens, including the 308-foot-tall Armstrong Tree, which is believed to be about 1,400 years old. If craning your neck is too strenuous, relax at one of the picnic tables scattered among the trees.

The more adventurous can choose from any number of longer hikes up out of the redwoods to the oak and madrone forests on the ridges higher up and continue on into the **Austin Creek State Recreation Area,** which is north of the reserve.

One such hike is a relatively quick loop (2.2 miles) that illustrates the wide range of vegetation and microclimates. The **East Ridge Trail** climbs steeply from just behind the visitor center up to a warm ridge that ducks in and out of the sun before descending back into the redwoods (head down the hill at the first signposted trail junction or the hike will become a half-day ordeal). Once back in the redwoods it's an easy walk down the road or the **Pioneer Trail** back to the visitor center.

Redwoods are almost as common as vines in the Russian River Valley.

Another moderate loop is the 2.3-mile **Pool Ridge Trail,** which climbs 500 feet up a series of switchbacks before looping back down into the forest.

The reserve is open sunrise to sunset and there's a $4 day-use fee for cars. Alternatively, park at the visitor center (17020 Armstrong Woods Rd., Guerneville, 707/869-2958, open 11 A.M.–3 P.M.) and walk in on the road or a trail to avoid the fee. Dogs and bikes are not allowed on any trails. For more information, call 707/869-2015.

Austin Creek State Recreation Area

More adventurous outdoorsy types might want to drive straight through the Armstrong reserve up the steep, switchback road (no trailers and vehicles over 20 feet) to this 5,700-acre wilderness with 20 miles of hiking trails, chaparral and oak woodlands, rolling hills, meandering creeks, and scenic campgrounds (17000 Armstrong Woods Rd., 707/869-2015, day use $6).

The road ends at the **Bullfrog Pond** campground but stops at several trailheads on the way up, including the **Gilliam Creek Trail,** which dives down to Schoolhouse Creek and toward a handful of primitive, creekside campgrounds. The closest of these is almost four miles, so allow plenty of time.

Horseback riding is allowed on all of the Austin Creek trails, but unless you own your own horse the only option for getting on one is with **Armstrong Woods Pack Station** concession (707/887-2939, www.redwoodhorses.com), which operates by reservation only from down in the Armstrong Redwoods reserve. Short, two-hour rides to full-day trips are available year-round (weather permitting) from $60, and fully catered, overnight rides, with camping at one of Austin Creek's primitive campgrounds, costs $250. There's usually a four-person minimum for the rides, though if there are not enough riders booked there is also the option of a two-person private ride for double the normal price.

The Russian River

With the Russian River gently snaking through the vineyards and forests towards the sea, it's not surprising that **canoeing and kayaking** are popular summer activities here. The river flow is relatively smooth this far downstream, even in the winter when the water is higher and faster, so don't expect any adrenaline-pumping rapids. Do expect to have to slather on the sunscreen on a hot summer day, however, and not to care if you tip over and take an unexpected dip in the river.

The least strenuous way to experience the river's meandering pace is to rent a canoe at **Burkes Canoe Trips** (8600 River Rd., Forestville, 707/887-1222, www.burkescanoetrips.com, May–Oct., $50 a day). Paddle or simply float 10 miles downriver, stopping at the many secluded beaches along the way, to Guerneville, where courtesy shuttles run back to base every half hour all day long.

For a slightly more strenuous option involving real "sit on top" touring kayaks rather than the glorified aluminum cans that most places rent go to **Russian River Outfitters,** farther downstream in the old logging town of Duncans

Mills, about five miles west of Guerneville (behind the old railway depot building on Moscow Rd., 707/865-9080). From here it is six miles to the ocean at Jenner, where a shuttle can pick you up by prior arrangement, or simply paddle upstream to the beach at Monte Rio and back.

Single kayaks cost from $45 for a half day and doubles from $65. This less-populated section of the river downstream from Guerneville is where you're less likely to see garbage and old tires, and more likely to see some of the river's wildlife, including otters, herons, and an occasional turtle sunning itself.

Kayaks and canoes can also be rented for one day or more from **Kings Sport & Tackle** in Guerneville (16258 Main St., 707/869-2156, open daily). Single kayaks cost $30 a day, doubles are $45, and aluminum canoes cost $50. From Guerneville's Johnson's Beach it's four miles to Monte Rio downstream or eight miles to Forestville upstream. Make it a round-trip or pay $15 for the store to send a shuttle for pickup or dropoff (9 A.M.–2 P.M. only).

Fishing for the river's bass, bluegill, catfish, and winter salmon is also popular from a rented canoe or one of the many beaches, though a California fishing license is required. Two-day and longer licenses can be bought at Kings Sport & Tackle in Guerneville (which also rents fishing equipment) and most other tackle shops in the area. Also ask about the myriad rules and regulations. Barbed hooks can not be used, for example, and only artificial lures (no bait) are allowed during the summer.

Ballooning

While not as plentiful as in the Napa Valley area, there are still plenty of opportunities to take to the air in this part of the Wine Country, and, arguably, the aerial views of vineyards, mountains, rivers, forests, and the distant ocean are more impressive than in less scenically diverse Napa.

Taking to the air in Wine Country, of course, usually means ballooning, which entails getting up before the crack of dawn (balloons usually take off not long after sunrise), spending several hundred dollars, waiting

RUSSIAN RIVER BEACHES

It can get hot in this part of Sonoma in the summer—too hot for even a crisp, chilled chardonnay to provide relief. Luckily, the cool waters of the Russian River are a short drive away, though perhaps best experienced without being inebriated.

Native Americans had a good name for the river—Long Snake—and as it snakes its way down the Alexander Valley, past Healdsburg, and into the Russian River Valley there are ample opportunities to take a dip.

In summer the river is a relatively meek body of water compared to the swift torrent it can become in the winter and spring, fed by the rains and melting snow hundred of miles away in the mountains. Don't be fooled, though: It's still fairly cold with plenty of hidden obstacles underwater.

In the Alexander Valley west of Geyserville on Highway 128 is the **Geyserville Bridge,** with space for a few cars to park off the side of the road at both ends. The easiest way down to the river is a short trail at the southwest end of the bridge that leads down to a gravelly beach area and stretches for quite a ways downstream.

A better place for swimming is **Memorial Beach** at the southern end of Healdsburg, just across the Memorial Bridge. This is a more family-friendly beach with a swimming lagoon and concession stands for renting canoes. There's a $5 fee for parking in the lot, which can fill up quickly in the summer. Finding free parking any-

Take a dip in the cool Russian River on a hot summer day.

© PHILIP GOLDSMITH

around as the balloon is set up, and having little idea of which way it will actually drift once it does get airborne. Almost everyone thinks the reward, however, is worth it, as the initial adrenaline surge from lifting off yields to a sense of relaxation from being in a still and silent world thousands of feet above the stress of daily life.

Flights usually last about an hour, but expect the whole experience, including a complimentary post-flight brunch, to take up about half a day. Also expect to have to make reservations up to a month in advance during the summer.

Aerostat Adventures (707/433-3777 or 800/579-0183, www.aerostat-adventures.com, $210/person) flies from either the giant parking lot of J Vineyards & Winery or the Sonoma County airport near Santa Rosa. **Up and Away** (707/836-0171 or 800/711-2998,

www.up-away.com, $195/person) meets passengers at the Sonoma County airport, though balloons may take off elsewhere, depending on the weather. Both companies balloons fly year-round and usually carry 6–8 people, though private flights can also be arranged.

Golf

Stroll among the redwoods without donning hiking boots at the **Northwood Golf Club** in Monte Rio, just west of Guerneville where near the beach is tough. The best alternative is to park on 1st Street in Healdsburg and walk.

As the river winds its way down into the Russian River Valley, the beaches become more plentiful and some of the visitors less modest. Don't be surprised at the occasional nude sunbather, especially at some of the more secluded sunning spots.

The historic **Wohler Bridge** on Wohler Road (just off the southern end of the Westside Rd.) has a small parking lot and boat ramp at the north end of the bridge and some limited parking along the road. The beach here is a mixture of sand and gravel, and it's possible to walk farther up- and downstream for privacy.

Continue south on Wohler Road, turning right on River Road, and about a mile up on the right is the entrance to **Steelhead Beach** ($4 day-use fee). The large parking lot and boat ramp at the main beach hint at the spot's popularity for fishing and canoeing. A couple of half-mile trails from the parking area lead to a more secluded stretch of beach better for swimming.

Farther along River Road, just west of the junction with Westside Road, is **Sunset Beach** (also known as Hacienda Beach), a popular spot with locals but easy to miss. Look for tiny Sunset Avenue off the south side of River Road next to a cluster of old wooden buildings. Parking on Sunset is illegal unless you live there, but there's usually plenty of space on the wide shoulder along River Road. At the first bend in Sunset, a dusty trail off to the right leads down to a wide, gravelly beach and a good swimming hole.

Another good family beach is **Johnson's Beach** in the middle of Guerneville, just a few hundred yards off Main Street, where a makeshift dam is set up each summer to create a lagoon for swimming or paddling around in a rented canoe. It's crowded in summer, but the big parking lot is free and the food plentiful. The beach is also the site of the town's Fourth of July bash and the annual Jazz on the River festival.

(19400 Hwy. 116, Monte Rio, 707/865-1116 or 800/330-1167). The historic par-36, 9-hole course was conceived by members of the exclusive gentlemen's retreat, the Bohemian Club Grove, just across the road, designed by famous course architect Alistair McKenzie (who also designed the Augusta National course) and completed in 1928. Weekend greens fees start at $20 for 9 holes, $30 for 18.

Russian River Spas

The spa destination in the Russian River Valley is as alternative as its remote location on the Bohemian Highway just south of Occidental suggests. The mud baths at **Osmosis** (209 Bohemian Hwy., Occidental, 707/823-8231, www.osmosis.com, open daily) are of the dry variety, in which hundreds of enzymes are mixed with rice bran and ground up evergreen leaves to ferment the impurities out of the skin.

The warm, relaxing treatment is best enjoyed before consuming the local fermented grape juice, however, otherwise an early hangover might be the only result. The enzyme baths cost from $65 and include a pretreatment tea service in the peaceful Zen garden. Massages and facials are also available to complete the rejuvenation process.

ACCOMMODATIONS

The main city in these parts is Santa Rosa, and it has perhaps more rooms than any other town, although mostly in chain hotels. But the bohemian resort town of Guerneville and the surrounding area offer the widest range of accommodations, from so-called river resorts that have seen better days to some classier and reasonably priced inns and B&Bs.

As usual, camping is by far the cheapest

option, and there's plenty of the great outdoors to choose from, including the wilds of the backcountry and the relative comforts of the grounds of some of those resorts along the river.

If all else fails there are usually rooms to be found in the string of motels along the freeway and to the south in Sebastopol. Just be sure to drink a glass of wine to remember that this is indeed Wine Country and not some random freeway exit to Anywhere, U.S.A.

Under $100

The **Creekside Inn** (16180 Neely Rd., Guerneville, 707/869-3623, www.creeksideinn.com) is indeed right beside the creek otherwise known as the Russian River. It is just a few minutes' stroll to Guerneville's main street but also even closer to noisy Highway 116. Nevertheless, the rooms in the main house are cheap, starting at $90 for those with rather plain furnishings and increasing to $175 for the more sumptuously decorated suites that also have their own decks. The several acres of grounds also include a pool and eight cottages, from studios to two-bedrooms, starting at $130 a night.

Rather like a funky Guerneville version of an 1830s resort, **Fern Grove Cottages** (16650 Hwy. 116, Guerneville, 707/869-8105, www.ferngrove.com) offers equal measures of tranquillity and activity among the redwoods at the far western end of town. The collection of well-spaced cottages includes studio, one-bedroom, and two-bedroom accommodations starting at less than $80 a night, plus some twists including wet bars, hot tubs, and fireplaces. They are relative bargains, though the somewhat sparse decor is a reminder that they were originally built in the 1920s for a cheap family resort. On-site amenities include a pool, bar, and giant picnic area that's a hive of activity in the summer.

The **Rio Inn** (4444 Wood Rd., Guerneville, 707/869-4444 or 800/344-7018, www.rioinn.com) is a mock-Tudor pile that harks back to 1600s England but was actually built in the 1890s. It was once the main lodge of one

of the first of the big destination resorts in this region, and center of the music and dance scene in the tiny forest hamlet of Rio Nido from the 1920s right up the era of the Grateful Dead and beyond. The offbeat collection of rooms mix Ye Olde furnishings (with a heavy Victorian rather than Tudor influence) with modern conveniences and start at under $100 for the six smaller downstairs rooms. The four deluxe rooms upstairs cost upward of $130 a night. Common areas include a parlor, library, and pub, with a couple of friendly cats and plenty of pub games.

$100–200

In a pretty part of the valley en route to Armstrong Redwoods State Reserve is the very affordable **Retreat Resort and Spa** (14711 Armstrong Woods Rd., Guerneville, 707/869-2706 or 888/739-3529, www.retreatresort.biz). It's all minimalist and modern here, a refreshing change from the sometimes tacky older resorts of downtown Guerneville a mile away. The resort also hosts several major wine-related events and has its own wine-tasting program. Rates start at less than $150 for standard rooms and rise to around $200 for the small suites. Add around $100 to indulge in one of the many spa treatments, or simply lie by the pool for free.

A few miles west of Guerneville in Monte Rio is the **Village Inn** (20822 River Blvd., off Bohemian Hwy., Monte Rio, 707/865-2304 or 800/303-2303, www.villageinn-ca.com), a tastefully restored Victorian home set in the redwoods on the south bank of the river not far from the infamous Bohemian Grove, an exclusive country club for America's elite and powerful. All 11 rooms have private bathrooms and a view of something, whether trees or the river. The bargains here are 22, 24, and 26 (all $135 a night), which have club chairs and views of the river from their balconies. The cheapest rooms start at $95, while the most expensive deluxe king studio ($165) has a big private deck.

Standing sentinel at a sharp bend in Wohler Road just half a mile south of Wohler Bridge is the historic **M̄ Raford House** (10630 Wohler

Rd., Healdsburg, 707/887-9573 or 800/887-9503, www.rafordhouse.com), once part of a huge hop-growing estate in its Victorian heyday but now overlooking acres of vineyards. All six rooms have private bathrooms and are decorated in a tasteful and fairly restrained Victorian style. The smallest of the six start at $140 a night, while the biggest rooms ($175 and up) have their own fireplaces. The largest of all, the Bridal Room, also has a private covered porch overlooking the valley. Rooms at the front of the house have the best views but also a view (and the noise) of the road.

One of the larger non-chain hotels in Santa Rosa is the **Hotel La Rose** (308 Wilson St., Santa Rosa, 707/579-3200 or 800/527-6738, www.hotellarose.com), an imposing basalt stone building that's part of the historic Railroad Square development downtown, within walking distance of many of the city's sights and restaurants. The 49 rooms in the main building and Carriage House across the street (built in 1985) cater to the tourist and business crowd alike so are well equipped and business-like with minimal frills to the Victorian-style decor. Standard rooms start at about $130, and top floor rooms in both buildings are the most interesting with either vaulted or sloping ceilings.

Over $200

A bit like staying on a French country wine estate, the **Vintners Inn** (4350 Barnes Rd., Santa Rosa, 707/575-7350 or 800/421-2584, www.vintnersinn.com) sprawls amid 50 acres of manicured gardens and vineyards just a few miles north of Santa Rosa. It's ideally located for exploring the Russian River Valley, and quick access to the freeway (River Road exit) gives easy access to Healdsburg and beyond (though also some freeway noise). All 44 rooms and suites are cozy and luxurious, some with fireplaces and all with either balconies or patios. Special deals often push prices below $200 and breakfast is always included. Alternatively, indulge in a sumptuous brunch at the renowned **John Ash & Co.** restaurant, one of the eateries credited with starting the Californian "Wine Country cuisine" style of cooking that so many other restaurants now mimic.

A little off the beaten wine tracks is the neat, former railroad town of Occidental, and just off the main road on the edge of the forest is a delightfully rambling Victorian homestead that is now the ⚄ **Inn at Occidental,** a quirky yet luxurious bed-and-breakfast (3657 Church St., Occidental, 707/874-1047, www.innatoccidental.com). None of the 16 whimsical rooms and suites are alike, though all have fireplaces and are stuffed with odd pieces of folk art, as are many of the inn's common areas. Rates drop below $200 for a few of the smaller rooms during the winter, but most usually cost $200–300 a night.

A little piece of the Mediterranean landed in the redwoods just south of Guerneville in the form of the **Applewood Inn** (13555 Hwy. 116, Guerneville, 707/869-9093 or 800/555-8509, www.applewoodinn.com). Nestled around a manicured central courtyard are three salmon-pink villas, the oldest of which is the 1922 Belden House. It has the cheapest (and smallest) rooms, starting at under $200. The more modern Piccola Casa and Gate House, built since 1996, both contain the bigger and more expensive rooms costing over $300 a night. At those prices, the tranquil surroundings, swimming pool, in-room luxuries, and available spa therapies are to be expected. The big building at one end of the courtyard also houses an outstanding restaurant offering classy Mediterranean-influenced Californian food and an extensive local wine list. Alternatively, order one of the gourmet picnic baskets for $50 and head to the hills.

Just a stone's throw from the Russian River, tucked away in the woods just off busy River Road, is the **Farmhouse Inn and Restaurant** (7871 River Rd., Forestville, 707/887-3300 or 800/464-6642, www.farmhouseinn.com). Brightly painted cottages house the eight rooms that start at less than $200 a night for the smallest (rooms 3 and 5) and go up to more than $300 for the largest suite with its own fireplace and sauna. The inn started an expansion in 2005 that more than doubles

Northern Sonoma

the number of cottages and modernize the rather worn-out rooms. Expect prices to increase as a result.

Camping

There are plenty of resort campgrounds along the Russian River, but many cater to summer crowds and RVs, and usually charge a premium price for the extensive services and facilities they offer. In all cases, reservations are essential during the busy summer months.

One of the more reasonable is **Burkes Canoe Trips** (8600 River Road., Forestville, 707/887-1222), hidden in the redwoods right next to the river (and the road) just north of Forestville. The full-service campground, open May–October, has 60 sites for tents or RVs for $20 a night. This is also a popular place to rent canoes (see *Recreation*). The year-round **Hilton Park Family Campground** (10750 River Rd., Forestville, 707/887-9206, www.hiltonparkcampground.com) is one of the smaller of the riverside resort campgrounds, with 49 open or secluded sites for tents ($32 per night or $37 for the premium riverside sites) and small RVs ($42), all in a lush, woodsy setting. There are also eight "camping cottages" that just about sleep two people and have space for a tent outside, but cost a relatively expensive $65 per night.

The more scenic campgrounds are generally off the beaten track—well off the beaten track in the case of the primitive but scenic creekside campgrounds high up in the **Austin Creek State Recreation Area.** The road up into the park through Armstrong Redwoods State Reserve ends at the **Bullfrog Pond Campground,** with 23 sites ($15 a night), toilets, and drinking water. No vehicles over 20 feet long are allowed into the park, so the camping experience here is relatively free of humming RVs.

From Bullfrog Pond it's about a three-mile hike to the **Tom King Trail** and **Gilliam Creek Trail** primitive campgrounds, and about four miles to **Manning Flat** campground. A water purifier or filter is essential if you want to drink the creek water, which you probably will in the summer when it can get very hot. The required backcountry camping permits ($15 a night on a first-come, first-served basis), together with maps, can be picked up at the Armstrong Redwoods park office (17020 Armstrong Woods Rd, Guerneville, 707/869-2958, 11 A.M.–3 P.M.) on the way up into the Austin Creek area.

FOOD

The food scene in the Russian River Valley is one of the most varied in northern Sonoma, as would be expected from a place that is effectively the produce basket of Northern California's Wine Country.

It certainly has its share of pricey, stylish establishments, particular in the many inns hidden away in the woods. But since it's a down-to-earth, outdoorsy sort of place there are also plenty of cheap and homey establishments where the lack of an uptight reservation system can make the experience instantly relaxing.

Along the River

Being the hub of the region, Guerneville should be the first stop for those desperate for a quick and easy meal. There might be a bit of a wait in the busy summer months, particularly on festival weekends, but there are plenty of places to cater to the ravenous hordes.

This is also not a five-star resort town, so don't expect five-star restaurants. Instead most places are the caliber of the landmark **River Inn Restaurant** (16141 Main St., 707/869-0481), with its cozy booths, acres of Formica, hunks of ham, and piles of pancakes.

One of the few saviors of beer drinkers in this part of Wine Country is the **Stumptown Brewery and Smokehouse** just east of Guerneville in Rio Nido (15045 River Rd., 707/869-0705, lunch and dinner Fri.–Sun, dinner weekdays, closed Tues.), which serves juicy ribs, brisket, and sandwiches for less than $15. Its heady microbrews, like Red Rocket and Racer 5, will get you drunk as fast as their names suggest.

A California town would not be complete without its cheap Mexican restaurant, and one of Guerneville's most popular is the spacious **Taqueria la Tapatia** at the western end of town (16632 River Rd., 707/869-1821, lunch and dinner daily). It's right next door to **Spliffs Organic Espresso** (16626 River Rd., Guerneville, 707/869-2230). Only in Guerneville can hemp, organics, and coffee be inspiration for a name (and a big sign), though don't expect anything more potent than caffeine in the coffee.

Coffee, sandwiches, and other snacks are also available at the **Coffee Bazaar,** just round the corner from Main Street (14045 Armstrong Woods Rd., Guerneville, 707/869-9706, open 6 A.M.–8 P.M. daily). The cool cavernous hangout is about as laid-back as things get in this part of the world, and there's also a fascinating little used bookstore to browse through right next door.

Though Guerneville seems to be the town of big grills and bigger hunks of meat, the vegetarian restaurant **Sparks** (16248 Main St., Guerneville, 707/869-8206, lunch weekdays except in winter, lunch and dinner weekends, dinner entrées $12–17) does its bit to even things out with its gourmet, animal-friendly food.

Just south of Guerneville things get classier and more romantic at the **Ⓜ Applewood Inn** (13555 Hwy. 116, Guerneville, 707/869-9093 or 800/555-8509, dinner daily, dinner entrées $20–28). Seasonal dishes like braised rabbit with olives and Humboldt Fog cheese are inspired by local produce and classic French cooking. As would be expected, the wine list is a who's who of local growers and regularly wins *Wine Spectator*'s Award of Excellence. Although the place is open every night, it might close early during the winter if no one turns up.

East of Guerneville, the restaurant at the luxurious **Farmhouse Inn and Restaurant** (7871 River Rd. Forestville, 707/887-3300 or 800/464-6642, www.farmhouseinn.com, dinner Thurs.–Sun., dinner entrées $23–30) lets the veritable treasure trove of local produce do the talking, with dishes like oven-roasted bluenose sea bass, or roasted red kuri squash and mascarpone ravioli. At over $25 for most main courses, however, it will be the credit card doing the talking at the end of the evening.

Part of an eclectic little winery is the Greek-themed **Topolos at Russian River Vineyards** (5700 Hwy. 116, Forestville, 707/887-1562, lunch and dinner daily but closed Mon.–Tues. in winter, dinner entrées $12–21), just outside Forestville. Even simple lunchtime sandwiches get the Greek treatment (turkey club lavosh), and dinner dishes like chicken saltimbocca co-exist alongside more traditional grilled New York steaks. Make an appointment for a tour of the winery before lunch, then try some of the wines with a meal on the patio.

About a 15-mile drive west of Guerneville in the two-block hamlet of Duncans Mills are several restaurants that fill the gap between most of Guerneville's down-home eateries and the pricier, upscale dining at the local inns.

Seafood is a dominant theme at the **Blue Heron Inn** (hard to miss at 25300 Steelhead Blvd., 707/865-9135, lunch and dinner Tues.–Sun., dinner entrées $15–21). It has a tavern menu of appetizers and sandwiches, most under $15, and a bistro-style dinner menu with main courses like roasted game hen and gourmet fish and chips accompanied by wine or a decent selection of local microbrews.

Just over the main road on the town's only other block is the **Cape Fear Café** (25191 Hwy. 116, 707/865-9246, lunch and dinner daily, dinner entrées $16–24), where seafood meets soul food. Many dishes have a Cajun twist and the grits make a brunch here worth a drive.

A scenic place to grab a bite halfway between Guerneville and Duncans Mills is the **Village Inn Restaurant** in Monte Rio (20822 River Blvd., off Bohemian Hwy., Monte Rio, 707/865-2304, dinner Wed.–Sun., entrées $14–25). The beautifully restored building and its dining patio peek out from the redwoods onto the banks of the river. Most of the bistro-style main courses are well under $20 and can be washed down by wine from the award-winning list.

Away from the River

What was once the much-loved Willowside Café reopened in 2002 as **ZaZu** (3535 Guerneville Rd., Santa Rosa, 707/523-4814, dinner Wed.–Sun., brunch weekends, dinner entrées $16–25), a stylish, compact roadhouse about three miles east of Graton that serves California-inspired, Northern Italian cuisine. Enjoy familiar seasonal dishes with special touches, like flat-iron steak with Point Reyes blue cheese ravioli ($23), at copper-topped tables overlooking the vineyards.

In nearby Graton is the **Underwood Bar & Bistro** (9113 Graton Rd., just west of Hwy. 116, 707/823-7023, lunch Tues.–Sat., dinner Tues.–Sun.), where dark wood and a nickel-plated bar add some unique texture to the interior. The Mediterranean-inspired menu features tapas plates (the oysters are popular) and main dishes like Catalan fish stew and Moroccan-spiced lamb ($20).

Across the road (and sharing the same owners) is a rustic, local gathering spot, the **Willow Wood Market Café** (9020 Graton Rd., 707/823-0233, open daily until 9 P.M.), which also doubles as a country store. A well-priced breakfast, lunch, and limited dinner menu is available, and the polenta is legendary in these parts. It is becoming a victim of its own success, however, with lines that snake out of the door on the busiest lunchtimes, though the back patio provides a bit more space.

Sebastopol is chock-full of places to eat though many of them cater to Bay Area urban overspill and don't particularly stand out. A few are worth navigating the town's one-way system to visit, however.

Wine is the main attraction at the **Appellations Wine Bar** (6761 Sebastopol Ave. or Hwy. 12, in the Gravenstein Station mall, 707/829-7791, Tues.–Sun. nights), but the many small plates costing less than $10 might be enough to satisfy as you explore the fascinating wine list from the comfort of a booth in this gloriously decorated old rail car.

If something more filling is needed, the popular **Ⓜ K&L Bistro** (119 S. Main St., 707/823-6614, lunch Tues.–Sat., dinner Tues.–Sun., dinner entrées $15–25) serves classic French-style bistro food, including french fries that are probably the best in Wine Country. Equally suited to the relaxed, cheerful setting is K&L's famous mac and cheese.

The Occidental Italian

Picture-postcard Occidental would, at first glance, seem to be the sort of town teeming with celebrated chefs ready to turn its sleepy Victorian charm into the next big Wine Country food destination. Instead the rural counterculture is alive and well here and so, evidently, is the Italian culture. There are almost as many Italian restaurants here as organic-labeled eateries and services (organic housecleaning, anyone?).

Find mountains of cheap, Italian comfort food and surroundings in need of some updating at **Negri's** (3700 Main St., 707/823-5301, lunch and dinner daily), the historic **Union Hotel** (3731 Main St., 707/874-3555, lunch and dinner daily), which also curiously offers free overnight RV parking with dinner, and the **Howard Street Café** (3611 Main St., 707/874-2838, breakfast and lunch daily).

Even the tiny, organic **Naked Lady Café** (3782 Main St., 707/874-2408, dinner Wed.–Sun., brunch weekends) serves Italian-inspired dinners and brunches, including crispy pizzas

the unofficial mayor of Occidental

© PHILIP GOLDSMITH

from a wood-fired oven. Naked in this case refers to the simplicity of the organic food rather than the state of the owner.

The Santa Rosa Scene

With vast expanses of Wine Country to explore, there are few reasons to head into Santa Rosa. One, however, is the city's burgeoning restaurant scene, which might eventually persuade people to linger for longer downtown.

Some of the best restaurants are around the historic Railroad Square development near downtown. The location was obviously inspiration when naming **La Gare** (208 Wilson St., 707/528-4355, dinner Wed.–Sun.), which serves simple, reasonably priced French-Swiss food in a setting of starched white tablecloths (the French influence) and mountain ambience (from Switzerland).

Sassafras Restaurant & Wine Bar (1229 N. Dutton Ave. 707/578-7600, lunch weekdays, dinner daily, dinner entrées $16–23) adds some spice to a somewhat featureless setting in the Santa Rosa Business Park and combines an extensive menu of small plates, pizzas, and main courses (most less than $20), many with a Caribbean or Cuban twist. The huge wine list is dominated by Northern Californian wines.

One of the oldest of the destination restaurants in the area is **Mixx Restaurant & Bar** (135 4th St., 707/573-1344, lunch Mon.–Fri, dinner Mon.–Sat., dinner entrées $13–22), which mixes up Californian cuisine with some international edginess—an Asian hint here or Caribbean twist there—all accompanied by a wine list blessed by *Wine Spectator* magazine that emphasizes smaller Californian wineries. Or bring your own wine on Tuesday when there is no corkage fee.

As the French grape varietal syrah is becomes more popular in Northern California it seems only fitting that the French-American restaurant **Syrah** (205 5th St., 707/568-4002, lunch and dinner Tues.–Sat., dinner entrées $17–28) found its roots and is now a popular fixture in Santa Rosa with an impressive cheese menu. Not surprisingly, syrah and shiraz dominate the red wine portion of the wine list, but there

Northern Sonoma

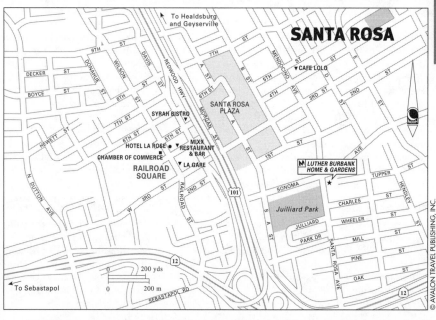

are plenty of other Californian and international wines to choose from, all well-priced.

One of the most popular new restaurants on the Santa Rosa scene is **Café Lolo** (620 5th St. 707/576-7822, lunch Mon.–Fri., dinner Mon.–Sat. until 9:30 P.M., dinner entrées $14–23). It would be at home almost anywhere in Napa or Sonoma with its cool, sophisticated decor and stylish Californian food inspired by local seasonal produce. The wine list does not include a huge number of locals but is otherwise well priced.

During the day, the schizophrenic **Creekside Bistro** (2800 4th St., Santa Rosa, 707/575-8839) belongs to all-American Hank, who flips burgers and pancakes, and pours coffee in a relaxed diner atmosphere that seems to best suit the bland suburban building. When Hank goes home in the evening, it becomes **Emile's Creekside Bistro** (dinner Wed.–Sun., entrées $14–20) and chef Emile Waldteufel takes things up a notch or two with his moderately priced French country dishes like confit of duck with baby spinach and gorgonzola, and stuffed ballottine of chicken. This is when reservations are recommended.

Just north of Santa Rosa, **Willi's Wine Bar** (4404 Old Redwood Hwy., just south of River Rd., 707/526-3096, lunch and dinner Wed.–Mon., dinner only Sun., $7–15) is another player in the burgeoning small plate scene, where sipping wine or cocktails is as much a part of the fun as eating. Willi's shares the same owners as Willi's Seafood and Raw Bar in Healdsburg and has a relaxed, new-age ambience that creates a perfect backdrop for the globally inspired small dishes, few of which are over $10. There are so many dishes to choose from that they almost outnumber the wines.

Picnic Supplies

There is no shortage of supermarkets, including organic ones, in most of the region's towns, but a few smaller stores are worth searching out for some more unusual options.

The **Korbel Delicatessen** (13250 River Rd., Guerneville, 707/824-7313, open daily), right next door to the winery's tasting room,

makes fat sandwiches and gourmet salads to go. Eat on the small deck outside or head off into the wilds. The **Kozlowski Farms** store in Forestville (5566 Hwy. 116, 707/887-1587, www.kozlowskifarms.com, open daily), hidden down a driveway a few yards north of Ross Station Road, has a deli and offers a different kind of tasting—the countless jams, jellies, sauces, and chutneys it makes.

The **Duncan's Mills Wine and Cheese Company** (25179 Hwy. 116, 707/865-0565) is the first little building on the north side of the road from Guerneville, next to the cows, and offers not only a great selection of local wines (with regular tastings) but also an equally impressive selection of local cheeses. Just a few yards farther, **Duncan's Mills General Store** (25200 Hwy. 116, 707/865-1240) is where your remaining picnic supplies can be found.

And in Guerneville, almost thumbing its nose at neighboring Safeway, is the little organic grocery store **Food for Humans** (on 1st St. at Mill St., 707/869-3612), an eminently better place to buy produce.

There is also no shortage of tranquil places to have a picnic, from the beaches of the Russian River to the shade of the redwoods at the Armstrong Redwoods State Reserve just north of Guerneville. Or head to one of the many picnic-friendly wineries and pick up a bottle of wine to go with lunch. Some of the better picnicking wineries include Davis Bynum, Hop Kiln, Iron Horse, and Foppiano.

Farmers Markets

With so many small towns in this agricultural region there's a farmers market almost every day of the week. In **Guerneville,** it's held on Wednesday afternoon (4 P.M.–7 P.M. May–Oct.) at the town square just off Main Street. On Fridays 4 P.M.–dusk (June–Oct.) it's **Occidental's** turn, downtown in front of the Howard Station Café. **Sebastopol's** farmers market is held on Sunday morning (Apr.–Sept., until 1:30 P.M.) at the Downtown Plaza, and **Duncan's Mills** has its own on Saturday (11 A.M.–3 P.M. May–Oct.) behind the Blue Heron Restaurant on Steelhead Boulevard.

INFORMATION AND SERVICES

The most important tool for visiting the Russian River Valley is the excellent, free map published by the **Russian River Wine Road,** an organization representing wineries and other businesses throughout northern Sonoma that is based in Healdsburg (707/433-4335 or 800/723-6336, www.wineroad.com). The map is pretty easy to find at all major wineries and covers all the major roads in the Russian River Valley and up into the Dry Creek and Alexander Valleys.

More detailed and specific information about the Russian River Valley can be found in the free guide published by the **Russian River Val-** ley Winegrowers Association (707/521-2534, www.rrvw.org), also widely available. Neither organization has offices open to the public.

Maps and other information about the region are available at the drop-in office of the **Russian River Chamber of Commerce** in the center of Guerneville (16209 1st St., at the old bridge, 707/869-9000 or 877/644-9001, www.russianriver.com. open 10 A.M.–5 P.M. Mon.–Sat., 10 A.M.–4 P.M. Sun.). There's also an outpost at the Korbel winery in the old station house that is now the ticket office.

Also worth noting is that there are virtually no gas stations west of Sebastopol and Guerneville, so fill up in Forestville or Sebastopol if you plan to venture out to the coast.

Dry Creek Valley

This compact valley is perhaps one of the easiest parts of the Wine Country to visit in a day, and certainly one of the easiest to get around in by car or bike.

At its southern end is the Victorian town of **Healdsburg,** with plenty of Wine Country frills but still relatively crowd-free even on summer weekends. It also has one of the highest numbers of downtown tasting rooms of all Wine Country towns, enabling visitors to sample a good cross section of the region's wine without ever having to drive anywhere.

Although Healdsburg is the only place to shop, stay, or eat, getting out of the town is recommended to discover some the charms of the valley. At its hotter, northern end, the Dry Creek Valley is dominated by the huge Lake Sonoma Recreation Area, which offers some of the best outdoor recreation in the county. Between Healdsburg and the lake are simply vineyards, barns, and small wineries full of character, many run by eccentric characters.

Although the wine industry got an early start here when French and later Italian immigrants planted grapes in the late 1800s, Prohibition killed it off and for much of the 20th century the valley was full of plum and pear orchards. It was not until the early 1970s that grape growing started to pick up again, and the 7,000 acres of prune orchards, with their bounty shriveling in the hot sun, are now long gone.

During that agricultural transition, little else apparently changed in the valley and the only development seems to have been winery related. Just two main roads run up the valley on either side of Dry Creek itself: West Dry Creek Road and the original Dry Creek Road, which eventually becomes Skaggs Springs Road and heads off over the coastal hills to the ocean. Apart from a couple of roads traversing the valley and cutting through the eastern hills to the freeway and Alexander Valley beyond, that's about it.

Development did significantly change one thing: the valley's eponymous creek. Dry Creek used to dry up to nothing more than a few puddles by the end of the summer, like many of the smaller creeks running down the valley sides still do. Since the dam that created Lake Sonoma was completed in the 1980s, however, Dry Creek has become wet year-round.

The Wines

Dry Creek is perhaps best known for its zinfandels, which can sometimes take on an overbearing, jammy style in the hotter parts of the

DRY CREEK AND ALEXANDER VALLEYS

© AVALON TRAVEL PUBLISHING, INC.

valley. But zinfandel vines do not dominate the valley as the wine's prevalence might suggest, accounting for about a quarter of the almost 10,000 acres of vineyards.

About 4,000 acres are planted with cabernet sauvignon and merlot, particularly on the cooler western hillsides, including renowned Bradford Mountain. The hotter valley floor with its richer, alluvial soils grows excellent sauvignon blanc and, increasingly, semillon. Other varietals hint at the valley's French and Italian heritage, with syrah and petite sirah coexisting with small amounts of sangiovese and carignane.

The ideal mix of growing conditions comes from the 1,500-foot coastal hills on the valley's western side and the lower hills on the eastern side that separate it from the Alexander Valley. These hillsides have thousands of acres of benchlands and canyons where growers can usually find just the right degree of heat needed for ideal ripening of most grape varietals. The hills also shield the valley from direct influence of the cold coastal air, yet just enough cool air and fog is funneled up from the Russian River Valley to prevent things from getting too hot.

At the far northern end of the valley, on the hot, rocky ridges overlooking Lake Sonoma, is the aptly named Rockpile appellation, established in 2002. Don't expect to be visiting wineries here, though, because there are none. In fact, there are few paved roads. The 200 acres of vineyards are planted predominantly with zinfandel and cabernet, producing intensely flavored wines for the few wineries lucky enough to own land here.

VALLEY WINERIES

Unless otherwise noted, the valley's wineries generally offer free tasting except for the more expensive reserve wines at some places.

Frick Winery

Proceeds from the sale of a '57 Chevy helped get Bill Frick started in the wine business in 1976 near Santa Cruz. He moved to this small hillside winery at the end of sleepy Walling Road at the far northern end of Dry Creek Valley in the late 1980s.

The six acres of estate vineyards are mainly planted to Rhône varietals, and owner Bill Frick is perhaps Dry Creek's most ardent Rhône Ranger. The 2,500 cases of wine produced each year include syrah, viognier, cinsault, and C-squared, which is a blend of cinsault and carignane.

The tasting room is open weekends noon–4:30 P.M., but by appointment only during the week (23072 Walling Rd., off Canyon Rd or Dutcher Creek Rd., Geyserville, 707/857-1980, www.frickwinery.com, free tasting).

Fritz Winery

Unlike many wineries in the valley, Fritz has actually become smaller with age after slashing its annual production by two-thirds in the mid-1990s as part of a business reorganization. Production has since crept up to almost 20,000 cases after a new vineyard was acquired in the Russian River Valley, but it is still well below 1995 levels.

© PHILIP GOLDSMITH

wineries galore in the Dry Creek Valley

The estate vineyards and other Dry Creek sources provide grapes for zinfandel, sauvignon blanc, and cabernet, including a rich cabernet from the tiny Rockpile appellation, and Russian River wines include chardonnay and pinot noir.

The winery building itself, buried in a hillside north of (and sometimes confused with) the Frick Winery, owes its Jetsons-like styling in part to the energy crisis of the late 1970s, when it was built. The patio and domed tasting room are above two levels of winery workings deep underground, so no pumps or coolers were needed, saving power and adding to its green credentials (24691 Dutcher Creek Rd., Cloverdale, 707/894-3389 or 800/418-9463, www.fritzwinery.com, open 10:30 A.M.–4:30 P.M. daily).

J. Pedroncelli Winery

It no longer sells jug wines like it did up to the 1950s, but Pedroncelli still produces some very approachable wines for the masses at the slightly ramshackle cluster of buildings on Canyon Road. None of the wines sell for more than $16, and most cost far less, so stock up for a picnic.

The winery has been a family affair since John Pedroncelli bought the rundown former Canota winery and 90 acres of vineyards in 1927. The 75,000-case production includes zinfandel, chardonnay, sangiovese, and cabernet sauvignon, all made in the style of easy-drinking, basic table wines.

Some more unusual wines include vintage port and a zinfandel rosé that is bone dry compared to the more common pink-colored zinfandel creations in supermarkets (1220 Canyon Rd., Geyserville, 707/857-3531 or 800/836-3894, www.pedroncelli.com, open 10 A.M.–4:30 P.M. daily).

Preston Vineyards

Zinfandel falls way down the list of interesting wines at Lou Preston's idiosyncratic establishment. Like Fritz, this is another of Dry Creek's incredible shrinking wineries. Founded in the mid-1970s, Preston's annual production eventually grew to 30,000 cases in the late 1980s but is now down to about 8,000.

This is probably to allow Lou and wife Susan to pursue their other varied Wine Country passions, from bread making (there's a commercial bakery on-site) to olive-oil production from the small olive grove at the winery, and even an annual bocce tournament on the winery's two bocce ball courts.

The organic wines are just as varied. Zinfandel is produced here but the list is dominated by Rhône varietals, including a highly regarded petite sirah, syrah, cinsault, carignane, mourvèdre, and an unusual blend of syrah and petite sirah (called, naturally, syrah sirah). Also worth trying are the spicy barbera, the grassy sauvignon blanc, and the cheery Guadagni Red jug wine, a blend of zinfandel, malvoise, and carignane made in tribute to the Guadagni family, which established some of the best of Preston's 110 acres of vineyards in the late 1800s (9282 W. Dry Creek Rd., Healdsburg, 707/433-3372, www.prestonvineyards.com, open 11 A.M.–4 P.M. daily).

Bella Vineyards

This rising star of the Dry Creek Valley was originally founded in the mid-1990s just up the road from Preston Vineyards as a grape supplier to other wineries, but owners Scott and Lynn Adams soon decided to start making wine themselves.

Bella is already well known for its zinfandels, including the rich, sweet late-harvest versions, all sourced from old vines and their rootstock relatives in the Dry Creek and Alexander Valleys. A limited-production Rhône-style blend of zinfandel, syrah, and grenache was added in 2000, followed by the first syrah bottling in 2001. But zinfandel still accounts for most of the 3,500-case annual production.

Newer still than the syrah are the pristine caves dug into the hillside and completed in 2004. They are a cool summer diversion at the hot northern end of the valley (9711 W. Dry Creek Rd., Healdsburg, 866/572-3552, www.bellawinery.com, open 11:30 A.M.–4:30 P.M. daily).

Michel-Schlumberger

This beautiful mission-revival building surrounding a tranquil courtyard is tucked away up Wine Creek Canyon surrounded by 100 acres of undulating benchland vineyards that create a multitude of different growing conditions, from the cool heights of Bradford Mountain down to the hotter canyon floor.

Zinfandel is notably absent from the wine portfolio. Instead, the cooler hillsides favor cabernet sauvignon, merlot, pinot blanc, chardonnay, and pinot noir. The cabernets, particularly the reserve, are outstanding illustrations that Dry Creek Valley is good for more than just zinfandel.

Some cheaper wines are sourced from Schlumberger's 90 acres of vineyards outside the valley, including a syrah and a basic red table wine. All told, the winery produces about 20,000 cases of wine a year. Tours of the winery and vineyards followed by wine tasting are offered twice a day by appointment at 11 A.M. and 2 P.M. (4155 Wine Creek Rd., off W. Dry Creek Rd., Healdsburg, 707/433-7427 or 800/447-3060, www.michelschlumberger.com).

Quivira Estate

There's nothing mythical about the vineyard-designate zinfandels and a bargain-priced sauvignon blanc made by this winery, named after a mythical place where Spanish explorers in the 1500s expected to find untold riches.

Those wines are Quivira's specialties, but it also makes several Rhône-style wines, including a syrah, a mourvèdre, and the Steelhead Red blend, taking total production to about 25,000 cases annually.

The mythical land of Quivira shows up on many of the 16th-century maps of the Pacific region collected by the Wendt family, which founded the winery in the 1980s. They are also heavily involved in local environmental projects, including the restoration of nearby Wine Creek, said to have got its name during Prohibition when it ran with the confiscated wine found by the authorities. Learn more on an appointment-only tour (4900 W. Dry Creek Rd., Healdsburg, 800/292-8339,

www.quivirawine.com, open 11 A.M.– 5 P.M. daily, tours $10).

Dry Creek Vineyards

Built in 1973 not far from Dry Creek itself, this ivy-clad winery is said to be the first winery built in the valley since the repeal of Prohibition. Some historians would beg to differ but the winery has, without doubt, played an important role in transforming the valley from prune orchards to vineyards.

Owner David Stare planted the valley's first sauvignon blanc vines and is now a cheerleader for the varietal, making the winery's fumé blanc a flagship wine along with its Heritage Clone zinfandel. Together those two wines account for almost half the winery's 100,000-case annual production.

A full range of other reds and whites are also made from grapes grown in the estate vineyards and throughout Sonoma, including chenin blanc, a meritage blend, and even a zinfandel grappa. The sailing theme on the labels and in the names of some wines hints at Stare's other passion, sailing.

A shady, grassed picnic area next to the parking lot might provide some relief from the summer sun (3770 Lambert Bridge Rd., Healdsburg, 707/433-1000 or 800/864-9463, www.drycreekvineyard.com, open 10:30 A.M.– 4:30 P.M. daily).

Ridge Vineyards

Not just the wines but the entire building itself is organic here. The new barrel and tasting rooms that opened in 2003 were constructed using only sustainable materials, though it's hard to tell.

The thick walls are made of rice-straw bales and a natural plaster, both chosen for their natural insulation properties. Recycled lumber was used for the framing, flooring, and siding, and even the facing on the tasting room bar is made of pieces of old oak fermentation tanks. To cap it all off, 400 solar panels on the roof provide most of the winery's power.

Ridge started buying grapes from the surrounding vineyards in 1972, eventually buying the property in 1991 to add to many other vineyards it owns throughout Northern and Central California.

Ridge is the king of zin, some years making more than 13 different bottlings that account for the majority of its 85,000-case annual production. Two-thirds of the zinfandel vineyards are in northern Sonoma, which makes the Lytton Springs winery the company's Zinfandel Central, though it also makes syrah, petite sirah, and grenache. Ridge has another winery in the Santa Cruz Mountains that is more famous for its outstanding cabernet (650 Lytton Springs Rd., Healdsburg, 707/433-7721, www.ridgewine.com, open 11 A.M.–4 P.M. daily).

Ferrari Carano

It might sound like it was established by one of the old Italian families of northern Sonoma, but it is actually the flagship winery of a hospitality empire built up by the Carano family since the 1970s. Sister businesses include the Eldorado Hotel and Casino in Reno and the Vintners Inn in Santa Rosa.

Nevertheless, the pink, Italianate mansion known as Villa Fiore (House of Flowers) and the acres of manicured gardens evoke a grandiose past. Equally grandiose is the huge, vaulted cellar that can house up to 1,500 barrels of aging wine and is part of an appointment-only tour.

The 160,000 cases of wine made each year are sourced from the 1,200 acres of vineyards that Carano owns throughout Sonoma, including its rapidly growing Alexander Valley mountain estate.

They include some highly rated chardonnays and a full range of reds from single varietals to blends including Siena, a combination of sangiovese and cabernet, and the Tresor bordeaux-style wine. The $3 tasting fee (unusual for Dry Creek) also covers the sweet muscat dessert wine, Eldorado Noir (8761 Dry Creek Rd., Healdsburg, 707/433-6700 or 800/831-0381, www.ferrari-carano.com).

Forchini Vineyards & Winery

The Forchini family has been growing grapes in the Dry Creek and Russian River Valleys since the 1970s but only started making wines in the mid-1990s, and production hasn't grown much since then.

The 3,000 cases of wine made each year use only about a quarter of the fruit from the family's 90 acres of vineyards (the rest is sold to other winemakers). The well-balanced Dry Creek cabernet sauvignon is, unusually, blended with 10 percent carignane; the zinfandel is a typically intense Dry Creek style; and the Russian River vineyards are represented by a big, rich chardonnay and more reserved pinot noir. The cheap and cheerful Papa Nonno blend, made in the style of easy-drinking Tuscan table wine, is primarily zinfandel and makes a great picnic wine.

The small tasting room in the main house is open weekends only (or during appointment during the week) and has a small deck overlooking the cabernet vines lining the driveway (5141 Dry Creek Rd., Healdsburg, 707/431-8886, www.forchini.com).

Seghesio Family Vineyards

Another of the old Italian family wineries that helped define the northern Sonoma wine industry over the last hundred years is about a 20-minute walk from Healdsburg Plaza in a building dating from the 1890s.

It is still very much a family affair, run by the grandchildren of founder Edoardo Seghesio, who arrived in the region from Italy in 1886, planted his first vines in 1895, and established the winery in 1902. The wines are very much Italian as well, sourced from 400 acres of vineyards throughout the Russian River, Alexander, and Dry Creek Valleys.

About two-thirds of the winery's 80,000-case production is just one wine—the excellent and bargain-priced Sonoma County zinfandel. At the opposite end of the zin scale is the limited production and age-worthy San Lorenzo. Sangiovese is the other dominant varietal, and wines include Omaggio, a cabernet sangiovese blend, and the limited-production Chianti Station, which is sourced from the oldest sangiovese vines in the United States.

Also represented are the Italian varietals barbera and the unusual arneis, a grape that has roots in the same Piedmont region of Italy as the Seghesios (14730 Grove St., Healdsburg, 707/433-3579, www.seghesio.com, open 10 A.M.–5 P.M. daily).

Wineries by Appointment

Up a long driveway off West Dry Creek Road, just south of Wine Creek Road, is where the fourth generation of Rafanellis now makes its limited-production wines at the **A. Rafanelli Winery** (4685 W. Dry Creek Rd., 707/433-1385). An intense zinfandel accounts for more than half the 11,000-case annual production, and the rest is cabernet and merlot sourced from the hillside vineyards. Look out over the vineyards and valley from a small seating area and vegetable garden next to the winery's old redwood barn.

After decades of making wine for other valley wineries, Rick Hutchinson started his own **Amphora Winery** (3901 Wine Creek Rd., 707/431-7767) in 1997 in a small barn just down the hill from Michel-Schlumberger. He makes just over 2,000 cases of vineyard-designate zinfandel, cabernet, syrah, merlot, and petite sirah. Pottery is Hutchinson's other passion, in particular the creation of the amphorae that inspired the name and appear on the wine labels.

There is more than the family's German heritage to the **Göpfrich Estate Vineyard and Winery** (7462 W. Dry Creek Rd., 707/433-1645). In addition to the limited production cabernet, zinfandel, and syrah wines from the Dry Creek estate, Göpfrich also sells limited quantities of fragrant, late-harvest German white wines including riesling, huxelrebe, and silvaner from its sister winery in the Rheinhessen region of Germany.

HEALDSBURG TASTING ROOMS

Being located at the junction of the three most important northern Sonoma appellations makes Healdsburg a good jumping-off point for visiting them all. Westside Road heads down into the Russian River Valley, Dry Creek Road to its namesake's valley, and Healdsburg Avenue heads north into the Alexander Valley.

But it's just as easy to ditch the car and sample wines from those appellations through the town's numerous downtown tasting rooms and wineries, all within walking distance from the plaza. There are more wineries represented here than most people can comfortably visit in a day, and it makes for a more relaxing way to taste the Wine Country than jumping in and out of a hot car.

Toad Hollow Vineyards

The toad in this hollow is actually owner Todd Williams, the half brother of comedian Robin who has sported the warty nickname since his youth. This downtown tasting room is the only public face of the Russian River Valley winery where you can taste its unusual selection of red, white, rosé, and sparkling wines at the gnarled redwood bar.

Toad Hollow is best known for its oak-free chardonnay, sourced from the 103 acres of estate vineyards, but also makes estate pinot noir, and merlot, a Central Coast zinfandel, and one or two unique (and uniquely named) wines including the popular Eyes of the Toad, a bone-dry pinot noir rosé, and a cheaper red blend called Erik's the Red, which is made from a staggering 15 different types of grape. The two sparkling wines are not local, however, but imported from France.

If the wines don't entertain, their colorful labels, painted by San Francisco artist Maureen Erickson, might. Serious wines sport a very conservative-looking toad while the fun wines see the toad in party mood (409A Healdsburg Ave., Healdsburg, 707/431-8667, www.toadhollow.com, open 10:30 A.M.–5:30 P.M. daily).

Rosenblum Cellars

Although the winery itself is in industrial Alameda just across the bay from San Francisco, Rosenblum is best known for its big, bold, highly praised zinfandels sourced from vineyards in the Dry Creek Valley and Rockpile appellations, hence the tasting room in Healdsburg next to the Oakville Grocery.

Zinfandels might dominate the 100,000-case annual output, but Rosenblum also makes

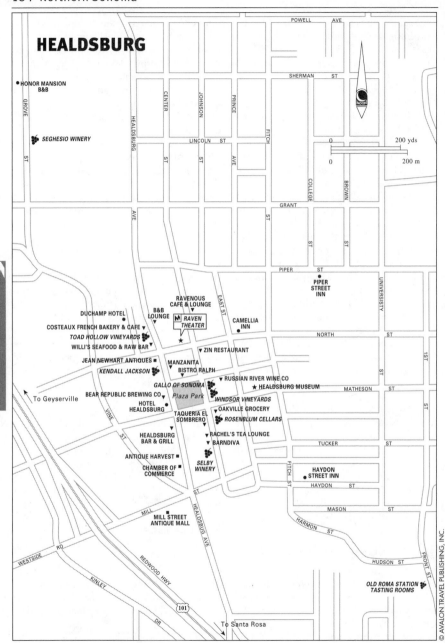

HEALDSBURG

- HONOR MANSION B&B
- SEGHESIO WINERY

POWELL AVE
SHERMAN ST
CENTER ST
JOHNSON ST
PRINCE AVE
FITCH
LINCOLN ST
HEALDSBURG AVE
GROVE ST
COLLEGE ST
BROWN ST
GRANT ST
PIPER ST
PIPER STREET INN
UNIVERSITY ST

0   200 yds
0   200 m

- RAVENOUS CAFE & LOUNGE
- DUCHAMP HOTEL
- B&B LOUNGE
- RAVEN THEATER
- CAMELLIA INN
- COSTEAUX FRENCH BAKERY & CAFE
- TOAD HOLLOW VINEYARDS
- WILLI'S SEAFOOD & RAW BAR
- ZIN RESTAURANT
- JEAN NEWHART ANTIQUES
- MANZANITA
- BISTRO RALPH
- KENDALL JACKSON
- GALLO OF SONOMA
- RUSSIAN RIVER WINE CO
- HEALDSBURG MUSEUM
- NORTH ST
- MATHESON ST
- 1ST ST
- To Geyserville
- BEAR REPUBLIC BREWING CO
- Plaza Park
- WINDSOR VINEYARDS
- HOTEL HEALDSBURG
- OAKVILLE GROCERY
- TAQUERIA EL SOMBRERO
- ROSENBLUM CELLARS
- VINE ST
- HEALDSBURG BAR & GRILL
- RACHEL'S TEA LOUNGE
- BARNDIVA
- TUCKER ST
- ANTIQUE HARVEST
- CHAMBER OF COMMERCE
- SELBY WINERY
- FITCH ST
- HAYDON STREET INN
- HAYDON ST
- MASON ST
- MILL ST
- MILL STREET ANTIQUE MALL
- HEALDSBURG AVE
- HARMON ST
- WESTSIDE RD
- REDWOOD HWY
- KINLEY
- HUDSON ST
- FRONT ST
- OLD ROMA STATION TASTING ROOMS
- 101
- To Santa Rosa

© AVALON TRAVEL PUBLISHING, INC.

a lot of other wines from vineyards all over California. These include some rich muscat dessert wines and the fun Coat du Bone blends sold under the Chateau La Paws label—a tribute to the veterinarian roots of founder Dr. Kent Rosenblum.

The tasting room is through a vine-draped pergola just a few yards down Center Street from the Oakville Grocery and shares its space with a small art gallery (250 Center St., Healdsburg, 707/431-1169, www.rosenblumcellars.com, open 10 A.M.–5 P.M., until 6 P.M. Fri. and Sat.).

Selby Winery

Down Center Street from Rosenblum, on the other side of the street, is the tiny tasting room of the Selby Winery, which has its production facility in a nearby warehouse.

The 10,000 cases of wine Selby makes each year come from vineyards all over Sonoma, with an emphasis on the nearby Russian River Valley, Alexander Valley, and Dry Creek Valley.

Wines include chardonnay, pinot noir, syrah, cabernet, zinfandel, a dry syrah rosé, and a juicy zinfandel port in convenient half bottles. All can be tasted free and there's a nominal $2 charge for tasting the reserve chardonnay and pinot noir (215 Center St. Healdsburg, 707/431-1288, www.selbywinery.com, open 11 A.M.–5 P.M. daily).

Gallo of Sonoma

It might be part of the largest privately owned wine company in California, and the largest landowner in Sonoma County, but Gallo of Sonoma has a remarkably modest, café-style tasting room on the plaza that opened in 2002.

Also remarkable is the fact that this is the only place that the public can taste Gallo's best wines, made under the Gallo of Sonoma label. None of the countless, historic wineries acquired by Gallo over the years, including the Frei Brothers winery in the Dry Creek Valley, are open to the public. A local supermarket is the place to try out Gallo's 57 other labels of cheap and cheerful wines, like Turning Leaf.

The premium wines poured here include the full range of reds, including the Italian varietals

barbera and sangiovese. Whites are represented by chardonnay and pinot gris, and some of the wines, most notably the cabernet and chardonnay, are available in more expensive vineyard-specific and estate forms.

The stalwart Sonoma County cabernet and chardonnay are consistently highly rated for their price (under $15). And with so many wines to taste, this is a good place for a horizontal tasting, sampling three wines of the same varietal that were sourced from different vineyards or made in different ways. Vertical tasting flights are also offered (320 Center St., Healdsburg, 707/433-2458, www.gallosonoma.com, open 11 A.M.–5 P.M. Sun.–Wed., 11 A.M.–7 P.M. Thurs.–Sat.).

Kendall-Jackson

If Gallo is the largest landowner in Sonoma County, then the Kendall-Jackson empire can boast the county's highest acreage of vineyards.

The Healdsburg tasting room of this Sonoma wine titan (337 Healdsburg Ave., Healdsburg, 707/433-7102, www.kj.com, open 10 A.M.–5 P.M. daily) is a giant but chintzy place that offers tastes of some of the bewildering array of wines for $2, including not only Kendall-Jackson wines but also some from the numerous other wineries the company owns in California and Australia. Tasting the reasonably priced reserves and other high-end wines costs $10.

If there is a specific wine not available for tasting here then it might be offered at the main visitor center, a French-style chateau next to U.S. 101 at the Fulton Road exit, a short drive south of Healdsburg (5007 Fulton Rd., 707/571-7500).

Windsor Vineyards

Windsor is better known as the first mail-order winery in the United States rather than for its wines. One mail order and tasting room offer that's popular is for free customized labels—buy three bottles of wine in this cavernous tasting room (though it has to be the same wine) and have your own words printed on the label. It's a great idea for an impromptu gift, though you have to keep the wording clean. Windsor doesn't own a wine-making facility, instead making its 210,000 cases of a staggering 45 different wines at the nearby Chateau Souverain winery in the Alexander Valley.

The wine is not expensive, though it's also not regularly seen on the pages of *Wine Spectator* magazine (308B Center St., Healdsburg, 707/433-7302, www.windsorvineyards.com, open 10 A.M.–5 P.M. daily, until 6 P.M. weekends).

Old Roma Station

Four small wineries have their tasting rooms huddled around this old station building on the southern edge of town and the edge of the Russian River (51–57 Front St., Healdsburg).

Open daily is the tiny tasting room of the boutique **Camellia Cellars** (707/433-1290, www.camelliacellars.com), which makes less than 2,000 cases a year of sangiovese, cabernet, and its "Super Tuscan" Proprietor's Blend.

Across the parking lot is the more spacious tasting room of **Huntington Wine Cellars** (707/433-5215), which makes a standard set of red and white wines from vineyards in northern Sonoma and Napa.

The big red barn houses two wineries that are only open without an appointment at weekends. **Sapphire Hill Vineyards** (707/431-1888, www.sapphirehill.com) produces several thousand cases of Russian River Valley chardonnay, syrah, pinot noir, and zinfandel. **Holdredge Wines** (707/431-1424, www.holdredge.com) produces less than a thousand cases of mostly pinot noir but also some syrah sourced from its Russian River Valley vineyards.

SIGHTS

Healdsburg has to rank as one of the more appealing Wine Country towns, with the right mix of history, modernity, shops, and wine, and a population of 11,000 that is large enough to prevent the town's economy lurching too far in favor of wine tourists. There is still plenty of Wine Country paraphernalia and often-voiced concerns that the town is being "St. Helena-ized," though it remains decidedly less frenetic than that smaller Napa Valley town. This could

be partly thanks to some of its active cultural counterweights, including the loose collective of local artists called Stark Raving Beautiful with the motto "Help Make Healdsburg Weird" and a desire to prevent the town from becoming a "Bourgeois Playland."

The town has a history as storied as any other in Wine Country. It was established in the mid-1800s by an enterprising former gold miner from Ohio, Harmon Heald, who eventually bought enough parcels of land to lay out the town around a Spanish-style plaza and sell plots to other businessmen. He bought the land from Captain Henry Fitch, who was granted most of the surrounding area by the Mexican government and whose name lives on in Fitch Mountain, the small hump at the bend in the Russian River just east of the town.

Healdsburg was incorporated in 1867 and boomed after the railroad arrived in 1871. Like many of the region's towns, it went through a slump brought on by the 1906 earthquake, the Great Depression, and Prohibition, but returned to prosperity after Prohibition when the region's agriculture and wine industry took off.

The modest-looking **Healdsburg Museum & Historical Society** (221 Matheson St., at Fitch St., 707/431-3325, www.healdsburg-museum.org, open 11 A.M.–4 P.M. Tues.–Sun., free), a few blocks from the plaza, is a treasure trove of information and photos illustrating the town's Victorian heyday and its Native American roots. Serious history buffs can also pour through the oral histories, official records, and newspapers going back to the 1860s.

Ask for a booklet about historic homes and visit some of the many Victorian buildings dotted around town. The library itself is in one of Healdsburg's most notable neoclassical buildings.

ENTERTAINMENT
 **Raven Theater**

Hats off to Healdsburg's fiercely independent Raven Theater (115 North St., 707/433-5448, www.raventheater.org) for keeping it real in the middle of Wine Country where so many other

The independent Raven Theater helps keep Healdsburg real.

Northern Sonoma

small towns have long since sold out to the mighty tourist dollar. Believe it or not there are four movie theaters squeezed into this historic building (though a couple are probably the size of the average living room), so there's usually a combination of mainstream, independent, and documentary films showing 3–5 times every day (admission $9, matinees $5).

There's also a varied mix of music and comedy, including some big showbiz names every now and then together with theater productions put on by local groups. Check the website for a full calendar.

Nightlife

A couple of local hangouts keep the bar scene in Healdsburg real, too, opening all day every day until 2 A.M. Both **John & Zeke's Bar & Grill** (111 Plaza St., 707/433-3735) and the **B&B Lounge** (420 Healdsburg Ave., 707/433-5960) have a no-nonsense attitude and shun wine-country frills for good old-fashioned bar room entertainment from jukeboxes, pool, darts, and the like.

At the other end of the drinking spectrum are places like **Barndiva** (231 Center St.,

Healdsburg, 707/431-0100) and **Willi's Seafood and Raw Bar** (4404 Old Redwood Hwy., just south of River Rd., 707/526-3096), where cocktails are often the drink of choice and the entertainment revolves around fancy food and people-watching.

The best place to escape the Wine Country scene and nurse a cold beer at a small, hole-in-the-wall bar is, ironically, right among the wineries of Dry Creek Valley. The **Dry Creek Bar** at the Dry Creek General Store (3495 Dry Creek Rd., at Lambert Bridge Rd., 707/433-4171) is open daily from 3 P.M. Grab a beer, sit outside, and watch the wine tasters drive by.

SHOPPING

Wine is about all you'll be buying in most of the Dry Creek Valley except in Healdsburg, a town of boutiques that is also known for its antique shopping. Most of the treasures have long gone and many of the old antique stores have gone, too, as rents increased, but it's still fun to rummage through the handful of stores that remain along Healdsburg Avenue just south of the plaza.

The barnlike **Antique Harvest** (225 Healdsburg Ave., 707/433-0223) is chock-full of one person's junk, or another's antiques. The **Mill Street Antique Mall** (44 Mill St., just off Healdsburg Ave., 707/433-7461, open daily until 5 P.M., or 6 P.M. on Sat.) is a cooperative boasting more than 20,000 square feet of floorspace that is home to numerous small, local dealers.

For both old and modern furnishings from France, visit **21st Arrondissement** (309 Healdsburg Ave., 707/433-2166). The name is a play on the 20 *arrondissements,* or districts, in Paris. This is the self-proclaimed 21st, according to owner Myra Hoefer, who makes regular trips to her other home in Paris to find goodies to fill the store. Another Francophile founded **Jean Newhart Antiques** (387 Healdsburg Ave., 707/473-9632, open 10 A.M.–5 P.M. daily). Like Myra, Jean Newhart regularly travels to France to stock up the store.

Classic and contemporary furniture at **Dovetail Collection** (407 Healdsburg Ave., 707/431-0111, open 11 A.M.–5 P.M. Thurs.–Mon.) is made by Northern Californian artisans, along with the jewelry, ceramics, and other unique gifts.

Other shopping highlights include the **Russian River Wine Company** (132 Plaza St., 707/433-0490, 9 A.M.–5 P.M. weekdays, 11 A.M.–4 P.M. Sat.), which sells wine from all over the area, not just the Russian River, and specializes in smaller producers. It also hosts wine classes and visiting winemakers some weekends. Right next door is the cool, tranquil space of the **Plaza Arts Gallery,** which showcases mainly contemporary art from its local resident artists.

RECREATION

Lake Sonoma Recreation Area

When the Army Corps of Engineers completed the Warm Springs Dam at the northern end of Dry Creek Valley in 1983, the resulting Lake Sonoma not only made Dry Creek's name obsolete by providing a year-round source of water but also became one of the best regional recreation areas.

Controversially, the lake flooded some sacred sites of the Pomo people, now represented in a small exhibition in the Milt Brandt Visitor Center (3333 Skaggs Springs Rd., Geyserville, 707/433-9483, open daily 9 A.M.–5:30 P.M., until 7:30 P.M. Fri. and Sat.) right at the end of Dry Creek Road. Despite protests during the drawn-out planning stages in the 1970s, the flood control, water supply, and recreation advantages created by the dam won the day, and it was finally completed more than 20 years after first getting approval.

The 17,000 acres of hot, oak-studded hills of the Lake Sonoma Recreation Area have more than 40 miles of trails for hikers, bikers, and riders, the region's best bass fishing, and plenty of open water (about 2,700 surface acres to be precise) for swimming and boating.

The main access points to the lake and trails are Stewarts Point Road just south of the bridge, Rockpile Road north of the bridge, and the grassy **Yorty Creek Recreation Area,** which is on the eastern side of lake and is accessible from Cloverdale (from S. Cloverdale Blvd., turn left on W. Brookside Rd., left on Foothill Rd., and right onto Hot Springs Rd.).

A couple of the easier and more accessible hiking trails start at the South Lake Trailhead (on Stewarts Point Road about a half mile south from its junction with Skaggs Springs Road, just before the marina turnoff). From there it's a quick jaunt up the hill to the **Overlook,** with great views of the lake. Or take the **South Lake Trail** for a longer hike, ducking in and out of groves of madrone and pine along the way. At about two miles head right; it's then about three-quarters of a mile down to the **Quicksilver campground,** where you can duck into the lake for a swim, if you come prepared. Alternatively, go left and stay on the South Lake Trail for as long as you want. Other trails start at another trailhead across the bridge off Rockpile Road. A trail map is available at the visitor center.

Mountain bikers will have to be content with just one loop on the **Half-a-Canoe Trail,** which starts at the No Name Flat Trailhead, about 1.5 miles north of the bridge on the left.

The loop is about 4.5 miles and mostly fire road with a short section of single-track.

You might notice that it gets hotter as you drive up Dry Creek Valley. Temperatures around the lake regularly top 100 degrees in the summer, so take plenty of water whatever you do (the lake water is not drinkable). Other natural hazards include the occasional rattlesnake, disease-carrying ticks, and poison oak. You might be lucky enough to see the odd jackrabbit, a wild pig, or a rare peregrine falcon.

Fishing

The **Congressman Don Clausen Fish Hatchery** (behind the recreation area visitor center) was built to beef up the steelhead, chinook, and coho salmon populations in the Russian River and its tributaries and to mitigate some of the detrimental effects caused by construction of the Warm Springs and nearby Coyote Valley Dams. Tours are offered during the January–April spawning season (call 707/433-9483 for information). The main fishing draw on the lake is the healthy stock of largemouth bass, which love the submerged trees that were left in the Dry Creek arm of the lake when it was flooded.

The bass record stands at just over 15 pounds, though most reportedly weigh less than 10 pounds. There are also smallmouth bass, catfish, crappies, sunfish, perch, and numerous other species, including some landlocked steelhead.

When the water is clearest during the summer, sight fishing is possible in the shallower waters close to the shore, as is bank fishing, particularly at the Yorty Creek Recreation Area. The lake is primarily a boat-fishing lake, however, and boats can be rented at the **Lake Sonoma Marina** (100 Marina Dr., 707/433-2200, $20–30 per hour for fishing boats, depending on season, or $40–50 per hour for larger powerboats), just off Stewarts Point Road about a half mile south of Skaggs Springs Road.

Other Water Activities

There are three places to launch boats on the lake—a trailer ramp at the Lake Sonoma Marina ($10 to launch), a big public ramp just across the bridge ($3), and a car-top launch area at Yorty Creek ($3). Check with a ranger for the boating rules. If fishing or high-octane boating doesn't appeal, paddleboats can also be rented at the marina.

Unless you're fortunate to be camping at one of the hike-in or boat-in campsites, there are not many places with decent shoreline access for swimming. The only official swimming beach is at the Yorty Creek Recreation Area.

ACCOMMODATIONS

Take one look at the expanses of vineyards and hills dotted with the occasional winery and it's pretty clear that the Dry Creek Valley is not a part of the world that's chock-full of hotels. Pretty much every accommodation option is in the town of Healdsburg, where Victorian frills still dominate the scene though some contemporary style has recently crept in. As would be expected in a premium Wine Country destination town, prices are not cheap regardless of style.

Under $100

Few options exist for those on a budget, even a Wine Country budget, other than chain hotels and motels. Cheaper lodging is available to the north in the Alexander Valley and south in the Russian River Valley, but the town of Healdsburg itself seems to work hard to retain its sense of exclusivity.

One of the better of the chain lodging options is the **Dry Creek Inn,** a Best Western property less than a mile from the plaza but perilously close to the freeway at the Dry Creek Road exit (198 Dry Creek Rd., Healdsburg, 707/433-0300, www.drycreekinn.com). Most of the bland rooms start at under $100 a night, even in peak season. A large pool and complimentary bottle of drinkable wine make the stay a little more bearable.

$100–200

This could be classified as the Victorian frills price category, into which fall the many small, family-owned inns and B&Bs in often historic houses. There might be some inflexibilities inherent to such small establishments (check whether smoking or pets are allowed, for example, and ask about the sometimes-strict cancellation policies), but the advantage is that the owners usually know the area like the back of their hands and can offer great local insights and, of course, a great local breakfast.

The ⋈ **Haydon Street Inn** (321 Haydon St., Healdsburg, 707/433-5228 or 800/528-3703, www.haydon.com) is on a quiet residential street about a 10-minute walk from the plaza and is one of the relative bargains in a crowded local field. The Queen Anne-style house was built in 1912 as a private residence and briefly used as a convent before becoming a B&B in the 1980s. The six rooms in the main house cost $125–200 a night, and all have private bathrooms (though across the hallway in the case of the Blue Room). Two additional, deluxe rooms are in a separate cottage on the manicured grounds and cost $215 a night.

There's a little more chintz on show at the **Camellia Inn** (211 North St., Healdsburg, 707/433-8182 or 800/727-8182, www.camelliainn.com), where flowers abound on the walls and fabrics inside the elegant 1869 house and also in the gardens, which contain more than 50 varieties of camellia, some planted by renowned horticulturist Luther Burbank, who was a friend of the original owners. Unusually for a small B&B, there is air-conditioning in all rooms and a small swimming pool. Four of the nine rooms have gas fireplaces. Rates start at $109 for the tiny budget room but jump to $179–239 for the queen rooms and the single suite. The Lewand family owns both the inn and the **Camellia Cellars** winery, which has a tasting room not far away on Front Street. Wine usually shows up in the Victorian parlor most evenings, and you can chat with the innkeeper and winemaker himself, Ray Lewand.

Other standouts in the crowded Victorian B&B scene include the four-room **Piper Street Inn** (402 Piper St., Healdsburg, 877/703-0570 or 707/433-8721, www.piperstreetinn.com) and

the six-room **Calderwood Inn** (25 W. Grant St., Healdsburg, 707/431-1110 or 800/600-5444, www.calderwoodinn.com), which is not far from the Seghesio Family Winery.

Over $200

In this price range, Victorian frills start to yield to more contemporary style, nowhere more so than at the ⋈ **Hotel Healdsburg** (25 Matheson St., Healdsburg, 707/431-2800, www.hotelhealdsburg.com), the centerpiece of the decidedly un-Victorian hunk of modern architecture that dominates the western side of the plaza. Strategically placed design elements and luxurious furnishings successfully soften the angular concrete minimalism of the interior, both in the rooms and the stark lobby area. Such New York style doesn't come cheap, however, even in sleepy Healdsburg. The smallest of the 49 rooms start at about $260 a night, though they include the usual luxury amenities, including DVD player, walk-in shower, and high-speed Internet. Add a tub and a few more square feet, and the rate jumps to more than $300. All guests have access to the tranquil outdoor pool and small fitness room, and the minimally named **The Spa** offers a wide range of spa treatments and massages for $100 and up.

Compared to the hotel's stylish interior, the expensive on-site restaurant, the **Dry Creek Kitchen,** has a rather bland expense-account atmosphere, and its culinary popularity has waned somewhat in recent years.

Even more luxury, tranquillity, and contemporary style can be found at the even more expensive **DuChamp Hotel** (421 Foss St., Healdsburg, 707/431-1300 or 800/431-9341, www.duchamphotel.com), a short walk from the plaza and voted one of the top 25 hot new hotels by *Condé Nast Traveler* in 2001. Where the Hotel Healdsburg sometimes feels like it's trying a bit too hard to be hip, the DuChamp feels effortlessly chic, from the low-key minimalism of the six pool- and creekside villas (starting at $300) to the unique furnishings of the four cottage suites (starting at $275) with interiors inspired by the artists after which they're named (Man Ray, Miro, Picasso, and Warhol). It even has its own champagne label (made by Iron Horse Vineyards), which can be enjoyed on the private terrace of a few rooms or in front of the fireplace of the others. Private tastings can also be arranged at the nearby DuChamp Estate Winery (which makes only syrah wine).

A few Victorians offer some healthy competition to the high-end, modern newcomers, not least the **Honor Mansion** (14891 Grove St., Healdsburg, 707/433-4277 or 800/554-4667, www.honormansion.com). At this gloriously indulgent establishment the unusual antiques and period architectural features do the talking without an excess of applied frills, giving some rooms at the self-styled "resort inn" an almost artistic, contemporary feel. The 13 rooms and suites don't come cheap ($225–550 a night) but do come with all amenities, including CD players and VCRs, as well as some fun features ranging from double-headed showers and ornate, four-poster beds to private patios and giant fireplaces. There's even a two-story suite inside an old Victorian water tower. The three acres of verdant grounds contain include a swimming pool, koi pond, bocce and tennis courts, and a croquet lawn. The two- or three-course breakfast can be enjoyed out on the dining patio, weather permitting.

The town of Healdsburg might have a surplus of historic Victorian houses, but the Ⓜ **Madrona Manor**, just outside the town at the southern end of the Dry Creek Valley appellation, puts them all in the shade. This enormous pile of Victorian opulence is the centerpiece of an eight-acre hilltop estate dating from the 1880s, and not surprisingly its movie-set looks make it a very popular wedding location (1001 Westside Rd., Healdsburg, 707/433-4231 or 800/258-4003, www.madronamanor.com).

The elegantly furnished rooms and common areas contain plenty of genuine and reproduction antiques, and most amenities except for televisions, which is probably fine since no children under 12 can stay there anyway. Any bored adults can watch the fire burn or the sun set from the private decks of some of the

21 rooms and suites that are spread among five different buildings.

Summer rates start at just over $200 a night, with the cheapest in the Carriage House and main manor, and rise to more than $400 for the suites. Winter rates are sometimes as low as $170 a night. If the romantic setting, landscaped grounds, and swimming pool aren't enough to keep guests from ever leaving during their stay then the manor's renowned restaurant might be. It serves the sumptuous, complimentary breakfast and stylish, though pricey, dinners (on the big porch in the summer) with an outstanding wine list that leans heavily on the local appellations.

Camping

Lake Sonoma Recreation Area at the northern end of Dry Creek Valley is a tent-camping mecca, especially if you have a boat. There are more than 100 hike-in or boat-in primitive campsites along its 50 miles of shoreline, most of them on the Warm Springs arm of the lake. The most easily accessible on foot are the Island View or Quicksilver campgrounds, though the heat and terrain make the 2.5-mile hikes to them fairly strenuous during the summer months

Most of the campgrounds are small, with an average of about 10 tent sites. None have drinking water but all have fire rings and chemical toilets. Apart from the usual wildlife warnings (look out for rattlesnakes and ticks that carry Lyme disease), visitors should also keep an eye out for feral pigs, descendants of domestic pigs brought by early white settlers.

Also worth noting: Some campsites are located on lake areas designated for water skiing and the constant drone of power boats and jet skis can spoil an otherwise idyllic scene. More peace and quiet can be found near parts of the lake designated as wake-free zones (marked on the free map available at the visitor center). Island View is the quieter of the two most accessible hike-in campgrounds.

Reservations cost $14 a night during the summer months (877/444-6777, www .reserveusa.com). Even with a reservation, all backcountry campers must first get a permit from the hard-to-miss **visitor center** (3333 Skaggs Springs Rd., Geyserville, 707/433-9483), which also has trail maps. More information about the campsites is also available at the Army Corps website (www.spn.usace.army.mil/lakesonoma/index.htm).

For car campers, there's just one developed, drive-in campground: **Liberty Glen.** About a mile across the bridge from the visitor center, it has 95 sites for tents and RVs (no electrical hookups) that cost $10 a night (877/444-6777, www.reserveusa.com). Worth noting is that during the summer the gates to the site are closed to cars at 10 P.M., so don't plan on any late-night reveling.

FOOD

With Dry Creek largely devoid of shops and restaurants, it is left to Healdsburg to supply most of the food. Like the town's breezy, relaxed atmosphere, the culinary scene is also fairly relaxed. Restaurants generally never seem to be trying as hard as in some other Wine Country destination towns.

There are a few exceptions, and well-known regional chefs have had their eye on the place for some time. Some big-name establishments have taken hold here, like Manzanita with input from Bizou in San Francisco, but they lack the big-city attitude (and, reportedly, the polished big-city service). Dinner reservations, though usually not needed, are nearly always recommended, especially in summer.

Fine Dining

It's no surprise that almost half the wines available at **Zin Restaurant** (344 Center St., Healdsburg, 707/473-0946, lunch and dinner daily, dinner entrées $13–25) are zinfandels. More surprising is that chef Jeff Mall manages to match many of the dishes on the menu to one style of the wine or another, highlighting just how flexible the humble zinfandel grape really is. Of course, you don't need to be a zinfandel lover to enjoy the post-industrial interior, with its concrete walls and exposed beams,

or the elegantly understated but exquisitely executed dishes made with seasonal local produce. Wines from all northern Sonoma regions are represented, and in addition to the reasonably priced main courses there are cheaper blue plate specials on many days of the week, depending on what's available down on the farm.

Competing with Zin's industrial chic interior and casual atmosphere is the relative newcomer, **Manzanita** (336 Healdsburg Ave., Healdsburg, 707/433-8111, dinner Wed.–Sun., entrées $17–26). The Mediterranean-style bistro food won't win awards for originality here in the Wine Country, but the reasonably priced, crispy pizzas and other favorites, like lasagna and cassoulet ($15–25), are made with flair and the requisite laundry lists of local, seasonal produce.

Bistro Ralph (109 Plaza St., Healdsburg, 707/433-1380, lunch weekdays, dinner daily) is everything a cozy local bistro should be, with whitewashed brick walls, white-clothed tables, and giant plates of fries for $5. Owner Ralph Tingle kicked off Healdsburg's culinary resurgence with this bistro in the early 1990s, and it still serves sophisticated Californian food in a relaxed, if cramped, environment right across from the leafy plaza. Dinner main courses start at $15 and quickly escalate, but lunch (weekdays only) remains a relative bargain.

The big red barn housing **Barndiva** (231 Center St., Healdsburg, opposite the police station, 707/431-0100, lunch and dinner Wed.–Sun.) looks very Wine Country from the outside, but the interior is more big city than big barn. This being a rural part of the world, the clientele doesn't quite match the contemporary interior, but it's still a fun and unusual scene. Barndiva opened in 2004 and bills itself primarily as a cocktail lounge, though one that also serves stylish, Asian-influenced food and a huge selection of wine from a menu best examined while sober. The small plates of food ($7–12) are listed according to mood, the wines by their flavor profile. It takes a while to decide whether you're in a spicy, passionate mood or are feeling light and clean, but it's a fun diversion.

Another newcomer to the small-plate phe-

BEER BEFORE WINE

It's hard to imagine a time before vineyards in the Wine Country, but another type of vine was once the mainstay of the agricultural economy in the Russian River Valley. From Sebastopol to Healdsburg, and up into Mendocino, hops rather than vines once lined the roads and covered the hillsides. All that is left to remind us now are the tall hop kilns that rear up over the landscape, some long since converted into wineries.

The conditions were perfect for hop growing. Rich alluvial soils and the cooling influence of the fog favored the hop vines just like they favor chardonnay and pinot noir grape vines today. Hops were first planted in the region around 1880, and by 1930 almost three million pounds were harvested each year. That's enough to make more than 100 million gallons of beer, by some estimates.

The small green fruit, resembling a miniature pine cone, was harvested, dried (or "toasted") in the giant kilns, and used to make beer. A resin-like substance from the hops called lupolin is what gives beer its distinctive bitter taste.

Market forces, disease, and, ironically, the invention of a local grower all spelled doom for the local hop industry. After World War II, demand and prices for hops plummeted as the public started to prefer less bitter beer (call it the Budweiser effect). Adding to growers' misery, downy mildew infected the soils in the 1950s, killing the hops.

The final nail in the hop growers' coffin was the invention of an automated hop harvesting machine in the 1940s by Santa Rosa grower Florian Dauenhauer, which quickly made the small, hand-harvested lots that were common in Sonoma far less economical. Growers sought out bigger lots elsewhere in California and the Pacific Northwest that could be easily machine harvested, and by the 1960s the Sonoma hop industry was dead.

All that is left of the beer-related industry these days is handful of brewpubs, though you'll have to ask where they get their hops from. In Healdsburg, the **Bear Republic Brewing Company** (345 Healdsburg Ave., Healdsburg, 707/433-2337) is right behind the Hotel Healdsburg and has a quiet, sunny outdoor patio. In Guerneville, the **Stumptown Brewery** (15045 River Rd., Guerneville, 707/869-0705) offers such potent-sounding microbrews as Red Rocket and Death and Taxes. In Santa Rosa, the **Third Street Ale Works** (610 3rd St., Santa Rosa, 707/523-3060) challenges drinkers to get their mouths around names like "Drunken Weasel" Dunkelweizen and Goat Rock Doppelbock.

nomenon is **Willi's Seafood and Raw Bar,** a few blocks north of the plaza (403 Healdsburg Ave., Healdsburg, 707/433-9191). This is a sister establishment to the popular Willi's Wine Bar just south of Healdsburg and suffers from the same pleasant problem—there are just too many of the small plates of food to choose from. Most are under $10, so just try them all if you're peckish. This is also the place to experiment with food and wine pairing. Although the decoration in the dining room is straight from Cuba, the inspiration for the food seems to come from all over the world.

An unassuming house opposite a strip mall a block from the plaza is home to the flagship of perhaps one of Healdsburg's most success-

ful restaurant partnerships, Joyanne and John Pezzolo. Their **N Ravenous Café & Lounge** (420 Center St., Healdsburg, 707/431-1302, lunch and dinner Wed.–Sun.) was moved here from its previous, pint-sized location next to the Raven Theater (they transformed that former space into an equally successful lunch spot, Ravenette). Inside, the Ravenous Café feels as homey as the exterior suggests and serves generous portions of sophisticated bistro food from the ever-changing menu, though the trademark Ravenous Burger is always on the menu. The corkage fee is only $10, as opposed to $15–20 at most other places.

If you want a Victorian setting for dinner there is probably no better option than the restaurant at **Madrona Manor** just outside Healdsburg (1001 Westside Rd., Healdsburg, 707/433-4321, dinner daily, entrées $17–30). Eating here is as much about the sumptuous, five-room Victorian setting and candle-lit table decorations as the food, though the very expensive and stylish modern cuisine gets rave reviews.

Casual Dining

Although most of Healdsburg's many bistros serve very reasonably priced lunches, there are plenty of even cheaper places to grab a quick bite. The younger sister to the Ravenous Café is **Ravenette,** an eight-table, lunch-only café in the annex of the Raven Theater (117 North St., 707/431-1770, open Wed.–Sun.).

At the other end of the spectrum is the spacious **Healdsburg Bar & Grill** (245 Healdsburg Ave., Healdsburg, 707/433-3333), with as many tables inside its saloon-style interior as outside on its shady patio. As its name and the giant outdoor barbecues suggest, this is paradise for lovers of big hunks of chargrilled meat.

There's more saloon-style dining and food at the **Bear Republic Brewing Company,** right behind the Hotel Healdsburg (345 Healdsburg Ave., Healdsburg, 707/433-2337), though the many microbrews are the main attraction and can be enjoyed right next to the stainless steel brewing tanks on the patio outside.

As trendy bistros have come and gone, the tiny **Taqueria el Sombrero** (245 Center St., Healdsburg, 707/433-3818) has been doling out its authentic Mexican food to locals since the 1970s, which is probably the last time the interior was furnished. The Hat, as el Sombrero is better known, is just yards from the corner of the plaza dominated by the **Oakville Grocery** (124 Matheson St., Healdsburg, 707/433-3200, open 7 A.M.–7 P.M. daily, until 8:30 P.M. Fri. and Sat.). Go there for deli food with that added Wine Country flair (and price) to stock up for a picnic or eat at one of the shaded tables on the large patio overlooking the plaza.

Adding some European flair to the deli scene is the **Costeaux French Bakery & Café** (417 Healdsburg Ave., Healdsburg, 707/433-1913, open 6:30 A.M.–6 P.M. Tues.–Sat., until 4 P.M. Sun.). It sells the usual crusty bread and other bakery fare together with some tasty breakfasts and deli lunches that can be enjoyed on the big patio next to the sidewalk, a few blocks north of the plaza and considerably calmer than Oakville's. It also offers a light dinner and wine on Friday and Saturday evenings.

Escape the Wine Country and pretend you're in the English countryside for a few hours at **Rachel's Tea Lounge** (239A Center St., 707/473-0743, open 10:30 A.M.–4 P.M. Tues.–Sun.). Besides a nice cup of tea and pastries, Rachel sells packaged tea and all sorts of tea-related paraphernalia.

Picnic Supplies

The **Oakville Grocery** (124 Matheson St., Healdsburg, 707/433-3200) is also picnic central, and has just about everything needed, including wine, for either a gourmet, alfresco feast or just some simple bread and cheese. Also don't forget the sandwiches and bread available at the **Costeaux French Bakery** (417 Healdsburg Ave., Healdsburg, 707/433-1913).

Less Wine Country luxury but equally good sandwiches and other deli food can be found a few blocks east on Center Street at **Anstead's Marketplace & Deli** (428 Center St., 707/431-0530), a place more popular with lunching locals than the Oakville Grocery.

If you're heading up to the Alexander Valley or Dry Creek Valley, then **Big John's Market** is on the way (1345 Healdsburg Ave., just north of W. Dry Creek Rd., 707/433-0336, open 8 A.M.–8 P.M. daily) and is a bakery, deli, and grocery store all in one.

Once in the Dry Creek Valley there's really only one place to buy food, and that's the **Dry Creek General Store** (3495 Dry Creek Rd., at Lambert Bridge Rd., 707/433-4171, open 6 A.M.–6 P.M. daily, from 7 A.M. on Sun.), which has existed in some form or another since the 1880s and continues to supply modern-day picnickers and peckish winery employees with deli sandwiches and groceries. Locals also like to hang out at the neighboring **Dry**

The Dry Creek General Store is the center of the action in this sleepy valley.

© PHILIP GOLDSMITH

Creek Bar to sip a cool beer while contemplating the wine business. The bar opens at 3 P.M. and usually closes whenever the last person falls off a stool.

Farmers Market

If you're after something really fresh, the **Healdsburg Farmer's Market** is held on Saturday mornings (9 A.M.–noon May–Nov.) in the parking lot of the Plaza Park (North St. and Vine St.), a few blocks west of the plaza itself. Those in the know say it's one of the best farmers markets in this part of Sonoma.

INFORMATION AND SERVICES

Comprehensive information about the wines and the winemakers of the Dry Creek Valley is available from the **Winegrowers of Dry Creek Valley** (www.wdcv.com, 707/433-3031). The association does a sterling job of ensuring the area's wineries get national attention and organizes the sell-out Passport Weekend event, a two-day party involving nearly all the valley's wineries on the last weekend in April.

Wine buffs can do even more research at the **Healdsburg Public Library** (Piper St. and Center St., 707/433-3772, closed Sun.), which houses Sonoma County's **Wine Library,** a small annex crammed with every conceivable wine book, including plenty on local and California wine history.

More information about the Healdsburg and its amenities can be found at the **Healdsburg Chamber of Commerce & Visitors Bureau** (217 Healdsburg Ave., 707/433-7562, www.healdsburg.org, open daily), a few blocks south of the plaza.

The Alexander Valley

Most people speeding north on the freeway might glimpse vineyards as they cruise past the Alexander Valley. Some might even stop to visit some of the valley's biggest wineries that are close to offramps, including Geyser Peak, Clos du Bois, and Chateau Souverain.

However, finding the true character of this part of the Wine Country, and many of its smaller wineries, requires a little more time navigating U.S. 128, which runs from Geyserville around some rather alarming 90-degree bends down into the rustic Chalk Hill and Knights Valley appellations. From there it's only a short drive to Calistoga at the northern end of the Napa Valley.

The 20-mile-long Alexander Valley stretches from Healdsburg in the south to the cow town of Cloverdale in the north. In between there is only one town of note: the hamlet of **Geyserville,** which for years has been destined to become the next big Wine Country resort town, only to stubbornly remain its old sleepy self.

Geyserville wasn't always so quiet. Back in the late 1800s the nearby geysers drew visitors far and wide and the influx of money helped build the town's grand Victorian homes. Now, the only signs of the area's underground hot water supply are the clouds of steam sometimes visible from the 19 geothermal plants in the hills east of Geyserville (an area known simply as The Geysers). The area is one of the world's largest geothermal energy sources.

As with many other parts of the Wine Country, this valley was once dominated by cattle pasture and fruit orchards. The cows still hold sway around **Cloverdale** and farther north where dairies are still more common than wineries, but the wineries are increasing.

Cloverdale marks the end of Northern California's big wine lands and the beginning of the outposts of Mendocino County's more modest wine lands, most notably the Anderson Valley, but also around Hopland and Ukiah farther up

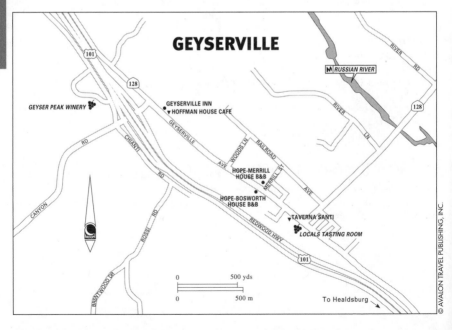

U.S. 101. How many Wine Country visitors will venture this far beyond Napa and Sonoma is yet to be seen, but Cloverdale optimistically opened its Wine and Visitor Center in 2000, clearly anticipating the move from the edge of the Wine Country to the center of the action as it shifts northward.

The Wines

The Alexander Valley is the northernmost appellation in Sonoma and also one of the hottest. Some cool, fog-laden air creeps in past Healdsburg to the southern part of the Valley, but it doesn't creep far. Summer temperatures in Geyserville can often be 10 or 20 degrees higher than in Healdsburg just a few miles south.

The ripening power of the heat, together with the gravelly soils deposited by the river, makes this a natural place to grow cabernet sauvignon. Alexander Valley cabernets are characterized by soft tannins and lush fruit, with a hint of chocolate flavor, making them perhaps the easiest drinking in California, if not the most complex. Other varietals grown here include chardonnay, which ripens easily to make rich and flavorful wines, along with merlot, zinfandel, and increasingly syrah and sangiovese.

The appellation expanded in 1990 to include the vineyards creeping up the hillsides, particularly on the eastern side of the valley where the mountains climb to more than 2,500 feet. As growers experiment with the cooler hillside vineyards, subtler styles of wine are being created than the blockbusters from the baking valley floor.

At the southern end of Alexander Valley, east of Santa Rosa, is the Chalk Hill appellation, which derives its name from soils that contain chalk-like volcanic ash, similar to those at the northern end of the Napa Valley. It's directly in the path of the Russian River Valley air cooler and is mostly contained within the easternmost part of the Russian River appellation. The few wineries here are perhaps best known for some tangy chardonnays.

Sandwiched between the eastern parts of Chalk Hill and Alexander Valley, with the border of Napa County to the west, is the Knights

© PHILIP GOLDSMITH

a busy day in Geyserville

Northern Sonoma

THE ITALIAN CONNECTION

It is not by chance or climate alone that there is a preponderance of Italian names among the wineries of the Dry Creek and Alexander Valleys. In the 1880s, an Italian immigrant called Andrea Sbarboro, who had a financial background, had the bright idea of starting a sort of grape-growing cooperative, or colony, to provide worthwhile work and lodging to the many other Italians arriving by the boatload in San Francisco.

He and his financial backers, including several Swiss businessmen, bought about 1,500 acres of land just south of Cloverdale and called the place Asti, after the town in the Piedmont region of Italy that was (and still is) famous for its wines. The Italian-Swiss Agricultural Colony, later shortened to Italian-Swiss Colony, was born.

The idea was that workers recruited to work there contributed a small portion of their salary each month in exchange for food and lodging, and to buy shares in the venture, thus making some money for Sbarboro and giving workers a sense of ownership.

Things didn't go quite to plan. Workers were suspicious of Sbarboro's financial intentions and did not want to share the risk, and the falling price of grapes soon meant the colony had to also build its own winery to remain viable.

But the colony and its winery eventually became a huge success. By the turn of the 20th century it was both profitable and said to be the biggest producer of table wine in California. By 1910 it was making more than 14 million gallons of wine a year.

Early generations of many local wine families came to work at the colony. Edoardo and Angela Seghesio met there, and Ed went on to create the Seghesio Family Vineyards in the early 1900s, for example. Ferrari, Martini, and Rossi are other Italian names once associated with the colony that have been influential in the local wine world over the last century.

Pietro Rossi was Sbarboro's first winemaker, and the Rossi family bought the winery during Prohibition, keeping it alive as the Asti Grape Products Company, and then re-entered the commercial wine business after repeal. It was eventually sold in the 1940s and after changing hands a few more times was finally bought by Fosters Wine Estates in 1988.

Although it is no longer open to the public (though it reportedly might be soon), the old winery at Asti has been well preserved. Some of the old grandeur of the buildings and grounds can still be seen by peering through the giant iron gates on Geyserville Avenue, just before the road crosses the freeway into Cloverdale.

Valley appellation, a primarily grape-growing region with just a couple of small wineries.

Millions of years ago the Russian River ran down the Alexander Valley, through Knights Valley, and into the Napa Valley, depositing gravelly soils ideal for growing grapes. Knights Valley soils are also part volcanic, deposited during the volcanic eruptions that eventually changed the course of the river westward to its present-day path through the Russian River Valley.

Completely shielded from the cool ocean air, Knights Valley is the hottest of Sonoma's appellations, providing ideal conditions for sauvignon blanc and cabernet sauvignon. Look for the Knights Valley appellation in the wines from Napa Valley's Beringer, which owns about half the vineyards here.

WINERIES

From the north end of the valley at the historic Asti winery, home of Italian-Swiss Colony (no longer open to the public), the Alexander Valley stretches southeast, past Healdsburg down to the Chalk Hill Road.

Most major wineries are on Geyserville Avenue, which runs parallel to the freeway between Healdsburg and Cloverdale, and on Highway 128, which runs southeast from Geyserville.

Pastori

One of the northernmost wineries open to the public is also one of the quirkiest and among the smallest in the valley. The primitive, cinderblock tasting room of Pastori, squeezed into one of the old warehouses at the side of the road, is a throwback to the old days of wine making when locals would come and fill up their jugs for a couple of bucks.

Frank Pastori is one of Sonoma's old-timers, and his family has been making wine here since the early 1900s. If the tasting room is open at all (it seems to have no regular hours) he's likely to be the only one there and will happily spin yarns about the good old days of wine making and perhaps try to convince you that white wine is "not real wine."

He offers good old prices for his zinfandel wine and port, and jug wines (bring your own jug). Don't expect much more than basic table wines but do expect an unusual Wine Country experience (23189 Geyserville Ave., Cloverdale, 707/857-3418, open whenever there's someone there).

Silver Oak Cellars

Just the other side of the freeway from Pastori is a temple for red-wine lovers, the Sonoma outpost of Silver Oak, which makes just one wine—cabernet sauvignon.

If you like cabernet, you'll undoubtedly like Silver Oak's powerful, velvety version that some say has an unusual aroma from being aged for years only in American oak barrels. This is a French-barrel-free zone.

The 50,000 cases made here are produced from the winery's 200 acres of vineyards in the Alexander Valley, Russian River Valley, and Chalk Hill appellations. A further 10,000 cases are made at Silver Oak's Napa winery.

Die-hard fans line up each year to buy the new release despite its ready availability, a testament to the loyalty of Silver Oak fans and the quality of the wine. Some less adoring fans, however, think this cult status makes the wines more expensive than they perhaps deserve to be.

The Alexander Valley cabernet is $60 and the Napa version is over $100. Not surprisingly there's a $10 tasting fee, though you can keep the glass. Also worth tasting is the more moderately priced port that's only available at the winery (24625 Chianti Rd., Geyserville, 800/273-8809, www.silveroak.com, open 9 A.M.–4 P.M. Mon.–Sat., appointment-only tours at 1:30 P.M.).

Geyser Peak Winery

Just down Chianti Road from Silver Oak is the giant, ivy-clad home of one of the region's biggest wineries, owned, along with nearby Canyon Road Winery, by Jim Beam Brands, a company more commonly associated with whiskey.

There has been a winery on the site since 1880, but the Geyser Peak name dates from 1911. Through the 1980s it was a bulk wine producer, making up to a million cases of cheap wines a year, and only became known for premium wine in the late 1990s. It now proudly boasts being named Best U.S. Wine Producer at the 2003 International Wine & Spirit Competition.

A dizzying selection of wines makes up the 350,000-case production, including cabernet, merlot, zinfandel, shiraz, sauvignon blanc, and chardonnay, nearly all available as regular, reserve, and vineyard-designate wines. The cheaper wines in particular can be good value, but the winery is perhaps best known for its concentrated Alexander Valley cabernets and red blends.

The giant tasting room is big enough to cope with the vast number of wines and crowds. Lower end wines can be tasted free, while reserve tastings start at $7 for four wines (22281 Chianti Rd., Geyserville, 707/857-9400, www.geyserpeakwinery.com, open 10 A.M.–5 P.M. daily).

Trentadue Winery

In keeping with the Tuscan heritage of the founding family, Trentadue was one of the

COURTESY OF TRENTADUE WINERY

Trentadue Winery, a sangiovese specialist

first wineries in this region to grow sangiovese grapes and now produces a cluster of sangiovese-based wines.

The flagship La Storia Cuvée 32 wine (Trentadue is Italian for the number 32) is a blend of sangiovese, merlot, and cabernet. Sangiovese even makes its way into the Old Patch Red blend, named for a 100-year-old block of zinfandel vines.

Trentadue also makes some of the best-value wines in the valley. The limited-production La Storia wines regularly score over 90 points in wine magazines yet start at well under $30. The cheaper Trentadue wines are rarely above $20. Many of the wines are produced in small lots, however, so they sell out quickly.

About a fifth of the winery's 20,000-case production is merlot, but sauvignon blanc, viognier, zinfandel, cabernet, pinot noir, and sangiovese are also made here. You can also taste a flight of the red and white ports in the Mediterranean-style tasting room for $5, the same price as the reserve wine tasting (19170 Geyserville Ave., Geyserville, 707/433-3104 or 888/332-3032, www.trentadue.com, open 10 A.M.–5 P.M. daily, tasting free or $5).

Chateau Souverain

Under the freeway from Trentadue is one of the grand wineries of the valley with some gloriously over-the-top architecture evoking both a French chateau and the hop-drying kilns that were once part of the Sonoma landscape.

Chateau Souverain was originally a Napa Valley winery when it was established in 1944 but moved to the Alexander Valley when its founder sold to the Pillsbury food company in 1973. The current winery, built in 1974, was called Souverain Cellars by Pillsbury, renamed Chateau Souverain by the next owner, Nestlé, in 1986, and now belongs to the multinational Fosters Wine Estates.

It may have an unsettled history, but there's nothing unsettled about the wines, which include consistently high-scoring Alexander Valley cabernet and merlot, together with chardonnay, sauvignon blanc, viognier, syrah, and zinfandel. Some grapes are sourced in the Dry Creek Valley and elsewhere in Sonoma County.

All told, Souverain produces about 300,000 cases of wine, more than a third of which is cabernet and chardonnay. Winemaker Ed Killian also keeps the best grapes for the Winemaker Reserve cabernet, merlot, and chardonnay wines, available only at the winery and well priced considering their reserve status (400 Souverain Rd., Geyserville, 888/809-4637, www.chateausouverain.com, open 10 A.M.– 5 P.M. daily, $3 tasting fee).

The winery also has an excellent restaurant, the **Alexander Valley Grille** (707/433-3141), which serves sumptuous brunches, lunches, and dinners in its cavernous dining room or outside on the large patio overlooking the vineyards.

Jordan Vineyard and Winery

While Judy Jordan focuses on bubbly and pinot noir at the J Winery in the Russian River appellation, father Tom crafts rich cabernet sauvignon and chardonnay at this chateau-style winery just north of Healdsburg, making about 90,000 cases in total of eminently drinkable wine.

Two-thirds of the production is the cabernet, which has a style that highlights this area's ability to produce soft and forward red wines. Although the winery is open daily, tours and tastings are by appointment only, Monday–Saturday (1474 Alexander Valley Rd., Healdsburg, 707/431-5250 or 800/654-1213, www.jordanwinery.com).

Simi Winery

Brothers Pietro and Giuseppe Simi came from Tuscany in the 1860s and set themselves up as winemakers and traders in San Francisco before moving to the current site just north of Healdsburg in 1881.

Back then the winery was called Montepulciano after the Simis' Tuscan homeland. The Simi name was adopted after repeal of Prohibition, but by the 1970s the family connection had ended and the winery was bought by a subsidiary of multinational conglomerate Constellation Brands in the 1990s.

In its heyday, the winery boasted Sonoma's first public tasting room—a 25,000-gallon redwood tank set up at the side of the road by Isabelle Simi Haigh, the second-generation owner of the winery. It was evidently a roaring success, but the current tasting room is a more modern affair inside the historic stone cellar building that dates from the late 1800s.

The winery is best known for its chardonnay, sourced from the 120 acres of Russian River Valley vineyards, and its cabernet from 600 acres of Alexander Valley vineyards. Those two wines alone account for more than two-thirds of the 300,000-case annual production and garner consistently good reviews. Other wines in the portfolio include sauvignon blanc and merlot.

Tastings are $5 ($10 for reserve wines), and $3 extra buys an informative tour of the gardens, which include a stand of redwood trees planted by Isabelle Simi. Tours are offered twice daily at 11 A.M. and 2 P.M. (16275 Healdsburg Ave., Healdsburg, 800/746-4880, www.simiwinery.com, open 10 A.M.–5 P.M. daily, $5 tasting fee).

Stryker Sonoma Winery

The name is appropriate considering this new winery is housed in one of the most striking buildings in the Alexander Valley, a contemporary glass, wood, and concrete structure that won an architectural award in 2002.

The huge, glass-walled tasting room overlooks 26 acres of estate vineyards that provide the grapes for the 7,000 cases of wine made each year, mainly cabernet, merlot, zinfandel, and chardonnay. All are available only at the winery and through the website (5110 Hwy. 128, Geyserville, 707/433-1944 or 800/433-1944, www.strykersonoma.com, open 10:30 A.M.– 5 P.M. daily, free tasting).

Sausal Winery

Some of the first zinfandel vines planted in the valley are part of Sausal's 120 acres of vineyards, and the winery takes full advantage of them. The bulk of the 10,000 cases of wine made here each year is zinfandel, and much of that is made using grapes from these old vines. Wines range from the affordable Private Reserve down to cheap, summer-drinking Cellar Cats Red, named for the winery's two feline residents, which is perfect for a picnic in the shade of the old oak trees on the grounds.

This is still the Alexander Valley, however, so a rich, age-worthy cabernet sauvignon gets a look in, too. And the sangiovese is a nod to the Italian heritage of the family that now owns the winery.

Leo Demostene, son of a first-generation Italian immigrant, bought this former prune and pear farm in the 1950s and started making bulk wine after working for many years at Abele Ferrari's historic Soda Rock Winery and marrying Ferrari's daughter, Rose. The current winery, which includes a converted prune dehydrator, was completed in the 1970s after Leo's death by the current Demostene generation (7370 Hwy. 128, Healdsburg, 707/433-2285 or 800/500-2285, www.sausalwinery.com, open 10 A.M.–4 P.M. daily, free tasting).

Alexander Valley Vineyards

It shares the name of the historic valley for good reason. The founders of the winery bought a large chunk of the original homestead of Cyrus Alexander, the mountain man who became a ranch manager and finally a landowner credited with planting the valley's first vineyards in 1846.

Whether Alexander ever made wine from those grapes is not known, but today's vineyards provide the grapes for the 100,000 cases of mainly red wines the winery produces.

About half that volume is cabernet and merlot with another quarter accounted for by chardonnay and the two decadent zinfandel blends, Sin Zin and Redemption Zin.

Other varietals include chardonnay, pinot noir, sangiovese, syrah, and viognier, together with some interesting red blends and the flagship wine called Cyrus, a bordeaux-style wine honoring the winery's namesake.

Historical sites pepper the current estate, including a wooden schoolhouse built by Alexander in 1853, and the Alexander family gravesite up the hill behind the winery. Educational tours of the expansive wine caves are also available by appointment (8644 Hwy. 128, Healdsburg, 800/888-7209, www.avvwine.com, open 10 A.M.–5 P.M. daily, free tasting).

Field Stone Winery

Built from stones unearthed during construction in 1977, this small winery cut into a dusty valley hillside was one of the first of a wave of modern underground wineries built in the Wine Country, and it had a tumultuous early life.

A former mayor of Berkeley, Wallace Johnson, founded the winery to test his newly invented mechanical grape-harvesting system, but he died just two years later. The winery then passed to his daughter, Katrina, and son-in-law, the Reverend John Staten, giving it a unique claim of being the first (and perhaps only) winery managed by a Presbyterian minister.

Grapes from the 50 acres of estate vineyards, together with some from the Russian River Valley and Mendocino, go into the 10,000 cases of wine made each year.

Reds include cabernet, merlot, sangiovese, and a reserve petite sirah, while whites include a limited-production viognier, sauvignon blanc, chardonnay, and gewürztraminer. Some of the proceeds from the sale of the Convivio line of lower-priced wines are donated to a local clinic serving local farm workers.

Oak trees shade two small picnic areas outside the small tasting room, sometimes shared with the local wild turkeys, and staff might be willing to take you on an impromptu tour if it's not too busy (10075 Hwy. 128, Healdsburg, 707/433-7266 or 800/544-7273, www.fieldstonewinery.com, open 10 A.M.–5 P.M. daily, free tasting).

Locals Tasting Room

Opened in 2003, this charming tasting room cooperative on Geyserville's main street pours wines from six of northern Sonoma's boutique wineries (Geyserville Ave. at Hwy. 128, 707/857-4900, www.tastelocalwine.com).

They include the Russian River region's **Crane Canyon** and **Eric Ross** wineries, Dry Creek's **Peterson Winery** and **Martin Family Vineyards,** and the intriguing **Sauvignon Republic Cellars,** itself a cooperative of four regional winemakers dedicated to producing the best examples of this varietal from vineyards all over California.

Wineries by Appointment

Among the 14 varietals grown on the 320 acres of Alexander Valley vineyards owned by the Robert Young winery, chardonnay dominates, and this is what the winery is best known for. In fact, there is a **Robert Young** (4960 Red Winery Rd., Geyserville, 707/4331-4811, www.ryew.com) clone of the chardonnay grape. Much of the rest of the estate is planted with cabernet (the Young family was the first to plant cabernet in the Alexander Valley in 1963) and merlot, which go into the flagship Scion blended red wine. Only about 4 percent of the grapes are used to make the 4,000 or so cases of wine. The rest are sold to other wineries.

You might miss the turnoff from Highway 128 to Chalk Hill Road, but you won't miss the striking modern gates of the **Lancaster Estate** (1500 Chalk Hill Rd., Healdsburg, 707/433-8178 or 800/799-8444, www.lancasterestate.com). Lancaster offers a tour of the state-of-the-art wine-making facility and caves before retiring to what seems like a private salon for tastings of the bordeaux-style red wines that range from the limited production Nicole's Vineyard to the primary Lancaster Estate wines.

Make sure to get detailed directions to **Medlock Ames** (13414 Chalk Hill Rd., Healdsburg, 707/431-8845, www.medlockames.com), about a mile off the Chalk Hill Road down what seems like an endless dirt driveway. Take a wrong turn and you might end up in a neighbor's driveway. Take the right turn and you'll find the new stone and glass winery surrounded by manicured gardens.

Medlock Ames was started by two thirty-something friends with money to invest and a passion for the Wine Country lifestyle. Newly minted winemaker Ames Morrison and moneyed business partner Chris Medlock James have produced limited production merlot and cabernet from the 55 acres of organic vineyard since 1999. The current 2,000-case production could eventually reach 15,000 cases, as an informal tour of the huge but relatively empty barrel room reveals.

SIGHTS

Cloverdale Historical Museum

The modest museum is actually the meticulously restored Gothic revival-style Gould-Shaw Victorian house and headquarters for the nonprofit Cloverdale Historical Society (215 N. Cloverdale Blvd., Cloverdale, 707/894-2067, open 11 A.M.–3 P.M. Fri.–Sun. Nov.–Feb., Thurs.–Mon. Mar.–Oct.).

The house itself is one of the oldest dwellings still standing in Cloverdale, and almost everything in it, from the iron crib to the pump organ, is from the same era, donated or borrowed from other historic homes in the area. It also houses the society's research center, with archives going back to the late 1800s, and you can pick up a guide for a short walking tour of some of the other historic Victorian homes in the town.

ENTERTAINMENT

If you can ignore the ugly concrete scar it creates halfway up the otherwise unspoiled hillside, the **River Rock Casino** (3250 Hwy. 128, Geyserville, 707/857-2777, www.riverrockcasino.com, open 24 hours) provides one of the more unusual recreational opportunities in the Wine Country. That's if you call winning or losing money a recreation.

The casino is jointly owned by a Nevada gaming company and the Dry Creek Band of the Pomo Indian tribe, which has suffered at the hands of white people since the first settlers arrived in the 1800s. The Pomo tribe's 85-acre Dry Creek Rancheria, on which the casino is built, is a far cry from the vast territory of mountains and valleys in the region they used to call home.

The casino has sweeping sunset views over the vineyards of the Alexander Valley, as well as the usual array of modern amenities to help visitors part with their money, including restaurants, bars, 1,600 slot machines, and 16 tables. It's also easy to find—the entrance is right off Highway 128 about three miles south of the bridge over the river, just past the red barn on the left.

RECREATION

Some of the best outdoor pursuits can be found in the neighboring Dry Creek and Russian River Valleys, but the Alexander Valley and Chalk Hill areas do have their own unique possibilities.

Although most opportunities to float on the river are focused south of Healdsburg, the stretch of Russian River between Cloverdale and Healdsburg is long, straight, and probably one of the easier to navigate. **Trowbridge Canoes,** at the Alexander Valley RV Park (800/640-1386, www.trowbridgecanoe.com, Fri.–Mon. only) rents two-person canoes for $100 a day from April through September. Included in the price is a shuttle back to base from Healdsburg.

Safari West

Cruising around the Alexander Valley in a rental car might not exactly bring to mind the savannas of Africa, but try telling that to the cheetahs, zebras, and giraffes that happily laze away in the sun just over the hill from many of Chalk Hill's wineries.

The Chalk Hill appellation is the unlikely setting for the 400-acre Safari West wildlife preserve, which contains a wide variety of endangered species from around the world, including many from central Africa, which evidently has weather similar to northern Sonoma.

This is not a zoo or safari in the regular sense of the word, however. Instead, it started out as a private ranch and preserve in the late 1980s, dedicated to saving endangered species from around the world. Humans were only admitted in 1993.

Seeing these magnificent animals (not the humans) requires a reservation for one of the private or group tours that set off three times a day (twice a day in winter). The group Safari Trek on a big towed trailer costs $25 and lasts about 90 minutes. The longer Safari Adventure on a customized old jeep costs $58 (on Porter Creek Rd. at Franz Valley Rd., 707/579-2551 or 800/616-2695, www.safariwest.com).

The more adventurous might consider sleep-ing overnight in one of the luxurious tent cabins ($225 for two people, extra guests $25) or cottages ($300 for two). Lunch and dinner are available at the on-site café; wine is served but antelope burgers are not.

Because it's a working preserve, visitors get easy access to the wildlife experts that work there and who are happy to reel off fascinating facts about the animals. This little corner of wild Africa in Sonoma also provides a welcome escape from the wilds of Wine Country tourism.

ACCOMMODATIONS

The Alexander Valley has more places to stay than its rural setting and tiny towns might suggest. Most of the B&Bs are clustered up at the far northern end of the valley in the cowtown of Cloverdale, but there are a few worthwhile places to consider around Geyserville to the south.

Under $100

With all the B&Bs in the valley costing well over $100 it is once again left to the motels to accommodate those with tight budgets or an aversion to Victorian inns. The biggest concentration of motels in this area (all totally unexceptional) is just off the freeway on Cloverdale Boulevard (take the Citrus Fair Dr. exit) and includes the **Cloverdale Oaks Motel** (123 S. Cloverdale Blvd., 707/894-2404), the **Vineyard Valley Motel** (721 N. Cloverdale Blvd., 707/894-0707), and the **Garden Motel** (611 N. Cloverdale Blvd., 707/894-2594). Best Western and Holiday Inn also have properties in the area.

$100–200

At the lowest end of the price range is the conveniently located **Geyserville Inn** (21714 Geyserville Ave., Geyserville, 707/857-4343 or 877/857-4343, www.geyservilleinn.com), a modern two-floor building resembling an upscale motel at the northern edge of Geyserville. Request an east-facing room to get a view of the vineyards and mountains rather than the freeway, which is a little too close for comfort.

The smaller of the 38 rather plain rooms often cost less than $100 a night; $120–140 gets one of the larger rooms with fireplace or balcony. Next door is the homey **Hoffman House Café,** which serves breakfast and lunch every day.

Driving through Geyserville, it's easy to miss two bargain B&Bs among the homes along the main road, but slow down and the historic elegance of the two Victorian-style **Hope Inns** becomes more obvious (21253 Geyserville Ave., Geyserville, 707/857-3356 or 800/825-4233, www.hope-inns.com). The richly decorated interiors were restored in painstaking detail by the Hope family in the 1980s and put many of the historic Healdsburg B&Bs to shame.

There are eight rooms ($130–250) in the **Hope-Merrill House,** an 1870 Eastlake-style Victorian that features silk-screened wallpapers, coffered ceilings, and original woodwork. This is where the dining room (where breakfast is served), pool, and registration desk are located. Across the street is the Queen Anne–style **Hope-Bosworth House,** which has four rooms ($130–180) featuring the more restrained furnishings of that period. Only one room, the sumptuous Sterling Suite in the Hope-Merrill House, has a television, though others have some features that more than compensate, from fireplaces and chaise lounges to whirlpool and claw-foot tubs.

The huge brick fireplace in the lobby of the **Old Crocker Inn** (1126 Old Crocker Inn Rd., Cloverdale, 707/894-4000 or 800/716-2007, www.oldcrockerinn.com), just south of Cloverdale, gives a hint of the Wild West roots of this charming lodge. It was built by railway magnate Charles Crocker, founder of the Central Pacific Railroad, in the early 20th century as a grand summer house, and the current owners have re-created the rustic character that it must originally have had—an odd blend of the Wild West and Victoriana.

The biggest room is the namesake Crocker room with a massive mahogany four-poster ($195 a night). The other four rooms in the main lodge building ($145–185) are named after Crocker's railroad partners. There are

also three small cottages, two of them able to comfortably sleep four people ($175–235). All the rooms have old and modern features alike, including claw-foot tubs, gas fireplaces, TVs, and Internet access. The peaceful five-acre property also has an outdoor pool and feels like it's far from the madding crowds of the Wine Country. The complimentary gourmet breakfast is served in the lodge's spacious dining room.

Camping

The valley's main campground is the **Cloverdale KOA Wine Country Campground** next to the hamlet of Asti (1166 Asti Ridge Rd., across the River Rd. bridge from Geyserville Ave., 707/894-3337). It might be part of the KOA chain, but it is a clean, easily accessible, and family-friendly option when the sites at nearby Lake Sonoma in the Dry Creek Valley are full. It also has a well-stocked fishing pond, bicycles for rent, and a big swimming pool.

There are 47 tent sites that cost from $34 and over 100 RV sites from $38 a night. Reserve at 800/368-4558 or online (www.winecountrykoa.com). The rustic little one- and two-room Kamping Kabins ($58–80) might also be an alternative if the local B&Bs are full too, though you have to supply your own bedding.

FOOD

Most valley dining options are in nearby Healdsburg, but there are some notable exceptions, particularly **N Taverna Santi,** right in the heart of Geyserville (21047 Geyserville Ave. 707/857-1790, www.tavernasanti.com, dinner daily, lunch Thurs.–Mon., dinner entrées $15–40). It might seem strange to have a white-tablecloth bistro in a one-street town that most tourists whiz right through, but Santi has flourished since it opened in 2000, a testament to its superb Italian food.

Despite the white tablecloths, the interior and back patio feel relaxed and there's a refreshing absence of overbearing design elements. The same can be said for the food from the short

© PHILIP GOLDSMITH

the Alexander Valley's gourmet picnic stop

menu, from Italian classics like osso bucco ($22) to the less familiar chicken cooked under a brick ($18). The wine list also has plenty of Italian in it, with wines from Italy itself or Italian varietals produced by local wineries.

A little farther north on Geyserville Avenue is the **Hoffman House Café** (21712 Geyserville Ave., Geyserville, 707/857-3264, daily until 3 P.M.), with a big outdoor patio and a reputation for great brunches. It also sells gourmet boxed lunches, ideal for picnics.

For more food on the go, and some of the best picnic supplies around, the bright yellow and green  **Jimtown Store** (96706 Hwy. 128, at Alexander Valley Rd., Healdsburg, 707/433-1212), with its bright red vintage pickup truck parked outside, is a valley fixture and seems to sell a bit of everything, including its own label wine. The boxed lunches alone are worth a detour, and include a fat, gourmet baguette sandwich, cookies, salad, and fruit, all for less than $11.

INFORMATION AND SERVICES

More information about this area's wines together with a comprehensive winery map can be found on the **Alexander Valley Winegrowers Association** website (www.alexandervalley.org).

More information about the history and businesses of Cloverdale and Geyserville can be obtained from their respective chambers of commerce. The **Geyserville Chamber of Commerce** is not open to the public but has an excellent website at www.geyservillecc.com and can also be reached at 707/857-3745. The **Cloverdale Chamber of Commerce** (105 N. Cloverdale Blvd., 707/894-4470, www.cloverdale.net) also contains the **North Coast Wine & Visitor Center** (open weekdays 10 A.M.–3 P.M., weekends 11 A.M.–2 P.M.), which has maps, guides, and discount vouchers for anyone planning to explore northern Sonoma and Mendocino wineries.

The South and East Bays

Think of wine regions within an easy drive of San Francisco or Oakland and either Napa or Sonoma will jump to mind. Pity then the poor, forgotten Santa Cruz Mountains and Livermore Valley to the south, two regions steeped in just as much wine-making history and producing wines that are as well respected as those from more famous appellations.

The Santa Cruz Mountains are doing just fine and actually don't need any pity. They have plenty of Silicon Valley money to the east, some of Northern California's best redwood forests in their cool, damp heights, and fabulous beaches to the west, resulting in a curious cultural blend of capitalists, hippies, mountain folk, and surfer dudes Within Northern California's Wine Country only the Russian River Valley can boast a similar degree of scenic and cultural diversity.

Clinging to the eastern and western slopes of the Santa Cruz Mountains are a few hundred acres of vineyards. Some face east and others west, some at high elevations and others at lower altitude, some warm and others exposed to chilling ocean winds. It all creates a patchwork of growing conditions ideal for

Must-Sees

Look for **M** to find the sights and activities you can't miss and **N** for the best dining and lodging.

M **Picchetti Winery:** This rustic, historic winery is set amid hiking trails in the hills above Silicon Valley. Just watch out for the energetic peacocks (page 211).

M **Testarossa Vineyards:** It's a pretty walk from downtown Los Gatos to this pinot specialist on the hilltop, housed in a former Jesuit Novitiate (page 214).

M **Hakone Japanese Gardens:** A little piece of Zen in the already serene hills above Saratoga (page 216).

M **David Bruce Winery:** Perched on a mountain ridgeline, this is the winery that helped put Santa Cruz pinot noir on the map (page 226).

© PHILIP GOLDSMITH

the Santa Cruz Beach Boardwalk

M **Roaring Camp and Big Trees Railroad:** Though crowded in the summer, the old steam trains of Roaring Camp are a unique way to experience the area's redwood forests (page 228).

M **Big Basin Redwoods State Park:** Experience the mountain forests firsthand with a half-day hike, or simply visit the Nature Lodge and stroll the short Redwood Trail (page 229).

M **Bonny Doon Vineyard:** It's a little out of the way, but a lot of fun and home to a staggering range of unusual varietal wines (page 234).

M **Santa Cruz Beach Boardwalk:** This seedy but fun combination of sun, sea, sand, and thrill rides is a great family attraction (page 236).

M **Wente Vineyards:** The grandfather of Livermore Valley wineries helped revitalize the valley's threatened wine industry (page 247).

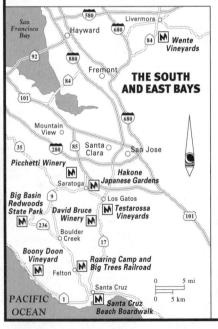

THE SOUTH AND EAST BAYS

a wide variety of grapes. The notoriously fin-icky pinot noir grape thinks much of the land is heaven, but there are fine growing areas for chardonnay, cabernet sauvignon, and other grapes, too.

Small mountain wineries happily craft lim-ited-production wines with a greater sense of place than many in other appellations. A lim-ited supply of local mountain grapes often means making wine from regions farther south along the Central Coast, giving visi-tors the chance to compare great wines like pinot noir and chardonnay from prime coastal growing regions in both Northern and South-ern California.

The Livermore Valley might be a little more desperate for attention than the mellow moun-tains of Santa Cruz. Subdivisions of bedroom communities have overtaken the valley and very nearly pushed out grape growing alto-gether in the 1990s. Only some of the biggest wineries managed to stem the loss of vine-yards, convincing the city of Livermore that the wine industry is worth having around in the long term.

Now those wineries would really like visitors to prove them right, discovering that there's far more to see than suburban strip malls and tail-gating cars on the freeway.

Wine-Making History

The Santa Cruz region is one of the oldest grape-growing regions in Northern Califor-nia. It got a head start on the more famous Napa and Sonoma regions for two reasons: It was the earliest area to be tamed by the missionaries, and the wines could be easily transported over land to the bigger cities of San Francisco and Oakland. Early Napa and Sonoma wineries had to ship wines across the bay to San Francisco. Heavy logging in the 1800s cleared large swaths of the forested mountainsides, making way for agriculture and viticulture. By the early 1900s, there were thousands of acres of vineyards to serve the burgeoning Bay Area population, but the boom ended abruptly.

The rise of the Napa and Sonoma wine

industries, where flat valleys were easier to farm, combined with the double whammy of the phylloxera infestation and Prohibi-tion to all but wipe out the once-flourish-ing wine business here. By the 1940s, only a handful of small wineries remained and virtually no intact vineyards. Nevertheless, the mountain wine industry hung on and is flourishing again, albeit in an altogether more compact and specialized form than in its Victorian heyday.

Today there are only about 300 acres of vine-yards in the Santa Cruz appellation, though hundreds more surround its fringes. The small acreage, together with low yields of fruit from the rocky mountain soil, means that nearly every winery in this region has to use grapes from elsewhere in California to make commer-cial quantities of wine. The Central Coast re-gion is one of the most common sources.

Some estate wines carry the Santa Cruz Mountains designation, however, mainly pinot noir, cabernet sauvignon, and chardonnay—the three main varietals grown here. As the ge-ography suggests, they tend to have an earthy, sometimes austere flavor compared to wines from the hotter Napa and Sonoma Counties. Cooler weather is one reason, but the soil's thinness is another big factor in the unique taste of the area's wines. Mountain soils tend to be thin and rocky to begin with, and the more than 50 inches of rain that fall here every year has washed out much of the goodness over the millennia, leaving infertile though mineral-rich earth.

The chardonnay in particular is a total con-trast to some of the buttery fruit bombs farther north, but even the cabernet sauvignon grown on the hottest ridgelines can taste angular, just like the rocky surroundings. Palates more used to the plump Napa or Sonoma wines in gen-eral might find it hard going in these moun-tains. In this case, stick to the pinot noir, a varietal that finds life as comfortable here as in Carneros or the Russian River Valley, or the zinfandel, a varietal that is easy enough to ripen even up in the mountains, though it's still sparsely planted.

PLANNING YOUR TIME

Exploring the Santa Cruz Mountains, you might begin to realize why the area doesn't show up on nearly as many radar screens as Napa or Sonoma. In fact, you might wish you *had* radar to help navigate the often widely spaced wineries that leave little in the way of signage to indicate where they actually are.

Even when there are signs, you might be concentrating more on how to avoid flying off the narrow mountain road. But when you do eventually find the wineries, you'll have a rewarding and often intimate experience. Just don't come expecting the sort of Wine Country frills found in the towns and large wineries of Napa and Sonoma—this area is about small producers making serious wine surrounded by some serious scenery.

Many of these Santa Cruz wineries are clustered on the eastern slopes of the mountains around **Los Gatos** and **Saratoga.** They are generally closer together (though no less easy to find) than those on the west-facing slopes of the mountains leading down toward the city of **Santa Cruz.**

Forget about driving from winery to winery, or trying to cover them all in a hectic day. Instead, accustom yourself to slow but scenic mountain roads and let the great outdoors lure you out of the car (and lower your blood pressure). Driving from Saratoga up over the mountains to Santa Cruz can take up to two hours, depending on the route, even without stopping. Throw in a few wineries and a bit of outdoor exercise en route, and it can easily turn into a half- or full-day trip.

On the other side of the San Francisco Bay, by contrast, the **Livermore Valley** is much more suited to quick exploration. Wineries are close together and the roads are flat and relatively straight. Make a single day of it and hit five wineries to get a good taste of what the valley's wines are all about. Or stretch one visit into a weekend, incorporating a few more wineries plus some golf or hiking.

Virtually all wine events for the Santa Cruz Mountains region are organized by the Santa Cruz Mountains Winegrowers Association (831/688-6961, www.scmwa.com), including the notable **Wineries Passport Program** ($25 admission, but all tasting is free), which runs on four weekends during the year (usually the third Saturday of January, April, July, and November) and is the only way to visit the many small wineries not otherwise open to the public. Plan wisely so you don't spend the whole day driving the mountain roads.

The association also organizes other annual events, including the **Vintners' Festival** (also $25), an arts, music, wine, and food celebration on the first and second weekends in June, and recently started the **Pinot Paradise** event in April ($30 admission), which sells out fast given this wine's newfound popularity.

Los Gatos and Saratoga

The contrast could not be greater between these two towns edging the wealthy Silicon Valley suburbs and the rest of the Santa Cruz Mountains region. In some respects, Los Gatos and Saratoga have more in common with the Wine Country towns in Napa and Sonoma than they do with their western neighbors. Expensive restaurants, boutique shopping, Victorian history, and million-dollar homes are the norm here, made all the more desirable by their proximity to the lush mountains viewable from almost every vantage point.

The mountains, not the wine industry, made these towns. As loggers cleared the mountains, the eastern mountain towns sprang up to serve the lumber industry. Once the trees were largely gone, the area became a summer playground for the San Francisco elite. Today, the area is still a playground for the rich, as local real estate prices and the Ferrari dealership in Los Gatos illustrate. Ironically, this same scenery is helping to preserve the remaining wine industry from encroaching development as the mountains act as a natural buffer to the spreading suburbs.

Although many of the wineries in the hills north of Saratoga share the landscape with ostentatious, private McMansions, the land is not under the same development pressure as some smaller wineries in the thick of suburbia closer to San Jose. Nevertheless, some of the rural charm that makes many wineries in Napa and Sonoma so individual is missing.

The Wines

As far as wine-growing conditions are concerned, the Santa Cruz Mountains appellation can really be divided into two sections. The eastern side of the mountains, along the ridgeline and down into Saratoga and Los Gatos (at the border of the Santa Clara AVA), is largely shielded from the cold ocean wind and fog. This is where much of the cabernet sauvignon tends to be planted, so it can fully ripen in the longer hours of sunshine and warmer temperatures. Chardonnay is also common in this area, and one of California's best chardonnay producers, Mount Eden Vineyards, is close to Saratoga.

Although the Santa Cruz Mountains AVA is home to relatively small wineries and tasting fees are rare, they tend to be a little more common among wineries closer to urban areas. Those that do charge are noted; the rest are free. Winery opening hours also tend to reflect the lack of tourist traffic in the area. A few are open all week, but many open only on weekends or by appointment.

WINERIES

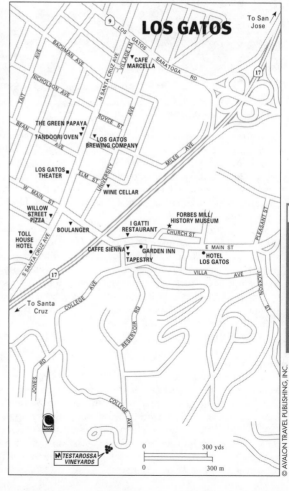 Picchetti Winery

This historic and rustic winery in a handful of old barns about a half mile up Monte Bello Road

is one of only a few still surviving in some form or another from the area's pre-Prohibition wine heyday. Picchetti was first established in the 1890s by Italian immigrant Vincent Picchetti and even managed to survive Prohibition by replanting much of the original vineyard with fruit and by raising livestock, only to fall victim to economic conditions in the 1960s when the winery was sold.

It was leased in 1998 from the Mid-Peninsula Open Space District—its caretaker since the 1960s—and wine production started there

© PHILIP GOLDSMITH

Los Gatos is the gateway to the mountains.

again after the necessary equipment upgrades. Now it makes about 9,000 cases of wine, though most from other vineyards elsewhere in the Santa Cruz Mountains, together with some Central Coast and Sonoma area wines. The exception is a zinfandel made from 110-year-old vines.

Since it is still owned by and located in the Mid-Peninsula Open Space District, plenty of hiking trails head off into the wooded hills around the winery. A trail map is usually available right near the parking lot, but watch out for the many amorous peacocks strutting around the area (13100 Monte Bello Rd., Cupertino, 408/741-1310, 11 A.M.–5 P.M. daily, www.picchetti.com).

Ridge Winery

Ridge is about a 3.5-mile drive up twisting Monte Bello Road from Picchetti, but it feels like driving to the top of the world, and the views east across San Jose and the bay are spectacular. Although it is not the oldest winery in these parts, Ridge is one of the biggest names in Santa Cruz due to its almost cult-like cabernet sauvignon sourced from its ridgetop Monte Bello vineyard right above the modest redwood winery building.

Grapes were first grown here in the 1880s, but those original vineyards, like many others in the region, were abandoned during Prohibition. The current 80-acre Monte Bello vineyard was first planted in the 1960s and rises from an elevation of 1,300 feet up to 2,600 feet (you pass some on the drive up here). It now provides grapes for Ridge's famous cabernet, considered by some to be one of California's best, and also for what is regarded as one of the best chardonnays in the Santa Cruz Mountains, often compared to the chardonnay made by neighboring Mount Eden from vineyards along the same mountain ridge.

Ridge also makes some equally good cabernet and chardonnay from grapes grown elsewhere in the Santa Cruz Mountains, and both are a more palatable price. To confuse matters, Ridge also owns the former Lytton Springs winery up in the Dry Creek Valley and hundreds of acres of vineyards in Sonoma County, so its portfolio of wines stretches far beyond the cabernet, chardonnay, and small quantities of zinfandel made here. Many of these, together with the Santa Cruz Mountains wines, can be tasted on weekends when the tasting room is open, though public tasting of the Monte Bello wines is limited to a couple of special pre-release weekend events in March and May. Call the winery for more information (17100 Monte Bello Rd., Cupertino, 408/867-3233, www.ridgewine.com).

Fellom Ranch Vineyards

This is one of the wineries established right after the end of Prohibition in the 1930s by Roy Fellom, then state senator; it borders the famous Monte Bello vineyards of Ridge Winery, which alone makes people sit up and take note.

The original vineyard 2,000 feet up in the mountains has long since been replanted with cabernet sauvignon and merlot that now supply grapes for the bargain-priced cabernet made here. It may not share the fame of the Monte Bello cabernet made by Ridge next door, but it shares some of the same characteristics and costs only $20. Fellom also makes a worthy zinfandel from a vineyard in Saratoga, brining its total production up to about 1,500 cases, though tasting the wines requires some perseverance.

During the summer the winery can be visited only by appointment, while in the winter months visitors seem to be actively discouraged, except on the Passport weekends organized by the Santa Cruz Mountains Winegrowers Association (17075 Monte Bello Rd., Cupertino, 408/741-0206, www.fellom.com).

Mount Eden Vineyards

This is another post-Prohibition success story, established in the 1940s by the controversial wine industry figure Martin Ray, known for producing some phenomenal wines and for his attempts to reform the industry's wine labeling practices, which won him as many enemies as friends. After getting legally tangled with investment partners, Ray was forced to sell the winery, and it was bought by another group of investors that renamed it Mount Eden in 1972.

Since then, Mount Eden has gained a reputation for producing one of the best chardonnays in the mountains from its vineyards

on the ridgeline, hailed by some critics as the best chardonnay in California. It also makes a chardonnay using grapes from Wolff Vineyard about a hundred miles south in the Edna Valley, and the contrast between the two is a fascinating example of just how different this wine can be depending on where the grapes are grown and how they're handled.

The estate chardonnay is taut and full of mineral and citrus flavors, a style designed to mellow with age, while the version from the warmer, more fertile Edna Valley has more of the tropical fruit flavors and creaminess that people normally associate with Californian chardonnay.

Mount Eden's other wines, including an estate cabernet sauvignon and pinot noir, are less highly regarded but still some of the best examples in this region. The pinot in particular has been receiving some rave reviews in recent years. Total production is about 15,000 cases, about half of which is the Central Coast chardonnay.

The winery can only be visited by appointment, but it is a worthwhile trip to make not only for the wines but also for the view east across the sprawl of Silicon Valley and the sight of the multimillion dollar homes that have sprung up in the hills over the last decade. Tours need to be booked about a week in advance and are offered only on weekdays during regular business hours (22020 Mt. Eden Rd., Saratoga, 888/865-9463, www.mounteden.com).

Cooper-Garrod Vineyards

The stables right near the entrance to Cooper-Garrod give away the ranching roots of this small winery. The land was bought in the late 1800s by the Garrod family and planted with fruit orchards right up until the 1970s when the last apricot and plum trees were pulled out to make way for vines. The Coopers entered the picture through marriage.

About 3,000 cases of wine are now made from the 28 acres of vineyards, and the tasting room is the old Fruit House, where those apricots and prunes were once stored. The wines include some fine estate chardonnay and some ripe cabernet sauvignon and cabernet franc.

The ranching heritage is not entirely forgotten, either. The **Garrod Farms Riding Stable** offers horseback rides by appointment on weekend afternoons in the nearby hills, followed by a private tasting at the winery. Call 408/867-9527 for information and reservations (22645 Garrod Rd., off Mt. Eden Rd., Saratoga, 408/867-7116, www.cgv.com, weekdays noon–5 P.M., weekends 11 A.M.–5 P.M.).

Savannah-Chanelle Vineyards

Savannah-Chanelle's tasting room in a big redwood barn a few miles west of Saratoga on Highway 9 is one of the few open to the public in this area but also one of the few to charge a tasting fee ($5) for regular tasting. The winery makes a huge number of different wines, most from vineyards outside the Santa Cruz region. It is best known for its pinot noir.

Seven different versions of pinot account for about 80 percent of the 6,000 cases of wine made here and include several vineyard designates. Grapes come from vineyards up and down California, including the Santa Lucia Highlands down near Monterey, farther south along the Central Coast, and in Marin County up north.

The only estate wines up until 2004 were the few hundred cases of zinfandel and cabernet franc. The winery's first estate-grown pinot noir (the 2002 vintage) was released in 2005, and future releases should be worth checking out considering the vast experience the winery now has with that varietal (23600 Congress Springs Rd./Hwy. 9, Saratoga, 408/741-2934, www.savannahchanelle.com, 11 A.M.–5 P.M. daily, tasting $5).

Testarossa Vineyards

It's a pretty half-mile walk (or a five-minute drive) from downtown Los Gatos up the College Avenue hill to the old Jesuit Novitiate that now houses this rapidly growing pinot noir specialist, though don't go expecting to taste Santa Cruz pinot noir. Instead, Testarossa makes pinot from almost every other important growing region along the Central Coast of California, as far south as Santa Barbara.

In fact, Testarossa makes no Santa Cruz wines at all. The four vineyard-designate pinots and six vineyard-designate chardonnays come from as far south as the Santa Rita Hills near Santa Barbara and as far north as the Santa Lucia Highlands just south of Monterey. A couple of vineyards in the Russian River Valley were added in 2004 and will probably increase total production above the 10,000 cases made a year earlier.

Although the wines are pricey by Santa Cruz standards, with most costing $30–60 a bottle, they regularly get high ratings from critics and should be on the tasting list of any pinot or chardonnay lover. Cheaper wines are made under the Novitiate label, harking back to the small wine-making operation that the Jesuits once had. A small display about the history of the Novitiate and its wine-making legacy can be seen in the historic cave that leads to the big, modern tasting room (300-A College Ave., Los Gatos, 408/354-6150, www.testarossa.com, 11 A.M.–5 P.M. daily, tasting $10).

SIGHTS

Los Gatos and Saratoga are two of the most historically fascinating towns in Silicon Valley, thanks to the neighboring mountains that shaped the industrial and agricultural history of the region. Much of that history has been preserved, though there are some exceptions. Most notably, the Old Town of Los Gatos is now more accurately the New Old Town, after the shopping center that grew up in the old Victorian **University Avenue School** was "remodeled" by the enterprising city in the late 1990s (at least it wasn't renamed Ye Olde Town).

Los Gatos sits on what was once the main gateway from the coast at Santa Cruz to the Bay Area (a route down which U.S. 17 now runs). Early Spanish pioneers from the Santa Cruz mission used it as a shortcut to San Francisco and, legend has it, coined the area's original name, La Rinconada de Los Gatos (little corner of the cats), from the large number of mountain lions seen drinking at what is now Los Gatos Creek.

Downtown Los Gatos

With the supply route established, industry flourished in both Los Gatos and Saratoga, helped along by the gold rush supply business in the mid-1800s. Logging up in the mountains during the late 1800s was followed by fledgling vineyards and other agriculture on the freshly cleared mountainsides. Where there are now subdivisions and McMansions stretching toward San Jose, there were once hundreds of acres of prunes, apricots, and other fruits.

Los Gatos Creek

You can now walk along Los Gatos Creek without fear of mountain lions on **Los Gatos Creek Trail.** The trail runs from **Lexington Reservoir,** a popular boating and fishing lake south of town, north past Vasona Lake (another popular summer fun spot) to **Los Gatos Creek County Park** and beyond. Sadly, it also runs within earshot of a freeway for much of its length. Access the trail at East Main Street just before it crosses the freeway to West Main Street (look for the sign near Caffé Siena) and head south for a mile to the reservoir. Alternatively, go north a few yards to Church Street and see the site of the old **Forbes Mill,** built

in 1854 by Scottish entrepreneur James Forbes in order to cash in on the demand from hungry gold miners for flour. It was the first commercial building here and the catalyst for the eventual creation of the town, though only one wall remains today.

In the small storage annex built for the mill in 1880 is the **History Museum of Los Gatos** (75 Church St., at E. Main St., 408/395-7375, www.losgatosmuseum.com, noon–4 P.M. Wed.– Sun., $2 donation). Exhibits cover local history and related history of the surrounding region, including the history of the Ohlone Native Americans who once called the area home.

Historic Los Gatos

From the history museum at the Forbes Mill, head across the freeway on Main Street to visit several of Los Gatos's finest historic buildings, including: the modest 1902 **Opera House** building (140 W. Main St.); the ornate renaissance revival **First National Bank** building dating from 1920 (W. Main St. at N. Santa Cruz Ave.); the art deco **Bank of Italy** building from the 1930s (160–170 W. Main St.); and the 1891 **La Canada Building** (1–17 N. Santa Cruz Ave.), with its circular bay window and pointy-roofed turret. These buildings are all part of a short walking tour, maps of which are available from the Los Gatos Chamber of Commerce (see *Information*).

Turn the corner from historic Main Street onto North Santa Cruz Avenue and you're suddenly thrust very much into the 21st century. Boutiques, restaurants, and an increasing number of chain shops (to the dismay of locals) line the five blocks down to the Los Gatos–Saratoga Road. Look for the art deco **Los Gatos Theater,** which dates from 1915 and was remodeled in 1929, and the hard-to-miss **Coggeshall Mansion** (115 N. Santa Cruz Ave.), a turreted Victorian house said to be haunted and now home to an unexceptional seafood and steak restaurant.

Historic Saratoga

About the time James Forbes was grinding his flour in Los Gatos, the town that would become

© PHILIP GOLDSMITH

The South and East Bays

Saratoga was growing around a mountain pass tollgate on what is now Big Basin Way. The tollgate settlement was later named McCartysville after the man who drew up the first town plan and sold off lots for as little as $10 (now those lots would sell for about 100,000 times that). The Saratoga moniker didn't come about until 1865, when a mineral spring in the hills above the town inspired the residents to copy the name of the more famous upstate New York spa town.

Villa Montalvo

In its heyday, Saratoga became a magnet for wealthy San Franciscans looking to escape that city's summer fog, including Senator James Phelan, who built Villa Montalvo (15400 Montalvo Rd, off Big Basin Way., Saratoga, 408/961-5800, www.villamontalvo.com) up in the hills in 1912. The ornate Mediterranean mansion, with formal gardens, an arboretum, and hiking trails spreading over 175 acres of land, is now open to the public every day until 5 P.M., until 7 P.M. on weekdays April–September. Parking and admission to the park are free.

Villa Montalvo is also a popular arts center, offering residencies for artists, plus regular art and sculpture shows inside or on the grounds. As one of Silicon Valley's most popular concert venues it attracts some big-name musicians, from pop to classical. There's a concert virtually every weekend of the year (on two or three nights a week during summer) either in the Carriage House Theater or at one of the two outdoor venues. Contact Villa Montalvo for a schedule and book a restaurant well in advance if you plan to eat in Saratoga before a concert. A free shuttle runs from nearby West Valley College (14000 Fruitvale Ave., off Saratoga Ave. in Saratoga) on concert nights when parking at the villa is limited and costs $25.

M Hakone Japanese Gardens

Shortly after Phelan had settled down in his summer retreat, San Francisco art patrons Oliver and Isabel Stine bought 18 acres of land above Saratoga for their own summer home.

Regular trips to Japan led them to gradually transform the hillside into what is now the Hakone Japanese Gardens (21000 Big Basin Way, Saratoga, 408/741-4994, www.hakone.com, daily until 5 P.M., $7), up a steep driveway just west of Saratoga village.

The idea of crowds of visitors wandering around these very Zen gardens might not seem to be very Zen, but there are still plenty of peaceful spots to be found among the maples, pavilions, and ponds, which are said to be the oldest residential Japanese gardens in the western hemisphere. It is actually a series of separate gardens rising up the hillside with spectacular views. The Kizuna-En bamboo garden is designed to represent Saratoga and its sister city in Japan, Muko-Shi. The classic, gravelly Zen Garden is designed for meditation, the lush Hill and Pond Garden for strolling, and the mossy, damp Tea Garden for soothing away your worries before witnessing the arcane and intricate Japanese tea ceremony.

EVENTS

The big annual blowout in Los Gatos is the **Fiesta de Artes** art and wine festival, usually held in the second weekend of August along Main Street and at the Town Plaza. Many local wineries and restaurants take part in this sweaty street fair along with local arts and crafts vendors and live music.

In July and August, Los Gatos hosts the free **Jazz on the Plaza,** six concerts on consecutive Wednesday evenings at the Town Plaza. The summer also flushes out the thespians in the **Los Gatos Shakespeare Festival.** The outdoor performances are held on several evenings a week during July at Oak Meadow Park on the corner of Blossom Hill Road and University Avenue. Ticket prices and the schedule are usually posted in the spring. Contact the Festival Theatre Ensemble for more information or tickets (408/996-0635, www.festivaltheatreensemble.org).

Saratoga has its annual shindig in September, usually the evening of the third Saturday. The annual **Celebrate Saratoga** event downtown on Big Basin Way features local restaurants, wineries, and entertainment.

RECREATION

There's almost no end to the number of parks on the eastern slopes of the Santa Cruz Mountains, despite the proximity of urban areas. Within a few minutes of Los Gatos or Saratoga you can be lost in the woods or embarking on a half-day hike up to the mountain ridges high above.

Castle Rock State Park

On the warm eastern slopes of the mountains, Castle Rock State Park (15300 Skyline Blvd., 2.5 miles south of U.S. 9, Los Gatos, 408/867-2952) sits between Saratoga and Big Basin, with 32 miles of trails crisscrossing its 3,600 acres, though mountain bikes are prohibited on all of them. Hike the Skyline to the Sea Trail into neighboring Big Basin and on to the ocean, or take the 5.5-mile loop via the Saratoga Gap Trail, past Castle Rock Falls to the trail camp, then back on the Ridge Trail, stopping off at Goat Rock for a view seemingly of the world.

Sanborn-Skyline State Park

Down the mountains from Castle Rock is Sanborn-Skyline State Park (16055 Sanborn Rd., off Hwy. 9, Saratoga, 408/867-9959). The hostel, campground, and acres of grassy picnic meadows bring most people here, but it also has some good half-day hiking trails up to some fine views and is far more accessible than the state parks deeper in the mountains. Hike up to Skyline Boulevard on the ridge and cross into neighboring Castle Rock State Park via the Sanborn and Skyline Trails, stopping off for some fine views at Indian Rock and Summit Rock. It's a steep climb that rises about 1,000 feet in three miles.

Stevens Creek County Park

Most accessible of all is Stevens Creek County Park (11401 Stevens Canyon Rd., Cupertino, 408/867-3654), which you will probably drive through in search of many of the eastern mountain wineries. At the center of it all is Stevens

© PHILIP GOLDSMITH

Another hiker you might meet on the trails of Picchetti Ranch.

Creek Reservoir, right at the turn off Monte Bello Road that leads up to the Picchetti Winery and Ridge Vineyards.

This is primarily a fishing lake, but there are also numerous short trails and picnic sites in the surrounding 1,000 acres of dry oak woods and canyonland. The Picchetti Winery is where some of the trails start, and maps are usually available at the winery's parking lot. Most of the other trails and picnic areas are directly off Stevens Canyon Road, which runs past the reservoir. Maps are also available at the official park entrance just north of the reservoir, though it's tempting to simply pull over at one of the many small parking lots along the roads and head off into the woods for a picnic or short hike.

ACCOMMODATIONS

Although lacking the sort of cozy B&Bs that dominate the accommodation scene up in the Santa Cruz Mountains and along the coast, the warmer eastern hills and slopes of this part of the Wine Country around Los Gatos and Saratoga have plenty of no-nonsense and well-priced places to stay, all on the doorstep of both urban sophistication and woodsy wilderness.

The two towns are on quiet periphery of the Silicon Valley sprawl yet only a 20-minute drive to San Jose (traffic permitting). As a result, many hotels, however cheap, are often popular with visiting business travelers looking to escape the nearby urban and suburban bustle. Midweek rooms might therefore be a little harder to come by (even in the middle of winter), but weekend rooms, by contrast, might be more plentiful—the opposite pattern to much of the rest of Wine Country, where weekenders dominate. It also results in far more uniform room rates, with fewer, if any, weekend or summer price spikes compared to, say, the city of Santa Cruz.

Under $100

Considering the amount of rain that falls in these mountains during the winter, camping is out of the question between November and May for all but the hardiest souls. But there is alternative budget accommodation available at the **Sanborn Park Hostel** (15808 Sanborn Rd., Saratoga, 408/741-0166 or 408/741-9555, www.sanbornparkhostel.org, closed Sun.–Wed. Jan.–Mar., no credit cards, three-night maximum stay) just outside Saratoga in Sanborn-Skyline State Park. It is as equally blessed with redwoods and wildlife as the nearby campsites, with miles of hiking trails weaving through the 3,600 acres of surrounding parkland. The Savannah-Chanelle winery is also within easy walking distance. The driveway to the hostel is off Sanborn Road just before the "one-lane bridge" (if you reach the park entrance you've gone a bridge too far). Simply follow that driveway up past a murky-looking pond to the log cabin-style hostel.

A drawback of such serenity is that the log-cabin style hostel is about three miles west of the nearest civilization in downtown Saratoga and really only accessible by car. Luckily, the kind hosts will shuttle guests to and from the town, but then you're on your own. Still, at only $16 a night ($14 for Hostelling International members), you can rent a car and dine out in style for less than a weekend stay at some local hotels. Or save more money and cook your own meal in big kitchen. The 39 hostel beds are spread among six bedrooms with shared bathrooms, and a few private family rooms are also available.

$100–150

When Joe DiMaggio and Marilyn Monroe stayed here in the 1950s, the **Garden Inn** (46 E. Main St., Los Gatos, 408/354-6446 or 866/800-4906, www.gardeninn.us) in downtown Los Gatos was probably one of the swankiest joints in the then-sleepy village. Now the stars of Silicon Valley are more likely to visit the swanky car dealership next door to pick up their Rolls, Bentley, or Aston Martin. The inn shows its age a bit, but downtown location and price outweigh any decorative disadvantages of the plain but comfortable and well equipped rooms arranged around the quiet courtyard and patio area. Rates start at $110 year-round for the basic rooms, rising to $160 for executive suites, equipped like a home away from home. Cheaper rates, especially for the suites, might be available on the website.

The **Saratoga Oaks Lodge** (14626 Big Basin Way/Hwy. 9, Saratoga, 408/867-3307 or 888/867-3588, www.saratogaoakslodge.com) is not far from the site of a former tollgate on the main road a few blocks from downtown Saratoga. The tolls to stay in this modern, airy hotel today are pretty good deals. The most basic queen and king rooms start at $120 a night, though the more luxurious and secluded rooms and suites in cottages up the hill among the trademark oaks cost $190–240. All the rooms are modern, with refrigerators and microwaves; some rooms have fireplaces and steam baths.

Over $150

The **N Inn at Saratoga** (20645 4th St., Saratoga, 408/867-5020, www.innatsaratoga.com) is a stone's throw from just about everything Saratoga has to offer yet seemingly in the middle of nowhere in its quiet, creekside setting. The decor inside is neutral, both in terms of color and any great sense of design, leaving Mother Nature to put on the main show outside the big windows or balconies in every room. The creek, neighboring Wildwood Park, and abundant patios and other outdoor nooks create a sense of tranquillity, complemented by a broad range of amenities and services, including free Internet access, exercise room, VCRs and refrigerators in every room, and evening wine receptions. Rates start at $160 for standard queen rooms (request a creek view) and quickly rise to $250 for junior suites and $400 for the mammoth full suites.

Two hotels vie for both high-end business and discerning private travelers in downtown Los Gatos, both offering central locations, quality restaurants, and modern luxury. The **Toll House Hotel** (140 S. Santa Cruz Ave., Los Gatos, 408/395-7070 or 800/238-6111, www.tollhousehotel.com) is the least attractive of the two from the outside but is smack in the middle of the downtown action and underwent an extensive renovation in 2004, which

equipped its rooms with luxuries like featherbeds, DVD and CD players, and Aveda bath products. Guests can also use the nearby Los Gatos Athletic Club or eat on the huge patio of the hotel's Three Degrees restaurant. Rates are $170–190 in the winter and $190–230 in the summer for standard rooms or bigger Select rooms with patio or balcony, though discounts are often available. Suites have accommodated the likes of Ray Charles and the Doobie Brothers over the years.

The **N Hotel Los Gatos** (210 E. Main St., Los Gatos, 408/335-1700 or 866/335-1700, www.hotellosgatos.com) is the more modern of the two buildings, a faux-Mediterranean pile built around patios and a small pool on the edge of the downtown area. The 72 rooms sport more contemporary, edgy furnishings than those at the Toll House but have the same high level of amenities, and the hotel is also home to Kuleto's Restaurant, a destination in its own right. Rates start at $170 for standard rooms if booked online (nondiscounted rates are often over $200) and jump to $300 and higher for the suites, many of which have fireplaces and balconies or patios. Packages that include treatments at the on-site Preston Wynne Spa are also available.

Camping

The closest place to camp near civilization is at **Saratoga Springs** (22801 Big Basin Way, Saratoga, 408/867-9999, www.saratoga-springs.com), the creekside site of a former Victorian resort just a few miles up Big Basin Road (Hwy. 9) from Saratoga. For total wilderness head farther into the mountains because this campground is geared up for family fun, with a video arcade, playground, laundry facility, swimming pool, and weekly rates available. Of the roughly 60 sites, about half are for RVs, with full hookups, and half are for tents only and up to six people. RV sites are $32 a night or $199 a week, tent sites are $25 or $150 for the week.

Only a mile up Sanborn Road from Big Basin Road and Saratoga Springs is **Sanborn-Skyline County Park** (16055 Sanborn Rd., off Hwy. 9,

Saratoga, information 408/867-9959, reservations 408/355-2201 or www.gooutsideandplay.org), a 3,600-acre park that climbs up the eastern slopes of the mountains. It is home to the Sanborn Park Hostel and plenty of campsites, with showers and restrooms. Kids will enjoy a short nature trail and science center. Nine sites for RVs up to 30 feet long with hookups are available year-round (reservations required). The 33 tent sites are set in up in a wooded area overlooking the park's huge meadow and are open from late March through October. They are technically walk-in sites, but most are only a few hundred yards from the parking lot, and hand carts are provided to help schlep camping gear from the car up the hill.

Hardcore campers will probably prefer the more primitive, hike-in campsites in **Castle Rock State Park** (15000 Skyline Blvd., Los Gatos, information 408/867-2952, $10 per night), a 3,600-acre wilderness strung along the crest of the mountains just a few minutes' drive from the hubbub of Silicon Valley. From the main overnight parking lot on Skyline Boulevard (U.S. 35, 2.5 miles south of U.S. 9), the Castle Rock Trail Camp is about a 2.5-mile hike along the Saratoga Gap Trail and is the bigger of the two, with 19 sites sheltered by oak and madrone trees. It's also the highest elevation at about 2,400 feet, so it get chilly at night.

The smaller Waterman Trail Gap campground is about a four-mile hike beyond at a slightly lower elevation in redwood forest along the Skyline to the Sea Trail. There is a parking lot far closer, at the junction of U.S. 9 and 236 just north of Big Basin Redwoods State Park, but no overnight parking is allowed there. Both campgrounds have vault toilets and drinking water, but campfires are only allowed at Castle Rock, and even then only outside peak fire season. Reservations (call 831/338-8861) are required at Waterman Trail Gap and are recommended at the Castle Rock Trail campground, particularly in summer.

FOOD

There are some classy dining options in the Los Gatos and Saratoga area, where some of the

South Bay's best restaurants cater to the moneyed crowds of Silicon Valley. It's new money, however, so don't be surprised to see patrons at pricey restaurants wearing more in the way of Tommy Bahama than Georgio Armani, as one newspaper put it.

Downtown Los Gatos

Modest digs are often a sign that bistros are going to be unpretentious and worth visiting, and this is certainly the case with **I Gatti** (25 Main St., Los Gatos, 408/399-5180, dinner daily, lunch weekdays, closed Mon., dinner entrées $13–25), on Main Street just east of the freeway overpass. The bistro is small but comfortable thanks to well-spaced tables and warm earth tones throughout, and it cooks up some interesting modern twists on Italian comfort food without losing sight of solid Italian traditions.

A little more experimental with its bistro fare is **M Tapestry** (11 College Ave., Los Gatos, 408/395-2808, dinner daily, large plates $16–25), in a little craftsman cottage tucked behind Caffé Siena just off Main Street. It offers both small, appetizer-sized plates and large plates of true California fusion food, taking fresh, California ingredients and creative inspiration from all over the world (often from Asia). Sometimes it works, other times it's too complicated for its own good. The smallish wine list is equally international in its inspiration.

One of the few constants in the ever-changing Los Gatos restaurant scene is the popular **Café Marcella** (368 Village Ln., Los Gatos, 408/354-8006, lunch Tues.–Sat., dinner Tues.–Sun., dinner entrées $14–27) just off the top end of North Santa Cruz Avenue. Try the double-cut pork chop, a specialty here, or any of the Mediterranean-inspired pastas, and look out for an occasional Asian influence in some of the daily specials. The huge wine list is dominated by California, Italy, and France, and includes a good selection from the Santa Cruz Mountains.

Those looking for a romantic but nonthreatening place to eat should try the **Wine Cellar** (50 University Ave., Los Gatos, 408/354-4808, lunch and dinner daily, dinner entrées $18–

38). There are no white tablecloths or other fancy trappings in sight, but the basement setting and warm, earthy decor create a relaxed, cozy atmosphere in keeping with the modern American bistro food, though some of the more complex dishes reportedly fall flat. Serious fondue lovers should avoid the cheesy dip here and head to La Fondue in Saratoga instead. The wine list is dominated by Californian wines but there are few from Santa Cruz.

Vietnam meets California at the cozy **Green Papaya** (137 N. Santa Cruz Ave., Los Gatos, 408/395-9115, lunch and dinner daily except Mon., dinner entrées $13–25). This is no generic noodle house, more a classy Asian bistro. Try the signature green papaya salad or one of the clay pot dishes, classic Vietnamese with Californian flair. Or try more American dishes with an Asian slant like the rib-eye steak with fragrant basmati rice.

The **Tandoori Oven** (133 N. Santa Cruz Ave., Los Gatos, 408/395-1784, lunch and dinner daily, under $10) is just what a casual Indian restaurant should be—cheap, spicy, and with a menu chock-full of double-vowelled dishes from Northern India. For something more American try one of the wraps made with tasty naan bread.

Pub grub and microbrews are the all-American draws at the **Los Gatos Brewing Company** (130G N. Santa Cruz Ave., Los Gatos 408/395-9929, lunch and dinner daily). The pub menu of burgers, pizzas, and pastas is reasonably priced though there's a large dinner menu of steaks and other grilled meats that pushes the $20 mark.

Pizza lovers should head to **Willow Street,** with a big outdoor patio overlooking the plaza (20 S. Santa Cruz Ave., Los Gatos, 408/354-5566, open daily). Pizzas from the wood-fired oven, burgers, steaks, and daily specials are not usually much more than $10, many less than that.

A quick and cheap Mexican fix is never more than a few blocks away thanks to several colorful Los Gatos locations of **Andalé Mexican Restaurant** (6 and 21 N. Santa Cruz Ave., Los Gatos, 408/395-8997, lunch and dinner daily, breakfast weekends, under $10).

Downtown Saratoga

The Basin (14572 Big Basin Way, Saratoga, 408/867-1906, dinner daily, entrées $14–26) thrives in the Saratoga restaurant field, having carved out a popular niche with its earth-friendly menu that draws strongly on fresh organic or wild local ingredients, including hormone- and chemical-free meats. Dishes can best be described as Californian comfort food with plenty of Mediterranean influences.

Huddled together on the same few blocks at the edge of the village are three of Saratoga's best restaurants, the Plumed Horse, Gervais, and Viaggio, all equally praised and equally expensive. The **Plumed Horse** (14555 Big Basin Way, Saratoga, 408/867-4711, dinner Mon.–Sat., dinner entrées $24–55) is the grandfather of them all, serving stylish, traditional haute cuisine since 1952 in its stately surroundings with a wine list endorsed by *Wine Spectator* magazine. The **Crazy Horse** lounge next door has occasional live music and a much cheaper bistro menu of small plates and salads ($7–15), together with a big wine list and plenty of fruity cocktails.

Neighboring **Gervais** (14560 Big Basin Way, Saratoga, 408/867-7017, dinner Mon.–Sat., lunch Thurs.–Sat., dinner entrées $21–32) is no new kid on the block either. It has been around since the late 1970s and now serves its contemporary, French-inspired food in homey and simple cottage surroundings or outside on a small patio. The wine list is dominated by California and France, though with very few local wines. **Viaggio** (14550 Big Basin Way, Saratoga, 408/741-5300, lunch weekdays, dinner daily, closed Mon., dinner entrées $18–30) is the newest of the trio with a big patio and a strong Italian slant to its Mediterranean bistro food. The international wine list has a decent selection of local Santa Cruz wines and can be sampled at the wine bar too, along with a small menu of appetizers.

Fondue never really goes out of style, which is just as well because **La Fondue** (14510 Big Basin Way, Saratoga, 408/867-3332, dinner daily, about $30 a person) adds some wacky character to Saratoga's increasingly upscale dining scene. The dark interior is a fantasyland of castles, lairs, and medieval chambers where diners loom over pots of bubbling cheeses and sauces like time-traveling sorcerers. There is a staggering number of combinations of cheeses, sauces, meats and vegetables to choose from, not to mention chocolate fondue for dessert. Because eating the vast volumes of food takes many hours there are usually only two sittings a night, so reserving a table a couple of weeks in advance is essential, though you might luck out on the night. Worth noting is that on Monday and Tuesday there is no corkage charge.

The casual, rambling café **M Blue Rock Shoot** (14523 Big Basin Way, Saratoga, 408/872-0309, open daily) is in a hillside house that is hard not to feel instantly at home in thanks to its rustic atmosphere and countless private nooks upstairs, downstairs, and outside. Buy cheap coffee, beer, wine, pizza, or sandwiches on the main floor, then get lost somewhere inside with good book. Live music (with cover charge) on Friday and Saturday nights showcases local musicians and livens up the otherwise mellow atmosphere.

Picnic Supplies

A relaxing, sun-drenched hangout with a small selection of sandwiches and other small eats—as well as a good breakfast spot—is **Caffé Siena** (26 E. Main St., Los Gatos, 408/399-2830, open 7 A.M. to late afternoon daily) at the quieter end of downtown.

Quick lunches, sandwiches, and other deli foods perfect for a picnic can be found at **Boulanger** (145 W. Main St., Los Gatos, 408/395-1344) on the plaza. There's usually plenty of seating inside and out.

Farmers Market

Build your own meal from scratch with ingredients from the **Los Gatos Farmers' Market** (408/353-4293) every Sunday morning next to the Town Park Plaza. It operates all year and is probably one of the few farmers markets to have its own oyster bar.

INFORMATION AND SERVICES

This side of the mountains, the **Los Gatos Chamber of Commerce** (349 N. Santa Cruz Ave., 408/354-9300, www.losgatosweb.com) is the source of information, listings, and guides for the busy town. Similar information is available for Saratoga from the **Saratoga Chamber of Commerce** in Saratoga village (14485 Big Basin Way/Hwy. 9, 408/867-0753, www.saratogachamber.org).

The weekly newspapers, usually available in cafés and on the street, are worth picking up for up-to-date event and entertainment listings. *Metro* is the weekly paper for Los Gatos, Saratoga, and other Silicon Valley towns, though its territory also stretches to Santa Cruz. The *Los Gatos Weekly Times* is a more news-oriented weekly but also has some listings.

GETTING THERE AND AROUND

Access to Saratoga and Los Gatos area wineries from the north is via I-280, a pretty and remarkably traffic-free freeway that runs along the eastern edge of the coastal mountains from San Francisco down to San Jose (reached from San Francisco International airport via I-380).

From I-280, take U.S. 85 south at Cupertino and exit on Saratoga Ave. to reach Saratoga village at Big Basin Way (U.S. 9), or continue on to U.S. 17, taking that road west for one junction to the Los Gatos exit. Turn left at the top of the offramp and cross back over the freeway to get to one end of downtown Los Gatos at East Main Street, or head north from the freeway and turn left at the lights onto Santa Cruz Avenue to get to the other end. It's about four miles between Los Gatos and Saratoga along the Los Gatos–Saratoga Road via Monte Sereno.

U.S. 85 also links to U.S. 101 when coming from the south, and those coming from San Jose and the East Bay can get straight onto U.S. 17 from I-880.

Parking in Los Gatos and Saratoga is usually a relatively simple affair, which is lucky because a car really is the best means of getting around in this area. Some of the wineries north of Saratoga can prove tricky to find when navigating the winding roads through the hills and woods. Pay close attention to directions and geographical features on any map as many of the roads will not be clearly named when you reach a junction.

The San Lorenzo Valley

The heart of the Santa Cruz Mountains is actually a valley—the San Lorenzo Valley, which leads southwest down to the ocean at Santa Cruz. To the east, Skyline Boulevard runs along the ridgeline, high enough that it's possible to see both the ocean and the bay peeking through the trees at certain points.

From Skyline Boulevard, it's easy to see how the giant Big Basin Redwoods State Park got its name. The top portion of the San Lorenzo Valley really does look like a giant basin when viewed from the ridge above, one that is brimming with the dark green redwood forests surrounded by edges of parched ridgelines.

Down in the San Lorenzo Valley it still feels like you're in the mountains. Small, one-street former logging towns like **Boulder Creek** and **Ben Lomond** lie against a backdrop of forested mountain slopes where Bigfoot sightings are common, if some residents are to be believed. At the other end of the valley is the small town of **Felton.** Closer to Santa Cruz some urbanization is a little more evident, though there's still an easy-going mountain culture. All these mountain towns have an eclectic culture born of the waves of development over the centuries, from early loggers to Victorian resorts, bible camps, and a more recent influx of artists.

The Wines

The western slopes of the mountains tend to be planted more to chardonnay and pinot noir, though other varieties like syrah are also now gaining ground. Wherever they are grown, grapes only just ripen here. Any cooler and the winemaker's job would be even harder than it already is.

During the summer, a sunny day in the mountains can rapidly turn into a fog-shrouded afternoon as the cool marine air rushes up the western slopes of the mountains and spills over the eastern ridge, often burning off before it has chance to descend into the warm Silicon Valley. Most of the vineyards are at the higher elevations of the western slopes, areas that the fog takes longer to reach and remain warmer for longer. Chardonnay needs the warmth to ripen, though pinot noir can be happy up high or slightly lower down the slopes.

Closer to the ocean the lower elevations can be so cool that growing vines is a struggle. The Ben Lomond subappellation covers many of these lower slopes, and despite its large geographical size (38,000 acres) it contains very few vineyards, so don't expect to see it named on many bottles.

WINERIES

As is the case farther east, most wineries offer free tasting, but their opening hours vary considerably, so bear that in mind when planning a tour.

Ahlgren Vineyard

Hewlett and Packard famously started their business in a Silicon Valley garage, and so did the Ahlgrens back in the 1970s, moving to a custom-built winery in the hills only when their garage wine-making operation started to outgrow its suburban location.

The winery now has a bit more space, though it is still a delightfully homespun operation tucked under the cabin-style home in the hills. Production has grown to about 2,000 cases a year, all made with grapes bought from vineyards locally and as far away as Paso Robles and Livermore. Considering so few cases are made, the portfolio holds a remarkable number of wines.

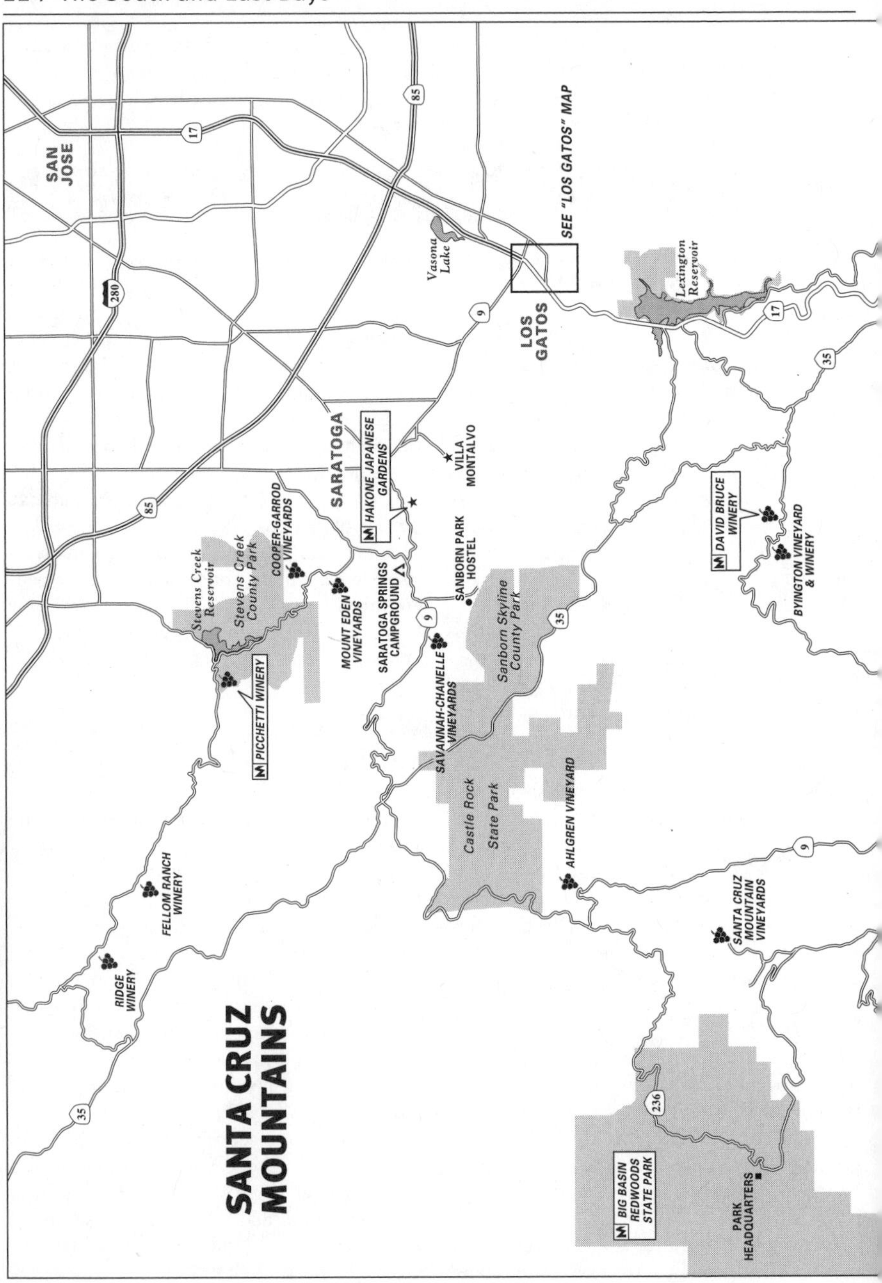
SAN JOSE
SEE "LOS GATOS" MAP
Vasona Lake
Lexington Reservoir
LOS GATOS
SARATOGA
HAKONE JAPANESE GARDENS
VILLA MONTALVO
COOPER-GARROD VINEYARDS
Stevens Creek Reservoir
Stevens Creek County Park
MOUNT EDEN VINEYARDS
SARATOGA SPRINGS CAMPGROUND
SANBORN PARK HOSTEL
Sanborn Skyline County Park
PICCHETTI WINERY
SAVANNAH-CHANELLE VINEYARDS
DAVID BRUCE WINERY
BYINGTON VINEYARD & WINERY
Castle Rock State Park
AHLGREN VINEYARD
FELLOM RANCH WINERY
RIDGE WINERY
SANTA CRUZ MOUNTAIN VINEYARDS
SANTA CRUZ MOUNTAINS
BIG BASIN REDWOODS STATE PARK
PARK HEADQUARTERS
280
85
17
9
35
236

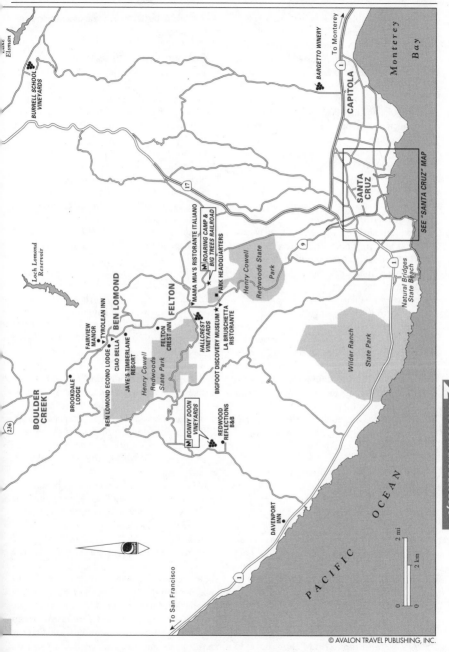

To Monterey

BARGETTO WINERY

Monterey Bay

CAPITOLA

Lake Elsman

BURRELL SCHOOL VINEYARDS

SANTA CRUZ

SEE "SANTA CRUZ" MAP

17

Loch Lomond Reservoir

9

Henry Cowell Redwoods State Park

Natural Bridges State Beach

MAMA MIA'S RISTORANTE ITALIANO

ROARING CAMP BIG TREES RAILROAD

PARK HEADQUARTERS

FELTON

FAIRVIEW MANOR

TYROLEAN INN

BEN LOMOND

CIAO BELLA

BEN LOMOND ECONO LODGE

JAVE'S TIMBERLANE RESORT

Henry Cowell Redwoods State Park

FELTON CREST INN

HALLCREST VINEYARDS

LA BRUSCHETTA RISTORANTE

BIGFOOT DISCOVERY MUSEUM

Wilder Ranch State Park

BROOKDALE LODGE

236

BOULDER CREEK

BONNY DOON VINEYARDS

REDWOOD REFLECTIONS B&B

DAVENPORT INN

PACIFIC OCEAN

To San Francisco

1

0 2 mi

0 2 km

The South and East Bays

The most notable wines come from the local Bates Ranch Vineyard and include cabernet sauvignon, cabernet franc, and extremely limited-production merlot. Another cluster comes from vineyards down near Monterey, including a chardonnay, syrah, and pinot noir.

Being such a tiny operation run literally out of an oversized garage it's hardly surprising that the winery is only open Saturday afternoons. But it's a unique experience very much in keeping with the low-key atmosphere of Santa Cruz winemakers (20320 Hwy. 9, Boulder Creek, 831/338-6071, www.ahlgrenvineyard.com, open noon–4 P.M. Sat.).

Hallcrest Vineyards

Most wineries in these mountains farm organically, but Hallcrest takes organic a step further into the production process and makes a range of cheaper wines under the Organic Wine Works label that are even free of sulfites, the preservatives added to wines in tiny amounts to prevent them from spoiling too quickly.

Those wines are not quite up to the standard of the regular Hallcrest label, which graces several vineyard-designate pinot noirs, a chardonnay, and a cabernet sauvignon blend, all from Santa Cruz appellation vineyards. These can usually be tasted side by side with the organic wines, most of which cost well under $10 a bottle but none of which are from the Santa Cruz area, probably because the grapes are too expensive to grow here for wines that are not likely to last for long.

Like the rest of the winery, the cozy tasting room with its large picnicking deck (with a view) dates from the 1940s when it was built by a San Francisco lawyer, Chaffee Hall, making this one of the oldest wineries in the mountains. The winery continued to operate under various owners until the Schumacher family bought it in 1987 and restored the Hallcrest name. They now make about 10,000 cases of organic wines and 5,000 cases of the Hallcrest label. The organic winery workings and pretty grounds with plenty of grassy picnic spots can be further explored on an appointment-only tour that costs $5 (379 Felton Empire Rd., Felton, 831/335-

4441, www.hallcrestvineyards.com, noon–5 P.M. daily).

David Bruce Winery

Regarded as the king of pinot noir in these mountains, David Bruce founded his winery up here on top of the world in 1964, supplementing his main profession as a dermatologist after being inspired by the wines of Martin Ray (now Mount Eden).

He has been somewhat of a pioneer since then, credited with being one of the first winemakers in the 1960s to make both a white zinfandel (later turned into a huge commercial success by Sutter Home) and a late-harvest zin that critics didn't quite know what to make of. He also planted some Rhône grape varietals like grenache long before most other wineries in California.

But his pinot noir is what won him the most fame and accolades over the years, and seven pinots are now made alongside cabernet sauvignon, chardonnay, syrah, sangiovese, and petite sirah. Not surprisingly, pinot noir accounts for about two-thirds of the 60,000 cases of wine made each year.

As is the case with most wineries on the wild slopes of the mountains, the estate vineyards here at about 2,200 feet are tiny, covering just 16 acres. More than half those acres are planted to pinot noir, and that goes into the limited-production flagship wine, though another Santa Cruz bottling is made using some estate grapes and fruit from other small vineyards nearby.

If you hit the winery on the right day you might be able to taste a Santa Cruz pinot noir beside versions from one or both of the other two great pinot-growing regions in Northern California—the Russian River Valley and Carneros. Other wines usually available to taste include the highly regarded chardonnay from the estate and other Santa Cruz vineyards, and a cabernet sauvignon from the hotter Santa Clara appellation farther east. Although the gray, metal winery building and dark tasting room are nothing special to look at the wines and the views easily compensate (21439 Bear Creek Rd.,

Los Gatos, 408/354-4214 or 800/397-9972, www.davidbrucewinery.com, noon–5 P.M. weekdays, 11 A.M.–5 P.M. weekends).

Byington Vineyard & Winery

Just beyond David Bruce on Bear Creek Road, this huge winery with its sweeping views to the ocean was built in the late 1980s in a style that's part chateau, part McMansion. It now makes about 20,000 cases of wine a year from its modest estate vineyard and a chunk of land down near Paso Robles on the Central Coast. It is also one of the few Santa Cruz wineries big enough to cater to large gatherings and does a roaring trade in weddings and meetings.

Pinot noir and chardonnay dominate the production, both made in three styles using grapes from either the estate, Central Coast, or up in Sonoma. There is also a cabernet sauvignon worth trying from the renowned Bates Ranch nearby in the mountains, and a red blend called Alliage, made predominantly with Sonoma grapes (21850 Bear Creek Rd., off Hwy. 17, Los Gatos, 408/354-1111, www.byington.com, 11 A.M.–5 P.M. daily, tasting free, tours $10).

Burrell School Vineyards

The white wooden fence marks the gate to the old schoolhouse that is now the home of this producer of some fine estate wines. The schoolhouse itself dates from the 1890s and had the distinction of being the first in the district to get both a flagpole and a bell, which features prominently on the Burrell School labels.

Owners Dave and Ann Moulton started their winery here in 1973 and now make a few thousand cases of predominantly red wines, most notably the estate merlot and a pinot noir sourced from several vineyards in the Santa Cruz appellation. The other estate wine is chardonnay, which has the typical Santa Cruz acidity that could do with a year or two to mellow.

A couple of wines are made from Santa Clara grapes, most notably the syrah, and one unusual blend worth trying is the Valedictorian, made from the estate merlot, a Santa Cruz cabernet sauvignon, and a Santa Cruz cabernet franc. Most can be tasted in the old Teachers Carriage House on the grounds either at weekends or by appointment during the week (24060 Summit Rd., Los Gatos, 408/353-6290, www.burrellschool.com, 11 A.M.–5 P.M. weekends).

Santa Cruz Mountain Vineyards

The winery is probably justified in sharing the same name as the mountains and the appellation because its vineyards are on the site of the those planted by pioneer George Jarvis in the 1860s, though he used to make brandy from his grapes.

When he established this winery in the early 1970s, Ken Burnap also bought a small pinot noir vineyard planted by David Bruce, and pinot noir is still the mainstay of the 2,500-case production today. Besides the estate version, which is a fine example of a Santa Cruz pinot, the winery makes another pinot bottling, cabernet sauvignon, merlot, and syrah, all using grapes from other Santa Cruz Mountain vineyards.

A fun wine worth trying just for its bargain price is the Bobcat Red, a blend of syrah, merlot, and cabernet franc from Central Coast vineyards. But perhaps the most talked-about wine made here is the petite sirah, which Burnap has labeled by what he says is its correct name, durif. DNA testing over the years has shown that much of what is called petite sirah in California is actually one of three different grape varietals, so the name durif is not likely to take off until the genetic confusion is sorted out.

In 2004, the winery moved from its original site to a new location in Boulder Creek a few miles west, as the crow flies, and tastings are by appointment only (830 Memory Ln., Boulder Creek, 831/335-4242, www.scmvwine.com).

Bargetto Winery

By just a few years, this is the oldest operating winery in the Santa Cruz Mountains, though technically it's just outside the appellation's boundary. Italian immigrants Philip and John Bargetto first started making wine before Prohibition and resumed commercial production in 1933 after repeal. The third generation of Bargettos now runs the winery, and it has grown to make about 25,000 cases of wine a year.

The bulk of Bargetto's wines are sourced from its 50-acre Regan Vineyard east of the winery and include pinot noir, chardonnay, merlot, and a handful of Italian wines including dolcetto, pinot grigio, and the pricey La Vita blend of three Italian grapes. Most of the wines are reasonably priced at under $20 a bottle and do not suffer from the over-oaking or over-extraction typical in many other cheap chardonnays or pinots. Most can be tasted free in the rustic tasting room or outdoors on a tasting patio, but the La Vita and a few library wines will cost $5.

For some true overkill, try the unusual mead-style dessert wines Bargetto also makes, either pure mead or the same sickly sweet honey wine with fruit such as raspberries, apricots, or olallieberry added. They are bottled under the Chaucer's label and are an acquired taste. Tours are also available by appointment (3535 N. Main St., Soquel, 831/475-2258, www.bargetto.com, noon–5 P.M. daily).

SIGHTS

Ⓜ Roaring Camp and Big Trees Railroad

For a taste of the redwood forests and mountain scenery without struggling up and down rocky trails, why not let an old steam train do the puffing and wheezing as it hauls passengers up and down the valley.

The narrow-gauge railroad of the Roaring Camp and Big Trees Railroad once transported logs from the first sawmill established west of the Mississippi in 1842. The settlement was named Roaring Camp for the alcohol-fueled excesses of its residents. Steam trains now run over old-fashioned wooden trestle bridges in a loop up Bear Mountain, through towering stands of the redwoods that were saved from the Roaring Camp axes. During the winter there's just one train a day on weekends (12:30 P.M.);

in spring and fall there are four trains on weekend days and one on weekdays (at 11 A.M.), and in the summer (mid-June through Aug.) there are four trains daily. Judging by the size of the parking lot it can get as busy as Grand Central Station during rush hour. The fare is $18 or $12 for kids.

Roaring Camp Railroad also runs the **Santa Cruz, Big Trees, and Pacific Railway,** a less glamorous diesel-powered train that runs from Felton down the San Lorenzo gorge to the Santa Cruz Beach Boardwalk. If you're in Santa Cruz, hop on the **Redwood Express** for a stress-free way to enjoy a picnic up in redwood country. And if you're already among the redwoods and want to visit Santa Cruz, avoid the hassle of parking and traffic, pack the sunscreen, and take the **Suntan Special.** It's an hour-long spectacular train ride from the redwoods to the beach.

Trains run daily June–August and on weekends in spring and fall, leaving the Beach Boardwalk daily at 12:30 and 4:30 P.M., and departing Roaring Camp at 10:30 A.M. and 2:30 P.M. Roundtrip fare is $20, or $15 for kids. The Roaring Camp Railroad is on Graham Hill Road, off Highway 9, in Felton (831/335-4484, www.roaringcamp.com).

Bigfoot Discovery Museum

Where there are mountains there are Bigfoot sightings, and in the Santa Cruz Mountains it's no different, despite ever-advancing urbanization. The last alleged sighting of a giant, shaggy Pacific Coast Bigfoot was as recent at 2004, and the species (for want of a better word) is celebrated at the **Bigfoot Discovery Museum** (5497 Hwy. 9, 831/335-4478, www.bigfootdiscoveryproject.com, open 11 A.M.–6 P.M. Wed.–Sun., donation requested), housed in a modest collection of huts next to the main road in Felton.

The photos, artifacts, and other information gathered here about worldwide Bigfoot sightings is the culmination of a life of amateur research by Michael Rugg, who has lived in the area since the 1950s and is as passionate about Bigfoot as he is his countless arts and crafts pursuits.

Where there are ancient forests there will be the myth of Bigfoot.

Whether Bigfoot will ever be discovered by science is open to debate, though the fact that a previously unknown species of monkey was found in the jungles of southern Africa in 2005 certainly suggests it's still possible, at least in theory. The truth is out there, somewhere deep in the forests of the Santa Cruz Mountains.

RECREATION
Big Basin Redwoods State Park

This was California's first state park, established in 1902 thanks to the efforts of the Sempevirens Club, whose early conservationists managed to save 3,800 acres of old-growth redwoods from the axes that cleared most of the other mountain slopes. The park has since expanded to encompass 18,000 acres of forest and chaparral stretching from 2,000 feet up in the mountains down to the coast.

This wild area was once the domain of grizzly bears, but now the biggest animals found here (though you rarely see them) are mountain lions, coyotes, and foxes. Deer are usually more visible, as are the raccoons and hundreds

of bird species. More than 80 miles of trails offer a bewildering array of ways for hikers and bikers to see the animals, forest, flowers, and waterfalls. Mountain bikes are only allowed on fire roads, however, not any of the tempting single-track.

Be sure to pick up a map at the visitor center in the park headquarters (21600 Big Basin Way in Boulder Creek, U.S. 236 off U.S. 9 about 12 miles west of Saratoga, 831/338-8860, open 9 A.M.–5 P.M. daily). Also ask about the free **guided hikes** and **wildflower walks** offered at certain times of the year and be sure to check out the small **Nature Lodge** museum near the park headquarters to learn more about the park and its natural history.

The easiest hike, more of a stroll, is the half-mile jaunt around the **Redwood Trail** loop close the park headquarters. It's the quickest way to see the famous trees, including the tallest of them all, the 329-foot-tall Mother of the Forest, but you won't experience the wilderness that the park is known for.

All other trails head deep into the park, so you'll have to double back if you don't have more than a couple of hours to spare. Good half-day hikes include the **Meteor Trail** to the park's best lookout, Ocean View Point at 1,600 feet (though you'll see nothing but clouds if it's foggy). From the park headquarters, head north on the Skyline to the Sea Trail, through the redwoods along Opal Creek and past the historic Maddocks Cabin site (turn back here if you're short on time) before turning left at the two-mile point up the Meteor Trail, which climbs steeply to a fire road. Turn left on the fire road and the lookout point is only a few hundred yards farther. It's about 5.5 miles to the lookout and back.

Longer hikes include the 12-mile slog to three spectacular waterfalls: **Berry Creek Falls,** 70 feet of vertical water framed by lush ferns and forest; freefalling **Silver Falls;** and the **Golden Falls** cascading over sandstone rock. Take the Skyline to the Sea Trail west from the park headquarters up over the ridge and down to the creek, following it until you round a bend and can't miss the Berry Creek

Falls. At this point, head north on the **Berry Creek Falls Trail** to the other two waterfalls, sticking your head into the path of the cascading Silver Falls water if you're overheating. Either return the same way or, just north of Golden Falls past the Sunset camp, take a right on the **Sunset Trail** to loop back toward park headquarters.

That **Skyline to the Sea Trail,** a jumping-off point for so many other trails in the park, is itself a great 11-mile hike all the way down to the ocean at Waddell Beach. Either have someone pick you up at the end, or camp at one of the trail camps along the way.

Henry Cowell Redwoods State Park

At the other end of the San Lorenzo Valley is Big Basin's little brother, Henry Cowell Redwoods State Park (101 N. Big Trees Park Rd., Felton, 831/335-4598), with equally impressive redwoods and 20 miles of hiking trails set in the San Lorenzo River canyon. Park headquarters is off Highway 9 just south of Felton, and there are numerous trail heads along Highway 9 farther south and at the campground, which is accessed from Graham Hill Road south of Felton.

As at Big Basin, there's a short **Redwood Trail** loop from the park headquarters for instant big-tree gratification, but it's worth continuing along the **River Trail** for a longer hike into the middle of the park, linking with other trails that could keep you occupied all day. Worth noting is that the **Santa Cruz, Big Trees, and Pacific Railway** (see *Sights*) runs right through the middle of the park from Felton along the river on its way down to Santa Cruz, an ideal way to experience the park for those without the time, inclination, or wet-weather gear to explore it on foot.

ACCOMMODATIONS

Under $100

The **Ⓝ Brookdale Lodge** (11570 Hwy. 9, Brookdale, 831/338-6433, www.brookdalelodge.com) has a storied history, playing host to film stars and politicians (including president Herbert Hoover) during its heyday in the 1930s

and '40s. Now it's a bit of a faded star but still a fascinating and well-priced place to stay up in the redwoods, not least because of the mountain brook running right through the middle of the main dining room, a sight that has to be seen to be believed. The motel-style standard rooms start at $60 midweek and $80 on weekends in the winter, $80–100 during the summer. Suites and cottages are $110–200 a night, depending on season. Any strange sounds you hear during the night could either be your neighbors the other side of the thin walls or the ghosts said to haunt the lodge, including a nine-year-old girl who drowned in the dining room brook in the 1970s.

The **Ben Lomond Econo Lodge** (9733 Hwy. 9, Ben Lomond, 831/336-2292, www.stayintheredwoods.com) is a slightly shabby motel with clean but unremarkable rooms furnished in classic (not classy) motel style, but the location, the price, and decent-sized outdoor pool more than make up for the spartan interior comforts. It actually looks a bit like a motel plucked from beside a freeway offramp and dropped into the middle of the redwoods next to a creek, just a block from the few blocks that comprise downtown Ben Lomond. Queen rooms start at $70 in the winter and $100 during the summer, though are slightly higher at weekends. There's also a two-bed cabin with a kitchen that costs $160–250 depending on season and time of the week.

$100–200

The mountains tend to be the domain of rustic inns and resorts, but there are a couple of cozy B&Bs worth investigating. Not far from the Bonny Doon winery in the hills above Santa Cruz and Davenport is the tiny **Ⓝ Redwood Reflections B&B** (4600 Smith Grade, off Bonny Doon Rd., Santa Cruz, 831/423-7221), with three cozy but private rooms costing $90–159 a night including a breakfast that will keep you going all day. Snuggle up in the hot tub, next to the fire, or in front of the TV on windswept winter days. If the weather's better, strike out on the hiking trails, take a swim in the pool, or walk the mile to the Bonny

Doon winery, where there always seems to be a party going on. One of the rooms is a converted ice cream parlor full of kitschy paraphernalia collected by the owners over the years for their kids.

In a more central mountain location is the **Fairview Manor** (245 Fairview Ave., off Hwy. 9, Ben Lomond, 831/336-3355, www.fairviewmanor.com). The five rooms, all with private bathrooms, are by no means luxurious but cost $130–140 a night, a great price for the location in the redwoods next to the San Lorenzo River in Ben Lomond.

Jaye's Timberlane Resort (8705 Hwy. 9, Ben Lomond, 831/336-5479, www.jayestimberlane.com) is a resort in the rustic rather than the pampering sense of the word, featuring 10 simple cabins set among seven acres of redwoods and tarmac. The cabins themselves have either one or two bedrooms, a bathroom, and small kitchen, with wood-paneled walls, a fireplace, TV, and furnishings that have seen better days. You won't be knocking together a four-course dinner to go with your favorite Santa Cruz pinot, or luxuriating in a foaming, candlelit bath, but for the price ($80–150 a night, depending on season) and location these compact little dwellings are a pretty good deal.

Over $200

At the other end of the B&B scale is the stylish **Felton Crest Inn** (780 El Solyo Heights Dr., Felton, 831/335-4011 or 800/474-4011, www.feltoncrest.com), on a quiet, private road off the main highway. Four sumptuously furnished rooms, each on a separate floor, have down comforters, TVs and VCRs, and a couple come with Jacuzzi tubs and private decks. Prices range from $225 for the bottom floor room up to $295 for the Penthouse on the top floor with vaulted ceilings. Relax on the main deck or in hammocks among the redwoods, or head down one of the forest trails that leads into neighboring Henry Cowell State Park.

Camping

In the middle of the Santa Cruz Mountains

are some of the Bay Area's best campsites, most notably in **Big Basin Redwoods State Park** (21600 Big Basin Way, off Hwy. 9, Boulder Creek, 831/338-8860), California's oldest state park, containing towering redwoods and towering views from its loftiest points (see *Recreation*).

The camping options are almost endless. The 146 campsites ($20–25) include 31 for RVs up to 27 feet long (no hookups) and 74 tent-only sites. There are also a handful of hike-in trail camps throughout the park, two group campsites, horse camps, and hike and bike camps. The main camping area has restrooms, showers, and a small grocery store. The park gets very popular with backpackers and Bay Area weekenders during the summer, so make reservations through Reserve America (www.reserveamerica.com or 800/444-7275).

Families or the tentless might consider one of Big Basin's 41 tent cabins ($50), canvas-roofed hunts that sleep up to four people and sit on their own little campsites with picnic tables and fire rings. Bring your own sleeping bag or rent linens from the concession that runs the cabins (800/874- 8368, www.bigbasintentcabin.com). Despite being glorified campsites, the tent cabins have a two-night weekend minimum during the summer.

Toward Santa Cruz is the smaller (but equally pretty and packed with redwoods) **Henry Cowell Redwoods State Park** (101 N. Big Trees Park Rd., off Hwy. 9, Felton, 831/438-2396). The entrance to the campground is on Graham Hill Road (off Hwy. 9) on the other side of the park from the headquarters. There are 112 campsites for tents or RVs (no hookups) that cost $20–25 a night, plus showers and restrooms. Unlike Big Basin, this campground is closed during the winter (Nov.–Mar.). Reserve sites the rest of the year through Reserve America (www.reserveamerica.com or 800/444-7275). Anyone not feeling energetic enough to hike the miles of trails in this and Big Basin park can take an easy 15-minute hike from the campground to an observation deck with views to Santa Cruz and the ocean.

FOOD

Restaurants in the San Lorenzo Valley have a few things in common, like the fact that most are along Highway 9 and have a typically rustic feel to the food and the interiors. But if you're anticipating big hunks fit for a lumberjack you're in for a few surprises, courtesy of the more sophisticated artist community that thrives in the woods.

Boulder Creek

The **Boulder Creek Brewing Company** (13040 Hwy. 9, Boulder Creek, 831/338-7782, open daily) has the sort of hearty menu needed to fuel long hikes in nearby Big Basin Redwoods State Park. Load up on carbs and protein with the burgers, pizzas, burritos, and pastas, or order one of the bulging sandwiches to go for a mountain picnic. Wash it all down with one of the internationally inspired microbrews.

If you prefer your protein from vegetarian sources, the **Blue Sun Café** (13070 Hwy. 9, Boulder Creek, 831/338-2105, open daily until 3 P.M.) offers an extensive breakfast and lunch menu, including sandwiches that are tasty enough to make even a meat eater think twice.

Ben Lomond

They might not have redwoods in Bavaria, but that didn't stop German native Dieter Seider from re-creating a cozy Bavarian meat shack in the middle of Ben Lomond, the **Tyrolean Inn** (9600 Hwy. 9, Ben Lomond, 831/336-5188, lunch weekdays, dinner daily, closed Mon., dinner entrées $14–27). Dieter will have you doing the polka while waiting for the bratwurst, sauerkraut, and countless other less-pronounceable German staples. And as if an excuse were needed to down a half gallon of hefeweizen there seems to be some sort of beer festival going on every month.

If German kitsch is not your style then how about some Italian kitsch? Ben Lomond has that too at **N Ciao! Bella!!** (9217 Hwy. 9, Ben Lomond, 831/336-9221, www.ciaobellabenlomond.com, dinner daily, dinner entrées $9–23). This is part restaurant,

part Broadway musical, and totally wacky. The food is Italian comfort and pretty good but that's more or less where the Italian connection ends. Everything else (including the exclamation points in the name) screams roadhouse on acid in the land of Oz, right from when you drive up to the riotous exterior and park in a space "Reserved for Elvis" to the jaw-dropping moment the wait staff get up on stage to perform an impromptu Broadway rendition. It's loud but a lot of fun (generally adult fun, however).

Felton

Head down the road for reasonably priced Italian food in more traditional surroundings at **Mama Mia's Ristorante Italiano** (6231 Graham Hill Rd., off Hwy. 9, Felton, 831/335-4414, dinner daily, entrées $12–22). It's the original restaurant in a small South Bay chain and still turns out down-home Italian pizza, pasta, and meat dishes on checkered tablecloths, earning a loyal following from Boulder Creek to Santa Cruz.

Closer still to Santa Cruz, the restaurants get a little more sophisticated in Felton, not least **La Bruschetta Ristorante** (5447 Hwy. 9, Felton, 831/335-3337, lunch and dinner daily, dinner entrées $14–22). The rustic Sicilian food (including plenty of bruschetta appetizers) has influences from North Africa, Greece, and other parts of Europe, typical of food from this southern Italian island thanks to its position smack in the middle of the Mediterranean Sea. Try to get a table out on the big brick patio under the oak trees.

INFORMATION AND SERVICES

The first stop for all wine-related information should be the **Santa Cruz Mountains Winegrowers Association** (831/688-6961, www.scmwa.com), which has information about all the region's wines and wineries on a free map, usually available in winery tasting rooms. The website has information about the regular wine events the association arranges, including the regular Passport weekends, often the only way to visit some of the smaller wineries not listed in this chapter. Some of the non-wine-related listings on the website tend to be a little out of date, so take them with a pinch of salt, but the map is an essential tool for exploring the widely spaced wineries in the mountains.

For more information about the various state parks up in the mountains, visit the **California State Parks** website (www.parks.ca.gov).

GETTING THERE AND AROUND

Anyone planning to visit wineries in the Santa Cruz Mountains should really only consider driving, since most wineries are in the middle of nowhere and accessible only by car. Even intrepid bike riders will quickly give up on any ideas of biking between wineries once the distances and inclines become clearer.

The mountain wineries can be accessed from U.S. 9, which runs between Santa Cruz and Saratoga, via the San Lorenzo Valley towns of Felton, Ben Lomond, and Boulder Creek. Alternatively, U.S. 17 slices through the mountains and provides access to the handful of wineries north and south via Summit Road, just southwest of Los Gatos.

Travel south on Summit Road past the Burrell School and neighboring wineries, and the road eventually becomes the Old San Jose Road before descending to the coast and U.S. 1 at Soquel, just east of Santa Cruz. Go north on Summit Road for faster access to the David Bruce Winery and Byington Vineyard before descending on Bear Creek Road to Boulder Creek. Summit Road also links up with Skyline Boulevard, which runs along the ridgeline of the mountains above Los Gatos and Saratoga, eventually intersecting with U.S. 9.

Although distances between towns in the mountains are not huge (and gas stations are common in the San Lorenzo Valley), some of the roads can be tortuously slow, especially the southern end of Skyline Boulevard and U.S. 9 as it climbs from Saratoga up to the ridge.

Santa Cruz

The seaside surf town of Santa Cruz is a fascinating mix of sleaze and staid middle-class culture that only a historic port town on the edge of the wealthy Bay Area could be. It attracts millions of visitors every year in search of a hedonistic beach lifestyle and boardwalk entertainment, and the city's main beach is still the center of action, if not the prettiest part of town. Away from the sand the city of 55,000 feels more like a small suburban town, sprawling lazily around the San Lorenzo River with only Pacific Avenue lending any sense of a lively downtown area.

The seed of modern-day Santa Cruz was the mission, established here in the late 1700s and around which a small trading post built up. The trading post eventually became a port serving the mountain lumber business and trades associated with the gold rush before the pleasures of the climate and location were recognized by Victorian society and Santa Cruz was transformed into the resort town as tourism overtook the dwindling logging and fishing industries.

Despite its religious and Victorian heritage, Santa Cruz became famous in the 1960s for being a low-key counterculture town, attracting surfers and the fringes of the San Francisco hippy scene. The city is home to the most progressive campus of the University of California and a city council that has been equally progressive, regularly taking a position on international political situations and passing socially conscious legislation, including a minimum wage that is almost double that required under state law.

More recently, money has moved in as overspill from Silicon Valley is lured by relatively cheap property prices and the pleasant summer climate. As money gains influence, the laid-back vibe of Santa Cruz is increasingly being challenged with new rules and regulations to bring order to what many perceive as chaos. The city introduced a stringent law to ban aggressive panhandling, and the signs posted at regular intervals along Pacific Avenue downtown list plenty of other activities now deemed antisocial that could get you in trouble.

Santa Cruz is one of the best surfing spots in Northern California, and riding the waves along the city's beaches has been a pastime since the 1930s when the sport was introduced from Southern California. Some world-class surfing events are held here each year, including the O'Neill Cold Water Classic every fall.

WINERIES
Bonny Doon Vineyard

It seems to be a constant party down at Bonny Doon, a winery on the cool lower slopes of the mountains just outside Davenport, up the coast from Santa Cruz. The tasting room atmosphere makes a refreshing change from wine snobbery of some other big Santa Cruz wineries. It's also a place where the merchandise can be almost as much fun as the wine, especially if based on the wacky wine labels created by four different artists over the years, including Chuck House and Ralph Steadman, who's perhaps best known for the illustrations in Hunter S. Thompson's drug-fueled epic *Fear and Loathing in Las Vegas*.

Bonny Doon doesn't have to worry about the art eclipsing what's actually in the bottles. Known as a hippy boutique winery in its early days in the 1980s, it now turns out several hundred thousand cases of wine a year, and founder Randall Grahm has trailblazed a path (often a very wide path) along which the rest of the Californian industry has (sometimes) followed, from his unique approach to marketing to the recent use of screw-caps on some wines.

He is very much Santa Cruz's "Rhône Ranger," having planted a bewildering array of poetically named Rhône grape varietals over the last few decades and making wines with bizarre-sounding names that win critical praise not only for their quality but also their bargain prices.

Try Le Pousseur, a powerful syrah blend; the fruity Il Fiasco sangiovese from the Monterey

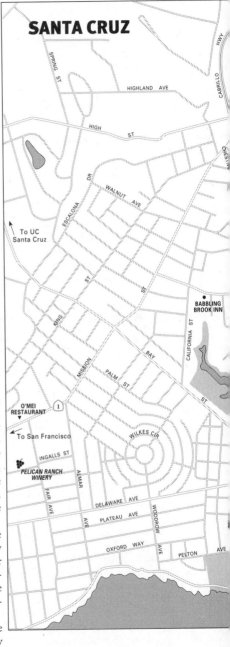

SANTA CRUZ

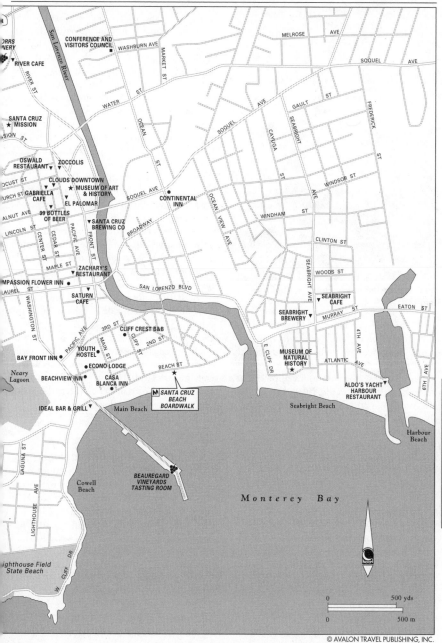

CONFERENCE AND VISITORS COUNCIL

MELROSE AVE

WASHBURN AVE

SOQUEL AVE

MARKET ST

RRS NERY

RIVER CAFE

RIVER ST

San Lorenzo River

WATER ST

GAULT ST

OCEAN ST

SOQUEL AVE

CAVIGA

SEABRIGHT

FREDERICK ST

SANTA CRUZ MISSION

SSION ST

OSWALD RESTAURANT

ZOCCOLIS

LOCUST ST

CLOUDS DOWNTOWN

MUSEUM OF ART & HISTORY

URCH ST

GABRIELLA CAFE

EL PALOMAR

WALNUT AVE

99 BOTTLES OF BEER

LINCOLN ST

SANTA CRUZ BREWING CO

PACIFIC AVE

SOQUEL AVE

CONTINENTAL INN

WINDSOR ST

WINDHAM ST

CEDAR ST

CENTER ST

FRONT ST

BROADWAY

OCEAN VIEW AVE

CLINTON ST

MAPLE ST

ZACHARY'S RESTAURANT

SEABRIGHT AVE

WOODS ST

MPASSION FLOWER INN

SATURN CAFE

SAN LORENZO BLVD

SEABRIGHT CAFE

LAUREL ST

WASHINGTON ST

PACIFIC AVE

3RD ST

CLIFF CREST B&B

2ND ST

SEABRIGHT BREWERY

MURRAY ST

EATON ST

YOUTH HOSTEL

MAIN ST

CLIFF ST

4TH AVE

BAY FRONT INN

ECONO LODGE

BEACH ST

MUSEUM OF NATURAL HISTORY

ATLANTIC AVE

6TH AVE

Neary Lagoon

BEACHVIEW INN

CASA BLANCA INN

SANTA CRUZ BEACH BOARDWALK

ALDO'S YACHT HARBOUR RESTAURANT

IDEAL BAR & GRILL

Main Beach

Seabright Beach

Harbour Beach

LAGUNA ST

E CLIFF DR

BEAUREGARD VINEYARDS TASTING ROOM

Cowell Beach

Monterey Bay

LIGHTHOUSE AVE

W CLIFF DR

ighthouse Field State Beach

MOON

| 0 | 500 yds |
| 0 | 500 m |

The South and East Bays

© AVALON TRAVEL PUBLISHING, INC.

Don't let the laid-back vibe of Santa Cruz fool you.

© PHILIP GOLDSMITH

area; the Madiran Heart of Darkness, made with the French regional grape tannat that few people in France have probably heard of; or the peppery Clos de Gilroy, made from grenache grown in the region just south of here that's better known for its garlic. In all there are usually more than 20 wines available for tasting at the rustic tasting room.

The wines themselves are no longer made here ever since the winery bought an operation over in the Livermore Valley, but a distillery on the site turns out some mind-blowing grappa (10 Pine Flat Rd., Santa Cruz, 831/425-4518, www.bonnydoonvineyard.com, 11 A.M.–5 P.M. daily).

Downtown Tasting Rooms

In the height of summer, when tourists throng the beaches and boardwalk, Santa Cruz might not feel much like a wine town, but there are a handful of tasting rooms in the city pouring local wines as a reminder that there's a great wine region up in the nearby hills.

Storrs Winery (303 Potrero St., off River St., 831/458-5030, www.storrswine.com, noon–

5 P.M. daily) specializes in Santa Cruz appellation wines, including chardonnay, zinfandel, and pinot noir, but also makes fruity riesling and gewürztraminer from the warmer Salinas Valley to the south—about 10,000 cases in total. The tasting room is near the center of town in the Old Sash Mill, a former lumber mill now home to small businesses and cafés.

The view is as good a reason to visit the **Beauregard Vineyards** tasting room (831/425-7777, www.beauregardvineyards.com, open 1–6 P.M. daily) as the wine. It's near the end of the wharf and has almost 360-degree views of the ocean and beaches from its second-floor location above Marini's Candies. Beauregard is best known for its crisp chardonnays (perfect for the wharf's fish) sourced from its vineyards in the subappellation of Ben Lomond up in the mountains. Those same vineyards also provide grapes for a zinfandel and merlot, and there's a fine pinot noir from the Central Coast area.

The **Pelican Ranch Winery** has a tasting room on the western side of the city (402 Ingalls St., Ste. 21, 831/426-6911, www.pelicanranch.com, open noon–5 P.M. Fri.–Sun.). Moderately priced chardonnay from the Santa Cruz region is poured alongside pinot noir, as well as syrah from the Central Coast region. This is a new urban winery, started in 1997, and it makes about 1,000 cases of vineyard-designate wines a year.

SIGHTS
 Santa Cruz Beach Boardwalk

It may be old and quaint, with tamer rides compared to some bigger and more modern theme parks, but the Santa Cruz Beach Boardwalk (400 Beach St., 831/423-5590, www.beachboardwalk.com, open daily Memorial Day through Labor Day, weekends and holidays the rest of the year) is about the most fun adrenaline junkies can have on a trip to Wine Country short of an illegal bungee jump out of a balloon over the Napa Valley.

Unfortunately, the city has not realized the full potential of the prim beachfront site, and the road that runs along the beach in front of the boardwalk is a seedy-looking mix of cheap

BEACH BLUBBER

The Santa Cruz beach boardwalk might not conjure up images of deserted California coastline where animals can freely frolic, but just a few miles north the human influence wanes and nature reclaims the coast. At **Año Nuevo State Park** nature reclaims it in a big way.

The park is home to a large colony of northern elephant seals, monsters more of the beach than the deep that can weigh up to 2.5 tons and grow up to 16 feet long. In December every year they haul their blubbery masses out of the water, not so much to frolic as simply to wallow on the rocks and sand in preparation for the breeding season.

Immobile as they might look, get too close to an irritable male and you might discover that they have quite good acceleration, though little stamina for a chase. Be aware that it's illegal, however, to harass them, and you shouldn't get closer than 25 feet. During breeding season from mid-December to the end of March, docent-led tours are the only way to get near the breeding colony. Call 800/444-4445 for reservations.

Although the seals live most of the rest of the year in the water they do come ashore to molt. Watching them roll and flap around on land it's easy to see why their terrestrial excursions are rare and fairly brief. The giant, mature males of the species, with their long, trunk-like snouts, molt July–August, smaller females and juveniles April–May, and younger males somewhere in between.

With the huge numbers of these blubber torpedos that haul out onto the beach it's also hard to believe that elephant seals were once hunted almost to extinction. By the end of the 1800s only 50–100 were believed to be left, and they were down in Mexico. By the mid-1990s an estimated 2,000 pups were born in California, and there were about 2,000 seals in the Año Nuevo colony. So if you're here in the breeding season you might just be witnessing several thousand tons of elephant seals strutting their stuff.

fast-food restaurants, shabby motels, and acres of decaying asphalt parking lots. Ignore the mess out front and head through the gates to the boardwalk and it's a different world.

The half-mile-long stretch of former beach boardwalk (it's now asphalt) along the city's main swimming beach is the West Coast's answer to Atlantic City or Coney Island. It has more than 30 rides, some that hark back to its Victorian beginning, others that will keep kids entertained for hours, and still more that have the potential to rearrange your internal organs. Cruising the boardwalk and inhaling the aromas of greasy seaside fast food are free but the rides are not, though they are thankfully cheap and cost $2–4. To make a day of it, buy an unlimited-ride wristband for $27.

There are a dozen rides for kids, including the **Charles Looff Carousel** ($2.40), a candy-colored piece of spinning history with a 342-pipe organ and 70 hand-made horses dating

from 1911. Charles's son, Arthur Looff, was the man behind the **Giant Dipper** roller coaster ($3.90), a soaring wooden structure built in 1924. It might lack the inverted thrills of modern coasters but has a certain stomach-churning Victorian ambience (and great views from the top) that has kept it rolling for more than 80 years. Both the Looff rides are registered as National Historic Landmarks.

The **Hurricane** is a compact, twisting steel rollercoaster opened in 1992 that offers two minutes of even greater twists and turns, creating forces of up to 4.5G that seem to never let up. There's talk that it might be replaced by a new coaster sometime soon.

Those in search of more G-force fun should check out the newest attraction called **Double Shot** ($3.90), and we're not talking tequila. It's certainly a descriptive name—riders rocket up a 125-foot-high tower, hang at the top a while to appreciate the views, then plummet back to earth. Drinking tequila beforehand is not recommended.

If a Hurricane is not enough, there are four other stormy rides to batter and twirl you around, including **Cyclone, Whirlwind,** and the upside-down experience of the **Typhoon.** There are many more opportunities to be flung around in mechanical contraptions plus plenty of more sedate amusements like miniature golf and the nearby **Boardwalk Bowl** (115 Cliff St., 831/426-3324, www.boardwalkbowl.com, open year-round).

For more information on all the rides and arcade games on the boardwalk, together with a full list of events throughout the year both outdoors and in the **Cocoanut Grove** casino and ballroom, visit www.beachboardwalk.com or call 831/426-7433.

Santa Cruz Mission

The history of Santa Cruz has been punctuated by earthquakes that literally reshaped the city over the last 200 years. The original mission building around which the city was built eventually fell foul of the shaking ground.

Built in 1794, that original **Misión de Exaltación de la Santa Cruz** was quickly overshadowed by the Spanish colony of Branciforte, which was built across the San Lorenzo River in 1797 and quickly turned into a den of iniquity that proved more of a lure for the Ohlone Native Americans than religion did. The mission was abandoned in the early 1800s after being looted by the rowdy residents of Branciforte who were actually supposed to save its contents and ship them inland away from the threat of pirate attacks. An earthquake in 1845 demolished half the run-down mission and its bell tower. Another in 1857 finished the job. Now there's a just a replica, built in the 1930s, standing near the site of the original.

Historic Districts

Earthquakes destroyed the original mission, and more recently the 1989 Loma Prieta earthquake damaged large swaths of other parts of the city that dated from the post-mission period, especially some of the famed Victorian

© PHILIP GOLDSMITH

the Santa Cruz Mission

homes. In fact, one of three National Register Historic Districts was de-listed in 1991 due to the loss of so many old buildings downtown, particularly along Pacific Avenue.

The two other historic districts are still largely intact and enough to keep any Victorian fanatic happy, however, including the **Mission Hill Historic District** on the site of the original Branciforte settlement. Here and along both **Walnut Avenue** (between Center St. and Rincon St.) and **Ocean View Avenue** (south of Broadway St.), gabled Queen Anne–style homes rub shoulders with ornate Italianate or Gothic revival–style buildings, many built with money from the logging industry that fueled a citywide building boom in the mid- to late 1800s. Pick up information about historic walking tours from the Santa Cruz County Conference and Visitors Bureau (1211 Ocean St., 831/425-1234 or 800/833-3494).

Museums

The **Santa Cruz Museum of Art and History** in the McPherson Center (705 Front St., at Cop-

"SEABIRD INVASION HITS COASTAL HOMES"

So screamed the headline of the *Santa Cruz Sentinel* on August 18, 1961. The previous night's event will go down in the annals of Santa Cruz's strange history (annals that are, by now, bulging)—a nighttime invasion of swarms of suicidal seabirds that slammed into houses and cars while vomiting the remains of anchovies, sending terrified residents running indoors and leaving the stench of rotting fish on the streets in the morning.

It is thought that swarms of sooty shearwaters that had happily been gorging on anchovies were startled and rose in a giant flock, became disoriented in the thick, dark ocean fog that regularly envelops the coastline, and flew toward the nearest light they saw, which happened to be the streetlights, house lights,

and car headlights along the northern Santa Cruz Bay shoreline. Pity the poor residents who then came outside to investigate the thud of birds against their windows only to have even more birds fly straight toward the beams of their flashlights.

As if the event itself wasn't strange enough, it occurred just two years before Alfred Hitchcock released his film *The Birds*. Hitchcock reportedly had a copy of the story sent to him, and it may well have inspired the scenes of menacing birds attacking terrified residents when *The Birds* was filmed in Bodega Bay just north of San Francisco. The Santa Cruz seabird incident did not, however, inspire Hitchcock's movie outright—it was already in the making, based on a Daphne DuMaurier novel.

per St., Santa Cruz, 831/429-1964, www.santacruzmah.org, 11 A.M.–5 P.M. Tues.–Sun., $5) was established in 1996 by the merger of the city's history museum and art museum (another result of the 1989 earthquake). Permanent exhibits include *Where the Redwoods Meet the Sea,* which highlights the history of Santa Cruz County from the Native Americans to present-day industries, and there are always several temporary exhibits of art, photography, or history.

The modest **Santa Cruz Surfing Museum** packs more than 70 years of local surfing history into the Mark Abbott Memorial Lighthouse at Lighthouse Point on West Cliff Drive (701 W. Cliff Dr., Santa Cruz, 831/420-6289, open noon–4 P.M. Wed.–Mon.). See the giant redwood surfboards used in the early days of surfing and a modern board that was attacked by a shark, plus hundreds of photos and memorabilia from a century of wave riding. The museum is right across from the famous Steamers Lane surfing spot.

The surfing museum is affiliated with the **Santa Cruz Museum of Natural History** on the other side of town (1305 E. Cliff Dr., Santa Cruz, 831/420-6115, www.santacruzmuseums.org, 10 A.M.–5 P.M. Tues.–Sun., $2.50). Kid-friendly exhibits explore the history of the region and

its original natives, the Ohlone. Or stick your hands into the Tidepool Touch Tank, just one of the museum's nature and wildlife exhibits.

Outdoor Attractions

Visit the **Neary Lagoon Wildlife Refuge,** an urban oasis with a raised walkway that winds around the reeds and over the water. Entrances are located at the end of Chestnut and Blackburn Streets, and at the corner of Bay and California Streets. Watch out for the mean geese.

Birds are about all you'll see at Neary Lagoon, but there's often a lot more wildlife on display at the **Santa Cruz Wharf** (Beach St., opposite Front St.), hordes of colorful tourists aside. Sea lions usually haul themselves out of the water and wallow noisily on the wharf's beams, and anglers try their luck at catching some of the Monterey Bay's abundant sealife. If all else fails, just pick up some professionally caught fish at the market or try the usually mediocre seafood at one of the many restaurants.

EVENTS

Santa Cruz is hopping with events all year long, about which more information can be found at the Santa Cruz Conference and Visitors

The South and East Bays

Council (1211 Ocean St., 831/425-1234 or 800/833-3494, www.santacruza.org). On the last Saturday of February, the **Annual Clam Chowder Cook-Off** is held on the Beach Boardwalk and you can be the judge, too (tasting kits $7, 831/420-5273).

The free **Jazz on the Wharf** is held on a Sunday in early March (usually the first weekend), and the Santa Cruz Wharf plays host to several other annual events. They include **Woodies on the Wharf** in late June, a celebration of classic surf wagons; **Art on the Wharf** in mid-July; and **Halloween on the Wharf** on the obvious date.

Big names play at the **Santa Cruz Blues Festival** on Memorial Day weekend (www.santacruzbluesfestival.com, $35–60), so tickets usually sell out fast. Despite the name it is held a few miles south of the city at the Aptos Village Park. Alternatively, visit the **Boulder Creek Art, Wine & Music Festival** up in the mountains, where local blues and jazz bands will provide the entertainment to accompany your culinary indulgences in the redwoods. Contact the Boulder Creek Business Association (831/338-7099, www.bcba.net) to check if the event is still happening—in 2005 the state highway agency tried to shut it down because it involves consumption of alcohol on a state road, Highway 9.

On the first weekend in August, the **Cabrillo Music, Art, and Wine Festival** is the city's outdoor food, wine, and entertainment summer blowout, held on Church Street outside the Civic Auditorium.

Surfing is a big draw all year, and the Steamers Lane surf break off Lighthouse Field State Beach is the usual venue. The world's largest **Kayak Surf Festival** is held every year at Steamers Lane in mid-March, and late May brings the longboarders out at the **Annual Longboard Club Invitational,** the oldest and longest-running surfing event on the West Coast, organized by the Santa Cruz Longboard Union. The **O'Neill Cold Water Classic** is held in mid-October, ironically the time of year that the sea is warmest in these parts. Visit www.oneillcwc.asglive.com for photos

and more information about this world-class surfing event.

RECREATION

Santa Cruz Beaches

Santa Cruz is all about beach life, so visiting one of the city's beaches is a must, whether on a crowded summer weekend when bodies can be packed like sardines on the shore, or in winter when a few lone surfers brave the ocean chill to catch some of the storm-generated waves. Be warned that even in the summer the sea feels like it could induce mild hypothermia. You'll quickly understand why the surfers wear wetsuits year-round.

The city's **Main Beach** is the long stretch of sand right in front of the Beach Boardwalk and gets the most crowded in summer with families, local teens, and San Jose outsiders. This is the best people-watching beach. Slightly quieter, though not by much, is **Cowell Beach,** on the other side of the wharf from Main Beach. This is where novice surfers tend to congregate, providing some amusing entertainment for landlubbers. For some more impressive surfing action head southwest to **Lighthouse Field State Beach** off West Cliff Drive. The headlands overlook the renowned Steamers Lane surf break, which tends to pick up the most steam in the winter months.

Right at the end of West Cliff Drive is the beautiful cove of **Natural Bridges State Beach** (2531 W. Cliff Dr., $6 parking fee), famous for both its natural sandstone arch (there's just one now—the other two collapsed from natural causes in the early 1900s and 1980) and for the more than 100,000 monarch butterflies that overwinter here between October and February before embarking on their long spring migration of up to 2,000 miles. On cold, wet days the butterflies huddle together, forming colorful clumps that hang from the eucalyptus trees along a trail that leads around the **Monarch Butterfly Natural Preserve.** Docent-led tours are offered when the butterflies are in town, on weekends at 11 A.M. and 2 P.M.; call 831/423-4609 for more information. There

© PHILIP GOLDSMITH

Santa Cruz beaches, where Wine Country meets the sea.

are even events to celebrate the arrival and departure of the butterflies—the Welcome Back Monarchs day is on the second Sunday of October and the Migration Festival is on the second Saturday of February. Those folks in Santa Cruz certainly know how to party. Down near the shore there are hundreds of tidepools to explore at low tide, as well as the ever-present seals, sea lions, and seabirds.

This being a counterculture city, there has to be at least one clothing-optional beach, and it's a few blocks south of Natural Bridges. Look for access down to the tiny **2222 Beach** right opposite the house at 2222 West Cliff Drive.

Many of the quieter beaches frequented more by locals are southeast of Main Beach and the wharf, across the mouth of the San Lorenzo River and accessed from East Cliff Drive. **Twin Lakes State Park** actually encompasses three beaches that locals call Seabright, Harbor, and Schwan Lake. **Seabright Beach** is perhaps the prettiest and most easily accessible from downtown. It is between the mouth of the San Lorenzo River and the harbor entrance. **Harbor Beach** on the other side of the harbor

entrance is smaller but with plenty of restaurants and cafés along its edge, and farther east is a stretch of beach in front of **Schwan Lake,** a good bird-watching spot.

Wilder Ranch State Park

A couple of miles north of Santa Cruz on the coast road, Wilder Ranch State Park (1401 Old Coast Rd. on the west side of Hwy. 1, 831/423-9703 or 831/426-0505, $6 day-use fee) boasts 7,000 acres of forest, chaparral, marshes, and meadows together with 34 miles of hiking and biking trails. This is more than simply a hiking destination, however. It was once a working ranch and still is to a certain extent. The land was bought by dairy farmer D. D. Wilder in 1871 but was also the site of the rancho that once supplied food to the mission in Santa Cruz.

Victorian farmhouses, several barns, and an old adobe said to be roofed with tiles from the long-gone mission have been restored and are now central to the living history events and demonstrations that go on year-round. There are still about 900 acres of agricultural land in the park (brussels sprouts anyone?), some of it still plowed using horses, as shown by docents dressed in period costume who also demonstrate many other Victorian farming practices. If the hard farm life is too exhausting, go for a stroll out to the bluffs overlooking the sea, or duck through the tunnel under U.S. 1 and start hiking for the hills.

ACCOMMODATIONS

The city of Santa Cruz has about as much in common with rustic mountain wineries as seawater has with a fine pinot noir. Santa Cruz became a beach resort town in the late 1800s and has never looked back, which means there are plenty of hotels and B&Bs to accommodate the hordes of summer tourists and surfers that still throng the beaches and boardwalk today.

The city provides plenty of guilty tourist pleasures yet is still only less than a half-hour drive from many mountain wineries. Expect the usual price manipulation typical of hotels

The South and East Bays

in tourist destinations—a jump in rates during the summer plus sometimes unreasonable minimum stay and cancellation requirements. Be sure to check all the details when you book.

If Santa Cruz is booked up or simply too brash for your tastes, there are some notable places to stay a little farther north or south.

Hostels

Serious bargain hunters or those who have blown their travel budget on cases of wine might want to check out the **Santa Cruz Youth Hostel** (321 Main St., Santa Cruz., 831/423-8304, www.hi-santacruz.org). It's everything a hostel should be—clean, cheap ($18 a night plus $3 temporary membership fee for non-members), centrally located, and with a bit of history to boot. The dorm-style rooms plus a couple of family rooms are in the Victorian Carmelita Cottages, built to house sea captains awaiting their next vessel. Reservations are essential in the summer, and there's a small fee for parking.

Under $100

Other bargain-priced accommodations tend to be of the motel variety, with just about every chain represented. As this a resort town, however, a bargain-priced establishment in Santa Cruz will be less than luxurious for prices that can top $100 in the summer.

A central location a few blocks from the beach and some low prices make the motel-style **Bay Front Inn** (325 Pacific Ave., Santa Cruz, 831/423-8564, www.bayfrontinnsc.com) a relative bargain in the crowded motel scene. The 38 rooms cost $50–70 during the week, $20 higher at weekends, and suites are available for less of a bargain at $225. Don't expect luxury at this price.

The **Beachview Inn** (50 Front St., Santa Cruz, 831/426-3575 or 800/946-0614, www.beachviewinn.com) is even closer to the ocean, with views of the beach over the rooftops of neighboring buildings, and just a little pricier. Rates range from $60 for the smaller motel-style rooms with one bed up to $110 for the larger rooms with two beds, some with Jacuzzis. Summer rates are $80–190 a night. All rooms have cable TV and air-conditioning.

The **Econo Lodge Boardwalk** (550 2nd St., Santa Cruz, 831/426-3626) is a couple of blocks from the boardwalk and offers clean but typically sparse motels rooms with one or two beds for rates that yo-yo wildly depending on the season. From fall through spring they start at $55–80 depending on the month and shoot up to over $125 in peak summer season, which runs July–September.

The **Continental Inn** is a little off the beaten track but still fairly central, about six blocks from the boardwalk and downtown area (414 Ocean St., Santa Cruz, 831/429-1221 or 800/343-6941, www.continentalinn.net). The rooms are clean and fairly well equipped for a glorified motel, with some big-hotel amenities like free high-speed Internet access, irons, and hair dryers. Rates start at $75 in winter and $95 in summer for the queen rooms and run up to $160 for suites.

$100–150

The **Casa Blanca Inn** (101 Main St., at Beach St., Santa Cruz, 831/423-1570 or 800/644-1570) has 39 rooms ranging from spacious and uniquely furnished to gussied-up motel rooms, all in a prime oceanfront location. Amenities include microwaves and refrigerators, fireplaces and Jacuzzis in some rooms, and ocean views in all but six of the rooms. Rates are as varied as the rooms themselves, ranging $78–200 in low season and $125–250 in high season. The inn incorporates the 1918 Cerf Mansion, which contains some of the better rooms.

The **Compassion Flower Inn** (216 Laurel St., Santa Cruz, 831/466-0420, www.compassionflowerinn.com) is a reminder that Santa Cruz is not only a tourist mecca but also a center of California's thriving counterculture. The inn is a self-declared hemp and medical-marijuana friendly B, B&B, or "bed, bud, and breakfast" inn, as its owners like to call it. Hemp fabrics adorn the rooms (no, not the tokable variety), marijuana-leaf motifs are everywhere, and there's a resident guru to help make your stay a spiritual one. Don't expect to buy your stash here though—it's a bring-your-own-pot establishment, and a doctor's note is needed to smoke openly, thanks to Santa Cruz's own ordinance legalizing medical marijuana. Pot aside, the inn is also a luxurious place to stay, with five rooms in the meticulously restored 1860 Gothic-style Victorian house. The cheapest Hemp and Passion Flower rooms ($115 weekdays, $125 weekends) share a bathroom. Rates for the larger room and the suite are $135–175 a night.

About nine miles north of Santa Cruz, the artist-friendly coastal hamlet of Davenport offers a refreshing change of pace (if you can ignore the cement plant on the edge of town), and the 12-room **Davenport Inn** is about the biggest business on the main drag (31 Davenport Ave./Hwy. 1, Davenport, 831/425-1818 or 800/870-1817, www.davenportinn.com). Each room is furnished in an eclectic mix of art and antiques, and many have ocean views from their first floor balcony. Rates range from $115 for the smaller rooms to $155 for Captain Davenport's Retreat, with French doors offering views that any seafaring captain would appreciate. An off-season discount of 10 percent is often available in the chilly winter months. The inn is above the New Davenport Cash Store (which replaced the old one that burned down in the 1950s), a bar and restaurant. All are owned by the same artist couple, so the decor in the restaurant hints at the look of many of the rooms.

The **Terrace Court Motel** (125 Beach St., Santa Cruz, 831/423-3031, www.terracecourt.com) is right opposite the beach above a surf shop.

$150–250

The **Cliff Crest Bed and Breakfast Inn** (407 Cliff St., Santa Cruz, 831/427-2609, www.cliffcrestinn.com) is an Easter-egg blue Queen Anne Victorian house a few blocks from the beach and boardwalk with five rooms, all tastefully decorated with antiques that the owners, an artist and chemical engineer, have collected over the years. The smallest Pineapple and Apricot rooms might leave you feeling a bit claustrophobic but are the cheapest at $175

in winter, $195 in summer. The three larger rooms are $195–245 depending on the season, though some midweek specials are often available in the winter.

Touting itself as the biggest and oldest B&B in Santa Cruz, the **M** **Babbling Brook Inn** is also one of the most unusual places to stay in the city (1025 Laurel St., Santa Cruz, 831/427-2437 or 800/866-1131, www.babblingbrookinn.com). The rustic collection of buildings is centered around a log cabin that incorporates foundations from a grist mill built here in the 1700s and a tannery that dated from the 1870s, all set in an acre of lush gardens through which the namesake brook babbles. Most of the 13 luxurious rooms are named after historic artists and have fireplaces, whirlpool tubs, featherbeds, and sofas. The cheapest is the elegant Contessa room ($179–200, depending on season), named after the Countess Florenzo de Chandler, who bought the property in 1924 and made a few additions. Other rooms cost $179–235 a night, including a generous breakfast.

Over $250

Romantics who want to escape the bustle of Santa Cruz could head a few miles east to Capitola where the **Inn at Depot Hill** (250 Monterey Ave., Capitola, 831/462-3376 or 800/572-2632, www.innatdepothill.com) offers some of the area's most luxurious and intimate accommodations. The upscale B&B is in a former railroad depot, where eight rooms have been transformed into geographic time capsules that transport guests to old England, France, Holland, Italy, and even Japan without leaving any modern amenities like whirlpool tubs, stereos, or TVs behind. The English cottage decor of the Stratford-on-Avon room offers the cheapest getaway at $230–250. Other rooms run from $255 up to $355 a night, though winter specials can sometimes push the rates closer to $200.

FOOD

For a big city there are surprisingly few fine dining opportunities in Santa Cruz, particularly compared to towns like Saratoga or St. Helena that are more in the thick of Wine Country. Many upscale restaurants have tried and failed to gain traction with the laid-back residents who seem to prefer low-key and well-known eateries rather than upscale upstarts. A lively café scene thrives off the student population, and if you can't decide what to eat it's worth heading for tree-lined Pacific Avenue, which is the commercial center of the city.

Beachfront Dining

Casablanca Restaurant (101 Main St., at Beach St., Santa Cruz, 831/426-9063, dinner daily, entrées $15–30) has a tough time living up to one of the best restaurant views in the city, overlooking the ocean and wharf from its perch in the eponymous hotel. The meat-heavy menu is not terribly adventurous, perhaps not wanting to upstage the venue or put off hotel guests, but dishes are still high quality.

Anyone who happens to be in Santa Cruz the same month they were born and likes free food should call the **Ideal Bar & Grill** (106 Beach St., Santa Cruz, 831/423-5271, breakfast, lunch, dinner daily, dinner entrées $16–28), a hopping indoor-outdoor scene at the foot of the wharf. One random day a month (call for the date), anyone born that month gets a free prime rib meal. Yes, it's totally free. Just have identification to prove your birthdate and buy a drink or appetizer to go with the meal. If it's not your day there are plenty of other deals throughout the week, including $10 prime rib on Fridays and $10 lobster dinners on Wednesdays. Live music at this beachfront bar can be loud, but that's half the fun.

If the sun's shining, leave the downtown crowds behind for a breakfast or lunch listening to the waves and clanking of boat rigging at **Aldo's Yacht Harbor Restaurant** (616 Atlantic Ave., off Seabright, Santa Cruz, 831/426-3736, 7 A.M.–4 P.M. daily, open later in summer, lunch entrées under $10), perched above the water at the Santa Cruz Harbor. Seafood is the starring feature whatever the time of day, from the seafood scramble at breakfast (washed down with famously strong coffee) to

a seasonal local catch at lunch. Or just stare out to sea over a cool beer and dish of calamari.

Downtown Santa Cruz

Everything is cozy charm at the star of the small Santa Cruz bistro scene, **Ⓜ Gabriella Café** (910 Cedar St., at Church St., Santa Cruz, 831/457-1677, lunch and dinner daily, brunch weekends, dinner entrées $12–20). Flowers bloom outside the modest bungalow, white-clothed tables are squeezed into every nook, and a hand-scribbled menu features a modest selection of simple but beautifully executed, Italian-inspired dishes (including thin, crispy pizza) incorporating seasonal produce from local organic farms. The wine list is equally well stocked with local productions from the Monterey and Santa Cruz regions.

A little more full of itself is the hip bistro **Ⓜ Oswald** (1547 E. Pacific Ave., Santa Cruz, 831/423-7427, dinner Tues.–Sun., entrées $16–25). Owner and chef Eric Lau has been creating French-influenced California cuisine with seasonal local produce and fish between these brick walls for over a decade. Try to reserve the banquette table in the corner or up on the mezzanine for some good people-watching while sipping a local wine.

California-Asian fusion food gets the modern hipster treatment at **Clouds Downtown** (110 Church St., Santa Cruz, 831/429-2000, lunch and diner daily, dinner entrées $13–23). It's a draw for both the cocktail crowd as well as diners who can tolerate the high decibels for the menu of surf and turf dressed up with Asian-inspired finery.

Prices at the popular veteran Chinese restaurant **O'Mei** (2316 Mission St., Santa Cruz, 831/425-8458, lunch weekdays, dinner daily, dinner entrées $10–20) have crept up in recent years, but the quality of the food makes it a worthwhile destination to discover how much better gourmet Chinese food is over the take-out variety, and how well it can go with fine wine. The dominant style is Sichuan but there are influences from all over China. Regulars rave about the red oil dumplings.

Highly praised Mexican food in a slightly

more luxurious setting than the average taqueria is served at **El Palomar** (1336 Pacific Ave., Santa Cruz, 831/425-7575, lunch and dinner daily, dinner entrées $8–20) in the beautifully restored Palomar Inn Hotel downtown on the main drag. The hotel has long since gone residential, but the restaurant occupies the former lobby and atrium patio.

The place to go downtown for breakfast is **Zachary's Restaurant** (819 Pacific Ave., Santa Cruz., 831/427-0646, breakfast daily until 2:30 P.M.), a funky Santa Cruz institution with lines snaking out of the door at weekends. Try Mike's Mess, a plateful of eggs scrambled with all sorts of good stuff and topped with cheese, sour cream, and tomatoes.

A convenient place to grab food to go is the downtown deli and diner **Zoccolis** (1534 Pacific Ave., 831/423-1711, open daily until 6 P.M.). None of the gourmet sandwiches and daily pasta dishes cost more than $10 and there are nearly 20 different salads to choose from.

Cafés

The **River Café** (415 River St., Santa Cruz, 831/420-1280,. 10 A.M.–6 P.M. Tues.–Sat, 11 A.M.–5 P.M. Sun.) is part artisan cheese shop and part tiny eatery. Bring your own wine and sit on the outside patio for a late lunch of salad and a plate of some of the dozens of sheep, cow, and goat cheeses, or simply stock up for a picnic in the mountains.

Breakfasts are well worth the sometimes lengthy weekend line at the popular and homey **Seabreeze Café** (542 Seabright Ave., Santa Cruz, 831/427-9713, breakfast and early lunch daily, no credit cards). For under $10 meat eaters and vegetarians alike can fill up for the day. Check the board for sumptuous daily specials.

Day or night, the vegetarian world is spinning downtown at Santa Cruz's quintessential **⋈ Saturn Café** (145 Laurel St., Santa Cruz, 831/429-8505 open daily, late morning to early morning, under $10). Have a lunchtime burger with choice of veggie or vegan patty and all the usual fixings, a midnight sandwich named after one of our neighboring planets, or an af-

ternoon snack from the cheap eats menu for less than the cost of parking downtown.

Many of Santa Cruz's downtown cafés sell light meals (plus good, earth-friendly coffee) and are generally strung along the parallel Pacific Avenue and Cedar Street, plus some of the cross streets. Many also offer free wireless Internet access. Try the **Santa Cruz Coffee Roasting Company** (1330 Pacific Ave., 831/459-0100), **Cafe Bene** (1101 Cedar St., 831/425-0441), **Café Pegolesi** (418 Cedar St., 831/426-1775), and **Lulu Carpenter's** (1545 Pacific Ave., 831/429-9804).

Brewpubs

Because Santa Cruz is a big student and party town there are plenty of temples to beer, all open daily until late. The most bewildering array (including 40 on tap) and some fine burgers are at the aptly named **99 Bottles of Beer on the Wall** (110 Walnut Ave., Santa Cruz, 831/459-9999). Drink all 99 (not necessarily in a day) and win a T-shirt.

A couple of other brewpubs offer more in the way of crazily-named local microbrews. **The Santa Cruz Brewing Company** (516 Front St., Santa Cruz, 831/429-8838) is a wannabe English pub in a former warehouse offering 13 microbrews to accompany its gourmet pub grub. Farther south, the **Seabright Brewery** (519 Seabright Ave., Santa Cruz, 831/426-2739) concocts some quality pale ales and stouts that can be sipped over some basic pub fare on the outdoor patio.

INFORMATION AND SERVICES

Information about both the city and county of Santa Cruz is available at the **Santa Cruz County Conference and Visitors Council,** a little off the beaten path in Santa Cruz (1211 Ocean St., 831/425-1234 or 800/833-3494, open 9 A.M.–5 P.M. Mon.–Sat., 10 A.M.–4 P.M. Sun., www.santacruzca.org). There's useful city information in its free visitor guide, as well as information about sights and wineries further afield in the county. Also worth checking out for more detailed information about

Santa Cruz itself is the City of Santa Cruz website maintained by **Santa Cruz City Hall** (www.ci.santa-cruz.ca.us).

The weekly newspapers, usually available in cafés and on the street, are worth picking up in either side of the mountains for up-to-date event and entertainment listings. *Good Times* covers Santa Cruz and up into the mountains, and *Metro* is the weekly paper for Los Gatos, Saratoga, and other Silicon Valley towns, though its territory also stretches to Santa Cruz. The *Los Gatos Weekly Times* is a more news-oriented weekly but also has listings.

GETTING THERE

Driving to Santa Cruz from either San Francisco to the north or San Jose to the east involves navigating through or around the mountains, and will likely take longer than the mileage might suggest. If you're in Saratoga, U.S. 9 is going to be by far the quickest route, slow as it might feel, and it meets U.S. 1 in Santa Cruz just a few blocks from the mission just up the hill from the downtown area.

From San Francisco and points north, the slow and pretty route is on the Pacific Coast Highway (U.S. 1), but faster routes use U.S. 17, which runs past Los Gatos and through Scotts Valley. This is the main road across the mountains but it's by no means quick. It twists and turns like any mountain road and is often clogged with rush-hour traffic, beach traffic, or traffic backed up by one of the regular rain-induced spinouts in winter.

From the south, U.S. 1 also heads straight into Santa Cruz and can be picked up easily from U.S. 101 just north of Salinas.

Greyhound (425 Front St., 831/423-1800) offers daily bus service from San Francisco or Los Angeles via either San Jose or Monterey.

GETTING AROUND

Biking as a means of winery touring might be out of the question in the mountains, but in the city of Santa Cruz you might be wishing you had a bike when searching for parking down-

The bicycle is king in downtown Santa Cruz.

town or at the beach, especially in summer—or when you discover just how efficient the parking and traffic cops are.

The bicycle is king in earth-friendly Santa Cruz and they seem to be the main mode of transport for the students at the University of California at Santa Cruz. If you're in Santa Cruz for a few days, leave the car at the hotel and rent bikes (and locks). It need not be as strenuous as it sounds.

Try out an electric bike from **Electric Sierra Rentals** (302 Pacific Ave., at W. Cliff Dr. a few blocks from the wharf, 831/425-1593 or 877/372-8773, www.electricrecbikes.com). There are electric versions of mountain bikes, beach cruisers, and tandems starting at $10 an hour or from $35 a day. They have a range of about 20 miles, making them perfect for puttering around town, but speed demons take note—you won't get more than 20 mph out of them. Electric Sierra Rentals also rents more traditional human-powered bikes for $25 a day.

On crowded summer weekends you can usually find free parking at the County Government Center (701 Ocean St.), and hop on the **Santa Cruz Beach Shuttle,** which runs about every half hour during daylight hours down to the wharf and boardwalk and back.

The Livermore Valley

During the summer months it's hard to believe that this hot, dry, and thoroughly suburbanized valley was actually once awash with water as creeks from the surrounding hills drained down into a natural basin before they were dammed, creating reservoirs such as the Del Valle Regional Park—a positive recreational oasis in the hills north of Livermore.

The heat and the gravelly, well-drained soils left behind by the once-flowing waters were identified early on in California's wine-making history as a perfect combination for growing wine grapes. The first vines were planted here in 1844, before even the Napa and Sonoma wine industries had gotten started. It would be more than 50 years until Livermore's first nonagricultural industry—brick making—got its start.

Despite these ideal growing conditions—some say they are as good as parts of the Napa Valley—Livermore wine has never really hit the big time. Without the marketing muscle that a big-name appellation like Napa or Sonoma provides, wineries must squeeze more out of their vineyards to make cheaper, but lower quality, wines that will sell. They're stuck in a wine marketing catch-22.

That might change in the future if the current resurgence of wine making in the area can bring in the accolades and the dollars. As urban sprawl ate into the vineyards during the 1960s, '70s, and '80s, the number of vine-covered acres fell dramatically. Now they're on the rise again thanks to agricultural protections put in place in the early 1990s, and the number of wineries has slowly increased to 24 today, though that's still far below the 50 or more that existed back in the valley's Victorian wine heyday.

The Wines

As anyone who has driven through the valley in July or August and stepped out of their air-conditioned car at a gas station will know, the Livermore Valley gets very hot in the summer. In terms of the way grape-growing climates are measured, this is a Region III climate, which is about the same as the Alexander Valley, the upper Napa Valley, and Tuscany.

Consequently this is a land of big, fruity wines, predominantly chardonnay and cabernet sauvignon these days, but also plenty of other whites including some sauvignon blanc and semillon, which once dominated the vineyards here.

The valley's wineries generally don't charge for tasting (unless noted), though you'll typically have to pay to taste some reserve or library wines. Other than a few giants like Concannon and Wente, most wineries here are small family affairs and many open only on weekends.

WINERIES

Cedar Mountain Winery

Located on a rise at the eastern end of the valley, Cedar Mountain's estate vineyard is exposed to a little more of the cool breezes from the bay than the valley floor below and is a pretty backdrop for the opera concerts held here in the summer.

The cooler temperatures and longer growing season might explain how it has become known for producing some fine red wines, including its proprietary blend of cabernet sauvignon and merlot called Duet.

Most of the 4,000 cases of wine are reds and include a regular and reserve cabernet, merlot, and a zinfandel made from Amador County fruit from the Sierra foothills. The lone white wine is chardonnay, made in a typical warm-climate style with lots of tropical fruit flavors and a creamy texture (7000 Tesla Rd., Livermore, 925/373-6636, open noon–4 P.M. weekends).

🅜 Wente Vineyards

Considered the patriarch of the Livermore Valley wine scene for more than a century, Wente now owns large swaths of the vineyards here and a handful of the wineries, but its sheer size and financial muscle have helped many of the

The South and East Bays

LIVERMORE

GREENVILLE RD

LAWRENCE
LIVERMORE
NATIONAL
LABORATORY

S VASCO RD

PURPLE
ORCHID B&B

RD

POPPY RIDGE
GOLF COURSE

CEDAR
MOUNTAIN
WINERY

TESLA

VINEYARD INN AT
CRANE RIDGE

WENTE VINEYARDS
ESTATE TASTING
ROOM

MINES   RD

580

EAST AVE

BUENA VISTA AVE

STONY RIDGE
WINERY

CONCANNON
VINEYARD

ST

WENTE   ST

PORTOLA

ST

AVE

LIVERMORE AVE

MARINA

AVE

ARROYO   RD

WENTE
VINEYARDS

COURSE AT WENTE VINEYARDS/
WENTE VINEYARDS RESTAURANT/
VISITOR CENTER

Del Valle
Regional
Park

RIATA DINER
AND TAVERN

ST

COLLEGE AVE

ARROYO   RD

BLVD

WETMORE   RD

ZEPHYR'S
GRILL & BAR

P ST

N ST

CASA OROZCO

ST

HOLMES

ST

N MURRIETA BLVD

CONCANNON

E VINEYARD AVE

THOMAS COYNE
WINERY

84

ISABEL AVE

FENESTRA
WINERY

1 mi

1 km

STANLEY   BLVD

84

COMFORT INN/
HAMPTON INN/
COURTYARD BY
MARRIOT

580

To Pleasanton,
Oakland, and San
Francisco

To Pleasanton

VINEYARD   AVE

MITCHELL KATZ
WINERY

© AVALON TRAVEL PUBLISHING, INC.

VINEYARDS VS. SUBDIVISIONS

The strip malls and seemingly endless miles of subdivision that devoured thousands of acres of vineyards since the 1950s met their match in the valley's wine-making juggernaut, the Wente family.

The family has been instrumental in helping prevent the Livermore Valley from being concreted over and has helped many of the valley's small producers make a go of wine making. In some respects, the Wentes are to Livermore today what the Mondavis were to the Napa Valley in the 1960s and '70s.

In the early 1990s, with pressure from the Wentes, the South Livermore Plan was hatched by local officials. In it was the requirement that for every new home built, the developer had to plant one acre of vineyards. It also allowed wineries to be built on 20-acre parcels of land instead of the larger 100 acres required before.

The plan seems to be working. New wineries are springing up, and existing wineries have been buying land to expand vineyards at knockdown prices from local developers. Since 1993 the number of acres of vineyards has more than doubled to about 5,000, according to some estimates. That still makes the Livermore Valley a small wine-growing region compared to most in California, but it's heading in the right direction.

valley's other players by providing them with a powerful voice in California.

Carl Wente first came to California from his native Germany in 1880, working briefly for Charles Krug up in Napa before being drawn to the booming Livermore Valley, where he and some partners bought a modest 25 acres of land in 1882. By the turn of the century, Wente had transformed his business into the biggest winery in the valley, a title the winery still holds today.

After Prohibition, the Wente winery continued to go from strength to strength, acquiring more land, making the first chardonnay in California in the late 1930s, and putting

on its most recent growth spurt in the last 20 years with the acquisition of local wineries, including Murietta's Well, Ruby Hill, and the historic Cresta Blanca winery. Cresta Blanca was the first to be established in the Livermore Valley and is now home to Wente's restaurant and visitors center.

The original winery is the place to come to taste the wines, however, not least because it is still free (the visitor center charges $4) and has a fairly well-stocked deli. Tours are offered four times a day.

Wente was a chardonnay pioneer in the valley, so it's no surprise that this is the wine it is best known for today. It makes more than 60,000 cases of chardonnay ranging in scale from the bargain-priced Vineyard Selection and buttery Riva Ranch Reserve, right up to the limited-production small-lot versions available only at the winery and the Nth Degree chardonnay, which is literally managed to the Nth degree from vineyard to barrel to create a wine that tastes more like a caramel apple.

The hundreds of thousands of cases of other wines include about a dozen other varietals, ranging from some decent reserve cabernet sauvignon down to the ubiquitous white zinfandel (5565 Tesla Rd., Livermore, 925/456-2305, www.wentevineyards.com, 11 A.M.–4:30 P.M. daily).

Concannon Vineyard

Just a year after Carl Wente came to the valley to start his winery, James Concannon arrived here from Ireland by way of Boston and San Francisco and bought 47 acres of land, eventually building a winery in 1895 that has operated continuously ever since. It made sacramental wine during Prohibition and was run by successive generations until it was sold in 1982.

After changing hands several times during the 1980s, the winery was bought by a group of investors led by the Wente family to help prevent developers from paving over the vineyards. It was eventually sold again in 2002 to The Wine Group, owner of a handful of small wineries in Northern California, which expanded the range of wines and 60,000-case

The South and East Bays

production to include the Select Vineyards label made using Central Coast grapes, and some additional high-end wines.

Concannon was the first winery to make a petite sirah in California (in the 1960s) since Prohibition and the wine is probably what the winery is best known for today. It's also one of the few Livermore wineries to make it.

The flagship wine here is the Heritage petite sirah, still a relative bargain at $36 and worth tasting along with the white Assemblage wine, a fine bordeaux-style blend of sauvignon blanc and semillon. Other estate wines include a red Assemblage blend, cabernet sauvignon, viognier, and syrah. Just about every other major varietal is available, most from Central Coast regions including the Edna Valley and Monterey.

There's plenty going on outside the tasting room. Picnicking is positively encouraged, and occasional events take place during the summer on the big lawn outside the winery. Tours are offered on some weekends (4590 Tesla Rd., Livermore, 925/456-2505 or 800/258-9866, www.concannonvineyard.com, 11 A.M.–4:30 P.M. daily).

Stony Ridge Winery

This is another winery that makes some of the valley's more unusual wines. It originally operated in the historic Ruby Hill Winery before changing owners and location, eventually ending up in its current low-rise stucco and tile-roofed home in the 1990s.

The emphasis here is on Italian varietals. A sangiovese, a nebbiolo made with grapes from the Sierra foothills, and the proprietary white blend Orobianco are all made along with the more traditional Livermore Valley wines, including good cabernet sauvignon and merlot, plus chardonnay. An interesting port made from sangiovese and cabernet is worth trying.

The Italian theme continues in the small restaurant in the winery, which makes some good panini that can be enjoyed at one of the shaded plastic tables on the big patio outside or perhaps while tossing balls on the bocce court (4948 Tesla Rd., Livermore, 925/449-0458,

www.stonyridgewinery.com, open 11 A.M.–4:30 P.M. Thurs.–Sun.).

Fenestra Winery

Another relatively recent winery that at one point used the old Ruby Hill Winery is Fenestra, established in the 1970s by chemistry professor Lanny Replogle, who now applies his chemistry knowledge to the art of fermenting grapes. The winery eventually settled in another historic home, the old wooden, Victorian-era George True winery, abandoned in the 1960s, and now makes about 7,500 cases of an eclectic mix of red and white wines, most poured in the warehouse-style tasting area.

One of the most unusual is the Semmonay blend of semillon and chardonnay, two varietals that are also bottled as standalone wines. Fenestra also makes a crisp sauvignon blanc, a varietal ideally suited to the Livermore climate (like semillon) but long since overtaken by the more popular chardonnay.

Reds include a fine cabernet sauvignon, merlot, syrah, and pinot noir, all from the Livermore Valley, plus a petite sirah from vineyards in Lodi, just north of here, which also supply the Portuguese grapes used to make Fenestra's traditional port. Although it's only open weekends, there's usually some sort of fun event happening at the winery during the summer. Check the website for information (83 Vallecitos Rd., Livermore, 925/862-2292, www.fenestrawinery.com, open noon–5 P.M. weekends).

Thomas Coyne Winery

This is probably Livermore's leading boutique winery, and it occupies perhaps one of the most picturesque sites in the valley (and a great picnic spot), where old barns are framed by orchards and the hill in the distance. The winery and other barns here date back to the 1880s, when Bordeaux native Alexander Duval established his Chateau Bellevue winery, though he became more famous for cloistering his daughter, who later escaped to marry her lover.

Like Lanny Replogle, Coyne is another former chemist (the valley evidently attracts them), who established this winery in 1994. He now makes about 4,000 cases of wine a year, including a merlot, syrah, and pinot blanc from the nearby Detjens vineyard. Many of the other wines are sourced from vineyards outside the valley, most notably a mourvèdre from Contra Costa County and a Sonoma County cabernet sauvignon (51 E. Vallecitos Rd., Livermore, 925/373-6541, www.thomascoynewinery.com, noon–5 P.M. weekends).

Mitchell Katz Winery

The old Ruby Hill winery, home to many of the valley's small wine-making startups over the decades, burned down in 1989 but was resurrected in 2002 by one of the valley's rising stars, Mitchell Katz.

The impressive winery building with its driveway lined with palm trees is a replica of Ruby Hill and even uses some of the bricks and architectural features of the old structure that survived the fire, and the best way to appreciate it is probably with an appointment-only tour.

Wine-making here is on a much smaller scale than the building, with about 4,000 cases made a year, though a spacious tasting room and event center also help fill the 16,000 square feet.

Those 4,000 cases include a lot of wines. Standouts include chardonnay, cabernet sauvignon, and zinfandel from the Livermore Valley, and a petite sirah from the surrounding Ruby Hill vineyards, named for the color of the soil. The sauvignon blanc and some of the cheaper red blends are also popular (1188 Vineyard Ave., Pleasanton, 925/931-0744, www.mitchelkatzwinery.com, noon–5 P.M. weekends).

SIGHTS

Don't start worrying about radioactive grapes, but one of the government's foremost nuclear research facilities is right here amid the vineyards. The **Lawrence Livermore National Laboratory** (7000 East Ave., Livermore, 925/424-6575, www.llnl.gov) has been responsible for developing and refining some of the most lethal thermonuclear warheads in history over the last half century, and for designing the X-ray lasers that were to be used in the now-defunct Star Wars missile defense system. It has been responsible for some more peaceful milestones, however, in areas like atmospheric research and astrophysics.

Since much of what the laboratory does is top secret, visitors cannot tramp around as they would at a winery. However, the lab's **Discovery Center** is just outside the gates on Greenville Road at the end of East Avenue, a stone's thrown from many wineries. Appointment-only tours are offered on Tuesdays and Thursdays. Just don't expect much comment about how they plan to clean up their radioactive legacy on the site.

ENTERTAINMENT AND EVENTS

Livermore lacks the cultural infrastructure of other parts of the Wine Country, but the city and its wineries do manage to create some semblance of wine culture.

The **Livermore Valley Opera** (925/960-9210, www.livermorevalleyopera.com) has limited performances of classic operas in its spring and fall seasons, usually around mid-March and mid-October, held at the Livermore Performing Arts Theater (600 Maple St., tickets $45). In June there is also an **Opera in the Vineyard** performance outdoors at the Cedar Mountain Winery on Tesla Road.

Pretty much the only theatrical and musical performances in town are sponsored by the **Del Valle Fine Arts** group (925/447-2752, www.delvallefinearts.org) and take place usually once a month in the First Presbyterian Church of Livermore at 4th and South L Streets downtown. Tickets cost $15.

If the limited cultural attractions are not to taste then there's always that stalwart of suburban entertainment available—bowling. The **Granada Bowling Center** has been family run since 1964, like most of the wineries around here (1620 Railroad Ave., daily until midnight, $4.50 plus $4 for shoes). It's a fairly standard setup but there are few places in Wine Country where bowling could even be considered after wine tasting.

More normal winery-related events include the **Holidays in the Vineyards** celebration, on the first weekend in December, when the valley's wineries throw open their doors and celebrate the holiday season with arts, crafts, music, and plenty of food. A similar excuse for wineries to celebrate with food, wine, and other events is the **Annual Harvest Wine Celebration,** held over the Labor Day weekend.

RECREATION
Del Valle Regional Park
Up in the hills just south of Livermore is this 4,000-acre summer activity paradise with 28 miles of trails and a huge lake to cool off in. The park is about 10 miles south of Livermore and reached via Mines Road, which starts almost opposite Stony Ridge Winery, and then Del Valle Road. The day-use fee is $6, and the park is open from dawn to 9 P.M.

The biggest attractions in the summer might be the two swimming beaches, both of which are just a short walk from the parking lots at the boat launch (turn right at the entrance) or the **Rocky Ridge Visitors Center,** which also houses a small exhibit about the park, its nature, and its history.

Fishing in the lake for trout, catfish, and bass is also popular, though you'll need a permit, and just about every other lake-related activity is also available. Those without their own boat can rent kayaks and sailboards at the **Windsurf Del Valle** concession in the park (925/455-4008, daily during the summer, weekends during the winter, kayaks $18/hour, sailboards from $16/hour).

Many of the trails that start at both parking areas wind along the shore of the lake to three hike-in campgrounds, and two other campgrounds are accessible by road within the park. Camping permits can be bought at the park entrance.

Golf
Livermore is a golfer's paradise, with several championship courses designed by some of golf's biggest names. The biggest name in Livermore

wine teamed up with Greg Norman to create the **Course at Wente Vineyards,** an 18-hole championship course surrounded by vineyards (5050 Arroyo Rd., next to the Wente Visitors Center, 925/456-2475, www.wentegolf.com). Rates start at $60 midweek during the winter and rise to $95 for weekend morning tee times, though the rates do include golf cart and practice balls.

Golf widows need be widows no more. The 27-hole, par-72 **Poppy Ridge Golf Course** (4280 Greenville Rd., Livermore, 925/455-2035, www.poppyridgegolf.com/Livermore) was named as the most women-friendly golf course by *Golf for Women* magazine.

ACCOMMODATIONS

There are few options for staying in Livermore beyond chain hotels and motels, but one of the most luxurious alternatives is the **Purple Orchid Inn Resort and Spa** (4549 Cross Rd., off Tesla Rd., Livermore, 925/606-8855 or 800/353-4549, www.purpleorchid.com, rooms $150–260, suites $380). The inn looks like a giant log cabin—in fact it's touted as the world's biggest residential log structure—but is crammed with enough luxury features to justify its high prices. These include a full spa and stunning views from the rooms, plus in-room amenities like a fireplaces and Jacuzzi tubs. As the only such resort in the area it tends to book up fast, so plan ahead.

The **Vineyard Inn at Crane Ridge** (5405 Greenville Rd., Livermore, 925/455-8085) is about a small as a B&B gets, with just two rooms costing $199 and $225 a night. Both have Jacuzzi tubs, balconies, and fireplaces, and guests are treated to wine from the neighboring White Crane Winery.

Just east of Livermore in Pleasanton is another notable B&B, the **Evergreen Inn** (9104 Longview Dr., Pleasanton, 925/426-0901, rooms from $135). Although it looks like a family home from the outside, the four rooms inside are well appointed and come with a hearty breakfast. There's also a hot tub on an outside deck for guests to use.

Those having no luck finding rooms in the handful of B&Bs might have to resort to a chain hotel, in which case the biggest concentration can be found along Constitution Drive downtown. The include the **Comfort Inn** (2625 Constitution Dr., 925/606-6200, rooms from $70), the **Courtyard by Marriott** (2929 Constitution Dr., 925/243-1000, rooms from $80), the **Hampton Inn** (2850 Constitution Dr., 925/606-6400, rooms from $80), and the **Hilton Garden Inn** (2801 Constitution Dr., 925/292-2000, rooms from $90).

FOOD

The Livermore food scene is a strange combination of chain restaurants, undistinguished independents, and an increasing number of upscale, Wine Country-style restaurants that mimic the California cuisine of some of the best Sonoma and Napa eateries and are slowly but surely putting the city on the culinary map.

One little piece of Napa that landed in Livermore is the **M Wente Vineyards Restaurant** (5050 Arroyo Road, Livermore, 925/456-2450, lunch and dinner daily, dinner entrées $20–40). It has all the Wine Country requisites—high-quality food, scenic surroundings, the spin-off cookbook, and high prices. Some of the seasonal produce used in the food is supplied by Wente's own organic garden.

In downtown Livermore, **Zephyr's Grill & Bar** (1736 1st St., Livermore, 925/961-1000, lunch and dinner daily, dinner entrées $17–34) is a stylish new indoor-outdoor restaurant offering a traditional steak and chop menu with an impressive Californian wine list. If you must dine outdoors, be warned that you might literally be rubbing shoulders with people passing by on the sidewalk.

The destination Mexican restaurant in town is the Livermore outpost of the East Bay's small **Casa Orozco** chain (325 S. L St., Livermore, 925/449-3045, lunch and dinner daily, dinner entrées $12–16). It specializes in hearty country food beyond the normal tacos and burritos, though those stalwarts are available too.

Some good down-home cowboy food can be had at the **Riata Diner and Tavern** (190 S. J St., Livermore, 925/294-9170, lunch and din-

ner Tues.–Sun., dinner entrées $9–22), named after the braided rawhide ropes used by *vaqueros* before the days of plastic. This is a meat-lover's paradise, with tri-tip, ribs, and steaks galore, plus a small nod to non-meat eaters with a few fish dishes. There's also a good deli, with sandwiches starting at $5, including the tri-tip stuffed Trailhand, which should keep any wannabe trailhand going all day.

Like Livermore, neighboring Pleasanton is undergoing something of a food renaissance as well. Its Main Street is the center of most of the action, but slightly off the beaten path and worth seeking out is **Claude & Dominique's** (210 Rose Ave., off Main St., 925/462-0100, dinner Tues.–Sat., entrées $18–26) a French bistro that might not look terribly authentic from the outside but serves a veritable greatest hits of French country cooking, from escargots to coq au vin and chateaubriand.

INFORMATION AND SERVICES

Livermore is part of the Tri-Valley area, which incorporates the neighboring towns of Dublin, Pleasanton, and San Ramon, and is served by the **Tri-Valley Convention and Visitors Bureau,** source of a wide range of listings and services (260 Main St., Pleasanton, 925/874-9253 or 888/846-8910, www.tivalleycvb.com).

For specific wine-related information, contact the **Livermore Valley Winegrowers Association** (3585 Greenville Rd., Ste. 4., Livermore, 925/447-9463, www.livermorewine.com).

GETTING THERE

Livermore is best known to many nonresidents as a town along the freeway to somewhere else, so the freeway is the best way to get here. From Oakland and San Francisco to the west, and the Central Valley to the east, I-580 runs straight past Livermore. From Sacramento and San Jose, I-680 connects with I-580 just west of Livermore. The best exit to take from the freeway is North Livermore Avenue, which runs through the downtown area to the first wineries about three miles south.

Know
Northern California
Wine Country

The Land

GEOLOGY

Some 150 million years ago, probably long before vines had evolved from the primordial jungles, what we today know as Wine Country was at the bottom of a giant ocean, lapping up against the volcanoes that formed California's Sierra Nevada mountain range about 100 miles east of today's Napa Valley.

In fact, much of modern-day California did not come into existence until the tectonic plates that make up the earth's crust had played a game of planetary bumper cars for long enough, eventually pushing up the sea floor, creating mountains, and shifting and splitting ancient continents to create the map of the world we recognize today.

From a winemaker's point of view, the geological history of California is part of what makes this area of the world such a great wine-growing region. The ancient soils, valleys, and mountains combine into some of the most perfect places on earth to grow grapes.

Franciscan Formation

The tectonic plate that made California is the Farallon plate, immortalized in the tiny Farallon Islands that lie a few miles off the coast of San Francisco. As the plate collided with the massive North American continental plate just west of the Sierra Nevada, it dived underneath at what is called the subduction zone, feeding molten rock to the prehistoric volcanoes that built up the mountains we know today (and are still building the mountains farther north at Mount St. Helens in Washington).

Geologists believe that as those mountains got bigger and heavier from spewing out lava they literally squashed the earth's crust over the course of millions of years, eventually forcing up an adjacent bulge under the ocean, much as pushing the edge of your finger into mud will cause the mud around it to bulge up.

That big undersea bulge then acted like a giant spatula, scraping off big chunks of the

Farallon plate at the subduction zone. Eventually those scrapings built up enough to rise out of the ocean and create much of today's coastal California, including the Wine Country. These geological scrapings are known as the Franciscan formation and form the underlying bedrock from northern to southern California.

Fire and Water

The mountains and valleys of coastal California are altogether more recent additions to the Franciscan formation, recent at least in terms of geological timelines. About five million years ago, fissures in the bedrock opened up all over the land and spawned violent volcanoes that spewed out lava, ash, and giant boulders, rearranging the surface of the land and blanketing it with deep layers of volcanic rock and ash.

In the Napa Valley, evidence of these ancient volcanoes is easy to see. Mount St. Helena is an ancient volcano that once blew its top, flattening nearby trees that were buried, fossilized,

Some mission cacti are as old as Sonoma's mission itself.

and eventually resurfaced in the area where Calistoga's Petrified Forest is today. Nearby, Calistoga's hot springs, geyser, and the volcanic mud that visitors submerge themselves in are reminders of the cauldron that still bubbles deep underground, and just southeast of Calistoga is an area called Glass Mountain, so called because of the lumps of the black, glass-like volcanic rock, obsidian, found in the soils.

While the volcanoes were adding their own ingredients to what would become the complex mix of soils in the Wine Country, the now famous San Andreas fault had started to blend them and the Franciscan soils together.

The mountains and valleys of Napa and Sonoma were formed in the last three million years as the Pacific plate, another giant chunk of the earth's crust under the Pacific Ocean, slid northward along the San Andreas fault, eventually breaking up the Farallon plate in front of it. As it moved, it slowly compressed the edge of the neighboring North American continental plate and buckled the land on the other side of the San Andreas fault line over millions of years, pushing up ridges of the Franciscan bedrock through the deep volcanic deposits covering it to form many of the mountain ranges that today define Northern California's Wine Country.

The Mayacamas Mountains between the Napa and Sonoma Valleys, for example, were formed by this buckling, as was the coastal range of mountains on which the best Santa Cruz wines are grown. The plates are still moving today, ever so slowly, and the only reminders we have of this ongoing evolution of the planet's geology are the occasional earthquakes that rattle California.

The Franciscan and volcanic soils were further mixed up over the millennia by rivers and streams that carved their way down through the rocks, picking up sediment and dumping it miles away. The resulting patchwork of Franciscan, volcanic, and sedimentary soils is a winemaker's dream and helps explain why Northern California's Wine Country can turn out so many diverse styles of wine. Napa Valley alone is said to have up to 150 types of soil.

CLIMATE

The soils aren't everything, of course. The mountains, hills, and valleys that make the geographical patchwork of Wine Country also create a patchwork of climates, sheltering some areas from cool ocean winds, funneling the cool air to others, and exposing different slopes to different amounts of sunshine throughout the day. Throughout the Wine Country and indeed much of the greater San Francisco Bay Area, microclimates are the norm. A cool, murky August morning can become hot and sunny in just a half hour. Even within one sunny valley the temperature can vary widely in just 20 miles.

The average maximum temperature in the city of Napa in July and August (the hottest months of the year) is about 82°F, according to historical climate data. In St. Helena, halfway up the Napa Valley, it averages about 89°F, and in Calistoga, far away from the cooling influence of the San Francisco Bay air, it averages 92°F. Carneros, meanwhile, is right next to the bay and usually only reaches the mid-70s at best.

Elsewhere in Wine Country, the extremes are just as great. On the eastern side of the Santa Cruz Mountains, sheltered from the ocean air, Los Gatos swelters in average high temperatures of 86°F in July, while on the other side of the mountains Santa Cruz relaxes in 74°F. In northern Sonoma, Cloverdale in the Alexander Valley bakes in average temperatures of nearly 92°F in July, while down in the fog-bound Russian River Valley, Occidental chills out at about 75°F.

For a winemaker, different climates are measured using a method called heat summation (also known as the Winkler Scale), which categorizes climates into regions on a scale from 1 to 5 depending on how hot the average daily temperature is during a vine's main growing season from April to October. Different grapes grow and ripen best in each climate region.

If California were a country, it would be one of the few on earth that have areas corresponding to all five growing regions. Northern

California's Wine Country alone contains four of the five regions (though some say it has only three), which means there's an ideal climate for almost any type of grape.

Winemakers also have an easier job here than their colleagues in many other parts of the world, particularly in Europe, because rainfall is almost nonexistent for much of the summer, allowing the grapes to ripen in the plentiful sun and avoid being infected by mildew. Most rain falls between November and April, and apart from the rare summer thunderstorm or late spring showers it is generally dry from late May through October.

Fog

One of the defining aspects of the weather along the Northern California coast is the fog, not a mental fog brought on by drinking too much wine, but the damp, chilly marine fog that creeps—sometimes charges—inland from the cold Pacific Ocean throughout the summer though every gap it can find in the hills.

Perhaps no aspect of the weather in Wine Country is more important. It takes the edge off the sometimes vicious summer heat and sun, keeps the nights cool, and slows the ripening of grapes in many places to a perfect tempo. It also generates the damp conditions in which California's famous coastal redwoods thrive—nowhere more so than in the Russian River Valley, which is essentially a fog freeway, providing a direct channel from the ocean through the coastal hills and inland.

The factors that generate the fog, however, actually start hundreds of miles away in the Central Valley of California.

As the temperature rises there during the summer, so does the hot air, lowering the atmospheric pressure near the ground. Something has to replace all that rising air and even out the pressure. Imagine, then, a giant sucking noise as air is pulled in from the ocean to do just that.

And because the ocean is so cold, thanks to some chilly northern currents, it actually condenses water from the air (much like icy weather does to your breath), forming a deep

bank of fog that sits, menacingly, just off the coast until it is dragged into action.

Many additional factors have recently been found to influence fog formation, from weather over the Rocky Mountains to the currents in the South Pacific. But all they care about in the Wine Country is that the fog helps make a great bottle of wine.

THE COMBINATION

The combination of diverse soils and diverse microclimates offers just about everything a winemaker could want. There are very few grapes that have not been able to grow somewhere in California.

The French have a term for the unique place that a grape is grown: *terroir.* It describes the combination of every geological, geographical, and climate-related aspect of a particular site you can think of, from the soil, slope, and elevation to sun exposure, wind levels, and temperature patterns. There is no equivalent word in English, but if there were it would likely have been coined in California, which is the land of a million *terroirs.*

Terroir explains why grapes grown in one vineyard will make a wine that tastes different from that made from grapes in a neighboring vineyard. So-called vineyard-designate wines sourced from specific vineyards take advantage of that difference. There can even be a difference in the wine made from different sections, or blocks, of an individual vineyard.

It explains, for example, why Stag's Leap Wine Cellars can make distinct wines from specific blocks of its vineyards, and why Stags Leap District cabernets as a whole taste different from those produced in the Rutherford District just a few miles up the road.

Best Soils and Climate

Almost without exception, the best soils for growing wine grapes are well drained and relatively infertile. Drainage is important to prevent the vines and grapes from getting too damp and potentially rotting, and also to encourage the vines to grow deep roots in search

© PHILIP GOLDSMITH

Produce is apparently as good as the wine in Sonoma.

of a stable source of water for the long, dry summers in California. Some of the oldest vines have been known to send roots down as deep as 100 feet.

Fertility (or the lack of it) is a less important factor, though it's not by chance that some of the world's great vineyards thrive on fairly barren, rocky land, including steep mountainsides where even native plants struggle to grow.

Ultimately, grape growers are trying to produce a stressed vine, one that has to relentlessly search for water and survive on meager nutrients. Not exactly the aim of most gardeners, who water and feed their plants to make them as big and lush as possible.

The theory goes that a stressed vine will produce fewer and smaller grapes but they will have a far more concentrated flavor. That same principle (taken to an extreme) explains why a small, shriveled raisin has a far more concentrated and powerful flavor than a big, plump Thompson seedless grape, which was probably grown with the aid of plenty of watering and fertilizer.

Climate plays an equally important role in how a wine turns out, determining how quickly

a grape ripens and the level of ripeness it is ultimately able to reach. Temperatures during the day and night are affected by sun exposure, wind patterns, and countless other factors. Climate helps explain why a cabernet produced from vineyards on the west-facing slopes of a valley side that gets sun much of the warmest part of the day will taste slightly different from that made from a vineyard on an east-facing slope that might get less sun because the morning sun is blocked by the fog.

Appellations

The diversity of growing conditions is recognized around the world by defining geographical regions based on their specific soils and climate that distinguish the wines made there from those made everywhere else. In the United States, such regions are called **American Viticultural Areas,** or AVAs, though many people simply call them appellations, after the French word meaning almost, but not quite, the same thing.

An appellation describes a geographical place, like an entire state or even a country. A viticultural area describes a unique growing region only. An appellation can be an AVA, but not all are. California is an appellation, for example, and contains the Napa Valley AVA.

The federal Alcohol and Tobacco Tax and Trade Bureau (TTB) is the arbiter of AVAs and dishes them out only when wineries in a specific area have been able to prove that theirs is a unique place to grow grapes. Such proof usually comes in the form of an analysis of soils, climate, and physical features of the land. The petitioning and granting of an AVA takes many years, as is typical of most federal government processes.

The first AVA was established in 1980 in, of all places, Augusta, Georgia, and they are still being established today. The biggest in America in terms of area is the Ohio River Valley, covering 26,000 square miles in parts of four different states. The smallest is Cole Ranch in Mendocino County, California, covering about a quarter square mile.

In Northern California there was a rush to get AVA status in the early 1980s by most of the major wine regions, and today there are 89 in California (a figure that is constantly growing). The first AVA was the Santa Cruz Mountains, created in early 1982, followed shortly thereafter by the Sonoma Valley in the same month and Livermore Valley later that year. In 1983 the Napa Valley and Dry Creek Valley gained their AVA status.

There can also be AVAs within AVAs, often called subappellations (again a technically incorrect term in some cases but often used anyway). The Napa Valley AVA, for example, contains a patchwork of 14 smaller AVAs, each producing its own distinctive style of wine. The appellation of Sonoma County contains 11 AVAs, some of which overlap. If defining the land is so complicated it's no wonder that the wines are so varied.

History

Northern California is widely regarded as the historic center of the state's wine industry, but it was not always so. In the early 1800s, Southern California was where all the wine-making action took place.

CALIFORNIA'S EARLY WINE INDUSTRY

Spanish Missions

California's missions played a crucial, though controversial, role in California's history, including its wine-making history. Their inexorable march northward from Mexico to Northern California blazed a trail through the wilderness and introduced important wine-making skills through their demand for sacramental wines. They also marked the beginning of the end of the lifestyle and culture of the region's traditional Native American tribes, which had lived off the land for thousands of years.

The most important mission in Northern California from the wine industry's perspective was the 21st California mission and the

last one ever built—Mission San Francisco de Solano in present day Sonoma. It was established by Father Jose Altimira, who arrived in the Sonoma Valley in 1819. Once the mission had been dedicated in 1924, the missionaries quickly set about their religious purpose. With the aid of the Mexican army the natives were converted to Christianity whether they wanted to be or not. Within six years the mission had also established a big farming operation, with 4,000 sheep and 2,000 cattle, and had planted some of the region's first vines.

That new mission was founded not only to continue the spread of Christianity but also to provide food for the ailing missions in present-day San Francisco and San Rafael, which were struggling to sustain themselves. It was also the first and only mission in California created under Mexican rule, and it's likely that part of its purpose was to help prevent any expansion of a Russian trading outpost established nearby on the Sonoma coast at Fort Ross.

Just three years later trouble rode into town in the form of a 25-year-old Mexican army

© PHILIP GOLDSMITH

Guerneville's historic bridge

lieutenant, Mariano Guadalupe Vallejo, who was sent north from the Presidio in San Francisco to rattle some sabers at the Russians and establish a military post at Sonoma. Vallejo would remain in Sonoma for the next half century and play a pivotal role in the creation of modern California.

When the missions were secularized by the Mexican government in 1835, Vallejo's garrison at Sonoma was well established and had created a Mexican-style plaza (present day Sonoma Plaza) as a parade ground. He was ordered to take over the mission, and he promptly started to divide the buildings and land between friends and relatives. Meanwhile, the garrison and the town started to grow in importance and Vallejo was promoted to colonel, the highest rank he ever reached (despite this he somehow became commonly known as General Vallejo, a title that sticks to this day). He started living the good life, amassing land and planting vineyards as the military importance of his garrison in peaceful California slowly dwindled.

Across the mountain in the Napa Valley, meanwhile, pioneer George Yount is said to have taken time from battling grizzly bears and Native Americans to plant a few acres of cuttings from Vallejo's vines in 1838.

The Bear Flag Revolt

It was around this time that more American settlers were crossing the mountains to Northern California and letting everyone know about it. The Mexican government became mildly apoplectic and tried to round up these American illegals and dissuade others from coming to California, a strange reversal of roles when compared to today's flow of Mexican migrant workers into California. Near Sacramento, Captain John Sutter was welcoming the new immigrants at his fort, riling the Mexican government even more. Not helping matters was the arrival of U.S. Army captain John C. Frémont in California on a mapping expedition.

As the tensions rose, Vallejo tried to stay neutral, walking a fine line between supporting various parties in the increasingly fragmented Mexican government and remaining friendly with the new American immigrants.

Soon tensions boiled over. In 1846, word came that Mexican general Castro was planning to drive out the Americans at Sutter's fort. Some of the settlers believed that Vallejo, who had met with Castro several times, was part of the plan to re-exert Mexican authority, and they launched a preemptive attack on Vallejo's small garrison at Sonoma.

A ragtag group of about 30 men rode the 120 miles from Sacramento to Sonoma on the night of June 13, 1846, and barged into Vallejo's unprotected residence, La Casa Grande, to arrest him. He was taken the next day to Sacramento, where he remained under arrest until August. That day the members of the raiding party made a flag for their newly declared California Republic, and that Bear Flag replaced the Mexican emblem over Sonoma Plaza.

The U.S. Navy, which had a ship off the coast, soon stepped into the power vacuum created by the Bear Flaggers and raised the Stars and Stripes over Sonoma Plaza on July 9, 1846,

THE BARE FLAG

The flag of the great State of California, symbol of strength, courage, and freedom, started out as a crudely painted rectangle of fabric incorporating a woman's red petticoat. At least, that's one version of events back in 1846 when it was first raised over Sonoma Plaza.

The ragtag group of men behind the short-lived Bear Flag Republic needed something for their symbol. A loose committee finally decided that it should incorporate a bear, symbolizing strength and courage, and a star, inspired by the newly minted flag of Texas. So the saddle stitchers and painters in the group set about making their new flag.

One member supplied the red fabric that some say was part of his wife's petticoat, although others maintain it was actually a flannel shirt. This was sewn to some bleached fabric onto which was painted the bear, the star, and the words "California Republic," the bear apparently looking more like a squat pig.

When finally it was done, the paint still wet, the flag was raised and flew for the 25 days it took for the U.S. Army to march into town. The original handmade Bear Flag that was replaced by the Stars and Stripes on July 9, 1846, was eventually destroyed in the San Francisco earthquake and fire in 1906, but in 1911 the design was adopted as the official state flag and today flies above almost every public building in the state.

claiming California for America with little in the way of a fight. Coincidentally, a few months earlier, U.S. president James Polk had declared war on Mexico after his request to buy Texas and California had been rejected. News of the war didn't reach California until mid-July. Two years later when the war was over, California and other Southwest states were officially ceded by Mexico.

The Early Wine Boom

When Vallejo was released he returned to Sonoma and over the next decade became a big player in the region's politics. As Northern California's importance and wealth grew during that period, helped by the Gold Rush, the entrepreneurs and immigrants that would shape the region for the next 100 years arrived by the boatload.

By now, the missionaries and General Vallejo

California's state flag was first raised in Sonoma Plaza, about where this statue stands today.

had shown that the valley was well suited to growing just about everything, including grapes. The catalyst for the eventual agricultural boom was a series of land grants that divided up the millions of acres that Vallejo and his cronies had amassed while running the area during Mexican rule.

The land was snatched up by names that would eventually become a big part of modern

Sonoma history, including Agoston Haraszthy, a Hungarian immigrant who planted some of the earliest European vineyard cuttings and is credited with dragging the California wine industry from its missionary roots into the modern era through his Buena Vista Winery in the Sonoma Valley.

Over in the Napa Valley, in 1844 Edward Bale was granted a huge swath of land near present-day St. Helena by way of marriage to Vallejo's niece. He planted some vines, and friend Charles Krug, a Napa wine pioneer, made wine for him. And in northern Sonoma, Captain Henry Fitch was granted 48,000 acres of land around present-day Healdsburg, about a quarter of which he later gave to Cyrus Alexander (after whom Alexander Valley is named) in recognition of the help that the former mountain man had been in managing Fitch's huge acreage.

Up at the northern end of the Sonoma Valley, in 1859, Scotsman Charles Stuart bought some of Vallejo's land and named his home and ranch Glen Ellen, after Ellen, his wife. The name was eventually usurped by the town that developed, and Stuart's ranch was renamed Glen Oaks. It still exists today. Captain Henry Boyes was another beneficiary of Vallejo's land and would go on to establish his mineral baths, Boyes Hot Springs, another name that eventually became a town.

By 1876, the Sonoma Valley alone was producing 2.3 million gallons of wine a year, and Northern California had overtaken the south as the biggest wine-producing region in the state. Around this time many of the immigrants that would shape the Napa and Sonoma wine industry had started to arrive from Europe, lured by the early successes of pioneering winemakers in the Napa and Sonoma Valleys, like Krug, Jacob Gundlach, and the Beringer brothers.

Outlying areas like the Alexander Valley and Dry Creek Valley were being planted with vines; the Italian Swiss Colony, a wine-making cooperative, was established near Cloverdale; and down in Santa Cruz the first vines were planted on land freshly cleared of redwood forests.

Then the scourge of phylloxera struck. A small aphid-like insect attacks the roots of vines and slowly kills them by preventing the plant from absorbing water and nutrients. Phylloxera wiped out many vineyards in Europe in the late 1800s but is actually native to the United States. In fact, California's wine industry was doing so well in the late 1800s in part because of the European devastation. It would only be years later, after most Californian vineyards had been decimated, that vines with resistant rootstock were replanted in Northern California by Gundlach, one of the Sonoma Valley's early wine pioneers.

Not long after Northern California's wine industry had started to recover from phylloxera and was once again booming, it took another economic hit, one from which it barely recovered.

Prohibition

The 18th Amendment of the United States Constitution, which ushered in the era of Prohibition in 1919, was born not out of government meddling but of the increasingly powerful temperance movement, which had its roots in the puritanical beliefs of the country's founding fathers and in public disgust at the increasing drunkenness of American society during the 1800s.

By some estimates, average Americans was drinking almost three times the amount of whiskey and other spirits in the mid-1800s as they do today. The more people drank the more temperance movements tended to spring up all over the country in response. Eventually, the so-called Drys gained increasing political clout, passing laws in many states that banned public drinking and finally getting the Volstead Act, and with it Prohibition, passed in Congress. Winemakers had hoped that, being a gentleman's drink, wine would be exempt from the legislation, but in the end the commercial production, sale, and transportation of any form of alcoholic drink was banned.

As with every piece of legislation, it doesn't take long for people to find the loopholes and to take advantage of weak enforcement. Bootleggers and gangsters set up a huge underground liquor network, and the wine industry got in on the act. Despite all commercial wine being banned, there were more acres of vineyards in existence during Prohibition than before it, and the price of grapes actually increased even as the quality of the grapes generally declined. Grape juice concentrate or bricks of compressed grapes were shipped all over the country, sometimes even accompanied by yeast tablets, for individuals to make their own wine behind the closed doors, which was perfectly legal.

Although many vineyards flourished, wineries did not and many closed. The few that remained open did so by making sacramental wine, which was still legal (as wine historians like to say, a lot of people found religion during Prohibition) or wine for government functions, also legal. After all, leaders still had to be able to entertain foreign dignitaries with fine wine even when the rest of the country made do without.

In many ways, Prohibition marked the end of one chapter of California's wine-making history. In some areas like the Santa Cruz Mountains and Livermore Valley, virtually all the wineries closed, never to reopen. Fruit trees replaced vines in many of today's wine-making valleys and held sway until relatively recently.

In Napa and Sonoma, a handful of wineries continued to operate during Prohibition making sacramental wines, including Beringer Vineyards (the oldest continuously operating winery in the Napa Valley), Beaulieu Vineyard, Buena Vista Winery (its Carneros facility is the oldest continuously operating winery in California), and Sebastiani Vineyards. Still others turned to farming or supplying grapes until Prohibition was repealed, then resumed wine making, while a few wineries continued to make wine and store it in the hope that Prohibition would soon end.

It took 14 years to come to an end and was finally repealed in 1933, when the 21st Amendment was passed by Congress. In those 14 years, California's wine industry had been gutted. Most wineries had closed, important wine-making skills had been lost, and the public had lost the taste for fine wines, instead preferring homemade hooch.

The Modern Era

In some ways the wine industry took several steps back after repeal, turning out bulk wines of far lower quality than the world-class wines made by the new European immigrants some 30 years before in the early 1900s. The few big wineries that did survive, especially those in the Napa and Sonoma Valleys, continued to make high quality wines, so the art of wine making in the region was not totally dead. It just took many decades for it to once again dominate California's wine industry.

One of the key figures who helped start the modern age of fine wine making was Robert Mondavi in the Napa Valley. His father, Cesare Mondavi, was one of the many producers of bulk wine in the Napa Valley after Prohibition, and his two sons, Robert and Peter, were already getting some experience helping run the bulk business. When Cesare bought the old Charles Krug winery in 1943, the family's attention increasingly turned to fine wines, but following a family feud after Cesare's death, Robert was forced out of the family business.

With wine already in his blood, he started his own Robert Mondavi Winery in 1966, which was also the first winery built in Napa since the repeal of Prohibition. It proved to be one of the catalysts for the growth in the fine wine industry in the region, and Mondavi is often cited as one of the figures who proved that a dream of starting a great winery could become reality. He also rode on the growing wave of popularity of fine wines, and in the following decade hundreds more wineries were established by dreamers hoping to catch the same wave, including many of today's biggest wine-making names. In 1970 there were an estimated 240 wineries in all of California, a figure that had barely changed for decades. By the end of the 1970s that number had more than doubled to over 500.

The Paris Tasting

The reputation of California's modern wines was cemented at an international wine-tasting event in Paris in 1976. British wine writer and critic Stephen Spurrier, already familiar with the

ORGANIC WITH VOODOO

Organic farming is relatively common these days, especially in environmentally conscious California, and a good proportion of wineries follow some if not all of the organic farming techniques required to become certified organic. An increasing number of wineries are taking things a step further and dabble in the world of biodynamic farming, described by one organic winemaker in the Sonoma Valley as "organic with voodoo."

Biodynamic farming has its roots in the early 1900s teachings of an Austrian philosopher and scientist, Rudolf Steiner, who believed there was a spiritual connection between the environment and the wider cosmos that had to be preserved. The spiritual element is what baffles many people, but on a practical level biodynamic farming has a little less voodoo than it sounds.

Where organic farming focuses on ensuring specific physical activities like fertilizing and pest control are done in an environmentally friendly way, biodynamic farming requires that the entire farm be considered a living system, kept in perfect natural balance and connected to all the natural rhythms of the earth.

To be certified organic by state and federal regulators, wineries cannot use certain things like synthetic pesticides and fertilizers, plastic containers and corks, and certain wine additives (organic wine-making principles are actually surprisingly tolerant of many other slightly unnatural practices). Biodynamic principles require altogether more proactive actions and are certified only by a nongovernmental body, the Demeter Association. Certain composts, for example, have to be made using specific natural ingredients and applied to the soil at certain times of the year, plants must be planted in line with the rhythm of the sun and moon, and all plants and animals, from crops to weeds, livestock to insects, must be treated as one living, integrated ecosystem.

It's a bit like stepping back in time hundreds of years to an age before modern farming techniques were developed, an age when farmers had to work with whatever nature provided and crop rotation was considered the height of farming technology.

From a wine-making point of view, biodynamics is appealing because it is the only way that wines can be guaranteed to express the true, unadulterated natural characteristics of the land on which the grapes are grown, or the *terroir*.

Many organic wineries already use some biodynamic principles in some of their vineyards and are happy to leave it at that. After all, few wine buyers understand what goes into biodynamic wines, so the cost and approximate two-year time span it usually takes to have a winery certified biodynamic is often not worth it from a marketing standpoint. In the long run, however, it has been shown that a successful biodynamic farm or winery can actually save money by letting nature do much of the work of tending to the vines. Some also argue that biodynamic wine tastes better, though that's a more subjective test.

Frog's Leap Winery and Robert Sinskey in the Napa Valley are examples of part organic (certified), part biodynamic (uncertified) wineries. One of the trailblazers of biodynamic farming in Northern California's Wine Country is Benziger Family Winery in the Sonoma Valley, which has been certified biodynamic since 1994.

More information on biodynamic farming can be found at the **Demeter Association** in Oregon (541/998-5691, www.demeter-usa.org) and the Michigan-based **Biodynamic Farming and Gardening Association** (888/757-2742, www.biodynamics.com). More information on what makes a wine organic is available at the San Francisco–based **Organic Grapes into Wine Alliance** (www.organicwine.com).

rising quality of California's wines, suggested a taste-off between what he regarded as the best Californian and best French wines in an event to celebrate the American bicentennial.

Five Californian chardonnays and five cabernet sauvignons were pitted against the same number of French white burgundies and red bordeaux wines. The all-French panel of esteemed judges had to taste blind in case the French national disdain for New World wines at the time influenced their conclusions. Having set all this up, Spurrier must have been pretty confident the Californian wines would do well, and they did.

The tasting panel placed a 1973 cabernet sauvignon from Stag's Leap Wine Cellars in the Napa Valley at the top of the reds, followed by the five bordeaux and the remaining Californian reds. The Californian whites did even better. A 1973 Chateau Montelena chardonnay was judged to be the best white wine, and two other Californian chardonnays were placed in the top five (from Chalone Vineyard and Spring Mountain Vineyards).

The shockwave of the French being beaten at their own game reverberated around the wine world. The French were gutted. California winemakers never looked back.

CALIFORNIA'S MODERN WINE INDUSTRY
Economy
The wine industry is to the Napa and Sonoma Valleys and large parts of northern Sonoma what the movie business is to Los Angeles—an integral part of the cultural and social fabric. Everyone seems to have some link to the wine business, whether directly or indirectly, and given the industry's sheer size it's hardly surprising.

If California were a country it would be the fourth-largest producer of wine in the world after Italy, France, and Spain. The state's wine industry made 522 million gallons of wine in 2004, according to the Wine Institute, or more than 90 percent of all the wine produced in the United States. That makes California's wine industry about a $16 billion industry in terms

of retail sales, but it brings a lot more money to the state in other ways.

An estimated 14 million tourists visit the state's almost 1,300 wineries each year, and the wine industry employs more than 200,000 people. All told, the value of the wine industry to California's overall economy was estimated at more than $45 billion in 2002, according to one research report.

Napa and Sonoma dominate California's wine industry, though not by sheer size (Santa Cruz and other parts of Northern California's Wine Country are bit players by comparison). Together, the two counties contain almost half of all the wineries in the state even though they account for less than a fifth of the state's total acreage of wine-grape vineyards. The important factor is quality. Huge quantities of cheap wines are churned out in the Central Valley of California, but Napa, Sonoma, and other important Northern California wine regions produce a big proportion of the state's premium wines, which sell for premium prices.

Consumption Trends
Luckily, the rest of the world likes to drink wine because Americans apparently don't. Although an impressive 688 million gallons of wine were consumed in the United States in 2004, much of it made in California, per capita consumption is only just over two gallons, or about 11 bottles per year.

Per capita consumption in the United States is actually less today than in the mid-1980s but has been increasing again recently. Still, by 2001 people in the United Kingdom were drinking about twice as much wine on average than their U.S. counterparts, the Germans three times more, and the French a whopping seven times more wine. Even Slovakians and Swedes drink more wine than the average American.

It's not that Americans in general don't drink much wine, just that most Americans don't drink any at all. Nearly all the wine consumed is drunk by less than one-fifth of the population. A wide range of factors might explain the country's low rate of wine consumption, including its puritanical roots, the legacy of Prohibition, and even climate.

One important factor is simply that the American population does not have a great wine-making legacy. Wines have only been made in California in commercial quantities for 150 years, which might seem like a long time but is a blink of an eye when you consider that the Romans fueled their orgies with the stuff some 2,000 years ago. Moreover, the waves of new American immigrants from Central America and Asia also tend to have had little exposure to wines.

Europeans have been making wine for thousands of years, and it is as much a part of the culinary culture in many European countries there as, say, apple pie is in the United States. American consumers tend to view wine as a special occasion drink, something to be enjoyed once in a while rather than every day.

While it's true that high-quality wine might be a little too expensive for most people to open a bottle every day, consider that wine in an open bottle can remain fresh for 4–5 days if stored correctly. If you prefer to save an expensive wine for a special occasion, consider stocking up with "house wine," which still tastes good but at a price far more inviting for an everyday drink.

Chardonnay remains the most popular wine, even though that popularity has waned slightly in recent years. Merlot, white zinfandel, and cabernet sauvignon were not far behind in popularity. Those four varietals together accounted for just over half the wines sold in American food stores in 2004, and for the first time red wines outsold white in that year.

The Power of Marketing

Take a trip to wineries in Napa and Sonoma and you'd be lucky to find any wine for sale at under $20, which might give the impression that wine is generally an expensive drink. But those pricey wines account for only a fraction of the wine made in California. A trip to the local supermarket will confirm that most wine sold in the United States is of the cheap and cheerful kind, usually in big 1.5-liter bottles

or casks. In fact, about two-thirds of the wine sold in the United States in 2004 cost less than $7 a bottle, which represents about the same bang for the buck as beer.

So-called premium wine costing over $7 a bottle is where the big money is for the wineries, however, so that's where the marketing dollars tend to get spent. It's also the fastest-growing segment of the wine industry in the United States.

Wineries in the best wine-making regions of Northern California have high costs to recoup for sure. Land for vineyards in the Napa Valley costs about $120,000. It then costs a further $25,000–50,000 an acre to prepare and plant it with vines. Add the costs of managing that vineyard and actually making, bottling, and distributing the wine, and some wine prices start to seem a teeny bit justified.

But it's also in a winery's best interests to try to wean consumers onto the expensive stuff because they'll then probably be consumers for life. Research shows that once your palate is used to a $50 cabernet you're highly unlikely to be taking a trip to the local supermarket to pick up a jumbo bottle of $5 generic red wine to go with dinner. You'll buy as much of the $50 wine as you can afford.

It's a tough balancing act for the wineries from a marketing point of view. On the one hand they want to lure new premium wine consumers into the fold by promoting their wines as an easy entry into some sort of elite Wine Country lifestyle. But as wineries push pricey wines and all the pretensions that go along with them onto non-wine drinkers, they risk scaring the uninitiated away altogether.

The industry sometimes doesn't seem to help itself either. One new winemaker in Sonoma recounted that he asked some industry colleagues how he should price his new wine. They told him not to price it too low or no one would take it seriously. It goes to show that price is not necessarily a firm measure of quality, just one of many indicators.

Fortunately, the wine industry sometimes gets some marketing help from unlikely places. Touting the health benefits of moderate amounts of wine has always been a surefire, if temporary, way to get more Americans to drink the stuff.

More recently, the Oscar-winning 2004 movie *Sideways,* a comedy drama that follows two aging bachelors on a voyage of self discovery through the Santa Barbara Wine Country, did wonders for sales of pinot noir. As the movie's characters waxed lyrical about the joys of a good pinot, American consumers apparently decided to discover the joys themselves, and sales of pinot noir in California jumped by a third in the year leading up to the 2005 Academy Awards compared to the previous year, according to statistics from A. C. Nielson, which monitors sales at retail outlets. Although Santa Barbara pinots were the stars of the movie, Northern California's pinots benefited just the same.

Wine and Health

In 1991, CBS aired a *60 Minutes* program titled "The French Paradox," which reported that the French population has a far lower incidence of heart attacks than the American population despite getting less exercise, eating more fatty foods, and smoking more. According to some medical experts, this apparent health paradox could be explained by the fact that the average French person drinks a lot of wine.

The American wine industry could not have asked for better publicity. In the month following the broadcast, wine sales reportedly jumped by 44 percent compared to the same period a year earlier. Although the sales spurt didn't last, and research has since suggested that the French paradox is far more complex than can be explained simply by higher wine consumption (though drinking wine has been shown to have health benefits), the wine industry gained a new marketing angle for its wines.

Wine and some other alcoholic beverages have been shown to indeed have health benefits. In the case of the French paradox, however, it is thought that the health benefits have as much to do with overall lifestyle and food consumption patterns as they do with drinking wine.

Low stress (the French take far more vaca-

tions than most Americans) and a Mediterranean diet rich in fish, fresh vegetables, and oils, for example, could be factors. Regular wine drinkers also tend not to be binge drinkers, avoiding all the potential health hazards associated with overconsumption of alcohol.

The jury is still out on whether alcoholic beverages, and wine in particular, have direct effects on long-term health. Statistical studies performed all over the world suggest that moderate wine drinkers (those that drink 1–2 glasses a day) seem to suffer from lower rates of heart diseases and certain cancers, but no one yet knows exactly why or what other factors might be involved.

Some research has focused on a family of chemicals found in the skins of red grapes (and therefore only in red wines) called polyphenols, which are believed to be natural antioxidants. Some polyphenols have specifically been shown to reduce the likelihood of arteries getting clogged in laboratory tests.

Several studies place the emphasis more on lifestyle than red wine specifically. In one study published in the science journal *Nature* in 2005, researchers in Denmark tested cholesterol levels in subjects who drank red wine, grape-skin extract, or water over a four-week period. They discovered that levels of "good" cholesterol increased only in those who drank the wine, showing that the alcohol content was more important to health. However, the study did not find a link between the polyphenols in grape skins and improved health. Because drinking other alcoholic drinks such as beer does not seem to have the same health benefits, researchers deduced that other factors give wine drinkers a healthy advantage, suggesting instead it was lifestyle related.

Although all the focus has been on the beneficial effects of drinking wine, there are some less well-publicized downsides to drinking wine, even in moderate amounts (other than overindulgence and alcoholism, which is not specific to wine).

As anyone who has drunk several glasses of a Napa cabernet with dinner will probably have discovered, red wine stains teeth. But it does more than just this temporary cosmetic damage. The acids in both red and white wines wear away the protective enamel on teeth (white wines are the worst offenders), making them more susceptible to decay. For wine tasters who often swill hundreds of wines around in their mouths each week it is a very real problem, and regular fluoride treatment is often recommended to replace minerals lost from the teeth.

But even for the occasional wine drinker there can be an effect, not least because wine is consumed over several hours, giving those acids plenty of time to start working on the teeth. The recommendations to prevent damage include drinking plenty of water to help dilute the acidity and get your saliva flowing, and eating cheese at the end of the meal. Cheese neutralizes acids and might even harden the enamel weakened by the wine's acid.

UNSUNG HEROES

They pick the grapes, prune the vines, and sometimes help manage the vineyards, but the workers toiling away during the long, hot summers in Northern California are largely the unsung heroes of the wine industry, ensuring winemakers have the best vines and grapes to work with but rarely remembered when the cork is pulled.

As is the case in much of the rest of the state's agricultural sector, most of these workers are migrants from Latin America. They do the work that locals usually won't touch for the money offered, which in many cases is barely above the state's minimum hourly wage. And by all accounts, migrant workers are more productive.

The political debate continues over their legal status—it's a thorny issue that will probably never be fully resolved. But without question they are valuable competitive assets for California's winemakers and the state's agriculture industry as a whole.

Despite the low wages paid to workers, it still costs almost double the amount per ton to harvest grapes and maintain the vines by hand than by machines. Increasing mechanization has drastically reduced the number of vineyard workers in the last few decades, but they remain a critical part of the wine industry, particularly in the premium growing areas like Napa and Sonoma, where hand picking of the valuable grapes is much preferred over letting a machine bludgeon its way through the vines. Steep mountain vineyards in Northern California also pose problems for machines and require the human touch to manage and harvest them.

By some estimates, 98 percent of the vineyard workers in California are from Mexico, so it's no surprise that after decades of toiling in the vineyards an increasing number of Mexican-American families are cashing in on the skills, knowledge, and contacts they have developed.

Since the early 1990s, more than a dozen Mexican families have started their own wineries in Sonoma and Napa. Former migrant worker Reynaldo Robledo, for example, started working in California's vineyards in the 1960s, later established his own vineyard management company, and finally realized his dream to make his own wine. He founded the Robledo Family Winery in Carneros, which became the first Mexican-American winery to open a public tasting room in 2003.

His story and those of the numerous other newly minted Mexican-American wine-making families are just part of the latest chapter in California's wine industry, an industry that owes a historical debt to immigrants from all over the world, from the Victorian pioneers like Charles Krug and Samuele Sebastiani to the Gallo and Mondavi families, who helped put California's wine industry on the international map after Prohibition.

Wine 101

CALIFORNIA GRAPE VARIETALS

The diversity of California's wine industry and the multitude of growing conditions are perfectly by the vast number of grape varietals grown in the state. There are more than 30 types of red wine grapes grown in almost 300,000 acres of vineyards, and 25 types of white wine grapes grown in almost 200,000 acres of vineyards. It's a dizzying array of varietals but is dominated by just a handful.

Certain grapes will only grow in certain conditions, while others will grow anywhere. Chardonnay, for example, is the everyman's grape, able to grow happily almost anywhere in the Wine Country. Pinot noir is fussy and will only grow in a narrow range of cooler climates and make good wine in an even narrower range.

Red Wine Grapes

Cabernet sauvignon is by far the most important red wine grape in California, accounting for about a quarter of all red grapes grown in the state. It is easy to ripen in the Californian sun and capable of making both powerful, tannic wines in hotter climates to lighter, more austere wines in cooler mountain regions, all of them usually capable of long-term aging if they are well made and all having the telltale aromas of cassis (black currant), blackberry, cedar wood, and leather.

Merlot is the second most widely planted red wine grape in California, though its popularity peaked in the 1990s and is now waning. It is usually blended with cabernet sauvignon in bordeaux wines but in California is often made into an easy drinking wine that is less tannic and more plump than most cabernet sauvignons. Sometimes its more subtle flavors can be lost, resulting in a bland wine, but a well-made merlot has just as much structure as other reds.

Zinfandel is not far behind merlot in terms of total acreage planted and is often considered a California native, though recent genetic studies have shown it probably originally came from southern Europe. The grape ripens almost too easily in hot Californian sun, leading to high sugar levels and even higher alcohol levels in the resulting wines that can sometimes overpower even the powerful berry aromas and flavors.

Pinot noir is a distant fourth in terms of acreage due to its finicky nature, which limits the areas where it can be successfully grown. It is said to have the most complex flavors and be able to communicate the unique properties of the *terroir* like no other grape, but only if grown in the right conditions—not too hot yet just warm enough to ripen the grapes sufficiently. Classic pinot flavors and aromas include cherry, raspberry, strawberry, violet, and any number of earthy overtones. Cooler parts of California are some of the few areas of the world where great pinot noirs are made, the most famous being the Burgundy region of France. It is also one of the most important grapes for making champagne.

Syrah is the rising star of California's red wines and the fifth most-planted red grape in the state. Its traditional home is the Rhône region of France, and it is often made into Rhône-style wines in cooler parts of California, exhibiting telltale black pepper and chocolate flavors and an almost purple color. It makes a much denser, more powerful wine when grown in hotter climates, including parts of California and in Australia, where it is commonly known as **shiraz,** named after the Persian (now Iranian) region of Shiraz where the grape is believed to have originated.

White Wine Grapes

Chardonnay is the king of white grapes in California. It accounts for almost 100,000 acres, or more than half the total acreage planted with white varietals. It grows almost anywhere and can be made into wines of a multitude of styles to suit almost every palate, depending on the wine-making process. Over-oaking is a common fault of Californian chardonnays, as is an overreliance on high levels of malolactic fermentation, which give the wines a sweet, slightly bland flavor. Chardonnay is also one of the most important champagne grapes.

Chenin blanc is the grape that chardonnay eclipsed, and the acreage planted to this varietal in California has been declining steadily since the 1980s. It makes an equally easy-drinking (some say plain) wine as chardonnay, full of fruity flavors.

Sauvignon blanc is one of the most important white grape varietals in Bordeaux, where it is usually blended with semillon, and it is growing in popularity in California. In cool climates like its home in France and parts of California it makes a refreshingly crisp, aromatic wine, often with unusual aromas of grass and herbs. In warmer climates it makes a heavier style of wine from which winemakers sometimes coax richer, more tropical fruit flavors. These richer styles of wine are often called **fumé blanc** but are still made from the same sauvignon blanc grape.

Viognier is an increasingly fashionable white varietal that exploded onto the California wine scene in the 1990s. In 1992 there were just 100 acres planted of this varietal. By 2002 there were 2,000 acres. It does well in California's warm climate, where it ripens enough to create full-bodied, elegant wines with a distinctive exotic, floral aroma and rich texture.

Riesling is regarded as the king of grapes on its home turf in Germany and is increasingly popular in California thanks to its ability to make different styles of wine depending on the climate and wine-making process. Some rieslings are too sweet and lack structure, but the best wines have a unique balance of acidity, tropical fruit flavors, powerful aromas, and a lightness that makes them some of the most complex in the white wine world.

HOW WINE IS MADE

For thousands of years civilizations have made wine, and the chemical process of fermentation that turns the sugar in grape juice into alcohol in wine is the same as it's always been. The actual process of making wine has changed drastically, however, particularly since the science behind

© PHILIP GOLDSMITH

viognier grapes

HOW MANY GRAPES IN A GLASS?

Understanding the wine-making process is a bit easier if it's brought down to a personal scale—how many grapes go into the bottle of wine you're drinking. The Sonoma County Grape Growers Association has helpfully worked it out for us.

An average vineyard yields about 5 tons, or 10,000 pounds, of grapes per acre. All those grapes make about 13.5 barrels of wine, which is 797 gallons, or 3,985 bottles.

Do the math and it turns out that one bottle of wine is made using about 2.4 pounds of grapes, so one glass comes from just under 10 ounces of grapes.

This is little more than a back-of-an-envelope calculation, however, and will depend on all sorts of factors, from the type of grape to the style of wine being made.

The Napa Valley Vintners Association has slightly different figures. It says a ton of grapes makes on average 720 bottles of wine, so each bottle contains about 2.8 pounds of grapes. It also helpfully calculates that one average vine plant produces enough grapes to make 4–6 bottles of wine each year.

fermentation was first discovered in the mid-1800s. Since then wine making has become ever more refined to get the best out of particular grapes and to make different styles of wine, some for aging and others for mass consumption.

The year that appears on a wine bottle, known as the wine's vintage, is the year that the grapes are harvested and wine making begins. The processes used to make red and white wines are similar but with a few important differences. One of the most important is that red wines are made by fermenting the juice in contact with the skins of the grapes. The skins contain the pigments that make red wine red; juice from virtually all grapes, whether red or white, is relatively colorless. Cut a red grape in half and the flesh inside looks almost identical to that of a white grape.

Grapes are brought from the vineyards to the crush pad at the winery, where they are unloaded onto a conveyor and fed into a **crusher-destemmer,** a machine that will chop off the stems but let the grapes through, gently crushing them in the process so the juice can seep out. In the case of the best grapes destined for more expensive wines, human sorters often pull out withered, unripe, or otherwise unworthy grapes and stems from the conveyor so only the best get through. Once grapes are crushed and destemmed, the wine-making process begins.

Although red and white wine-making techniques differ in many ways, they both involve a fermentation stage during which naturally occurring yeasts, often supplemented by the addition of other yeast strains for certain flavor characteristics, get to work on the grape juice and turn the naturally occurring sugar into alcohol. Fermentation can be carried out in giant wooden tanks (the old fashioned way), temperature-controlled stainless steel tanks (the modern way), or even open-top concrete tanks (old-fashioned but still widely used in California for some wines, like pinot noir).

Almost as important as the type of fermentation vessel used is how the wine gets in and out of it. A lot of modern wineries use standard food-grade pumps and pipes to move the wine between each stage of wine making. The more traditional method of moving the liquid around is gravity flow—literally letting gravity do the work. This is how it used to be done before the age of modern pumps and electricity. Many old (and an increasing number of modern) wineries are designed around the gravity flow principle, whereby each stage of the wine-making process is at a progressively lower level of the winery. Purists argue that gravity-flow wine making minimizes the amount of contact the wine has with processing equipment and the heat it generates.

Californian wine making differs from that in some other parts of the world in that winemakers cannot add any sugar to the wine. Luckily, the weather is hot enough that ripening grapes to their necessary sweetness is not a problem. Very little else can be added to wines either, except for yeast and clarifying agents.

The one chemical that is sometimes used in wine making is sulfur dioxide, and this is responsible for the statement on wine labels that a wine "contains sulfites." Sulfur dioxide is added to wines before bottling to prevent the growth of bacteria that could spoil the wine, and it is also sometimes added at the beginning of the wine-making process to kill naturally occurring yeasts, some of which might impart slightly funky flavors to a wine. In most cases, however, natural yeasts are an important part of the wine-making process, though often supplemented by other strains of yeast, all of which create wines with slightly different characteristics.

Making Red Wine

After destemming and crushing, the grapes are either pumped or flow by gravity into the fermentation vessel, where fermentation begins and will usually keep going for a couple of weeks.

During fermentation the grape skins, seeds, and remaining small pieces of stem float to the top and form a thick crust that has to be constantly broken and remixed with the fermenting wine to ensure all the pigments in the grape skins and the other desirable chemicals like tannins are leached out of this "cap" of crud. These days the wine from the bottom of the fermentation tank is usually pumped the over the cap and filters back down through it, or a giant, mixer-like system keeps all the skins and stems constantly circulating through the fermenting wine.

Traditionally, the cap was broken up and pushed back down into the wine by hand using a big wooden paddle, and this punching-down technique is still used in some smaller wineries today, especially to produce pinot noir—a wine that requires more work to extract the color from the grape skins.

Once the winemaker determines that enough pigment and tannins have been extracted from the skins and fermentation has gone on long enough, the liquid is transferred into barrels or stainless steel storage tanks. This is known as the free-run juice and goes into the best wine. Sometimes the free run is blended with some of the more concentrated and tannic press wine, generated when the leftover skins and other mulch in the cap are pressed to extract all the remaining juice, which is then stored separately. In some cases fermentation is stopped by chilling the wine and filtering out the yeast, but fermentation will also stop naturally when alcohol levels rise high enough to kill the yeast—usually about 15 percent by volume.

The blending of the free-run wine and the press wine is just part of the important **blending** process. Wines from different vineyards, sometimes from different parts, or blocks, of the same vineyard, are usually made and stored separately and will have slightly different characteristics. They are blended together at a later stage by the winemaker, often together with small quantities of wines made from different grapes, to make the final product.

Most of the premium wines made in Napa, Sonoma, and Santa Cruz are aged in oak barrels once they have been blended—the barrels you often see stacked on giant racks in caves or cool storage rooms of wineries. This barrel aging not only lets the wine continue to develop its taste and aroma through ongoing chemical reactions but also imparts new flavors and aromas that come from the barrels themselves. It is also when most red wines undergo **malolactic fermentation,** which is not fermentation at all but a bacterial reaction that converts the tart malic acid in a wine to the softer lactic acid.

Buying the barrels and storing them is expensive and reserved for the best wines that can command premium prices. Cheaper wines made to be drunk right away are bottled straight from the stainless steel tanks in which they were blended. Sometimes oak chips are added to those tanks to impart some of the important oaky flavors.

Before wines are bottled or left to age in barrels they are purified using a process called **fining,** which uses a coagulant to remove all the particles of dead yeast, excess tannins, and other crud suspended in the liquid. The coagulant can be anything from types of clay to egg whites or gelatin and is simply dropped into the wine, where it attaches itself to particles and pulls them down to the bottom of the barrel or tank. In fine wines that need to age further, the freshly cleaned wine is siphoned off into clean barrels to ensure this gunk does not interfere with the aging process, a process known as **racking.** After usually six months or a year (longer for the very best age-worthy wines) the wine from barrels will be bottled, often after being filtered to remove the last of the sediment. Cheaper wines stored in stainless steel tanks are usually bottled soon after fining.

Some more expensive red wines are made without the crusher-destemmer step; instead, whole bunches of grapes with the biggest stems removed are left to ferment using the yeasts naturally occurring on the skins. The grapes eventually burst and allow the fermented juice to escape.

Making White Wine

White wine production leaves out many of the steps involved in making red wines and is an altogether quicker process. The speed of the wine making and the fact that most Californian white wines are not aged for long (if at all) before bottling explain why a bottle of white wine often has a much more recent vintage date on the label than a red.

Winemakers don't want white grape juice to sit in contact with grape skins and stems for long because that would introduce all sorts of bitter flavors, so the grapes often go through not only the crusher-destemmer but also a press, which gently squeezes the juice out. The first juice out of the grapes is the best and is often reserved for the best wines, much like the best olive oils are the "first cold pressed." The last juice to be squeezed out picks up some of the bitterness from the skins, seeds, and stems and is destined for cheaper wines.

Most Californian white wines are fermented in giant stainless steel vessels, and fermentation is carefully controlled using giant refrigeration jackets wrapped around the outside of the tanks to ensure a wine retains some sweetness—white wines, even dry whites, generally contain more residual sugar than most reds. Because of this

extra refrigeration the fermentation time for white wines is generally longer than that of reds. During fermentation, dead yeasts and other particles, known as the **lees,** will slowly drop to the bottom and are sometimes left in contact with the fermented wine to add distinct yeasty, toasty aromas.

Once fermentation is complete, the wine is fined and filtered and either bottled or transferred to barrels for some aging, which adds the oakiness that Californian chardonnays are so famous for. It then often undergoes some degree of malolactic fermentation, which turns a crisp white wine into a rich, buttery-tasting one. If a winemaker does not want malolactic fermentation to occur, the wine undergoes some additional filtering and might also be treated with sulfur dioxide to kill the bacteria responsible for the reaction.

Making Champagne

The cool climate of Carneros and the Russian River Valley is ideally suited for growing the two most important champagne grape varietals, chardonnay and pinot noir. A few other grapes are also often used, including small amounts of pinot blanc and pinot meunier (producers of the Spanish sparkling wine, cava, use totally different grapes more suited to the local Spanish climate).

Most Californian champagne-style wines are blends of both pinot noir and chardonnay, with some exceptions. A blanc de blancs champagne is made only from chardonnay grapes and has the lightest, most delicate style. A blanc de noirs is still a white wine but made exclusively from dark-skinned grapes like pinot noir, giving it a fuller body. Somewhere in between the two is rosé, or pink, champagne, which is made by adding a small amount of red wine to the white blend.

The key to making champagne is to bottle the wine while it is still fermenting so the yeast will continue to do its work and generate both alcohol and the all-important gas that creates the fizz, carbon dioxide (carbonic acid).

The fizziness was likely discovered by accident when the cold winters of the Champagne

FIVE FIZZY FACTS

Champagne making is a high-pressure business: The pressure inside a champagne bottle created by the dissolved carbon dioxide gas (carbonic acid) is about 90 pounds per square inch, or about three times the pressure in a car tire. That's why the glass of champagne bottles is so thick and the cork can shoot so far.

Champagne isn't just for celebration: More than 80 percent of sparkling wine sales occur between November and January, but it is a style of wine that can be enjoyed at any time of year and with a wide range of foods. Try it instead of chardonnay at the beginning of a meal.

Not all bubbles are created equal: The more expensive the champagne, the smaller the bubbles and the smoother and creamier it feels in your mouth. The priciest French champagnes barely taste fizzy at all. The cheapest supermarket sparklers feel like fizzy water or soda in your mouth.

Champagne gets you tipsy more quickly: The carbonation in sparkling wine is thought to relax the valve between your stomach and small intestine, where alcohol is absorbed by the blood more quickly. So while still wines stay in the stomach longer, champagne enters the small intestine more quickly and really does go to your head faster.

Better champagne glasses make for better bubbles: The tall, slender champagne glasses, known as flutes, help keep the wine sparkling for longer and show off the bubbles better. Most good-quality flutes have a small etching at the bottom that encourages the bubbles to form. That's why you'll usually see a long, straight line of bubbles rising from the very bottom of the glass.

region stopped barrel fermentation in its tracks before the wine was bottled. Once the wine was bottled and the weather warmed up, fermentation started again, only this time inside the sealed bottle, where the carbonic acid had nowhere to go. As pressure built up the corks popped off (and the fizzy wine was drunk by people assuming it had gone bad) or the bottles simply exploded.

English merchants taking delivery of barrels of French wine were likely the first to experience this peculiar exploding wine phenomenon. At the time, back in the late 1700s, England was also home to a state-of-the-art glass-blowing industry, so once the wine sellers understood what was going on with the wine they were able to develop bottles thick enough to contain it.

The full potential of this new style of fizzy wine was quickly realized and modern champagne production began. The biggest challenge for the early champagne houses was to remove the sediment of dead yeast and other by-products of fermentation from the bottle without

losing the fizz, otherwise the champagne would end up murky.

The process developed in 1805, known as méthode champenoise, is still largely unchanged today. Bottles of half-made champagne are stored neck down in large racks and were traditionally turned on an exact schedule over many months to get the sediment to work its way down to the cork, a process known as riddling. Today, of course, it's all done by computer-controlled machines (despite what many champagne houses would have you believe).

Then comes the process of disgorging, during which the sediment is carefully removed. In today's automated version, the neck of the bottle is frozen, and when the cork is removed, the compressed gas in the wine shoots the frozen plug of muck out. Finally comes dosing, when the bottle is topped off with wine and some sugar (more sugar for the sweeter wines, less for the dry styles) before being recorked and allowed to continue fermenting in peace.

It's a precise and expensive process, which is why it's reserved for the high-end champagnes.

Cheaper sparkling wines are today more likely to be made in large, stainless steel tanks that are pressurized to keep the carbon dioxide dissolved in the wine before it is filtered and bottled.

Making Port

Dark, juicy ports have become increasingly popular in recent years, and some sort of port can now be found at most wineries. Not all of it is good, however. Some is nothing more than an overly sweet red dessert wine that has about as much complexity as concentrated grape juice. Others approach (though do not yet reach) the sophistication of the best ports made in the country where they were invented—Portugal (the name is derived from the Portuguese coastal city of Oporto).

Traditional ports are made using the Portuguese grape varietals tinta barroca, tinta roriz, tinto cao, and touriga, though a lot of Californian ports use more common regional varietals, particularly zinfandel and syrah.

It is made in pretty much the same way as red wine to start with, but the fermentation is stopped in its tracks when the wine is poured into a fortified spirit like brandy, which has enough alcohol to kill the yeast that was happily minding its own business turning the wine's sugar into alcohol. The result is a half-fermented wine still containing plenty of unfermented sugar but with a high alcohol level (usually around 20 percent) thanks to the addition of the brandy.

Because fermentation of red wine is stopped halfway, the winemaker has to work hard to ensure that enough color has been extracted from the grape skins before the wine is poured off into the brandy. In Portugal that is still often achieved by the age-old custom of crushing the grapes with bare feet to thoroughly grind up the skins. Not many Californian wineries will admit to that.

The best ports in the world are aged for many years in barrels, but many Californian ports are made to be drunk relatively young, though they can also be aged in the bottle just like regular wines.

Wine Barrels

Oak was traditionally used for making barrels because it was strong, had a fine grain and so was watertight, and was plentiful in the forests of Europe. Early winemakers also discovered that wines picked up some pleasant flavors and smells when stored in oak barrels, which is why oak has remained the most desirable wood to use when aging wines.

Most barrels used in wine making today are made of oak, but not all oak is the same when it comes to making wine. Just as different varietals of grape have different flavors and smells, so different types of oak have different characteristics that a winemaker can manipulate.

French oak is the most highly prized because of the soft, subtle flavors it gives a wine. It is also the most expensive. A typical French oak barrel costs a winery $500–600, compared to about $200–300 for a barrel made from American oak, which tends to add more pronounced flavors to a wine. As French oak is priced out of the market, the oak from Eastern Europe, particularly Hungary and Slovakia, is becoming more popular and has some of the some of the same characteristics as its French cousin but for far less cost to the winery.

Some of the most distinctive flavors and smells added to a wine by aging it in oak barrels include vanilla, leather, tobacco, cloves, and cedar. Those flavors will be stronger the newer the barrel is. Wineries often age wine in a mixture of new and old barrels, both to save money and to get the right mixture of strong and mellow flavors from the oak. They will also often use a mixture of American and European oak to get the right balance of flavors and aromas.

When barrels are made (an art in itself) they are usually **toasted** by lighting a fire inside the half-finished barrel to create a thin layer of burnt wood. This toasted wood imparts its own set of flavors and smells to the wine, including the rich, chocolate, caramel, and nutty characteristics typical in barrel-aged wines, particularly reds.

The Wine-Making Year

A winegrower's year is a busy one, and January

is about the only time they can take significant time off for a well-earned vacation. Most of us have more flexible vacation time and can choose when to visit Wine Country based on all sorts of factors, including the weather, the scenery, events, and where the winegrowers are in their year-long process of creating great wines.

January: The vineyards are bare, the weather is cool and wet, and the Wine Country is at its quietest. This is also the time of year that the vines are pruned. Straggly bare stems are cut back to the thick, gnarled trunk of the vine.

February: More vineyard maintenance and pruning are carried out, but the wet weather has by now started all the wildflowers blooming, including the bright yellow wild mustard that fills the rows between vines and colors entire vineyards yellow in many parts of the Wine Country between now and April.

March: New vines are planted and bottling lines at wineries spring into action, bottling wines designed to be drunk young (like many whites) that were made the previous year.

April: Buds are open on the vines and the new growing season begins in the vineyard as the weather finally starts to dry out and warm up. The danger of late frosts often gets the giant wind machines going to keep the air moving and prevent ice from forming on the delicate shoots.

May: Vines are now growing vigorously and wineries are gearing up for the summer rush of tourists.

June: The vines are tied to the wires and posts of the trellises to make sure the grapes get as much sun as possible later in the year. The vines also start flowering, so rain is an unwelcome, though rare, disruption. Bottling of older wines begins before the heat of summer sets in.

July: Flowering is over and grapes are starting to form. Spraying with organic or other chemicals starts to safeguard the developing grapes from pests and diseases.

August: This is the first month that red grapes will really start to look red as they continue to grow. Some pruning of excess leaves sometimes takes place to ensure grapes are not shaded and can fully ripen. Smaller, less well-developed clusters of grapes might also be cut off so the vine can concentrate all its energy and nutrients into the remaining grapes. Wineries start to clear space for the imminent harvest.

September: The first harvesting begins, with the earliest ripening grapes in the hottest areas picked first (in particularly hot years or those with an early summer, harvesting sometimes starts in August). Most grapes in Northern California's premium growing regions are picked by hand, usually by migrant workers. This is the best time to surreptitiously taste just how sweet wine grapes are if you see any dangling over the shoulder of country roads. Wineries themselves are hives of activity as tons of grapes start to be brought in by truck.

October: Harvesting finishes and the vineyards start to look a little more bare, though the vines will keep their leaves for another month or so. The crush is well underway at wineries, and steel tanks rapidly fill up with wine.

November: The vineyards start to turn shades of red and yellow as the weather starts to cool and the leaves finally drop when the nights get cold enough. In wineries, the wine is starting to be transferred from the fermentation vats into barrels to begin aging.

December: Many wineries offer barrel tasting of new wines, and the winemaker will start to plan the blends that will ultimately be bottled.

Reading Wine Labels

Thanks to strict labeling regulations overseen by the federal Bureau of Alcohol, Tobacco, and Firearms it is tough for wineries to mislead consumers about what goes into a bottle of wine, but there is a little more to a wine's content than might meet the eye.

The year on the bottle is the **vintage date** and indicates the year in which at least 95 percent of the grapes that went into the wine were harvested.

Usually underneath the vintage is the **appellation of origin,** which is where the dominant grapes in the wine were grown. It is usually a geographical area (appellation) like California or Sonoma County or a specific American Viticultural Area (AVA) such as Rutherford, Napa Valley, or Dry Creek Valley. In the case of an appellation, at least 75 percent of the grapes in the wine must have come from that area. In the case of an AVA at least 85 percent of the grapes must be from the place identified on the bottle.

The type of grape the wine is made from, or **varietal designation,** is usually displayed above or below the appellation of origin. If a specific grape varietal is identified (cabernet sauvignon or sauvignon blanc, for example) then at least 75 percent of the grapes the wine is made of must be that named varietal. That leaves a lot of leeway for winemakers to blend small quantities of other grapes into a wine to add to its character; sometimes these blending grapes will be identified in tasting notes, other times not.

If less than 75 percent of the grapes in a wine are one varietal, then a winery will either simply call it red or white wine or will come up with a snappy and unique name to describe the blend. Such a wine is known as a **proprietary wine** or blend.

The final words to look for on labels are **estate bottled,** which means that all of the grapes in a wine came from land owned or controlled by the winery, and the wine was made and bottled on the winery premises. So-called estate wines tend to be among the winery's best and most expensive.

HOW TO TASTE WINE

The involved process of thoroughly smelling and tasting a wine is one reason why aficionados love the stuff and a big reason that novices tend to be intimidated. Some people seem to regard wine almost as an intellectual pursuit. Others just like the taste or want to get drunk.

On one level, it seems ludicrous to spend so long detecting every nuance of flavor in a wine. After all, when a plate of food arrives in a restaurant we don't sit for five minutes smelling it to try to detect every ingredient and how

they were cooked. Then again, there is probably no other drinkable liquid on earth that can pack as many complex aromas and flavors into a glass as wine can, and certainly no other food product that can reflect so completely the place that it came from.

With the magic worked by winemakers, simple grape juice can be transformed into wines that mimic the smells and tastes of a remarkable range of fruits, vegetables, and countless other substances. Grapes actually contain many of the same chemicals that give other fruits and vegetables their distinctive smells. Wine reviews often read like a shopping list for the produce department at a local supermarket.

Wine appreciation cannot be taught. It has to be learned. One reason that many people are confused by those slightly pretentious-sounding reviews is that they cannot actually recognize the smell of many of the substances with which a wine's smell or taste is compared. Someone who has never smoked a cigar, for example, is not gong to understand what a reviewer is referring to when he describes a cabernet sauvignon as having an aroma of "cigar box." Everyone knows what chocolate tastes and smells like, though, so a "chocolaty" cabernet will instantly ring a bell in most people's minds.

The sort of diverse smell and flavor database that critics use takes time (and an extremely varied diet) to develop. Patience is the best way to learn—it takes a while to develop a palate that can detect the subtle nuances of wine and years to build up a useful tasting memory that you can draw on to recognize and describe wines or their aromas.

When in doubt simply listen to how everyone else describes the wine, or just ask whoever is pouring the wine at a winery what exactly you are supposed to be smelling or tasting. On a few occasions you might not get much help from a harried staffer, but usually they are happy to give a quick description.

Alternatively, an intensive wine-tasting course (see *Opportunities for Study*) can shorten the process of learning all the smells and tastes by setting out every imaginable fruit, vegetable, and other organic substance in dishes, allowing students to directly match aromas from the foods to the aromas in wines (something you can also do at home with whatever you have in your kitchen). Some courses are listed below for anyone interested.

Of course, the world of smells and tastes is unique to each individual. There are some fairly standard categories of the basic flavors and aromas of wines. Beyond them, it's fine to make up your own comparisons and the more recognizable they are the better. Take the description "wet dog." It is clearly not in any textbook but was probably inspired by a critic walking his dog that morning in the rain. It's a smell that any dog owner will instantly recognize (though it's also a smell that indicates the wine is not even fit for a dog to drink).

For fun, make up your own personal wine descriptions every day—pinot noir can sometimes smell a little like a traffic jam on the St. Helena Highway on a hot summer afternoon. Alternatively, just ignore all the fancy words and simply say "it smells and tastes good."

Critics don't always agree with each other, illustrating just how subjective the art of describing wines really is. Take these three excerpts from reviews in three major wine magazines of a 2001 merlot from Pride Mountain Vineyards. All three have a few common threads but they could equally be describing totally different wines:

Possesses gorgeous aromas of creosote, damp earth, sweet black cherry as well as currant fruit, and a chocolaty aftertaste.

Rich in spicy currant, exotic spice, and ripe blackberry fruit, turning spicy and exhibiting pretty mocha-scented oak.

Smoky aromas of black raspberry, coffee, and nutty oak. Lush, fat, and sweet, with layered flavors of black raspberry and sweet oak.

Looking at Wine

How a wine looks in the glass can give some clues about what you're about to drink. Try to look at it against a white background (the tasting room menu, for example). Overall the wine should be crystal clear and a bright, vivid color. Any hint of cloudiness is generally not a good sign.

White wines range from a pale yellow in young and light wines like sauvignon blanc to a darker gold in some heavier whites like some styles of chardonnay that have been aged in oak. White wines darken as they age; a hint of brown might be a sign of a well-aged wine, but for most Californian whites it's usually the sign of a wine that's past its prime.

Red wines have a much wider range of colors, ranging from deep red in the case of cabernet sauvignon to deep purple in a young syrah and a paler brick red in pinot noir. The color of red wines fades as they age and the pigment molecules react with other chemical components of the wine, so the deeper the color the younger the wine.

Smelling the Wine

Wine glasses are designed to concentrate the aroma of a wine and channel it straight to your nose. Most of what we taste is actually what we smell, so smelling a wine is the key to enjoying it and discovering its complexities.

Professionals smell the wine to learn more about it, such as the main grape varietals it contains and the region it came from, especially in blind tastings that are designed to be as objective as possible. Most people smell wine just to enjoy and appreciate the glorious aromas before drinking it. Trying to identify them is really nothing more than a bit of fun that might one day be useful if someone asks you to identify a wine with no label.

Swirl the glass to help release the aromas and then take a deep sniff and try to identify all the aromas. Take as many sniffs as you want. Some wines have an intense smell, others more subtle ones.

Most of the up-front smells are the aromas that come directly from the fruit in the wine, and such fruity smells are the biggest category of aromas in the world of wine tasting. Another big category of aromas is vegetative, which roughly translates as anything that smells like it came from a plant, whether grass, bell pepper, or tobacco, and there are also floral aromas.

Classic aromas for white wines include bell pepper, apple, grapefruit, apricot, peach, honey, and melon. For red wines there might be aromas of any number of berries, cherries, raisins, plums, licorice, and black pepper.

Some of the more subtle, underlying smells come from the barrel, yeasts, and other winemaking factors, and these are collectively known as the bouquet. The older the wine, the more pronounced the bouquet will be. Classic bouquet smells include vanilla, oak, nuts, butterscotch, and chocolate.

Wine aromas are supposed to be pleasant, but sometimes bad smells creep in and are an indicator of a wine gone bad. Most are pretty obviously bad, like the rotten egg smell of hydrogen sulfide, the vinegary smell of oxidized wine, or the sherry-like smell of cooked, or maderized, wine.

A corked wine—one that has been contaminated by mold on the cork—can sometimes be harder to detect. Often the characteristic musty or mildewed smell is so fleeting that it might be missed and quickly overpowered by other aromas. Another indicator of mold contamination is a strong smell of wet cardboard.

Tasting the Wine

Taking a sip of wine will be the ultimate test of whether to buy it or not. Most wine smells pleasant enough (unless you have an aversion to fruit or the wine is bad), but not all wines will taste good to everyone.

Our taste buds can only detect four fundamental tastes—sweet, sour, bitter, and salty—but those four are enough to determine whether a wine is in balance and ultimately good to drink.

The amounts of alcohol, tannin, residual sugar, and acid in a wine can all be detected by swirling it around in your mouth for about 10 seconds, making sure it coats every part of your mouth to hit all the different taste buds. More aromas than you initially smelled might also be detectable once a wine is in your mouth.

The sum of these tastes is more important than each one individually. How they all merge together is a reflection of a wine's balance, yet another highly subjective measurement of overall quality. Some people prefer sweeter wines; others prefer a little more acidity to make their mouth water. Some don't like the astringency of tannins while others like the backbone they can give to a powerful wine. Generally, however, people describe a wine as balanced when all these tastes are about equal to each other.

Aftertaste (the pleasant kind) is almost as important as the main taste. Poor wines have no aftertaste, and once the wine is swallowed that's your lot. Good wines leave your taste buds tingling for anywhere from a few seconds to almost a minute.

Another aspect of a wine that is worth noting is its body. Much like water will feel lighter in your mouth than milk, a light-bodied white wine will have a difference presence in your mouth than a full-bodied red like a zinfandel.

The Aroma Wheel

To help people recognize a wine's aromas, an educator at the University of California at Davis created the Aroma Wheel, which broadly categorizes aromas and bouquets, then subcategorizes them and gives specific examples. If you smell something fruity, for example, the wheel will break down fruity smells into categories such as citrus, berry, and tropical fruit, then break each of those subcategories down further into examples of specific fruits.

Aroma Wheels are often sold among the wine paraphernalia in the tasting rooms of large wineries but can also be bought online (along with Aroma Wheel T-shirts for those who live for wine) at http://wineserver.ucdavis.edu/Acnoble/waw. That website also includes information on how to use the wheel.

WINE AND FOOD

Probably as intimidating to many people as the smelling and tasting of wine is the question of how to match a wine with food, or vice versa. Like everything else to do with wine it ultimately boils down to personal taste and personal experience. Some winemakers in Bordeaux reportedly drink nothing but red bordeaux with everything.

Learning from scratch how your favorite wine interacts on your palate with your favorite foods will increase your appreciation for both the wine and the food. Along the way you'll probably discover the few combinations that really are best avoided and a few others that make your taste buds sing.

There really are no rules to pairing food and wine, despite what some connoisseurs might say. Instead, think of any advice you are given as merely guidelines that will help make the voyage of discovering your favorite food and wine combinations quicker and easier.

These guidelines are constantly in flux. Cuisine trends change and so too do wine-making trends. The old adage of white wine with fish and red wine with red meat is somewhat irrelevant. It all depends on the style of a particular wine, how the meat or fish is prepared, and what goes into the accompanying sauces and dishes.

One general guideline to pairing food and wine is that a wine should have some of the same basic taste characteristics as the food, otherwise it will become overpowered. Acidic foods pair well with acidic wines, sweet foods with sweet wines, and so on.

An acidic dish like a vinaigrette-drenched salad, for example, will go best with a crisp white wine like a young sauvignon blanc (white wines are typically more acidic than reds). A less acidic wine will lose out to the tartness in the food and taste flat. The same principle explains why a plump, sweet port or muscat goes well with sweet desserts.

For a thoroughly educational experience, try drinking just one wine, white or red, with a multiple-course meal to see how its taste dramatically changes with each course. The basics of food and wine interaction very quickly become evident.

A Napa cabernet, for example, will be perfectly balanced with a steak but will taste like grape juice when drunk with that vinaigrette salad dressing (the acid in the salad dressing overpowers the acid and tannins in the wine and leaves just the sweet fruit flavors). It will taste like a hunk of wood when drunk with a fruit tart at dessert because the sweet fruit overpowers the fruit in the wine, leaving just those woody tannins to dominate.

Some of the simplest foods can prove to be the hardest to find a good wine match. Cheese, for example, does not (as many people believe) go terribly well with many red wines. Try port for rich cheeses like Stilton or a dry white wine like sauvignon blanc for sharper cheeses like goat cheese.

Wine in Restaurants

If you've ever wondered how restaurants can justify charging more than $40 for a wine that you just bought in a tasting room for $20, the answer is fairly simple even if hard to swallow sometimes.

The markup helps restaurants cover their overhead costs, especially those related to the wine. It pays for the salary of a sommelier (so make sure you use his services), some of the salaries of the wait staff, spoilage of wine (by

© PHILIP GOLDSMITH

Food is never far away in the Wine Country.

some estimates about 5 percent of all restaurant wines spoil before being opened), the cost of storing wine (wine cellars cost a lot of money), and all sorts of other costs of doing business, from the electricity bill to broken wine glasses that can cost a restaurant thousands of dollars a year to replace.

In general, cheap wines have higher markups than expensive wines. Those from well-known regions or made from popular grape varietals also tend to have higher markups because they're guaranteed sellers.

One way to save money on wine in restaurants is to bring your own. Corkage fees (the fee charged by the restaurant for you to bring and open your own wine) vary but are generally about $15 in Wine Country restaurants. It sounds pricey but is worth considering if you plan to drink an expensive wine. Some places offer free corkage on certain days of the week, however, and many others offer free corkage on one bottle of your own wine for every bottle you buy from their wine list. Ask about the corkage policy of the restaurant when making a reservation.

Having ordered a bottle in a restaurant there is yet another wine ritual to go through. The smelling and tasting ritual is all about finding those wines you like; this restaurant ritual is all about finding those wines that you don't want to drink.

When a server brings a bottle of wine to the table and shows it to you like some trophy, double-check that it is in fact the wine you ordered. Take note of the vintage because it's not uncommon for a restaurant to receive new wines and forget to update its wine list.

When the wine is opened, the cork will often be handed to you or placed gingerly on the table. It might make a nice souvenir but is actually given to you to check whether it's in good condition. A good cork should feel springy and soft. A dried out and hard cork suggests that the wine was not stored well and should be a warning to pay close attention when you taste the wine. Don't bother smelling the cork—it will just smell of cork. And don't bother doing anything with synthetic corks, other than perhaps bouncing them off the ceiling.

Finally, the server will pour a tasting-room quantity of wine into your glass. The idea is to check that the wine is the right temperature and that it is not oxidized or corked. If you simply don't like it, you're stuck with it, though many wines will sometimes taste a bit rough when first opened. Always give the wine a few minutes in the glass before drinking to let it open up and show off its full range of aromas and tastes.

White wines tend to come chilled but red wines can sometimes feel like they have been stored above a hot oven in the kitchen. In those cases it's fine to ask for an ice bucket to cool the bottle down. After all, red wine is generally best drunk at 60–70°F, not 85°F.

AGING WINE

The whole point of aging wine for some people is to make it more valuable. For most of us, however, aging wine is all about making it taste better after a few years of "development." Youthful wine is like a youthful person—brash, unsure of itself, and a bit awkward. Like us, a wine mellows, gets more complex, and becomes a more well-rounded individual the older it gets. At least that's the theory.

As wine ages it undergoes a complex chemical process that only scientists fully understand. For the rest of us, the aging of wine is a process full of mystery and myths. One common myth is that all wine gets better as it ages. Sadly, that's not true, so don't start stocking a cellar with $10 bottles of cabernet. A poorly made wine that is not in balance when young will not turn into a finely balanced masterpiece after a few years.

A wine has to almost be designed to be aged by the winemaker. Moreover, a wine capable of aging for a decade or more might taste a little unappealing when young. A wine made to be drunk young will probably taste flat and generally awful after 10 years.

Another myth is that age-worthy wine gets better and better as it gets older. While that's almost true for some of the most famous bordeaux wines, most modern wines are created to

BOTTLE SIZE MATTERS

If you're wondering how the regular wine bottle came to be the size it is (750 milliliters and probably the only beverage in the United States measured in metric units), it is because this was the approximate size a Victorian glass blower could blow with one deep breath. The size was then standardized by European winemakers. There are some bottles smaller—the half bottle and the split, or quarter bottle handed out on some airlines—but most people tend to notice the bigger bottles on display at some wineries.

Bigger bottles are actually better when it comes to aging fine wine. Aging is directly affected by how much of the liquid is exposed to the small gap between the wine and the cork, known as the ullage. The lower the proportion of wine there is in contact with the ullage, the longer the aging process will be. Since even giant bottles generally have necks almost as narrow as regular bottles, they also have a proportionately smaller ullage. Big bottles don't stop at the common Magnum size either. There are some true giants that hold enough wine to keep a big party going all night long.

Bottle sizes are named after mythical kings. No one really knows why, but the theory is that such names convey greatness, grandeur, and longevity. They increase in size as follows:

Magnum: 2 standard bottles (1.5 liters)

Jeroboam: 4 bottles (3 liters)

Methusela: 8 bottles (6 liters)

Salamanazar: 12 bottles (9 liters)

Balthazar: 16 bottles (12 liters)

Nebuchadnezzar: 20 bottles (15 liters)

And the biggest bottle ever? It was a one-off creation that held 130 liters of wine, the equivalent of 173 regular bottles or 1,200 glasses of wine, commissioned by the American Morton's Steakhouse chain in 2004 to celebrate its 25th anniversary. That giant bottle was 4.5 feet tall and filled with Beringer Private Reserve cabernet sauvignon, a quintessential steak wine that is also a quintessentially expensive Napa Valley wine. The retail value of the wine in that bottle was a staggering $17,000, and the bottle eventually sold at auction in late 2004 for almost $56,000, giant corkscrew not included.

---

be drunk relatively young and will reach a peak after a certain number of years then go downhill fast. Wineries don't help matters by making sweeping statements that a wine will "continue to improve for 10–15 years." It all depends on how it's stored. In many cases that wine will be barely drinkable after 10 years unless stored under almost perfect aging conditions.

Unfortunately, winemakers and wineries are the only sources of information on how a wine might age, because there are no hard and fast rules. One way to get a fairly good idea of how a particular wine will age is to taste some so-called library wines, those from previous vintages that are kept by wineries in part so they

themselves know how their wines change with age. Most good wineries either offer library tasting to the public for a fee or will happily oblige if it will likely result in the sale of a case of expensive wine.

In California, virtually no white wines are made to be aged and should be consumed within a couple of years. Some that are more age-worthy tend to be chardonnays from mountain vineyards like those on Mt. Veeder in the Napa Valley, and those in the Santa Cruz Mountains.

It's harder to determine which Californian red wines will age well. In very general terms, good quality red port will happily age for the longest, followed by a decent cabernet sauvignon, syrah, zinfandel, merlot, and finally pinot noir, which is often at its peak after a couple of years.

Price can also offer a hint at a wine's aging potential, though this test sometimes falls foul of overpricing. A $100 bottle of Napa Valley cabernet will probably only be bought by serious collectors, for example, who are unlikely to crack it open that night but will instead cellar it for years to either enjoy themselves or sell for a profit to another collector. Winemakers and wineries often have that sort of buyer in mind when they craft the style of wine.

STORING WINE

Research has shown that most American consumers drink wine very soon after buying it, so storage is not a big issue. Aging wines, even for a few years, however, requires a little care to ensure it does not spoil. A pretty iron wine rack on top of a fridge opposite a sunny kitchen window will be useless for anything but short-term storage.

Wine likes to be dark, still, and kept at a fairly constant temperature somewhere from 50–70°F, conditions found in most basements or even a dark interior closet in many homes. The most ideal storage conditions will also be cool (below 60°F) and damp (over 60 percent relative humidity), though these last two requirements can be tough to achieve without digging your own cave or buying some sort of specially designed storage cellar.

Although excessive heat makes wines age a little too fast to achieve their full potential, a constantly fluctuating temperature is the biggest enemy. As the temperature goes up and down during the day the wine will expand and contract in the bottle, causing the cork to move in the bottle neck and potentially suck in air. That air will oxidize the wine and spoil it.

If a wine is stored in very low humidity the cork might also dry out and expose the wine to air. Keeping the cork moist so it retains a good seal with the neck of the bottle is the main reason for storing wine sideways.

SHIPPING WINE

The 21st Amendment to the U.S. Constitution ended Prohibition in 1933 but still plagues the wine industry today because it allows states to continue to regulate the sale and distribution of all types of alcoholic beverages.

Since repeal, a patchwork of rules and regulations unique to almost every state has evolved. If you plan to buy wine at a Californian winery or on the Internet and have it shipped to your home state you might be out of luck, although an important U.S. Supreme Court decision in May 2005 on interstate shipping laws is likely to eventually reshape the archaic laws right across the country.

Before May 2005, there were 23 states that banned any direct shipping of wine and other alcoholic drinks to consumers from out of state (Alabama, Arkansas, Connecticut, Delaware, Florida, Indiana, Kansas, Kentucky, Maine, Maryland, Massachusetts, Michigan, Mississippi, Montana, New Jersey, New York, Ohio, Oklahoma, Pennsylvania, South Dakota, Tennessee, Utah, and Vermont). Even buying the wine yourself and sending it home in a FedEx box to avoid having to carry it was illegal. Many of those states allow shipments from producers within the state, however, and some allowed wine shipments from out of state as long as it came through designated in-state distributors.

That discrimination between in-state and out-of-state wineries was the basis of the May 2005 Supreme Court decision that struck down such shipping laws in both New York and Michigan. The court ruled that such discrimination against out-of-state businesses was in violation of the Commerce Clause of the U.S. Constitution, which ensures free trade between states. Although the ruling only affected two states, by definition it called into question the laws in the other 22 states that similarly ban out-of-state wine shipments.

Importantly, however, the Supreme Court left the 21st Amendment untouched in its ruling, so many of those states are still free to enact legislation to either ban or put restric-

© PHILIP GOLDSMITH

This truck's days of delivering wine are over.

tions on all distribution of alcoholic beverages, whether from within or outside the state.

They could go the route of the 13 states (Alaska, Arizona, Georgia, Louisiana, Nebraska, Nevada, New Hampshire, North Carolina, North Dakota, Rhode Island, South Carolina, Texas, Virginia, and Wyoming) that, along with the District of Columbia, allow direct shipping but with restrictions. Though all stop short of an outright ban, the restrictions vary state by state and can be complex. Some allow shipment of only limited quantities of wine, others leave the rules up to each individual county within the state, and still others limit shipments from individual wineries. These rules also change regularly. Texas, for example, lifted many restrictions on shipments in May 2005 as a result of an earlier lawsuit.

The remaining 13 states allow wine shipments from out of state but only on a reciprocal basis, meaning that shipments are only allowed from states that in turn allow shipments to be made to them.

Luckily, California wineries are on top of the ever-changing situation and will generally be able to ship wine for personal consumption to the following states: California, Colorado, Hawaii, Iowa, Idaho, Minnesota, Missouri, North Carolina, North Dakota, Nebraska, New Hampshire, New Mexico, Nevada, Oregon, South Carolina, Virginia, Washington, West Virginia, Wisconsin, and Wyoming. Expect at least New York and Michigan to be added to that list, but be sure to ask your favorite winery about the latest laws because everything might well have changed by the time this book is published.

International shipping tends to be prohibitively expensive and involves considerable taxes, though some wineries will oblige. If you plan to take wine overseas yourself, be sure to check the liquor import laws of the countries in question.

WINE CLUBS

Chances are that you will be told about a winery's wine club while at the tasting room bar. Every winery has a wine club of some sort, and many dream up fancy names to make them sound more exclusive (some actually are exclusive and have long waiting lists to join).

Wine clubs are an important marketing tool for wineries, and can be one of the only distribution channels for small, boutique wineries. They can also be a great way for visitors to the Wine Country to get discounts on their favorite wines even if they live hundreds of miles away or when the wines are not widely distributed. Make sure you read the rules carefully, however. The small print sometimes commits new members to more than they anticipate.

When new members sign up to a wine club and hand over a credit card number they often get an on-the-spot discount on wines (this club discount varies, but it's generally 10–30 percent). More importantly for the winery, the new club members have also agreed to buy at least one (sometimes more) wine club shipment in the future before they are able to cancel their membership. Those shipments contain wines that the winery chooses, not the customer, and are subject to often sizable shipping fees that can more than offset the club discount (if you live near the winery you can usually avoid shipping fees by collecting the wine yourself).

Wine club shipments are usually made once every three or four months and there's often a choice of different tiers of membership, offering different styles (red or white) or quantities of wine in each shipment. There are also plenty of other "exclusive" membership privileges, from discounts on gifts to free reserve wine tastings, some more worthwhile than others.

OPPORTUNITIES FOR STUDY

Where better to get some professional wine training than in the heart of Wine Country? It's easy to learn a lot just by visiting wineries and talking to the staff, but to really come to grips with wine it might be worth taking one of the short courses at the Culinary Institute of America just north of St. Helena.

They don't come cheap and last several days but will quickly get your wine knowledge up

Learn about food and wine at the Culinary Institute in Napa.

to professional levels. The best introductory course are **Mastering Wine** (level 1), a five-day crash course in everything wine for $1,000, and **Sensory Analysis,** a two-day course for $450 that focuses only on developing your sensory skills to appreciate wine. For a full catalog of these and other courses, together with schedules, contact the Culinary Institute at 707/967-2568 or browse the Professional Wine Studies Program online at www.ciaprochef.com.

A less formal crash course in wine making and wine appreciation is offered through the popular **Wine Boot Camp** program organized by Affairs of the Vine. The one-day courses ($400) take place at one or more wineries in a different wine region each month, with much of the education provided by winemakers and other experts. Students even get to try their hand at making a wine blend. For more information and a calendar, contact Affairs of the Vine at 707/874-1975 or www.winebootcamp.com.

© PHILIP GOLDSMITH

Getting There

BY AIR

There are four major international airports within a few hours' drive of most parts of Northern California's Wine Country. San Francisco International Airport, Oakland International Airport, and San Jose's Norman Y. Mineta International Airport all serve the cities surrounding the San Francisco Bay Area, and Sacramento International Airport serves its namesake city and parts of California's Central Valley.

The biggest airport by far is **San Francisco International,** known locally as SFO (650/821-8211, www.flysfo.org). It is served by 28 airlines at last count, about two-thirds of which are international carriers. All major domestic U.S. airlines serve SFO (United Airlines has by far the largest number of flights), as do a number of low-cost carriers, including Southwest Airlines, ATA, and JetBlue.

Driving from SFO to Napa or Sonoma takes about 1.5 hours if traffic is good but involves hitting San Francisco city streets for a few miles to reach the Golden Gate Bridge. In rush hour, add at least a half hour to that. Driving to the Santa Cruz region is faster. It takes about a half hour to reach Los Gatos, an hour to Santa Cruz.

The Oakland and San Jose airports get their "International" name tag from just a handful of international flights, and most of the airlines serving them are domestic. Flying into either can often be cheaper than going to SFO, but the drawback is that direct flights from major U.S. cities tend to be less common and connections might be necessary.

Oakland International Airport (510/563-3300, www.flyoakland.com) is just across the bay from San Francisco and is served by four of the big domestic airlines (United, American, Delta, and Continental) as well as major low-cost carriers (JetBlue, Southwest, and America West) and a handful of charter airlines. Driving time from Oakland's airport to Napa and the eastern side of the Santa Cruz Mountains is about an hour. Driving to Healdsburg in northern Sonoma can take more than two hours. This is the closest airport to the Livermore Valley—about a half hour away.

San Jose's **Norman Y. Mineta International Airport** (408/277-4759, www.sjc.org) is served by the six major domestic airlines and low-cost carriers including Southwest and ATA. The airport is about a 45-minute drive south of SFO, putting it very close to destinations in the Santa Cruz Mountains but farther from Napa and Sonoma.

Sacramento International Airport is smaller than the three Bay Area airports and is really only an option for those visiting Napa, about a 1.5-hour drive.

BY RAIL

The days of being able to easily get to much of Wine Country by train are long gone. About 100 years gone to be exact. Railroads that brought Victorian visitors to Sonoma's lush forests and Calistoga's spa resorts were driven out of business by the car, which has since come to dominate transport in the state of California and Wine Country.

Oakland is the only major Bay Area city served by rail service these days (technically Emeryville, right next to Oakland) via Amtrak's California Zephyr service from Chicago and Denver. The service is not for those with limited vacation time, since it takes several days to cross the West, and to get from Emeryville to parts of the Wine Country requires transferring onto Amtrak bus services.

From the Emeryville station (5885 Horton St.) there are connecting bus services to San Francisco and some of the bigger Wine Country towns, including Napa and Healdsburg. There is both an Amtrak bus and train service (from Sacramento on the Capitol Corridor service) to San Jose and a connecting bus service to Santa Cruz.

Times and frequencies of all these services vary depending on the day and season, so contact Amtrak for more information (800/872-7245, www.amtrak.com).

BY BUS

Most major cities in Wine Country can be reached by a combination of long-distance and local bus services (and Amtrak bus service outlined above). Many of the smaller towns and most of the wineries, however, are off the beaten path and can be reached only with your own four wheels (or two), though it's certainly an option to go to Napa, Healdsburg, or Sonoma by bus and rent a bicycle for a couple of days of touring.

Getting to those cities by bus might take a while. The long-distance **Greyhound Lines** buses serve only the major Bay Area cities of San Francisco, Oakland, and San Jose, plus the two Wine Country cities of Santa Cruz and Santa Rosa. For more information about these service and for schedules, contact Greyhound (800/231-2222, www.greyhound.com).

Local bus service from Santa Rosa on the **Sonoma County Transit** bus network connects to Guerneville, Healdsburg, Glen Ellen, and Sonoma. San Francisco is the best place to head for using Greyhound Lines for connections to Napa via the Vallejo ferry and local **Vine** bus service. More information on all these connection possibilities can be found in each destination chapter.

Getting Around

BY CAR

Almost everyone gets around by car in California and it's no different in the Wine Country, where public transportation links are even thinner on the ground than in urban areas. With so many people in cars, congestion is a constant problem.

The San Francisco Bay Area was ranked the second most congested part of the nation in 2005, beaten only by (where else) Los Angeles, and rush hour on the area's freeways has been stretched to two or three hours at each end of the day, even on weekends: 7–10 A.M. and 4–7 P.M., expect slow freeway traffic at almost any major intersection, bottleneck, or bridge.

Up in the Wine Country the roads are smaller but will also often be congested during rush hour and especially on summer weekends when visitors from local cities flock to their favorite wineries.

The worst roads are in the busiest parts of Wine Country—U.S. 17 between Santa Cruz and San Jose, U.S. 12 between Sonoma and Kenwood in the Sonoma Valley, and U.S. 29 between Napa and St. Helena in the Napa Valley. In northern Sonoma, the U.S. 101 freeway

through Santa Rosa tends to get clogged during the rush hours almost every day, though mercifully the roads from the freeway into the Russian River Valley are far quieter, except sometimes the River Road (U.S. 116) through Guerneville, which can be a traffic jam on hot summer weekends or when there's an event in town.

You can help the traffic flow by making sure you know where you're going and driving at the same clip as other drivers. If you're being tailgated by more than one car on a narrow, winding road, pull over at the nearest turnout or turnoff to let the faster traffic pass. And on two-lane roads with a center turn lane, use that lane both for turning left to avoid holding up traffic behind you and also to merge into traffic when turning onto that main road.

Gas in the San Francisco Bay Area is some of the most expensive in the nation due to a combination of higher state and local taxes, higher costs for gas stations, and tight supply of the special, cleaner-burning formulation that is required in the state. The most expensive gas by far is in San Francisco. Some of the cheapest is in the most unlikely places off the beaten track, like Forestville in the Russian River Valley and Kenwood in the Sonoma Valley. Although there's sometimes no rhyme or reason to explain the difference in prices between one gas station and the next, Arco usually offers the cheapest gas and will sometimes be matched by other local gas stations. The prevalence of gas stations generally means you'd be hard pressed to run out of gas anywhere in the Wine Country, though don't set off on a drive over a winding mountain road if the gas warning light is already on.

Much of the Wine Country is within easy reach of a freeway. From San Francisco, Napa and northern Sonoma can be reached by taking U.S. 101 north out of the city and over the Golden Gate Bridge ($5 toll, payable southbound only). About a 20-minute drive north of the bridge is U.S. 37 East, which connects with U.S. 121, which leads to Carneros, the Sonoma Valley, and the Napa Valley. Continue on U.S. 101 to Santa Rosa (about 45 minutes from the bridge) for jumping off points to the Russian River Valley, and drive a further 15 minutes for Healdsburg, the Dry Creek Valley, and Alexander Valley.

Driving from downtown San Francisco to Napa is often quicker via I-80 East, which crosses the Bay Bridge ($3 toll, payable westbound only) then turns north and crosses the Carquinez Bridge about 25 minutes later ($3 toll, payable northbound). Shortly after is the American Canyon Road exit, which leads to the southern end of the Napa Valley.

The Santa Cruz Mountains wine region is best reached via I-280 South from San Francisco rather than the more congested and less scenic U.S. 101.

Rental Cars

All the major car-rental companies are represented at the three main Bay Area airports, and most also have locations in downtown San Francisco, Oakland, San Jose, Santa Cruz, Santa Rosa, and Napa. Prices vary wildly though they tend to be more expensive in California than in other parts of the nation. Deals are always available, and it's worth noting that four-day rentals usually cost the same as weekly ones.

For current prices and availability contact **Alamo** (800/462-5266, www.alamo.com), **Avis** (800/831-2847, www.avis.com), **Budget** (800/527-0700, www.budget.com), **Dollar** (800/800-3665, www.dollar.com), **Enterprise** (800/736-8222, www.enterprise.com), **Hertz** (800/654-3131, www.hertz.com), and **Thrifty** (800/847-4389, www.thrifty.com). You can also get some good deals and make reservations through major online travel agencies, including **Orbitz** (ww.orbitz.com), **Travelocity** (www.travelocity.com), and **Expedia** (www,expedia.com). Check whether there are any discounts from your airline, too.

Always check what your own car-insurance policy, credit cards, or travel insurance will cover before renting a car so you don't buy unnecessary (and often pricey) car, medical, or personal possession insurance at the rental counter. Liability insurance is required by law for all drivers in California, so if you have no car insurance of your own you'll have to buy it from the rental company. Credit cards will generally not cover it.

BY BIKE

Biking is a potentially fun way of seeing parts of the Wine Country but one that few people seem to try, if the lack of bicycles on the roads of Sonoma and Napa is anything to go by. Choose your location well, however, and the rewards of experiencing the warm air and all the unique smells of Wine Country are many. Plan badly and you'll be cursing all day long.

The roads in much of Wine Country can make biking more exciting than you'd like. Small roads tend to be winding and narrow, with the ever-present danger of inattentive (or drunk) drivers failing to see cyclists or give them enough clearance. While accidents seem to be few, close shaves are more common, so be well aware of approaching cars and always cycle in single file as close to the edge of the road as possible.

Make sure you wear a helmet and don't plan on drinking much. Biking drunk is technically illegal, but more importantly it increases your risk of having an accident, whether from being hit by a car or running off the road down a ravine.

Drinking and strenuous exercise is also a recipe for dehydration and heatstroke. Hot summer days might not be the best time to go biking in much of the Wine Country except in the cooler parts of the Russian River Valley and down in Carneros. If you do go in the summer, plan on taking a picnic and whiling away the hottest mid–late afternoon hours somewhere off the bike. Spring and fall are the best times to venture out on two wheels. Winter is out, unless you like wet-weather riding or happen upon one of the occasional warm, dry spells.

Best Bike Tours
Some of the best places to see wineries by bike include the Dry Creek Valley, a relatively flat and compact area crammed with small wineries, many just a few minutes' ride from Healdsburg's bike shop. Healdsburg is also the jumping-off point for rides down the Westside Road into the Russian River Valley and into

the Alexander Valley, though distances are longer and wineries farther apart.

The handful of wineries and historic sites around the city of Sonoma are also perfect for a bike tour. They are close together and only a short ride from Sonoma's main bike-rental shop near the downtown plaza. From Sonoma it is a slightly longer ride down into Carneros, but once you're there the flatlands and wetlands are fun to explore on a bike. Wineries here tend to be farther apart, however, and the weather can be on the cool and murky side, even in summer.

The Napa Valley has some good areas for biking, but the size of the valley and the crowds mean you'll have to plan a route carefully to avoid traffic and long distances. Try sticking to the Calistoga area, for example, or the wineries along the Silverado Trail in the Rutherford appellation, just a few minutes' ride from St. Helena.

The Santa Cruz Mountains are not terribly bike friendly. Steep climbs and long distances between wineries make touring by bike for the most intrepid only. The city of Santa Cruz, however, is a perfect place to ditch the car and hop on a bike to see the city for a day.

Tips for Travelers

CONDUCT
Despite seemingly endless official rules and regulations there's a refreshing anything-goes attitude to life in Northern California. The multicultural population is so used to bizarre behavior by its fellow citizens that people barely bat an eye at characters who might leave outsiders staring in disbelief.

Californians might be tolerant of the stranger members of their society, but they are not necessarily as liberal and laid-back as people would like to believe. This is a hardworking state. People work hard to attain their personal Californian Dream and then work hard to keep it. They work hard to stay in shape and just as hard to enjoy themselves, whether through outdoor recreation or indoor wining and dining. All that hard work has cre-

ated a multitasking population that is ironically under so much stress that it even works hard to try to unwind.

Wine Country is generally a wealthy enclave in a wealthy part of California, a place where money talks and lifestyle is everything. Like the rest of California, it's also a place of sharp economic contrasts. Migrant workers in the vineyards harvesting grapes are at one end of the economic scale, corporate winery executives are at the other. As is the norm in California, each group seems to happily tolerate the other.

Dress
California virtually invented business casual attire, and it's rare to see a shirt and tie, especially in Wine Country. About the only places that require you to pay attention to

what you wear are golf courses (collared shirt and appropriate shoes) and a handful of top restaurants (smart casual for women, jacket and tie for men).

Otherwise you can get by wearing just about anything, though you'll have to wear something because public nudity is illegal (though on some beaches officials usually turn blind eye), and establishments of all kinds will generally not serve the shoeless or shirtless.

Smoking

Smokers will find California's environment far from tolerant. Smoking is banned in all bars and restaurants in the state and is usually not allowed in or near public buildings either. That includes many hotels and inns, which either have a property-wide no-smoking policy or will only allow smoking in outdoor areas.

Despite the rather stringent ban there are a few bars where you might see people light up, probably because the bar owner tacitly approves (and risks a fine). In such cases offended nonsmokers would do well to keep quiet because any outsiders complaining may quickly find the wrath of the bar's local patrons bearing down on them.

Tipping

As is the case in the rest of the nation, tipping is a voluntary but necessary practice in restaurants, bars, taxis, and for services given by valets or hotel concierges. A 15 percent tip is average, though more is normal in this land where money talks. Most restaurants will automatically add a standard 18 percent gratuity to the bill for parties of over six or eight people. If that's the case you have no obligation to add any further tip when signing the credit card slip, even though there will still be a spot for one.

Tipping is definitely not necessary in winery tasting rooms. In fact you risk offending the generally well-paid staff if you do try to slip them a fiver, however helpful they have been. If you feel a strong urge to return a favor, simply buy a bottle or two of wine.

ACCESS FOR DISABLED TRAVELERS

California is one of the most progressive states in the county when it comes to access for people with disabilities, and its state laws often go beyond the requirements of the federal Americans with Disabilities Act, which requires that all new public buildings must be handicapped-accessible and older ones must be retrofitted if "readily achievable."

Major wineries that are open to the public without an appointment, together with museums and other sights, all generally have wheelchair access ramps and restrooms for the disabled. Appointment-only wineries often stay appointment-only partly because of the prohibitive cost of meeting the various building and safety codes required for commercial public buildings, including access for the disabled. Small B&Bs and inns often do not have to comply with the strict laws because their historic buildings cannot easily be made handicapped-accessible.

The Wine Country is ostensibly a rural area, so access for the disabled is always going to be far from universal. One organization that can help the those with disabilities plan visits within Northern California and the Wine Country is **Access Northern California** (1427 Grant St., Berkeley, 510/524-2026, www.accessnca.com). It has specific information on accommodations and sights with access for the disabled. Also contact local chambers of commerce or visitor centers for more specific information.

TRAVELING WITH CHILDREN

Most, but not all, of the activities in the Wine Country are geared toward adults. Wineries generally allow children onto the premises, but anyone under 21, California's legal minimum drinking age, cannot taste any wines. And wineries without wine tasting tend to be pretty boring places, especially for kids.

If there are children in tow, careful planning can avoid tears of boredom and frustration. Some wineries offer educational tours that can be fun for kids and adults alike. Others have other attractions, ranging from art to historic cars, though in all cases double-check that children are welcome.

Plenty of sights and museums have something to offer inquisitive young brains. Copia in Napa, for example, has a whole set of educational and interactive exhibits geared towards kids. The Petrified Forest or Old Faithful geyser near Calistoga will delight and amaze children (though not necessarily adults), as will an adult-supervised ride in a canoe on the Russian River or a ride on one of the narrow-gauge railroads at either Train Town in Sonoma or through the redwoods at Roaring Camp in the Santa Cruz Mountains.

For emergency entertainment for thoroughly bored kids, drive down to the Santa Cruz Boardwalk and plant them in the seat of a roller coaster. If that doesn't get them excited, nothing will.

Also worth noting is that a lot of higher-priced B&Bs and resorts do not allow children under a certain age, and some do not allow children at all. The reasons vary—in some cases the policy is to protect precious antiques, in other cases simply to ensure that the peace and tranquillity guests are paying top dollar for is not shattered by screaming kids. Always check the policy on young guests when booking a room.

TRAVELING WITH PETS

Wine Country might not be terribly kid-friendly, but it is most definitely not dog-friendly. Dogs are actively discouraged or banned in many wineries, even those that have their own resident winery pooch. They are also not allowed in rooms of many lodgings, though a few hotels and motels will accepts pets for an additional nightly fee. On many hiking trails, dogs are either not allowed at all or must be on a leash at all times.

Worse still (from the dog's point of view), the hot summer weather makes cars thoroughly uncomfortable places to be even for short periods of time. Dogs should never be left for long periods in a car in the California sun, even with the windows slightly cracked.

MAPS

Beware the cartoonish maps in many of the free magazines that blanket the Wine Country. Many of them are highly inaccurate for anything other than determining the approximate location of wineries and other major sights. Even for that purpose they can sometimes be unreliable, putting wineries on the wrong side of the road, for example, or giving little idea of distances involved. As road maps they should certainly not be relied on. Many small roads are missing from them, and other roads turn out to be dead ends or are misnamed.

The most reliable road maps for planning a trip covering Wine Country are published by the veteran map companies. Most of these maps don't have wineries or other sights marked on them but are good for general navigation, especially when used in conjunction with this book or the winery maps published by local wine associations in each region (listed at the end of each chapter).

The **American Automobile Association** (AAA) publishes a specific *Sonoma and Napa Wine Country* map as well as more detailed road maps for Napa, Sonoma, and the greater San Francisco Bay Area. They are available from your local AAA office and are free for members. Check www.aaa.com for your local office and to order maps online.

Rand McNally publishes several excellent road maps covering the Wine Country, including *North Bay and Wine Country* and *South Bay and Peninsula Cities,* as well as another map for the greater Bay Area that includes some but not all of the major wine regions. Rand McNally maps are usually available at bookstores and can also be ordered online at www.randmcnally.com.

Health and Safety

DRINKING AND DRIVING

Driving (and even biking) under the influence of alcohol is a serious offense in California. Both state and local police are well aware that visitors to Wine Country might have overindulged, and they will often be on the lookout for erratic driving in popular wine-tasting areas on busy weekends.

The blood alcohol limit for driving in the state is 0.08 percent, a level you can reach very quickly in a tasting room. Most wineries will pour about one ounce of wine per taste (some might be stingier, but use one ounce as a guideline), which means that by visiting one winery and tasting (and swallowing) four wines you will already be well on the way to that limit.

People weighing less than 150 pounds who taste another flight of four wines at another winery in a two-hour period will likely be at their legal limit already. Those over 150 pounds will have a little more leeway, but not much.

The penalties for a DUI conviction are severe, including a fine ranging $200–7,000 and time in jail, not to mention the potential loss of your driving license and a big jump in insurance premiums if you are able to get it back. If you are a driver involved in an accident that causes bodily harm while your blood alcohol over the legal limit the penalties are even stiffer.

Trying to calculate how much can be drunk before reaching the limit is a notoriously inexact science. It depends not only on how much alcohol is consumed but also the person's weight, gender, metabolism, and how much food he or she has eaten over the previous few hours. Drinking a lot of water while tasting might ward off headaches but will do little to lower the blood alcohol level.

The only way to guarantee you are safe to drive is to drink no wine at all. Instead, use a designated driver or, if that's not an option, learn to spit wine out after smelling the aromas and swirling it around your mouth. If you really want to experience the lingering aftertaste of a $100 cabernet, then swallow just one wine out of all those you taste. There are usually plenty of spitting containers on tasting room counters. Just double-check that it's not the water jug you're about to empty your wine into.

OUTDOORS

The Wine Country might be all about luxury pampering, but the wilds here are also a major draw for visitors and can be just as wild as anywhere else in California. Experiencing the Wine Country is as much about experiencing the great outdoors as the wine but there are some basic outdoor rules to be aware of, particularly if you've had some wine. Even a few tastes of wine can be enough to potentially impair your usually good outdoor judgment.

On the hiking or mountain-biking trail, make sure you know where you're going, and never go alone in case you get into trouble. Also be aware that many of the trails in Wine Country might start off in cool, damp woods but will often climb up to scrubland with little shade and often searing heat in the summer. Sunscreen, sunglasses, and a hat are mandatory in California during the summer, far less important during the winter. Luckily, most large wineries sell baseball caps should your bare head be overheating.

On the water, whether the Russian River or the many lakes, take the usual water-safety precautions. Don't jump in unless you know what's under the water, especially in the Russian River where all sorts of treelike debris washed downstream during the winter and spring might lurk just below the surface of the often-murky water. Always wear a lifejacket when in a boat, and avoid doing anything on or in the water when you've had too much to drink.

Lyme Disease

Potentially the most dangerous animal for outdoor hikers in many parts of California, particularly parts of the Wine Country, is also one of the smallest. The diminutive deer tick, which thrives in most lowland hills and meadows, can transmit Lyme disease, one of the most common vector-transmitted diseases in the United States.

The good news is that Lyme disease is easily treated with antibiotics if caught early. The bad news is that it can be difficult to detect early, with many of the early symptoms (including fever, aches and pains, headaches, and fatigue) often mistaken for other ailments. If left untreated, Lyme disease can develop into a serious degenerative illness, and the longer it goes untreated the harder it is to cure with antibiotics.

The best protection is to wear long pants and sleeves to avoid picking the ticks up in the first place. Plenty of insect repellent also helps. If you are bitten by a tick and it is still attached, do not try to pull it off with your fingers because the head will likely stay embedded. Remove ticks with tweezers by grasping the tick's head parts as close to your skin as possible and applying slow steady traction. Do not attempt to get ticks out of your skin by burning them or coating them with nail polish remover or petroleum jelly.

Always check for ticks after being outdoors in woodland or grassy meadows and watch for the telltale circular rash that usually appears around tick bites from three days to a month after being bitten. Also be aware that any flu-like symptoms might be a sign of Lyme disease. If in any doubt, see a doctor.

Wildlife

Much of California's other wildlife is not a great danger for visitors to the Wine Country. Mountain lions, also known as pumas or cougars, do live in many of the hills and forests around urban areas, especially those where deer (their favorite prey) are common, but they are rarely seen and usually stay well away from humans, especially big groups of noisy humans (one reason to never hike alone).

Attacks by mountain lions are extremely rare. In fact you're more likely to get struck by lightning. Sightings are more common, though still relatively rare. If you do happen across a lion on a hiking trail and it doesn't instinctively run the other way try to make yourself look as large as possible to scare it, then slowly back away. Mountain lions are big cats—males can weight up to 150 pounds and grow up to eight feet long from head to tip of the tail—but they'd rather not pick a fight with something their own size. In the rare instance a lion does attack, fight it with whatever comes to hand, like rocks and sticks. It's a strategy that has saved plenty of victims.

One thing you should not do is turn and run—mountain lions can run faster. Dogs should be kept on a leash (it's the law in most wilderness areas) to avoid agitating mountain lions, and also for the well-being of the dog, which would be easy prey. If you see a big cat in the brush next to the trail do not try to approach it. Remember that you are trespassing on their territory, so if you let them get on with their lives you'll likely be left alone.

Another animal that can do some damage to humans but is rarely seen is the western diamondback rattlesnake, the most common of the eight varieties of rattler found in California. The snakes are brown with a triangular head and a dark diamond pattern running down their backs. They also have that distinctive rattle that should be a warning to walk the other way if you hear it.

Rattlesnakes live throughout the Wine Country, preferring hot rocky or grassy areas. When tromping through such areas always be aware of where you're stepping, and if climbing on rocky ledges make sure you can see where you're putting your hands. If you are bitten, the venom is rarely fatal but can lead to a few days of discomfort and requires a visit to the local hospital.

Snakes will usually head other way when they hear anyone approaching, but if you do see one and it refuses to budge, back off and give it a wide berth. Also be especially alert for rattlers in the spring when the snakes are just emerging from hibernation and tend to be groggy, hungry, and mean.

Poison Oak

Poison oak is a deciduous shrub, usually 2–6 feet tall, with glossy leaves resembling those of a real oak tree. The leaves are arranged in clusters of three and are tinged a rusty red color in the late summer and fall. Those leaves and stems contain an oil, similar to that in poison ivy, called urushiol, which causes an allergic skin reaction in an estimated three-quarters of the population, even after only brief exposure.

Even in the winter the bare stems remain just as dangerous to passing skin, and burning even a small amount of poison oak on a campfire generates dangerous smoke that, if inhaled, can lead to a potentially fatal inflammation of the lungs.

The plant is common all over California, particularly in lowland woods and meadows, and you will almost certainly encounter it alongside hiking trails. It is particularly abundant after wet winters. Learn to identify it and avoid it if at all possible.

Wear long pants and sleeves and wash both clothes and skin as soon as possible if you even *think* you have been in contact with poison oak. Rashes can take a few days to appear, but once they do you're stuck with them and they'll likely grow. The oil from hiking boots and clothes can also rub off on skin and cause a rash, so wash these too if you think they have been contaminated.

If you do get a rash, do not scratch it and make sure it is covered because the oozing sores can spread the toxins to other parts of the body. Mild rashes will usually go away in a few days. The more badly afflicted could be driven mad for many weeks by a growing rash, and some might require treatment with anti-inflammatory steroids, though the application of readily available hydrocortisone cream is the usual treatment.

Some specialized cleansing products that will neutralize the toxic oils are worth using if you're highly allergic. They are sold under the Tecnu brand name and are available at most pharmacies.

Dehydration and Heatstroke

Dehydration is a perennial enemy for about half the year in much of the Wine Country, whether from tasting too much wine or from any sort of exertion in the heat. Most of Northern California is warm from May to November and can get downright hot from July to September, especially in the inland valleys.

Parts of the Russian River Valley, Carneros, and coastal regions will often be cooler because of fog and cool ocean breezes, but even these areas can heat up quickly in the summer when the sun comes out or the breezes die. The other half of the year from November to May is the rainy season, though even in November, April, and May there can be some very warm spells of weather.

Drink plenty of water, especially if hiking but even when frolicking on or in the water on a hot day. For serious hiking in hot weather at least a half quart of water per hour is recommended (in small doses, not all at once). Wear a hat to help prevent both sunburn and heatstroke, a potentially fatal condition created when the body overheats, causing symptoms including headache, confusion, and muscle cramps.

The water you do drink should always come from a bottle or a tap. Most of California's rivers and lakes contain parasites and bacteria that play havoc with digestive systems. If camping at a primitive site near water, consider taking a water filter so you don't have to carry all your water in with you.

Glossary

acetic: All wines contain a minuscule amount of acetic acid (vinegar), but bad wine will have enough (over about 0.1 percent) to actually start smelling of vinegar. Not a good thing.

acid/acidity: The natural acids (citric, malic, tartaric, and lactic) in a wine create a tartness that is supposed to act as a counterpoint to sugary sweetness, balancing the wine.

aftertaste: The flavors that linger on your palate after swallowing the wine. The longer the aftertaste the better—sometimes you can still taste wines almost a minute after swallowing.

aging: The process of storing a wine in barrels or bottles for a few months to many decades so it develops character and more desirable flavors. White wines tend to turn from a greenish hue in young wines to a yellowish caste/tone to a gold/amber color as they age. Reds usually have a purple tone when young, turning to a deep red (bordeaux wines and cabernet, for example) or a brick red color (burgundy wines and pinot noir, for example), detectable at the surface edge in a wineglass as they age.

alcohol: The colorless and flavorless chemical created as a byproduct of fermentation that gets you drunk but also acts as a preservative for the wine. The higher the sugar content of the grape when picked, the higher the alcohol content of the wine. Californian red wines tend to have alcohol content of over 13 percent, sometimes as high as 16 percent in the case of some zinfandels.

angular: Describes a tart wine with a sharp edge to its taste. The opposite of round, soft, or supple wine.

appellation or AVA: The specific area a wine comes from. Technically, appellation is a French term and in California the correct

terminology is American Viticultural Area or AVA. To be classified as an AVA by the federal Bureau of Alcohol, Tobacco, and Firearms (BATF), an area must have unique soil, climate, or other growing conditions that will distinguish its wines from those grown in other areas. When an AVA, such as Napa Valley or Carneros, is named on the label, at least 85 percent of the grapes must have come from there (100 percent in Washington and Oregon). There can also be AVAs within AVAs. The Napa Valley, for example is a single AVA that contains 13 other AVAs, also called subappellations.

approachable: An approachable wine is easy to enjoy and generally made to be drunk without aging.

aroma: The initial scent of a wine that comes from the fruit or smells like fruit. As wine ages, some of the fruit-related smells dwindle and are replaced by more complex fermentation-related smells, referred to as the bouquet.

aromatic: Describes wines that have a strong flowery or spicy character.

astringent: The rough, puckery taste that most people describe as sour and that often comes from a high tannin content. Astringent wines normally mellow with age.

austere: Slightly hard and acidic wines that seem to lack depth of flavor. Such wines may soften a bit with age and develop more subtle complexity than fuller wines. Austere wines are often from cool growing regions, especially mountain areas.

Bacchus: The Roman god of wine and a name sometimes seen in jokey marketing material.

balance: A balanced wine is what winemakers strive to make, one in which no flavor or aroma overpowers another. Acid balances the sweetness, fruit against oak and tannin. You'll know a balanced wine when you taste one.

barrel: A wooden vessel used to store wine before it is bottled, made of oak and charred (toasted) on the inside to impart specific flavors and color to the wine. On any winery tour you'll likely pass racks of oak barrels (sometimes called *barriques*) that are usually the standard size of 59 gallons or about 225 liters. American oak barrels cost more than $200 new. Highly prized French oak barrels cost more than $500 each. Barrels are usually used and reused for several vintages, then end up as planters or are discarded.

barrel fermenting: The fermentation of wine in barrels to impart specific flavors and texture. It often gives a richer flavor to white wines, though is sometimes overused and will make a wine "over oaked." In red wines, barrel fermenting will impart more tannins to the wine so it can age for longer. The increasingly common alternative is to age wines in stainless steel or concrete vats.

big: Wine with a big, robust, and full-bodied character, usually because of high alcohol content. Dry Creek Valley zinfandel is an example of a big wine.

bitter: One of the four basic tastes that your taste buds can detect. Some wines are supposed to have slight bitterness, but too much is a bad thing. It comes from unripe grapes or from too many stems being crushed with the grapes (that's why many wineries destem grapes first).

blanc de blancs: Sparkling wine or champagne made purely from white grapes like chardonnay. Other sparklers might contain the juice from the red pinot noir grape and are called blanc de noirs.

blending: The mixing of different types of wine (cabernet, merlot, or syrah, for example) or of wines made from the same grape but from different vineyards. Blending different wines is part of the winemaker's art and is done to create a wine of particular character, much like different shades of paint are blended to create the desired tone.

body: How heavy the wine feels in your mouth, a perception created by the alcohol, glycerin, and sugar content of a wine. An Alexander Valley cabernet sauvignon is a full-bodied wine, while a Santa Cruz chardonnay is lighter bodied.

bordeaux blend: A wine (usually red) made from a blend of some or all of the main grape varietals used to make wine in the French region of Bordeaux—cabernet sauvignon, merlot, cabernet franc, malbec, petit verdot, and carmenère in the case of red wine; sauvignon blanc, semillon, and muscadelle in the case of white. See also *meritage.*

botrytis: A gray fungus (also known at noble rot) that attacks grapes in humid conditions, shriveling them up like raisins and concentrating the sugar and acid content. Wines made from affected grapes are sweet and complex, often sold as dessert wines.

bouquet: Often confused with the aroma, the bouquet refers specifically to the scent in a wine that comes from the aging process in either the barrel or bottle, rather than from the fruit.

brawny: Term used mainly to describe young red wines (especially in California) with high alcohol and tannin levels.

briary: An aggressive, prickly taste in young wines, sometimes described as "peppery."

brix: A measure of the sugar content in a grape, used to determine when grapes should be harvested. The final alcohol content of a wine is often related to the brix reading of the grapes when harvested.

brut: Refers to a dry (but not the driest) champagne or sparkling wine with less than 1.5 percent residual sugar.

burgundy: A catch-all term to describe red and white wine from the Burgundy region in France. Real red burgundies are usually pinot noir. Cheap Californian burgundies are usually misusing the term for totally unrelated wine.

buttery: An obvious taste often found in good white wines, particularly Californian chardonnay.

cava: A sparkling wine from Spain made in a similar style to champagne but using different grapes.

Champagne: A region in northern France best known for production of sparkling wine by a very specific method, known as the méthode champenoise, using chardonnay, pinot noir, and pinot meunier.

chaptalization: The addition of sugar to wine before or during fermentation to increase the final alcohol content. It is legal in France, where cooler weather often means grapes do not have enough sugar when harvested, but not legal (and not necessary) in California.

charmat method: The process of making cheaper sparkling wines (like those costing $5 at supermarkets) by carrying out the secondary fermentation (the one that creates the bubbles) in large steel vats under pressure rather than in the bottle like the more expensive méthode champenoise used to make fine champagnes.

chewy: Usually used to describe powerful tannins in red wines like zinfandel that give it an almost viscous mouthfeel, making you almost want to chew it before swallowing.

citrus: An aroma and flavor reminiscent of citrus fruits, especially grapefruit, in many white wines, particularly those from cooler growing regions like Carneros and the Russian River Valley.

claret: An old English term used to describe red wines from Bordeaux. In France "clairet" is a particular bordeaux that is produced like red wine but the wine must stay in contact with the skins for the first 24 hours during its making.

clone: A genetic variation of a grapevine. In a wine and vineyard context, usually the specific genetic type of vine picked to match the local growing conditions or the desired style of wine.

cloudy: Used to describe a wine that is a little hazy when viewed through the glass rather than crystal clear. Except in some rare occasions, a cloudy wine is not a good thing and might have an unpleasant smell, too.

complex: The ultimate flattery for winemakers is to call their wines complex. Everything from the aroma to the long aftertaste is in balance and harmony.

cooked: Leave wine in a hot car for a day, open it, and it will probably taste odd. It's been cooked (see *maderized*).

cooperage: All the containers a winery uses to store and age wine, including barrels, vats, and tanks.

corked: The most common fault of restaurant wine, it is the brief taste or smell of wet cardboard in a wine that is caused by bacteria in a contaminated cork interacting with chemicals in the wine. It can often be very subtle, so many people might not realize a wine is corked, and it is harmless to drink.

creamy: The silky taste and texture of a white wine that has undergone malolactic fermentation. Often accompanied by the faintest smell of creamy foods like crème brûlée.

crisp: A definite but not undesirable tartness and acidity usually used to describe white wines and often accompanied by the aroma of citrus fruits. White wines from cool climates like Carneros are often crisp.

crush: Literally the crushing of the grape skins to release the juice and start the fermentation process. Crush is the term also used to describe the process of harvesting and transporting the grapes of a particular year prior to making the wine.

cuvée: A French term to describe the blend of wines from different grapes and different years that is used to make champagne and sparkling wines.

decanting: The slow and careful pouring of aged red wine into a broad, shallow glass container to ensure the sediment from aging stays in the bottle and to then allow the wine to breathe, or start to release its aromas, before drinking.

demi-sec: A slightly sweet sparkling wine or champagne containing 3.5–5 percent residual sugar.

dessert wine: A sweet red or white wine usually drunk in small amounts with dessert. The sweetness of desserts would mask the much smaller amount of sugar in a normal wine and make it taste bitter or acidic. Sweet dessert wines are often made from "late harvest" grapes, picked when they are riper and their sugar content is higher. The botrytis fungus can also be used to make these sweeter wines.

dry: Describes a red or white wine that has been fermented until less than 0.2 percent of the natural sugars remain. Although a dry wine will not taste sweet, it might still taste fruity.

dumb: My favorite wine term—it means literally a wine with nothing to say. Flavors and aroma might have been muted by over-chilling a white wine or simply because a red wine is at a certain stage of aging when it is in between youthfulness and adulthood (often when about 5–6 years old).

earthy: Fine pinot noir is always earthy, possessing an aroma and/or flavor that could have come straight from the ground. Think of what a handful of damp soil smells like and that's the earthiness. Different soil smells a different way, and the pros can often detect the type of soil or region a wine comes from simply by recognizing the smell of that earth. Or so they say. A lot of wines have the potential to be earthy, but other aromas and flavors often mask the distinctive smell.

elegant: How to praise a well-balanced and graceful wine. The opposite would be rustic.

enology: The science and study of wine making, often spelled oenology outside the United States. An *enophile* is someone who loves wine.

estate bottled: Refers to wine made from vineyards that are both owned by the winery and in the same appellation or AVA as the winery. In addition, the entire wine-making process from fermentation to bottling has to occur at that winery. Non-estate wines are made from grapes bought from other growers or grown in another appellation.

fat: Describes the texture of a full-bodied wine with lots of fruit. A full-bodied wine without enough acidity to balance the fruit is often called flabby.

fermentation: The process that turns grape juice into wine. A biochemical process in yeast cells converts the sugar in grape juice into alcohol and carbon dioxide. Usually that gas is allowed to simply escape, but in the secondary fermentation process used to make sparkling wines it is retained in the wine under pressure and released as the bubbles when a bottle is opened.

filtering: The easy way to remove particles from a wine to ensure it is clear before being bottled. Pumping wine through filters can, however, damage the flavor of a wine. Fining is a more laborious but better way to clarify wine.

fining: The process of adding a natural, non-reactive substance like gelatin or crushed eggshell to a tank of wine to slowly remove suspended particles as it falls to the bottom. It takes longer than simple filtering.

finish: Also sometimes called the aftertaste, this is the lingering impression of the wine on your palate after swallowing. It might be long or short (or absent), acidic or sweet. Generally, a longer finish denotes a better wine.

firm: A wine that has some acidic astringency, much like firm, unripe fruit. Like unripe fruit, a firm wine is usually young and will ripen with age, mellowing its acidity. But sometimes it won't.

flat: Wines with too little acidity are said to be flat and uninteresting.

flowery: A white wine that has an aroma reminiscent of flowers.

forward: A forward wine is one that has all its best aromas and flavors right up front and screams "drink me now." You'll usually hear the term "fruit forward" used to describe cheap red wines in which the fruity flavors overpower all others (if there are even others present).

fruity: A generic term used to describe whatever aroma and flavor comes from the grape itself. Strangely enough, wine does not usually smell of the one fruit used to make it but of everything from grapefruit to honeydew melon depending on the type of grape and how the wine was made. Fruity wines are not necessarily sweet wines.

funky: Believe it or not, this is a real wine-tasting term used to describe an certain unidentifiable yeasty aroma that some wines have. You'll have to be a professional wine critic to recognize the smell. Most people simply call any unidentifiable smell or taste "funky." Just don't do it in front of a winemaker.

grassy: Sauvignon blanc is often described as grassy. Imagine the smell of freshly cut grass. Too much grassiness is not a good trait.

green: Another term often applied to sauvignon blanc. It describes the slightly leafy taste of a wine made with underripe fruit.

hollow: When there's really nothing between the first, initial taste of a wine and the aftertaste. Something's missing in the middle for any number of reasons.

horizontal tasting: No, not drinking wine while lying down but tasting the same type of wine from the same year but from different wineries. It's fun to line up a horizontal tasting of, say, cabernets from different Napa Valley appellations to learn how different growing conditions affect wine.

hot: You'll know a hot wine when the back of your throat burns after swallowing as though you just downed a shot of vodka. It's caused by too much alcohol in the wine and not enough of everything else. This is a normal character of fortified wines like port and sherry but a no-no in regular wines like cabernet sauvignon. Cheap, high-alcohol zinfandels are often hot.

jammy: Word most often used to describe Californian zinfandel. Imagine the taste of a spoonful of blackberry jam.

late harvest: Picking grapes as late as possible so their sugar content is as high as possible to make a sweeter wine, usually a dessert wine.

lean: More body would be good, sort of thin in the mouth, often too much astringency, sometimes a compliment for certain styles.

lees: The leftover yeast and other crud that falls to the bottom of barrels or fermentation tanks or is removed by fining. It is also sometimes called mud. Makers of white and sparkling wines sometimes leave it in the bottle so it can impart a yeasty, toasty flavor and smell to aged wines. That technique is called fermenting wine *sur lies.*

legs: Spot the novice wine taster cracking jokes about "great legs." Swirl wine around the glass, then stop and watch clear rivulets cling to the side of the glass. They are the legs, and how fat or long they are actually has nothing to do with the quality of the wine. Instead they have everything to do with how much alcohol and glycerin there is in the wine, what the temperature is, and even how clean the glass is.

length: Pretty much the same as finish, namely how long the flavors and aromas of a wine last on the back of your throat after swallowing. The longer the better.

maderized: What might happen to your wine if you leave it in a hot car for too long. It is a distinctive brown color and smell caused by exposure of wine to excessive heat and oxygen. Also sometimes called oxidized. Even if you haven't smelled the Portuguese fortified wine madeira, you'll know when a wine has maderized. It doesn't smell like wine anymore.

malolactic fermentation: A secondary chemical process (not technical fermentation at all) that nearly all red wines undergo and white wines are sometimes put through to give them a smoother, less acidic flavor (often described as creamy or buttery). It converts the harsh-tasting malic acid that naturally occurs in wine into the softer lactic acid plus carbon dioxide. Wineries often use the process to make a more popular style of easy-drinking chardonnay, though sometimes they overdo it and create a wine that lacks any sort of acidity at all and is just flat.

meritage: Californian wines have to contain at least 75 percent of one grape varietal to be labeled as such, but some of the best red wines are blends of some of the five varietals used in bordeaux wine with no grape in the majority. Californian winemakers, not wanting to use the term bordeaux blend, instead came up with a new term to describe blended red wines: meritage. It remains an uncommon term, however, and most wineries instead come up with their own proprietary names for their blends.

mouthfeel: How a wine feels rather than tastes in your mouth. Use any description you want. Ones I use too much include velvety and soft.

musty: A flaw that makes a wine smell like your grandmother's dank old attic. It is caused by mold getting into the wine sometime during the wine-making or bottling process.

nonvintage: Most wines are made with grapes harvested in a single year (vintage). Nonvintage wines are made by blending wines made in different years and have no year on their label. Some cheap red wines are nonvintage and made by using up surplus wine from different years. The best champagnes are also nonvintage so the winemakers can make sure the wine is of consistent high quality every year.

nose: The most important tool for wine tasting but in most cases used to describe the overall smell of a wine, a combination of the aroma and bouquet.

oaky: The taste or smell of freshly sawn oak, toast, or vanilla that comes from aging wine in oak barrels that have usually been charred, or toasted, on the inside. A hint of oakiness in red wines is considered a good thing and is a matter of taste in white wines. Oak aromas and flavors should never overpower the fruit in a wine, as they do in some "over-oaked" chardonnays. There's an entire vocabulary used to describe oak smells and tastes, all of which depend on factors ranging from where the oak tree was grown to the size of the wood's grain.

open-up/opening-up: Some bottled cellar-aged red wines possess the peculiarity that, when the cork is first pulled and the wine poured, the full flavors do not immediately make an appearance. However, after the passage of several minutes in an open glass goblet, the wine develops unsuspected flavor characteristics that can verge on the sublime. This phenomenon is referred to as "opening-up". Conversely, these flavors can disappear just as fast in just 30 minutes, leaving a subsequent impression of a flat, stale, "over-the-hill" and/or mediocre wine.

overripe: A grape precondition necessary for making certain styles of Californian zinfandel wines. Left on the vine to dry in the sun, certain grape varietals will develop the desirable "raisiny" character and concentrated sugar necessary for making specialty wines such as the Hungarian tokay.

oxidized: As soon as a bottle of wine is opened it is exposed to the oxygen in the air and starts to oxidize, usually a good thing for an hour or two. If it has been exposed to air for too long, however, either due to a leaky cork during storage or from being left open on a kitchen counter for a week, it will start to smell like cheap sherry and turn brown. At that point it is oxidized. With excessive heat as well it will become maderized.

peppery: A term that usually goes hand-in-hand with spicy to describe the slightly pun-gent quality of wines like gewürztraminer and some styles of syrah.

phylloxera: A small aphid-like insect that attacks the roots of vines and slowly kills them by preventing the plant from absorbing water and nutrients. It wiped out many vineyards in Europe in the late 1800s but is actually native to the United States, where it has periodically ravaged California vines, particularly in the early 1900s. Most vines are now grafted onto resistant rootstock, though some are not and limited outbreaks still periodically occur.

Pierce's disease: A virus that infects grapevines and kills them in 1–5 years. It is spread by a leafhopper-type insect called the glassy winged sharpshooter. Though the disease is not yet endemic in Northern California's vineyards, authorities are worried it could soon be and have imposed strict plant quarantine laws to prevent its spread.

plump: Almost a fat wine but not quite.

pomace: The mashed-up residue of skin, seeds, stems, and pulp left after grapes are pressed to release the juice. In California it's often used as fertilizer. In Italy they distill it to make grappa.

racking: A traditional method of wine clarification that involves transferring wine from one barrel to another to leave sediment and other deposits behind.

reserve wine: The term "reserve wine" actually means nothing in California thanks to the total lack of official definition. In general, a reserve wine is made from the best grapes (they are reserved specially) and often aged for longer to create a higher quality wine than a winery's normal offerings. In practice the term is often as much about marketing as good wine. Some wineries give their best of the best wines other labels like "special selection."

residual sugar: The percentage, by weight or volume, of the unfermented grape sugar that remains in wine when it is bottled. The driest wines have less than 0.5 percent residual sugar, though many have slightly more to give them a fuller flavor.

rootstock: The roots of a grapevine, which often come from a different species than the leaves. Many vines are a combination of two different plants. The stems and leaves might come from one, and they are grafted, or grown onto, roots from another chosen either for its suitability for certain growing conditions or resistance to disease.

rough: If a wine feels like it's taking the lining off your throat with its tannins, it's described as rough. Some rough wines smooth and mellow with age.

Rutherford dust: A slightly mineral flavor said to be present in some of the classic cabernets grown in the Rutherford appellation of Napa Valley.

sediment: The small quantity of particulate matter often found at the bottom of well-aged red wines generated during the aging process. Sediment includes a lot of the phenols that give wine its color, so as a wine gets really old the color literally starts dropping out of it. Sediment is harmless but best left in the bottle for presentation's sake.

soft: A wine that has low acid or tannin content that has little impact on your taste buds.

sommelier: The person responsible for the wine cellar, wine service, and wine list in a restaurant. If you have no clue which wine to order, ask to speak to the sommelier and he or she can usually help.

sour: Almost a synonym for acidic. Implies presence of acetic acid plus excess acid component. (It is also one of the four basic taste sensations detected by the human tongue.)

spicy: Almost a synonym for peppery, but it implies a more nuanced flavor suggesting delicate Indian spices rather than those that get up your nose.

supple: A red wine with a mouthfeel that lies somewhere between lean and fat. Usually an easy drinker.

tannin: The reason many people don't like red wines. Tannin is a naturally occurring chemical (a phenol) in grape skins, seeds, and stems, and the wood of barrels. It gives red wines their "backbone," helps preserve them, and has an astringent taste. Young wines, particularly those meant for aging, can be highly tannic but will mellow and soften with age. Other overly tannic wines taste rough or harsh and might never mellow. White wines generally contain very little tannin.

tartaric acid: If you ever see what looks like small shards of glass in a bottle of white wine they are probably crystals of tartaric acid, a harmless acid that is in all white wines and can crystallize under certain conditions.

terroir: A French term for all the environmental characteristics of a vineyard, including every conceivable nuance of the soils, climate, and geography. The *terroir* is said to give the grapes grown there a unique flavor profile, and the best wine experts in the world can identify (allegedly) the exact vineyard that the grapes in a wine came from.

tobacco: A common description of a flavor often found in cabernet sauvignon that refers to the smell of fresh tobacco leaves. Cigar box is a common term often used in its place. Like all those flavor descriptions, it's easier to identify if you have actually experienced the smell firsthand by smelling and smoking a cigar.

ullage: The small gap between the wine in the bottle and the cork. It should be almost nonexistent and is formed by the evaporation of wine through the cork or cork leakage. If the ullage gets too big it will contain enough oxygen to start oxidizing the wine.

vanilla: A desirable aroma and taste component of many red wines that comes from the compound vanillin in oak barrels. Newer barrels have more vanillin than older barrels. Smell a bottle of vanilla essence used in cooking to help identify the subtle equivalent in a wine.

varietal: A wine made from a particular type of grape, such as pinot noir, chardonnay, cabernet sauvignon, and so on, that shows the distinct characteristics of that type of grape. A varietal wine must contain more than 75 percent of the grape variety identified on the label. Blended wines made from more than one type of grape, such as many European wines identified more by their region than the grape (bordeaux and chianti, for example), are not varietal wines.

vertical tasting: Tasting a number of different vintages of one varietal of wine from the same winery, starting from the youngest and working to the oldest. Vertical tasting can help identify the best years for a particular wine and show how it changes as it ages.

vineyard-designate: Describes a wine that is made using grapes from a single, named vineyard only. These wines are usually more expensive and higher quality than those made with grapes from multiple vineyards.

Vitis vinifera: The main grapevine species behind all the great wines of the world, and one that is often grafted onto rootstock from other *Vitis* species. All the major varietal grapes are members of the *Vitis vinifera* species, including chardonnay, cabernet sauvignon, pinot noir, sauvignon blanc, and so on.

vintage: The year grapes are harvested, which is the year on the bottle label. Making the wine and bottling it often takes several more years, so a 2003 wine might not be released until 2005 or beyond.

yeast: Single-celled fungi that use enzymes to turn the natural sugars in grape juice into alcohol and carbon dioxide gas (and energy for themselves) through a biochemical process called fermentation. Different wild and genetically modified yeasts are used by winemakers, each performing differently and imparting a slightly different flavor to the wine. Wild yeasts often live naturally on grape skins, and winemakers will simply rely on them. A few wild yeasts can, however, give an undesirable "yeasty" odor to wines.

Suggested Reading

CUISINE

Don't expect to lose weight with cookbooks from the Wine Country, though there's usually plenty of advice on pairing food with wines between their covers. Wine Country cuisine is all about using the freshest local produce, and recipes in many of the Wine Country cookbooks tend to rely heavily on the kind of ingredients you might not necessarily find in your local supermarket. Still, they make a nice reminder of what to strive for in re-creating an idyllic Wine Country lifestyle and will probably be a fun reminder of memorable meals in the Wine Country restaurants that inspire many of them.

Bernstein, Sondra. *The Girl and the Fig Cookbook.* Simon & Schuster, 2004. Simple recipes that reflect the culinary fun to be had in the Sonoma restaurant, from liquid meals of martinis through to full French-inspired bistro meals, not all requiring the trademark figs.

Brown, Carrie, and John Werner. *The Jimtown Store Cookbook.* HarperCollins, 2002. The Jimtown Store is the little store that could, hidden away in the heart of the Alexander Valley but still managing to compile a no-nonsense collection of classically stylish yet simple Wine Country recipes that cross all culinary borders.

Chiarello, Michael, and Penelope Wisner. *The Tra Vigne Cookbook: Seasons in the California Wine Country.* Chronicle Books, 1999. The landmark St. Helena Italian restaurant is beautiful to look at and so is this book, though some of the recipes might have you out in the woods hunting for a particular wild mushroom that happens to be in season.

Jordan, Michele Anna, and Faith Echtermeyer. *The New Cook's Tour of Sonoma:*

150 Recipes and the Best of the Region's Food and Wine. Sasquatch Books, 2000. A sort of greatest hits of Wine Country cooking, with recipes from all over Northern California and profiles about the people behind the famous produce of the region that defines the cuisine.

Keller, Thomas. *Bouchon.* Artisan Press, 2004. If you can't afford to eat at French Laundry or would rather spend $200 on a case of wine, then buy this giant cookbook from the little bistro opened by the same owners just down the street in Yountville and learn how to make some simple yet sophisticated bistro-style food to go with your new wine purchase.

Pawlcyn, Cindy. *Mustards Grill Napa Valley Cookbook.* Berkeley: Ten Speed Press, 2001. One of the more digestible Wine Country cookbooks from this famous Yountville restaurant, with plenty of relatively simple recipes based on hearty American fare with twists of sophistication.

Sone, Hiro, and Lissa Doumani. *Terra: Cooking from the Heart of Napa Valley.* Berkeley: Ten Speed Press, 2001. This cookbook from one of St. Helena's best restaurants contains often sophisticated and tricky recipes drawing on French, Italian, and Japanese cuisine, but it helps makes their preparation as simple as possible with plenty of handy kitchen tips.

Wente, Carolyn, and Kimball Jones. *The Casual Vineyard Table.* Berkeley: Ten Speed Press, 2001. The Livermore Valley gets in on the cookbook action with this compilation of Wine Country recipes that can be prepared in an hour or less, all from the kitchen of the giant Wente Winery.

HISTORIC LITERATURE

Fisher, M. F. K. *The Art of Eating,* 5th edition. Wiley, 2004. One of the Sonoma and Napa Valleys' most famous writers, who ended up living in Glen Ellen, Fisher was also one of America's most well-known food writers in her later years. This compilation of five of her books is a collection of autobiographical information and musings on food preparation, consumption, and nutrition. She was described by John Updike as "the poet of appetites."

London, Jack. *The Valley of the Moon.* University of California Press, 1999. Although not one of this prolific Victorian author's most well-known books (such as *The Call of the Wild*), this is a clear homage to the beauty of the Sonoma Valley, a mythical nirvana to the story's two protagonists, who try to escape their harsh working-class roots in Oakland for a simple country life. The story mirrors the life of London himself, who eventually moved from Oakland to live in the Sonoma Valley, a place he adored. Originally published in 1913.

Russack, Benjamin, ed. *Wine Country: A Literary Companion.* Berkeley: Heyday Books, 1998. A collection of essays, poetry, travelogues, and fiction from almost two dozen writers spanning more than a century, all about or inspired by, the Wine Country of Napa and Sonoma. Includes works from Jack London, Robert Louis Stevenson, M. F. K. Fisher, Ambrose Bierce, Ursula Le Guin, and many other heavyweights.

Stevenson, Robert Louis. *The Silverado Squatters.* Wildside Press, 2004. The Victorian author is better known for his classic book *Treasure Island* but spent a few days of his honeymoon in a cottage at the abandoned Silverado mine just outside Calistoga. He wrote an entertaining account of the colorful characters he met and places he visited in the surrounding area, including early wineries and some sights still there today. Originally published in 1884.

NAPA VALLEY

Conaway, James. *The Far Side of Eden.* Mariner Books, 2002. James Conway picks up where his previous book, *Napa: The Story of an American Eden,* left off to chart the rise and impact of new money in the Napa Valley's recent social and wine-making history through the boom years of the 1990s.

Conaway, James. *Napa: The Story of an American Eden.* Houghton Mifflin Company, 1990. With a compelling narrative style, author and journalist James Conway tells the story of the key people, families, and politics that helped make the Napa Valley what it is today—a land of dreams, obsessions, money, and wine.

Lapsley, James T. *Bottled Poetry: Napa Winemaking from Prohibition to the Modern Era.* University of California Press, 1997. An entertaining analysis of the people, dreams, and marketing savvy that helped make Napa the great wine region it is today. More businesslike in its approach and style than Conway's books but still as readable.

Mondavi, Robert. *Harvests of Joy: How the Good Life Became Great Business.* Harcourt, 1998. No family has had more of an impact on the modern wine industry of the Napa Valley, and indeed California, than the Mondavis, and Robert Mondavi in particular. Here the man himself gives the inside information on what makes it all tick.

O'Rear, Charles. *Napa Valley: The Land, the Wine, the People.* Berkeley: Ten Speed Press, 2001. *National Geographic* photographer O'Rear paints a picture of life in the Napa Valley through hundreds of color and black & white photos of the people and places that make it a unique place.

Swinchatt, Jonathan. *The Winemaker's Dance: Exploring Terroir in the Napa Valley.* University of California Press, 2004. A dense book for wine or science enthusiasts only that explains how the Napa Valley came to be the way it is and how its geology and geography make it such a unique place to grow grapes.

SANTA CRUZ MOUNTAINS

Beal, Chandra, and Richard Beal. *Santa Cruz Beach Boardwalk: The Early Years.* The Pacific Group, 2003. Early photographs and thoroughly researched history bring the Victorian era of the Santa Cruz Beach Boardwalk to life and explain how this seaside playground was so important to the development of the city of Santa Cruz.

Beal, Richard. *Highway 17: The Road to Santa Cruz.* Pacific Group, 1990. Tells the story of the Santa Cruz Mountains through the history of the most important road in the region, which follows the route of early missionaries who sought and found an easy way to get to the San Francisco Bay.

Young, Casey. *Mountain Vines, Mountain Wines: Exploring the Wineries of the Santa Cruz Mountains.* Mountain Vines Publishing, 2003. Part coffee-table book and part travel guide, this large-format color book details 50 large and small wineries of the Santa Cruz Mountains with glorious photography and more facts and figures than the usual coffee-table book.

SONOMA COUNTY

Barry, Jennifer, Robert Holmes, and Mimi Luebbermann. *Sonoma: A Food and Wine Lovers' Journey.* Berkeley: Ten Speed Press, 2003. A coffee-table book with glorious photographs but also plenty of travel facts and recipes that highlight the food as well as the wine of this bountiful part of the world.

Deutschman, Alan. *A Tale of Two Valleys: Wine, Wealth and the Battle for the Good Life in Napa and Sonoma.* New York: Broad-

way, 2003. *Vanity Fair* contributing writer Deutschman continues where James Conway left off with his book *The Far Side of Eden,* chronicling the flood of dot-com wealth into both the Napa and Sonoma Valleys and the changes it wrought in Wine Country society. His style is more brash than Conway's and might not be to everyone's liking.

TRAVEL AND RECREATION

Brown, Ann Marie. *Foghorn Outdoors 101 Great Hikes of the San Francisco Bay Area.* Emeryville: Avalon Travel Publishing, 2003. 2nd edition. The perfect companion for any avid hiker visiting the Wine Country or even just the Bay Area includes some of the best short and longer hikes in Napa, Sonoma, and the Santa Cruz Mountains, with thorough descriptions of each trail and directions to trailheads.

Diller, David. *Mountain Biking Santa Cruz.* Extremeline Productions, 2003. Widely regarded as the best guide to one of Northern California's best mountain-biking areas, with detailed descriptions, maps, and photos to help both novices and experts alike get the most out of this "fat-tire fantasyland" of more than a dozen parks and other open spaces.

Taber, Tom. *The Santa Cruz Mountains Trail Book,* 9th edition. Oak Valley Press, 2002. An essential guide to the hundreds of miles of hiking and biking trails in the numerous parks and preserves of the Santa Cruz Mountains, constantly updated since it was first published in 1976.

WINE REFERENCE

Kolpan, Steven, Brian Smith, and Michael Weiss. *Exploring Wine: The Culinary Institute of America's Guide to Wines of the World,* 2nd edition. Wiley, 2001. This giant tome is a crash course in wine making, wine appreciation, and the wines of the world with the added authority of being from the Culinary

Institute, which offers some of the most highly regarded wine and food education courses in the country. That probably explains the unbelievably comprehensive chapter on pairing food and wine that, like many chapters, tends to read more like a textbook.

Kramer, Matt. *Matt Kramer's New California Wine.* Running Press, 2004. Food and wine writer Kramer explains what has shaped and continues to shape the modern Californian wine industry with plenty of facts and information about key wineries and wines from every California wine-making region, including Napa, Sonoma, Santa Cruz, and Mendocino. A vital book for California wine enthusiasts.

MacNeil, Karen. *The Wine Bible.* Workman Publishing, 2001. A book to be found on many winery office desks, not least because MacNeil and her husband are Napa Valley winemakers themselves. It has an altogether more chatty, approachable style than the Culinary Institute guide and contains information on just about every wine and wine-related term you will come across, although it sometimes lacks depth.

Sullivan, Charles. *A Companion to California Wine: An Encyclopedia of Wine and Winemaking from the Mission Period to the Present.* University of California Press, 1998. Learn just about everything there is to know about California's wine industry, from its history to key facts and figures, in this fascinating reference book.

Internet Resources

All the following Internet resources are either totally free or at least have some useful information that is free. They supplement the more specific regional Internet resources listed in each destination chapter. Most major magazines are not included in this list because they have subscription-based websites.

WINE

Damn Good Wine
www.damngoodwine.com

A blog offering irreverent wine reviews and wine information.

Vines.org
www.vines.org

A free, if slightly clunky-looking site that is a giant database of all things wine. Its encyclopedic format is not ideal for browsing, but it will likely have an answer to any specific question you can throw at it.

Vinography
www.vinography.com

An entertaining and sometimes brutally honest blog from a well-informed San Francisco wine enthusiast.

Wine Business Online
www.winebusiness.com

All the latest industry news, events, jobs, and other business-related wine information for industry insiders.

Winefiles
www.winefiles.org

An authoritative, searchable database of wine, wine making, wine history, and grape growing from the Sonoma County Wine Library.

The Wine Institute
www.wineinstitute.org

The main lobbying organization for the national wine industry with all the background you could want on wine-related laws, regulations, and statistics.

RECREATION

Bay Area Hiker
www.bahiker.com

Maps, photos, and information about some of the best hikes in the Bay Area and Wine Country from the author of a popular regional hiking book.

MTB Live
http://mtb.live.com/mtb-sfbay

Links to trail maps and information about most of the outstanding mountain-biking locations in the greater Bay Area, including much of the Wine Country.

Index

183, 185–186; transportation 153; wineries 179–186
Dry Creek Vineyards: 181
Dublin: 253
Duckhorn Vineyards: 72
Dutton Estate Winery: 11, 160

E
earthquakes: 257
East Bay:*see* Livermore Valley
East Ridge Trail: 166
economics of wine: 266
educational tours: 15
Ehlers Estate: 72–73
elephant seals: 237
Eric Ross winery: 202
estate bottled wine: 277
Etude Wines: 143

F
Fallen Bridge Trail: 129
Farallon plate: 256
farmers markets: Calistoga 105; Healdsburg 195; Los Gatos 222; Napa Valley 47; Russian River Valley 15, 176; Sonoma Valley 138; St. Helena 86; Yountville 59
Far Niente winery: 14, 53–54
fauna: 229, 239, 294
Fellom Ranch Vineyards: 213
Felton: 9, 223, 232
Fenestra Winery: 250
fermentation: 271–276
Ferrari Carano: 182
ferries: 27
festivals: Carneros 147; Livermore Valley 251–252; Los Gatos 216–217; Napa Valley 38–39; Northern Sonoma 164–165; Santa Cruz 239–240; Santa Cruz Mountains 210; Sonoma Valley 126
Fetters Hot Springs: 110
Field Stone Winery: 202
First National Bank (Los Gatos): 215
First Presbyterian Church: 36
fishing: 128, 167, 189, 218, 252
Fitch, Henry: 263
fizziness: 274–275
flora: 229, 295
fog: 258
food:*see specific place*
food pairings: 280–281
Foppiano Vineyards: 155, 157

Forbes Mill: 215
Forchini Vineyards & Winery: 182
Forestville: 153, 154
Franciscan formation: 256–257
Frank Family Vineyards: 31, 88–89
Frank Johnson Vineyards: 158
Freemark Abbey: 71–72
Freixenet: 141, 145
French Paradox: 268
Frick Winery: 179
Fritz Winery: 179–180
Frog's Leap Winery: 8, 21, 31, 63, 265
fumé blanc: 271

G
Gallo of Sonoma: 185
gambling: 203, 238
gardens:*see* botanical gardens
Gary Farrell Wines: 159
gasoline: 288–289
gay/lesbian travelers: 163
geologic history: 256–257
Geyser Peak Winery: 199
Geyserville: 197
Geyserville Bridge: 168
Gilliam Creek Trail: 167, 172
Glass Mountain: 257
Glen Ellen: general discussion 6, 109, 110; food 135–136; sights 8, 12; wineries 116–119; *see also* Sonoma Valley
Gloria Ferrer: 6, 145
Goat Rock: 217
Golden Falls: 16, 229
Gold Ridge Experiment Farm: 162
golf courses: 42, 55, 80–81, 130, 168–169, 252
Gondola Servizio: 36
Goodspeed Trail: 128
Goosecross Cellars: 15, 31, 49
Göpfrich Estate Vineyard & Winery: 183
grape-to-bottle ratio: 272
grape varietals: 270–271
Graton: 11, 153, 154
Gravenstein Highway: 153, 155
Grey Pine Trail: 128
Greystone Winery: 15, 78–79
Guerneville: general discussion 7, 152, 153, 154; accommodations 170; entertainment 163; food 172–173; sights 9, 11
Gundlach Bundschu Winery: 6, 9, 15, 107, 113–114
Gunsight Rock Overlook: 128

Parks and Reserves

Acknowledgments

You've never heard gossip like the gossip in the wine country. That's one secret I learned during the year I spent researching this book, visiting hundreds of wineries and tasting hundreds of wines while listening to entertaining stories from the folks that make, pour, or sell the stuff. Those folks come from a tight-knit community of growers, winemakers, vineyard workers, and a cast of thousands working in tasting rooms and behind the scenes (winery dogs included) who all seem to have a tale, a tip, some advice, or some gossip for a hapless writer with wine-stained teeth and a funny accent.

I'm grateful to all of the hundreds of people I met along the way who helped me tap into that sprawling wine country grapevine and taught me more than I ever thought I'd know about wine. In particular, Miryam Areas, Kate Jones, and Michael Coates all introduced me to some fascinating wine industry movers and shakers in Sonoma and Napa.

I appreciate the time given by all my interviewees, including Steve Ledson, Bruce Cohn, Jeff Bundschu, Peter Marks, Tammy White, and especially Bob Benziger, who redefined the term mover and shaker with a white-knuckle ride through the Benziger vineyards in a golf cart, during which I miraculously managed to keep the wine in my glass.

Thanks also to the patient folks in Avalon's editorial, cartography, graphics, and marketing departments, who must have thought I was slumped in a wine-induced stupor as deadlines came and went. Special thanks to my long-suffering editor, Sabrina Young, and also to Rebecca Browning, without whom this book would probably not exist and I'd be writing about something far less interesting.

Closer to home, Nicole Phillips patiently listened to my frustrations, shared my dreams, endured my frantic all-night writing sessions, smiled gamely through endless winery visits, and managed to develop a wine palate more finely tuned than mine will ever be. Heartfelt thanks, Nicole, and I look forward to sharing a 2029-vintage Stags Leap cabernet with you some day.

I should also mention the great British wine critics including Hugh Johnson, Jancis Robinson, and Malcolm Gluck who helped pique my interest in wine decades ago in my home country. Their uniquely British combination of skepticism, humor, and objectiveness helped demystify a subject that too many people still find intimidating. I hope their columns and books inspire many more people to explore the world of wine.

This book is dedicated to all future wine drinkers.

www.moon.com

For helpful advice on planning a trip, visit www.moon.com for the **TRAVEL PLANNER** and get access to useful travel strategies and valuable information about great places to visit. When you travel with Moon, expect an experience that is uncommon and truly unique.

HANDBOOKS | METRO | OUTDOORS | LIVING ABROAD

U.S.~Metric Conversion

1 inch	=	2.54 centimeters (cm)
1 foot	=	.304 meters (m)
1 yard	=	0.914 meters
1 mile	=	1.6093 kilometers (km)
1 km	=	.6214 miles
1 fathom	=	1.8288 m
1 chain	=	20.1168 m
1 furlong	=	201.168 m
1 acre	=	.4047 hectares
1 sq km	=	100 hectares
1 sq mile	=	2.59 square km
1 ounce	=	28.35 grams
1 pound	=	.4536 kilograms
1 short ton	=	.90718 metric ton
1 short ton	=	2000 pounds
1 long ton	=	1.016 metric tons
1 long ton	=	2240 pounds
1 metric ton	=	1000 kilograms
1 quart	=	.94635 liters
1 US gallon	=	3.7854 liters
1 Imperial gallon	=	4.5459 liters
1 nautical mile	=	1.852 km

To compute Celsius temperatures, subtract 32 from Fahrenheit and divide by 1.8. To go the other way, multiply Celsius by 1.8 and add 32.

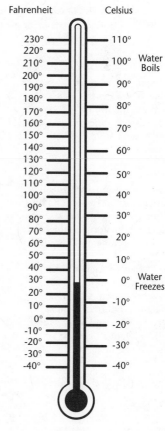

Keeping Current

Although we strive to produce the most up-to-date guidebook humanly possible, change is unavoidable. Between the time this book goes to print and the moment you read it, a handful of the businesses noted in these pages will undoubtedly change prices, move, or even close their doors forever. Other worthy attractions will open for the first time. If you have a favorite gem you'd like to see included in the next edition, or see anything that needs updating, clarification, or correction, please drop us a line. Send your comments via email to atpfeedback@avalonpub.com, or use the address below.

Moon Handbooks Northern California Wine Country
Avalon Travel Publishing
1400 65th Street, Suite 250
Emeryville, CA 94608, USA
www.moon.com

Editor: Sabrina Young
Series Manager: Kathryn Ettinger
Acquisitions Editor: Rebecca K. Browning
Copy Editor: Deana Shields
Graphics Coordinator: Tabitha Lahr
Production Coordinator: Darren Alessi
Cover Designer: Kari Gim
Interior Designers: Amber Pirker
Map Editor: Kat Smith
Cartographers: Suzanne Service,
  Kat Kalamaras, Kansai Uchida
Cartography Manager: Mike Morgenfeld
Proofreader: Donna Leverenz
Indexer: Judy Hunt

ISBN-10: 1-56691-880-4
ISBN-13: 978-156691-880-0
ISSN: 1556-4053

Printing History
1st Edition—January 2006
5 4 3 2

Avalon Travel Publishing
An Imprint of
Avalon Publishing Group, Inc.

AVALON
publishing group incorporated

Some photos and illustrations are used by permission and are the property of the original copyright owners.

Front cover photo: © Charles O'Rear/CORBIS

Printed in Canada by Transcontinental

Text © 2006 by Philip Goldsmith.
Maps © 2006 by
Avalon Travel Publishing, Inc.
All rights reserved.